The Idea of the City in Late Antiquity

The city was one of the central and defining features of the world of the Greek and Roman Mediterranean. Challenging the idea that the ancient city 'declined and fell', Andrew Wallace-Hadrill argues that memories of the past enabled cities to adapt and remain relevant in the changing post-Roman world. In the new kingdoms in Italy, France, and Spain, cities remained a key part of the structure of control, while to contemporary authors, such as Cassiodorus in Ostrogothic Italy, Gregory of Tours in Merovingian Gaul, and Isidore in Visigothic Spain, they remained as crucial as in antiquity. The archaeological evidence of new cities founded in this period, from Constantinople to Reccopolis in Spain, also shows the deep influence of past models. This timely and exhilarating book reveals the adaptability of cities and the endurance of the Greek and Roman world.

ANDREW WALLACE-HADRILL is Emeritus Director of Research and Honorary Professor in the Faculty of Classics at the University of Cambridge and Emeritus Fellow of Sidney Sussex College. He is a Roman cultural historian and his books include *Suetonius: The Scholar and His Caesars* (1983), *Augustan Rome* (1993), *Houses and Society in Pompeii and Herculaneum* (1994), *Rome's Cultural Revolution* (2008), and *Herculaneum: Past and Future* (2011). Former Director of the British School at Rome, he has directed archaeological projects at Pompeii and Herculaneum. This book is the result of his project on the Impact of the Ancient City, which received funding from the European Research Council.

Praise for *The Idea of the City in Late Antiquity*

With exciting literary arguments that challenge the assumption of urban 'decline and fall' in the post-Roman West, Andrew Wallace-Hadrill illuminates the continuous bustle of activity in centres like Seville, Marseille, and Ravenna. No seventh-century collapse here, but a lively, highly readable story of proud city dwellers adapting to a new medieval world, in what is also an admirable and compelling homage to his father.

Judith Herrin, Emerita Professor of Late Antique and Byzantine Studies, King's College London, and author of Ravenna: Capital of Empire, Crucible of Europe *(2021)*

Andrew Wallace-Hadrill's book, *The Idea of the City in Late Antiquity*, is a welcome addition to our understanding of the resilience of urban life in the face of the collapse of Roman imperial power in the West. The 'idea of the city' is explored primarily through the words of the men who lived into post-Roman times, and mostly in the West. Tracing changes to what it meant to live in a city, even as its physical fabric changed or decayed, opens up new avenues to appreciate the human construction of social, economic, and religious life in the post-Roman world. Wallace-Hadrill demonstrates that the human dimension – not just the physical remnant – is paramount for anyone interested in urbanism, whether ancient or modern. Scholars as well as students will benefit from reading this finely nuanced study of how late Romans used the idea of the city to restore and recreate new and enduring communities.

Michele R. Salzman, Distinguished Professor of History, University of California, Riverside, author of The Falls of Rome: Crises, Resilience, and Resurgence in Late Antiquity *(2021)*

The Idea of the City in Late Antiquity

A Study in Resilience

ANDREW WALLACE-HADRILL

University of Cambridge

Shaftesbury Road, Cambridge CB2 8EA, United Kingdom

One Liberty Plaza, 20th Floor, New York, NY 10006, USA

477 Williamstown Road, Port Melbourne, VIC 3207, Australia

314–321, 3rd Floor, Plot 3, Splendor Forum, Jasola District Centre,
New Delhi – 110025, India

103 Penang Road, #05–06/07, Visioncrest Commercial, Singapore 238467

Cambridge University Press is part of Cambridge University Press & Assessment,
a department of the University of Cambridge.

We share the University's mission to contribute to society through the pursuit of
education, learning and research at the highest international levels of excellence.

www.cambridge.org
Information on this title: www.cambridge.org/9781009527071

DOI: 10.1017/9781009527118

© Andrew Wallace-Hadrill 2025

This publication is in copyright. Subject to statutory exception and to the provisions
of relevant collective licensing agreements, no reproduction of any part may take
place without the written permission of Cambridge University Press & Assessment.

When citing this work, please include a reference to the DOI 10.1017/9781009527118

First published 2025

Printed in the United Kingdom by CPI Group Ltd, Croydon CR0 4YY

A catalogue record for this publication is available from the British Library

Library of Congress Cataloging-in-Publication Data
Names: Wallace-Hadrill, Andrew, author.
Title: The idea of the city in late antiquity : a study in resilience / Andrew Wallace-Hadrill,
University of Cambridge.
Description: Cambridge, United Kingdom ; New York, NY : Cambridge University Press,
2025. | Includes bibliographical references and index.
Identifiers: LCCN 2024023328 | ISBN 9781009527071 (hardback) | ISBN 9781009527118
(epub)
Subjects: LCSH: Cities and towns, Ancient – Mediterranean Region.
Classification: LCC HT114 .W35 2025 | DDC 307.760937/09015–dc23/eng/20240928
LC record available at https://lccn.loc.gov/2024023328

ISBN 978-1-009-52707-1 Hardback

Cambridge University Press & Assessment has no responsibility for the persistence
or accuracy of URLs for external or third-party internet websites referred to in this
publication and does not guarantee that any content on such websites is, or will remain,
accurate or appropriate.

To the memory of my father

Contents

List of Figures [*page* viii]
Preface [xi]

1 The End of the Ancient City? [1]

2 In Praise of the City [33]

3 The City in Question [74]

4 The City Revived? Cassiodorus and Ostrogothic Italy [115]

5 The City Embattled: Procopius and Justinian's Urban World [158]

6 The City and Its Records: The Ravenna Papyri [196]

7 The City of Bishops: Gregory of Tours and Merovingian Gaul [236]

8 The Grammar of the City: Isidore and Visigothic Spain [271]

9 The Fabric of the City: The Idea Embodied [314]

10 Decline and Resilience [373]

Bibliography [398]
Index [432]

Figures

2.1 The Avezzano Relief: relief representing a walled city [*page* 36]
2.2 Ambrogio Lorenzetti, Allegorie e Effetti del Buono e del Cattivo Governo in città e in campagna, 1338, Palazzo Pubblico, Siena [36]
2.3 Corpus Agrimensorum, Hyginus Gromaticus, centuriated city and country [38]
2.4 Fall of Icarus, detail with imaginary city from House of Sacerdos Amandus, Pompeii [39]
2.5 Imaginary city, fresco from house on Colle Oppio, Rome [40]
2.6 Iconographia Rateriana, bird's eye view of Verona [40]
2.7 The Madaba map of Jerusalem, Church of St George, Madaba, Jordan [41]
2.8 Personification of Antioch, Vatican Museum [42]
2.9 Cassiodorus' monastery at Vivarium [56]
3.1 Heavenly Jerusalem in Psalm 48 [92]
3.2 The amphitheatre of Tarragona and Sta Maria del Miracle [113]
4.1 Octagonal dome of the 'Orthodox' bapistery with the baptism of a bearded Christ in the River Jordan [124]
4.2 Octagonal dome of the 'Arian' baptistery, with the same scene as in the Orthodox bapistery, but a beardless Christ [124]
4.3 Mosaic representation of Theoderic's Palace from Sant'Apollinare at Ravenna [125]
4.4 Mosaic representation of Classis from Sant'Apollinare at Ravenna [125]
4.5 Detail of the representation of the Palatium from Sant'Apollinare. The hands of deleted courtiers are visible against the columns [126]

List of Figures ix

4.6 Justinian flanked by Bishop Maximian from S. Vitale at Ravenna   [126]
4.7 The Mausoleum of Theoderic at Ravenna   [127]
6.1 Example of papyrus from Ravenna archive   [217]
6.2 Civitates in Gregory the Great's *Registrum*   [220]
7.1 Civitates in the Notitia Galliarum   [240]
7.2 Civitates in Gregory of Tours   [241]
8.1 Cities in Isidore   [298]
9.1 Sauvaget's diagram showing supposed breakdown of a colonnaded street into a suq   [315]
9.2 Sauvaget's plan of Latakia/Laodicea showing contemporary (1930s) street plan and placement of classical colonnades   [316]
9.3 Plan of present-day (2010s) Latakia with hypothetical ancient street grid   [317]
9.4 The centre of Aleppo in the nineteenth century, according to Sauvaget, showing 2/3 rows of shops in former classical colonnaded street   [319]
9.5 Corner of the Forum of Iol Caesarea/Cherchel showing supposed traces of stalls   [322]
9.6 Plan of Constantinople with contours to show the seven hills   [328]
9.7 Street plan of Constantinople as a regular grid according to Berger   [329]
9.8 Plan of Constantinople showing principal streets and monuments   [330]
9.9 Eastern tip of Constantinople with monumental complex   [331]
9.10 Peutinger Map (Codex Vindobonensis 324), detail of Constantinople with the column of Constantine   [335]
9.11 View of Constantinople from manuscript (MS Canonici Misc 378 fols 84r-87r,) of the *Notitia Urbis Constantinopolitanae*   [337]
9.12 Plan of Justiniana Prima   [345]
9.13 Photo of circular Forum and colonnades of Justiniana Prima   [346]
9.14 Hypothetical initial plan (a) and plan as constructed (b) according to Vasić   [347]
9.15 Plan of Dara/Anastasiopolis   [349]
9.16 Plan of Zénobia-Halabiya   [351]

9.17 Plan of Resafa/Sergiopolis   [353]
9.18 Golden tremissis of Reccopolis. Obv. stylised head of Leovigild facing right with paludamentum, LIVVIGILDVS REX; rev. cross on four steps, RECCOPOLIS CONOB   [357]
9.19 Reccopolis and hinterland, with route of aqueduct   [358]
9.20 Reccopolis with results of geophysical prospection   [359]
9.21 The Acropolis (Upper City) of Reccopolis, with results of excavation and geophysical prospection   [359]
9.22 View from Royal Palace of Reccopolis over Tagus valley   [360]
9.23 View of housing in Reccopolis and road leading to acropolis   [361]
9.24 Plan of Umayyad ʿAnjar (Lebanon)   [364]
9.25 View of central dome of the octagon of the Aachen Palace Basilica   [371]
9.26 View of the central dome of the octagon of S. Vitale in Ravenna   [371]
10.1 Stylised representation of the four ecosystem functions   [375]
10.2 Plan of ancient Antioch after Justinian   [380]
10.3 Plan of Ottoman Antioch   [381]
10.4 View of southern end of Antioch viewed from Mt. Silpius   [382]
10.5 View of Antakya hotel/museum   [383]
10.6 Plan of ancient Mérida   [386]
10.7 View of temple of Diana area   [387]
10.8 View of bridge and Alcazaba of Mérida   [388]
10.9 Porch of S Eulalia, constructed in the sixteenth century from remains of Roman temple of Mars   [388]
10.10 Plan of Naples in the seventh century   [390]

Preface

The landscape of the Greek and Roman classical world was characterised by a dense network of cities – cities, by all means, which, compared to those of the modern world, seem surprisingly small. Cities too which, while contrasted with the countryside around them, also embraced it, in communities which combined city and country. To these Greeks and Romans it seemed self-evident that without cities there could be no form of human society, at least beyond the barbarian 'other'. This book explores the question of how such an idea of the city survived the partial collapse of unified imperial control in the fifth century AD.

It is often argued, or assumed, that the Greek and Roman version of 'the city' did not survive the system's collapse in the western Mediterranean. The case was made most explicitly by my former colleague and friend Wolf Liebeschuetz in his *Decline and Fall of the Roman City* (2001): he pointed not only to material decline, but to the collapse of the political structures which for him defined the ancient city. In challenging his narrative, I do not argue that his picture is wrong so much as partial. Indeed, many of the physical and institutional structures of earlier antiquity may have crumbled, but, alongside the indicators of collapse, there was survival, reconstruction, reinvention, adaptation – in a word, resilience. The phenomenon of the city is too complex to be reduced to a tick-box list of key features. The idea of the city proved tenacious and persistent, as powerful a legacy as the Latin language or Roman law. In this book, I set myself the task of re-examining some of the writers between the fifth and seventh centuries who had most to say about cities and charting the resilience of an idea.

What made this book possible was the exceptional opportunity of a European Research Council Advanced Grant to pursue the theme of 'The Impact of the Ancient City'.[1] The project set itself the ambitious – if not over-ambitious – goal of exploring that impact across the Mediterranean from antiquity to the present. We wanted a balance between work on the Latin-speaking Western Mediterranean and the Greek-speaking East;

---

[1] Formal acknowledgement is due to the ERC Advanced Grant no. 693418, 'The Impact of the Ancient City'.

between those whose skill was working with authors and texts – that is to say, on the 'idea of the city' – and those working on physical realities, archaeological in character; and between those working on antiquity or the early medieval period and those working on more modern material. The group set itself the goal of meeting once a week, to hear papers by a member of the group or a visitor. The result was that we all became used to learning about and discussing material far beyond our own core competences. Hence, in this book a classical historian, who has rarely ventured as far as, yet alone beyond, the fourth century AD, focuses on a period of Late Antiquity that stretches from the fourth to the seventh centuries, and in some cases beyond. If this foray beyond familiar territory at times seemed rash, I was given courage by the support of a remarkable research team, whose periods range from the early Middle Ages to the modern period. But, more to the point, rash or not, it was a duty. The entire spirit of our project was that we were not allowed to shelter behind the cosy barriers of disciplinary specialisation. Of course, that carries risks: those truly at home with the period and the authors I discuss will recognise the hand of the newcomer, and even at times that of the over-enthusiastic convert.

I have tried to compensate for the limitations of my own knowledge by leaning on the friendship of those more expert than myself. My first debt is to my colleagues in the project. Javier Martínez Jiménez, an archaeologist specialising in Visigothic Spain, and Sam Ottewill-Soulsby, an early medieval historian of ideas, both encouraged me in the reading of authors like Isidore of Seville; accompanied me to several Spanish cities, especially Mérida and Reccopolis; and made many useful suggestions on my drafts. To Javier Martínez Jiménez I am specifically indebted for a series of maps, and to Sam Ottewill-Soulsby for advice on much else, including *laudes urbium*. Suna Çağaptay, an archaeologist working on the transition from Byzantine to Ottoman, sparked my interest in Constantinople and Antioch by leading fieldwork trips. Louise Blanke, an archaeologist working with Alan Walmsley on Jarash in the post-antique period, helped me explore the potential of resilience theory. Ed Zychowicz-Coghill, a medieval Arabist, showed me in Spain and Turkey how interconnected were the Islamic and Christian worlds; a thousand pities that the political situation prevented us from visiting 'Anjar together. Sofia Greaves, a Classicist who chose to study nineteenth- and twentieth-century Italy, taught me not only about the impact of classical models on modern urban planning but also about the impact of urban planners on the modern image of the ancient city. Tom Langley, who joined our group while working on his doctorate on the Cappodocian fathers, showed me the rich potential of patristic writing for often contradictory views of the city. Among my colleagues, I owe an especial debt to Elizabeth Key Fowden, whose knowledge of the Eastern Mediterranean stretches from the Late Antique period to the Early Modern. From the outset, she helped me formulate the project, and insisted on questioning many assumptions, particularly that we can meaningfully talk about 'the ancient city' (whose antiquity?). She alone among my colleagues read the whole book in draft, making numerous incisive comments. In particular, she made me think about the western Mediterranean emphasis of this book. Naturally, this is partly the result of the divisions of labour within the project, with my focus on the West balanced by hers on the East. But it is also the result of the different trajectories of West and East in Late Antiquity, with the fragmentation of power into separate kingdoms in the West contrasting with the continuity of imperial power in Constantinople: one result is that the exercise of looking back to the past for models is rather different in West and East. I should emphasise that this book is far from offering a report on the findings of the project as a whole, but represents my own personal contribution to it.

In addition to an exceptional team, I have been fortunate in the willingness of friends to guide me in areas they know far better than I do. My colleague Robin Osborne persuaded me to recast the first chapter. Arjan Zuiderhoek added helpful comments on the same chapter. Mark Vessey steered me through St Augustine and Salvian of Marseille. Andrea Giardina's research group at the Scuola Normale di Pisa, whose edition of the *Variae* puts our understanding of Cassiodorus on a new basis, and among them especially Fabrizio Oppedisano, Pierfrancesco Porena, and Ignazio Tantillo, invited me for stimulating discussions. Geoffrey Greatrex put his unrivalled knowledge of Procopius at my disposal. Federico Marazzi brought me up to speed on sixth- and seventh-century Italy. Ian Wood, whose friendship goes back to our time as doctoral students, when he was supervised by my father, helped me generously with Gregory of Tours. To two friends in particular I owe an especial debt, for reading and commenting on the first draft in its entirety: Bryan Ward-Perkins and Rosamond McKitterick. At a late stage, Caroline Goodson helpfully surveyed the final draft. Between them, these friends rescued me from a thousand errors, great and small, made helpful suggestions, and pointed to gaps in my bibliography. It is thanks to them all that my footnotes give an appearance of learning that belies the limits of my own knowledge. Their suggestions have made this a better book. Had I followed them all, it would have been even better, but I might have ceased to recognise my writing as my own.

A further process of redrafting followed the comments of the readers for Cambridge University Press. They persuaded me both to spell out my argument more explicitly and to cut back some of the less pertinent discussion. Some may still feel I have expanded too much in my discussions of authors. But here I remain obstinate in maintaining we should not simply mine authors for relevant arguments, but try to understand their ideas on cities in their broader context. I have experienced much frustration in reading the literature on this theme at the way that texts are reduced to bare references in footnotes, as if they were simply a quarry for 'facts' or a repertory of opinions. Doubtless, had I been briefer about each of these authors, I would have left space for the many others whom I have decided not to pursue. My aim is not to be exhaustive, but to think about the chosen authors in greater depth. My hope is that among my readers will be those who, like myself, had little previous knowledge of these texts: I wish to share with them my enjoyment.

It may come as a surprise to those who know my previous work on Roman cities that I devote so much space to authors and texts, and so little to archaeological evidence. I have not changed my view that texts and archaeology are most fruitfully read together. However, my focus here is not on the materiality of the city, but on how it was constructed in what contemporaries had to say about it. The archaeology of the Late Antique city has become a vast and fruitful field, but it is beyond the scope of this book to contribute to it. I have tried to compensate for my neglect in Chapter 9, which, rather than looking to the physical remains for evidence of the crumbling of the classical city, and the transformations of the medieval, looks at new cities founded in the period as evidence for the idea of the city which they incorporate.

My last and deepest debt is closer to home. I have moved into territory, especially towards the end of the story, on which my own father was a master, though I could no longer consult him as I would have liked, a feeling which came on me most strongly when I reached Gregory of Tours. When he died, only too prematurely, nearly forty years ago, he left me his books on Late Antiquity. For decades they have looked reprovingly from my shelves, at my neglect of a period I had told him I wanted to work on. It has therefore been a solace and a joy to work through his copies of a series of authors – Orosius, Augustine, Salvian, Cassiodorus, Procopius, Gregory of Tours, and Isidore in particular – who felt like house guests I had too long neglected and could finally meet and get to know. When I first, as a sixth-former, became excited by Roman history, my father suggested I read Gibbon; this I did over a summer vacation, the same in which I first visited Rome. It set me on a path with many twists and turns, but which at last finds me in the world of Gibbon. To my father's inspiration I owe more than I can express. He was always suspicious of the work of Classicists working on the post-classical period and would have found much to question here. Nevertheless, it is to his memory I dedicate this book.

1 | The End of the Ancient City?

> Yet do you think, brothers, that a city consists in its walls not its people?
>
> (*An putatis, fratres, civitatem in parietibus et non in civibus deputandam?*)
>
> (Augustine, *de excidio urbis Romae*)[1]

The sack of Rome by Alaric and his Gothic troops in AD 410 sent ripples of horror round the Roman world: it may be seen to symbolise if not the end, then at least the beginning of the end of Rome, both as a city and as the centre of an empire. Augustine of Hippo, in his reflections *On the Sack of Rome* written shortly after the event, struggled to make sense of the wrath of God.[2] Why, if God promised Abraham to save a city from destruction for the presence of fifty, or even of ten just men, did he allow Rome to be sacked? His answer is that Rome was in fact spared. The news was horrendous: slaughter, burning, plundering, and the torturing of people (2.3).[3] But it was not like Sodom, which was entirely destroyed: many left Rome and would return; many who remained escaped or took refuge at altars (2.2). We should rather give thanks to God that he spared the city from a far worse destruction. You should realise, he insists, cities are about people, not about walls.

Augustine's reflections may introduce two of the central concerns of this book. One is that cities are, in modern terms, resilient, capable of recovering from disaster. A good proportion of the population, and indeed of the buildings, survived the three days of ransacking by Alaric's Gothic troops. Rome recovered, to be sacked again in 455 by Gaiseric's Vandals, and to recover and be sacked again, perhaps most damagingly, in 472 in civil conflict by Ricimer's Gothic troops. Worse was to come in the following century in the protracted struggles between Belisarius and the Ostrogothic forces under Totila. The cumulative impact on the imperial capital was severe, but the city showed the capacity

---

[1] Translated in Atkins and Dodaro, *Augustine: The Political Writings*, pp. 205–213.
[2] See, eloquently, Peter Brown, *Augustine of Hippo*, pp. 287–298; 'his whole perspective implied a belief in the resilience of the empire as a whole' (p. 295).
[3] See Salzman, 'Apocalypse then?', for the exaggeration of reactions.

to recover.[4] A central aim of this book is to explore the capacity of cities to survive the multiple shocks that came with the collapse of Roman imperial power in the West and to remain the basis of the urbanism of the early medieval world.

The second theme implicit in Augustine's reflections is that to understand a city, you must look beyond its fabric. That 'men not walls make a city' was an ancient proverb, as Augustine flags. The proverb, as we will see, can be traced back to archaic Greece and the lyric poet Alcaeus. It was intentionally paradoxical, for it was the defensive circuit of the city that defined its image (Chapter 2). The agreed definition of the city was in terms of human society, not urban fabric. Augustine developed his understanding of the city at length in his *City of God* (*de civitate Dei*), discussed here in Chapter 3. His definition of a *civitas* started from Cicero's definition of the state in his *Republic* as 'a multitude of humans bound together by shared justice and common interests' (*de Republica* 1.39). That contrast between physical fabric and human society is reflected in the snappy definition offered by Isidore, writing in Visigothic Spain in the seventh century: 'the town [*urbs*] is the walls themselves, the city [*civitas*] is not stones but inhabitants' (*Etymologies* 15.2.1).

This point brings out a fundamental ambivalence that affects all discussion of the city, ancient or modern. Are we talking about the urban centre and its physical structures, which in the case of antiquity leave such imposing remains, but which are subject to destruction and decay, or are we talking about the human community and the whole bundle of ideas, social hierarchies, legal and institutional structures, economic practices, and shared beliefs and customs which define it? It is tempting to treat the cities of antiquity as a case apart, on the grounds that the *civitas*, as opposed to the *urbs*, comprehended the countryside and its inhabitants, farms, villages, and small towns in a way not always true of the medieval and modern European city, though elsewhere globally the pattern is widespread.[5] But even if you restrict your focus to the built-up centre, the same ambivalence is there. As Henri Lefebvre taught us, space is constituted not only physically, but by the practices and activities within it.[6] A city as an empty stage is nothing: it is defined by the human activities it supports, places of work, places of meeting, the rituals and processions that

---

[4] The successive sacks of Rome are discussed by Salzman, *The Falls of Rome*, with an emphasis on the theme of resilience.
[5] See Zuiderhoek, *The Ancient City*, p. 43 citing Marcus and Sabloff, *The Ancient City*, pp. 3–26. I am grateful to the author for this point.
[6] Lefebvre, *La production de l'espace*; see Filippi, *Rethinking the Roman City*, pp. 3–4.

make it not rigid but a 'moving city'.[7] But the relationship is mutual and continuous: the stage set is constructed for the drama to be performed on it and to facilitate action, and as the drama develops, so the set is changed. The city is an ever-changing stage set for the performance of an ever-changing drama. Action defines physical setting, and physical setting defines action.

In this sense, it is hard to draw a clear line between the city as physical structure and the city as idea, or complex bundle of ideas, practices, institutions, economic forces, social relations, and beliefs. The lamentations over the decay and destruction of cities in Late Antiquity focus on the physical because it makes a powerful symbol.[8] But to destroy a city effectively requires not only the demolition of its structures, but the extermination or displacement of its inhabitants, as Chosroes knew when he destroyed Antioch (ineffectively, as it turned out).[9] Even inhabitants can be replaced if the city has an ongoing function in a wider network, and cities always form part of a network.[10]

The focus of this book is on the idea of the city, not its fabric. This is not remotely to suggest that the physical realities of the city are less interesting or important. Thanks, above all, to the urban archaeology of the last generation, we have a far clearer picture of the processes of physical transformation which cities across the former Roman Empire underwent in the period after its collapse. This book simply addresses a different question: whether the entire idea of the city changed forever at the end of antiquity, or whether it in some form continued to underpin the cities of the post-antique world.

Liebeschuetz and the Fall of the Ancient City

To speak of 'the end of the ancient city', as many do, is not only to point to the crumbling or transformation for other purposes of its fabric, but to the dismantling, or transformation to other forms, of its ideas, institutions, social and economic structures, and ideological systems. The most explicit argument along these lines was developed by Wolf Liebeschuetz in his

---

[7] See the chapters in Östenberg, Malmberg, and Bjørnebye, *The Moving City*; processions are also a central theme of Dey, *The Afterlife of the Roman City*.

[8] Lamentations over cities were memorably discussed by Cracco Ruggini and Cracco, 'Changing fortunes'; see also a balanced discussion by Brogiolo, 'Ideas of the town'.

[9] Brogiolo, 'Ideas of the town', pp. 111–112; on Antioch, see Chs. 5 and 10.

[10] Cf. Osborne and Wallace-Hadrill, 'Cities of the ancient Mediterranean'; on Greek cities as a network, Malkin, *A Small Greek World*.

Decline and Fall of the Roman City. Building on his earlier study of Antioch, his book is outstanding for its deep scholarship, the rare attention given by a historian to archaeological as well as written evidence, and its coverage of both the Eastern and the Western Mediterranean. As a survey of the post-antique city (in what he defines as 'late Late Antiquity') his work will continue to command respect. For Liebeschuetz, the evidence of decay or transformation of the physical fabric runs parallel with the abandonment of the institutions which for him define the ancient city, which he identifies as the rule of cities by municipal councils drawn from a hereditary elite of landowners, together with the rise of an intolerant religion, in the form of a particular brand of Trinitarian Catholicism, seen most starkly in the political power of the bishop.[11] This book takes a very different perspective.

Liebeschuetz's title, with its deliberate echo of Gibbon's *Decline and Fall*, was designed to be provocative, a pushback against the emphasis on 'transformation' most closely associated with the inspiring works of Peter Brown.[12] Over that choice there is continuing controversy, though in his text Liebeschuetz speaks of 'transformation' so frequently that one may doubt his paradigm is incompatible with that of Brown.[13] But where his argument has been a good deal less controversial, and is entirely in line with previous scholarship, is in the assumption that the ancient city did indeed come to an end. Here he agrees with Max Weber, Moses Finley, and his own doctoral supervisor, Hugo Jones, only parting from them in their analysis that the causes of the demise were economic rather than political.[14] Rejecting the characterisation of the ancient city as a 'consumer city', in contrast to the 'producer city' of the Middle Ages, he uses archaeological evidence both to reinforce the role of commerce in antiquity and to counter the picture of economic decline at the end of antiquity. For Liebeschuetz, the underlying causes were political: the collapse of a landowning class (the 'curials'), spurred by local patriotism to lavish their wealth on the embellishment of the urban centre.[15]

In the pages that follow, I wish not merely to challenge this analysis and the importance it attributes to the supposed demise of a 'curial' elite, but to

---

[11] Liebeschuetz, *Antioch*; *Decline and Fall of the Roman City*. His ideas were promptly debated in Krause and Witschel, *Die Stadt in der Spätantike*.

[12] Here his argument is partially akin to that of Bryan Ward-Perkins, *The Fall of Rome*. Ward-Perkins' principal target is Walter Goffart: see esp. pp. 7–9 and 174; reference to Peter Brown (pp. 3–4) is altogether less polemical.

[13] Admirably surveyed by Humphries, *Cities and the Meanings of Late Antiquity*; for earlier surveys, Lavan, 'The late-antique city'; Grig, 'Cities in the "long" Late Antiquity'; see also Salzman, *Falls of Rome*, pp. 13–16.

[14] Liebeschuetz, *Decline and Fall*, p. 8.   [15] Ibid., p. 4.

question the assumption which he shared with Weber, Finley, and Jones – and, indeed, the mainstream of ancient historians – that the 'ancient city' (in the sense used in classical scholarship of the city of Greco-Roman antiquity) came to an end at a certain point, whether for economic, political, or other causes, and that the cities of the world after antiquity belong to an entirely different category. As Moses Finley put it with characteristic force in what is perhaps the most influential single paper on the ancient city:

> Unless and until the kind of concrete investigation I have suggested demonstrates that, allowing for exceptions, Graeco-Roman towns did not all have common factors of sufficient weight to warrant their inclusion of a single category and their differentiation from both the oriental and the medieval town, I hold it to be methodologically correct to retain the ancient city as a type.[16]

Alarm bells should start ringing when he speaks of 'the oriental town' as a type. 'Oriental' is only too easily a code-word for 'Islamic'. Naturally, writing today, nearly half a century later, Finley would never have fallen into the trap of speaking of 'the oriental', in which he was following the lead of Max Weber. Those working on the Islamic world have stressed how unhelpful it is to see 'the Islamic city' as a category and how unhelpful is Weber's idea of the 'Oriental' city.[17] It is neither the case that cities across the Islamic world and across time have been typologically similar, nor that any characteristics they have in common have been the result of Islamic religion, except quite obviously in the presence of mosques. Islamic cities have often been characterised by their willingness to accept the presence of religiously diverse communities within them, something that cannot always be said of the 'Christian' city. In a word, the assumption that the oriental or the Islamic is typologically other risks being an exercise in Orientalism of the type decried by Edward Said.[18] But if we cannot share Finley's confidence that the ancient city was typologically different from the oriental city, is it any more helpful to make a type out of the medieval?

My question is not how or whether the city of antiquity declined and fell, but how it informed and shaped the cities that followed. What does it mean to speak of 'the Roman city' or 'the ancient city'? Cities are subject to

---

[16] Finley, 'The ancient city', p. 23.
[17] Abu-Lughod, 'The Islamic city'; Raymond, 'The spatial organization of the city'; Bennison and Gascoigne, *Cities in the Pre-Modern Islamic World*; Liverani, 'Power and citizenship'.
[18] Weber's observations on 'the Oriental city' have attracted particularly sharp criticism: see Zubaida, 'Max Weber's "The City" and the Islamic city'; Turner, 'Revisiting Weber and Islam'.

constant change, and there is no doubt that the period we now call 'Late Antiquity', between, say, the fourth and eighth centuries AD, is one of profound change. The Roman Mediterranean before this period may be characterised as a world of cities.[19] But the Christian and Islamic worlds after this period are also worlds of cities. In antiquity, the idea of the city was the principal way of thinking about human society; did it remain so after antiquity? My focus will be not on the physical structures, though these undoubtedly mattered, but on the idea of the city – that is, what contemporaries thought the city was and how and why it mattered.

The Invention of 'the Ancient City'

These questions require that we go back to basics and interrogate the modern historiographical invention of 'the ancient city'. Where does the idea of 'the ancient city' in the abstract, as a sociological phenomenon that can be studied as such, come from, and why do we still cling to it? The answer seems to be that it is a nineteenth-century invention. It is not the sort of idea you can find in Edward Gibbon.[20] He may have entitled his great work *The History of the Decline and Fall of the Roman Empire*, but in many ways the story he told suggested that in fact there was no end: the narrative proliferates into the stories of the successor kingdoms in the west, of Byzantium and Islam in the East, and then of the Renaissance in the West. His story was of the fall of an empire, not of a city, though on this he was remarkably ambivalent. His inspiration, he tells us, came from sitting on the steps of the Capitoline in Rome and listening to the chants of 'the bare-footed friars', and his first idea was 'circumscribed to the decay of the city rather than of the empire';[21] his last chapter (71) is an account of the fate of Rome in the Middle Ages and early modern periods. Even here, despite the laments of the humanist Poggio with which he opens his picture of decay, he is unwilling to join others in blaming 'the Goths and Christians', despite his story of 'the triumph of barbarism and religion', and prefers to blame 'the domestic hostilities of the Romans themselves' in

---

[19] This much is standard: see, most recently, Woolf, *The Life and Death of Ancient Cities*, which has the merit of placing the cities of antiquity in a broader and longer timeframe.

[20] Cited here in the seven-volume edition by J. B. Bury (1896–1900). The last part of chapter II of *Decline and Fall* (vol. 1, pp. 43–50) enumerates the cities of the empire, but stops short of offering 'the city' as an abstraction, or as a phenomenon peculiar to the Roman Empire.

[21] Gibbon, *Memoirs of my Life and Writings*, vol. 1, p. 82; cf. the last sentence of his work, ch. 71, vol. 7, p. 325: 'It was among the ruins of the Capitol that I first conceived the idea ...'

more recent times.[22] The City of Rome may stand in Gibbon as a metonym for the empire; but for the City, as for the empire, the story goes on. Gibbon's greatest achievement was to show the limitations of his title.[23]

In the nineteenth century, antiquity acquired a new relevance for the city. The rapid expansion of European cities brought by industrialisation and colonialism also brought crises of health and social order. One response was in transformations of the infrastructure: the opening of broad avenues both to improve air circulation in densely packed urban plans and to make social control more easy, associated with the name of Baron Haussmann; at the same time, water supply was improved by new aqueducts, and sewage disposal transformed by the creation of new drainage systems, as by Bazelgette in London or Haussmann in Paris.[24] In both cities, as in Naples, the Romans were felt to provide a model of a better-ordered city. Naples built a new aqueduct to save itself from the horrors of cholera,[25] and though in both construction and route it was significantly different from the ancient Roman aqueduct, it was advertised as a recreation of the Roman. What was now perceived as tangled chaos was laid at the door of the 'medieval city', or 'the Islamic city'. The liberation of Greece from Ottoman domination was rapidly followed by a conscious policy of 'de-Ottomanisation': tangled quarters were replaced by the new model of well-ordered city plans. Thessalonike is a late but spectacular example of this process: after the great fire of 1909, blamed on the narrow and crowded streets of the Ottoman city, a new rectilinear plan was introduced by the French archaeologist and urbanist Ernest Hébrard, which 'recreated' the plan of the classical city.[26]

It is possible, even likely, that the new way of thinking of 'the ancient city' as an abstract conception with a strongly positive value originated not among historians but the architects, engineers, and planners concerned with their contemporary cities.[27] Nevertheless, as far as the historical profession is concerned, it had a precise moment of formulation. In his fundamental essay on the ancient city, Moses Finley pointed to Numa Denis Fustel de Coulanges and his *La Cité antique* of 1868. Fustel was a historian equally at home in antiquity and the Middle Ages. The teacher

---

[22] Citations from ch. 71, vol. 7, pp. 308, 313. [23] Fowden, 'Gibbon and Islam'.
[24] See Greaves, 'Roman planning as a model'; 'Ildefonso Cerdà and the Eixample grid plan'.
[25] Snowden, *Naples in the Time of Cholera*.
[26] See Cormack, 'Exploring Thessaloniki'; Bakirtzis, 'Perceptions, histories and urban realities of Thessaloniki's layered past'.
[27] See Greaves, 'Ildefonso Cerdà and the Eixample grid plan'.

of Durkheim, he pioneered a sociological approach: he wanted to analyse 'the ancient city' as a phenomenon with specific characteristics and an internal coherence. He identified the key factor as religion.

Religion and the Ancient City

Religion is the first of the four elements that have been variously identified as giving 'the ancient city' (of the Greco-Roman world, that is) a distinctive identity that separates it from later cities; each of these four – religion, the economy, politics, and topography or urban fabric – has its own history. It is not easy to see whether in his formulation of a *'cité antique'*, Fustel de Coulanges was drawing on earlier authors.[28] He consciously favoured ancient sources and rarely cited modern ones. He was an admirer of Aristotle's *Politics*, and his ability to set out analytically the components of the *polis* and the variants within a pattern. Indeed, in one sense it might be said that it was Aristotle who invented 'the ancient city' as an abstraction. But Aristotle did not regard himself as examining a culturally bounded phenomenon – the city of the Greeks at a certain time – but a universal in human experience. He sees the city as a natural human phenomenon: the family arises naturally from the bonds of affection between man and woman; the family generates the village (*kômê*), and the *polis* is formed by the association of neighbouring villages to form a self-sufficient unit (*Politics* 1.2). Aristotle thought indeed that the city had a beginning (in the family), but does not conceive the possibility of an end.

Fustel, on the other hand, very much sees the ancient city as a time-limited phenomenon, with a beginning, like Aristotle's, but an end produced by a change in certain crucial parameters. The idea of his that has attracted the most attention is the attempt to isolate an 'Aryan' tradition of family and property, in which India is deployed as evidence for the structures that Greece and Rome had in common. The city originates with the family, which is based on ancestor worship and the claim to ancestral property; family units aggregate into Greek *genê* and Roman *gentes*; these aggregate into larger groupings (*phratriai* or *curiae*), and these, in turn, into tribes, until eventually, like a set of Russian dolls, these aggregate into the city. Each of these groupings is characterised by a form of ancestral religion that marks it apart from others at its level, until you reach the *polis* with a form of religion that is unique to itself and exclusive of the members

[28] See the essay by Momigliano, 'The ancient city of Fustel de Coulanges'.

of any other *polis*. This is Aristotle with an important twist, not least because religion plays so small a part in the Greek philosopher's picture.

Modern study of the tribal divisions of the Greek city has inverted Fustel's picture of the relationship: tribes and the like are now seen not as the origins of the city, but as subdivisions formed by the city to organise itself.[29] To that extent, Fustel's thesis cannot be said to command assent today. But independently of his account of the origins of the city, which forms the first two 'books' of his exposition, he offers in the third book an analysis of the elements that comprised the city; unlike in Aristotle, these are seen not as universals of the city in general, but specifics that set apart the ancient city from anything modern. Indeed, he goes out of his way in his opening pages to spell out the danger, caused by classical education, of supposing that the institutions of antiquity can be revived and imitated today, including ancient ideas of 'liberty'. Looking back from the perspective of the Paris of Napoleon III to the French Revolution, he attributes the problems of the last eighty years to a misguided use of the past: 'To understand the truth about the Greeks and Romans, it is wise to study them without thinking of ourselves, as if they were entirely foreign to us' (pp. 3–4). His strictures would apply as much to Haussmann's sewers and avenues as to the revolutionary invocation of Roman *libertas*. It is precisely this urge to look at the ancient city as an alien phenomenon that turns it into a typology with an end as well as a beginning.

For Fustel, all the characteristics of the ancient city flow from its origins in the family and ancestor cult (chs 3–17). So, he claims that the city is formed deliberately, not by a process of growth: 'We are not to picture ancient cities as anything like what we see in our day. We build a few houses; it is a village. Insensibly the number of houses increases, and it becomes a city; and finally, if there is occasion for it, we surround this with a wall' (p. 126). This city is founded at one moment in time, as a religious act, and the founder, whether mythological or historical, is remembered and celebrated in cult. Each city has its own religious practices, its own calendar, and its own priesthood. Political power is founded in priestly roles. The city demands absolute devotion from its citizens, and the municipal spirit of patriotism is the highest duty.

What makes Fustel's analysis so fascinating is that it scores some good hits in pinpointing the distinctiveness of the ancient city, including his insistence on the importance of religion, while at the same time pushing his hypothesis to the limit and beyond. No historian today would subscribe to

---

[29] Starting with Roussel, *Tribu et cité*.

his characterisation of the *polis* even in archaic Greece, let alone the city throughout antiquity. He does so because he is indeed creating an ideal type. His ancient city is not to be confused with the reality of the ancient city, because he believes that it was undermined from the very start. A series of revolutions, which he discusses in the following 'book', demolished the basic principles on which both city religion and social structures were based. These revolutions go back to the archaic period of both Greek and Roman history. Religious ideas changed fundamentally, under the influence, first, of philosophy, and then of Christianity. Christianity is seen as the diametric opposite of city religion: it is universal in nature, so that it no longer matters to which city you belong, only what religion you practise. Simultaneously, the Roman Empire terminally undermined the independence of the cities that made it up. So, in the end, while the ancient city definitively comes to an end with Constantine's adoption of Christianity as a state religion, it only really existed in its purest form at some undefined moment in the Iron Age or the Archaic period. Ancient history is not so much the history of the ancient city as the history of its long dissolution.

While no ancient historian today takes Fustel's account of the origins of the city seriously, the enduring legacy of his work is the idea that there was such a thing as a typologically distinct ancient city. His vision of Christianity as the antithesis of city religion also lingers, as is apparent in Liebeschuetz. So, he can speak of 'a Christian sense of identity which replaced the older civic pride based on secular history and links with Rome' (p. 18): this could be Fustel, except that antiquity is now characterised not by civic religion but by secularity. Again, in his Summary and Conclusions, he put it like this:

> Plato and Aristotle wrote of the city as an institution that educated its citizens. The Christian late Roman city certainly produced a different kind of person from the classical city. The change can be summarised as an expansion of the sphere of religion at the expense of the secular. (pp. 414–415)

Here, too, we are offered a vision of a classical city defined not by city religion but by secularity. The common factor is the assumption that Christianity must radically change the classical city. Yet (as Liebeschuetz was well aware), the flood of imperial rulings of the fourth and fifth centuries which are used to define and shore up the municipal elite issue from emperors with a strongly Christianising agenda. Christianity thus plays an ambivalent role as what undermined the classical city, and what gave it new life.

The Economy and the Ancient City

Where Fustel had seen religion as the field in which the distinctive character of the ancient city could be isolated, Max Weber, in his essay of 1921, saw it as being the economy, and more particularly the relation between town and country. Weber makes use of Fustel, and invokes from time to time his ideas on *phylae* and such subdivisions of the *polis*.[30] But for Weber the only critical element was the economy, something Fustel gave space to only in so far as he was concerned with the religious origins of private property. From the outset, Weber's definition of the city was an economic one:

> Economically defined, the city is a settlement the inhabitants of which live primarily off trade and commerce rather than agriculture. (p. 66)

Such a definition could never have come out of Fustel, but Weber was talking about the city as a historical phenomenon, and about antiquity only as a subset of that. Above all, he was concerned to explain the rise of capitalism and the modern state:

> Yet neither modern capitalism nor the modern state grew up on the basis of ancient cities while medieval urban development, though not alone decisive, was a carrier of both phenomena and an important factor in their origin. (p. 181)

The explanandum is simultaneously why the medieval city led to modernity and why the ancient did not.

Weber's thinking is notoriously complex and dense, and Moses Finley warned that his views were not easily extrapolated from his text.[31] Yet paradoxically this leads Finley to simplify Weber's position, which is highly nuanced. Weber has a great deal to say about variations, particularly in the case of the medieval city, for which he gives an enormous amount of well-researched detail (far more than for antiquity). Finley was only interested in the broad contrast drawn between the ancient and the medieval – hence his emphasis on the Weberian 'ideal type'. Weber starts by establishing the contrast between the consumer and the producer city,

---

[30] Weber, *The City*, p. 96 on fraternal associations; 101 on clanless *plebs*; 144–149 on clans and noble families in a cultic community; 170–172 on tribes, curiae, etc.; 175 on tyrants fostering new cults; 205 on divisions into demes and tribes replacing phylae and phratries; 214 on clients, etc. On Weber see among much bibliography Wilfried Nippel, 'Webers "Stadt". Entstehung–Struktur der Argumentation–Rezeption'; Michael Sommer, 'Max Webers Fragment Die Stadt'.

[31] Finley, 'The ancient city', 13–14.

though at once he flags that individual cases do not necessarily conform to the types:

> Moreover, it hardly needs to be mentioned that actual cities nearly always represent mixed types. Thus, if cities are to be economically classified at all, it must be in terms of their prevailing economic component. (p. 70)

Having already defined the city as 'living off trade and commerce rather than agriculture', his producer city, typical of the Middle Ages, fits the profile comfortably. It is the ancient city that creates difficulties, because of the integration of city and landscape into a single unit and the presence of landowners living in the city. The 'rather than agriculture' element is in question, so the consumer city is introduced as what is almost an aberrant form of city.

A great deal of the rest of his essay is dedicated to nuancing the contrast from which it starts. In particular, he nuances the generalisation that the medieval city was primarily mercantile and not the residence of the landowning aristocracy by pointing to Italy and the Mediterranean:

> The presence of large acreages accessible to the urbanite is found more frequently as one turns attention *to the south or back toward antiquity*. While today we justly regard the typical 'urbanite' as a man who does not supply his own food need on his own land, originally the contrary was the case for the majority of typical ancient cities ... The full urbanite of antiquity was a semi-peasant. (p. 71 [emphasis added])

So far it is the exceptionality of antiquity that is stressed, but 'the south' hints at a medieval exception, later spelled out:

> In many Mediterranean area such as Sicily a man living outside the urban walls as a rural worker and country resident is almost unknown. This is a product of century-long insecurity. By contrast in old Hellas the Spartan polis sparkled by the absence of walls, yet the property of being a 'garrison-town' was met. Sparta despised walls for the very reason that it was a permanent open military camp. (p. 75)

Here roles are inverted: medieval and modern Sicily and unspecified other zones of the Mediterranean become cities inhabited by landowners, ancient Sparta an example of the opposite. These are offered more as exceptions that point to the rule. Later, Italy as a whole is seen to break the pattern:

> The cutting of status connections with the rural nobility was carried out in relatively pure form only in the civic corporations of Northern Europe. In the South, chiefly Italy, the reverse occurs when, with the mounting power

of the cities, rural nobles took up urban residence. This latter phenomenon also appears in augmented form in Antiquity where the city originated precisely as the seat of nobility. Thus the ancient and to a lesser extent, the southern medieval European city form a transitional stage between the Asiatic and the North-European cities. (p. 95)

By now it is becoming clear that the ideal type of the medieval city is essentially a northern European, and not so much a Mediterranean, phenomenon. It raises the question of whether in antiquity itself northern European cities conformed to the Mediterranean model, but while Weber makes great efforts to differentiate medieval cities, he generalises about ancient cities without looking for variants. As he comes to discuss the 'patrician city', he concedes that in both antiquity and the Middle Ages, patricians may be found resident within cities:

> It cannot be too often re-iterated that the urban residence of the nobility had its economic cause in urban economic opportunities. The exploitations of these opportunities in every case produced the power of the patriciate. Neither the ancient Eupatrid patrician nor the medieval patrician was a merchant. (p. 153)

Again, the contrast between antiquity and the Middle Ages is dissolving, and the thesis that the urban residence of landowners was an impediment to the emergence of commerce is modified. The nobility might indeed live in the city, and might indeed profit from the opportunities of trade it generated, only with the exception that they did not overtly take part in trade as merchants.

As he turns to outline the bigger picture in his final chapter, awareness of the contrast between Northern Europe and the Mediterranean again surfaces:

> It is in these respects [i.e., the location of the city within the total political and social organisation] that the typical medieval city was most sharply distinguished from the ancient city. The medieval city, in turn, may be divided into two sub-forms with continuous transitions between them but which in their purest forms approximate ancient city forms. The Southern European city, particularly of Italy and South France, despite all the differences, was closer to the ancient polis than the Northern European city, that is of North France, Germany and England. (p. 197)

Recent research supports Weber's caution in drawing distinctions between the ancient and the medieval city in the Mediterranean.[32] The more nuanced the distinctions become between the periods, the harder it is to

---

[32] That the Italian city remained the residence of the elite throughout the Middle Ages is stressed by Wickham, *Early Medieval Italy*, pp. 80ff.; cf. p. 86: 'We do not have to identify a historical

set up the 'consumer city' with its resident landowning elite as a phenomenon limited to antiquity, as does Finley.

Weber's typological distinction, albeit qualified at a significant point, coincided with that of Henri Pirenne, a historian for whom he had little time. Pirenne's *Medieval Cities: Their Origins and the Revival of Trade* of 1928, as its title indicates, was not primarily concerned with the ancient city. In looking for the origin of the medieval city, he needed to account for the demise of the classical city. Famously, as in his *Mohammed and Charlemagne*, he saw the Arab conquest of the eastern and southern Mediterranean as the great historical turning point. He regarded, not without reason, Merovingian Gaul as an extension of Gallo-Roman practice: the city did not yet change in its nature. The collapse comes, somewhat surprisingly, under Charlemagne, with a collapse of Mediterranean trade as a result of Islamic dominance over the sea. Paradoxically, he sees this collapse as the chance for the city to invent itself in a new form, with a focus on commerce and the rise of a new merchant class that would pave the way to later capitalism. He thus coincided with Weber in seeing the medieval city as a new beginning, almost cut off from the city of antiquity. While a historian of the medieval Low Countries, such as Adriaan Verhulst, would agree that, in this area at least, there was minimal continuity with the Roman past,[33] it is among archaeologists that the sharpest doubts about Pirenne's thesis have been raised.[34] The idea that Mediterranean trade was cut off and that Charlemagne's reign marks a deep break with the past has lost its traction, even if the case for a transformation of the European economy and patterns of trade is strong.[35]

Politics and the Ancient City

In different ways, Fustel de Coulanges and Max Weber sought to identify the 'essence' of the ancient city, whether in city-based religious practices or in the economic relationship of town and country. In both, Aristotle's *Politics* hover somewhere in the background. Yet neither addresses what

---

break in the economic base of our cities, now landownership, now commerce (let alone industry); now aristocratic, now bourgeois', going on to refer to Weber.

[33] Verhulst, *The Rise of Cities*.
[34] Hodges and Whitehead, *Mohammed, Charlemagne and The Origins of Europe*. The European project on *The Transformation of the Roman World* explored many related issues. For a more recent survey, Bonnie Effros, 'The enduring attraction of the Pirenne thesis'.
[35] For a radical reassessment of the Pirenne thesis, see McCormick, *Origins of the European Economy*.

Aristotle himself clearly regarded as the essence of the *polis*: its political systems.³⁶ Aristotle's *polis* is a community of *politai*; and he defines the *politēs* by his participation in politics:

> A citizen without further qualifications is defined by nothing more than sharing actively (*metechein*) in judicial office (*krisis*) and political office (*archê*). (*Politics* 1275a22–24)

That was, of course, a very Athenian perspective, for no city carried the ideals of participation quite so far as Athens. It is also a distinctly masculine point of view. As has been vigorously pointed out by Josine Blok, women were *politai* just as much as men, and the definition of citizenship offered in the court cases where it is disputed is the right to participate in the religious life of the city: the *hiera kai hosia*.³⁷ Fustel of course was well aware of this definition, and his emphasis on family cults, and his insistence that the non-citizen was excluded from the religion of the *polis*, reflects this reality. But whether you focus on the all-too-masculine public life of 'politics' or on the religious rituals that embrace all members of the family, it is participation in the life of the *polis* that is the essence.

We might indeed object that a definition like this refers not to the city as urban phenomenon but to the city-state, and that this is a separate issue. But the integration of town and country into a single community means that this distinction can never quite hold. On the Aristotelian model, the countryman, whether peasant or landlord, must make constant use of the urban centre, whether as a market or as a political centre in which to exercise rights of voting and, indeed, to hold magistracies, or for access to justice, or for access to the religious festivals of the city. The Parthenon is not just an urban monument, but the centre of the greatest festival of the community as a whole, rural as well as urban, the Panathenaia. It follows that the essence of Athens as an urban centre is the product of Athens as the centre of a city-state.

The historian who took this point most seriously was A. H. M. (Hugo) Jones, the predecessor of Moses Finley in the chair of ancient history at Cambridge.³⁸ His ideas of the city were worked out over the span of an exceptionally productive career, which started with two linked volumes,

---

[36] See Zuiderhoek, *The Ancient City* (esp. pp. 78–93) for a sophisticated recent discussion giving emphasis to politics.

[37] Blok, 'A covenant between Gods and men'; Blok, *Citizenship in Classical Athens*, pp. 1–24. See also my paper, 'Civitas Romana'.

[38] Remarkably, Finley does not cite Jones' works on the Greek city in his essay, though their views on the agrarian dominance of the ancient economy were close.

The Cities of the Eastern Roman Empire (1937) and *The Greek City from Alexander to Justinian* (1940), later followed by his massive history of the *Later Roman Empire 284–602* published in 1964.[39] What these impressive works have in common is a determination to expand Roman history beyond what was then the traditional scope of the Oxford ancient history syllabus on which he was trained, ignoring the Hellenistic period and terminating with the death of Trajan. His initial focus on the Greek East made it easier for him to ignore the potential terminus of 476 as the end of the Roman Empire in the West. He saw the real break as coming with Justinian (or his successor Maurice). That enabled him to take the story up to the eve of the birth of Islam and the Arab conquests of the seventh century, which, not unlike Pirenne, he implicitly took as ushering in an entirely new world. In starting his *Greek City* with Alexander, he was pushing out into the relatively little-studied Hellenistic world; his *Later Roman Empire*, in starting with Diocletian, rightly identified the then nascent period of 'Late Antiquity' as the most neglected field.

It is perhaps the paradox of Jones' work that in trying to expand the study of ancient history beyond the confines of the 'classical' world, one which might be seen to end in the East with Alexander and in the West with Diocletian, he nevertheless retained many of the values of the classical world. His *polis* is that of Aristotle, written before his pupil Alexander changed that world by his eastern conquests. Jones's studies of the Greek city start from the observation that 'the Greek city' as a phenomenon saw an unprecedented period of expansion as a result of Alexander's conquests. The creation of hundreds of new Greek cities, in areas previously not urbanised or not Greek, and the continuous process of city foundation that was taken up by Alexander's successors, and then by the Romans, especially the Roman emperors, who were every bit as keen as the Hellenistic monarchs to have their names immortalised in new city foundations, continues to the very end of his period: Justinian was the most prolific founder of new cities of them all.

Even as the number of cities multiplies (*Cities of the Eastern Roman Empire* catalogues some 899 cities in the eastern provinces of the empire, though it leaves out the more eastern foundations in central Asia that fell outside Roman rule), so their adhesion to an Aristotelian model fades. The chapters on 'Internal Politics' (part III) spell out the long decline from an Aristotelian ideal. At first, the semblance at least of democracy and autonomy is preserved by Alexander. His successors follow his lead and,

---

[39] See Lavan. 'A. H. M. Jones and "the cities"'.

whatever their tactics of maintaining control, 'there was one which they could not use, the formal limitation of political power to a small class' (p. 157). All citizens were assumed to have equal rights, even if their numbers were limited (p. 160). An essential principle of democracy, of limiting the power of magistrates, was preserved by limiting tenure of office to a year (p. 12). Nevertheless, in practice decision-making tended to be with the council (*boulē*) not the *ekklēsia* of all citizens, representing 'a distinctly oligarchic trend' since 'persons of standing and substance' tended always to be elected (p. 166). So democracy survives, but in a compromised form, 'tempered by a convention that the rich should have a virtual monopoly of office, provided they paid for it very liberally' (p. 168).

Roman conquest pushes this oligarchic tendency further. By the time the Romans arrive, democracy has lost its substance, 'but it remained a popular ideal' (p. 170). The Romans do what Alexander's successors could not: 'place power in the hands of the well-to-do' (p. 170). In Rome the senate and the magistrates dominated in a way incompatible with Greek democracy, and this became the new model. Membership of councils was limited to those of a certain property qualification, and the councils acquired the right of veto over assemblies. Councils became ever more dominant, and membership of the 'curial class' – those who served on the council (*boulē* = *curia*) – became hereditary (p. 176). The assent of the citizen body became more and more of a formality, and eventually the assembly ceased to meet, its voice replaced by chanted acclamations that were recorded (p. 177). The privileges of the curial class were enshrined in the laws which protected them (the *honestiores*) from the physical punishments to which the humble citizens (the *humiliores*) were subject (pp. 179–180). Not even the election of magistrates was a matter of free choice by the citizens, who, even if they got to vote, were presented by the council with a closed list (p. 181).

Despite the erosion of the rights of citizens, the ruling class still felt obliged to use their wealth for the benefit of their cities:

> The tradition of local patriotism indeed maintained itself for a surprisingly long period, all things considered. Men still in the third century AD took pride in their cities, and the great families still in many cases felt the traditional obligation to pay for their position by lavish expenditure. (p. 182)

Gradually, the financial burdens of holding office and council membership come to outweigh the advantages of prestige, and competition for office fades. Thus, membership of the *boulê* and the expenses it implies become compulsory. Jones here makes clear his increasing distaste at a process of decline by his choice of language ('degeneration'). His picture culminates with Libanius in fourth-century Antioch, who offers an idealised vision of how things used to be, and still ought to be:

> Libanius paints a picture of the council of Antioch as it was in the recent past which is very different. The councillors are all of ancient family: their ancestors have all held magistracies and liturgies for generations and have trained up their descendants to a proper sense of civic spirit. (p. 191)

By the end of this chapter on 'the Roman age', the process of decline is advanced: any semblance of democracy has gone, the ordinary citizen is separated from the class of 'curials' and has no vote, and it is only by a sort of hereditary inertia that the ruling class still bother to evince civic spirit and spend their wealth lavishly for the public benefit. The final collapse comes with Late Antiquity, here called 'the Byzantine age'. At this point Jones can turn not only to the complaints of Libanius, but to the rich sequence of imperial edicts preserved in the *Theodosian Code* (book 15). Spanning the years 312 to 438 (Theodosius' excerptors were only interested in the pronouncements of Christian emperors, and Catholic Trinitarians at that),[40] emperors issue a series of 192 increasingly indignant rulings about city councils, attempting to block attempts to evade their local financial obligations by those who sought exemption through imperial service, membership of the senate, and even the privilege of clergy.

This stream of imperial constitutions is taken to demonstrate the widespread and growing unpopularity of service on city councils, and, at the same time, the utter impotence of imperial pronouncements in the face of local evasion. The wonder is not so much that council service had become undesirable, but that the system managed to survive at all:

> These tasks were, now that the service of one's native city had no emotional appeal, felt to be exacting and tedious, and it is natural that many decurions aspired either to more interesting work in the higher grades of the public services. (p. 206)

Jones has charted the steady process, over the 800 years and more that separate Alexander from Justinian, first of a decline of the institutions that characterised the Aristotelian *polis*, from democracy and autonomy to the willing domination of the rich, to the conversion of the rich into a hereditary caste that was compelled to undertake local burdens; at the same time, he has traced a decline in morale, from the sort of competitive

---

[40] See Humphries, 'The rhetorical construction of a Christian Empire'.

euergetism that made the rich willing to support their cities, seen as a spirit of 'patriotism', to the surprising continuance of that patriotic spirit after the need to compete for local recognition had gone, to the final evaporation of that spirit.

We meet the same picture of ineluctable decline in the chapter on 'the Cities' in *The Later Roman Empire* (pp. 712–766), written twenty-five years later, except that now the story starts with the late empire, so that decline is already advanced when the story begins, with Libanius and the Theodosian Code. Jones now broadens his view to include the western empire, bringing into the picture the Germanic kingdoms which from the late fifth century replaced imperial administration (p. 748). He notes with interest that when Alaric II, Visigothic king of Spain, issues his law code based on that of Theodosius, the provisions affecting cities and their administration remain virtually unchanged, while the pen of Cassiodorus shows for the sixth century how meticulously the Ostrogothic regime enforced old rules intended to support cities and encourage curials. Italian archives, particularly from Ravenna, show the councils, *curiae*, and the local magistrates in action from 489 to 625 (p. 761). And though the general tone is one of ineluctable decline, he observes that this is far from the end of the story for cities in the East:

> The cities apparently continued to prosper economically, and the guilds maintained their membership without any need of governmental action. The archaeological evidence supports this conclusion and even suggests a revival of the towns in the fifth and sixth centuries. To take one instance, Gerasa, a largish city in Arabia, which had flourished greatly in the second century AD evidently fell on evil days in the third and shows little or no sign of revival in the fourth or early fifth. But from the latter part of the fifth century a dozen churches, many of them of some architectural pretensions, were erected and several public buildings repaired or re-erected: this activity went on uninterrupted down to the Arab conquest, the last church being dedicated under Phocas. (p. 763)

This passage is the more remarkable because of the rarity of references to archaeological evidence in a text almost entirely dependent on written sources. This might be taken as a sign of the new significance being awarded to archaeological data in the 1960s, did we not know that Jones' archaeological interests were more longstanding. In his obituary, Russell Meiggs recounts that the young Jones travelled widely, making repeated visits to Constantinople and Jerash (Gerasa), and was known to his friends as 'Jerash Jones'.[41]

As we have seen, it is Jones' thesis of progressive political decline and the loss of patriotic spirit by the landowning elite that forms the basis of Liebeschuetz's more detailed account of the same 'decline and fall'. While Jones' thesis incorporates an economic side, subscribing to the Weberian thesis of the 'consumer city' and assuming that the prosperity of classical cities was founded on the willingness of landowners to invest 'patriotically' in urban monuments and benefactions (what Paul Veyne called 'euergetism'), for Liebeschuetz, who rejects the 'consumer city', the matter is almost purely political and constitutional.

> This book's principal theme is political change. The discussion focuses on the end of city-government by the *curia*, and its replacement by another looser, and much less transparent form of oligarchic control. (p. 4)

He sees government passing to the hands of a group of 'notables': rich and influential figures who were free of the disagreeable burden of being members of the *curia*, as the end of any trace of constitutional government that would be recognised by Aristotle.

We will return the issue of the demise of the *curia* in due course (see Chapter 7). The relevant point here is to observe how 'constitutional' government forms the thread that gives supposed unity to the idea of 'the ancient city'. The *curia* is the last vestige of a political essence that marks the ancient city apart. There is nothing inherently wrong in following an Aristotelian line and giving primacy to politics over religion or the economy in our analysis of ancient cities. The problem lies in using it to set up an unbridgeable gulf between 'the ancient city' and later cities. Another way of looking at it – and one developed here – is to say that how cities were governed evolved continuously under the impact of imperial control, and that the elimination of the *curia*, or at least its reduction to a mere formality, was simply the next step in a process of continuous evolution. If we focus on the perspective of contemporaries, the gulf may seem more like a channel of communication.

Urban Fabric and the Ancient City

While Fustel de Coulanges, Max Weber, Moses Finley, and A. H. M. Jones put different emphasis on the importance of religious, economic, and political

---

[41] Meiggs, 'Arnold Hugh Martin Jones', p. 186.

factors, they agree that 'the ancient city' was a distinctive phenomenon which terminated at the end of 'antiquity'. They also (despite Jones' interest in Jerash) paid little attention to the physical form of the city; not until Liebeschuetz does archaeological evidence start to form part of the picture. But, for all that, the physical city is there in the background. Moses Finley opened his essay on 'The Ancient City' with a discussion of definitions, and turned at once to the much-quoted comment of Pausanias, in his second-century AD guide to Greece, questioning the city status of Panopeus in Phocis:

> no government buildings, no theatre, no town square, no water conducted to a fountain, and ... the people live in hovels like mountain cabins on the edge of a ravine. (10.4.1)

That suggested a definition of sorts:

> a city must be more than a conglomeration of people; there are necessary conditions of architecture and amenity, which in turn express certain social, cultural and political conditions.[42]

Yet one might use Pausanias to make exactly the opposite point. Bearing in mind the proverbial 'men not walls make a city', Panopeus shows that possession of the sort of public buildings which typify ancient cities was *not* after all a necessary part of the definition of a *polis*, whereas the independence and self-government to which Aristotle points were so. An archaeologist might conclude on the basis of physical remains that Panopeus was no city, whereas the inhabitants might claim that they were indeed a *polis*. In the end, Finley brushes off archaeological study of the fabric of cities impatiently:

> There is considerable publication about what is sometimes rather grandiloquently called 'ancient town-planning', and no one will dispute this is part of urban history, as are demography, drains and sanitation. But a town is more than the mere arithmetical total of layout and drains and inhabitants, and it is remarkable that the ancient city *qua* city has aroused so little interest. (pp. 7–8)

His list of those responsible for this 'grandiloquent' conception omits the ancient historian who might rate as the pioneer of the study of ancient town planning, Francis Haverfield.[43] The use of the expression 'town planning',

---

[42] Finley, 'The ancient city', p. 3.
[43] Finley, 'The ancient city', p. 8 note 11 cites Martin, *L'urbanisme dans la Grèce antique*; Wycherley, *How the Greeks built Cities*; and Homo, *Rome impériale et l'urbanisme dans l'antiquité*. Along with Haverfield, Ward-Perkins, *Cities of Ancient Greece and Italy* is a striking omission. For the discussion of town planning from Haverfield on, see Greaves and Wallace-Hadrill, 'Introduction', pp. 11–13.

by Haverfield at least, was largely due to the Town Planning Conference organised by the Royal Institute of British Architects (RIBA) in London in October 1910.[44] Intended to be a major international event, it deliberately looked at town planning past, present, and future. In the opening session, dedicated to antiquity, the Middle Ages, and the Renaissance, there were three papers on antiquity, by scholars of unquestionable authority: Professor Percy Gardner of Cambridge talked about Hellenistic Greek town planning; Francis Haverfield talked about the Romans; and Thomas Ashby, a pupil of Haverfield's and by then director of the British School at Rome, talked about Rome itself. A central theme of the work of Haverfield, an ancient historian by training and profession, was his commitment to the use of archaeological evidence. Indeed, he had played a crucial role (along with Percy Gardner and Thomas Ashby) in the foundation in 1901 of the British School at Rome, one aim of which was to put Classicists in touch with the physical remains of Roman antiquity,[45] and a decade later he was one of the founders of the Society for the Promotion of Roman Studies, which, like its Hellenic predecessor, sought to promote interest in physical remains as well as text. 'Town planning', a theme scarcely touched on by previous scholarship, suited his agenda well, for it allowed him to argue that the fundamental character of Roman civilisation was encapsulated in, and could be studied through, the remains of cities, and particularly their street plans. To promote this idea, he developed a line that seems to have gone down well with his audience.

> The great gift of the Roman Empire to Western Europe was town life, and during the Roman Empire the creation of new towns went on apace ... One central fact is plain: that all these towns assumed a definite form ... It was an old form – the familiar rectangular street plan ... The square and straight lines are indeed the simplest marks which divide man civilised from the barbarian.[46]

Haverfield stopped well short of claiming that Rome invented rectilinear planning (and he immediately offered an older Chinese example); his argument is rather that regular 'chess-board' city layouts, which he illustrated by Florence, Timgad, Silchester, and Caerwent, were both a symbol of Roman civilisation and a major legacy to the future. At the same time, he

---

[44] *Town Planning Conference London*. Discussed in greater detail by Greaves and myself in the introduction to *Rome and the Colonial City*, pp. 1–24. I am grateful to Sofia Greaves for underlining to me the significance of this conference.
[45] See Wiseman, *A Short History of the British School at Rome*, p. 3.
[46] Haverfield, 'Town planning in the Roman world', p. 124.

identified the loss of such planning with the fall of empire. He notes how rare it was for regular plans to survive into the Middle Ages, and takes Belgrade (Roman Singidunum) as the exception that proves the rule:

> Here on the high promontory which looks out over the lowlands of the Danube and the Save, is the 'old town' of the Servian capital, and this old town, grouped around the market-square, shows the regular streetage which I think we may safely connect with its Roman days. For once, the wave of barbarism, even the last and longest wave of Mahometanism, has failed wholly to efface it. (p. 129)

Haverfield could count on his audience to share his Orientalist take on Islam, and the assumption that it was represented in the sort of tangle of narrow streets that for them represented barbarism.

Interestingly, his prejudices were not shared by all contemporaries. His old pupil, Thomas Ashby, beneficiary and inspiring leader of the School which Haverfield did so much to create, spoke about Rome itself. In his quiet, non-conformist way,[47] he did not openly question Haverfield's celebration of regular streets so much as seek to show, through the topographical and historical factors that governed the development of Rome as a city, that there was no principle of planning at work here at least, in the greatest of Roman cities. In case his message was lost, Ashby concluded with a more explicit statement:

> There has been too much of a cult of the straight line and the right angle, not only in Rome since 1870, but in most other parts of the world, and I take it that one of the objects of the present Conference is to spread a different gospel among the nations. (p. 145)

His remark must have caused an uproar. His overt target was the post-Risorgimento expansion of Rome (as he was later to criticise Mussolini), but the message was clear. In the discussion, Professor Reginald Blomfield, secretary of the RIBA and one of Ashby's supporters in developing the British School as a base for architects, used his opening of the discussion as Chair to put him in his place:

> There is one remark in his [Haverfield's] Paper which struck me as admirable, and that was his reference to the straight line and the square as the distinguishing mark of civilised man as opposed to the barbarian. I think we may all take that as a motto for this Town Planning Conference. I notice that Dr Ashby disagrees with him, and I understand him to say

---

[47] See Hodges, *Visions of Rome*.

> that meandering lines are preferable; but I think he will find the principles of great architecture against him. (p. 177)

For all Blomfield's lordly put-down, Ashby, who knew his Italy a great deal better than Blomfield, could have pointed him to architects from Alberti on who celebrated the sinuous streets of an Italian hill town and their potential for opening up unexpected and striking vistas.[48]

As far as Haverfield was concerned, the battle was won in favour of the straight line and the rectangle, and he proceeded to elaborate his ideas in the slim volume that stands at the base of modern studies of ancient urbanism: *Ancient Town-Planning* (1913). He made good use of the conference, helping himself to Blomfield's discussion of Priene and Brinkmann's discussions of both the Renaissance and particularly the grid-like new towns of the thirteenth century. In the full version of the book, he is able to deploy many more examples, and to emphasise the gains of archaeology. But he also formulated the theme that so pleased Blomfield in even more explicit fashion:

> In almost all cases, the frequent establishment of towns has been accompanied by the adoption of a definite principle of town-planning, and throughout the principle has been essentially the same. It has been based on the straight line and the right angle. These, indeed, are the marks which sunder even the simplest civilization from barbarism. The savage, inconsistent in his moral life, is equally inconsistent, equally unable to 'keep straight', in his house-building and his road-making. (p. 14)

He was also able to spell out more explicitly the theme that grid planning ended with the end of the Roman Empire, even if some centuries later it was picked up as an enduring legacy. The end of antiquity is a catastrophic collapse:

> the Roman planning helped the towns of the empire to take definite form, but when the empire fell, it too met its end. (p. 140)

If the grid plan was the symbol and instantiation of civilisation, it could scarcely survive barbarian invasions.

> When, after 250 years of conflict, the barbarians triumphed, its work was done. In the next age of ceaseless orderless warfare it was less fit, with its straight broad streets, for defence and for fighting than the chaos of narrow tortuous lanes out of which it had grown and to which it now returned. (p. 140)

---

[48] See my 'Ancient ideals and modern interpretations', p. 51, on Alberti.

Haverfield's prejudices are very much of his time: there is a confident and unembarrassed Edwardian belief in the moral superiority of empire. He was not shy in drawing parallels between the Roman and the British Empires, and, as his inaugural lecture to the newly founded Roman society showed, he felt that the parallel showed the value of the study of the ancient world.[49] His views on the value of 'Romanisation' have been sharply criticised.[50] His views were what we now see as 'colonialist'. That was not only a British failing: the French in North Africa and Syria looked at the tangled streets of what they called the 'Islamic city' with equal distaste. Not only did their colonial authorities build new orthogonal towns alongside the old 'madinas', but their archaeologists sought to demonstrate how Islamic rule led to the breakup of the planned cities they had inherited.[51]

In Haverfield's picture, ancient rectilinear planning came to an end, later to be revived in the thirteenth century in the Terra Nova of Federico II and the *bastides* of France: his image of the ancient city is finite, with a beginning, middle, and end. Just as much as Fustel or Weber, he sees the 'ancient city' as a circumscribed entity with a specific character. He does not suggest that rectilinear planning is a Greco-Roman invention, as his Chinese example shows. Rather, such planning is a universal value, a hallmark of civilisation wherever it may be found. But the ancient world for him takes this universal value to a special level. Ancient civilisation is embodied in the city, and the values of the city are embodied in the orthogonal plan. So, the 'ancient city' as abstract idea achieves a concrete form, one which can be easily recognised on the ground by the archaeologist.

Haverfield's book thus locked into the scholarship an assumption that the ancient city was a distinct phenomenon with recognisable physical features. Subsequent books on ancient town planning modified some details and added new examples but did not challenge the underlying scheme. Ferdinando Castagnoli built up further the figure of Hippodamus as father of town planning;[52] John Ward-Perkins, director of Haverfield and Ashby's British School at Rome, took up the theme sixty years later, and in his slim volume on *Cities of Ancient Greece and Italy: Planning in Classical Antiquity* (1974) showed vividly how modern techniques of aerial photography could bring out the grid plans still visible on the ground. We may note that though Ward-Perkins mentions other urban

---

[49] Haverfield, 'An Inaugural Address'.
[50] Hingley, *Roman Officers and Gentlemen*; Freeman, *The Best Training Ground for Archaeologists*; Greaves and Wallace-Hadrill, 'Introduction', p. 10.
[51] See Ennahid, 'Searching for Rome'. [52] Castagnoli, *Ippodamo di Mileto*.

features, from monuments to drainage, the focus of the book is still on planning.

Ward-Perkins, like Haverfield, had an agenda in demonstrating the importance of archaeology in understanding the ancient city. He takes some pride in pointing out that we would not grasp the importance of orthogonal planning from the ancient texts: you need the archaeology to see it; hence, too, the dominance of image over text. He is explicit in his Introduction:

> Although this study of classical town planning concerns itself very largely with the formal layouts which are its most tangible surviving expression, it is as well to remember that this was not by any means the aspect of urban planning that bulked largest in the eyes of contemporaries. Questions of formal layout seem in fact to have been largely ignored or taken for granted by most Greek writers, or considered if at all for their relevance to the political and social problems which were their main interest... For town planning as such we are driven very largely to the study of surviving remains. (p. 8)

If, as he has just claimed, 'the history of the classical town is in a very real sense the history of classical civilisation itself', should we not be more perturbed that the ancient writers, who undoubtedly valued the city, showed so little interest in what is being offered as the ultimate expression of classical civilisation? The suspicion must surely lurk that the whole interest in street layouts – what Ashby called 'a cult of the straight line and the right angle' – is actually a modern obsession, retrojected onto antiquity, which is then recruited to give authority to one side of a modern debate.[53]

Haverfield and his Edwardian attitudes may be long gone. But the idea that the classical city was characterised by well-planned and orderly streets, and that these give way in the post-antique period to winding streets and urban clutter, persists. So, Averil Cameron puts it in her discussion of Procopius, who paints a strikingly classical picture of the streets of Justinian's new cities (see Chapter 6):

> All over the empire, archaeology shows that a transformation was occurring during the sixth century. The open spaces of the classical city – the baths, fora and public buildings which Procopius records, for instance at Justiniana Prima or Ras Kapoudia in North Africa, were giving way to the crowded and winding streets of the medieval souks; the houses were soon

---

[53] I develop this idea in 'Ancient ideals and modern interpretations'.

rather to be found huddling round the fortified citadel enclosing the bishop's palace and the main church.[54]

If we follow this vision, we may be persuaded that the classical city of antiquity is divided from the medieval city, whether Christian or Islamic, by an uncrossable gulf.

What Might 'The End of the Ancient City' Mean?

The four approaches to the 'ancient city' sketched here have in common the assumption that there was such a thing as 'the ancient city', the characteristics of which can be defined, and which had considerable duration over the best part of a millennium, from archaic Greece to the Antioch of Libanius, and which by a process of decline, irrespective of external pressures and changed conditions, came to an end at some unclear point in Late Antiquity, maybe with Constantine, maybe as late as the seventh-century Arab invasions of Syria.

Does it matter that these approaches have different perspectives and emphases – religious, economic, political, and physical – given that all four come to the same conclusion: that 'the ancient city' was distinctive and unique and came to an end in Late Antiquity? The danger is this: seen from the perspective of later history, it offers a simplified image of the city in antiquity, one that is fixed. Everything makes the city of antiquity different and unchanging: its religious pluralism, its economic model of town and country, its political constitution, and its physical structure. Yet when we look at each of these aspects in detail, the picture is more complex. If polytheism defines the ancient city, the Christianised city after Constantine no longer counts as 'ancient'. If we insist on the town/country relationship of the Weber/Finley model, we must not only ignore the abundant archaeological evidence for ancient urban commerce but must exaggerate and distort the contrast between antiquity and the Middle Ages. If politics defines the city, we must ignore the evidence of profound political differences between cities so carefully analysed by Aristotle and set up one particular variant propagated by imperial authorities as definitive. If straight streets and grid plans define the ancient city, we must not only explain their absence or limited importance in Athens, Rome, and Constantinople, but also account for the fact that some of the most orthogonal layouts, like that of 'Anjar, are post-antique and Islamic. The

---

[54] Averil Cameron, *Procopius*, p. 112–3.

simplified typology of 'the ancient city' understates its variety, its changes over time, and its ability to adapt to changing circumstances.

The flaw of these approaches is that they depend on a narrative of a lost ideal, except, indeed, with Weber/Finley, for whom the 'consumer city' is a model doomed to failure. That was built into Fustel's invention of the ancient city from the outset. His ideal – of a community built up in stages from a family unit which used shared cult to mark its property – never quite exists: almost from the outset, in archaic Greece and Rome, the ideal is compromised by an endless sequence of social changes and revolutions, which redefine social relations and undermine the religion which binds the community together. What the historical city offers us is a series of remnants of this lost ideal, from which we can reconstruct it, without ever having it simultaneously before our eyes. A. H. M. Jones's political city displays the same 'lost ideal' narrative. Somehow, the ideal stands just outside the narrative, in the Athens of the fifth and fourth centuries (he wrote separately on Athenian democracy). When the narrative opens, with Alexander, the democratic ideal only survives by lip service, and is rapidly eroded; its fate is sealed by Roman conquest (interestingly, Fustel too saw Roman conquest as a critical factor in the demise of his city); and as the Roman state tightens the rules, turning council membership into a hereditary obligation, so the city loses its soul, which is the principal of citizen participation. Yet 900 years stretch between the beginning and the end of this story of decline, and the wonder is that the city manages to retain the patriotic loyalty of its citizens for so long (Jones, like Fustel, saw the role of patriotic spirit as crucial).

Yet all these doubts, and all these difficulties, can be set aside if we cease to talk of 'the ancient city' and talk instead of the city in antiquity – that is, of antiquity as a chapter, or series of chapters, in a longer ongoing story of the city, not as a separate phenomenon. It is possible to think about the city in Classical Antiquity in the context of the phenomenon of urbanisation in a broader chronological and geographical context. As Greg Woolf argues in his account of ancient cities, seen in the context of the cities of Mesopotamia, the Indus Valley, and the Near East, Mediterranean cities are part of a longstanding and widespread phenomenon that is a recurrent feature of human societies, appearing in diverse guises. Mediterranean cities seem both relatively small and late in appearance. They may indeed have distinctive features, but that is no reason to cut them off from a longer history of city-making.[55] The city of antiquity is not a tale of a lost ideal, but

---

[55] Woolf, *The Life and Death of Ancient Cities*. I am grateful to the author for an advanced view of his text.

of a fundamental social, economic, political, and religious phenomenon that changes and develops constantly though time. There is no need to mark off uncompromising periods. The city of Late Antiquity is closer to the city of the early Middle Ages than it is to the city of archaic Greece. The very idea that a human structure should have a coherent duration for more than a millennium strains belief.

The deconstruction of the idea of 'the ancient city' proposed here is necessary in order to address the basic question of this book: how the idea of the city in antiquity affected the idea of the city in the subsequent period. Instead of seeing a collapse or abandonment of ideals, I am interested in continuities and adaptations. Rather than identifying the classical idea of the city with a particular phenomenon, city-governance by a council, city-cased polytheistic cult, or straight streets, we might allow for an evolving complexity; and rather than identifying the adaptations of the subsequent period as collapses of the old ideal, we might see them as adaptations driven by survival in changing circumstances. It is here that an approach focused on resilience may help.

Transformation and Resilience

Peter Brown, with his characteristic talent to evoke a world from an anecdote, used the story of the Seven Sleepers of Ephesus to encapsulate the transformation of the urban world of Late Antiquity.[56] As told by Gregory of Tours at the end of the sixth century on the basis of a Syrian original, the seven young men of Ephesus, persecuted as Christians by the emperor Decius, take refuge in a cave, where they fall asleep. The cave is blocked up and only unblocked by a local shepherd centuries later when Theodosius II is emperor. One of their number, Malchus, deputed to go to town to do their shopping, finds to his astonishment, being convinced that their sleep was simply overnight, that Ephesus is transformed, with a cross over the city gate, men praising Christ in the streets, and churches. At most two centuries separated the persecutions of Decius (who died in AD 251) from the reign of Theodosius II (408–450), but the world had changed profoundly: 'Don't you think you have entered a different city?', Gregory has Malchus exclaim.[57] The tale emphasises the difference brought by

---

[56] Peter Brown, *The Making of Late Antiquity*, p. 1; tellingly cited by Humphries, *Cities and the Meanings of Late Antiquity*, pp. 2–6.

[57] Gregory, *Passio Sanctorum Martyrum Septem Dormientium* ed. Krusch (*MGM SRM 1.2*) p. 401: Putasne, quia in aliam urbem ingressus es?

Christianisation. Yet this does not mean that the Ephesus of Decius in 250 was just the same as it had been since its foundation in the tenth century BC. Had our sleepers disappeared into their cave in the period of Persian control and woken up two centuries later, they might have been equally astonished to find the temple of Artemis ranking as one of the seven wonders of the world. They might have been equally astonished to wake up in Hadrianic Ephesus and find the city full of monuments of Roman taste, like the library of Celsus which tourists today so admire in reconstructed form. Eventually, the sleepers would wake again to find their city under Islamic control.[58] Cities never stand still; change is continuous, and the changes of Late Antiquity were simply the latest in a series.

One way of thinking about the longer-term history of the city is in terms of resilience. Resilience has become a fashionable idea: international movements encourage city authorities to adopt policies which will enhance their chances of bouncing back from natural and man-made catastrophes.[59] In its more sophisticated form, resilience theory is not just about the capacity of cities to recover from disaster and return to the *status quo ante*. It is about adaptation. Rather than a model of flourishing followed by decline and collapse, it sees in the natural world of ecology a cycle, in the form of a continuous loop, between growth and consolidation on the one hand, and adaptation in the face of crisis followed by new growth on the other. Critically, it sees the phase of adaptation as drawing on the past, using memory as a creative tool to build new structures. (The theory is explored in more detail in the final chapter.)

Cities are, or at least can be, resilient. They may be created in specific historical circumstances, but they gain a life of their own that transcends their origins. They respond continuously to changes in the environment. Sometimes those changes are deep shocks – what greater shock to a city than to be sacked? Sometimes they never recover. But the remarkable thing is how often they bounce back, changing themselves to respond to new circumstances, but simultaneously drawing on memories of the past as a resource. If cities are resilient, so is the idea of the city. We can identify long adaptive cycles whereby human societies move between phases of change and adaptation to consolidation to response to change and further adaptation, crucially drawing on memories of the past not from nostalgia but as a means of reformulation.[60] That theory has been fruitfully applied

---

[58] Foss, *Ephesus after Antiquity*.
[59] See the Rockefeller foundation-sponsored 100 Resilient Cities programme: Resilient Cities, Resilient Lives. The relevance of resilience theory is discussed in more detail in Chapter 10.
[60] Redman, 'Resilience theory in archaeology'.

to antiquity, whether by Alan Walmsley looking at Roman and post-Roman Syria, by Greg Woolf looking at the success of the surprisingly small but adaptive city of antiquity, or by Michele Salzman looking at the capacity of Rome and its ruling class to recover from successive shocks.[61]

My aim in the pages that follow is to explore some of the authors of Late Antiquity for whom the city provides an important focus and ask how they drew on past memories. My purpose is not to look at the city as a typology, but as part of a trajectory: a never-ending story in which earlier chapters influence later chapters, in such a way that they may indeed be new but make little sense without the chapters that precede. The question is not whether 'the ancient city' ended or was transformed, but which memories of the cities of antiquity continued to affect the cities which frequently continued in the same footprint. I shall explore a series of writers, chosen because they each have a good deal to say about the city.

My focus is on what contemporaries thought and wrote, their expectations, assumptions, and ideals, rather than on the urban fabric itself; exceptionally, I look at some of the striking number of new cities constructed between the fourth and eighth centuries because of the potential of a new layout, as opposed to a modified and adapted one, to illuminate an urban ideal. One rich source for ideals is the rhetorical tradition of 'praises of cities', *Laudes urbium*, that stretches from Late Antiquity into the Middle Ages: they may be poor guides to the realities of city life, but they are eloquent of a tradition of expectations (Chapter 2). Augustine and other Christian writers have too often been cast as the enemies of the city; a more careful reading of Orosius, Augustine, and Salvian suggests that the City of God, rather than displacing the earthly *civitas*, presupposes and builds on it (Chapter 3). I then explore four authors in whose writings cities are a recurrent theme: Cassiodorus, whose service of the Ostrogothic kings of sixth-century Italy put him on a hinge between the Roman imperial world and the new western world of successor kingdoms (Chapter 4); Procopius, whose histories, panegyric, and criticism of Justinian expose a sixth-century Mediterranean world to which the city remains central (Chapter 5); Gregory of Tours, whose accounts of a sixth- and seventh-century Gaul tormented by the squabbles of Merovingian kings still keeps the city centre stage (Chapter 7); and Isidore of Seville, whose works show a seventh-century bishop deeply involved in the politics of Visigothic Spain trying to show the enduring truth of the classical language of the city

---

[61] Walmsley, *Early Islamic Syria*; Woolf, 'Locating resilience in ancient urban networks'; Salzman, *Falls of Rome*, pp. 17–21 and passim.

(Chapter 8). Chapter 6 explores the potential of documentary papyri from Italy and Francia to illuminate the workings of city life. Resilience, and the process of drawing on memories of the past to adapt to the present, is a theme that runs throughout these chapters, and the final chapter draws together those threads.

2 | In Praise of the City

The idea that the ancient city was different in its essence from the medieval city, in religion, economy, politics, and physical form, is, as I argued in Chapter 1, an invention of modern historiography. There is little trace of it in the accounts of contemporaries, with the exception that the city was seen to have been transformed by Christianisation, though this took place before the end of antiquity with Constantine. The lack of any sense of caesura is tangible in two traditions of representation of the city which are richly documented from antiquity into the Middle Ages: the artistic tradition of depicting a city, and the rhetorical tradition of singing its praises. It is worth examining each of these in more detail. This chapter asks what contemporaries still valued about cities, what struck them as important. Particularly revealing is the lively tradition *of laudes urbium*: praises of cities. I shall examine this tradition to see how it reflects on the great divide between the ancient and medieval cities as constructed by modern scholars examined in Chapter 1: religion, as highlighted by Fustel de Coulanges; the economy, given pride of place by Weber and Finley; street plans and urban fabric, studied by Haverfield and his successors; and the political institutions emphasised by Jones and Liebeschuetz. First, however, it is worth reflecting on the artistic representation of the city.

The Image of the City: Walls Do Not a City Make?

It is sometimes suggested that walls were a feature of the Late Antique and medieval city, in contrast to the unwalled cities of the classical period.[1] Certainly, the instability of the later period led to still-visible walls circuits, like that of Rome itself.[2] The peace of the high empire allowed many cities to spread beyond their walls. But, for all that, walls remained fixed in the imagination as a defining feature of a city.

---

[1] See Tagliata, Courault, and Barker, *City Walls in Late Antiquity*.
[2] See Dey, *The Aurelian Wall*.

Proverbially, in Greek at least, it was not walls but men which made a city. Ancient commentators traced the thought back to the sixth-century lyric poet, Alceaus: ἄνδρες γὰρ πόλιος πύργος ἀρεύιοι – for men are the best wall of a city (122, 35 D). Sophocles, they thought, was echoing this in the *Oedipus Tyrannus* (56–57) when he said that 'neither a wall nor a ship was anything if empty of the men who dwelled within'. Equally, Thucydides had this trope in mind when he put into the mouth of his tragic figure, the general Nicias, who led the Athenians to catastrophic defeat in Sicily, that 'they, the army, *were* the city where they stood . . . for men made a city, and not walls or ships empty of men' (*Histories* 7.77). An Athenian hearing these words was likely to think also of Themistocles, the general who defeated Xerxes' fleet, and had advised the Athenians that the oracle urging them to trust in a wooden wall was referring not to the Acropolis (which they abandoned to be sacked) but to their navy, with which they defeated the Persians at Salamis (Herodotus, *Histories* 7.140–143). Such thoughts echoed down the centuries. The second century AD orator, Aristides, said that 'Themistocles showed that it was true what Alcaeus said of old, and many had repeated since, that neither stones nor wood nor the skills of architects made cities, but the men who knew how to save them.'[3] We have already met this thought in Augustine's essay *De excidio urbis Romae*: 'Do you really think, brothers, that a city is to be found in its walls not its citizens?' (see Chapter 1).

But from Alcaeus to Isidore, the proverb implied its own paradoxical opposite: that if you thought of a 'city', the first thing that came to mind was the walled settlement at its centre. It took the trauma of exile, or Persian invasions, or military defeat at Syracuse, or even the sack of Rome by Alaric, to remind you that when it came to the crunch, walls mattered less than the people they were supposed to protect. Plato in his *Laws* (6.778D–E) suggested that the ideal city would have no walls, since the courage of the inhabitants was the best defence. He was thinking of the wall-less Sparta. Aristotle, in the *Politics*, acknowledged that some thought that the ideal city should not have walls, because its citizens should come out to defend it. Aristotle reckoned this opinion to be old-fashioned and impracticable: it would not work against a superior enemy and could not

---

[3] Aristides, *On the four best Athenians* 2.273 (Dindorf). This was accepted as a verbal citation of Alcaeus in the Loeb edition by J. Edmonds of 1923 as frag. 30, but used more cautiously as a testimonial in the later edition by Campbell as frag. 426. Similarly Edmonds saw Aristides 1.821 as a fragment of Alcaeus (no. 28), whereas others reject it. But his translation – 'Not houses finely roofed or the stones of walls well-builded, nay nor canals and dockyards, make the city, but men able to use their opportunity' – has gained wide currency, especially on the internet, as a genuine Alcaeus quote.

survive the technological advances of modern siege warfare. What was needed was well-designed defences (*Politics* 7. 11, 1330b33–1331a9). Three centuries later, Vitruvius entirely concurred about the importance of well-designed walls (*On Architecture* 1.5).

Not only were city walls a practical necessity, ancient thought regarded them as the reason for the existence of the city.[4] So Cicero draws on what was a standard view of the emergence of civilisation, most clearly as an aside in his defence of Sestius: men once lived scattered across the landscape with no civil law until

> they congregated in a single place and converted people from savagery to justice and domestication. It was then that they fenced with walls (*moenibus saepserunt*) for shared benefit what we call *res publicae*, made gatherings of men that we call *civitates*, joined together their houses in what we call *urbes*, and discovered divine and human justice. (*pro Sestio* 91–92)[5]

Greek and Roman thought saw the city as the root of civilisation. Moreover, the invention of walled cities is assumed to be a universal human achievement, not something specific to Greeks or Romans. Indeed, 'first inventors' was a topic that fascinated some, and the elder Pliny offers an extensive list of the first inventors of all sorts of advances. Naturally there are many Greek names among these. However, Pliny observes, the Egyptians were there long before and their earliest city is called Diospolis: the City of God (*Natural History* 7.57). That reflects the general observation that Greek and Roman sources do not regard the city as something specific to their own civilisation, but as a universal human phenomenon which they too embrace. On the other hand, as the scheme of development implies, the city distinguishes them from the barbarian, and the lack of cities, together with the lack of technological advance, 'the arts', justice and legal systems, are a universal feature of barbarity. The city is the mark of civilisation, and walls are the mark of a city. That is reflected in ancient representations of the city.

Walls were indeed the defining feature of the city of the imagination.[6] A marble relief from Avezzano (perhaps first century AD and celebrating the draining of the lake under Claudius) shows vividly the distinction

---

[4] See the passages collected by Lovejoy and Boas, *Primitivism and Related Ideas in Antiquity*; Ottewill-Soulsby, 'First cities'.
[5] See also *de officiis* 2.3.15: urbes vero sine hominum coetu non potuissent nec aedificari nec frequentari ex quo leges moresque constituti.
[6] See Van der Graaff, *The Fortifications of Pompeii*, pp. 37–41.

between the countryside, with its trees and fields and animals, together with buildings, perhaps a villa and a sanctuary, and the city, perhaps Alba Fucens near which it was found, as an imposing wall circuit with a central gate, and behind it a regular grid of streets with densely packed houses (Figure 2.1). The tempting parallel is with Ambrogio Lorenzetti's *Allegory of Good and Bad Government*, painted for the Palazzo Pubblico of Siena in 1338/9 (Figure 2.2). To the left, the city, with its fine pinkish walls,

Figure 2.1 The Avezzano Relief: relief representing a walled city, Collezione Torlonia, Castello Piccolomini (Celano AQ), n. inv. 67504. Courtesy of the Ministero della Cultura, Direzione Regionale Musei Abruzzo; unauthorized use, reproduction or alteration is prohibited.

Figure 2.2 Ambrogio Lorenzetti, Allegorie e Effetti del Buono e del Cattivo Governo in città e in campagna, 1338, Palazzo Pubblico, Siena, photo Roberto Testi, © Comune di Siena.

containing a jumble of houses on several stories (no neat parallel roads here, for it is Siena). But it has what the Avezzano relief lacks: a busy scene of people enjoying the life of the well-governed city. To the right stretches the well-governed and well-tended countryside. The nobles ride out, perhaps to one of the villas glimpsed in the background, while the peasants bring their produce in to market and others till the fields. A river runs through the rolling Tuscan hills. Lorenzetti's image is more elaborate and, crucially, is peopled, for men not walls, one might say, make government, but the imagined contrast of town and country is remarkably similar.

We can find a different approach to representing the contrast of city and countryside in the illustrations in the manuscripts that accompany the works of the Roman land surveyors.[7] The manuscripts may be medieval, but they were evidently an essential accompaniment to the text and are likely to go back to the original editions. When cities are represented in these illustrations, they are invariably shown as a set of fortified walls, with nothing inside unless the roads that form part of the system. The most vivid example is preserved by the Vatican manuscript *Palatinus* 1564 (Figure 2.3). It shows a Roman colony, labelled as Colonia Augusta, set in a landscape of plains, mountains, rivers, and other settlements. All these elements are represented symbolically rather than realistically. The symbol for the Colonia shows a long wall of polygonal circuit (Vitruvius would approve) articulated by numerous towers with turrets. It is so distinguished from the neighbouring Oppidum, taken to be a native settlement predating the colony, smaller but also walled on a square plan. To the other side of the colony is a Praefectura, a unit of jurisdiction subject to the colony but beyond its territory, rendered as a small square fortress. Walls are thus the distinguishing feature of any settlement, not just a city: they formed a hierarchy in a landscape of sinuous rivers and equally sinuous roads.[8]

While depictions of cities are relatively common in medieval Italian art, as Chiara Frugoni's *A Distant City* showed, they are relatively rare in classical art.[9] But when we find them, it is the walls that mark out the city. A fine 'bird's eye' view from the house of Sacerdos Amandus in Pompeii shows Daedalus watching his son Icarus plunge to his death; in the background is a city, seen as a wall circuit with towers and

---

[7] See Campbell, *The Writings of the Roman Land Surveyors*.
[8] See Chouquer and Favory, *Les arpenteurs romains*, pp. 59–63; Tarpin, 'Strangers in Paradise'.
[9] See also Bertelli, 'Visual images of the town'.

Figure 2.3 Corpus Agrimensorum, Hyginus Gromaticus, centuriated city and country. From the Carolingian manuscript Palatinus 1564, by permission of the Vatican Apostolic Library, all rights reserved.

battlements, broken by gates, and a hint of buildings within (Figure 2.4). One of the most remarkable Roman depictions of a city was found on the walls of a building on the Colle Oppio in Rome, buried, together with Nero's Golden House, by Trajan's later construction of baths (Figure 2.5). Recovered in 2000, it caused a flutter of excitement in

Figure 2.4 Fall of Icarus, detail with imaginary city from House of Sacerdos Amandus, Pompeii, excavation photo of 1925, Courtesy Parco Archeologico di Pompei Archivio Fotografico.

Rome: was it the Eternal City itself? The answer proved to be negative, and, despite various suggested candidates, it may be no more than an imaginary city. The defining feature is the wall circuit, with battlements and gates. Beyond is the blue water of the sea or a river; within is a theatre in the left foreground, a temple, and other less distinct buildings.[10]

Again, we may be struck by a medieval parallel, in a depiction of Verona (Figure 2.6). Apparently commissioned by the tenth-century bishop of Verona, Ratherius (Rathier or Rather),[11] it may have been based on earlier depictions; the form in which it survives is as two eighteenth-century

---

[10] La Rocca, 'L'affresco con veduta di città'.
[11] Rather's complex career and mannered style is well brought out by Auerbach, *Literary Language and Its Public*, pp. 133–152. For more recent discussion, see van Renswoude, 'The sincerity of fiction'.

Figure 2.5 Imaginary city, fresco from house on Colle Oppio, Rome. Courtesy Eugenio La Rocca.

Figure 2.6 Iconographia Rateriana, bird's eye view of Verona. Copy by Scipione Maffei, cod. 106, Courtesy of the Fondazione Biblioteca Capitolare di Verona.

copies, one by Scipione Maffei, reassuringly similar, for the original is now lost. As in the Colle Oppio frieze, it is a wall circuit, with tall towers and battlements and a series of gates that define the city. Through it flows sinuously the river Atiesis (Adige), traversed by a handsome marble bridge, labelled Pons Marmoreus. A variety of buildings are picked out within the walls, including to the left (another coincidental parallel with the Colle Oppio frieze) Verona's famous Arena, labelled Theatrum, while on the steep hill on the far side of the river is the Roman theatre, this time labelled Arena Minor. There are of course churches, whereas the Colle Oppio shows temples, much alike at this scale, including some extra-mural sanctuaries. Whether or not this is a convincing representation of early medieval Verona, the pictorial language is strikingly similar. Above all, the city is unimaginable without its wall circuit.[12]

That much is true in representations on a smaller scale, like the famous image of Jerusalem on the sixth-century mosaic from St George's church in Madaba in Jordan: the oval circuit of walls describes the city, with battlements, towers, and gates; inside, the great colonnaded Cardo gives the horizontal axis, flanked by a cluster of churches and houses (Figure 2.7). At

Figure 2.7 The Madaba map of Jerusalem, Church of St George, Madaba, Jordan. FLHCAA1/Alamy Stock Photo.

---

[12] The image is the subject of detailed discussion in Arzone and Napione, *La più antica veduta di Verona*; contributors remain divided as to the date of the original.

an allegorical level was the tradition of personifications of the Fortune or *Tychē* of a city, most famously Antioch on the Orontes: a large female figure wears a mural crown, walls, battlements, towers, and a central gate (Figure 2.8). The *Tychē* of Antioch, the third-century BC original by Eutychides (his name evoked good fortune), was a much-admired piece: note that if the crowned head suggests the city of Antioch itself, the rest of her body, with the sheaf of wheat she carries, suggests the fertile territory; the rock on which she sits, Mount Sipylus; and the male figure at her feet, the river Orontes.[13] It well evokes the way a *polis* was conceived as the whole territory, the urban settlement its controlling centre.

Figure 2.8 Personification of Antioch by Eutychides. Cambridge Museum of Classical Archaeology, cast 1349 of original in Vatican Museum, photo Susanne Turner.

---

[13] See Richter, *Three Critical Periods in Greek Sculpture*, p. 22.

In a word, and despite Alcaeus and his imitators, it was precisely walls which made a city in the ancient imagination, and in a tradition that continued directly into the Middle Ages.[14] Indeed, there were examples of cities that did not have walls, such as (as we will see) Cassiodorus' native Squillace, but these were the exception that proved the rule. Equally, there were wall circuits around places that did not count as cities, typically defined as *castra*, forts. The two could be hard to distinguish: Strabo described Herculaneum as a fort, φρούριον (5.4.8), though by then in the late first century BC it was already an independent city, a *municipium*. They differed not only in size but in status, and, as Alcaeus or Isidore might have pointed out, what was lacking in a *castrum* was the larger human population, the *multitudo hominum* of the *cives* who made a *civitas*. A defensive circuit was not enough on its own to define a city, but it was the first thing that sprang to mind when you thought of a city.

Laudes Urbium

If we want to understand how ancient thinking about the city fed into that of the Middle Ages, the richest source is the tradition of Praises of Cities, *Laudes Urbium*. A longstanding tradition of work by medievalists, notably by Paul Oldfield, has gathered numerous examples of such 'praises' spanning the medieval period; it has also shown the deep roots of this tradition in classical literature, and especially in the rhetorical tradition.[15] With the earliest examples in Late Antiquity, and a modestly growing number between the eighth and eleventh centuries, concentrated in Italy (Verona, Milan, Aquileia, Modena, Naples) but also beyond (Metz and York), this becomes a flood in the twelfth and thirteenth centuries, again with Italy prominent, but with examples from France, Germany, England, Spain, and Portugal.[16] The peak coincides, for obvious reasons, with a period of exceptional growth and prosperity for European cities, and a growth, so

---

[14] *Pace* Cristina La Rocca, 'Urban change in Northern Italy', esp. 163–165, who follows Cracco Ruggini in seeing walls as a Late Antique phenomenon.

[15] Oldfield, *Urban Panegyric and the Transformation of the Medieval City*. The tradition has been of particular interest to Italian scholars studying the medieval city: notably Hyde, 'Medieval descriptions of cities'; Fasoli, 'La coscienza civica nelle "*Laudes Civitatum*"'; Frugoni, *A Distant City*, ch. 2; Romagnoli, 'La coscienza civica nella città comunale italiana'. Note also the useful student textbook of Fasoli and Bocchi, *La città medievale italiana*, which assembles many relevant passages. Ruth, *Urban Honor in Spain*, offers a thorough review of the classical background. More recently, see Welton, 'The city speaks'.

[16] Oldfield, *Urban Panegyric*, ch.1, for a roundup. Ruth, *Urban Honor*, adds numerous examples from Iberia.

it is argued, of 'civic consciousness', though the Lowlands, which certainly shared in the economic boom, but had more distant ties to the urbanism of the Roman past, does not share in this literary tradition.[17] Indeed, if there is a danger in casting the net ever wider, it is that every text that mentions cities is brought into the catch, like the splendid account by William of Malmesbury, which, in surveying the bishops of England, the *Gesta Pontificum Anglorum*, offers thumbnail sketches of a wide range of *civitates*, *oppida*, and *villae*, some of which, like Glastonbury, have little to be said for them ('a village situated in a secluded spot in the marshes ... It affords pleasure neither by its situation nor its beauty').[18]

What holds the majority of these *laudes* together, and provides a clear thread from antiquity into the Middle Ages, is the role of the rhetorical tradition in structuring them. Rhetorical prescriptions for how to praise an individual, and probably also a city, went back to Hellenistic manuals, and prescriptions for praising cities are found in Greek rhetorical manuals and Quintilian.[19] But instructions reach a new level of explicitness in the high empire, when training in epideictic rhetoric became a vital asset for civic life, and occasions multiplied, like arrivals of governors, city festivals, and so on, when florid praise was required both of individuals and of the cities themselves.[20]

The fullest examples we have are in the two treatises transmitted in the name of Menander Rhetor, though clearly by two different authors, neither of whom may actually have been called Menander.[21] Treatise I (p. 346, ll. 26ff.) sets out the basic four-part framework – position, origin, actions, and accomplishments – and elaborates on the first of these at some length. Position covers climate (heat, cold, seasons, including seasonal produce), proximity to the sea, plains, mountains, and rivers (urging wisely that if, for instance, the city is remote from the sea, one should stress the advantages for security of such remoteness). Treatise II focuses on how to greet an arriving governor. The speaker is urged to start with his own personal enthusiasm for the city he loves; move on to an encomium of the founder (unless he happens to be an

---

[17] Oldfield, *Urban Panegyric*, pp. 14–20. Verhulst *The Rise of Cities*, on the lack of connection of the urban tradition in the Lowlands with the Roman past.

[18] Edited and translated by Winterbottom, *Oxford Medieval Texts: William of Malmesbury*; for Glastonbury, book 2, ch. 91.

[19] Ps.-Dionysius, *Ars* 257.6–19, Quintilian, *Institutio Oratoria* 3.8. On this tradition, see Russell and Wilson, *Menander Rhetor*, pp. xi–xxxiv.

[20] On adventus ceremonies, see MacCormack, *Art and Ceremony in Late Antiquity*; Dey, *Afterlife of the Roman City*.

[21] Russell and Wilson, *Menander Rhetor* for text and commentary, pp. xi–xiii, on doubts about authorship.

unpopular emperor); next to praise the climate and situation, plains, rivers, harbours, and mountains; then to the hinterland and its crops; and then to the customs of the inhabitants – remembering all the time to repeat as a refrain his passionate love for the city.

There will have been many other variants on the theme, including the *Progymnasmata* of Hermogenes, which were abridged in Latin by Priscian and thus influential in the Latin west. Such instructions are found in an eighth-century Lombard manuscript, perhaps deriving from the rhetorician Theon:[22]

> The first praise of cities should furnish the dignity of the founder and it should include praise of distinguished men and also gods, just as Athens is said to have been established by Minerva: and they shall seem true rather than fabulous. The second [theme] concerns the form of fortifications and the site, which is either inland or maritime and in the mountains or in the plane. The third concerns the fertility of the lands, the bountifulness of the springs, the habits of the inhabitants. Then concerning its ornaments, which afterwards should be added, or its good fortune, if things had developed unaided or had occurred by virtue, weapons and warfare. We shall also praise it if that city has many noble men, by whose glory it shall provide light for the whole world. We should also be accustomed for praise to be shaped by neighbouring cities, if ours is greater, so that we protect others, or if lesser, so that by the light of neighbours we are illuminated. In these things also we shall briefly make comparison.

Given the rhetorical roots of the genre, one might be reasonably suspicious of how reliable a guide such *Laudes* could be to the historical realities of cities, or even of their underlying ideals. Exaggeration, at least in so far as it falls short of the absurd, is the standard fare of rhetoric. And even if we discount exaggeration, the concern might be that the tramlines of a prescriptive genre might lead to the reproduction of an outdated idea of the city that no longer made sense. But as Oldfield observes, no form of historical writing is without its difficulties, and the fact that encomium might form part of the performative ritual of civic life made it essential to adapt to changing realities. A set list of topics by no means dictates the use to which they were put, which proves to be remarkably varied and flexible.[23]

---

[22] *Rhetores Latini Minores* (ed. C. Halm, Frankfurt 1964), p. 587. I am grateful to Sam Ottewill-Soulsby for reference and translation. Cited by Fasoli, 'La coscienza cittadina'; Frugoni, *Distant City*, p. 54. Granier, 'La *renovatio* du modèle rhétorique antique', examines the manuscript tradition of this fragment, questioning direct influence on surviving compositions of the period.

[23] Oldfield, *Urban Panegyric*, ch. 2, pp. 36–60.

Two general observations about this long tradition of urban writing may be made at once. The first is a sense of continuity or community across time in the image of the city. The second is how explicitly later cities are praised with reference to antiquity. It is not just that the praises are written in Latin (there is a parallel Greek tradition too, of which similar points may be made)[24] with conscious reference to Classical texts (above all, of course, Virgil). It is that cities are presented as shaped by their histories. The Roman-ness, or at least antiquity, of their foundations, is brought out, and where there are no historical foundations to lay claim to, mythical foundations are invented that give them the antiquity they lack: Venice was founded not in Late Antiquity by refugees from Attila's sack of Aquileia (the Venetian myth), but by a Trojan ancestor, Antenor;[25] on the account of Geoffrey of Monmouth, London (despite the solid Roman origins of Londinium) was founded by Brutus, on that of William Fitz Stephen by King Lud who preceded the foundation of Rome.[26] Historical buildings from antiquity are not so much a forgotten layer of stratigraphy but part of the present reality. Just as the Arena of Verona with its opera festival is part of the physical reality of contemporary Verona, so the great 'labyrinth' was part of the reality of medieval Verona.

Above all, ancient Rome itself is the ultimate city against which to measure your city: it is a 'second Rome' – *altera Roma* or *secunda Roma*, a worthy competitor to ancient Rome, a claim made explicitly for Aachen, Milan, Naples, Pavia, Reims, Tournai, and Trier,[27] or, as in the case of Florence, a *parvula Roma*. In a word, antiquity is not so much a foreign country as a familiar part of the present landscape.

Unexpectedly, the surviving genre of city praises is not strictly classical, but picks up in Late Antiquity together with the rhetorical manuals. As Carl-Joachim Classen showed, there are plenty of passages in classical Greek and Latin literature which speak enthusiastically about ancient cities, but not according to the sort of formula recommended by the teachers of rhetoric. So Thucydides gives Pericles a memorable speech of praise for Athens, but in terms of its democratic institutions, not its physical reality. Rome is endlessly evoked by Latin poets, especially in its mythical foundations: contemporary reality is there to point a contrast.[28] The elder Pliny, by

---

[24] See Saradi, *The Byzantine City in the Sixth Century*, pp. 49–101. I am grateful to the author for advice and help.
[25] Oldfield, *Urban Panegyric*, p. 173. Beneš, *Urban Legends* well brings out the competitive invention of Roman origins in the creation of civic identity.
[26] Oldfield, *Urban Panegyric*, p. 179.
[27] See, for the theme, Hammer, 'The concept of the new or second Rome'; Oldfield, *Urban Panegyric*, ch. 8; Beneš, *Urban Legends*, p. 13.
[28] See Edwards, *Writing Rome*.

contrast, expatiates on the statistics of the physical city, the length of walls and roads, and the number of *vici* (*Natural Histories* 36.101–125), and so initiates a tradition of the *mirabilia Romae*, the wonders of Rome, which will lead to the Late Antique Regionary Catalogues of both Rome and Constantinople, and to the medieval tradition of the Einsiedeln itinerary or the *Mirabilia* of Magister Gregorius.[29] But though all these authors introduce key topics that characterise the *Laudes Urbium*, it is quite clear that they do not have a rhetorical model before their eyes, or at least not the model that was to become so influential.[30]

The *Antiochicus*, an explicit panegyric of his native Antioch by the fourth-century rhetorician Libanius, delivered in AD 356, is the traditional place to start;[31] rightly so, as it is an exceptionally clear example of the genre, though it is the only example of a Greek panegyric normally considered by historians of the medieval west, despite being part of a rich eastern tradition.[32] Libanius understood the rules of panegyric inside out: not only was he a performer of rhetoric (a 'sophist'), but a professor, paid by the city to teach his skills to students, and consequently immune from local tax burdens. After a career that saw him move from his native Antioch to Athens and to Constantinople, he returned in 354, shortly before giving this speech.[33] It is the longest and most detailed specimen of the genre, only matched in the thirteenth century by Bonvesin de la Riva's account of Milan, *De Magnalibus Mediolani*. But it sets out the topics which will recur in shorter form in city panegyric after panegyric.[34]

He starts (sections 1–11) by establishing his patriotic credentials. He has been asked by his city to make this speech, and, as a native, it is his patriotic duty to comply, though it is more of a challenge not to fall short of the occasion. The first topic he must address is countryside and climate (12–41). Antioch, needless to say, enjoys an ideal situation ('my native city is the fairest thing in the fairest land under the heaven', 16), with a temperate climate and fertile land, with wheat in abundance, and wine and olive oil to

---

[29] See McKitterick, *Rome and the Invention of the Papacy*, p. 62; Osborne, *The Marvels of Rome*; Walser, *Die Einsiedler Inschriftensammlung*.

[30] So Classen, *Die Stadt im Spiegel der Descriptiones und Laudes Urbium*, pp. 4–16. Ruth, *Urban Honor*, pp. 37–94, casts the net wider, but Classen's point holds.

[31] So Fasoli, 'Coscienza cittadina'; Oldfield, *Urban Panegyric*, p. 23. Classen, *Die Stadt*, pp. 18–22 notes Dio Chrysostom and Aelius Aristides as Libanius' predecessors in the Greek tradition. For an English translation of *Oration* 11, see Norman, *Antioch as a Centre of Hellenic Culture*.

[32] The Greek tradition is excellently studied by Saradi, *The Byzantine City*. On the hagiographical tradition, see her 'The city in Byzantine hagiography'.

[33] Liebeschuetz, *Antioch*, pp. 1–16.

[34] For text and Italian translation, see Chiesa, *Bonvesin da la Riva*; for discussion, see Oldfield, 'To destroy a city so great and remarkable'.

export. The proximity of the sea ensures that numerous merchant ships ply their trade; at the same time, not being situated on the coast saves Antioch from the bustle and vulgarity of a port city (34–41): precisely the sort of argument the first treatise of 'Menander Rhetor' urged.

The next topic is foundation and history, on which he expounds at length (42–162). After dealing with mythological background, he turns to the historical founder, Alexander's successor, Seleucus Nicator, though he cannot resist hinting that Alexander *would have* founded the city had he not been distracted by his campaign, and did at least built a fountain to celebrate the water sweet as his mother's milk (72–75). Seleucus selects the site, spurning the nearby Antigonia established by his rival, Antigonos the One-Eyed, in obedience to a divine portent: an eagle that takes the sacrificial meat and drops it where the city was to be built; foundations should be not merely of historical interest, but show divine intervention and approval (84–91). He has a good deal more to say about Seleucus and his successors (79–130), but, strikingly, passes in a single sentence (130) over the last four centuries of Roman control that had seen Antioch become the key for Roman campaigns in the East. What matters is not the recent past but the deep history that gives Antioch its identity.

Next, he turns to the inhabitants, the ruling elite of the council (*boulē*), the citizen population (*dēmos*), and the non-citizen immigrants (132–180). What he offers is, as he was well conscious, an ideal. The *boulē* is manned by men whose deep patriotism is reflected in their ancestral descent, grandfathers and great-grandfathers who had also been councillors. Such is their dedication to their city that they undertake municipal burdens even if exempted by imperial service (134–138) – a claim made more astonishing by the sequence of Libanian orations that complain to the emperor about rich people who try to evade local burdens through the imperial service, or worse, in the eyes of one on whom the teaching of Greek oratory conveyed exemption, by studying Roman law in Berytus.[35] Together with this ideal council goes an ideal citizen body, composed of fathers of families with furnished property (such is his rosy image of the citizen, 151), who cheerfully follow wherever the council leads – again, a bold claim in a city renowned for its riots. With sublime rhetorical skill, he turns an episode which might have undermined this picture to the city's credit: the usurpation of Eugenius (157–162). He depicts the population spontaneously putting down the usurper and his troops, working men leaving their workshops to fight, women hurling tiles from roofs. What goes unsaid,

[35] Liebeschuetz, *Antioch*, pp. 167–192, on the theme of the flight of councillors.

but was surely present to his audience, is that the council was considered by the emperor Diocletian to have been too tardy in its suppression of the revolt, and councillors including Libanius' own grandfather and uncle were heavily punished by confiscation of their estates. To this rosy picture is added that of immigration: you can find people from all over the world in Antioch, who chose this city in preference to the cities of their birth, so competing with the famous openness of Athens to immigrants (163–169). The consequence is a dense population (beyond counting, like the sands of the desert), though this places no strain on the food supply – a hopeful claim, in that food shortages were a principal cause of rioting (169–174). There is no problem billeting troops for the Persian wars, which makes our city the emperor's favourite city (177–180). Among the foreigners who flock to Antioch are students of rhetoric, Libanius' own students, and his city competes with Athens, which excels in philosophy as does Antioch in oratory (181–195) – Libanius speaks not without experience, having previously taught rhetoric in Athens.

Now Libanius turns to physical fabric (196–229), provocatively claiming that it is the largest city in the world – he says nothing here of Constantinople or Alexandria, let alone Rome (196). The feature to which he draws emphatic attention is the great colonnaded main street, forming a spine along its length – too long to measure, he claims, but its three kilometres were indeed impressive (196–202).[36] It is notable that he does *not* start the physical description of the city from its walls, as do so many *Laudes*, though he does indeed describe the circle of walls with pillars for battlements that surround the 'New City' on the island (204–206). This seems to be a deliberate rhetorical omission, following the principle of praising what is most distinctive in your city, and at the end, in comparing his city to others, he concedes that 'if she be inferior to any in respect of her walls, yet she surpasses that town in her supply of water etc.' (270). The colonnaded spine is the glory of the urban fabric. Libanius, no more than any other classical author, does not speak of a 'grid', but of a central route off which lead smaller alleys (he has no need to say 'at right angles'). He spurns cities which boast of a square plan, only possible in a city of small dimensions, whereas the sheer scale of Antioch means it has no single geometrical design (209). The great advantage of the colonnades is that they allow circulation in the city in all weathers (213–217). Compared to his enthusiasm for colonnades, his mention of the major monuments, hippodrome, theatre, and baths may seem surprisingly cursory (218–221).

[36] For maps of Antioch, see Chapter 10.

To the theme of the colonnade the speech will return, but first Libanius underlines a factor that the ancients regarded as essential for the health of a city: air circulation. The zephyrs blow gently along the main street, which he has said runs west to east (198) – more accurately, southwest to northeast – in such a way as to refresh all houses, the three-storeyed houses of the rich and the humble dwellings of the poor alike (222–226). Libanius may not know the debate among medical authorities that we find reflected in Vitruvius as to whether a city layout should minimise or maximise air circulation,[37] and, having misled us about precise orientation, he needs no Vitruvian anxieties about precise angles: the Zephyrs blow, and they are ideal.

So ideal is Antioch that it grows boundlessly: it is a permanent building site as new houses spring up in old vegetable gardens (227). Indeed, the city would be even larger were it not for three disastrous earthquakes: in consequence, he says, in remarkable anticipation of the excavations of the Princeton Expedition, wherever you dig in the city, you find remains of older buildings (229).[38] Just as his account of the foundation shows concern for historical depth, his description of urban fabric shows concern for stratigraphic depth. He now moves on to the suburbs (230–239). The town/country symbiosis of an ancient city comes out in his description of the villages around Antioch, populous enough to have markets of their own (230). In particular, he sings the beauties of Daphne, with its villas and streams and gardens, though what struck the Princeton Expedition was not the gardens but the mosaics. For Libanius, the most important thing about Daphne is its springs, which ensure a never-failing water supply for the city (240–248). The health of an ancient city depended on the twin factors of water supply and air circulation.

Comparison of the advantages of different quarters of the city allows Libanius to return to the colonnade and embrace the theme of commerce. There is not just one shopping quarter: the whole city is an enormous *agora* (249–259). No street is so mean that the inhabitants do not find shops nearby, and every luxury is available all over. The colonnade ensures that every house has a market stall facing it: not an inch of the colonnade is without a craft, and 'if anyone gets hold of a square yard or two on the edge, it straightaway becomes a tailor's shop or something like that, and they hang on to their stall like grim death' (254). The image of the city as a great

---

[37] Vitruvius, *de Architectura* 1.6.1–3. See my discussion in 'Ancient ideals and modern interpretations'.

[38] For the Princeton Expedition, see De Giorgi and Ager, *Antioch: A History*, and Chapter 10 of this book (pp. 380–1).

bazaar, and the competition for every square inch of public space, invites us to rethink the contrast with the suqs of the Islamic city (see Chapter 9).[39] Economic prosperity is further boosted by the river and lake, with a rich supply of fish: while the rich eat sea fish, the poor eat freshwater fish (260–262). The river promotes transport of the produce of the countryside to the town. It also links to the harbour, attracting traffic from across the Mediterranean, from Africa, Europe, and Asia, islands and highlands (263–264).

The speech winds up with a recapitulation of the theme that Antioch surpasses all other cities, touching too on the theme of diversity: everyone profits from being here, whether a financier, a professor of rhetoric, or a lover. There is something for all (268). Indeed, one may think of the speech as a whole as a demonstration of how the city unites diverse elements: economically it unites city and country, commerce and agriculture; socially it unites (or claims to unite) elite and masses, rich and poor (who all get to eat fish, a theme oddly recurrent in other *Laudes*); architecturally, it creates communication between public and private, the grand colonnades and monuments with the private housing, the rich in their three-storeyed buildings, the poor in their humble dwellings. One key element of diversity may be thought to be missing: that of religion. Antioch was a city of Christians and Jews as well as pagans; but it is only the pagan gods that are present in Libanius, whether in the city's foundation or the shrine of Apollo at Daphne. The Christian cult of St Babylas, to whom the Caesar Gallus built a sanctuary at Daphne in 351, which proved the source of major pagan–Christian rioting in Libanius' time, is buried in silence. His fellow Antiochene, John Chrysostom, would take a very different line, as would John of Antioch, patriarch of the city a century later.

Libanius' speech is helpful because it helps us to recognise recurrent topics in more compressed form in later writings. His virtual contemporary, Ausonius of Burdigala (Bordeaux), may count as a western mirror image of Libanius: also a teacher of rhetoric, and tutor to the future emperor Gratian, who rewarded him with the consulship of 379.[40] Later in life Ausonius took to writing, with considerable fluency, occasional poems, including some thematic series, like the twelve Caesars, or the Professors (teachers of rhetoric and grammar) of Bordeaux; of these, the most famous is his Ordo Urbium Nobilium, a rank order of the top Roman cities. At least, a rank order is what it professes to be, rather like the bureaucratic catalogues and lists so familiar from Late Antiquity, but

[39] See Liebeschuetz, *Antioch*, 55–56.   [40] See Green, *The Works of Ausonius*.

another way of thinking of it is as a praise poem of his own city, Burdigala, the last and certainly not the least in his Ordo. Among the twenty cities mentioned, we encounter typical elements of the *Laudes Urbium*.

Golden Rome tops the list, as almost goes without saying, and is dismissed in a single hexametre. Next, Constantinople and Carthage compete for second place: Carthage plays the card of antiquity, with Dido as founder and the Punic name of Byrsa, and Constantinople trumps with Constantine as founder, though this too in an ancient foundation, as Byzantium. Ausonius declares a draw, and we note the importance of the topic of foundation. Next Antioch and Alexandria compete, with matching Macedonian founders, Alexander and Seleucus – like each other in their tendency to riot, but contrasting in situation, one in the fertile recesses of the Nile valley, the other a bulwark against the Persians. Another draw. Trier takes sixth place as the major military base of the Rhine frontier: the features picked out are the walls that surround its long hill, the river Moselle slipping by (subject of Ausonius' finest poem), and the distant commerce it enables, *longiqua omnigenae vestans commercia terrae*.

Milan takes next place, and finally we have a list of buildings: cultured homes, *domus*, double walls, popular entertainments, circus and theatre, palace, mint and baths, and colonnades adorned with marble statuary (*marmoreis ornata peristyla signis*), and a city wall circuit with a great embankment. The shadow of Rome (*vicinia Romae*) does nothing to diminish the grandeur of the buildings. Capua comes in at number 8, though reliant mainly on its history, especially in the Punic wars, as an old rival to Rome (*Roma altera quondam*). Aquileia is famed for its walls and harbour, but especial credit is given to its role in the defeat of the usurper Maximus in 388. Ausonius forbears to mention that Maximus was responsible for the death of his pupil Gratian in 383. Arles, number ten, is the little Rome of Gaul, *Gallula Roma*: split by the Rhône, its bridge is its main street, *mediam plateam*, and its role is as a commercial hub for Gaul and Aquitaine.

Spain has been overlooked to this point: bringing in Seville (Hispalis), Corduba, Tarraco, and Braga in the next four places with five lines between them scarcely compensates. It is only too clear that Ausonius' focus is on Gaul and Italy. Athens is rather nonchalantly tossed in at fifteenth place, noting its double contribution to culture, to olive cultivation and Greek literature. Sicily is allowed two entries – Catania (Catina) and Syracuse – mentioned only for their mythical foundation. Ausonius can now return to Gaul and warms to his theme. Toulouse (Tolosa) deserves next place as his own alma mater (*altricem*): he picks out its situation, on the Garonne between the Pyrenees and the Cevennes, and its constantly growing population that expands it with four additional suburbs, *quadruplices urbes*. Narbonne (Narbo), to which twenty-one lines are dedicated, is the longest and the most enthusiastic entry so far. As the capital of Provincia nostra, Provence, and then Gallia Narbonensis, it covers a vast terrain. It rejoices in ports, mountains, and lakes. Its architectural assets include a temple of Parian marble that rivals the Capitoline. Its boast is a vast commerce that stretches to Africa and Sicily: her ships cross the whole world (*toto tibi navigat orbe cataplus*).

Narbonne is a mere warm-up act for Bordeaux, which, in bringing up the twentieth and last place, puts itself ambiguously at an inverted top position (*capite ... ancipiti*). Its forty-one hexametres make it twice the length of the lines for Narbonne, itself twice any other. And he starts with an apology to his *patria* that in a failure of piety he has not mentioned it before, despite its fame for wine, rivers, and people. The small size of the city prevented him mentioning it earlier, but now he can truly wax lyrical. Situation first: not the barbarous Rhine, but clement climes and rich and well-watered lands: the spring is long and the winters mild, and the vines covering the hillsides ripple like the waves of the sea. Then the urban fabric: foursquare walls with towers so high that their pinnacles reach to the clouds. The street layout is admirable, the disposition of the houses and broad streets, *plateae*, that deserve the name, while the crossroads correspond to the gates. A spring-fed stream flows through the town: the fountain house of Parian marble, with waters of medical properties, inspires Ausonius to fifteen lines of exclamation (more than he dedicates to most other cities in their entirety), including acknowledgement of the Celtic deity to which it is dedicated, Devona.

Finally, he can wind up with a detailed comparison – what the rhetoricians call a *synkrisis* – with Rome. Burdigala is his *patria*, yet Rome trumps all home cities:

> Haec patria est: patrias sed Roma supervenit omnes.
> Diligo Burdigalam, Romam colo; civis in hac sum,
> consul in ambabus; cunae hic, ibi sella curulis

(39–41)

He loves Burdigala, reveres Rome; is a citizen in one (Burdigala) but a consul in both (he held high office in his local senate as well as in Rome). One represents his cradle, the other his peak of achievement, his curule chair.

The ingenuity of this composition lies in distributing the classic topics of the *laus urbium* among all twenty cities, in accordance with the advice that if your city is famous for one thing and not another, then emphasise its advantages. You do not praise all cities for the same things, you look for local advantage. Bordeaux does not win on size, it is *exigua* and cannot match Toulouse for expansion; but its high walls and the regular layout of its streets are a model; it cannot match Trier or Narbonne for commerce, but it has climate and productive terrain, as generations of British wine-importers can testify; it cannot match Milan for magnificent buildings, yet its fountain house of Parian marble and its Celtic goddess are a proper source of pride. Above all, it is the poet's city, and patriotic pride is everything. Even though Rome claims a superior patriotic pride, it cannot touch the visceral affection for the place of your birth. Libanius would have agreed with the sentiment, as with Ausonius' list of points of praise of a city.

Libanius and Ausonius may stand for the survival of a classical ideal of the city, in both the Hellenophone East and the Latinate West, in the second half of the fourth century. Move on to the sixth century, when much has changed in the world of geo-politics, and urban ideals remain recognisably the same. Cassiodorus may stand as representative for Italy, no longer under Roman imperial rule, and partly transformed by Germanic conquests. Like the previous authors we have considered, Cassiodorus was rhetorically trained and competent in the extreme. Cities were at the heart of his concerns, and Cassiodorus has so much to say about cities in his *Variae*, the collection of official letters on varied topics, that he merits a chapter to himself (see Chapter 4). Here it is enough to consider his contribution to the *Laudes Urbium* tradition, one overlooked in most surveys of the subject.[41]

The last two of his twelve books of letters are different from the others, and for that reason get a separate preface, because they are written not on behalf of the royal court, but in his own voice as Praetorian Prefect (AD 533–538). That allows a more personal tone to enter some of the letters, and one feature of these last two books is a series of lyrical descriptions of a variety of Italian cities and areas. All of these letters offer material that would readily lend itself to a city panegyric, but that honour he reserves for his native city, Scyllaceum (Squillace). The occasion for letter 12.15 is a tax remission: the city attracts so many visitors that the provision of public hospitality has become a burden from which they need to be

---

[41] Not in Classen, *Laudes Urbium*, which misses little, nor in Frugoni, *Distant City*, or Oldfield, *Urban Panegyric*.

exempted. His intervention is excused by his patriotic affection, *patriotica ... affectione*. Here he consciously deploys the topics of panegyric. Foundation first, and the honour is attributed to Ulysses, fleeing from Troy – it seems pedantry to point out that there is no trace of its being more than a village dependent on Croton until the foundation of the Gracchan colony of Minervium in 129 BC. Next, situation: above the Adriatic Gulf (we would say the Ionian), it 'hangs from the foothills like a cluster of grapes' (*in modum botryonis*), a steep climb rewarded by gorgeous views (*voluptuose*) over the verdant fields and the dark blue of the sea. Situation means that it is blessed with the first light of the sun at dawn, and with that comes an exceptional quality of both light and air, giving it a better claim to be the *patria* of Phoebus than Rhodes (the rules of rhetoric require *synkrisis*). Not only does that mean temperate seasons, warm winters, and fresh summers. He turns to Hippocratic medical theory to argue that temperate climes produce temperate people: if your *patria* is hot, you will be fickle and sharp, if cold, sluggish and dim; and purity of air here leads to clarity of intellect, as in Athens. Situation by the sea also leads to an abundance of marine delicacies, and where the locals have created pools in the cliffs fed by river water, fish proliferate. Such are their numbers that they will come to you to feed on crumbs, and so (the rhetorician cannot resist the paradox), they feed before they become food. Artificial fish-cultivation was a Roman skill with a long history, and they knew that the mixture of fresh water with sea water produced an ideal environment for fish.[42] The Latin for such a facility was *vivarium*, and, by no coincidence, Vivarium was the name of the monastic community that Cassiodorus was later to found on this spot. In the *Institutiones* which he wrote to guide study at Vivarium, he describes the situation of the monastery and its gardens watered by the river Pellena, rich in fish (*piscosi amnis*): there he has made pools in the rocks where the multitude of fish may feed at liberty (*Institutiones* 1.29), charmingly illustrated in the earliest manuscript of this text, of the eighth century (Figure 2.9).[43]

Finally, Cassiodorus turns to the urban centre, and there is a surprise: it has no walls. But rhetoric must turn every disadvantage to an advantage. The absence of walls affords incomparable views over the countryside, and they can watch their harvests of grapes, grain, and olives pile up. It is a city that allows all the advantages of the country from within the town: it is somewhere between a rural city and an urban country villa, *civitatem credis*

---

[42] Marzano, *Roman Villas in Central Italy*, pp. 47–63.
[43] See the translation and introduction by Halporn and Vessey, *Cassiodorus: Institutions*.

Figure 2.9 Cassiodorus' monastery at Vivarium from the Bamberg MS of the Institutiones, Msc.Patr.61, fol.29v. Courtesy Staatsbibliothek Bamberg, photo Gerald Raab.

ruralem, villam iudicare possis urbanam. After this sprinkling of rhetorical fairy-dust, we can be swept away by the attractions of Squillace and feel no surprise that so many officials seek excuses for visits there at the city's expense. We can also understand why Cassiodorus himself sought refuge there when his long and difficult time as an official to the Ostrogothic court was terminated by its fall.

Just as Ausonius could turn to advantage the praises of his little city, *exigua Burdigala,* by underlining its strengths, including wine-production, Cassiodorus can use the advantages of views, climate, agrarian production, and pisciculture to offset any urban deficits his *patria* may suffer from. But the point is that though the strengths and weaknesses of each city may vary, the scale of urban amenities on which they are measured remains the same. For an almost contemporary view from the East, we may turn to Procopius, another author who has so much to say about the city that he deserves a chapter to himself (see Chapter 5). Here I shall look only at his venture into panegyric in the *Peri Ktismaton*, a work of undisguised praise of Justinian as founder of buildings and cities.[44] Procopius makes a suitable pair to Cassiodorus: he was, after all, with Belisarius as he invaded Italy, and Cassiodorus as Praetorian Prefect wrote letters about the defence of Italy. Procopius was no less rhetorically trained than Cassiodorus, but his style is very much less florid, and in his *Histories* positively Thucydidean.[45]

The aim of the *Peri Ktismaton* is to show off Justinian's tireless activity in founding churches, repairing neglected urban fabric, and building or renewing numerous cities and even more numerous forts (with these he can do no more than list, and the list is a very long one). One might perhaps have expected a major set-piece on Constantinople, considering the profusion of buildings Justinian was responsible for there, and above all the Haghia Sophia. But for a full-blown panegyric of Constantinople we need to look elsewhere, to Themistios or the *Patria Constantinopoleos*.[46]

It is in the more compact accounts of the building or rebuilding of other cities that we come closest to the urban panegyric. Libanius' Antioch had suffered a sequence of disasters, including plague and the comprehensive sack by the Persians under Chosroes I (Khosrau) in AD 540. This, Procopius had narrated at length in his *Histories* (2.8–9), but he passed over what Justinian did to restore the city. In his panegyric, Procopius makes amends. Chosroes had so thoroughly sacked Antioch, reducing it to dust and rubble, that house owners could not even identify the former locations of their houses to start reconstruction. Justinian has all the rubble removed, and the city rebuilt, as good as before if not even better. He rebuilds the defensive circuit of the walls on better lines (walls are an element that Justinian never neglects), and then re-establishes the street network:

> Next he laid it out with stoas and market-places, and dividing all the blocks of houses by means of streets, and making water-channels and fountains and sewers, all those of which the city now boasts, he built theatres and baths for it, ornamenting it with all the other public buildings

---

[44] Included among *Laudes Urbium* by Classen, *Laudes Urbium*, pp. 23–24; but see especially Saradi, *The Byzantine City*, pp. 71–78.
[45] See Kaldellis, *Procopius of Caesarea*.   [46] See Classen, *Laudes Urbium*, p. 87 n. 147.

> by means of which the prosperity of a city is wont to be shewn. He also, by bringing in a multitude of artisans and craftsmen, made it easier and less laborious for the inhabitants to build their own houses. Thus it was brought about that Antioch has become more splendid now than it formerly was. (ii.10)

In a few words, Procopius evokes a complete urban package: walls, streets, monuments, and even a workforce. That he exaggerates is clear; but does he mispresent the *type* of city Justinian was reconstructing, ignoring the shift to the winding streets of the 'medieval' city?[47] We are talking here more about ideals than realities; but it would be strange for Procopius to present to Justinian as an act of flattery an ideal to which he did not subscribe.

The same questions arise in his description of the building of Justiniana Prima, the new regional metropolis constructed at the site of the little village where the emperor was born (iv.1.17–27).

> In that place also he constructed an aqueduct and so caused the city to be abundantly supplied with ever-running water. And many other enterprises were carried out by the founder of this city – works of great size and worthy of especial note. For to enumerate the churches is not easy, and it is impossible to tell in words of the lodgings for magistrates, the great stoas, the fine market-places, the fountains, the streets, the baths, the shops. In brief, the city is both great and populous and blessed in every way – a city worthy to be the metropolis of the whole region, for it has attained this rank. It has also been allotted to the Archbishop of Illyricum as his seat, the other cities conceding this honour to it, as being first in point of size.

Excavations at the likely site of Justiniana do not wholly bear out Procopius' enthusiastic description, and it may be that Procopius, who had surely never visited the site, just had to use his imagination (see Chapter 9, pp. 343–8).[48] What we may take away from the passage is what he imagined an impressive city would look like. It looks back, indeed, to the formulas familiar from earlier descriptions of cities; but it also looks forward to how later generations would imagine their cities.

The world of Cassiodorus or Procopius still preserved significant elements of the classical system. The earliest of the texts seen (by those who wish to draw a line between the antique and the medieval) to belong to the medieval tradition are from eighth-century North Italy, the praises of Milan and of Verona, similar to each other in their unclassical verse form of the 'rhythmus'.[49] They are seen

---

[47] So Cameron, *Procopius*, pp. 111–112; cf Saradi, *The Byzantine City*, p. 72.
[48] Ivanišević, 'Main patterns of urbanism in Caričin Grad'.
[49] See Welton, 'The city speaks', pp. 23–24.

as part of a 'renewal' of interest, both in urban values and the tradition of *laudes urbium*, though Cassiodorus makes it plain that interest never flagged under the Ostrogoths, and the Lombards after them valued the potential of cities for the control of their kingdom.[50] The praise of Milan is closely dated by reference to the Lombard king, Liutprand (712–744), and bishop Theodorus (725–739), to the 730s.[51] Its hymnic quality suggests that it was for chanting, and one can imagine the faithful processing round the city singing on one of its patronal festivals. It splits into a series of three-line stanzas, each beginning with a successive letter of the alphabet – a trick favoured in some poetry of the period.[52]

Content as well as form marks a break with the classical, and the striking feature of both poems is the emphasis on local saints and bishops.[53] But there is a strong presence of traditional elements too, and the antique and the Christian are carefully balanced in the composition. The first eight stanzas described Milan in familiar terms:

> Alta urbs et spaciosa manet in Italia,
> Firmiter edificata opere mirifico,
> que ab antiquitus vocatur Mediolanum civitas.
>
> High and spacious is the city that remains in Italy.
> Solidly is it constructed, with amazing craftsmanship,
> Which from ancient times is named the noble city of Milan.

The next stanza looks at its rural setting in a well-cultivated and fruitful plain (2). The following three stanzas (3–5) look at its walls and towers:

> Celsas habet opertasque turres in circuitu –
>
> High and covered are the towers set around its circuit wall.

Statistics, as so often, are called for when talking of walls: these are twelve feet thick, built of ashlar blocks in the lower courses, and brick in the upper courses; the walls are pierced by nine gates, each protected by iron chains and portcullises. The next stanza (6) gives a brief glimpse of a well-paved town and its water supply:

---

[50] For the idea of 'renovatio', Granier, 'La *renovatio* du modèle rhétorique'; for Lombard interest in cities, Goodson, 'Urbanism as politics'.
[51] Latin text in Dümmler, *Poetae Latini*, pp. 24–26.
[52] See Raby, *A History of Christian-Latin*, pp. 19–27; Godman, *The Poetry of the Carolingian Renaissance*, pp. 30ff. On the context of the Lombard court of Pavia, Vocino, 'Between the palace', esp. pp. 261–266.
[53] Brogiolo, 'Ideas of the town', p. 123, stresses the unclassical elements.

> Foris valde speciosum habet edificium.
> Omne ambitum viarum firme stratum silice;
> Unda capit per ductorem limphe quendam balastris.
>
> Outwards is the town's construction well and truly fine to see,
> All its streets have solid paving firmly laid with basalt stone,
> While the aqueduct brings water to supply its heated baths.

As for monumental buildings, its glory is its churches, especially that of St Laurence, with its alabaster marble and gold and high towers (7). All of this qualifies Milan to be seen as a metropolis, the Queen of Cities and Mother of the Patria: *haec est urbium regina, mater adque patriae* (8). This odd phrase, '*mater patriae*', is a calque on the Greek metropolis, mother-city, though by using *patria* for city a tension is set up between maternity and paternity.

The remaining two-thirds of the poem turns to its shield of Christian protection. All the bishops of Italy recognise its supremacy (9), and the devotion of the population who hurry to church (10). We return to the theme of walls: the saints happily take their rest around the walls (*laetanter ibi quiescunt sancti circum moenia*), and their names are reeled off: Victor, Nabor, and Maternus and all their company (11–12). Indeed, there is not a city in the province which can boast more bodies of saints (13). Lucky indeed the city of Milan, to be able to rely on such defenders, *tales sanctos defensores* (14). Just as in the opening stanzas, where the walls, with their dimensions and gates, are the defence and the pride of the city, it is now the invisible army of saints which constitute its walls. That idea – of the power of saints to protect a city – is widespread in this period: Gregory of Tours describes how the Frankish army was persuaded to break off the siege of Zaragoza by the spectacle of a procession of the inhabitants parading in hair-shirts around the walls, carrying the tunic of their patron saint, St Vincent (*Histories* 3.29).

After such a picture of the walls and saints, the poem goes on to celebrate the city's musical tradition (15), its charity to the poor and to visitors (16), and its abundance of wine and meat (17: *vini copia et carnes adfluentur nimiae*). It is the royal seat of Liutprand, the Lombard king from 712 to 744 – a boast that overlooks the preference of Liutprand and his predecessors for Pavia (18). It is also the seat of the great archbishop Theodore (721–735). The physical vigour of the citizens (*viribus robusti cives*) means they can defeat the wicked gentiles, an allusion to Liutprand's expedition against the Saracens (20). The poem closes with prayers to Christ (21–24), in which the status of the poems as a hymn to be sung is made explicit: *Ymnum regi modolanter cantemus altissimo* (22).

The massive presence of saints and bishops may mark these praises off from classical predecessors, as might be expected in a Christian hymn; yet the function of the saints, to protect the city, and of the bishops, to raise its status in the province, align the verses with the patriotic aims of less religious *Laudes*. The praises of Verona follow a similar model and were surely composed under the influence of those of Milan, though they date to the end of the century, when Charlemagne's son Pippin is king (781–810).[54] They survive by chance, the interest of the tenth-century bishop of Verona, Ratherius, to whom is attributed the manuscript in which they survive alongside the image of Verona discussed earlier: the Iconographia Veronae. Like the Milan praise, that for Verona has an opening section which sets forth the physical realities and antiquities of the city, before going on to bishops and saints. The first stanza underlines the city's antiquity:

> Magna et praeclara pollet urbs haec in Italia
> In partibus Venetiarum, ut docet Isidorus,
> que Verona vocitatur olim ab antiquitus.
>
> Great and famous does this city flourish in Italy
> In the region of Venetians, Isidorus teaches us,
> Which from ancient times has always had Verona as its name.

What the learned citation of Isidorus is doing remains obscure. Isidore has a great deal to say about cities in the fifteenth book of his *Etymologies*, as we will see (Chapter 8), but Verona is a city he never mentions. On the other hand, since he describes a labyrinth in terms close to those of the next stanza, the reference may look forward.[55] But what he certainly stresses are the ancient roots of cities and their founders. At once the wall circuit is described: solidly walled in foursquare blocks, forty-eight towers gleam around, eight of which are particularly tall (2). It now, in remarkable language, turns to the remains of the distinctive classical monument of Verona: *habet altum laberintum*, it has a tall labyrinth of enormous circumference, and people will scarcely know how to escape from it unless they have a lamp and a ball of thread (3). We might think of this not as a deliberate amnesia about the function of an amphitheatre so much as an

---

[54] Latin text in *MGH Poetae Latini Aevi Carolini*, pp. 118–122. Translated in Godman, *Poetry of the Carolingian Renaissance*, no. 23; see also Stella, *La poesia Carolingia*. On the context of the Carolingian court of Verona, Vocino, 'Between the palace', pp. 264–266.

[55] Ward-Perkins, *From Classical Antiquity to the Middle Ages*, p. 227.

expression of wonderment, and a learned allusion to classical mythology and the role of Ariadne's thread in allowing Theseus to escape.

Next, we turn to the urban layout, and Verona boasts solid paving just as much as did Milan (3):

> Foro lato spatioso sternuto lapidibus
> Ubi quattuor in cantus magni instant fornices,
> plateae mire sternutae de sectis silicibus.
>
> With its broad and spacious forum pavemented with solid stone
> There in each of its four corners mighty arches stand,
> While the broad streets to our wonder in cut basalt pavers clad.

We may nurse doubts over how well the ancient paving of the forum and the streets was maintained into the late eighth century, but the ideal asserted is clear enough.[56] The poem remains with the theme of antiquities in listing the pagan temples of the city, but their names show that the poet is making it up, since they are the seven gods of the weekdays, from Luna to Sol (5). The next wonder is statuary, *scemata*, and the gleam of their gilded bronze (6). Next, the castle with its battlements and the stone bridges across the Atesis, so vividly depicted in the *Iconographia* as a *Pons Marmoreus* (7).

At this point the poem registers a disapproval of the pagan past: though built so well, the city was built by bad men (*malis hominibus*), who did not know the Christian religion and worshipped sticks and stones (*simulacra venerabant lignea, lapides*): it is to the credit of Verona that even the contributions of pagans were good ones (8). An account follows of the conversion of the world to the true faith (9–13). Now we can name the first eight bishops, from Eurepus to Zeno, who converted the city and worked many miracles (14–18). There follows a list of the saints who form a defence around the city and ward off its enemies (*circumvallata custodibus sanctissimis*) (19), and the remaining stanzas spell out the name of dozens of them, organised, like city gates, according to the cardinal points: to east, where they are particularly numerous (20–22), to south (23–28), and to west (29). Defended by such 'odour of sanctity' (*redolens a sanctorum corpore*), Verona is worthy of praise above all cities of Italy (30), and a *synkrisis* allows it to spell out the cities which join in its praise: Aquileia, Mantua, Brixia, Pavia, Rome, and Ravenna – an impressive list which quietly passes over Milan in favour of Rome (31). Its claim to glory is sealed as the seat of the king, *rex Pippinus piissimus* (32), a nice card to play against Milan's Liutprand.

---

[56] Ward-Perkins, *From Classical Antiquity*, p. 185.

What is impressive about both poems is that, though in an idiom seemingly designed for liturgical use, the classical features of city praises, of walls and streets and monuments and rich landscapes, are integrated with the new Christian elements. The saints are not there to replace the old walls, but to strengthen them. Nor can we take the use of 'rhythm' rather than scansion as a collapse of Classical learning. For reassurance that the old idiom is still alive, we can turn to Alcuin and his praise of York.[57] His 'Verses on the Saints of the Church of York' is a small epic: 1,657 well-turned hexametres taking the story of the church down to the election as Archbishop in AD 780 of his teacher Ecgbert and before his departure for Francia and the court of Charlemagne in 782. He opens, after a due invocation of poetic inspiration, with the praises of the city itself (15–45). His urge is to sing of his *patria* (16, *patriae . . . dicere laudes*), his cradle (17, *veteres cunas*), in grateful verses of the famous city of York (18, *Eboricae gratis praeclarae versibus urbis*). Founded first by the Romans, high with walls and towers (19, *muris et turribus altam*), it gathered together native Britons to act as an emporium for land and sea (24, *ut foret emporium terrae commune marisque*), and at the same time to be a military base, an ornament of empire and the terror of foreign arms. He expands on its function as a harbour for ships coming from far across the ocean (28–29). Next he turns inland, to the river Ouse with its fish (30, *piscosa . . . Ousa*), watering the fields, its banks covered in flowers, and beyond it the countryside lovely with woods and hills (31–32). It is a fine and healthy place to live, and its fertility allows numerous farmers (*coloni* – it was of course a Roman colony). It attracts settlers from far and wide who come in the hope of profit, 'seeking wealth from a wealthy land', and both profit and a home (37, *lucrumque laremque*). Alas, the Romans had to withdraw to defend their homeland, and control of the city passed to the idle Britons (41, *gens pigra Britonum*). The rest, as they say, is history, largely based on Bede.

Alcuin had a deep Classical training, and brief though his picture of York is, we see the familiar topics ticked off: foundation, walls, fertility of land, trade – even the fishy river, without which no city is complete. These topics might be thought a lingering trace of Classical influence, yet what is striking is how constant they remain in the dozens of *Laudes* that are

---

[57] Latin text in *MGH Poetae Latini Aevi Carolini*, 169ff. Translation in Godman, *Poetry of the Carolingian Renaissance*, pp. 4–7. On the author, Bullough, *Alcuin*; on the close ties between Alcuin's praise of York and the continental tradition of *Laudes Urbium*, Coates, 'The bishop as benefactor', esp. 547–556. On the poets of the Carolingian court, McKitterick, *Charlemagne*, pp. 139–140.

produced in increasing numbers over the following centuries. They have been excellently set out by Paul Oldfield, and there is no need to recapitulate in detail. A glance is enough at Sigebert of Gembloux, whose life of Bishop Theoderic I of Metz opens, as so often with such Lives, with a praise of his city, Metz (Mettis), dated between 1050 and 1060:

> Praecluis urbs salve, tellus praenobilis ave,
> Urbs populosa nimis, tellus praefertilis agris.
> Mel at lac manans, cum vino pane habundans,
> Mercibus exundans, auro gemmisque redundans.
>
> Hail, famed city, greetings most noble land,
> city too populous, land most fertile with fields,
> dripping milk and honey, abundant in bread with wine;
> flowing over with commerce, awash with gold and gems.

Just like Alcuin's York, Metz is equally rich in agriculture and in trade, and Sigibert goes on to name some lands which Metz outcompetes, including Attica's sweet Hymettus – competition, one takes it, to the honey of Metz. The walls are described at length, higher than those of Babylon, and impregnable to all manner of siege engines. As for the houses, he is looking at the palaces of Rome, and the theatre is like the labyrinth of Daedalus (echoes here of Verona). The river Moselle ensures both beauty and defence. The four gates look out to the four quarters (25, *anatolen, dysin, mesembrian, arcton* – all Greek names). When he sees the church of St Stephen, he floats up to heaven with the heavenly choirs. New walls are rising too, thanks to the defender of the city (*patriae columen*), Bishop Adelberus. He goes on to pick out a Roman ruin: the aqueduct with six hundred arches (54–61); even today, the ruins maintain our admiration: *laudem structurae retinent hodieque ruinae* (61). The past both frames and is part of the fame of the present.

Rome remains the measure of all things, as the late twelfth-century praise of Tournai makes emphatically clear:

> Nobilibus fundata viris velut altera Roma,
> Urbibus immensis immensior esse videbar,
> Non quia post Romam mea sit structura locata,
> Sed quia cum Roma non sunt mihi prospera fata.[58]
>
> Founded by noble men like a second Rome,
> I seemed vaster than vast cities,

---

[58] *Versus de Dignitate et Antiquitate Urbis Tornacensis*, 1–4, text in *MGH Scriptores XIV*, ed. G. Waits (1883), p. 357. See Oldfield, *Urban Panegyric*, pp. 177–178.

> not because my building was placed after Rome,
> but because with Rome my fate is not prosperous.

Rome manages to be a model not only for greatness, but for dignity in decline.

As a final example we may take the thirteenth-century praise of Milan, the *de Magnalibus urbis Mediolani* of Bonvesin de la Riva, written in Latin prose in AD 1288, of a length that exceeds even Libanius on Antioch (seventy printed sides).[59] Bonvesin (born in the 1240s, died before 1315) was a professor of Latin (*doctor grammaticae*) and wrote both in Latin and the 'vulgar tongue', being one of the most prolific authors in the latter from Lombardy. He chose to write his Praise of Milan in Latin – a choice that possibly restricted his audience but acknowledged the debt of the genre to previous writing in Latin. He knew his rhetorical rules, and yet he illustrates better than most how following those rules need not impede an author from taking a fresh and contemporary approach. In some ways the feel of it is strikingly 'modern', not least in his liberal deployment of statistics. It represents a Milan flourishing after two centuries of boom, and the great experiment of Communes in North Italy. And yet, its themes are deeply familiar. The classical tradition and the respect for the name of Rome is still present: three times he calls Milan a 'secunda Roma'.

The work is lucidly divided into eight chapters. The first four concern the physical aspects of the city, its situation (I), its buildings (II), its inhabitants (III), and the fertility of its lands (IV); the second four concern its virtues, fortitude, a military history (V), faith, a religious history (VI), liberty (VII), and dignity, as the seat of emperors, etc. (VIII). All these topics are familiar from the *Laudes* tradition but are worked out in unparalleled detail. On situation (I) he is brief but pursues the rhetorical topic of the happy medium between heat and cold, thanks to its situation away from the coast, and the abundance of rivers; he notes that the city itself is supplied not by aqueducts but cisterns, providing water of outstanding freshness. On buildings, in place of the usual generalised praise of housing, he can specify that there are 12,500 '*ostia com ianuis*', houses with independent openings on the main street (II.1), and 60 sheltered walkways on the *plateae* (the porticoed facades typical of north Italian cities) (II.2). The civic centre is described with its dimensions, the *curia* (palazzo comunale) with its four *campanili* and the lodgings for magistrates (*potestates*) and judges (II.3). The city is circular in plan (II.4) – a somewhat later plan shows it as a perfect circle. It is protected by a magnificent wall and rampart

---

[59] For an excellent edition, Chiesa, *Bonvesin de la Riva*.

(II.5); there are 6 principal gates with double towers and 10 secondary posterns. There are 200 churches in the city alone, with 480 altars, and, above all, the church of S. Lorenzo founded by Galla Placidia (or Patricia as he chooses to call her) (II.7). There are 36 churches dedicated to the Virgin Mary alone, plus another 240 in the county (II.8). Finally, a count of the 120 *campanili* in the city (II.9), before moving on to the county (*comitatus* = *contado*), with its 50 burghs, including Monza, a city itself in all but name, in which not only peasants but many nobles live (II.10), as well as villas, castles, and the *plebes* (*pievi* – English 'hundreds', more or less) into which the county is subdivided (II.11) and 2,500 fine churches (II.12). He sees both city and county as full of beautiful houses.

The next chapter (III) is a fascinating count of inhabitants. As a member of the Order of Umiliati, Bonvesin had access to official statistics, some of which were administered by his Order.[60] Having praised in general the health, stature, and good deportment of the people, as well as the clarity of their dialect (*ydioma*), although he notices the objection that some think them marred by their civil discord (III.1), he offers an estimate of the population at 200,000 within the city, excluding members of religious orders; to his calculations he will return (III.2). He starts with the religious orders: 9 canonaries plus the cathedral, 94 chapels, 6 monasteries and 8 nunneries, and 10 hospitals for the poor, the Umiliati, Augustinians, and so on, all of which add up to some 10,000 persons (III.3–11). The lay inhabitants are harder to calculate, he admits, but 'after long research' he reckons the total for the county to be 700,000 (III.12). Within the city there are 115 parishes, each with between 500 and 1,000 inhabitants (III.13); but the best index of the population is the amount of grain consumed: more than 1,200 *moggi* of grain brought for milling each day, implying 200,000 inhabitants in the city itself (III.14). It is clear both that he has access to revealing city statistics and that there was no census of the number of inhabitants, which has to be inferred. He then breaks down the population by rank and trade. The city fields 40,000 foot soldiers (the text is damaged and the number may be 20,000) (III.15); 10,000 mounted cavalry between city and county (III.16); 120 experts in civil and canon law, 1,500 notaries, 600 postmen, 6 trumpeters, 28 doctors, 150 surgeons, 8 professors of grammar, 14 teachers of Ambrosian chant, 70 elementary teachers, and 40 copyists (III.17–26); then we move to trades: 300 bakeries, over 1,000 wine-taverns, 440 butchers, more than 30 fishmongers (he lists the varieties of fish on sale, a subject to which he will return with enthusiasm), 150 hotels, 80 furriers

---

[60] On the Order, Andrews, *The Early Humiliati*.

(which, as he remarks, points to the sheer number of men who kept horses), and in excess of 30 makers of the brass bells to be hung on horse harnesses. As to artisans in general, haberdashers, costumiers, shoe-makers, and other traders, these are beyond count (III.27–33). One point he wants to emphasise is the high number of the members of the nobility who live both within the city and outside it: these include numerous *Valvasores*, a word which he falsely derives from the Latin *valvae*, doors, as being the doorkeepers of the Roman emperors when they resided in Milan: his Latin etymology wantonly obscures the feudal term of 'vassals'.[61] In addition to them there are the *capitanei* who head the *pievi*, and numerous other noble families devoted to hunting and falconry (III.34).

This is (for its day) an astonishingly minute analysis of the social composition of the city. His emphasis is always on diversity, the myriad trades and occupations that make it up; he is emphatic that the nobility are to be found alike in city and county, as are the knights who made up a crucial second order of nobility in communal Italy.[62] There is no especial emphasis on a merchant class, though they are undoubtedly present: merchants and knights, vintners and lawyers, religious orders and laity all rub shoulders. The city is deeply integrated into its surrounding countryside, the contado, and on this he expands in the next chapter (IV). We are offered a loving panorama of the richness of country produce: grain, pulses, and beets which feed rich and poor in the winter (IV.1), the diversity of fruit and nuts, including the prized chestnuts and *nespole* (IV.2–4); garden produce of vegetables and herbs (IV.5); meadows rich in hay, 200,000 cartloads of which are produced each year (IV.6); vines producing outstanding wines (who would deny Lombardy its *Nebbiolo*?), which are grown interplanted with other crops (IV.7–8); woods (IV.9); olives producing a 'compost', excellent with broad beans (IV.10); meat of all sorts :with the aid of the butchers, he calculates 70 animals butchered each day (IV.11); milk, honey, wax, ricotta, butter, cheese, eggs; the fishmongers have supplied him with the remarkable statistic that 7 *moggi* (around 1,000 litres) of prawns are consumed each day in the city (IV.12). This takes him on to a well-loved topic: fish. Thanks to the lakes and innumerable rivers, Milan consumes more than four mule-loads of fresh fish each day (IV.13). The streams also drive the mills, over 900 in number, and each mill can produce enough for 400 people a day; there is enough for the dogs to eat, too (IV.14). There are imported goods: salted fish, silk, cotton, salt, pepper, and exotic

---

[61] See the commentary of Chiesa, *Bonvesin de la Riva*, p. 214.
[62] Vigueur, *Cavaliers et Citoyens*; Wickham, *Sleepwalking into a New World*.

spices are brought in by the merchants; the quantity of salt is 65,830 *sextarii* (a sextarius or *staio* is one-sixth of a mule load) (IV.17). All of this builds up to a picture of the market in the city strongly reminiscent of Libanius' Antioch: there are four great annual markets, and twice weekly local markets in different areas of the city, a *forum comune* in which not only in specific places but throughout the main streets, *plateae*, people cry their wares; and, equally, there are markets in the burghs and villages of the county (IV.18). Bonvesin conjures up a charming picture of people crowding to the markets and festivals: handsome men, 'whether noble or not', gaggles of small children at play, elegant mothers and daughters who look like so many princesses (IV.19).

We may pass more swiftly over the remaining chapters. A historical sketch gives the cities long and tormented record of wars, sieges, and sackings, (V) notably the sack of the city and the levelling of its walls by the emperor Frederick Barbarossa: 'Alas, Milan, famous city ... Where now is the highest and most solid wall that once surrounded you? Where are your wonderful towers?' (V.7). Chapter VI on the city's faith, demonstrated by its defence of the church in the time of the hated Frederick, states:

> I have never read or heard that this city rebelled against Rome, but it was a most faithful ally and supporter. That is why in antiquity it was called a second Rome, whence the Romans wrote
>
> Rome secunda, vale, regni decus imperiale
> Urbs veneranda nimis, plenissima rebus opimis
>
> Hail, second Rome, imperial glory of the reign,
> City too much to be venerated, most full of rich things.

These hexametres are passed off as a bit of ancient verse (VI.1). He notably says nothing of Milan after the death of Barbarossa in 1250: the Milan of his own lifetime was tormented by the struggle for power between the Visconti and the della Torre.

Chapter VII asserts Milan's attachment to liberty, but our author has run out of steam and gives little chapter and verse. It is perhaps a wise silence: the Visconti had established a *signoria* in 1277, but it was still contested at the time of writing.[63] The final chapter (VIII) is more substantial and offers proofs of dignity as a seat of power and of church influence. Roman credentials are displayed again, with a claimed seat for emperors from

---

[63] Chiesa, *Bonvesin della Riva*, pp. 19–22.

Nerva to Maximian making it a *secunda Roma* (VIII.1). Perhaps the most remarkable feature of this chapter is the admission, generally to be excluded from a panegyric, that Milan has two defects: its lack of a port and its lack of civil concord. In both he contradicts earlier assertions that Milan was better for being away from the coast (I. 2), and that the inhabitants were well-behaved (III.1). But now his line is that without these defects, Milan would be superior to all other cities in the world: it would be not only a second Rome, but superior to the seat of the Popes (VIII.10). That allows him to conclude with a heart-felt exhortation to his *concives*, fellow citizens, not to waste energy on civil discord and feuds (VIII.15). That exhortation had a sharp contemporary relevance.

Continuities and Ruptures

To take the *Laudes Urbium* tradition as a reliable picture of the realities of changing urban life would be rash indeed. The entire point of panegyric is to present reality through a rosy filter: it tells us more about how the writer would like the world to be than how it really is, and the rhetorical training that informed this tradition made no bones about this imperative. What is clear is that there is a substantial continuity in the articulation of urban ideals. That medieval cities should sound like Classical ones is no surprise when their writers – imbued with education in the classical literary tradition, and continuing to use the language(s) of antiquity, words like *civitas*, *cives*, *urbs*, *patria*, and so on, which already come with an ideological charge – then hold up ancient Rome as the gold standard of urbanity. Nevertheless, the following of a literary tradition always leaves room for innovation: conservatism is a choice, not the effect of inertia. Modern historians have long seen a deep rupture between the ancient and the medieval city: the question is how and why contemporary voices choose to present the ruptures we perceive. In Chapter 1 we looked at four different ways that modern scholars have seen this rupture: in religion, in economics, in urban planning, and in political institutions. On each of these, the *laudes urbium* tradition has light to cast.

First, economics, the aspect which has been most influential. Max Weber and his interpreter, Moses Finley, offered a typological contrast between the consumer city of antiquity and the producer city of the Middle Ages. A crucial element of the argument was the changed relationship of town and country: in antiquity *asty* and *chora*, *urbs* and *territorium* are integrally linked, and the fact that the great landowners predominantly chose to reside in the city where political relationship were built acted as a retardant to the emergence of an independent commercial class. In the Middle Ages, this relationship is reversed, city and country are separated, the great landowners no longer inhabit and dominate the city, and a new commercial class emerges, crucially for the emergence of modern capitalism.[64] Whatever truth there may be in this picture, it is one that you could not without great difficulty detect mirrored in the *Laudes* tradition. Compare Libanius' Antioch with the Milan of Bonvesin de la Riva, and the countryside and its rich produce remain integral to the presentation of the city. The same thing can be seen in Praise after Praise, with fertile plains and fish-filled rivers held up as assets that parallel the buildings of the city. Just where the great landowners live is a question harder to extract from these texts: it is only when Bonvesin starts to deploy statistics to analyse the inhabitants of Milan that we can be confident that the nobility are to be found in city as well as countryside.

Of course, our picture is skewed. This literary tradition strongly favours Italy, especially North Italy, and is thinner for north-eastern Europe, and specifically the Low Countries, that played a crucial role in the transformation of commerce. Weber, as we have seen, was conscious that Mediterranean, and specifically Italian cities, did not fit his sharp consumer/producer contrast. More recent historians of medieval Italy are well aware that though there were feudal barons based in castles in the countryside, beneath them a significant slice of the landowning nobility was city based.[65] As Chris Wickham has put it recently:[66]

> the leadership of medieval Italian cities was not ever exclusively commercial, whether mercantile or artisanal, unlike the picture often painted for northern Europe. Most of Italy's major landowners lived in cities – that was the basic reason why Italian cities were so much larger, more powerful, and more socio-politically complex than those of the rest of Latin Europe, and had been for centuries – and they always had a central role to play in city politics.

That helps to explain why the *Laudes* do not suggest a new ideal of an urban, mercantile economy in a way that might have been perceived more sharply in the cities of Flanders. A pattern of urbanism which, though far

---

[64] I attempted to discuss this in 'Elites and trade in the Roman town'; *Houses and Society*, pp. 119–121; and, more recently, 'Back to M. I. Finley's ancient city'.
[65] See Jones, *The Italian City-State*, pp. 73–74; 'At the darkest point of the dark age Italy, in Carl Hegel's time-honoured phrase, remained "a land of cities".'
[66] Wickham, *Sleepwalking into a New World*, p. 8.

from unchanged, was not so dramatically different from that of antiquity made it easy to draw on the language of antiquity in expressing ideals.

For the archaeologist or architectural historian, it is the change in urban planning that seems to mark the deepest rupture. Here, again, the *Laudes* do nothing to flag a contrast. The wall circuit, with its towers and battlements, continues to symbolise the city. The sort of relationship between the city's gates and the quarters of the winds that concerned Vitruvius remains a medieval obsession: maybe the use of Greek wind names to describe the gates of Metz (*anatolen, dysin, mesembrian, arcton*) is a remote echo of the sort of Greek medical theory that Vitruvius drew on. Gates continue to be represented as aligning with the main streets. The finest example is in Lucian's Praise of Chester, *de laude Cestrie*, of the late twelfth century, which has 'four gates from the wind's four quarters' and 'two excellent straight broad streets [*plateae*] like the blessed cross, meeting and crossing each other, which then out of two become four, with their heads in the four gates'. As Keith Lilley has vividly shown, the classical grid becomes an image of the heavenly Jerusalem, so transmuting a classical ideal into a Christian one.[67] But to find a new reason for praising a city for its regular and ordered layout is not the same as acquiring a new ideal. Broad streets and solid paving continue to be an ideal, however implausible we may find it, in Milan and Verona in the eighth century or Chester in the twelfth. The boom from the twelfth to the fourteenth centuries in new towns built on a grid pattern, from the Bastides of France to the new cities planted in Wales by Edward I of England, suggests that, in terms of planning, the ideal of the regular layout was alive.[68] The central *forum* or *agora* is held typical of the classical city, its abandonment and building over of the post-classical: again, the well-paved *fora* of Milan and Verona in the eighth century, and the 'well-placed *forum* in the centre of the city for wares for sale' of twelfth-century Chester suggest that even if the *forum* lost its political function, it retained its symbolic usefulness as the heart of the city.

Politics is an area in which rupture clearly occurred, and even if the new *comuni* of Italy with their *consules* projected continuity of a sort with antiquity, Aristotle would have been hard put to accommodate most medieval cities to his *Politics* (though we may register a revival of interest in Aristotle with Thomas Aquinas, and specifically in the *de regimine principum* with the *Politics*). The Late Antique system of local government by the landowning elite as *curiales* certainly broke down, though it took

---

[67] Lilley, *City and Cosmos*.
[68] Lilley, *City and Cosmos*, and Boerefijn, *The Foundation, Planning and Building of New Towns*.

a surprisingly long time to do so.[69] When it comes to expressing ideals in the *Laudes*, the central concern is not political institutions but rather the big underlying question of the relations of rich and poor and the maintenance of civil concord. The focus is on the *cives*. Just as Libanius was desperately anxious that the citizen body should prove obedient to their Council and avoid civil conflict, Bonvesin knows that civil conflict is the weak point of Milan. The crucial new element, naturally absent from classical rhetoric, is the presence of the bishop, and not only as a spiritual figure. It is no coincidence that so many *Laudes* are incorporated into Lives of Bishops, as in Alcuin's account of York, or famously in William Fitz Stephens' Life of St Thomas. In both the Milan and Verona *Laudes*, lists of bishops keep company with saints as the protectors and glory of their cities. It is surely in the area of religion that the most significant rupture is seen.

That much is made explicit, in a rather charming way, in the Verona Praise, in the explanation that the pagan monuments were built by bad men, who had, however, the defence of not having heard the gospel. It was possible to respect the achievements of the pagan past, whether a great amphitheatre or 'labyrinth', or even, as at Metz, an aqueduct with hundreds of arches, while taking pride in a present where great cathedrals are the principal boast. And from this point of view, Fustel de Coulanges was right: if the ancient city was defined and held together by its local religious practices based on ancestors and the hearth, then the arrival of Christianity marked the end of the ancient city. From another point of view, the interesting question is not what impact Christianity had on the city, but what impact the city had on Christianity. The rise to local influence and power of the bishop flags a church that is not, as Fustel saw it, 'universal' and above local ties, but rooted in the civic structures of antiquity. The principle that to be a *civitas* you need to have a bishop, and, equally, to have a bishop you need to be a *civitas*, such as we see in the praise of Dijon by Gregory of Tours (Chapter 7, pp. 236–238), implies that the power of the bishop is also a mode of carrying forward the power of the city. Nor does cult become entirely 'universalised', despite insistence on Trinitarian doctrine: each city has its own specific collection of saints, some local products, some imported, and thus its unique calendar of festivals and processions. In those processions, the city of antiquity continues, and the *Laudes* make this clear.

Above all what emerges from the *Laudes* is the importance of civic patriotism. Long ago, Gina Fasoli deployed the *Laudes* to support the

---

[69] Liebeschuetz, *Decline, passim*. See Chapter 6 for detailed discussion.

argument that the *comuni* of Italy emerged from a growing *coscienza cittadina*, which she saw expressed in the Praises. Chris Wickham is sceptical over the importance of this vague idea of 'civic conscience'. Whether or not we agree that it played an important role in a movement which some have seen as a return to the values of the classical city, we can certainly see the same *coscienza cittadina* alive in the classical sources. From the moment that Libanius expresses the challenge of adequately doing his civic duty in praising his city, it is explicit that to praise a city is an act of patriotism. Cassiodorus can even use patriotism to justify his use of his power as Praetorian Prefect to exempt his native city from fiscal burdens. Ausonius knows that everyone will understand when he says he is torn between Rome and Bordeaux.

It is in the nature of cities to be diverse, even when following a common model. The rhetorical tradition assumed that there were enough common factors to encompass all this diversity. Equally, there is diversity across time and place: there is no reason to expect the *comuni* of North Italy to be like the cities of mercantile Flanders or the cities of antiquity. What they all have in common is the assumption that, whoever the rulers – Roman emperors, Gothic kings, Lombard and Frankish dynasties, or even Popes – the city remained an essential structuring principle of human society. To your city you owed your loyalty, and from it you derived your identity. What the tradition on *Laudes Urbium* best illustrates is the transmission of that idea. It enabled them to talk as if the world had not, after all, entirely changed.

3 | The City in Question

The Riot at Calama and Two *Patriae*

In AD 408, just two years before Alaric's troops sacked Rome, there was an ugly riot in Calama in North Africa. Calama (modern Guelma in Algeria) is 65 kilometres inland from the coastal city of Hippo Regius (Bône) where Augustine was bishop; not only proximity but also the fact that his friend and future biographer Possidius was bishop there meant that Augustine was closely connected with the incident; this is known through an exchange of letters with Nectarius, a leading citizen of Calama and spokesmen of the pagans there (*Letters* 90, 91, 104, 105).[1] As Augustine sees it (91.8), the pagan population is much at fault. Despite a freshly issued law of the emperor Honorius of the previous year banning pagan festivals (reiterating a longstanding ban), the people of Calama had celebrated theirs on the 1st of June, dancing flagrantly through the streets and past the Christian church. When the priests reproved them, they started to stone the church. Eight days later, the bishop lodged a complaint with the city authorities, to which the people responded with a second stoning of the church. Undeterred by a sign from heaven in the shape of a hailstorm, they proceeded to stone it a third time, set it on fire, and chased the staff, succeeding in killing one servant; they were heard by the bishop, hidden in a cranny, calling for his blood too. Nobody intervened to prevent the rioting except a foreigner (*peregrinus*), thanks to whom the survivors were able to escape.

The episode encapsulates some typical features of the Late Antique city. It was up to the city authorities, the *ordo decurionum*, to maintain order and respect for the law. After the first disorderly episode which the bishop reported to the *ordo*, they had the responsibility to intervene, both to stop the celebration of an illegal pagan festival and to ensure the safety of the church and its personnel. Their failure to intervene leads to worse damage

---

[1] For a translation, Atkins and Dodaro, *Augustine: The Political Writings*, pp. 1–22. On Nectarius, see Rebillard, *Christians and Their Many Identities*, pp. 82–84, arguing that though he pleaded the case of the pagans, Nectarius was himself a Christian.

to property and the loss of life. Nectarius writes to Augustine because he is very nervous at the official response. Rightly so. The imperial authorities in Late Antiquity were intolerant of rioting and their response could be nothing if not heavy-handed: under Diocletian they had responded to rioting at Antioch with heavy punishment for members of the city council, some of whom were executed, while Libanius' grandfather had his property confiscated; and in 387 they responded to another riot, the 'Riot of the Statues', in which imperial images were torn down, thus briefly depriving the city of its status as *civitas*, reducing it to a *vicus*.[2] The riot of 390 in Thessalonike led to a bloody massacre ordered by Theodosius, for which Ambrose forced him to do penance. And, indeed, Nectarius anticipates brutal treatment if Augustine does not intervene: 'with tears in his eyes', he conjures up the image of men dragged off to torture and returning to their wives and families with the shame of wounds and scars (103.4). In view of the repeated complaints in this period that curials were subjected to the physical punishments, beatings, and torture legally reserved for the humble, *humiliores*, it is clearly the punishment of the members of the ruling order that Nectarius fears. He accepts that the guilty should be punished and the costs of repairing the church met, but fears punishment for his friends in the *ordo* unless Augustine intervenes. But in what sense were they innocent, Augustine objects, when it was their failure to take action that allowed the rioting? Why did it take a visitor, a *peregrinus*, to bring the rioters to their senses? This was surely the function of the curials: their acts of liberality (albeit involuntary) to their fellow citizens in paying for public feasts, subsidised bathing, performances in the theatre and amphitheatre, and the like were designed to engender that sort of respect from the populace that Virgil evokes so vividly in the opening of the *Aeneid*, when he compares Neptune calming a storm to the effect of a man of respect, *pietate gravem ac meritis*, on a turbulent crowd (*Aeneid* 1. 148–153).[3]

Here we have the Late Antique city at its dysfunctional worst. The ruling council, landowners with the hereditary requirement to serve their city, are expected to implement the laws that come from the imperial centre. Honorius, son of the Trinitarian zealot Theodosius I, is caught in the midst of negotiations with Alaric and his Goths, soon to allow his general Stilicho to fall to court intrigue (22 August 408), triggering the sequence of events that ended with the sack of Rome. Honorius has caved in to the pressure of the bishops to outlaw pagan festivals. But at a local level, they

[2] Liebeschuetz, *Antioch*, pp. 104–105; Browning, 'The riot of AD 387 in Antioch'.
[3] On this traditional Roman model of crowd control, see Nippel, *Public Order in Ancient Rome*, pp. 4–16.

are not so easy to stop; after all, festivals were a principal way in which the population could benefit from the generosity of the rich and generate a sense of communal spirit. The new law caused anger, which the curials may well have shared. But the bishops, whether Augustine or Possidius, were unrelenting in their pressure on the imperial authorities to stamp out paganism. Nectarius' pleas fall on deaf ears.

And yet Nectarius and Augustine have much in common. Nectarius, at the opening of his first letter, plays a winning card by appealing to Cicero.[4] Or, rather, he appeals to the sense of *caritas patriae*, affection for your home city, the only thing that rightly trumps affection for parents (90.1). Though he himself grows old and cold, the warmth of his affection for his city, *dilectio et gratia civitatis*, grows by the day – which is why he wants the colony of Calama, in which he was born and has held office, to flourish. Augustine at once catches the allusion: he understands and applauds the warmth of his *patriae caritas* but urges him to look more carefully at that book *de Republica*, from which he has drunk his patriotic affection, *affectum amantissimi civis*, and note the virtues of frugality and restraint it urges (91.3). By cruel irony, we do not have a full text of Cicero's *de Republica*, though it is the work to which Augustine most frequently refers, and we do not have the passage he refers to; but, from the parallel discussion of the *patria* in the *de Legibus*, we recognise the Ciceronian argument.[5]

The way in which both a pagan leader and a Christian bishop reach back to Cicero for a definition of the city is a good illustration of how memory of the past can be drawn on in the process of change. As resilience theory envisages, memory of the past serves not as a form of nostalgia but as a resource that enables adaptation. This is precisely what Augustine is engaged in. Cicero, as we have seen, saw that there were two *patriae*: the city of your birth and the city of your citizenship, the *communis patria* of Rome, to which a higher duty and a higher affection was due. Augustine subtly adapts the theory of the twin *patriae*. Augustine longs to recruit Nectarius to citizenship of a higher city, *supernae cuiusdam patriae*, for the love of which he labours (91.1). Nectarius gets his point: Augustine wants to convert him to the cult of the supreme God, *exsuperantissimi Dei*, and to look to the heavenly *patria*, not the one surrounded by some wall circuit, *muralis gyrus*, nor the universal citizenship of the philosophers, but the one shared by the worshippers of the Great God who follow his rules. Among

---

[4] On Augustine's use of Cicero, see Dodaro, 'Augustine's secular city', and his *Christ and the Just Society*.

[5] See O'Daly, *Augustine's City of God*, pp. 24–26.

Nectarius' three *patriae*, the first, the walled city, stands for both Calama and Rome, but he understands well that the heavenly *patria* transcends the claims of Rome, even though Augustine is happy enough to work through the emperor and his legislation to bring that into being.

Those, from Fustel de Coulanges to Liebeschuetz, who see Christianity as the ideology which undermined and displaced ancient ideals of the city and citizenship might read this incident as part of an assault not just on paganism but on the essence of the city itself.[6] From an alternative point of view, the exchange rather illustrates how the Ciceronian idea of the city remained central to Christian as well as pagan thinking and how a new ideology was able to transform and thereby transmit core ideas. This chapter will explore how three closely connected Christian authors – Orosius, Augustine, and Salvian of Marseille – grappled with the ideas both of city and of citizenship in a period of challenge and gave them new relevance.

Citizenship in Imperial Legislation

From a 'catastrophist' viewpoint, we might take this exchange as marking the end, or at least a beginning of an end, of 'the ancient city'. Some have seen the appeal of Christianity as flowing into a void left by the loss of meaning of Roman citizenship and the collapse of Ciceronian civic conscience. But that does no justice to the subtlety of Augustine's thinking and the ambivalence of his position. Before attempting to tangle with the *de Civitate Dei*, it is relevant to ask what sort of appeal *civitas Romana* still held by Late Antiquity. It used to be the common assumption that Roman citizenship progressively lost content and meaning as citizenship spread across the empire, and that the 'universal' grant in AD 212 by Caracalla of citizenship to all inhabitants of the Roman world (the 'Constitutio Antoniniana') deprived it of the last vestiges of distinctiveness.[7] So Nicholas Sherwin-White, in his classic *The Roman Citizenship*, brings his narrative to an end with the Antonine Constitution, while Claude Nicolet, in his *World of the Citizen in Republican Rome*, argued that already Augustus had deprived the citizenship of any real meaning, except as

---

[6] So Liebeschuetz, *Decline and Fall*, p. 349 ('as the concepts of city and citizenship lost their meaning') and passim. Lidia Storoni Mazzolani ends her book on *The Idea of the City in Roman Thought* with Augustine, as if that was the end of the story.

[7] I have discussed this in detail in '*Civitas Romana*'. See now Rose et al. (eds.), *City, Citizen, Citizenship*, excellently demonstrating the continuing importance of the idea.

a status marker.[8] That depends on giving a strictly Aristotelian definition of citizenship as participation in the politics of the city; what it overlooks is the rest of the bundle of activities and rights which Fustel de Coulanges rightly identified as part of the package of citizenship, including sharing in the common worship of the city, and participation in the festivals, rituals, processions, and common meals that were characteristic of city life. In this sense, citizenship was a 'performance'.[9] Indeed, to judge from the fragmentary summary of Caracalla's edict that survives in a papyrus (*P. Giessen* 40), the motivation offered for the extension of the citizenship was to allow everyone to share in the common worship of the gods and give thanks for Caracalla's safety (he represented his murder of his brother Geta as survival of an assassination attempt).

If citizenship is also about common worship, then it is about identity. But there is more to it than this. It is about sharing in Roman legal structures, and those included the right to inherit from a Roman citizen. Since ownership of property was the prime, if not the only, form of wealth, testamentary rights were of critical importance.[10] On the other hand, if now all free persons shared in Roman citizenship, they were all equally entitled to inherit. To that extent, what was once a privilege was now the norm (it is calculated that before the Constitution, only a third of the population of the empire were enfranchised).[11] The best test of the value of a legal status is to ask what the consequences were if you were deprived of it. As Fustel saw, citizenship was an exclusive club to which the outsider could not belong, and the worst punishment a city could inflict was exile (deprivation of citizen rights). The punishments of deportation and relegation continued to be used in imperial legislation after AD 212: you could still be deprived of your citizen rights, and that included being deprived of your property. Citizenship was not automatic: you had to be inscribed in your local roll of citizens, *politographesthai*, a metaphor favoured by Christian authors before Augustine who saw membership of what Paul had called the *politeuma en ouranois* as analogous to citizenship.[12]

That Roman citizenship was never literally 'universal' is shown by the exceptions. Under a law brought in by Augustus, a slave who had been

---

[8] Sherwin-White, *Roman Citizenship*, pp. 264–287; Nicolet, *The World of the Citizen*, pp. 383–398.
[9] Duplouy, 'Citizenship as performance'.
[10] See Bresson, 'Fifty years before the Antonine Constitution'.
[11] Myles Lavan, 'The spread of Roman citizenship'.
[12] So Rapp, 'City and citizenship as Christian concepts', esp. 159–161; Paul, *Letter to the Philippians* 3.20, ἡμῶν γὰρ τὸ πολίτευμα ἐν οὐρανοῖς ὑπάρχει.

subjected to the formal punishment of a flogging or torture could never become a Roman citizen. Instead, the status of *dediticius*, on analogy to a surrendered enemy, was devised. It used to be thought that the Giessen papyrus mentioned this category as an exception; alternative readings are now preferred. Even so, late Roman law codes make clear that the status survived as one excluding citizen rights.[13] So did the status of 'Latin' (or 'Junian Latin') for a freed slave without citizen rights. You could be reduced to 'Latinity' as a punishment. So Constantine ruled:

> If a man should lose the dignity of Roman citizenship and thereby become a Latin and if he should depart from life while in the said status, his entire savings (*peculium*) shall be vindicated by his patron. (*Codex Theodosianus* 2.22.1)

Nor were freed slaves the only ones who could lose citizen rights. A longstanding instrument of Roman law was the declaration of a citizen as *infamis* (language that still survives among the Sicilian mafia). Certain categories were automatically regarded as *infames*: prostitutes, pimps, gladiators, actors, and bar-keepers among them.[14] While remaining citizens, they were excluded from certain aspects of public life, such as holding office or the ability to appear as a witness (Roman legal transactions commonly required seven witnesses, and bundles of documents from a little city like Herculaneum show what a role such witnessing played in social life).[15] In the Later Empire, branding with *infamia* becomes an ever heavier exclusion. So Constantine decreed a severe penalty for elite members who married 'loose women':

> Senators or those with the rank of *perfectissimus*, or those who in cities have held duumviral and quinquennial office or the distinctions of priest or *flamen* of the province shall be subjected to the stain of *infamia* and be foreigners (*peregrini*) outside Roman law if they marry a slave girl or daughter of a slave girl or freedwoman or daughter of a freedwoman, whether of Roman or Latin status, or an actress or daughter of an actress or an innkeeper or daughter of an innkeeper or a humble and abject women or daughter of a pimp or a gladiator, etc., etc. (*Codex Theodosianus* 4.6.3)

Just what being reduced to 'peregrines' outside Roman law meant is not clear, but it explicitly included a ban on passing property to the offspring of

---

[13] The status of *dediticius* was only removed from the statutes by Justinian, *Codex Justinianus* 7.5.1.
[14] See Gardner, *Being a Roman Citizen*, pp. 110–154.
[15] Wallace-Hadrill, *Herculaneum*, pp. 142–145.

any such marriage, and attempts to find loopholes were fiercely chased up under the threat of torture. More broadly, *infamia* was used as a penalty for a variety of legal offences, including punishment for judges themselves who delayed execution of sentence or allowed the condemned to be spirited away by clerics.[16]

Of course, exclusion from public privileges and property rights was especially hard for members of the upper order. It affected people of all statuses, and this became especially important as the blot of 'infamy' was directed against heretics. In the sixteenth book of the Theodosian Code, as intolerance of religious deviance became more marked under Theodosius I and his successors, the pressure is ramped up against non-Catholics, such as Arians, Manicheans, Donatists, and a multiplicity of other sects.[17] So in AD 381:

> If any Manichaean man or woman from the date of the law as previously and originally issued by Our Fathers, has transmitted his own property to any person whatsoever, by the execution of a testament or under any title of liberality whatever or any kind of gift, or if any one of the aforesaid persons has become enriched by the bestowal, through any form whatever, of an inheritance upon which he has entered, inasmuch as We forthwith deprive the aforesaid persons under the perpetual brand of just infamy of all right to make a will and live under Roman law, and since we do not permit them to have the right to bequeath or take any inheritance, the whole of such property, after due investigation conducted by our fisc, shall be appropriated to its resources. (16.5.7, Gratian, Valentinian and Theodosius, AD 381)

If Manicheans were the worst of heretics, those who apostatised from Catholicism to the pagan religion were scarcely better. Valentinian, Theodosius, and Arcadius decreed in AD 391:

> If any persons who have won distinction or been born to high rank deviate from the faith and blinded in mind abandon the worship and practice of the sacrosanct religion and have taken part in sacrifices, they should lose rank in such way that ejected from their place and standing they should be branded with perpetual infamy and be numbered not even among the lowest of the low. (16.7.5)

The Eunomians seem to have been less objectionable, and the constitutions vacillate between condemning and partially tolerating them. A decree

---

[16] *CTh* 9.40.15: see Lafferty, *Law and Society in the Age of Theoderic*, p. 90.

[17] See Humfress, 'Citizens and heretics'; Flierman and Rose, 'Banished from the company of the good'.

of AD 399 by Arcadius and Honorius in overriding a previous decision spells out what was at stake:

> For the Eunomians We remit the penalty of being deprived of testamentary capacity and of having their status changed to that of foreigners (*pegrinorumque mutandae condicionis*). We permit them to have the unrestricted power to make gifts from their own property as they wish, and to receive property in turn as a gift from others. (16.5.36.1)

On the other hand, if they persist in having gatherings and electing supposed bishops, 'they shall be deported and have their goods confiscated' (16.5.36.3). The main feature of the status of *peregrinus* seems to be incapacity to make wills or inherit under Roman law, and it is to be distinguished from deportation and confiscation, which is a more severe punishment.

The imperial pronouncements do not hesitate to use language of a highly coloured nature. Heretics are regularly condemned as raving madmen:

> The madness (*dementia*) of heretics shall not attempt further to perpetrate the criminality which they have devised nor to hold unlawful councils. (16.5.24)

Madness, like membership of infamous professions, compromised the rights of Roman citizens. The *furiosi* and *dementes* lacked the capacity to engage in any legal act.[18] By rhetorically defining heretics as insane, by implication their rights as Roman citizens were forfeited.

It is not just a question of the legal rights of citizenship, but of the right to live in cities. Expulsion from Rome to beyond the hundredth milestone was a traditional Roman way of controlling undesirable cults, including astrologers. Theodosius II and Valentinian III latch on to such traditional terms instructing the City Prefect of Rome:

> We command that Manicheans, heretics, schismatics, astrologers and every sect inimical to the Catholics shall be banished from the very sight of the City of Rome, in order that it may not be contaminated by the contagious presence of the criminals ... Unless they return within that time [twenty days] to the unity of communion, they shall be expelled from the City as far as the hundredth milestone and shall be tormented by the solitude of their choice. (16.5.62)

---

[18] Gardner, *Being a Roman Citizen*, pp. 167–172.

It could be not just Rome but all cities from which heretics were exiled:

> Those persons, however, who are not devoted to the aforesaid doctrines [i.e. of Trinitarian Catholicism] shall cease to assume, with studied deceit, the alien name of true religion, and they shall be branded upon the disclosure of their crimes. They shall be removed and completely barred from the threshold of all churches, since we forbid all heretics to hold unlawful assemblies within the towns. If factions should attempt anything, We order that their madness (*furor*) shall be banished and that they shall be driven away from the very walls of the cities (*ab ipsis urbium moenibus*), in order that Catholic churches throughout the whole world may be restored to the orthodox bishops who hold the Nicene faith. (16.5.6.3)

It is the cities of the empire that are the stronghold of bishops, and within their walls the orthodox doctrine must reign supreme.

This small sample of the flood of measures directed against heretics (sixty-six measures), apostates (seven), Jews (twenty-eight), and pagans (twenty-four) shows clearly that citizenship and its rights still had plenty of meaning. Just as the earlier emperors had used citizenship to reward the loyal, later emperors use its removal to punish the disloyal. Not only the legal gap between free and slave, and among freedmen between Romans and Latins, but also that between citizen and *peregrinus* still matter and could be deployed as a weapon in the imperial armoury. And since the tendency of the legislation was to deprive heretics and pagans of their civil rights (in the case of Jews, the rights of a traditional religion were still respected, provided they did not encroach on Christian space), it meant that progressively it was more the case that to be a Roman citizen was to be a Catholic Christian following the Nicene creed.

Orosius Against the Pagans

If before turning back to Augustine, we look at his younger friend, Orosius, we find that the categories of citizen and Christian have virtually merged. Originally from Spain, perhaps Braga, Orosius fled to Africa from barbarian raids in the second decade of the fifth century and took refuge in Hippo. Augustine, at the time working on his great refutation of pagan criticisms, set the young Spanish presbyter the task of research into Roman history and refuting the pagan case that the sack of Rome was the consequence of abandoning the old religion. Compared to Augustine's long and highly sophisticated answer to the pagans, Orosius had what sometimes seems a naively optimistic response: Roman history was a long story of brutalities and catastrophes survived, and unpleasant though the sack of Rome might have been, horrors were simply part of what was to be expected:[19]

> Did not my eyes fill with tears as I reviewed the past in order to prove that calamities have recurred in cycles through the ages? ... As I pondered over all this, did I not make the terrible experiences of my ancestors my own? ... And yet, if I may speak of my own story, how for the first time I saw those strange barbarians ... I slipped through the clutches of those who with stones and spears pursued me over the sea, I would that I could move my audience to tears. (3.20)

He can offer an example close to home of the repetitive horrors of history. Already in the reign of Gallienus in the mid third century, there had been a scourge of barbarian invasions, sent as divine punishment for the persecution of Christians:

> Throughout the various provinces, there exist today poor and insignificant settlements situated in the ruins of great cities which still bear evidences of their names and tokens of their misfortunes. Our own city of Tarraco in Spain is one of these, and we can point to it to console ourselves over our recent misery. (7.22)

So barbarian invasions are nothing new, and the consolation is that things could actually be worse: God is on the side of the Roman city, as could be seen in the way he got the barbarians to spare the Christians in Rome (7.39).

Orosius could still be remarkably cheerful about the advantages of being a Roman citizen in a Christian Roman Empire. After his flight from Spain to Africa, he takes comfort in the reflection that as a Roman he can take refuge anywhere in the empire:

> The width of the East, the vastness of the North, the great stretches of the South, the largest and most secure settlements on great islands, all have the same law and nationality as I (*mei iuris et nominis*), since I come there as a Roman and Christian to Christians and Romans. I do not fear the gods of my host. Neither do I fear that his religion will bring death to me. Nor am I afraid of any place where a native may do whatever is lawful and a stranger (*peregrino*) may not do whatever is lawful, where my host's law

---

[19] See Fear, *Orosius Seven Books of History*. The translations cited below are those of Raymond, *Seven Books of History against the Pagans*. For a sympathetic reading of Orosius' 'optimism' as a rhetorical strategy, see Van Nuffelen, *Orosius and the Rhetoric of History*. On the gap between Orosius and Augustine, Markus, *Saeculum*, pp. 2, 161–162; Brown, *Augustine of Hippo*, p. 296; Merrills, *History and Geography in Late Antiquity*, pp. 35–39, 62–64, 97–99.

will not be my own. One God, who established the unity of this realm in the days when he willed himself to become known [Orosius regards the Pax Augusta as providentially co-incident with the birth of Christ] is known and feared by all. The same laws, which are subject to God, hold sway everywhere. Wheresoever I go, stranger though I be, I need harbour no fear of sudden assault as a man without protection. Among Romans I am a Roman; among Christians, a Christian; among men, a man. The State comes to my aid with its laws, religion through its appeal to the conscience, and nature through its claim of universality. For a time I enjoy any country as if it were my own (*utor temporarie omni terra quasi patria*) because that native land, which is my real home and I love (*illa quam amo patria*) in not wholly on this earth.[20]

There is, for Orosius, a complete coincidence between Roman law and identity on the one hand and Christianity on the other. If Augustine felt himself more a citizen of the *civitas Dei* than the *civitas terrena*, for Orosius, thanks to divine providence, they overlap entirely. Indeed, he believes that even the Goths have understood the necessity of the rule of Roman law, and cites an acquaintance from Narbo whom he had met in Bethlehem, who had heard the Visigothic king Athaulf (Adolf) repeatedly say that when he understood that the barbarians were so lawless that a state could only be established by Roman laws, he had abandoned the ambition to obliterate the Roman name and create a Gothia in the place of Romania (7.43). On this irrepressibly cheerful note Orosius ends his history by challenging the reader to find any equally fortunate period from the foundation of the world to the present day (7.43).

Orosius' praise for Rome – and, specifically, the ideal of citizenship – has more than a trace of the panegyrical to it. Indeed, it has close parallels with a passage of a contemporary poet, Claudian – one that has been described as 'perhaps the most eloquent eulogy of Rome in all ancient literature'.[21] The court poet of Honorius and fervent supporter of his general, Stilicho, Claudian was a writer known to and seemingly admired by both Orosius and Augustine, though each laments his stubborn paganism.[22] On the occasion of Stilicho's elevation to the consulship in 400, Claudian wrote an extensive panegyric in three epic 'books'. The third contains a fulsome panegyric of Rome (*On Stilicho's Consulship* 3. 130–160).[23] After praising

---

[20] Orosius 5.2: *inter Romanos, ut dixi, Romanus, inter Christianos Christianus, inter homines homo legibus inploro rempublicam, religione conscientiam, communione naturam.*
[21] Cameron, *Claudian*, p. 236.
[22] Orosius, *Histories* 7.35, *paganus pervicacissimus*; Augustine, *Civ.Dei* 5.26, *a Christi nomine alienus*; see Cameron, *Claudian*, p. 191.
[23] Cameron, *Claudian*, pp. 352–354, offers full text and translation.

the size and beauty of the *urbs*, the seven hills of which rival the seven zones of the heavens, he turns to Roman citizenship:

> Haec est in gremium vistos quae sola recepit
> Humanumque genus communi nomine fovit
> Matris non dominae ritu, civesque vocavit
> Quos domuit, nexuque pio longinqua revinxit. (150–153)

> She alone has received the conquered into her bosom and like a mother not a mistress protected the human race with a common name, summoning those whom she has defeated to share her citizenship and drawing together distant races with bonds of affection.

Like Orosius and, as we will see, Augustine, Claudian celebrates the extension of citizen rights to the conquered as a quality of the Roman Empire that distinguishes it from other empires. A quite specific benefit of this is the freedom to travel:

> To her rule of peace we owe it that the world is our home, that we can live where we please, and that to visit Thule and explore its once dreaded wilds is a sport; thanks to her all may drink the waters of the Rhône and quaff Orontes' stream, thanks to her we are all one people. (154–159)

Just as Orosius, born in Spain and moving thence to Africa then Palestine, Claudian spoke from personal experience: born in Egypt speaking Greek, he moved to Rome and established his remarkable mastery of Latin poetical language. Critics have suggested that nothing in Claudian's praise of Rome is original and that all its topics drew on an extensive tradition of panegyric; if so, his skill is 'not so much a personal historical judgement of the Roman achievement, as Claudian's skill in assembling the *topoi* of a genre'.[24] This may be so; but it is striking that three authors writing within a few years of one another, and aware of each other's writings, should focus on the gift of citizenship as the hallmark of the Roman Empire.[25]

The City of God

Augustine, by contrast with Orosius, sees little cause for optimism in the things of this world: his hopes are pinned on the world to come. One of the

---

[24] Cameron, *Claudian*, p. 354.
[25] Claudian is cited also by Sherwin-White, *Roman Citizenship*, pp. 465–468, noting the traditional panegyrical elements. Surprisingly, he omits to cite the lines on citizenship; nor does he mention the parallel with Orosius.

themes of his exchange with Nectarius of Calama was a re-reading of Cicero's *Republic*. In his *de Civitate Dei* (always translated as the *City of God*, though the Latin equally conveys *Citizenship*) he picks up that theme, amplifies it, and elaborates it.[26] The Gothic sack of Rome in the interim has given a sharper edge to the reproofs of the pagans, who can now maintain that Rome 'fell' precisely because the cults of the gods who had always protected it had been banned. Like Orosius, he can point to the sackings of cities that were a constant theme of Roman history; unlike Orosius, his argument is not that things could be worse, but that the pagan gods have shown themselves to be utterly indifferent to the fates of cities and the sufferings of their worshippers. The Roman Empire was won at the cost of the sackings of numerous great cities,[27] which were never spared. Marcellus wept at the prospect of the sacking of Syracuse; Fabius Maximus, in sacking Tarentum, did not rescue the cult images of the gods ('let us leave them their angry gods'). He might have added Scipio Aemilianus weeping at the sack of Carthage, or Mummius at that of Corinth. Of all the examples of sacked cities he adduces, Troy is the most powerful.

Augustine deploys Virgil to heighten the drama and emotional effect.[28] As he points out, his pagan audience were 'imbued' with the text of Virgil from their earliest years, as was Augustine himself (for the metaphor of 'imbued' he aptly cites Horace on wine jars 'imbued' with odours).[29] What goes in early, goes deep. Virgil's description of the sacking of Troy is pitiless and shows the gods powerless to protect it. Aeneas sees Priam, not only king but high priest, staining with blood the fires of his own sacrificial altar.[30] The shrine of Juno, the Trojans' great protectress, is used by the Greeks to store their spoils. Later, he waxes satirical at the failure of the very gods that Aeneas brought with him from Troy to protect either Troy or Rome. Long before the Gothic sack was the Gallic sack (of the fourth century BC), when only the honking of the geese on the Capitoline saved that sacred hill. Rome was saved by geese, not gods. And where were those

---

[26] The classic study of the *City of God* is Markus, *Saeculum*. For some more recent views, Wetzel, *Augustine's City of God*; Vessey, *A Companion to Augustine*. For the author's life, the classic remains Brown, *Augustine of Hippo*; more recently, O'Donnell, *Augustine: A New Biography*.

[27] *Civ.Dei* 1.6: tot tantasque urbes ut late dominaretur expugnatas.

[28] On Augustine's use of classical literature, see the comprehensive review of Hagendahl, *Augustine and the Latin Classics*. On Augustine's use of Virgil, MacCormack, *The Shadows of Poetry*, esp. on his comparison of the sack of Rome to Troy (pp. 159–174).

[29] 1.3: Horace, *Epistles* 1.2.69f.: *quo semel est imbuta recens servabit odorem/ testa diu*. On the 'bookishness' of Augustine's text, see Vessey, 'The history of the book'; further, Clark, 'City of Books: Augustine and the World as Texts'; Strousma, 'Augustine and books'; Shanzer, 'Augustine and the Latin classics'.

[30] 1.2, sanguine foedantem quos ipse sacraverit ignes.

gods in the hour of need? Buzzing off like a swarm of flies (*tamquam muscas*). Just as Virgil described, they fled, 'abandoning shrines and altars, the very gods by whom the empire stood'.[31] They even allowed Troy to be sacked a second time, by the brutal partisan of Marius, Fimbria (85 BC); again the gods did nothing, for all their acute hearing and rapidity of movement (3.7–8). In the sack of Rome, by contrast, those who took refuge in Christian shrines and basilicas were spared by the Christian Goths, even the pagans who pretended to be Christians to save their own lives. Where else could one read of the sack of a city in which such mercy was shown, when the rules of war allowed no quarter (1.6)?

If there is a Classical author with whom Augustine is equally 'imbued' as with Virgil, it is Cicero. It is not to be forgotten that Augustine started his career as a teacher of rhetoric (like Ausonius and Libanius). The *Republic* (only one among the many Ciceronian texts cited) plays a key role in the strategy of the *City of God*. This text offers a definition of the 'city', albeit the *res publica* rather than the *civitas* – the slide between *politeia* and *polis* is pervasive in ancient thinking.[32] Definitions, says Augustine, are most useful in debate, and Scipio Aemilianus, Cicero's principal spokesman in the *Republic*, which is staged as a historical discussion set in the previous century, defines as follows. The *respublica* is the *res populi* (linguistically, there is no disputing that) and the *populus*, crucially, is defined 'not as any gathering of a large number of people, but as a gathering associated by legal consensus and shared benefits'.[33] Here justice, *iustitia*, emerges as a defining feature of the city.[34] The three types of constitution, in Aristotelian terms kingship (*basileia*), aristocracy, and *politeia*, without justice are perverted into tyranny, oligarchy (in Latin, *factio*), and popular tyranny (Aristotle calls this *demokratia*): without justice, there is no longer a *populus*, held together by common bonds of law and mutual benefit, so there is no longer a *res publica* (*Civ.Dei* 2.21). Not only justice but also morality are needed for the community. Scipio cites the most famous of lines by Rome's first epic poet, Ennius:

> Moribus antiquis res stet Romana virisque
>
> Rome's state stands by ancient morals and by men.

---

[31] 1.23, citing *Aeneid* 2.351f.: excessere omnes, adytis arisque relictis/ Di quibus imperium hoc steterat.

[32] Ando, 'The children of Cain,' discusses Augustine's use of the slide of meanings in *civitas*; cf. Conybeare, 'The city of Augustine'.

[33] 2.21: coetum iuris consensu et utilitatis communione sociatum, = Cicero, *Republic* 2.42.

[34] See Dodaro, *Christ and the Just Society*, pp. 4–5 and 10–17, on his redefinition of *iustitia*.

Thus, *mores* are a crucial element in the Roman state, though the historians – and particularly Sallust, who is here much cited – show the Roman republic suffering a moral collapse. But Cicero, now speaking in his own voice not that of Scipio, sees the Rome of his generation as having lost that which once made it great:

> Our generation which inherited the republic like a masterpiece of art, but faded with age, not only neglected to restore its original colours, but did not even bother to preserve its shape and outlines.[35]

Here is a confession which plays straight into Augustine's hands: the collapse of Roman morality and justice predates the birth of Christ. The pagan gods have done nothing whatsoever to promote morality; on the contrary, they demand festivals and theatrical performances which are an open incitement to immorality. The Romans themselves admit this by their classification of actors as *infames*. Cicero elsewhere concedes how as aedile he had celebrated the games of Flora, and as consul has celebrated ten days of festival to placate the gods in the crisis of the Catilinarian conspiracy. For Augustine it was self-evident that such festivals were obscene and immoral (2.27),[36] and it gives him a chance for his favourite play on words between morals and walls (one might almost say murals). The fall of *morum* precedes the fall of *moenium*.[37]

As for the justice that is a defining element of the *res publica*, Scipio in Cicero's *Republic* describes it as a form of musical harmony, of high notes and low notes, of the high and low in society. This harmonious concord in a city is the closest and strongest bond of safety in any constitution, and 'without justice it cannot exist'.[38] That opens the way for Augustine to demonstrate through Roman history as narrated by Sallust the disintegration of concord, the struggle of the orders, the civil and social wars, and the corruption of Rome by luxury and avarice, marking the collapse of justice and concord in the Republican Roman state. Rome fell while its walls were still intact (2.22). Later, as he tries to explain the City of God, he returns to the theme: did Rome ever truly have a *res publica*? Justice is not, as Plato's

---

[35] 2.21.

[36] See, further, Herdt, 'The theatre of the virtues'; Lim, 'Augustine and Roman public spectacles'. More broadly on Christian attitudes to spectacles, Lugaresi, *Il teatro di Dio*.

[37] 2.27: *qui non obponerentur defensores obpugnationibus moenium, nisi prius fierent expugnatores morum bonorum*; cf. 1.33, (Scipio) *neque enim censebat ille felicem esse rem publicam stantibus moenibus, ruentibus moribus*; 2.2 *omnis non murorum sed morum monumenta adque ornamenta ceciderunt.*

[38] 2,21 *eam esse in civitate concordiam ... eamque sine iustitia nullo pacto esse posse* = Cicero, *Rep.* 2.42.

Thrasymachus suggested, the imposition of the advantage of the powerful on the weak. But to deny the worship of the true God, as for centuries of persecution of Christians, is to deny each man his deserts, *suum cuique*, and thus to deny justice (19.21–22). Augustine's pagan critics, who doubtless abandoned reading this blockbuster many books back, might have reasonably retorted that it was in that case scarcely just to deny pagans their worship. But for Augustine, the only just city is the one united harmoniously in the worship of the true God.

There is one further essential element which Augustine takes from Cicero's *Republic*, and that is self-sacrificial loyalty to your *patria* (your home *city* not your home*land*). As often, a citation from Virgil flags raised emotional intensity. Brutus, who sacrificed his sons for the state, is the emblem of patriotism:

> Vicit amor patriae laudumque immensa cupido
>
> Love of the city won and the immense desire for praise. (*Aeneid* 6.823)

The Romans are driven by liberty and hunger for fame; how much more so should one be prepared to free the world of the works of the devil? A roll call of republican heroes further exemplifies this *amor patriae*: Torquatus, who executed a son for military disobedience, Camillus who twice saved Rome; Mucius who held his hand in the fire, and so on (5.18). If that is the Roman devotion to the republic, the good of the people, the good of the home city, the common weal,[39] surely the Romans give an example of the love owed to the city above.[40] He urges the pagans to convert. Again, Virgil catches the emotion:

> *Sanguine nobis*
> *Hanc patriam peperere suo.*
>
> With their blood they won us this home city. (*Aeneid* 11.24f.)

He exhorts the pagans to become members of this heavenly *patria* and to be added to the number of its citizens – a true asylum (contrasted to the asylum of Romulus) which offers remission of sins. So the City of God trumps the City of Rome. If for Cicero the natural feelings of patriotism felt for your place of birth were trumped by the love owed to Rome, now it is the heavenly city to which the Romans are to be recruited as newly enrolled citizens, trumping all other claims on their loyalty.[41]

---

[39] 5.18: *rem publicam, id est rem populi, rem patriae, rem communem.*
[40] 5.16: *quanta dilectio debeatur supernae patriae.*
[41] 2.29: *ad quam patriam te invitamus et exhortamur, ut eius adiciaris numero civium, cuius quodam modo asylum est vera remissio peccatorum.*

To demolish the pagan gods, Augustine turns to a close reading of Varro's *Antiquities, Human and Divine*. This work, unlike Varro on the *Latin Language* (in part) and *Agriculture*, is lost to us, and we have to rely on Augustine's report, extensive as it is. We rely on him too for Cicero's words of high praise for his contemporary:

> We, he says, who were foreign residents (*peregrinantes*) in our own city and like lost visitors, were brought back home by your books, so that finally we could recognise who and where we were. (6.2)

That is a key passage for Augustine's construction of the idea of a celestial citizenship. The Romans are *peregrini*, outsiders to Roman citizenship, in their own city because they do not recognise their own gods, to whom Varro's antiquarian researches re-introduce them.[42] The idea that Roman identity is bound up in Roman religion, and that this religion is bound up in the physical fabric of their city ('not a stone of the city but is full of the sense of the divine', as Livy's Camillus puts it; 5.51) might seem an insuperable obstacle to Augustine's attempt to strip Rome of its ancestral gods. But he turns it to his advantage. Just as Cicero sees Romans as *peregrini* for lack of knowledge of their gods, but ones who could be reincorporated through recovered knowledge, Augustine sees Romans as *peregrini*, pilgrims waiting to discover through the true god the true city.[43]

Throughout the first ten books Augustine is engaging closely with Classical literature: not just Virgil, Cicero, Sallust, and Varro, his principal witnesses for antiquity;[44] Plato and the neo-Platonists, Apuleius, Plotinus and Porphyry, for pagan philosophy; but also (among others) Terence (despite his disapproval of the stage, he loves this dramatist),[45] Horace, Lucan, the satirist Persius (but not Juvenal), the histories of Pompeius Trogus (but not Tacitus or Suetonius), and Aulus Gellius. That is part of a strategy to win round the pagans who loved the same literature.[46] But when it comes to describing the City of God, of necessity he turns to the Bible, and his tone changes to one of faithful exegesis, of texts which must by definition contain the truth, but may need subtle and allegorical interpretation to tease out their true meaning. The last twelve books are a minute exegesis of biblical texts relevant, in his vision, to the City of

---

[42] On his use of Varro, see Vessey, 'The history of the book', 20–24.
[43] I have discussed Varro's *Antiquities* in *Rome's Cultural Revolution*, pp. 231–237.
[44] See bibliography cited above. Vessey, 'The history of the book', p. 22, notes that Virgil, Cicero, Salust, and Terence were the staple of the contemporary schools of grammar and rhetoric.
[45] At *Confessions* 1.16 he admits his early fondness for Terence; ibid. 3.1.1, on his early passion for the stage at Carthage.
[46] So Brown, *Augustine of Hippo*, pp. 304–305.

God. And though the idea of the City of God, *politeuma en ouranô*, was already explicit in the Pauline epistles which he revered, it is to the Old Testament that he turns for authority.[47]

The biblical authority for the 'City of God' lies in particular in the Psalms, on which Augustine had already written 'discourses' bringing out the theme.[48] At the outset of the eleventh book, the first of the sequence on the theme, he states that the scriptural authority is to be found in the Psalms (11.1): 'Glorious things are spoken of thee, O City of God (*civitas Dei*)' (Ps. 87.3); 'Great is the Lord, and greatly to be praised in the City of our God (*in civitate Dei nostri*), in the mountain of his holiness' (Ps. 48.1); 'There is a river, the streams whereof shall make glad the City of God (*civitatem Dei*), the holy place of the tabernacles of the most High' (Ps. 46.4). Of course, to the psalmist, whom Augustine identifies as David, the city was Jerusalem with its hill, Mount Zion; as Psalm 48 continues (Figure 3.1):

[11] Let mount Zion rejoice, let the daughters of Judah be glad, because of thy judgements.
[12] Walk about Zion, and go round about her: tell the towers thereof.
[13] Mark ye well her bulwarks, consider her palaces; that ye may tell it to the generation following.
[14] For this God is our God for ever and ever: he will be our guide even unto death.

Augustine, to whom allegorical or 'mystical' readings were second nature, sees it not just as Jerusalem, but as the Heavenly Jerusalem, not the human city which God loves, but as God's own celestial city. With this authority under his belt, he sets about the task of tracing the Heavenly City, its origin, progress, and end, throughout the Old Testaments, whether or not it is explicitly mentioned. In his vision, there is from the outset an antithetical pair of two cities, one heavenly, one terrestrial. And he warns repeatedly that they form no simple opposition, for they are deeply entangled one with another: *in hoc saeculo perplexas ... invicemque permixtas*.[49]

The heavenly city must go back to the very Creation of the world, populated by God's angels; undeterred by the failure of *Genesis* to mention here either the City or even angels,[50] he pins it down to the first day of

---

[47] Paul, *Letter to the Philippians* 3.20. See Rapp, 'City and citizenship'. On Augustine's constructive misreading of the bible, see Ando, 'The children of Cain'.
[48] Brown, *Augustine of Hippo*, p. 314. Augustine, *Enarrationes in Psalmos*.
[49] 11.1; cf. 1.34 *perplexae quippe sunt istae duae civitates in hoc saeculo invicemque permixtae*; 10.32 *quas in hoc saeculo perplexas diximus invicemque permixtas*.
[50] No angel appears in the text until *Genesis* 16.7. But Ambrose, *Hexameron* 1.18.19, already thought that angels existed when God created heaven and earth.

Figure 3.1 Heavenly Jerusalem in Psalm 48. The Harley Psalter BL Harley MS 603, 27v. Courtesy of the British Library Board.

Creation, when God separated light and dark, thereby separating the celestial city of light, and its contrary city of dark, inhabited by fallen angels or devils.[51] What originates in heaven is then reflected on earth with the first men,[52] though we are to take note that there are not four cities, two in heaven and two on earth, but just two conjoined in heaven and earth, the heavenly belonging to good angels and men, the earthly to fallen angels and evil men (12.1), or the men who live by the flesh as against those who live by the spirit (14.1). The children of Adam and Eve, Cain and Abel, are the founders on earth of the heavenly and terrestrial cities (15.1).[53] Cain, who kills his brother Abel, foreshadows the Roman founder, Romulus, killing Remus (15.5). Cain is explicitly said by *Genesis* to have founded the first city, named after his son, Enoch;[54] This Augustine identifies as the model of the terrestrial city. The knotty problem of who were the inhabitants of

---

[51] 11.7 *lucis nomine significata est sancta civitas in sanctis angelis et spritibus beatis*. 11.11–20 for the fallen angels. Augustine had already written a twelve-book commentary on Genesis.

[52] 11.34 *de duabus istis diversis inter se adque contrariis societatibus angelorum, in quibus sunt exordia duarum et in rebus humanis civitatum.*

[53] Both the originality of Augustine's use of the city of Cain, and its later influence, are brilliantly demonstrated by Ottewill-Soulsby in 'First cities in Late Antique Christian thought' and 'Hunting diligently through the volumes of the Ancients'.

[54] 15.8, citing *Gen*. 4.17: *erat aedificans civitatem in nomine filii sui Enoch*.

that first city is solved by invoking the extraordinary length of lives of men of those days, which gave time to the original family to populate a city (15.10–15). Abel, effectively the first on earth to found the heavenly city, is followed by Seth, so that two cities run alongside each other, the heavenly one of those who are *peregrinantes* on earth, foreigners not citizens, headed now by Seth, and the terrestrial city of the sinful fratricide Cain (15.15). But God allows men freedom of will, which means there is no clear distinction of the heavenly and terrestrial cities on earth: the beauty of their daughters proves irresistible, and they intermarry (15.22). This is what he has always warned about the cities being mixed and entangled. The thought that the angels might have carnal knowledge of terrestrial women is rapidly dismissed (15.23).

Once Augustine has established the principle of antithetical pairs – light and dark, young and old, heavenly and terrestrial – his intertwined cities can be seen flowing through history. Having taken this down to the reign of King David, the Psalmist, he calls a halt on the grounds of excessive material (17.1), and notes that methodologically neither a purely historical not a purely allegorical interpretation of the Old Testament works, and that you have to mix methods (17.3), so giving himself the best of both worlds.[55] When he returns to the narrative element of his exposition in book 20, it is to show what *Revelations* has to say about the end of the two cities. The Last Judgement is depicted as an epic showdown between the two cities, in which the forces of the heavenly city finally defeat and obliterate those of the terrestrial city. We might be in the final scenes of *The Lord of the Rings*.

A pagan, at least one not imbued like Horace's wine jar with the texts of the scriptures, might find the last twelve books less penetrable than the first ten. But they could not miss the sustained attack on Roman imperialism. In the first five books, as we have seen, he rebuts the pagan accusation that disasters have fallen on Rome as a consequence of the suppression of pagan cults. Orosius, who lacked Augustine's rhetorical cutting edge, was content to demonstrate that there were plenty of miseries and disasters in the pagan past. Augustine goes considerably further. By establishing the Ciceronian definition of the state as dependent on justice and concord, he demonstrates that Rome lacked these essential requisites. How come, if Numa established Roman religion and the peace symbolised in the closure of the temple of Janus, that Rome was thereafter continuously at war (3.9)? Was it

---

[55] He is also consciously avoiding repetition of what he had already written in the *Enarratio in Psalmos*.

not, as Virgil saw, that as Rome 'gradually deteriorated and lost its gleam the madness of war and love of possession took over'?

> Deterior donec paulatim at decolor aetas
>
> Et belli rabies et amor successit habendi?[56]

Sallust thought that initially the Rome of the kings was without *cupiditas*, greed. But he conceded that prosperity brought envy: how different it would have been if the doors of the temple of Janus had remained closed and Rome had not been continuously at war with its neighbours (3.10). Sallust dated the lust for domination, *libido dominandi*, to the growth of empire in Asia under Cyrus, in Greece with the Spartans and Athenians; but Augustine can see the same lust in Rome's war with Alba in the regal period (3.14). Upon the establishment of the Republic, on Sallust's own account, the patricians started to oppress the plebs and innumerable riots, seditions, and civil wars arose: the Roman historians are so attached to freedom of speech that they do nothing to cover up the ills of their city, *mala civitatis* (3.17). Then, with the Punic wars, things got even worse: how many great and noble cities (*urbes*) were destroyed and how many *civitates* were lost (3.18)!

Augustine gradually establishes not merely that pagan cult did nothing to protect Rome from misery, but that Rome was marked from the start by lust for empire, appropriately in a city founded by a fratricide. The pagans attributed the growth and duration of Roman Empire to these gods: but what human happiness could there be in a story of calamitous warfare and bloodshed driven by greed (*cruenta cupiditate*) (4.3)? Justice, as Cicero saw, is the key ingredient: take justice away and what are kingdoms but brigandage on a large scale – *remota itaque iustitia quid sunt regna nisi magna latrocinia*? *Latrocinium* is as negative a term as you could ask for: a 'terrorist organisation', in modern terms. He cites the anecdote of Alexander's exchange with a pirate, who points out that the difference between them was that he, the pirate, operated with a single small ship, Alexander with a large navy (4.4). The Romans regarded pirates and rebel slaves with equal horror: Spartacus and his gladiators were the most frightening encounter which Rome had with their like: Where did the gods stand if a small band of gladiators could make the empire tremble (4.5)?

The Romans are not unique in building an empire on imperial desire, *cupiditas imperii*. Ninus built an empire in Assyria which lasted, according

---

[56] *Aeneid* 8.326–327, cited at *Civ.Dei* 3.10.

to Pompeius Trogus, 1,240 years (4.6). If Ninus could build such an empire without the gods of Rome, why should they be given credit for Rome's empire? Nor should we assume that the Roman Empire is now lost, afflicted rather than changed: given that even before Christian times it has recovered from affliction, no more should we despair now: who knows what the future will bring except God? (4.7).

To what, then, should we attribute the extent and duration of Roman power? Neither the sort of Felicity whom Romans turn into a goddess, nor the sort of fate which astrologers attempt to discern are satisfactory explanations (5.1). Augustine now brings Sallust and Virgil to bear witness on the moral qualities on which empire was built, the love of glory and honour flourishing before ambition and avarice took their place (5.12). It was the will of God that the Roman Empire should be larger and broader than the Assyrian, and he granted this to men who were motivated by honour, praise, and glory in what they did for their *patria*, and repressed their desire for money and other faults (5.13). Here Horace is brought into play, advising how to contain love of praise (*Epistles* 1.1.36), and the rewards for overcoming the lust for domination:

> Latius regnes avidum domando/spiritum
>
> You will reign more broadly by taming your greedy/spirit. (*Odes* 2.2.9f.)

It is thus moral qualities (*mores*) rather than the pagan gods which earned the Romans their empire.

Augustine can see much that is positive in the empire. Not only is it the reward for virtues, but it offers a model to the citizens of the eternal city, from which they are pilgrims on earth. By contemplating the example of how they have been inspired by glory to love their earthly city, they can learn the love of the city above for life everlasting (5.16).[57] By such turns of phrase, Augustine makes explicit that the *civitas Romana* is his model for the *civitas superna*. He now offers what Nicholas Sherwin-White recognised as one of the most remarkable passages of praise of the Roman citizenship, even though in his view, as we have seen, Roman citizenship had lost its meaning with the Antonine Constitution.[58] Augustine's praise for Roman citizenship is unambiguous:

---

[57] Markus, *Saeculum* 45–71 shows the complexity of the relationship between Rome and Augustine's *civitas terrena*.
[58] Sherwin-White, *Roman Citizenship*, pp. 461–463; he also notes how Augustine draws on the technical and legal language of Roman citizenship. For the engagement of bishops with Roman law, see Humfress, *Orthodoxy and the Courts in Late Antiquity*.

> Did the Romans ever hurt any of the peoples whom they had conquered and gave laws to, except insofar as this happened through the immense slaughter of wars? If this had happened by mutual agreement, it would have enjoyed greater success; but there would have been no glorying in triumph. For neither is it the case that the Romans too did not live under the laws they imposed on others. Had all this been done without Mars and Bellona, in such a way that there would be no room for victory, and nobody fought in order to celebrate victory over another, would the Romans and other peoples not have shared one and the same terms? Especially should it rapidly happen, as later was done in the most welcome and humane fashion, that all those who belonged to the Roman empire should receive the common bond of citizenship and be *Romani cives*, and that thus all should have what had previously been the privilege of a few. (5.17)

The extension of citizenship to the subject peoples of the empire is precisely what makes *civitas Romana* a model for imaging the *civitas Dei*. One notes that Augustine's commendation is strongly qualified: the lust for domination which is typical in his view of all empires and the lust for military glory are the fatal flaws of the empire – had it been done by agreement, *concorditer*, it would have been so much better.

Alas, only too many Romans in their greed for power became beasts of cruelty and luxury, and none more so than Nero (5.19). It is striking that at this point Augustine passes over the obvious tactic of exploring imperial history: Tacitus would have given him as much material as Sallust did for the Republic, and the fleeting mention of Nero, hated by Christians as the first of the great persecutors, acknowledges as much. It is a deliberate tactic to set the debate in Rome's remote past.[59] By passing over the pagan emperors, and indeed the story of Christian persecutions, he allows himself the panegyrical praise of the Christian emperors with which the book concludes. Christian emperors control their lust for power and luxury (5.24). Constantine could found in his New Rome a city that was the ally and daughter of Rome, *civitatem Romano imperio sociam, velut ipsius Romae filiam*, but free of pagan religion, and enjoy a long and successful reign (5.25). Passing swiftly over the interval, including Julian, he turns to Theodosius, whose praises by Claudian he echoes: *O nimium dilecte Deo*, one loved too much by God (5.26). He is held up as the model, unlike the republican Romans, of how to behave in civil war, and his shocking massacre in the circus at Thessalonike is turned to his credit by the public penance imposed on him by Ambrose. By now Theodosius is dead, and his

---

[59] See Brown, *Augustine*, p. 304.

sons and soon his grandsons are in power, but that in itself made a panegyrical tone mandatory.[60] Nevertheless, it helps Augustine make his point: that Roman imperial rule has its benefits and its downsides, which are mitigated by the Christian faith of its emperors. One might read the praise of Theodosius as qualified by a hint of a threat: an emperor who does not submit to the church, *ecclesiastica cohercitus disciplina*, might forfeit the praise.

The end of the fifth book of this *magnum opus et arduum*[61] is perhaps as far as a pagan critic might be expected to read, unless they followed the discussions of Varro and Apuleius in the next five. The theme of the Roman Empire is now dropped, to re-emerge only in the fifteenth book. Cain, the first founder of the earthly city, was a fratricide, which reminds us that Rome was founded by the fratricidal Romulus. There is a difference: while Cain and Abel represented the earthly versus the heavenly cities, Romulus and Remus were competing for control of the earthly city and the glory of domination, *dominandi gloria* (15.5). They set Rome on its course of lust for power. In book 18 he takes up the theme of historical empires (18.2). Assyria and Rome have been the most important empires, and Assyria built Babylon as the first Rome.[62] Babylon, he has already argued, is to be identified with the tower of Babel, that symbol of pride and, importantly, of linguistic unity, a unity which God deliberately disperses (16.4). Augustine is very interested in the relationship of empire and language.[63] Linguistic diversity is the principal mechanism by which human societies are alienated from each other. In the hierarchy of family, city, and world, it is shared language that holds groups together, diversity that separates them. This is why Rome as an imperial city imposed on its conquered peoples not only obedience but also its language, in the interests of peace within the society – something, he adds a little surprisingly, that has given rise to an abundance of interpreters.[64] By contrast, the celestial city, during its peregrination on earth, calls out its citizens from all peoples and binds together its peregrine society in all languages (*in omnibus linguis peregrinam colligit*

---

[60] On the similarity of this passage to the panegyric of Pacatus, see Kelly, 'Political history: The later Roman Empire'.

[61] For the phrase, *Civ. Dei* 1 praef. 1, echoing Cicero, *Orator* 33: see Shanzer, 'Augustine and the Latin classics', p. 169.

[62] 18.2: *Babylonia quasi prima Roma*, picked up at 18.22: *condita est civitas Roma velut altera Babylon*.

[63] Burton, 'Augustine and language', discusses Augustine's limited competence in languages other than Latin.

[64] 19.7 at enim opera data est, ut imperiosa civitas non solum iugum, verum etiam linguam suam domitis gentibus per pacem societatis inponeret, per quam non deesset, immo et abundaret, etiam interpretum copia.

societatem), and does not mind about diversity in ways, laws, and institutions; far from breaking up this diversity, it welcomes and preserves it, provided only that all are united in the religion of the true God (19.17).[65] We may be struck by how post-colonialist his position is, both in his fundamental rejection of the egotistical thrust of imperialism and in his vision of linguistic and cultural diversity.

He can now return to the Ciceronian theme of justice. Linked to the theme of the difficulty of attaining justice is a devastating critique of torture in the Roman judicial system (19.6). We cannot help thinking of the pleas of Nectarius to spare the innocent of Calama from being subjected to judicial inquisition. The judges, he now argues, are under pressure to establish guilt and innocence. This leads them to torture innocent people because the judges are unsure of their innocence. How can one look without tears filling one's eyes at the judge who subjects the accused to torture for fear of killing an innocent man, and so kills him, and never discovers whether he was innocent or not? Augustine fully bears out the accounts in a historian like Ammianus of the brutality of late Roman judicial inquisition.

There is a further twist to add. The Romans not only deified Romulus but also imposed the cult on the conquered. The city grew on their ancestral religion, which they had imbibed like a mother's milk, and so drenched the subject populations in their opinions that they not only believed but professed that Romulus was a god, rather than give offence to the city of which he was founder (22.6D). The fear of causing offence, however slight, was enough to compel cities under Roman law to worship Romulus as a god; and yet they deterred people from worshipping Christ by the most brutal martyrdoms (22.6H). What is odd about this passage is that there is very little sign of a cult of Romulus, let alone its imposition, across the empire. The passage makes more sense if Romulus is taken to stand for the cult of emperors, which drew on the model of the deification of Romulus and which was heavily involved in the persecution of Christians.

Where, then, does this massive and subtle treatise leave the ancient city and citizenship? It has been assumed too often that it marks the end of Roman citizenship and the ancient ideal of the *civitas*.[66] That does little justice to Augustine's nuance and ambivalence. He is highly critical of

---

[65] See Markus, *Saeculum*, pp. 70–71 on this passage.
[66] For instance, Sherwin-White's *Roman Citizenship*, though his narrative ends with Caracalla, has Augustine as the last of the 'retrospective panegyrists' (pp. 461–468). In a parallel pattern of thought, Marrou, *Saint Augustin et la fin de la culture antique*, puts Augustine at the end of the educational tradition of antiquity.

Roman imperialism, the unificatory design of which goes against God's design; nevertheless, he openly welcomes the idea of universal citizenship and uses it as the model for his *civitas Dei*. He does not think that the days of the empire are numbered, believing the matter to be in God's hands, but he is anxious that emperors should, like Theodosius, listen to the church. The *civitas Dei* is indeed opposed to the *civitas Romana*, as heavenly to terrestrial; but, as he repeatedly says, the cities are entangled, and the people of the Roman Empire who follow the true faith are already members of the *civitas Dei*, peregrinating on earth, and also capable of using the best in Roman history and its values of self-sacrificial devotion and patriotic love, *amor patriae*, on which to model their greater devotion to the heavenly kingdom. Paradoxically, the *civitas Dei* actually needs earthly cities from which to recruit its own members. One type of *amor patriae* is the seedbed of the other. It is not the *civitas*, the large grouping of people held together by legal consensus and mutual benefit, that is at fault, but the *dominandi cupido* that drives empire. That leaves plenty of room for the ideal of the city to survive, especially of one that listens to bishops.[67]

Salvian of Marseille: Cities and Barbarians

Augustine did not complete the text of the *de Civitate Dei*, which he had begun in 413, until 425. Honorius, ineffectual emperor of the West, died in 423, and, after the usurpation of the primicerius John, was succeeded in 425 by the grandson of Theodosius the Great, Valentinian III, accompanied by his mother, the formidable Galla Placidia, whose so-called mausoleum is one of the finest monuments of Ravenna. Palace intrigue triggered the rebellion of the military commander of North Africa, Count Bonifatius, a friend of Augustine's, who rashly invited the assistance of the Vandal army, then in Spain. They arrived, under their new king, Gaiseric, in the summer of 429, and by the next year were besieging Hippo. Augustine died during the siege, but before the fall and sack of the city, in August 430. Mercifully, his library survived the sack, thanks to the loyal Possidius.[68] Only Carthage held out against the Vandal army, to fall in 439. North Africa, and specially Africa Proconsularis, covering modern Tunisia and Algeria, was one of the most densely urbanised areas of the Roman world, and the Vandal conquest undoubtedly did damage to its urban fabric,

---

[67] Ando, 'The children of Cain', p. 65, concludes that for Augustine the *civitas* is social not physical; nevertheless, the two are 'imbricated' in Roman thought.

[68] On whom see Hermanowicz, 'Possidius on Augustine'.

though in fact cities survived under Vandal rule.[69] Meanwhile, other Germanic armies devastated Gaul. If the sack of Rome in 410 had been traumatic, by the 440s the scene of destruction had spread over many more cities, and the court at Ravenna had lost control of Africa, most of Gaul, and Spain.

Salvian of Marseille[70] was a priest, originally from the north-east of Gaul, who took refuge from barbarian invasions (as such he at least experienced them) in the relative safety of Provence, the area always closest to Roman control, in what was still one of the great port cities of the Mediterranean: Marseille.[71] His treatise *De Gubernatione Dei* (*On the Governance of God*), written twenty years after the *de Civitate Dei* in the 440s, has a great deal to say about both Roman citizenship and Roman cities. I am not concerned here with Salvian's theology, whether he was a Pelagian or a Semipelagian, nor with whether he agreed or disagreed with Augustine.[72] The personality of Salvian as a writer has been brilliantly illuminated by Peter Brown, underlining his particularity and specificity, the mid-level Gallic landowner displaced by Germanic invasions from his native city (not Trier, but nearby) to take refuge in the still civilised 'Romania' of south Gaul, and protesting sharply about the fiscal abuses that affected not only the peasants but also mid-level landowners like himself.[73] Here I wish to focus only on what he has to say about cities and citizenship, a theme little discussed despite its evident interest: for, not only does he offer an analysis of the late Roman city, but, unlike Augustine, a template for how the city can be made a better place here on earth, not just in some heavenly Jerusalem of the theological imagination.

Salvian, who evidently benefited from the best Gallic training in Roman rhetoric, sets out to prove a paradoxical thesis about divine providence. In answer to the accusation that God seems to have favoured the barbarians and heretics over the Catholic faithful of the Roman cities, he shows that

---

[69] The classic study of North African cities is Lepelley, *Les Cités de l'Afrique romaine*. For the immediate context, Klingshirn, 'Cultural geography'. On Roman persistence in Vandal Africa, Conant, *Staying Roman*. For the impact of Vandal conquest, Wickham, *Framing the Early Middle Ages*, pp. 636–644; for the Islamic period, Fenwick, 'From Africa to Ifrīqiya'.

[70] I cite Salvian's *De Gubernatione Dei* in the translation of Sandford, *On the Governance of God*. On Salvian, see Maas, 'Ethnicity, orthodoxy and community in Salvian of Marseilles'; Gray, 'Salvian, the ideal Christian community'; Elm, 'Salvian of Marseilles *On the Governance of God*'. The fullest study of Salvian is Badewien, *Geschichtstheologie und Sozialkritik im Werks Salvians*.

[71] On Marseille, Loseby, *Marseille in Late Antiquity and the Early Middle Ages*.

[72] On the relationship between the authors, see O'Donnell, 'Salvian and Augustine'; Lambert, 'Uses of decay', arguing that Salvian is simply independent of Augustine.

[73] See Brown, *Salvian of Marseilles*; and, more broadly, *Through the Eye of a Needle*.

the Romans have brought the divine wrath upon their heads by ignoring the basic precepts of Christianity, whereas the Arian barbarians have proved the moral superiors of the Romans. It is an argument directed not, as Augustine or Orosius may have done, against pagan Romans who thought that it was Christianity that had ruined the empire. His audience, as he states explicitly, is the Christians themselves. (1.1 cum *Christianis agimus*, we are dealing with Christians, he says, though many are infected with pagan unbelief, *incredulitatis paganicae*.) Later, at 3.1.5, he asks whether to address himself to Christians or pagans, and, on the grounds that it is a waste of time to try to convince pagans, concludes it is enough to prove his case to Christians. And while Augustine may be thought more subtle in supposing that divine retribution did not always manifest itself here on earth, but could wait for the Final Judgement, and that the ways of God are unknowable, Salvian has a simpler scheme of divine retribution for the wicked in the here and now. That is not simply a difference of theological position: while Augustine has limited desire to improve the *civitas terrena*, which, after all, is doomed to failure because founded by Cain not Abel, Salvian actually believes in the *civitas terrena* and wants to reform it. The threat of divine wrath here and now, in the shape of barbarian invasion and devastation, will persuade his fellow Christians to reform their behaviour.

The task he has set himself is to convince Roman Christians that they have been more deserving of God's wrath than barbarians. But at this point some definition of terms is needed, and Salvian cheerfully offers it (4.13):

> I know it seems to most men intolerable that we should be called worse than barbarians ... Since, then, some men think it unsupportable that we should be adjudged to be worse, or even not much better than barbarians, let us consider in what way we are better, and in relation to which of the barbarians. For there are two kinds of barbarians in the world, that is heretics and pagans. To all of these, as far as the divine law is concerned, I declare that we are incomparably superior; as far as our life and actions are concerned, I say with grief and lamentation that we are worse.[74]

Salvian's definition of the barbarian in purely religious terms, as heretics or pagans, might seem to create a source of confusion. Surely there were heretics and pagans who were also Roman? For a moment he seems to concede that his identification of Romans with Catholic Christians and barbarians with non-Catholics (Arians) and pagans needed modification.

---

[74] Salvian, *de gub.Dei* 4.13.

> However, as I have said before, let us not make this statement of the whole body of Romans without exception.[75]

Will he concede that there were Romans who were pagans? He has already decided that pagan Romans are of no relevance to his argument, and the exceptions are *good* Christians like monks:

> For I except first of all those men who have devoted themselves to a religious life, and then some laymen who are equal to them; or, if that is too much to say, at least very like them in their upright and honourable actions. As for the rest, all or practically all are more guilty than the barbarians. (4.13)

It is irrelevant to Salvian's argument whether there are heretics and pagans among the Romans, because he is trying to show that God is punishing not unbelievers, but those who, despite the privilege of sharing in revealed truth, continue to behave against God's command. The barbarian invasions are punishment for *disobedience*, not for disbelief.

We are thus offered a vision of the Roman world formed, as Peter Brown nicely puts it, of concentric circles.

> Gaul was ringed by an outer fringe of unconverted, pagan barbarians– Saxons, Huns, Franks, Gepids and Alamans. They were a supremely nasty lot ... Next came an anomalous grey zone. Goths and Vandals were not pagans. They were Christians. They were Arian heretics ... They erred in good faith. Only the Catholic, Roman Christians of Salvian's time had no excuse. They could expect no mercy.[76]

Salvian does not argue for a moment that the barbarians were innocents:

> The nation of Saxons is savage, the Franks treacherous, the Gepids ruthless, the Huns lewd – so we can see that the life of all barbarians is full of vice. (4.14)

But they don't know any better:

> And why is it strange that the barbarians have this degree of vice, since they know not the law and God, when a majority of Romans, who know that they are sinning, take the same attitude? (4.14)

At this point, he takes a racist swipe worthy of Juvenal at some of the barbarians within – the Syrians, a good example of Romans who ought to know better:

> Not to speak of any other type of man, let us consider only the throngs of Syrian merchants who have seized the greater part of all our towns – is

---

[75] Ibid. [76] Brown, *Salvian of Marseilles*, p. 11.

their life anything else than plotting, trickery and wearing falsehood threadbare? They think words practically wasted that do not bring some profit to the speaker. Among these men God's prohibition of an oath is held in such high esteem that they consider every sort of perjury actually profitable to them. What wonder is it then, that the barbarians, who do not know that falsehood is a sin, practise deception? (4.14)

Salvian plays neatly to some ancient Roman prejudices: against Syrians and against tradesmen of all sorts, with the Platonic definition of *kapeleia* as the middleman's structural need to lie to make a profit. He assumes, we note, that these Syrian traders are Christians and should know better.

Having thus warmed to his theme, Salvian brings it to the boil in the fifth book. The barbarians, he recapitulates, are either pagans or heretics. The heretics cannot help their heresy, for they have been given incomplete and falsified versions of the scriptures by unscrupulous men:

> The barbarians, indeed, lacking the Roman training or any other sort of civilized education, *Romanae immo humanae eruditionis expertes*, knowing nothing whatever unless they have heard it from their teachers, follow blindly what they hear. (5.2)

Here the old topic of Rome's *mission civilisatrice*, of bringing education and *humanitas* to the conquered, is turned on its head. The fact that these barbarians have not been civilised and Romanised means also that they are innocent of true Christianity, and therefore innocent of breaking God's word. The antithetical pairs of Roman versus barbarian, civilised versus uncivilised, Catholic versus heretic and pagan entirely coincide. But now at last he concedes that there are heretics and pagans within:

> All those of whom I speak are either Vandals or Goths, for I say nothing of the multitude of Roman heretics, and shall not compare them with either Romans or barbarians, since their lack of faith makes them worse than the Romans, and their disgraceful lives than the barbarians. That the men I speak of are Romans, far from helping us, makes our case even worse. It is easy to estimate what the whole Roman state deserves, when part of the Romans offend God by their way of life, part by their lack of faith and their way of living also. Add that the very heresies of the barbarians spring originally from the false teaching they received from the Romans, and the inception of heresy among them becomes another heavy charge against us. (5.3)

By a sleight of hand, he has turned the exception into a confirmation of his definition, that Romans are Catholic Christians. If there are still pagans and heretics among the Romans, and ones who teach the barbarians the wrong

Christianity, that is an internal failure of the Romans, who *ought* all be Catholics.

The ultimate test is the form of society. One might expect the Romans to have a good form of social organisation, the barbarians not. But ever since Tacitus' *Germania*, the Romans have had a suspicion that the barbarians may have a good form of social organisation which they have lost:

> Now almost all barbarians, at least those who belong to one tribe, under one king's rule, love one another, whereas almost all the Romans are at strife with one another. What citizen is there who does not envy his fellows? Who shows complete charity to his neighbours? All are indeed far from their neighbours in affection, however near in place; though living side by side, they are far apart in spirit. While this is a most grievous wrong, I wish it were true only of citizens and neighbours.

Salvian has added a crucial dimension to his definition of Romans: they are citizens, *cives*. That implies they live in cities, *civitates*, not in tribes like the barbarians, that their manners are civilised and civil. But corruption and extortion mean that they no longer behave like *cives*:

> What a situation is this, how savage, how rooted in the same impiety we deplore, how alien to barbarians and familiar to Romans, that they proscribe one another by mutual exactions. My last words, perhaps, give a wrong impression, for it would be much more tolerable if each man endured what he himself had inflicted on others. The present situation is harder to bear, for the many are proscribed by the few, who use the public levies for their individual gain, and convert the bills of indebtedness to the public treasury to their private profit. Nor is it only the highest officials who do this, but the least too in almost equal measure; not only the judges, but their obedient underlings as well. For what cities are there, or even what municipalities and villages, in which there are not as many tyrants as curials? (5.4)

Here are Salvian's perhaps most famous words: *Quae enim non modo urbes sed etiam municipia atque vici, ubi non quot curiales fuerint, tot tyranni sunt?* On the heels of the citizen, the city has entered into the picture, in its full settlement hierarchy of cities, towns, and villages, and with its characteristic social hierarchy of *curiales*. Salvian lays the blame squarely at the feet of the rich: it is the curial class which, by abusing its role of tax collecting, reduces the rest of the citizen body to misery. The consequence is that they do not even wish to be citizens any longer.

My interest here is not to explain 'the fall of the Roman empire', but to watch how the concept of citizenship is morphing in Salvian's hands. The consequence of the brutal extortions by the rich is a series of paradoxical inversions – the Romans flee to the barbarians and no longer wish to be Romans:

> Meanwhile the poor are being robbed, widows groan, orphans are trodden down, so that many, even persons of good birth, who have enjoyed a liberal education (*liberaliter instituti*), seek refuge with the enemy to escape death under the trials of the general persecution. They seek among the barbarians the Roman mercy, since they cannot endure the barbarous mercilessness they find among the Romans (*quaerentes apud barbaros Romanam humanitatem quia apud Romanos barbaram inhumanitatem ferre non possunt*). (5.5.21)

It is precisely the quality of Roman civilisation, *humanitas*, that has collapsed. The Romans have become barbarous and uncivilised, the barbarians offer the new *humanitas*. The force of this word is underlined by his suggestion that it is also people of education, *liberaliter instituti*, who flee in pursuit of the new humanity. The very qualities that most distinguished the educated Roman like Salvian himself from the barbarian are now to be found among the barbarians. Salvian evidently knew what he was talking about: his intervention with the monks of Lérins on behalf of a male relative from Cologne who was of respectable parentage is complicated by the fact that the mother has voluntarily, and not as a slave, gone over to the barbarians (*Letter* 1).

At this point, further distinguishing elements of Roman versus barbarian obtrude.

> Although these men differ in customs and language from those with whom they have taken refuge, and are unaccustomed too, if I may say so, to the nauseous odour of the bodies and clothing of the barbarians, yet they prefer the strange life they find there to the injustice rife among the Romans. So you find men passing over everywhere, now to the Goths, now to the Bagaudae, or whatever other barbarians have established their power anywhere, and they do not repent of their expatriation, for they would rather live as free men, though in seeming captivity, than as captives in seeming liberty. (5.5)

The body odour, strange clothing, and non-Latin language of the barbarian might put them beyond the pale, but freedom is an overriding consideration.[77] *Libertas* is a defining characteristic of the Roman citizen

---

[77] Salvian's Gallic predecessor Sidonius Apollinaris, as Rosamond McKitterick reminds me, commented adversely on the smell of Burgundians who poured rancid butter in their hair: Sidonius, *Poems* 12, 7, *infundens acido comam butyro*.

even more important than language, clothing, and personal care (how sweet the Roman must have smelt, oiled and scented from the public baths!) That *libertas* is now to be found with the barbarians is the worst collapse of citizenship imaginable. And this point Salvian spells out vividly:

> Hence the name of Roman citizen, once not only much valued but dearly bought, is now voluntarily repudiated and shunned, and is thought not merely valueless, but even almost abhorrent. What can be a greater proof of Roman injustice than that many worthy noblemen to whom their Roman status should have been the greatest source of fame and honour, have nevertheless been driven so far by the cruelty of Roman injustice that they no longer wish to be Romans? The result is that even those who do not take refuge with the barbarians are yet compelled to be barbarians themselves; for this is the case with the greater part of the Spaniards, no small proportion of the Gauls, and, in fine, all those throughout the Roman world whose Roman citizenship has been brought to nothing by Roman extortion.[78]

In speaking so of the value of the Roman citizenship, Salvian surely has in mind St Paul, and the officer who had bought his citizenship for a great price (*Acts* 22.28). Has this valuation of the citizenship already been rendered worthless by the Constitutio Antoniniana? Evidently not for Salvian, for whom *civitas* is still tied up with a bundle of values, of education, language, city living and *libertas*, the rule of law and freedom from abuse. The Christianity which should have reinforced those values and not replaced them has not done its work.

There is a further twist of the knife in Salvian's lamentations over the inversion of the values of Roman citizenship. Romans take refuge with either the barbarians or the Bacaudae. Just who the Bacaudae were – a sort of Robin Hood movement attested in Gaul from the late third century onwards – can be left to others.[79] What interests me here is the account Salvian gives of their relationship to Roman citizenship. He maintains that they were citizens forced by the tax system to abandon citizenship:

> I must now speak of the Bacaudae, who, despoiled, afflicted, and murdered by wicked and bloodthirsty magistrates, after they had lost the rights of Roman citizens (*ius Romanae libertatis*), forfeited also the honour of the Roman name (*honorem Romani nominis*). We transform their

---

[78] Salvian, *de gub.Dei* 5.5: *itaque nomen ciuium Romanorum aliquando non solum magno aestimatum sed magno emptum nunc ultro repudiatur ac fugitur, nec uile tantum sed etiam abominabile paene habetur.*

[79] On whom see Drinkwater, 'The Bacaudae of fifth-century Gaul'.

misfortunes into crime, we brand them with a name that recalls their losses, with a name that we ourselves have contrived for their shame! We call those men rebels and utterly abandoned, whom we ourselves have forced into crime. For by what other causes were they made Bacaudae save by our unjust acts, the wicked decisions of the magistrates, the proscription and extortion of those who have turned the public exactions to the increase of their private fortunes and made the tax indictions their opportunity for plunder? (5.6)

So much for the universal citizenship of the *Constitutio Antoniniana*. It was still possible for the free inhabitants of the Roman Empire to be deprived of their citizen rights, presumably as outlaws. They are classed as brigands, beyond the protections of Roman law:

Like wild beasts, instead of governing those put under their power, the officials have devoured them, feeding not only on their belongings as ordinary brigands would do, but even on their torn flesh and their blood. Thus it has come to pass that men who were strangled and half killed by brutal exactions began to be true barbarians, since they were not permitted to be Romans. They were satisfied to become what they were not, since they were no longer allowed to be what they had been; and they were compelled to defend their lives as best they could, since they saw that they had already completely lost their liberty. (5.6)

Salvian's vivid – indeed, lurid – account of the abuses of the poor by the rich has provided abundant fuel for the arguments of those, notably Geoffrey de Ste Croix, who wish to argue that the 'fall of the Roman Empire' was the result of internal, social ills, and not of external, barbarian pressure. One may be struck by the way Salvian's radical Christianity meshes with de Ste Croix's Marxism:

A particularly eloquent complaint is that of Salvian, a Christian priest in Southern Gaul ... Making some very severe strictures on the wealthy class of Gaul in his day, whom he compares to a pack of brigands, he says that the oppressed poor (and not only they) used to flee for refuge to the 'barbarians' ... Although of course I recognise that Salvian is prone to rhetorical exaggeration, like the great majority of later Latin and Greek writers, I agree with Ernst Stein that his *De Gubernatione Dei* is 'la source plus révélatrice sur la situation intérieure de l'Empire d'Occident ...'[80]

Beyond question, Salvian is rhetorical. Indeed, the whole work is undisguisedly a work of persuasion, and draws on the classical armoury of

---

[80] De Ste Croix, *The Class Struggle in the Ancient Greek World*, pp. 478–479.

persuasion to make its case, rejoicing in bloodthirsty exaggeration and pointed paradox. But behind the rhetoric is a constantly underlying assumption that citizenship has indeed a value, and that it is the conscious devaluation of citizenship by the powerful that has led to crisis. Against the Romans, who are characteristically citizens living in and around cities, there is a population of barbarians and Roman non-citizens, outlaws, people beyond the pale of urban civilisation. Salvian thinks that Christian values are compatible with the traditional legal values of Roman citizenship, and that if Romans were better Christians, they would end up treating each other in a manner that was not only Christian but civil – the behaviour expected in a civilised society.

The first five books of the *de Gubernatione* are no more than a warm-up for the next three, which examine in unsparing detail the fate of the cities of the empire. Salvian has given us his views on the treatment of the peasantry, but he is an urbanist through and through, and what disturbs him is the fall of cities. He reviews in succession the provinces of the west, starting close to home with eastern Gaul (book 6), proceeding to Aquitaine (beginning of book 7), and, with scarcely a word about Spain, on to North Africa, especially Carthage (books 7 and 8). The texture of the Roman world he depicts, in all its immorality, is deeply urban, of great cities, *urbes*, surrounded by lesser towns, *civitates*. Led by their urban elites, they cultivate a lifestyle recognisable to Tacitus' Agricola, on a knife edge between humanity and corruption, with education and Latin, porticoes, baths and dinner parties. Salvian knows these people because he is one of them:

> I myself have seen men of lofty birth and honour (*homines domi nobiles dignitate sublimes*), though already despoiled and plundered, still less ruined in fortunes than in morality; for, ravaged and stripped though they were, something still remained to them of their property, but nothing of their character ... It is sad to tell what we saw there; honoured old men, feeble Christians, when the ruin of their state was already imminent, making themselves slaves to appetite and lust ... They reclined at feasts, forgetful of their honour, forgetting justice, forgetting their faith and the name they bore. There were the leaders of the state, gorged with food, dissolute from winebibbing, wild with shouting, giddy with revelry, completely out of their senses, or rather, since this was their usual condition, precisely in their senses. In spite of all this, what I have next to say is still worse: not even the destruction of their towns put an end to their excesses. (6.13)

He speaks with the passion and authenticity of an eyewitness. He has seen the devastation of Trier, from the region of which he came:

> This (the unwillingness of cities to change their ways) can be quickly tested by the example of the greatest city of Gaul (*summa urbe Gallorum* – Trier), three times destroyed by successive captures, yet when the whole city had been burned to the ground, its wickedness increased even after its destruction. Those whom the enemy had not killed when they pillaged the city were overwhelmed by disaster after the sack; those who had escaped death in the capture did not survive the ruin that followed . . .
>
> Worse than all this, other cities (*civitates*) suffered from the destruction of this single town (*urbs*). There lay all about the torn and naked bodies of both sexes, a sight that I myself endured. These were a pollution to the eyes of the city, as they lay there lacerated by birds and dogs. The stench of the dead brought pestilence on the living: death breathed out death. Thus even those who had escaped the destruction of the city suffered the evils that sprang from the fate of the rest. (6.15)

And this is an author who, having witnessed the full brutality of a barbarian invasion, still thinks the Romans worse than the barbarians! Why? What Salvian is demanding is a radical change in the nature of the ancient city. And though sexual immorality features high on his list of pagan failings, nothing upsets him quite so much as spectacles and circuses. Here he is of course in a long line of Christian polemicists, but while others have declared *spectacula* to be immoral, it is Salvian who shows their visceral connection with the Roman city and its present woes. The circus and the theatre are emblematic of all that is worst about urban civilisation:

> And since indeed it would take too long to tell of all these snares, that is, the amphitheaters, the concert halls, games, parades, athletes, rope dancers, pantomimes and other monstrosities of which one is ashamed to speak, since it is shameful even to know of such wickedness, I shall describe only the vices of the circuses and theaters. (6.3)

It is in the case of Trier that the lesson was most painfully learnt. Trier was the finest city in Gaul and was sacked, so he says, three times by barbarians, but it perversely refused to learn the lesson: don't waste your money on spectacles! The folly of Trier comes to a head in its reaction to the third sack: the city authorities petition the emperor to restore the circus games:

> What followed these calamities? Who can assay such utter folly? The few men of rank who had survived destruction demanded of the emperors circuses as the sovereign remedy for a ruined city . . . Do you, O citizens of Trier, long for circuses when you have been plundered and captured, after

> slaughter and bloodshed, after stripes and captivity, and the repeated destruction of your ruined city? ... Do you then seek public shows, O citizen of Trier? Where, pray, are they to be given? Over the pyres and ashes, the bodies and blood of the dead? ... The remains of a most unhappy people lie on the graves of their dead, yet you ask for circuses; the city is blackened by fire, yet you put on a festive countenance; all things mourn, but you rejoice! (6.15)

The circuses and games had of course been a target of Christian polemic from Tertullian to Augustine and Quodvultdeus of Carthage.[81] Orosius too, as we have seen, has a very similar complaint about the sack of Rome, the new Sodom:

> they freely cried out, 'If we are given our circus back again, we have suffered nothing'. (1.6)

Salvian sees Carthage too as corrupted by a passion for games (6.12).

There is, as critics have not been slow to point out, an interesting contradiction in Salvian's account of spectacles, for he admits that numerous cities no longer had active circuses and theatres, whether because they were under barbarian control, and barbarians had no interest in such things, or because the fiscal crisis of the empire meant they could no longer afford such entertainment (6.8). Nowadays you had to go to Ravenna for the theatre, and Rome for circuses (6.9) But this, he claims, is just a temporary phenomenon: Romans *wanted* their spectacles, they were still addicted to them, even if they could not afford them, and the moment prosperity returned, they would resume their old ways. Trier's disgraceful request to the emperor for circuses is the proof that however much they have suffered, the old desire is still there.

This surely is at the heart of Salvian's argument. The cities of Gaul, not to speak of Spain and Africa, have suffered a devastating battering. What is the right model for the future? Not a reversion to a model of the pagan city in which spectacles were at the heart of how an urban community defined itself, but a city based on Christian values, though a city nonetheless.

As his exposition advances through western Gaul to Africa, we can continue to note the deeply urban texture of his Roman world. Aquitania, depicted at the start of book 7 as a paradise of vineyards, has cities that are no better than brothels. With the exception of a few holy men,

---

[81] See Van Slyke, 'The Devil and his pomp in fifth-century Carthage'; Lim, 'Augustine and Roman public spectacles'.

the people are adulterers who have sex with their slave girls, thereby demeaning their wives:

> Why should I speak of brothels? Even those I think are less wicked than the men of whom I spoke. For the prostitutes in them have not experienced the marriage bond, and so do not defile what they do not know; their shameless lives require atonement, it is true, but they are not liable to the charge of adultery. Add to this that such haunts are few, and few the prostitutes who have condemned themselves to a most unhappy life in them. Among the Aquitanians, on the other hand, what city in its richest and most elegant quarters was not practically a brothel? (*quae civitas in locupletissima ac nobilissima sui parte non quasi lupanar est*). (7.3)

This theme he takes up again with enthusiasm when he reaches Africa. Carthage should have been the model city, the *urbs* that was rival to Rome:

> There you would find all the appurtenances of the public offices, schools of the liberal arts, the studies of the philosophers, training schools in languages and ethics; there also were military forces and the powers that control the army, there was the office of the proconsul, there the daily judge and ruler of the province – in name, indeed, proconsul, but in power a very consul; there lastly were the administrators of the state properties, their honours differing from one another in rank and name – procurators, as I may call them, of the public streets and crossroads (*platearum et competorum procuratores*) – governing all the wards of the city and all sections of the people. (7.16)

This is a highly recognisable classical city, with its educational institutions, government structures, and attention to urban fabric. But within that fabric, for Salvian, a deep corruption lurks:

> What part of the city was not full of indecency, what street or bypath was not a place of shame (*quae platea aut semita non lupanar*)? Lust had so cut off most of the crossroads and streets with its snares, and entangled them with its nets, that even those who utterly abhorred such vices could scarcely avoid them. You might compare them to brigands lurking in ambush and snatching their spoils from passers-by; they so hedged in the paths, the winding roads and byways with their close-set traps, that scarcely anyone could be cautious enough not to fall into some of their treacherous snares, however many he escaped. All the citizens reeked, if I may use the expression, with the stench of lust, all inhaled the fetid odours of their mutual impurity. Yet this horrid condition inspired no loathing in them, for the same plague had infected them all. You would think the city a sink pot of lust and fornication, like the muck collected

> from the offscourings of all the streets and sewers (*caenum quasi ex omni platearum et cloacarum labe collectum*). What hope could there be in such a place, where, except for the temple of the Lord, there was nothing to be seen but filth? (7.17)

Rhetorical Salvian may be, but it is a rhetoric familiar to the classical city: sewers and cleanliness, public roads properly swept, were the aim of the Roman city, enjoined by the *lex Iulia municipalis*, and the perception that they were at risk both of physical and moral filth is nothing new.

Salvian likes to be specific about the moral failings of different cities. While the Aquitanians were tainted with adultery, the Carthaginians went in for homosexual prostitution and transvestitism. And, of course, the circus. As he has already explained in book 6 on the theme of spectacles, Carthage was particularly bad. As the Vandals devastated Africa, they persisted in their circuses, and all the immorality that went with it:

> The barbarians' arms clashed about the walls of Cirta and Carthage while the Christian congregation of the city raved in the circuses and wantoned in the theatres. Some had their throats cut without the walls, while others still committed fornication within; part of the people were captive to the enemy without, while part within the city were captive to their own vices. (6.12)

Salvian's account of the crisis of the fifth-century city seems to capture the city at a turning point: between the pagan city of the Classical era (if you want to think in such terms), and the Christian city of the Middle Ages. Many features of the classical city of the Roman Empire are still recognisably there. The ruling class, the *curiales*, still dominate the countryside as well as the town; and they consolidate their ties in classic urban dinner parties. On the one hand they exploit the peasants; on the other, they seek favour with the masses by staging spectacles in the circus and theatre. Spectacles are still, as Keith Hopkins described them, the 'glue' that held together a Roman community.[82] As magistrates their duty is to keep the streets free of the tide of moral and literal filth: no Roman city is thinkable without the brothel and the sewer (but then, how many cities in history have been without them?). It is possible to read Salvian as a rejection of the city entirely.[83] But it is equally possible to read him as a champion of reform. Salvian's demand to save the Roman world by higher standards of Christianity points to a new sort of city, dominated by the bishop, with

---

[82] Hopkins, *Death and Renewal*, pp. 1–30.
[83] So Markus, *The End of Ancient Christianity*, pp. 168–177 (I thank Mark Vessey for this reference).

Christian basilicas not circuses as the principal monumental form.[84] The Roman amphitheatre of Tarragona, its arena repurposed as a succession of churches, Visigothic and later, is an eloquent symbol of such a conversion (Figure 3.2).

Salvian wants change, but he still believes in being a Roman, and cares about the values of a citizenship from which St Paul benefited. For Augustine, the faithful were citizens of a heavenly city, but strangers, *peregrini*, here on earth, though they were called to imitate the values of the heavenly city on earth. Orosius, as we have seen, was in one sense more optimistic. As a Christian, he was not a *peregrinus*, an outsider to Roman law, but a citizen, free to travel safely across a vast Mediterranean empire, fleeing from Spain to Africa and even to Palestine. Salvian takes his argument a step further. Romans are distinctive from barbarians, who are not only uncouth, unwashed, uneducated, and ignorant, but either pagans or heretics. Salvian reminds Romans that citizenship is a bundle of values: it involves freedom and justice, mutual respect between citizens. The Catholic faith is not an alternative to the old Roman values but reinforces

Figure 3.2 The amphitheatre of Tarragona and Sta Maria del Miracle. Author's photo.

---

[84] Liebeschuetz, *Decline and Fall*, pp. 137–168, sees 'the rise of the bishop' as inimical to the values of the classical city.

them. In a word, he is capable of imagining that the cities of the empire, rather than being foreign to the *civitas Dei*, can be made stronger by its characteristics. That, for Salvian, is the best way to beat the barbarians.

The City Christianised

When Orosius, Augustine, and Salvian speak with such enthusiasm of *civitas*, the citizenship they take for granted is that of Rome, rather than the individual cities which made up Rome's empire. This 'universal' character made it an easy model for a *civitas Dei*, a citizenship of a universal (and Catholic) Christian community. But just as Roman citizenship did not render the local membership of individual cities superfluous, for they were the principal module through which citizenship was spread and maintained, so membership of a Christian community did not render local cities and citizenship irrelevant: as we will see, they formed the framework on which the administration of the church was based.

All three authors here discussed – above all Augustine, the master of Ciceronian rhetoric – were brought up in a highly classical tradition of thinking about the role of the city and citizenship in their world, and to that extent there is no surprise that they reflect classical Roman thinking. But they have in common a perception that, far from being rendered irrelevant by their faith, *civitas* remained a powerful way of thinking about society. Resilience theory underlines the importance of drawing on older elements of a system under challenge to adapt to a new system. That is one way of interpreting these responses to the intellectual crisis of the fifth century triggered by the sack of Rome. The ideas of the city and citizenship were indeed deeply entangled with the system of Roman imperial rule. These Christian authors were interested, in different ways, in disentangling and repurposing a set of ideas to retain their force in a post-imperial world.

4 | The City Revived?

Cassiodorus and Ostrogothic Italy

Few late Roman authors have so much to say about cities as Cassiodorus in his collection of official letters, the *Variae*.[1] A revealing introduction to his ideal of urbanism is a letter written in the name of the Ostrogothic king Athalaric around AD 527 to one Severus, probably the governor of Bruttium: it betrays both the ideal of urban living and the potential strain it might come under. The purpose of the letter is to require the official concerned to induce the local landowners (*possessores*) and councillors (*curiales*) to return to living in their cities, rather than on their rural estates, and for the most part of the year. They are now required to give a collateral guarantee that they will spend the greater part of the year in their cities.[2]

So, before he reaches the final paragraph with its legal detail (which is, to be honest, a touch vague), he sets out the case for living in cities. Taking a leaf out of Ambrose's account of the creation in the *Hexameron*, he turns to natural history for support.[3] Birds, too, like murmuring pigeons, have social habits and fly in flocks; only fierce raptors live alone (8.31.2–3). Since for Ambrose creation is providential, naturally the animal kingdom supplies moral lessons for humans; Cassiodorus can use that to found a standard imperial requirement in the laws of nature and, implicitly, of God. What he is careful *not* to say is that civilised Romans live in cities, and to live in the country is the mark of a barbarian; there were, after all, tens of thousands of Goths in Italy living off the land distributed to them at the rate of one third (see below).

The birds offer a second lesson on civilisation. After a lengthy purple passage about the richness and beauty of the Bruttian countryside

---

[1] After long languishing in neglect, Cassiodorus and his *Variae* have been rendered more accessible by the translation of Shane Bjornlie, *Cassiodorus, the Variae*, replacing the selection by Barnish, *Selected Variae*; and by the six-volume commentary edited by a team under Andrew Giardina, *Cassiodoro Senatore, Varie*.

[2] *Var.* 8.31.9. On this letter see the incisive commentary of Tantillo in Giardina, *Cassiodoro Varie* vol. IV, pp. 271–276.

[3] So Giardina, *Cassiodoro Varie* IV, 272–273; Zumbo, 'Sugli excursus zoologici nelle *Variae*'. Cf. Ambrose, *Hexameron* 5.14 (47) For birds of this sort there is no group life except that of conjugal relationship. This is the mode of life among the eagles and hawks. On the other hand, birds such as doves, cranes, starlings, crows, ravens, and even thrushes flock together for the most part.

(he understands, because he too has his acres), he urges the landowners of the advantages of living in town:

> For what kind of desire is it to abandon interaction with citizens, when they may observe that even some birds want to mingle with human society. For the swallows faithfully suspend nests in the dwellings of humankind, and the intrepid bird feeds its chicks amid the commotion of residents. It is, therefore, exceedingly disgraceful to educate the sons of noblemen in the wilderness, when one may see the birds entrust their offspring to human society. (*Var.* 8.31.7, trans. Bjornlie)[4]

Having established that even swallows are urbanites, and that the social bonds which for Cicero had characterised a *civitas* (see Chapter 3, pp. 76–77) are inbuilt into the order of nature, he can remind the landowners of why it is both natural and attractive to live in cities:

> Let the cities, therefore, return to their former dignity; let none prefer the allurements of the countryside to urban walls of the ancients. How is it possible to flee in time of peace from that place for which it is proper to wage war, lest it be destroyed? For whom would the assembly of nobility seem least pleasing? Who would not be eager for exchanging conversation with peers, visiting the forum, practising honest arts, representing one's own causes with the laws, being occupied occasionally with the draughts of Palamedes, going to the baths with companions, arranging dinners with lavish reciprocity? (*Var.* 8.31.7–8, trans. Bjornie, adapted)

There is much that is highly traditional here; but that does not mean it was not of contemporary relevance. The walls that traditionally protected a city had become highly relevant during a century in which invading armies had competed to sack cities, and Cassiodorus takes them for granted, even if he celebrates his own *patria*, Squillace, for its *lack* of walls and semi-rural aspect (see Chapter 2, pp. 54–56). The attractions of the city, the forum, courts, baths and dinner parties, are reminiscent of Agricola's attempts to persuade the British elites to take to city life.[5]

---

[4] I follow the helpful translation of Bjornlie, *Cassiodorus, the Variae* where indicated; occasionally I have adapted these. Where no translator is indicated, it is my own.
[5] Tacitus, *Agricola* 21: 'he exhorted them in private, and supported them in public, to build temples, fora, and houses ... Now it was time to educate the sons of the leading men in liberal arts ... Then our style of dress began to be respected and the use of the toga spread; gradually this extended to the softening effect of vices, porticoes and baths and elegant dinner parties.'

Cassiodorus will have been aware that it was an established requirement in Roman law for the local ruling class to live in their cities. In the pattern of the classical Roman city, substantial landowners could be expected to have both a country villa and a town house; early imperial legislation required that anyone serving on the city council should have a town house of a certain size, defined by so many tiles, though there is no evidence for this requirement at this period.[6] Valentinian and Valens, in AD 367, instructed the Prefect of Egypt to ensure that councillors should 'not vacate the cities and transfer their family *lares* to the country districts, an action which has been repeatedly prohibited by law', and two decades later Honorius and Arcadius, repeated the injunction, this time to the Praetorian Prefect, ruling that any councillor preferring their farm to the city would have that farm confiscated (*Codex Theodosianus* 12.18.1–2).[7] As often, Cassiodorus is reiterating an old requirement to live in the city, though he includes all large landowners and not just councillors in the requirement. But for him, the force of the law by itself is rarely enough: he wants to persuade and get people to see reason.

As Claude Lepelley showed, this letter is open to two opposite readings.[8] You could use this letter as evidence of the breakdown of the classical city. The rich landowners are shunning their urban responsibilities and hunkering down in the countryside in their villas. But equally striking is the survival of an ideal of urbanism, and the willingness of a Gothic king, albeit with heavy prompting from his spokesman, to support it. And though this ideal is directed in particular at the members of the local elite, the urban pleasures he evokes stretch beyond the elite: board games attributed to the mythical hero Palamedes, *Palamediaci ludi*, were a popular pursuit, as the numerous examples cut into paving in late antiquity attest.[9] Yet is this any more than a nostalgic echo of a long-lost past?

This letter has been seized upon by those arguing that there was a generalised crisis of the city in fifth- and sixth-century Italy, and that

---

[6] Lex Tarentina, Crawford et al., *Statutes*, pp. 301–312.
[7] Here and below the Codex Theodosianus (CTh) is cited in the translation of Pharr, *The Theodosian Code*.
[8] Lepelley, 'Un éloge nostalgique de la cité classique'. This letter is also the starting point for a thorough discussion of cities in Cassiodorus, together with texts, commentary, and French translation, by Valérie Fauvinet-Ranson, *Decor civitatis*, pp. 30–33; see also in brief, Fauvinet-Ranson, 'Les valeurs idéologiques'. See further Tabata, *Città dell'Italia*, pp. 124–126; La Rocca, 'Mores tuos'; Marazzi, 'Ostrogothic cities', pp. 108–109.
[9] See Purcell, 'Literate games'.

'ruralisation' was a widespread phenomenon.[10] That may indeed be the case, but this letter is an ambivalent piece of evidence. It is addressed quite specifically to the landowners of Bruttium, Cassiodorus' own territory. If it was part of a generalised crisis throughout Italy, we may ask why it was not issued as a generalised instruction, perhaps to the Praetorian Prefect, to all cities in Italy? Bruttium had long been far less densely urbanised than the north; and even Cassiodorus' own praises of Squillace suggest that such urbanisation that there was had a more rural feel to it. Indeed, we might suggest that the reason that the letter was addressed specifically to Bruttium was Cassiodorus' own awareness that it was a rural backwater compared to northern Italy and needed stimulus.

What is so risky is to use the *Variae* to establish 'facts', like the degree of urban decline in Italy. The story they tell is, rather, one of attitudes: of a tenacious affection for the values of the past, and the desire of the Gothic regime to present itself as the champion and defender of these values. 'Nostalgia' is one way to characterise this; and yet, in itself the term makes a value judgement in implying that the values of the classical past were no longer relevant. Seen from the point of view of resilience, we might rather be witnessing the use of memories of past values to forge a new future in a time of crisis. Cassiodorus is an eloquent spokesman for a set of ideas that is doubtless seen by the players to be under threat, but which in its articulation could serve a vital function: that of transmission of social memory. The message is consistent throughout the letters, and affects a wide range of areas: concern for urban fabric, for civic values, for the capital of Rome itself, and, above all, the overarching ideals of *civilitas*. Before turning to these, it is appropriate to set the author in the context of the Ostrogothic court and of his own role as its spokesman.

The World of Ostrogothic Italy

One might almost be lulled by the flowery rhetoric of Cassiodorus' letters, written in the name or in service of the kings of Italy, Theoderic and his successors, into ignoring the crackling tensions beneath the surface of Ostrogothic Italy.[11] That is precisely what they are designed to achieve.

---

[10] Especially Cracco Ruggini and Cracco, 'Changing fortunes of the city'; Noyé, 'Villes, économie et société dans la province de Bruttium-Lucania'; Wickham, *Framing the Early Middle Ages*, p. 603. See also Lepelley, 'Un éloge nostalgique'.

[11] On Ostrogothic Italy in general, see Moorhead, *Theoderic in Italy*; Amory, *People and Identity*; Arnold, *Theoderic and the Roman Imperial Restoration*,; Arnold et al., *Companion to*

Roman and Goth seem to live together in mutual respect. Yet many of the existing population of Italy must have regarded Theoderic and his Goths as an occupying army, alien in language, religion, and customs: worse, they had been rewarded with a third of the landed property of Italy.[12] The last Roman emperor in the West, Romulus Augustus, was sent into gilded retirement in 476 by his general Odoacer, who took the title and power of a king; Odoacer in turn was defeated, forcibly replaced, and some said murdered with his own hands by the Ostrogothic general, Theoderic, in 493, establishing a dynasty that lasted half a century.[13] Theoderic sought to present himself as a continuity with the Roman past, not a disruption, and Cassiodorus was the official Roman voice of continuity.[14] Yet tensions repeatedly emerged above the surface, most conspicuously in the brutal execution of the great philosopher Boethius for allegedly plotting with Constantinople for the overthrow of the Gothic regime, and later in the murder of Theoderic's daughter Amalasuntha, which gave Justinian his excuse for invasion. Cassiodorus represents not business as usual but the establishment on the ruins of imperial power of a form of kingdom that was to characterise Western Europe thenceforth. If the cities of the Roman empire can be seen as the product of imperial power and an essential tool for imperial administration, what would be their function under the new order? What did Gothic rather than Roman rule mean for cities? To appreciate the presentation of the city in the *Variae* it is helpful to look at Cassiodorus' role as a bridge builder between the Gothic court and Roman tradition, and to recognise the subtlety with which he crafts a voice that is simultaneously his own and that of the king.

Bridging the Gothic and the Roman

What indeed 'Goth' might mean is, like any ethnic label, far from a clear-cut business. But to say that something has soft edges is not to say it is soft

---

Ostrogothic Italy. On the cities of Italy in Cassiodorus, see Fauvinet-Ranson, *Decor civitatis*; Tabata, *Città dell'Italia*; Marazzi, 'Ostrogothic cities'. Recent work on Ostrogothic Italy is incisively reviewed by Costambeys, 'The legacy of Theoderic'. See now Dey and Oppedisano (eds.), *Justinian's Legacy* for fresh insights.

[12] What this third consisted in has been controversial since Goffart, *Barbarians and Romans*, suggested that not one third of land but of its revenues was settled on the Goths; balanced discussion in Lafferty, *Law and Society*, pp. 17, 221–224. Relevant is *Var.* 2.16, an encomium of Liberius, who carried out the settlement. See further Chapter 6.

[13] On this unedifying episode, Caliri, *Praestantissimus rex*, pp. 151–160.

[14] For the ideology and politics of the Ostrogothic court, Cristini, *La politica esterna dei successori di Teoderico*.

all through, and a Roman such as Cassiodorus had no doubt that there was a distinctive people, called Goths not just by Romans but by Goths themselves, who, like other ethnic groups, might have distinctive language, customs, and religion.[15] Indeed, we may speak of a process of 'ethnogenesis', the conscious creation of a group identity for people of diverse origin; and the twelve-volume *History of the Goths* of Cassiodorus, lost but supposedly abbreviated by the Gothic writer Jordanes,[16] is rightly recognised as a crucial step in this process.[17]

A central function of the Gothic court at Ravenna was to build bridges between the two communities, Gothic and Roman. Cassiodorus himself was surely chosen by Theoderic as a bridge builder, albeit benefiting from an insidetrack career thanks to his father, who as Praetorian Prefect was Theoderic's senior Roman administrative official. A curious autobiographical paragraph that goes under the name of the *ordo Generis Cassiodororum* outlines his early career and explains that it was a panegyric of Theoderic delivered while he was his father's *consiliarius* that won him promotion to the role of Quaestor Sacri Palatii, traditionally the role of the emperor's spokesman.[18]

Whatever this meant in practice, the role surely demanded a high level of linguistic competence. Cassiodorus' skills in Latin and Greek are beyond question: as he cheerfully describes himself in the *ordo*, he was *vir eruditissimus*, a man of the highest erudition; and the Gothic court set much store by its mastery of Latin grammar.[19] As Theoderic's successor, Athalaric, puts it in a letter to the senate, it was vital to promote the teaching of Latin grammar, *grammatica*, the art of faultless speaking:

> Barbarian kings do not employ this; it is only known among legitimate rulers. For other nations have arms and other assets; eloquence is only found to support the masters of the Romans. (*Var.* 9.21.4, trans. Bjornlie, adapted)

Athalaric draws a clear line between his own and 'barbarian' courts; eloquence in Latin made all the difference. As he personally appreciated,

---

[15] The radical position of Amory, *People and Identity in Ostrogothic Italy* seeing 'Gothic' as an ideological construct has been sharply criticised: for example, Heather, 'Merely an ideology?', pp. 33ff.; Liebeschuetz, 'Goths and Romans' defends the idea of the Goths as a *gens*; for an archaeological perspective, Christie, 'Ostrogothic Italy'.

[16] For the text, see Van Nuffelen and Van Hoof, *Romana and Getica*. On the author, see Goffart, *Narrators of Barbarian History*, pp. 20–111, with the critique of Liebeschuetz, 'Making a Gothic history'; Merrills, *History and Geography*, pp. 100–169, esp. pp. 101–115 on the relationship to Cassiodorus.

[17] So the argument of the 'Viennese school', esp. Wolfram, *History of the Goths* and Pohl, 'Telling the difference'.

[18] See Bjornlie, *Politics and Tradition*, pp. 159–162.

[19] On Cassiodorus' familiarity with Greek, see Garzya, 'Cassiodoro e la grecità'.

as grandson of Theoderic and just ten years old when he took over the throne under the watchful eye of his mother, Amalasunta, education was a vital asset in the court of Ravenna; and precisely the stylistic traits of Cassiodorus that we least appreciate – the erudition, allusiveness, fanciful arabesques and brightly coloured patches reminiscent of Ravenna mosaics – were what commended him to the court.

Linguistic skills flowed both ways: not only did Goths master Latin and Greek, but Romans close to the king needed to master Gothic. We must surely assume that Theoderic himself, brought up for a decade in Constantinople, knew Latin and Greek to some level, even if a fragmentary history that is otherwise complimentary to him describes him as *illiteratus*.[20] It is not easy to see how Cassiodorus can have done his job (let alone write the definitive History of the Goths) without fluent Gothic. He says nothing about himself or Theoderic on this score but underlines the critical importance of trilingual fluency in letters of praise of another Roman courtier, Cyprian, and of Amalasunta herself. Cyprian was, not unlike Cassiodorus, a Roman administrator whose father, Opilio, held the office of Royal Treasurer, *Comes Sacrarum Largitionum*, under Odoacer (*abiectis temporibus*, in a wretched period, he cannot resist adding, though what he is demonstrating is the continuity between the regimes; 5.41.5).[21] Now Theoderic is promoting Cyprian to the same rank, as a reward, he says, for a successful diplomatic mission to the Eastern court, during which he showed himself unabashed by the need to use Greek, thanks to his trilingual fluency, *instructus trifariis linguis* (5.40.5). The third language is of course Gothic: the need for constant diplomatic exchanges not only with Constantinople, but with other 'barbarian' courts, the Visigoths in Toulouse, the Vandals in Carthage, along with the Burgundians and Franks in Gaul, must have made knowledge of a Germanic language important, even though we may distrust Athalaric's assertion that barbarian courts, unlike his own, knew no Latin. A few years later, Athalaric promoted Cyprian to the patriciate, the highest Roman social rank, and again took the opportunity to praise his many skills. These are now reflected in the way he brings up his sons:

> Boys of Roman descent speak our language, excellently indicating the future loyalty offered to us, whose language they are now seen to affect. (*Var.* 8.21.6–7, trans. Bjornlie, adapted)

---

[20] Anonymus Valesianus 12.61: 'dum illiteratus esset, tantae sapientiae fuit ...' Note that all known Gothic soldiers spoke Latin: Amory, *People and Identity*, pp. 102–108.

[21] On Cyprian and his family, Amory, *People and Identity*, pp. 154–158.

For centuries Romans had valued bilingual fluency in Latin and Greek – 'in both our languages', as the emperor Claudius had put it.[22] But now *lingua nostra*, spoken by a Gothic king even when writing a letter in Latin, is Gothic, and it is a sign of genuine loyalty when a Roman official teaches his sons Gothic.[23]

Cyprian's Gothic loyalty had made him less popular in the final years of Theoderic's reign among the Romans who held him responsible for the downfall of Boethius and Symmachus, both accused of excessive contacts with the Byzantine court;[24] whatever the merits of that case, he was manifestly someone capable of using his linguistic versatility both to communicate with Byzantium and to retain the confidence of a Gothic court. Even more so, Theoderic's daughter Amalasunta was a powerful bridge-building figure. In AD 534, after the premature death of her son Athalaric, she decided to make her cousin Theodahad co-regent. Cassiodorus writes two matching letters in their names to the senate, announcing the appointment, in which each praises the other. Theodahad highlights Amalasunta's linguistic gifts (*Var.* 10.4.6); she was evidently a woman of outstanding intellectual ability, a worthy match to England's Elizabeth I. Cassiodorus later elaborates on these praises, this time not on behalf of Theodahad but in his own voice as Praetorian Prefect:

> For every kingdom most properly venerates her, to see her is respect, to hear her speaking is a wonder. In what language does she not prove most learned? She is learned in the brilliance of Attic eloquence; she shines in the pomp of Roman discourse; she glories in the wealth of her native speech; she surpasses all in their own languages, while she is equally inspiring in each ... Hence, a great and needed defence comes to diverse nations, because none need a translator in the presence of our wisest mistress's hearing. (*Var.* 11.1.6–7, trans. Bjornlie, adapted)

As all these passages make clear, to be a successful Gothic ruler required not only success on the battlefield, but an endless round of diplomatic contacts with the regimes that made up the fractured Roman world. Amalasunta continued her father's success in building these vital bridges, and it is of more than symbolic significance that it was her murder that occasioned the breakdown of relations with the eastern Roman court and gave Justinian the excuse he needed for invading Italy.

---

[22] Suetonius, *Claudius* 42, 'utroque sermone nostro'.
[23] See Amory, *People and Identity*, p. 107.
[24] See Bjornlie, *Politics and Tradition*, pp. 138–144; Heather, 'A tale of two cities', pp. 28–37.

If the aim of the court was to build strong bridges, nowhere encapsulates that urge so vividly as the court city of Ravenna. The modern visitor might be forgiven for imagining that this exquisite collection of buildings, with their bright mosaics, were the product of a single dynasty and will. Instead, we have the legacy of three sharply competing dynasties: the house of Theodosius, represented by his son Honorius, his sister Galla Placidia, and her son Valentinian III; then Theoderic and his dynasty, taking over the Roman palace to project themselves as heirs to Roman power, and no less connected to the eastern capital; and finally Justinian, taking over and deleting where he could the Gothic name. Yet there is a deep continuity of style and structure, from the exquisite mausoleum of Galla Placidia (whether or not her place of burial, a monument of her regime) and the 'Orthodox' baptistery, so-called in contrast to the Arian baptistery built by the Goths (Figures 4.1–4.2). If this is a statement of contrasting faiths, it would take the eye of theological refinement to distinguish the two, for the 'Arian' building models itself on its predecessor, in its octagonal form and its rich mosaic decoration, culminating in the scene of baptism in the cupola. If the fact that the 'Arian' Christ is beardless reflects, as is suggested, an Arian belief in the inferiority of son to father, this is the tiniest detail set against a deeply respectful sense of competitive imitation of the whole.[25] Once we reach Theoderic's great basilica, now named Sant'Apollinare Nuovo, immediately adjacent to his palace (the building that bears that name is actually later),[26] the counterposed images of his palace, PALATIVM, and of the naval base at CLASSIS, suggest for all the world the successor of Augustus, who built the first Palatium, and established the naval base at Classis (Figures 4.3–4.4). After Justinian's victory, any image of Theoderic could be excised, and the historian Agnellus tells us that his homonym, bishop Agnellus, inserted the two processions of male and female saints who flank the church.[27] The figures of Theoderic and his courtiers were removed from the mosaic representing his palace, though the ghostly hands and feet against the columns tell the tale of what is lost (Figure 4.5); the images of Palatium and Classis were too good to remove, and convincingly represented what Theoderic left to his successors.[28] Similarly, the images of Justinian and Theodora could be memorably imposed on the rich decoration

---

[25] For the shared visual language of the Arian and Orthodox traditions, see Carile, 'Production, promotion and reception' at pp. 62–63. The idea that the beardless Christ reflects Arian doctrine is shown as implausible by Urbano, 'Donatio, dedication, and *damnatio memoriae*'.

[26] On Theoderic's palace, see Johnson, 'Towards a history of Theoderic's building program', esp. pp. 80–92 on the palace; Dey, *Afterlife*, pp. 111–119.

[27] I am grateful to Bryan Ward-Perkins for putting me right on the processions.

[28] Urbano, 'Donatio, dedication, and *damnatio memoriae*', for the evidence of Agnellus' changes; further Jäggi, *Ravenna*, pp. 177–192.

Figure 4.1 Octagonal dome of the 'Orthodox' bapistery with the baptism of a bearded Christ in the River Jordan. Author's photo.

Figure 4.2 Octagonal dome of the 'Arian' baptistery, with the same scene as in the Orthodox bapistery, but a beardless Christ. Author's photo.

Figure 4.3 Mosaic representation of Theoderic's Palace from Sant'Apollinare at Ravenna. The figures of Theoderic and his court have been removed and replaced with curtains and blank golden fields. Flavio Vallenari / iStock / Getty Images Plus.

Figure 4.4 Mosaic representation of Classis from Sant'Apollinare at Ravenna. Author's photo.

of S. Vitale (Figure 4.6). It too was Theoderic's building, and what Justinian – or, rather, his archbishop, Agnellus – was deleting was not an alternative view of rule or an alternative religion, but the person of Theoderic himself. What Justinian did not delete was the massive structure of Theoderic's Mausoleum: in stark contrast to the glittering mosaics of his churches, his final resting place was of plain white stone, with understated decorative detail, and a monolithic capstone of exceptional dimensions (Figure 4.7).

Figure 4.5 Detail of the representation of the Palatium from Sant'Apollinare. The hands of deleted courtiers are visible against the columns. Author's photo.

Figure 4.6 Justinian flanked by Bishop Maximian from S. Vitale at Ravenna. Maximian was responsible for changes to the mosaics after the fall of the Gothic regime: the structure was built under Theoderic. Author's photo.

Figure 4.7 The Mausoleum of Theoderic at Ravenna. Author's photo.

This image of Theoderic as the heir of the Roman *Principes* (a word which could be safely used to gloss over the contrast between Imperator and Rex)[29] emerges not just from Cassiodorus, but from the cluster of accounts of the Gothic regime that survive. These include a panegyric by Ennodius, bishop of Pavia, and a match for Cassiodorus in rhetorical complexity,[30] as well as the fragmentary history of Theoderic's reign included in the compilation that goes under the awkward name of the Anonymus Valesianus.[31] Procopius, in his *Gothic Wars*, scarcely contradicts the image projected by Cassiodorus, and makes clear that the Goths regarded themselves as the faithful preservers of Roman tradition, and the injured party in a conflict started by those who called themselves Romans

---

[29] See Arnold, *Theoderic*, p. 75.   [30] See Marconi, *Ennodio*.
[31] Text and translation in the third volume of the Loeb translation of Ammianus Marcellinus. See the discussion of Bjornlie, *Politics and Tradition*, pp. 94–97.

but were truly Greeks (see Chapter 5). Perhaps the best confirmation of the picture offered by Cassiodorus is the legal compilation called the *Edictum Theoderici Regis*, the edict of king Theoderic. Long neglected, this has now been convincingly shown to be an authentic product of Theoderic's reign: a summary of the key elements of Roman law contained in the Theodosian Code, for the benefit of judges who knew the lengthy Roman Code less intimately than did Cassiodorus himself.[32] Closely following, and not overtly replacing, the imperial law code, it nevertheless has many small touches that accommodate to the situation of Ostrogothic Italy. It is explicitly addressed to both Romans and 'barbarians' (a term which Cassiodorus tended to avoid) and sets a model of how the two populations could live together under a single legal structure. It may indeed betray some of the economic pressures under which Italy laboured,[33] but that does not diminish the clear will of Theoderic to improve things through the rule of law.

The Voices of the Variae

In deciding to publish a selection of the correspondence he had drafted in a succession of government posts, Cassiodorus broke new ground in a long tradition of Latin literature. Sidonius Apollinaris had used his letters to frame the cultural life of late Roman Gaul, including his accounts of the court of the Visigothic king, Theoderic (this name was common among Goths, equivalent to German Dietrich), and an account of dining with the emperor Majorian.[34] Parading your links to people in power was no novelty.

The startling novelty is that the letters Cassiodorus decided to publish were (apart from the last two books, his official letters as Praetorian Prefect) not his own, but rather the official pronouncements he had drafted on behalf of the Gothic court. Of the twelve books of 'varied' letters, the first five are issued in the name of Theoderic (up to 526); the next two books, 6 and 7, are offered as standard letters, *formulae*, to be issued on appointment to a full range of government officials. Then books 8 and 9 are from Theoderic's successor, the young Athalaric (526–534); the letters of book 10 are mostly in the name of the next king, Theodahad (534–536), with

---

[32] Lafferty, *Law and Society in the Age of Theoderic the Great*.
[33] Lafferty, *Law and Society*, pp. 205–240.
[34] Sidonius Apollinaris, *Epistulae* 1.2 (Theoderic); 9.13 (dinner with Majorian. In general, see Harries, *Sidonius Apollinaris*.

only the last four from his successor, Witigis (536–540). The final two books, the separate status of which is marked by a second preface, are indeed letters sent in Cassiodorus' own name. His entitlement to write officially on behalf of the government derived from a sequence of offices: that of Quaestor Sacri Palatii, spokesman for Theoderic (507–511), then as Magister Officiorum, a role which he took over on the disgrace and downfall of Boethius, and continued to hold under Athalaric (523–528), and finally as Praetorian Prefect (533–540).[35]

Since Constantine, the *quaestor sacri palatii* was typically a lawyer capable of drafting imperial constitutions. What this meant in the Gothic court is conveniently spelt out for us by Cassiodorus' own *formula* for appointment to this role (*Var*. 6. 5). He stresses (speaking in the voice of the ruler), the unusual proximity of this office to the king:

> We retain the *Quaestor*, whom we deem to be the voice of our pronouncements, for our innermost counsel. This office is by necessity attached to our most private thoughts, so that it may speak what it knows that we feel: it resigns the opinion of its own will and thus willingly assumes the intent of our mind, so that what it pronounces would be judged more to come from us. Oh how difficult it is for the subject to adopt the speech of the ruler, to be able to pronounce what may be assumed as our own, and, being advanced in public distinction, to enact a noble falsehood! (*Var*. 6. 5.1-2, trans. Bjornlie)

This description beautifully encapsulates the ambivalence of voice. Here is Cassiodorus writing what he thinks the king should say in making an appointment: he writes with the king's voice ('the voice of our pronouncements', *nostrae linguae vocem*). If the quaestor's job is to be the voice of the king, that does not mean he should impose his own opinions (*arbitrium suae voluntatis deponit*): his job is to find the right expression for what he recognises as the king's will (*ut proprie dicere possit quod nos sentire cognoscit*). It is a form of ventriloquism: the puppet speaks, but everyone must know that it is truly the voice of the puppet-master – except that, in this case, it is actually the puppet who speaks, and we have to take it on trust that it is really what the puppet-master wants.

Cassiodorus, ever alert to paradox and ambivalence, seems to relish this complex situation – it is a 'noble falsehood', *gloriosam ... falsitatem*. He would smile if we asked him whether the letters as published genuinely

---

[35] Honoré, *Tribonian*, p. 9, concisely distinguishes the three offices: 'The functions of justice were therefore divided, so that, in broad terms, legislation fell to the quaestor, legal administration to the master of offices and the *scrinia*, and the execution of laws to the praetorian prefect.'

expressed the opinion of the king – or, rather, what he thought that opinion *ought* to be, what he would be well-advised to say. He would shrug and say there was no difference: royal pronouncements came out of discussion, possibly the checking of drafts, and his role was not to impose his own opinion but to help the king formulate an opinion which he would not regret. His job was to know Roman law inside out, so that the king made pronouncements compatible with tradition, while addressing contemporary issues. The Quaestor has to be a sort of photocopy of the king:

> And finally, it is fitting for the Quaestor to be the kind of official as would deserve to bear the likeness of the Princeps (*principis . . . imaginem*). For if we, as is usual, should happen to hear a case from the transcripts, what authority will a tongue have that is able to play the role of the royal presence in the hearing of others? (*Var.* 6. 5.4, trans. Bjornlie)

Intensely proud of his role, Cassiodorus adds a flourish: the quaestorship is

> the glory of letters, the temple of civility, the generator of every honour, the home of self-restraint, the seat of all virtues. (*Var.* 6. 5.5, trans. Bjornlie, adapted)[36]

'Temple of civility', *templum civilitatis*, goes to the heart, as we shall see, of the Cassiodoran value-system; but it is a value-system which is embraced enthusiastically by Theoderic. The Quaestor is more than a puppet, more than a photocopy: his role is hermeneutical, of interpreting what the king wants, or at least what he would want if well-advised. His opinion cannot really be disentangled from that of his sovereign.

Finally, he urges that the Quaestor, for all his power, must not get above himself, or cause embarrassment to his sovereign:

> Exercise the power of the *Princeps* with the rank of a subject. Thus glorified speak with our mouth, provided that you may hold yourself accountable to our court, where the blameworthy man receives a change of fortune and a praiseworthy man acquires the glory of good intention. (*Var.* 6. 5.6, trans. Bjornlie, adapted)

In a word: get it wrong and you'll be sacked, get it right and there is the prospect of promotion. The implication is that the Quaestor enjoys considerable discretion and may be expected to formulate opinions at times without close consultation and explicit approval: success or failure in the

---

[36] Here, as elsewhere, Bjornlie avoids translating *civilitas* as 'civility' (instead: 'civil harmony'); I have adapted his translations to make clear the use of the term.

role depends on the skill of giving a regal opinion in such a way that after the event, the king will not say he has got it wrong.

All this, of course, applies most strictly to Cassiodorus' period as Quaestor; it is striking that as *Magister Officiorum*, whose administrative duties are described in the following *formula* (6.6) and do *not* include acting as the royal mouthpiece, he nevertheless continues to write letters in the king's name: but then a king was at liberty to ask his officials what he wanted, and on more than one occasion they must have found it very convenient to put forward Cassiodorus as their spokesman when it was not strictly his job (as he puts it in his Preface, 'the Principes seem to set upon you those affairs from other offices which their own magistrates are unable to unravel, as though you were wrestling with an ordinary burden'; Pref. 7).

But at this stage, a secondary problem obtrudes: are these actually the letters as published at the time, or have they been subjected to significant editing in the light of later circumstances? Cassiodorus is quite open in both of his prefaces, to book 1 and to book 11.[37] Indeed, he has edited the letters. It is by no means at the request of the royal court that he publishes them, but rather of his learned friends; we cannot even assume that he had permission to do so, or that at the time of publication any Gothic king would have been in any position to stop him. It used to be assumed that he must have published while still in office with full access to the archives in Ravenna.[38] But that was superfluous if, as was standard practice from Cicero onwards, he kept copies of his own correspondence, in and out. A recent suggestion is that the letters were published after the fall of Witigis in 540, when Belisarius took both the king and other members of the court back with him to Constantinople. It might make sense that Cassiodorus should have been among them – he would be an ideal target for 'debriefing' – and in any case he was certainly in the eastern capital at some stage after the war.[39]

It could make a considerable difference for our interpretation of the aims of the collection just when and where it was pulled together. But this is speculative territory, and for now it is helpful to stick with what the author tells us explicitly. They seem to have been revised in Ravenna, as the army of Belisarius closed in on the Gothic position.[40]

---

[37] On the prefaces, see the discussion of Bjornlie, *Politics and Tradition*, pp. 189–199.

[38] See Bjornlie, *Politics and Tradition*, pp. 19–25.

[39] Bjornlie, *Politics and Tradition*; also O'Donnell, *Cassiodorus*, p. 106. On Cassiodorus' time in Constantinople, Barnish, 'The work of Cassiodorus after his conversion'.

[40] The later date suggested by Bjornlie; the traditional dating before 540 is defended by Porena, 'Gioco di ombre a Costantinopoli'. *Var.* 11, pref. 7 states that he wrote *de anima* after completing the letters; *de anima* 2 refers to his engagement with 'royal commands' as recent

As he describes it in the first preface, it was 'learned men', *diserti*, who pressed him

> to gather into one collection these words of mine which I had often supplied in offices for explicating the nature of public affairs, so that the coming generation might realise both the burden of my duties, which I had undertaken for public benefit, and the disinterested actions of a clear conscience. (Pref.1, trans. Bjornlie, adapted)

It is striking how he takes ownership of the letters. It is not a matter of republishing government correspondence, but of collecting together 'these words of mine', *dicta mea*. They were written *for* the kings, and *in the name of* the kings, but they were still his own words, and he took some pride in them. Indeed, the major preoccupation of the Preface is that his letters will prove to have been too hastily and inelegantly written, under the pressure of time and hard work. An author, he says, would do well to follow the advice of Horace's *Ars Poetica* and let his writings 'mature till the ninth year', but he has written when bombarded with high affairs of state. If he had had the leisure to take time over them, he would not have been doing his job. So, rather to our surprise, given the elaborate arabesques of his style, he is apologising for hasty and artless writing, with the implication that his main effort in editing them was to polish their style. This he can represent as a boon to future generations of officeholders like himself:

> But I have not been content to permit others to endure what I often experienced in bestowing offices; that is speeches written hastily and without polish, which were demanded so suddenly that it seemed hardly possible to write. And thus, I have included *formulae* for all the official posts in the sixth and seventh books, so that however late, I might take care for my own reputation. (Pref. 14, trans. Bjornlie)

We may take note of his confidence that precisely the administrative system with which he was familiar would continue into the future. Not just in his boiler-plate letters of appointment, but throughout, he is showing how it ought to be done. The very complexity of his style that causes us most problems is what he felt was needed all along in model correspondence from the royal palace.

The modern reader might have preferred more plain meaning and less charm of rhetoric, but that is not the taste of the sixth century. Cassiodorus goes on to draw a distinction between these books and the previous ones.

(*praeceptis regum quae nuper agebantur*). Walter Pohl argues that the last letter in the collection must date to 539: 'Social cohesion, breaks, and transformations in Italy'.

> And so I have combined two books from the tenure of my prefecture, so that I, who have acted as royal spokesman in ten books, should not be unknown for my own role, since it would be exceedingly absurd that I, who was known to have said so much on behalf of others, should fall silent concerning the office I attained. (*Var.* 11, pref. 6, trans. Bjornlie)

Again, he is concerned with the question of voice that he had raised so eloquently in this *formula* for the quaestorship. While the first ten books represent *dicta mea*, his own writing, but always on the behalf of the king, the last two books are his own words in his own authority as Prefect. That is why, despite the fact that the first preface had already set out the full breakdown of twelve books, he needs a new introduction, to Cassiodorus speaking for Cassiodorus. As if to drive home the point, he now offers us a thirteenth book, a treatise on the soul, *de Anima*, which certainly represents his own personal thinking, however much indebted to Augustine and others.[41] In subject matter and style, it has no connection to the twelve books of *Variae*; but the point is that like the last two books, it is all his own work, albeit written under the pressure of his flattering friends (pref. 7). The preface to the treatise itself repeats the thought of friends pressing him to write just when he had finished the *Variae* and had been 'welcomed into the peaceful harbour to which I had come perhaps without praise but at least free from care' (*de Anima* pref.1).

We may thus draw a line of distinction between the last two books of the *Variae*, which represent Cassiodorus' own voice, albeit modulated to conformity with the regime he served, and in which quite personal elements can be detected (we have already seen his patriotic praise of his native city of Squillace; see Chapter 2), in contrast with the first ten books, in the closely woven fabric of which it is vain to tease apart the warp of royal will from the weft of his own words, *mea dicta*. There is plenty of his own invention and style there; but that the regime approved of what he wrote is shown, exactly as he suggests, by the fact that they kept asking him to write and kept promoting him. Indeed, we may be struck by his successful survival at a court which passed through a series of crises: the supposed treachery of Boethius, despite being a senior member of the government as *Magister Officiorum*; the need for Athalaric to succeed while still a minor, leaving power with Amalasunta; Athalaric's untimely death, and Amalasunta's desperate strategy of marrying Theoderic's cousin, Theodahad, whose behaviour was questionable enough to have earned two letters of reproof penned

---

[41] See the helpful translation and notes by Halporn and Vessey, *Cassiodorus: Institutions*, pp. 237–283.

by Cassiodorus (*Var.* 4.39 and 5.12); the disgraceful murder of Amalasunta, confined on her island on lake Bolsena; the deposition of Theodahad by a member of his armed guard, Witigis, who then legitimised his claim by forcibly marrying Amalasunta's daughter, Matasunta (Cassiodorus actually penned a wedding speech); and, finally, the invasion of Italy by Belisarius. All these crises Cassiodorus survived, never himself disgraced or murdered; by that measure he represents the authentic voice of the Amal dynasty.

We may view, if we like, the *Variae* as a work of propaganda, or at the very least an exercise in Public Relations. But there are dangers in trying to be too specific about the occasion or target audience of such propaganda.[42] Whether issued before or after the fall of Witigis at Ravenna, the underlying message was consistent from the moment that Theoderic declared himself king of Italy: that he was the legitimate successor of the *Principes* who preceded him; that he respected, as they had done, the decisions and laws of his predecessors; that the presence of his Gothic army in Italy was not a threat to Roman stability, but its guarantor; and that he would do his utmost to ensure that Goths and Romans lived together in peace, respecting not the rules of barbarian violence, but of Roman law. That applied as much in AD 493 as fifty years later. Legitimacy resided in continuity, and that was the only potent argument against a hungry eastern emperor like Justinian who hoped to reclaim historical rule in the west. What is striking about Cassiodorus' articulation of this message in the *Variae* is its consistency and coherence. We may question again and again whether things were really as they ought to be in Italy, but not what Theoderic and his successors *claimed* they ought to be.

Ideals of the City in Cassiodorus

Cities for Cassiodorus are no mere incidental feature of Roman life: they lie at the heart of what distinguishes civilisation, the fabric of life of the Greek and Roman Mediterranean, from barbarity. One has only to read Jordanes' version of his *History of the Goths* to see the negative relationship between all barbarians and cities.[43] No barbarian tribe beyond the bounds of the empire makes settlements in what a Roman could call a 'city'; and once they

---

[42] Bjornlie, *Politics and Tradition*, passim, builds up a careful argument that the target audience was of middle-ranking bureaucrats in Constantinople, but this is speculation and seems unnecessarily restrictive. See Heather, 'A tale of two cities', pp. 19–37 at 27–28.

[43] For a recent edition, see Van Nuffelen and Van Hoof, *Romana and Getica*. Here quoted in the translation of Mierow, *The Gothic History of Jordanes*.

cross the border and enter the empire, their first engagement with cities is to sack them, for they know they are the treasure houses where the wealth of the Roman world is stored. The Sclaveni who inhabit the area between the Dnieper and the Vistula 'have swamps and forests for their cities', *paludes silvasque pro civitatibus habent* (35). Attila's chief settlement is unusual: 'a village, I say, like a great city', *vicum inquam ad instar civitatis amplissimae*. What gives it the semblance of a city is its extent, but what makes it a village is its wooden construction (178). Not all barbarians were equally awful: the Alans, though as effective in war as the Huns, did not share their sheer barbarity: 'unlike them in civilization, manners and appearance', *humanitate, victu, formaque dissimiles*; it was the squat heads and slashed cheeks on the Huns that struck terror into their enemies (126–128). Once they crossed the Roman frontier, barbarians, especially Goths, were capable of change. Fritigern and his Visigoths, once they had defeated Roman attempts to keep them on the far side of the Danube, found that:

> ...the Goths no longer as strangers and pilgrims (*advenae et peregrini*), but as citizens and lords (*cives et domini*), began to rule the inhabitants and to hold in their own right all the northern country as far as the Danube. (137)

But they have not yet become urbanised. A turning point is the visit of Alaric's predecessor, Athanaric, to Constantinople at the invitation of Theodosius in AD 381:

> As he entered the royal city, Athanaric exclaimed in wonder, 'Lo, now I see what I have often heard of with unbelieving ears', meaning the great and famous city. Turning his eyes hither and thither, he marvelled as he beheld the situation of the city, the coming and going of the ships, the splendid walls, and the people of divers nations gathered like a flood of waters streaming from different regions into one basin. (143)

The magnificence of the eastern capital was consciously exploited by Theodosius as a tool of diplomatic persuasion, and as a means to urbanise the barbarian. A Goth with a capital like that could make an impression, even on a Roman. Theoderic's years in the same city had the same effect. As his panegyrist, Ennodius, put it, 'Greece, foreseeing the future, raised you in the bosom of civility, *in gremio civilitatatis*' (*Pan.Theod.* 3). Cassiodorus, as we will see, was to pick up the idea of *civilitas*, with its connotations of cities, citizenship and civilisation, and turn it into the central virtue of the Gothic regime. Swamps and forests were in the past.

Throughout his letters, repeatedly and insistently, Cassiodorus, speaking both for the Gothic regime and in his own authority as Praetorian Prefect, presses the cause of urbanism, the repair of urban fabric, the maintenance of urban institutions and values, the patriotic duties of the citizen, *civis*, and the ideal which he deserves more credit for entirely reformulating, of *civilitas*.[44]

Urban Fabric

We may start with Cassiodorus' ideas about urban fabric.[45] One recurrent idea is that it is the duty of the good citizen to care about the urban fabric, its preservation and enhancement.[46] We first encounter Theoderic urging the citizens of Rome to show their love for the city by paying for building works. The king wants to be encouraged by a display of civic affection to improve the city:

> We are encouraged to make improvements to the city by the active zeal of its citizens (*affectuosis civium studiis*), since nobody is able to like what he knows the inhabitants do not love. For each person, his own native city (*patria*) is more precious. (*Var.* 1.21.1, trans. Bjornlie, adapted)

If they pay up, then his generosity will be redoubled. And, this being Cassiodorus, he urges them to follow the example of nature:

> The very birds roaming the sky love their own nests, the wandering beasts hasten to their thorny dens, delightful fish crossing watery fields seek with careful research their own hollows, and every kind of animal spends long hunting down a familiar refuge. What ought we to say now concerning Rome, which it is even more appropriate for her children to love? (*Var.* 1.21.3, trans. Bjornlie, adapted).

To Cassiodorus, civic spirit is natural, not a social construct, but part of the order of nature.

---

[44] I have discussed this theme in my paper, 'The cities of Cassiodorus'. This chapter travels over the same ground. Amory, *People and Identity*, p. 43, suggests that the ideology was developed by 'Theoderic and or his advisers'; maybe, but it is in the *Variae* that we can see the idea articulated.

[45] See Fauvinet-Ranson, *Decor civitatis*, pp. 197–227. The political importance of Theoderic's building activity is discussed by Saitta, *Civilitas*, pp. 103–138. For a full discussion of Theoderic's buildings, La Rocca, 'Mores tuos fabricatae loquuntur'; further, Bjornlie, *Politics and Tradition*, pp. 234–253; Lafferty, *Law and Society*, pp. 206–239; Arnold, *Theoderic and the Roman Imperial Restoration*, pp. 201–230.

[46] See Pergoli Campanelli, *Cassiodoro*, which argues, rather optimistically, that Cassiodorus anticipates the values of modern conservation; discussed in 'Antiqua in nitorem pristinum contineas' (2024).

A little later, Theoderic issues an edict to all Goths and Romans, instructing them to hand over all loose stone suitable for the repair of city walls. He is probably concerned here with the walls of Rome, but it is expressed as a general principle: city construction is a worthy object of regal care, because the repair of ancient cities is a credit to the age: *laus est temporum reparatio urbium vetustarum* (*Var.* 1.28). Hence, all should join in willingly. We may suspect other motives: in his anxiety to turn Ravenna into a great capital, Theoderic helped himself to building material stripped from elsewhere.[47] That a king sought to burnish his own image is no surprise, but the way Cassiodorus chose to represent it was as a common civic duty: Rome must willingly provide marble from the Domus Pinciana because it is the sign of the noblest citizen to seek to augment his home city: *nobilissimi civis est patriae suae augmenta cogitare* (*Var.* 3.10).[48] Similarly, the councillors (*curiales*) of the unidentified city of Estuni needed to understand that sending their marble slabs to Ravenna was a higher good, for it was far better for the material to support the cause of revival than to lie around as a painful memory of past times.

> It is our policy to construct new buildings, but more to conserve old ones, since it is no less a source of praise to create than to protect things. Hence we wish to put up modern buildings (*moderna*) without diminution of the previous; for whatever becomes inconvenient through another does not prove acceptable to our justice.
>
> So we gather that in your town columns lie around unused together with stones demolished by the envy of old age; and since there is no gain for things to lie around indecorously, they should rise up for a revived ornament rather than display mourning over the memory of bygone ages. (*Var.* 3.9.1-2, trans. AWH)

Again, the councillors of Catania are given a pat on the back for their civic devotion (*caritate civica*) in repairing the city walls, and are given permission to use the material from the collapsed amphitheatre for repairs.[49] So much is this a matter of principle that Cassiodorus includes in his book of model

---

[47] On the reuse of material, sometimes classified as 'spolia', see Dey, 'Politics, patronage and the transmission of construction techniques'; Dey, *Making of Medieval Rome*, pp. 109–110, 195–196. Ironically, the precious materials from the palace at Ravenna were later stripped out by Charlemagne for Aachen: see Nelson, 'Charlemagne and Ravenna' in Herrin and Nelson, *Ravenna*, pp. 239–252.

[48] Giardina, *Cassiodoro Varie* vol. II, 217–218, notes that the domus Pinciana was an imperial property.

[49] *Var.* 3.49.2 *Atque ideo suggestionis vestrae tenore comperto, quam caritate civica in communiendis moenibus suscepistis, absolutam huius rei vobis censemus esse licentiam.*

standard letters permission to someone offering to take over a ruinous public property for improvement at his own cost: 'Go on', he urges, 'and let what lay in ruins through careless antiquity take on a decorous aspect, for it is the mark of a good citizen to ornament his city' (*Var.* 7.44.1).[50]

Athalaric is only slightly less insistent than Theoderic on urban improvements. The councillors of Parma are sternly rebuked for failing to clean out their sewers.

> For this reason you should all agree to work on this most useful project, because a citizen has no spirit if he is not bound by gratitude to his city. (Var. 8.30.2)[51]

His grandfather Theoderic has provided water by an aqueduct, but the water supply was useless unless the drains were kept clear. The king issues an edict to stop his Gothic officials and soldiers from seizing the property of councillors: the state, the *res publica*, which the king defends is not just one city, but all cities, and for each citizen,

> To each and every citizen, his own city is the state.
>
> *Unicuique civi urbs sua res publica est.* (Var. 9.2.4)

One could of course argue that Theoderic's paraded concern with maintaining urban fabric is a mere mask, a pretence of continuing a tradition from the high empire that was no longer practicable in the changed circumstances of the sixth century.[52] The fifteenth book of the Theodosian Code preserves a whole string of imperial instructions in support of the repair and restoration of urban fabric, including rules against moving material from one city to another. The book opens with an edict of Constantine:

> No man shall suppose that municipalities may be deprived of their ornaments, since indeed it was not considered right by the ancients that a municipality should lose its embellishments, as though they should be transferred to the buildings of another city. (*Codex Theodosianus* 15.1.1, trans. Pharr)

Even disused temples enjoyed imperial protection. Arcadius and Honorius rule:

> All public buildings and buildings that belong to any temple, those that are situated within the walls of the city or even those that are attached to the

---

[50] See Dubouloz, 'Acception et défense des *loca publica*'.
[51] *Var.* 8.30.2 *civis animum non habet, qui urbis suae gratia non tenetur.*
[52] So La Rocca, 'Una prudente maschera'; see the reply of Marazzi, 'Ostrogthic cities', pp. 105–106.

walls ... shall be held and kept by decurions and members of the guilds. (*C.Th.* 15.1.41, trans. Pharr)

Theoderic uses the same language but is more lax about allowing buildings to be repurposed or demolished and ornaments to be transferred from one city to another.

There may always be a gap, sometimes substantial, between what a government claims to have achieved, or to wishes to achieve, and what it actually achieves. But what is interesting here is precisely the rhetoric which Theoderic and Cassiodorus thought suitable and effective. It was based on the assumption that the maintenance of urban fabric was a desirable end and a fundamental function of rule, an assumption borne out by centuries of imperial legislation on the theme.[53]

The citizen, then, is bound up with the fabric of the city, and Cassiodorus shows us the spectacle of a dynasty constantly attentive (or proclaiming itself to be so) to the repair and enhancement of the urban fabric, especially in Rome but also more generally across Italy. It is remarkable on how many of the principal types of urban monument they intervene.[54] There is some priority to defensive walls: in addition to Rome and Catania, as we have seen, measures are taken to repair the walls of Arles (3.44) and of Syracuse (9.14), where Gildila, the corrupt count of the city, is reproved for raising a special tax to finance the repair of the walls and then failing to repair them. This too is in line with earlier legislation, urging governors of provinces to ensure that

> municipal senates and inhabitants of each city shall build new walls or make the old walls stronger, and the expense thereof shall, of course, be arranged in such a way that the tax assessment shall be apportioned according to the ability of each man. (C.Th. 15.1.34, Theodosius, Arcadius and Honorius, AD 396, trans. Pharr)

An almost equally pressing concern is over aqueducts and drains. A pair of letters from Theoderic to Argolicus, the City Prefect of Rome, and to the Senate, announce the dispatch of an agent, Johannes, to sort out water problems. They must repair the splendid drains of Rome:

> Hence your Illustrious Sublimity should recognise that we have dispatched John on behalf of the splendid sewers of the City of Rome, which strike visitors with such amazement as to exceed the wonders of

---

[53] On imperial legislation protecting historical monuments see Janvier, *La législation du Bas-Empire Romain*.
[54] Fauvinet-Ranson, *Decor civitatis*, pp. 199–221.

> other cities ... For which other city dares compete with your heights, O Rome, when they cannot even offer a match for your depths? (Var. 3.30.1–2, trans. AWH)[55]

The drains of Rome are not a mere practicality of hygiene: they are the high point of Roman urbanism. The next letter turns to the aqueducts, where the problem seems to be that private landowners have been illegally tapping the public water supply to work their mills and water their vegetable plots (3.31).[56] The penalties for doing so will be fierce, as they will be for the robbing of metal and the theft of stone from temples and public buildings for private repairs. Later, we meet an edict addressed to all landowners, though those of Ravenna are specifically mentioned, on the importance of controlling vegetation around aqueducts. A little sermon follows:

> For what are now only shoots, would become, if ignored, even stronger. For such saplings which are dislodged with the ease of uprooting, later will hardly succumb to blows from axes. And therefore you ought to attend to this with shared haste, so that you may avoid with present diligence the troubles of future toil. For without opposition, this is the ruin of civil order, a sundering of buildings as though from a battering ram (*haec est enim civilis eversio, sine oppugnatione discidium*) (Var. 5.38.1, trans. Bjornlie)[57]

By contrast, an aqueduct in good repair provides liquid as pure as that fresh from a spring, and keeps the public baths impressive and swimming pools full of glassy water. So, again, his care goes beyond the mere issue of hygiene, and Cassiodorus' florid prose reminds us that urban amenities are the glory of urban culture. The theme is taken up again, as we have seen, in Athalaric's rebukes to the citizens of Parma.

Among aqueducts, pride of place must go to Rome. It is the duties of the *Comes Formarum*, the Count of the Aqueducts, as set out in the formula (*Var.* 7.6). In the wonders of Rome, beauty and utility come together, and never more so than with the aqueducts. Cassiodorus can give himself the chance here of a fine purple passage on the extraordinary engineering technique of the Roman aqueduct, in which human work competes with

---

[55] Giardina, *Cassiodoro Varie*, vol. II, 256, points to the echoes of Pliny's *Natural History* (36.104).
[56] Identical concerns go back to the *senatusconsultum* of 11 BC cited by Frontinus, *de aquis* 2.106, legislation reiterated by Constantine, *Codex Theodosianus* 15.2.1 = *Codex Justinianeus* 11.43.1.1.
[57] Similar regulations go back to the *senatusconsultum* of 11 BC cited by Frontinus, *de aquis* 2.126, legislation reiterated by Valentinian, *Codex Theodosianus* 15.2.2.

nature in terms of durability through the centuries, while slipping in a warning on the vital importance of maintenance.

> In the aqueducts of Rome both [beauty and utility] are outstanding, that the construction be wonderful and the health of the waters unique. For how many rivers are brought on man-made mountains, so that you would believe that the channels were natural, so solid is their stone, in that such water pressure can be endured for so many centuries. Hollowed mountains often collapse, and the courses of torrents are washed away; yet this ancient construction is not destroyed, so long as it is assisted by the hard work of maintenance.
> (*Var.* 7.6.2, trans. AWH)

Walls, water supply, and drains sound like the mere basics of urbanism. But we also find Theoderic concerned with the repair of storage facilities (*horrea*), though in this case he is decommissioning an imperial warehouse: the patrician Paulinus has undertaken to repair *horrea* in disrepair through their antiquity, and the king grants him total licence to repurpose for his own private use buildings in a city 'in which it is right that all buildings should gleam again, lest ruins spoil the sight of the many splendours of Rome, which is praised on the lips of the whole world'.[58] Similarly, Symmachus is praised at great length, and offered a financial subvention into the bargain, for his work in restoring buildings in Rome and its suburbs, and especially the theatre of Pompey. It is not enough for Rome to work: it needs to look good. By the time this letter was published, Symmachus had been executed by Theoderic for his loyal support of Boethius, an episode widely considered as a major blot on the record of the regime. Cassiodorus gives no hint of this: it is his policy to avoid controversy and emphasise the positive relations Theoderic had, both with Symmachus and with Boethius.[59]

One phrase of this letter in particular catches the eye: Symmachus is both a diligent imitator of antiquity and a noble institutor of the modern (*modernorum*).[60] This thought, and this phraseology, recurs in several guises in the *Variae*. It is not simply a matter of repairing and conserving antiquity, but of creating something new and up to date. The use of the

---

[58] *Var.* 3.29.1. Such privatisation of *horrea* was explicitly forbidden in *C.Th.* 15.1.12 (Valentinian and Valens, AD 364).

[59] *Var.* 4.51. Bjornlie, *Politics and Tradition*, pp. 170–171, suggests that the whole letter to Symmachus is a subsequent invention, containing a satirical attack on his fondness for theatres. Considering that Cassiodorus claimed to be related to Symmachus, it is unclear what he had to gain by mocking him; cf. Heather, 'A tale of two cities', pp. 28–29.

[60] *Var.* 4.51.2 *antiquorum diligentissimus imitator, modernorum nobilssimus institutor.*

word *modernus* is here quite significant.[61] If to us it might evoke a surprising modernism, that is actually in place. The word itself is not classical Latin. Cassiodorus' language is permeated with the Latin of Cicero and the younger Pliny, but every now and again he uses what we might think of as a neologism, or perhaps a late-Latinism, or even a modernism.[62] *Modernus* is also met in Ennodius' panegyric of Theoderic.[63] The formation of the word is authentic: *modernus* from *modo*, now, just as *hodiernus* from *hodie*. But, in this case, it carries a charge: there can and should be a nobility in the modern.

So, in praising Inportunus to the senate and elevating him to the patriciate, we hear that his family has decorated the modern age with antique morals:

> modernis saeculis moribus ornabantur antiquis. (Var. 3.5.3)

Theoderic is a believer in his modern age as well as antiquity. When the councillors of Estuni are ordered to supply building material for Ravenna, they are told that Theoderic's intention is to construct the new, to conserve the old (*nova construere, sed amplius vetusta servare*), and to erect the modern without diminution of the previous (*moderna sine priorum imminutione, Var.* 3.9.1). Cassiodorus himself, in drafting the formula for the appointment of the Palace Architect (*Var.* 7.5), enjoins on him the duty both of restoring the antique to its original glow and producing new work of similar antiquity; the antique and the modern are antithetical yet interlinked, the antique should be made new, and the new antique.[64] It has been suggested that Cassiodorus wrote his *Variae* as a critique of Justinian and his taste for innovation.[65] Neither Cassiodorus nor Theoderic, unless he was misrepresented, were opposed to innovation and modernism, but it had to go hand in hand with respect for and restoration of the antique. This seems to me highly relevant to the cycle of resilience: conservatism coupled with innovation is a crucial form of adaptation to changing circumstances.

---

[61] Cf. Moorhead, 'The word modernus'; Moorhead, *Theoderic in Italy*, pp. 427–428; Giardina, *Cassiodoro Varie politico*, pp. 43–44; La Rocca, 'Mores tuos', p. 12; Gardina, *Cassiodoro Varie*, vol. II, pp. 202 and 394.

[62] Zimmermann, *The Late Latin Vocabulary of Cassiodorus*, collects 'neologisms, words of foreign origin, Late Latin words and meanings' (p. vi) in the *Variae*; p. 56 for *modernus*.

[63] On the style, Fauvinet-Ranson, *Decor civitatis*, pp. 25–28.

[64] *Var.* 7.5.3: *antiqua in nitorem pristinum contineas et nova simili antiquitate producas*. Pergolesi Campanelli, *Cassiodoro*, pp. 27–81, sees in this and similar passages an anticipation of modern conservation theory – over-optimistically.

[65] See Bjornlie, *Politics and Tradition*, pp. 234–240, on *novitas* as a negative concept.

Before leaving the urban fabric, it is worth noting one other small feature: the recurrent concern for statues.[66] We meet it in Como, where a bronze statue has been removed: Theoderic will offer 100 *aurei* for information leading to its return (*Var.* 2.35). We meet it again in the list of the duties of the *comes Romae*: he should patrol the city at night against theft, and will find that statues are not totally mute, since, when they are struck by thieves, they seem to give a warning by their *tinnitus* (*Var.* 7.13.4). We see again how the city fabric is constantly at risk from people just helping themselves to stone and metal. But the point Cassiodorus wants to get across is that statues have an important value for the city. It is under his Prefecture that Honorius the City Prefect is instructed to repair the bronze elephants on the via Sacra – the perfect excuse for him to give a long excursus on the elephant (*Var.* 10.30).[67] But the underlying point is that that decorative or commemorative elements like bronze statues are an integral part of the fabric and dignity of the ancient city, and especially of Rome. In this too he follows the example of previous Principes. Over a century earlier, for example, Valentinian, Theodosius and Arcadius had warned off those who tried to help themselves to decorative elements from buildings:

> We gave assent to those persons who petition for public places, on condition that they do not remove anything useful, ornamental or advantageous to the municipality. Although we do not believe that any man exists who would connive at any surreptitious undertaking of petitioners, as against the advantages and ornaments of his municipality, nevertheless ... (*Cod. Theod.* 15.1.43, trans. Pharr)

Cassiodorus distinguishes himself from previous legislation not so much by the content of the law, as by the eloquent passion with which it is expressed.

Civic Values

A city cannot survive on fabric alone. It survives on an idea of urbanism, a set of institutions and a set of values.[68] And Cassiodorus as the voice of the Gothic regime is quite as keen on promoting those institutions and

---

[66] On the continued importance of statues in Rome, see Machado, *Urban Space and Aristocratic Power in Late Antique Rome*.

[67] Cassiodorus' elephants have attracted a flurry of recent discussion: Bjornlie, 'What have elephants to do with sixth-century politics?'; La Rocca, 'Cassiodoro, Teodato e il restauro degli elephanti'; Devecka, 'White elephant gifts'. I owe these references to Sam Ottewill-Soulsby, whose passion for elephants is second to none.

[68] See Scivoletto, 'Cassiodoro e la retorica della città'.

values as on preserving and improving fabric. At the top of his list of priorities is the ruling class of the city, the members of the *curia* or *curiales* (I will refer to them by the more familiar English term: councillors).[69] In the modern accounts of the Late Antique city which represent the city as being in a long decline, a key element is the supposed decline of the curial system (see Chapter 1, pp. 17–20).[70] Under the high empire, the rich, especially landowners, are supposed to have played a positive role in urban prosperity by voluntarily offering services (*munera*) to their communities in exchange for office and curial status. From the third century, membership of the *curia* progressively becomes both hereditary and obligatory, and there is an increasing volume of imperial legislation tightening the conditions of obligation as local elite members use imperial service and the church as excuses for evading their local duties. At the same time, councillors become responsible for tax collection, finding themselves in the curious position of both collecting and paying taxes in the form of local services. As Jones puts it, the legislation shows both 'that the imperial government considered the maintenance of the city councils essential to the well-being of the empire, and that many members of the city councils strongly disliked their position'.[71] The result, as he sees it, is the decline of both city councils and the city, though he shows that city councils persisted in the west until at least the seventh century under Visigothic rule, and in Francia as late as the eighth and ninth centuries (see Chapter 6).[72]

Four centuries is a remarkably long time for a decline, and another way of looking at it is to register surprise and interest that both Visigothic and Ostrogothic rulers made efforts to extend a system that was potentially unpopular among the rich. They might indeed have been keen on the continuation of cities without insisting on a very specific system of governance which was only developed in the Late Empire. Jones relies heavily on the law codes, from the Codex of Theodosius to that of Justinian; but since a function of the codes was to make the taxation system work, it is not all that much of a surprise to find emperors closing loopholes that permitted

---

[69] Under the early empire, these were referred to as *decuriones*; the word is still used in the law codes alongside *curiales*. Tabata, *Città dell'Italia*, pp. 41–71, for the administration of Ostrogothic cities and the role of the curiales; Fauvinet-Ranson, *Decor civitatis*, pp. 38–41.

[70] The thesis goes back to Jones, *The Greek City*, pp. 192–210, developed further in Jones, *The Later Roman Empire*, pp. 724–766, and thence forms the central thesis of Liebeschuetz, *Decline and Fall*.

[71] Jones, *Later Roman Empire*, p. 748.

[72] Liebeschuetz, *Decline and Fall*, p. 131. See further for Visigothic Spain, Churchin, 'Curials and local government'; Fernández, 'Aristocrats and statehood'. On the survival of the *Gesta municipalia* in Francia, see Barbier, *Archives oubliées du haut Moyen Âge*, and Chapter 6.

tax evasion. The value of Cassiodorus, in contrast to the law codes, is to reveal a little more of government thinking on this issue.

The importance of the councillors to the system of governance emerges at once from the sheer number of letters addressed by Cassiodorus to the *curiales* of cities across Italy, but also Gaul and Suavia (the formulations vary, sometimes also to *possessores,* landowners, sometimes also to *defensores,* but always to *curiales*).[73] This is simply how to get things done in cities, even if they also have governors (*comites*), who are typically Goths. The letters make clear that the government wishes to cherish and support the councillors. In the mid-fifth century, the emperor Majorian described the councillors as 'the sinews of the commonwealth and the innards of the cities'.[74] The language is cited by Cassiodorus.[75] An edict of Athalaric is eloquent. The health of a state depends on the health of its constituent parts, the cities:

> ... the Republic does not consist in the care of one city, but rather the provident protection of the entire *regnum* ... And therefore, being always watchful over divers cities, we have taken measures lest evils long endured should be able to burden the administration. (Var. 9.2.1, trans. Bjornlie)

The sickness takes the form of abusive treatment of councillors:

> The *curiales*, to whom the name was given with provident attention [i.e. indicating their care or *cura*, a false etymology], are said to be stricken with the most severe affliction, so that whatever has been chosen as a reason for distinction for them seems to have become instead an injury. Oh scandalous crime, oh intolerable evil! (*Var.* 9.2.1, trans. Bjornlie)

O importabile malum! *importabilis* proves to be another of those Cassiodoran late Latinisms, not met in classical literature. Any offender who has caused injury or loss to a councillor will be fined 10 pounds of gold, or flogged. Any soldier (by implication, a Goth)[76] depriving them of

---

[73] Tabata, *Città dell'Italia*, pp. 43–45, lists thirty-nine cities and two castella mentioned in the *Variae*: cf. Marazzi, 'Ostrogothic cities', p. 101. On the terminology, Cecconi, 'Honorati, possessores, curiales', with an important critique of the rigidly hierarchical definitions offered by Liebeschuetz; Tabata, *Città dell'Italia*, pp. 47–51, supports this interpretation.

[74] Majorian (457–461) Novellae vii.458 curiales nervos esse rei publicae ac viscera civitatum nullus ignorat. On Majorian's relationship with Rome, Salzman, *Falls of Rome*, pp. 162–166.

[75] Jones, *Later Roman Empire*, p. 748, n. 85, omits the parallel from Cassiodorus.

[76] See Amory, *People and Identity*, p. 21; Buchberger, *Shifting Ethnic Identities*, pp. 37–66.

their estates will be disciplined by a *iudex*. The councillors are urged to raise their spirits: they should live in a polity characterised by concord:

> Cranes know how to practice moral concord, among whom none seeks to be foremost, since they do not have ambition for inequity. (*Var.* 9.2.5, trans. Bjornlie).

Again Cassiodorus turns to Ambrose's *Hexameron* for evidence that concord and good government are part of the natural order: he even takes the Greek loan word, *politeia*, from this source.[77] A final flourish quotes the Roman law codes:

> Not in vain did antiquity call them the lesser senate, the sinews and innards of the cities. (trans. AWH)[78]

Cassiodorus, who, as an imperial administrator, was deeply versed in imperial legislation such as is preserved in the Codes, is evidently citing Majorian, and in calling him *antiquitas* attributes greater prestige to the idea.

In a closely comparable context, Cassiodorus sets out in one of his *formulae* the exceptional circumstances under which the Praetorian Prefect can order the sale of lands belonging to a councillor. Antiquity has prudently defined that the property of councillors should not be broken up easily. By whom, he asks, can the *urbium munia*, the services of the cities, be sustained, if the sinews of the cities (*civitatum nervi*) are cut off?[79] Again, Theoderic writes to Bishop Gudila about some men whom the councillors of Sarsina say belong to their number but have been reduced to slavery: how could men whom antiquity called the lesser senate be reduced to such a disgraceful condition?[80]

The overwhelming tone of Cassiodorus' letters about councillors is protective. The formula for the Praetorian Prefect attributes to him powers beyond those of any other government officer. He alone may flog the councillors, 'who are defined by law as the lesser senate'.[81] Libanius had vociferously protested against the flogging of councillors in the fourth

---

[77] On the debt to Ambrose *Hex.* 5. 50–52, see Giardina et al., vol. IV, 295. *Hex.* 5.47 is particularly close. On the *politeia* of cranes, *Hex.* 5.50: 'Let us begin, then, with those birds which have become examples for our own way of life. These birds have a natural social and military organization, whereas with us this service is compulsory and servile.'

[78] Ibid. 6: *non inaniter appellavit minorem senatum, nervos quoque vocitans ac viscera civitatum.*

[79] *Var.* 7.47.3: *a quibus enim urbium munia poterunt sustineri, si civitatum nervi passim videantur abscidi?*

[80] *Var.* 2.18.1: *quam videtur esse contrarium curionem rei publicae amissa turpiter libertate servire et usque ad condicionem pervenisse postremam, quem vocavit antiquitas minorem senatum?*

[81] *Var.* 6.3.4: *curiales etiam verberat, qui appellati sunt legibus minor senatus.*

century,[82] and here the power to flog them is restricted and exceptional. In several letters the councillors are seen as relatively small property owners who are in danger of exploitation by big landowners and their tax evasion. Theoderic writes to the senate to reprove senators for failure to pay taxes, thus landing the councillors in debt,[83] and in the next letter issues an edict against failure to pay tax by influential figures, *praepotentes*, which lands the councillors in debt (*Var.* 2.25).

A vivid illustration of a curial family which could no longer afford to carry out its duties concerns the family of a lady called Agenantia. Athalaric writes to his Praetorian Prefect giving him permission to remove Agenantia and her sons from the album of councillors in Lucania.[84]

> Therefore let your illustrious magnificence cause Agenantia, the wife of the leaarned Campanianus living in the province of Lucania, and their sons, to be immediately erased from the roll of the *curia*, so that posterity to come may not learn what is forbidden to interpose, since treachery is not perpetrated where a public record is not maintained. (*Var.* 9.4.2, trans. Bjornlie, adapted)

Such a proceeding is exceptional because 'the most sacred laws' have tied the councillors to their duties unless and only if released by the emperors (in practice, of course, it may have been much more common than he admits). The exemption from the curial role is clearly intended as a privilege (it is 'favour from the Princeps'), for which they have presumably petitioned on the grounds of poverty; yet Cassiodorus cannot resist adding a stern warning:

> Henceforth let them be counted among the populace of landowners, enduring no less the exactions that they themselves had inflicted on others. Now they will become troubled at the accustomed taxation; now they will dread the appearance of the collector. They will not know rights that come from holding authority. (*Var.* 9.4.2–3, trans. Bjornlie)

These letters might seem to bear out the idea that the councillors were under pressure, subject to abuse by those above them, and hatred by those below them, and that consequently the system was in decline. Maybe, but they also show that they were still regarded as essential for the functioning of cities, and cities as essential for the functioning of central government,

---

[82] See Liebeschuetz, *Antioch*, pp. 166 and 173 on the exemption from flogging and its limitation.
[83] *Var.* 2.24.4: *ne necesse sit curiali per multiplicem et inefficacem conventionis laborem in exiguis vestris illationibus sua potius damna suscipere.*
[84] Giardina, *Cassiodoro Varie* vol. IV, pp. 304–305 on the relationship of *curiales* and *possessores*. The latter must be non-curial landowners.

and consequently deserving of specific privileges and protection from above. Again, this is a contradiction Lepelley catches.[85] If the position of the councillors had since the third century become progressively less tenable, and their role in sustaining urban life in constant decline, we need to explain why not only emperors, but Ostrogothic kings three centuries later felt that their protection was so crucial. An opposite perspective, as we have seen (Chapter 3, pp. 104–108) is offered by Salvian of Marseille in his characterisation of the councillors as the oppressors of the cities in his bitter epigram *quot curiales, tot tyranni*.[86] The case of Agenantia illustrates both that the burden of responsibility could become intolerable to the families trapped in this role, and that from another perspective it put them in a position of power over their fellow landowners, and caused consequent resentment.

According to the thesis of Liebeschuetz, councillors progressively lost influence and found their role overtaken by that of bishops.[87] Is there any trace of this in Cassiodorus?[88] It is striking that *episcopi* do not feature in the regular lists of addressees of letters to cities. Bishops are addressed when the church is directly involved, like Gudila, who seems to have been complicit in freeing some councillors from their civic duties by making them fictitious 'slaves' of the church (*Var.* 2.18); their right of jurisdiction within the church is acknowledged (*Var.* 1.9), and they intervene directly in distributing compensation to communities for damage caused by passing troops (*Var.* 2.8). But we are in a rather different world from that described later in the sixth century by Gregory of Tours, when bishops indeed play a dominant role in the administration of cities of Francia (see Chapter 8). In this sense, the civic administration described by Cassiodorus is highly traditional, as indeed Theoderic intended it to seem.[89]

And so it would be without the omnipresence of the Goths, who live alongside Romans in their cities, are constantly urged by Theoderic to live in peace and amity, respecting the rules of civil society, and who benefit from their own officials, the *comites civitatum*, to whom the other city officials owe obedience and who exercise jurisdiction in all cases involving Goths.[90] As the

---

[85] Lepelley, 'La survie de l'idée de cité républicaine'.
[86] Salvian, *de Gubernatione Dei* 5.4: *quae enim sunt non modo urbes sed etiam municipia atque uici, ubi non quot curiales fuerint, tot tyranni sunt?* See Chapter 3.
[87] Liebeschuetz, *Decline and Fall*, pp. 137–168, 'The Rise of the Bishop'.
[88] Well discussed by Tabata, *Città dell'Italia*, pp. 160–168.
[89] Cf. Fauvinet-Ranson, *Decor civitatis*, pp. 41–44; on bishops and clerics in the *Variae*, cf. Saitta, *Civilitas*, pp. 65–88. Liebeschuetz, *Decline and Fall*, pp. 164–166 on bishops in Gregory of Tours.
[90] Tabata, *Città dell'Italia*, pp. 71–95, for thorough discussion of the *comitiva*; pp. 117–124.

formula for the *comitiva Gothorum* addressed to the *civitates* puts it, 'Since with God's help we know that Goths live intermingled with you', the *comes* is appointed to resolve disputes involving Goths.[91] It was perhaps this presence of a substantial body of people who did not count as Romans that made it so important to underline the persistence of Roman tradition. Critics in Constantinople, as emerged with catastrophic results at the end of Theoderic's reign, were only too open to scare stories of abuse of Romans by Goths.

SPQR

If Cassiodorus is protective of the city councillors as *minor senatus* of the *civitates*, it goes without saying that he was positive about the Roman senate to which he, like his father before him, belonged, and pride in which is revealed in his name of Senator.[92] As the first letter of the collection proclaims, from Theoderic to the emperor Anastasius, they are bound together by a shared vision of a unified Roman empire, and by love of the city of Rome, *veneranda Romanae urbis adfectio* (*Var.* 1.1.3).[93] Numerous letters to the senate expatiate on the reverence due to that body. Perhaps more revealing is when cracks begin to show, and above all in the relationship between the senate and the *plebs Romana*, because, as Theoderic repeatedly makes clear, it is not just the grandees of the senate he supports, but the Roman citizen body as a whole. Problems blow up in the first book over the circuses, with their factions, and the 'pantomimes', who seem to have been closely related to the factions and to have had the capacity to stir them to rioting.[94] *Variae* 1.20 introduces the theme with a disclaimer by the king as to whether a *princeps* really ought to trouble himself with the games when he has so many regal concerns – an idea that seems to echo a letter of Fronto to

---

[91] *Var.* 7.3: *cum deo iuvante sciamus Gothos vobiscum habitare permixtos*.

[92] On the vital role of the Roman aristocracy in building in the city of Rome, see Machado, *Urban Space and Aristocratic Power in Late Antique Rome*; Salzman, *Falls of Rome*; on the limits of action in Rome, Dey, *Making of Medieval Rome*, pp. 61–64.

[93] According to the Anonymus Valesianus 66, Theoderic on his visit to Rome promised explicitly to respect the laws of his predecessors. On Theoderic and Rome, see La Rocca, 'An arena of abuses'; Arnold, *Theoderic and the Roman Imperial Restoration*, pp. 201–230. On the senate, see La Rocca and Oppedisano, *Il senato romano nell'Italia ostrogota*.

[94] On circus factions the classic discussion is Cameron, *Circus Factions*; on Ostrogothic Rome, Tabata, *Città dell'Italia*, pp. 149–155; Fauvinet-Ranson, *Decor civitatis*, pp. 380–440, for full discussion of 'spectacles'; Ward-Perkins, *From Classical Antiquity to the Middle Ages*, pp. 92–118, on their continued importance in the Ostrogothic period.

Marcus Aurelius arguing that trivial though they may seem, the games are to be taken seriously by an emperor.[95] He calls on the patricians Albinus and Avienus to adjudicate which of two competing pantomimes should be the official pantomime of the greens. This fails to settle the dispute, and shortly afterwards we meet a letter about a row between the supporters of the Greens and the senators Theodorus and Inportunus that resulted in the death of a supporter. It seems that they responded to insulting chants by sending in armed men against those for whom they should feel citizenly affection (*civicus affectus*). It is one thing for a senator to respond to an insult from a passing man in the street, but mockery at the games is traditional and acceptable.[96] This is followed up by a string of angry letters. Theoderic tells the senate that if anyone's servant kills a freeborn citizen (*ingenuus*), he is to hand him over at once to justice, or incur a fine of 10 pounds of gold and the king's displeasure (*Var.* 1.30). The next letter is addressed to the Populus Romanus and urges that spectacles should be an occasion of sweet music not discord: *Romana sit vox plebis* (*Var.*1.31). Senators must not be insulted. The next is a lecture to the City Prefect Agapitus on the proper relations of Senate and Plebs: the tradition of popular insults has to be kept under control, and if any senator forgets the rules of civility (*civilitatis immemor*) and has a freeborn citizen killed, he is to be punished.[97]

Perhaps the most revealing letter about the plebs is one written by Cassiodorus as Praetorian Prefect on the issue of food distributions, *opsonia*, for the Roman people (*Var.* 12.11). The official in charge of the distributions must ensure that regal benefactions should not be tainted, like clear water polluted with mud, by corrupt agents. All fraud is serious, but fraud against the Roman people is intolerable (*importabilis* again). The people should receive the full amount granted and be kept happy. Nor should benefit fraudsters be allowed: the grant is aimed at full Roman citizens (*Quirites*): nobody of servile condition should sneak into the place of the freeborn (*non subripiat locum liberi fortuna servilis*), for it is

---

[95] *Var.* 1.20.1: *pars minima videatur principem de spectaculis loqui*; Cf. Fronto, *Principia Historiae* 2.17: 'It seems to be based on the loftiest principles of political wisdom, that the Emperor did not neglect even actors and the other performers of the stage, the circus, or the amphitheatre, knowing as he did that the Roman People are held fast by two things above all, the corn dole and the shows, that the success of a government depends on amusements as much as more serious things; neglect of serious matters entails the greater loss, neglect of amusements the greater discontent.'

[96] *Var.* 1.27.4–5: *teneatur ad culpam quisquis transeunti reverentissimo senatori iniuriam protervus inflixit, si male optavit, cum bene loqui debuit. Mores autem graves in spectaculis quis requirat?*

[97] *Var.* 1.32.2: si *vero senator civilitatis immemor quemquam ingenuum nefaria fecerit caede vexari.*

an offence against the majesty of the Roman people if the purity of its blood is contaminated by the company of slaves.[98] As Cassiodorus was doubtless well aware, Augustus had used similar words about purity and contamination to limit access to the corn dole.[99] In his determination both to defend the privileges of the Roman citizen and to keep abuses at bay, Theoderic followed long-established precedent.

Civilitas: An Old Idea Refreshed

Cassiodorus and his Gothic masters thus offer us a surprisingly traditional image of the SPQR. Both senate and people matter. The gulf between free citizen and slave matters. For a senator to use his slave to kill a citizen is not acceptable: it is an offence against *civilitas*. And it is this idea of *civilitas* which represents the most coherent and extensive bundle of values in Cassiodorus, and which lies at the heart of his thought about cities and citizenship. All who write about Cassiodorus are conscious of the centrality of this ideal, as they could scarcely fail to be, for the word cluster *civilis/civilitas/incivilis/incivilitas* recurs with astonishing frequency and in a wide range of contexts.[100] Some think the concept so vague as to be almost meaningless. So James O'Donnell, who has the merit of producing the first modern study of Cassiodorus as a whole, passes over the idea with some distaste:

> *Civilitas* is in fact part of a larger scheme of slogans that springs from the whole pattern of denatured language with which Cassiodorus loaded the *Variae*.[101]

He goes on to describe the slogan as 'linguistic spinelessness'. By contrast, I want to make a case for *civilitas* as a form of social memory in changed circumstances, of Roman ideals adapting to the new realities of Gothic occupation – in a word, of resilience at work.

---

[98] *Var.* 12.11: *non fiat Latialis pretio, qui civitatis illius non habet iura nascendo. . . . munera ista Quiritium sunt. non subripiat locum liberi fortuna servilis. in maiestatem populi Romani peccat, qui sanguinis illius puritatem famulorum societate commaculat.* This model of civic euergetism is in contrast to that of Christian charity: see Salzman, 'From a Classical to a Christian city'.

[99] Suetonius, *Divus Augustus*, 40.3: *Magni praeterea existimans sincerum atque ab omni colluvione peregrini ac servilis sanguinis incorruptum servare populum.*

[100] Discussion is extensive: see Scivoletto, 'Cassiodoro e la retorica della città'; Saitta, *La civilitas di Teodorico*; Amory, *People and Identity*, pp. 116–118; Bjornlie, *Politics and Tradition*, pp. 251–253; Arnold, *Theoderic and Roman Imperial Restoration*, pp. 126–130; Giardina, *Cassiodoro politico*, pp. 35–39.

[101] O'Donnell, *Cassiodorus*, p. 96.

The first point to make is that Cassiodorus' usage of the term is strikingly non-Classical. The root sense of *civilis* is that which takes places between citizens, above all the great opposites, civil law (*ius civile*) and civil war (*bellum civile*). However, in the early empire it acquires a new meaning as the behaviour of an emperor who, despite his apparently kingly status, behaves as if he were but a fellow citizen. Pliny, in his Panegyric of Trajan, a work familiar in Late Antiquity and transmitted in the manuscripts as the first of several later panegyrics (the *Panegyrici Latini*), describes how Trajan used to treat senators as if he were still just one of them, *unus ex nobis*; the danger of autocratic power is that its holder behaves as if above ordinary humans – indeed, almost divine, as Domitian was accused of doing. But it was Suetonius in his *Lives of the Caesars* who formulated this behaviour as an abstraction, the virtue of *civilitas*, of which Augustus was the first and a glowing example.[102] It is a significant coinage because it is expressive of a central feature of the system of power set up by Augustus: he reaffirmed the values of cities, citizenship, and the citizen society, legislated to redefine the citizenship, and used his power to extended the citizenship to non-citizens as a central way of rewarding supporters. Citizen numbers, on his own count, rose from approximately 4 to 5 million in the course of his reign. *Civilitas* thus expresses a core value of the Augustan system of power.

By the time we get to Cassiodorus, there is a new range of meanings, referring to the highest values of civility and civilisation. This usage is not encountered in earlier writers but is found in both Cassiodorus and his contemporary Ennodius, Bishop of Pavia and panegyrist of Theoderic.[103] Used by a panegyrist, it may be taken as a value willingly embraced by Theoderic. In its new formulation, *civilitas* was a value of a special relevance in Ostrogothic Italy. It is a word cluster that applies to human relations, between citizen and citizen, but also, and crucially, between Roman citizen and Goth.[104] Central to it is the rule of law (*ius civile*), and its opposite is the use of violence.[105] Thus, as we have seen, a senator who sends armed slaves against the Roman plebs is *civilitatis immemor*. This is simply not how citizens should treat each other. In the half dozen letters that concern the circus riots, *civilitas* is invoked in each. The use of violence

---

[102] See Wallace-Hadrill, '*Civilis princeps*'.
[103] Ennodius, *Panegyric of Theoderic* 3: *Educavit te in gremio civilitatis Graecia praesaga venturi*; 4, *quis hanc civilitatem credat inter familiares tibi vivere plena executione virtutes?*; 11: *video insperatum decorem urbium cineribus evenisse et sub civilitatis plenitudine palatina ubique tecta rutilare*; 20: *sed inter proeliares forte successus. civilitatis dulcedini nil reservas?*
[104] So Amory, *People and Identity*, pp. 43–85, perhaps underestimating other aspects.
[105] On Theoderic and law, see Lafferty, *Law and Society*.

by senators to defend their honour is simply incompatible with behaviour between fellow citizens. The senate should know because it is *ipsam civilitatis sedem*, the seat of civility.[106] Particularly instructive is Athalaric's general edict. Word has reached his ear of whisperings, *susurrationes*, that certain parties despise *civilitas* and choose to live with the savagery of beasts, until returning to rustic origins they regard human law as bestially odious.[107] Civility thus maps onto the developmental scheme by which man distinguishes himself from the beasts by living in cities under the law. Athalaric emphasises that all must live by the law, even those close to the royal family: they too must go through the courts and accept their judgements. The young king and his spokesman may be thinking of Theodahad, his cousin and successor, who is sharply criticised elsewhere (*Var.* 4.39). First on his list of some ten types of abuse is illegal seizure of property, 'under which civility can neither be claimed nor be a reality'.[108] He then throws in breaking up the marriages of others, bigamy, extorting corrupt payments, magic, and physical abuse of the poor. It is an extraordinary mixture, but the clear central theme is the rule of the law. The following letter, addressed to the senate, insists on the rule of law, *ius civile*, and wishes the king's own civility to be recognised.[109]

Civilitas covers the proper treatment, within the law, without violence and bestiality, of several groups of people. One notable group is the Jews.[110] No fewer than five letters concern synagogues, in Genoa, Rome, and Milan. The first to the Jews of Genoa (*Var.* 2.27) gives permission to preserve an ancient building by reroofing. The next reinforces all ancient legislation for the protection of the Jews:[111]

> The maintenance of the laws is the hallmark of civility (*custodia legum civilitatis est indicium*) and reverence for prior Principes also testifies to our sense of duty. For what is better than for a people to want to live under the precepts of justice, so that the assembly of many may be a union of free

---

[106] *Var.* 1.27.1: *Si exterarum gentium mores sub lege moderamur, si iuri Romano servit quicquid sociatur Italiae, quanto magis decet ipsam civilitatis sedem legum reverentiam plus habere?*

[107] *Var.* 9.18.pref: *diu est, quod diversorum querellae nostris auribus crebris susurrationibus insonarunt quosdam civilitate despecta affectare vivere beluina saevitia, dum regressi ad agreste principium ius humanum sibi aestimant feraliter odiosum.*

[108] *Var.* 9.18.1: *sub qua nec dici potest civilitas nec haberi.*

[109] *Var.* 9.19.3: *ut nostra civilitate recognita spes truculentis moribus auferatur.*

[110] See Tabata, *Città dell'Italia*, pp. 124–126; Saitta, *Civilitas*, pp. 89–99. Jews were similarly protected in Visigothic Spain: see Chernin, 'Visigothic Jewish converts'.

[111] *Var.* 4.33.1–2: *Custodia legum civilitatis est indicium et reverentia priorum principum nostrae quoque testatur devotionis exemplum … quatenus quod ad civilitatis usum constat esse repertum, perpeti devotione teneatur.*

wills? For this draws people from the life of a savage to a model of human concourse. (*Var.* 4.33.1, trans. Bjornlie, adapted)

On the basis of these worthy reflections, the Jews are permitted to use existing statutes so far as compatible with civility (*quod ad civilitatis usum constat esse repertum*). But the threat to civility is real: a few letters later we hear that there has been rioting in Rome and the synagogue burnt down; if anyone has complaints to bring against the Jews, they should bring them to the senate, but Theoderic wants everyone to live together peacefully (*Var.* 4.43). Along similar lines is a letter to the Jews of Milan, who have complained about physical assault and violence, and have invoked the king's protection: Theoderic agrees to protect civility, though he does observe that the Jews themselves must do nothing *inciviliter*.[112]

Thus, civility is not merely a matter of proper relations between Roman citizens under Roman law, though that idea is central, but is elevated into a general virtue of civilised life that distinguishes man from beast.[113] Hence – and this is what makes the idea so interesting – it applies to relations between Romans and Goths.[114] The stock-in-trade of a Goth is violence: they are soldiers, and their virtue is what protects Italy. But that violence is not to be turned against the unarmed civilian population. The contrast between Roman civility and barbarism is spelt out most clearly in a series of letters regarding the government of two recently acquired provinces: Gaul (i.e. southern Gaul) and Pannonia. Theoderic addresses all provincials of Gaul: they must learn to return after a long interval to Roman ways; they have been restored to ancient freedom, *antiqua libertas*, signalled by the wearing of the toga, *moribus togatis*, so must put off barbarity and mental cruelty. They must learn to live like settled people, unlike the random barbarians. He has sent them a governor to restore civil rule (*civilem regulam*).[115] Despite having seized the area from his Visigothic kin, Theoderic cheerfully represents their rule as barbaric in contrast to his own. Later, Wandil, as governor of Avignon, is urged to repress all violence: let our army live *civiliter* with the Romans, otherwise

---

[112] *Var.* 5.37.1: *Libenter annuimus quae sine legum iniuria postulantur, maxima cum pro servanda civilitate nec illis sunt neganda beneficia iustitiae, qui adhuc in fide noscuntur errare.*

[113] On this philosophical tradition, see Scivoletto, 'Cassiodoro e la retorica della città', pp. 328–334.

[114] *Civilitas* as a principle of relations between Romans and Goths is well discussed by Saitta, *Civilitas*, pp. 7–61; see also Amory, *People and Identity*, pp. 489–554; Barnish, 'Roman responses'.

[115] *Var.* 3.17.1: *atque ideo in antiquam libertatem deo praestante revocati vestimini moribus togatis, exuite barbariem, abicite mentium crudelitatem, quia sub aequitate nostri temporis non vos decet vivere moribus alienis.*

there is no point in freeing them (*Var.* 3.38.1). Ibba, his principal general in Gaul, is urged to restore certain property to the church of Narbonne: he should take care that as he is famous in war, he should be outstanding in civility, *civilitate eximius* (*Var.* 4.17.3).

A letter addressed to all barbarians and Romans in Pannonia (3.24) is a little more explicit about what barbarian ways mean: why, Theoderic asks, do they keep reverting to duelling (*monomachia*)?

> Why should you who do not have a corrupt judge return to trial by combat? You who have no enemy, lay aside the sword. Worse, you raise your arm against kindred, for whose sake it should happen one would rather die honourably. What use is the human tongue, if the armed fist settles litigation? Where is it believed that peace would exist, if there is resort to fighting in times of civility (*si sub civilitate pugnetur*)? (*Var.* 3.24.4, trans. Bjornlie, adapted)

They must learn to imitate the Goths who know how to fight externally and behave modestly internally.

That Goths did not always remember to live up to these standards in Italy is made crystal clear by a sequence of letters. The Goths of Picenum and Samnium are summoned to court for a donation, but they need to be reminded not to devastate the fields and crops through which they pass, because Theoderic pays his army to keep civility intact.[116] The passage of a Gothic army through the landscape was no joke, and later when Belisarius landed in Sicily, and the Goths were sent against him, Cassiodorus as Pretorian Prefect has to urge the landowners of Lucania and Bruttium not to take up arms to defend their territory, since they will be compensated for losses; they must not seize weapons to commit barbarity (*barbariem*), but continue with their patriotic cultivation (*patrioticus* is another Cassiodoran first).[117]

It was evidently a struggle not only to contain the violent urges of the Gothic rank and file, but to get those promoted to high positions to behave. We have already seen the letter in which Athalaric takes to task his governor of Syracuse, the Goth Gildila, for pocketing the money raised to repair the city walls. But he has also been interfering in the judicial process, and calling to his court arguments between Romans over which he had no

---

[116] *Var.* 5.26.2: *ideo exercituales gratanter subimus expensas, ut ab armatis custodiatur intacta civilitas.*

[117] *Var.* 12.5.5: *isti non desinant patrioticas possessiones excolere.* For the term, cf. 11.1.7: *patriotica responsione*; 12.12.5: *patriotica veritate*; 12.15.1: *patriotica affectione*; all passages from the last two books.

jurisdiction. He is told in no uncertain terms to back off and recognise that Goths were there as a defence force, not as judges. You defend the laws with arms and leave the Romans to litigate in peace, for the glory of the Goth is the protection of civility.[118]

Perhaps the most striking example of Theoderic's insistence on civility is the dressing-down he delivers to his nephew Theodahad (4.39, cf. 5.12). Domitius has complained that his lands have been seized by violence instead of taking the issue to court *civiliter*. Such greed is out of place in a man of Amal blood, when the family enjoys the purple.[119] Theodahad was to be Theoderic's successor but one, and people have asked why Cassiodorus included such a potentially embarrassing letter. But there is no better way of showing the Amal dynasty's attachment to the principle of *civilitas* than to show Theoderic teaching a member of his own family a lesson. After Theodahad's fall from grace and death, it was easy enough to make public this letter as a demonstration of how good Gothic kings thought.

Conclusion

The enthusiasm for cities and urban living repeatedly expressed in the *Variae* is a great deal more than nostalgia for a lost world. It lies at the heart of the credibility of Theoderic's bold experiment in setting up a form of government in which Gothic kings, potentially seen by the Roman population as 'barbarian' and incapable of civilised behaviour, present themselves as the legitimate successors of Roman emperors, the *Principes*. They did not import into Italy the sort of lifestyle Romans only too readily attributed to barbarians, for whom 'swamps and forests were their cities'. They grasped the importance simultaneously of the Roman civil law and of urban living. Many of Cassiodorus' letters suggest that the urban fabric of Italy was under considerable strain – but how could it be otherwise after a century in which invading armies had repeatedly ransacked cities? Both the stable agriculture and the network of trade on which the cities of Italy depended had been compromised. It took a real effort to encourage regrowth. The major contribution of Cassiodorus was to rearticulate these ideals. Because those ideals were highly traditional, some have dismissed his thinking as

---

[118] *Var.* 9.14.8: *Gothorum laus est civilitas custodita.*
[119] *Var.* 4.39: *Hamali sanguinis virum non decet vulgare desiderium, quia genus suum conspicit esse purpuratum ... Domitius itaque vir spectabilis ... dum civiliter oportuit recipi, si iure videbatur exposci.*

banal. On the contrary: it is a perfect example of resilience at work, reaching back to the memories of the past to adapt them to a changed situation. His reformulation of civic ideals was a model for the future. He was read in the later middle ages and helped form an idea of what Roman civility meant.[120]

---

[120] See Barnish, *Selected Variae of Cassiodorus*, pp. xxxiii–iv, on the abundant manuscript tradition.

5 | The City Embattled

Procopius and Justinian's Urban World

Procopius and Cassiodorus

The lives of Cassiodorus and Procopius intersected and coincided in a number of ways. Contemporaries, Procopius about fifteen years the junior of Cassiodorus, they illuminate the same world from different but convergent perspectives.[1] Procopius acted on the staff of Belisarius when Justinian's troops launched their attack against Ostrogothic Italy in 535: Cassiodorus was then, as Praetorian Prefect, the highest ranking official of the Gothic regime. In that sense, the two were on opposing sides; yet there was much about their education, culture, and attitudes which made them closer in sympathies. Procopius enjoyed a classical and rhetorical education every bit as refined as that of Cassiodorus and wrote Greek in a classicising and artificial Attic style quite as mannered as, if somewhat less tortured than, the Latin of Cassiodorus. Both may count as highly traditionalist in attitude. They admired the same figures and the same values. We have met Cassiodorus' admiration for Amalasunta, the multilingual daughter of Theoderic. Procopius too has high praise for this woman of 'exceptional intelligence and justice, who showed all too much masculinity in her nature', and sympathises with her insistence on a Roman and grammatical education for her son, Athalaric, much to the indignation of some Goths (*Wars* 5.2.3–17).[2]

No passage shows better the extent of Procopius' sympathy with a Cassiodoran viewpoint than his remarks on the Roman passion for conservation:

> Yet the Romans are lovers of their city (*philopolides*) above all the men we know, and they are eager to protect all their ancestral treasures and to preserve them, so that nothing of the ancient glory of Rome may be obliterated. For

---

[1] The classic study of Procopius is Cameron, *Procopius and the Sixth Century*, contested by Kaldellis, *Procopius of Caesarea*. Recent years have seen a number of useful conference proceedings and joint studies: *De Aedificiis: le texte de Procope*; Greatrex and Elton, *Shifting Genres in Late Antiquity*; Greatrex and Janniard, *Le Monde de Procope*; Lillington-Martin and Turquois, *Procopius of Caesarea*; Meier and Montinaro, *Companion to Procopius of Caesarea* for up to date (if sometimes repetitive) surveys.

[2] See Cooper, 'The heroine and the historian', casting doubt on Procopius' version.

even though they were for a long period barbarised (*barbaromenoi*), they preserved the buildings of the city and the most of its adornments, such as could through the excellence of their workmanship withstand so long a lapse of time and such neglect. Furthermore, all such memorials of the race as were still left are preserved even to this day, and among them the ship of Aeneas, the founder of the city, an altogether incredible sight. (*Wars* 8.22.5–7)[3]

Procopius makes clear that his values coincided with those of the Romans: patriotism is loyalty to your city and its ancient fabric, and it is this that 'barbarian' rule puts in danger, though only rule by the wrong sort of barbarian – the kind of Goth, for instance, who did not appreciate Amalsunta's promotion of Latin grammar. Cassiodorus might perhaps have complained that Procopius rather understated the effort put by his Theoderic into maintaining and restoring the monuments of Rome, but about the ideal aims they agreed. One may wonder what Cassiodorus would have made of Procopius' long excursus on the ship of Aeneas, the dimensions and construction of which he describes in almost epic detail, expressing surprise that none of the timbers had rotted over the course of so many years. It is evidently an eyewitness account, and Procopius will have had plenty of time on his hands for tourism during the siege of Rome. Did his guides really assert that this was the authentic ship of Aeneas, and would Cassiodorus himself have swallowed the story? There is a good case to be made that there was indeed a monumental ship shed, dating back to Augustus, and that its plan can be glimpsed on the marble maps of Rome, including the earliest, Augustan, version.[4] If so, the legend was a carefully cultivated one. The ship makes his point forcibly: that the Romans were so keen on conserving the past that even a wooden ship from a millennium and a half before might survive completely intact. And Cassiodorus would have been equally capable of such a learned, or pseudo-learned, excursus.

Procopius and Christian Belief

Born in Caesarea on the coast of Palestine, Procopius came from a city which archaeology confirms to have been flourishing in the sixth century.[5]

---

[3] Here and in the following I cite from the translation of Procopius in the Loeb Classical Library by H. B. Dewing (1914).
[4] See Tucci, 'Nave di Enea'; and Tucci, 'Dove erano il tempio di Nettuno e la nave di Enea?' at 39ff.
[5] On his life, see the bibliographic review of Greatrex, 'Perceptions of Procopius in recent scholarship', pp. 76–121, and now 'Procopius: Life and works', pp. 61–69. On Caesarea, see Greatrex, 'L'historien Procope'.

The foundation of Herod the Great, it was also a city of some cultural and religious diversity, with a substantial Samaritan population, which led to a series of uprisings in the fifth and sixth centuries (486, 529, 556), the first before his birth in around 500, the second two during his lifetime. It has been suggested that he was himself a Samaritan, though this is hard to sustain.[6] On the other hand, he devotes more attention to the Samaritans than any other ancient author, and in this surely reveals his local background.[7] On the face of it, Procopius should count as a Christian, though we may wonder how committed a Christian he was, and whether this attachment to classical values makes him a pagan, even a Platonist, though he implicitly flags that he is no pagan by his critical account of John of Cappodocia, who secretly practised the ancient belief 'which they now usually call *Hellenikē*' (*Wars* 1.25.10).[8] Procopius goes out of his way to make, *à propos* a legendary letter from Jesus to Abgar of Edessa, an unexceptionably orthodox statement about the nature of Christ (*Wars* 2.12.7–30), which may be taken as a profession of faith, or, to the more sceptical eye, an insurance policy against accusations of impiety.[9] At a period in which Samaritans, like heretics, were persecuted for their deviant views, it was wise for someone, particularly one in an official position in the Roman army, to give no hint of deviancy. Interestingly, he offers a model of the *bad* Samaritan in Arsenius, a favourite of Theodora, who converted to Christianity to keep his job at court but encouraged his Samaritan parents back in Scythopolis (Beth'Shean) in Palestine to attack the local Christian community (*Anecdota* 27.6–19). He also depicts a converted Samaritan who was challenged: Faustinus, who rose to senatorial rank, was condemned by the senate on the accusation of secretly reverting to Samaritan practices, though pardoned by the emperor (27.26–33).

Procopius gives no space in his narrative to doctrinal disputes, which played a significant role in Justinian's reign, and, early in the narrative of the Gothic Wars, he states very clearly his view of their futility:[10]

---

[6] Adshead, 'Procopius and the Samaritans'. Contra, for example, Kaldellis, *Procopius*, p. 227.
[7] Samaritans are mentioned at length in the *peri Ktismaton* (5.7.2–16); four times in the *Anecdota* (11.24,29; 18.34; 27.7, and 26–27); but not in the *Wars*.
[8] Cameron, *Procopius*, pp. 113–133, argues that he was a Christian, contested by Kaldellis, *Procopius of Caesarea*, pp. 165–173; Cameron, 'Writing about Procopius then and now', at p. 16, revises her view suggesting that pursuit of the author's beliefs is a biographical fallacy. For the sophistication of Procopius' views, Murray, 'Procopius and Boethius'. Stickler, 'Procopius and Christian historical thought' defends his stance as Christian.
[9] Discussed by Brodka, 'Prokopios von Kaisareia und die Abgarlegende'.
[10] See Conterno, 'Procopius and non-Chalcedonian Christians'.

> I will not even record the points of disagreement since I think it crazy folly to enquire what the real nature of God is. Humans cannot even understand human things fully, let alone what pertains to the nature of God. So I intend to keep safely quiet about such matters, simply so that existing beliefs shall not be discarded. I can say nothing about God except that he is totally good and has everything within his power. But let each say what he thinks he knows about this, both priest and layman. (*Wars* 5.3.6–9)

This viewpoint, while not in itself anti-Christian, certainly diverged from that of Justinian, who was prepared to throw the full force of imperial power behind doctrinal correctness. What is most striking is the view which Procopius expresses on Justinian's attempts to force people to change their faiths (*Anecdota* 11.14–33). There were many, he says, in the whole empire who rejected Christian orthodoxies, including so-called heretics like Montanists, Sabbatianists, and Arians; all of these he commanded to change their beliefs, and he confiscated the wealthy holdings of their churches; the result was widespread resistance (11.14–23). The Samaritans were similarly persecuted, causing general confusion. But while some, especially the countryfolk, took to arms, many put up a show of compliance:

> All who lived in my Caesarea and the other cities, regarding it as foolish to suffer ill for a senseless dogma, took the name of Christian in place of their current name, and by this pretence avoided the danger arising from the law. (11.25)

Both his sharp criticism of Justinian's attempts to impose orthodoxy by force, and his cheerful approval of the tactic of his fellow citizens ('*my* Caesarea' is a striking expression of civic identity) in simply pretending to convert, mean that any attempt to torture his text to disclose his true faith would require the subtle dialectic of the Inquisition.[11] That scholars have assumed diametrically opposed positions on the issue suggests the ambivalence of his writing. Here, again, his stance is reminiscent of that of Cassiodorus, or rather the Theoderic for whom he writes, in resisting Christian attempts to convert the Jews of Genoa: 'I cannot command your faith, for no one is forced to believe against his will' (*Variae* 2.27).[12]

---

[11] Kaldellis, *Procopius*, pp. 168–170, well brings out the contrast between Procopius' views and Justinian's intolerance. His argument that Procopius was a Platonist (pp. 94–117) pushes the text to the limits.

[12] Compare the letter of Theodahad to Justinian, *Var.* 10.26.4: 'For while divine authority permits various religions, we would not dare to impose a single faith. For we recall reading that we must sacrifice willingly to the Lord, not at the command of anyone compelling us: because he who attempts to do otherwise clearly resists heavenly ordinances.'

It is hard to believe that Cassiodorus, orthodox Christian though he was, would have approved of the decision of Justinian's Pragmatic Sanction of 554 to confiscate the property of the Arian churches of Italy.

The Shape of Procopius' Writings

Procopius' oeuvre falls into three parts, at first sight so different from each other that in the past scholars could deny they were written by the same author: the *Wars* (*Peri Polemon*), the *Secret History* (*Anecdota*), and the so-called *Buildings* (*Peri Ktismaton*, on the misleading title of which there is more to say). On the most recent accounts, they were published in close succession, with their composition overlapping: the first seven books of the *Wars* finished in 550/1; the *Secret History* drafted but not published in the same period, a first draft of the *Buildings* at the same time; the eighth book of the *Wars* around 553; and the final edition of the *Buildings* in 554 (rather than six years later, the other possibility).[13] As the most authoritative modern study of the author has shown, the three are in fact closely interrelated, and are best read as in dialogue with one another.[14] In the terms of classical rhetoric, the *Wars* are written in the factual tone of history; the *Secret History* in the polemical tones of invective; the *Buildings* in the flattering language of panegyric.[15] One might think of them as a great triptych altarpiece: the largest and central panel occupied by the eight books of the *Wars*, depicting, let us imagine, events on earth; to the left the *Buildings*, representing Paradise; and to its right the volume of *Secret History*, representing Hell. You are not invited to look at any panel in isolation, but in relation to the others. These contrasts are deliberate and effective: you cannot opt for the supposedly factual historical record of the *Wars* without allowing it to be undercut by the invective of the *Secret History* and, at the same time, using the panegyrical *Buildings* to bring out what is absent from

---

[13] There is ongoing dispute about the fine-tuning of these dates: see Greatrex, 'The dates of Procopius' works'. In favour of a later date for the *Buildings* is the mention of current works on a bridge over the Sangarius river, dedicated in 562: a date questioned by Greatrex, 'The date of Procopius' *Buildings*' but defended by Whitby, 'Procopius' *Buildings* and the panegyrical effect'.

[14] Cameron, *Procopius*, pp. 3–18; an argument elaborated rather than contradicted by Kaldellis, *Procopius*. See now Croke, 'The search for harmony in Procopius' works'.

[15] Gibbon, *Decline and Fall*, ch. 40: 'According to the vicissitudes of courage or servitude, of favour or disgrace, Procopius successively composed the *History*, the *Panegyric* and the *Satire* of his own times.'

the *History* and what a more optimistic account of Justinian might have included.[16]

It is in part a question of genre, for each of these forms (history, invective, and panegyric) were well-established literary traditions. No other author that we know attempted to set all three alongside each other in this manner, and for good reason. Tacitus famously declared that his own *Histories* would be *sine ira et studio*, without partisan anger or enthusiasm – that is, free from both invective and panegyric. That claim was possible for the simple reason that he wrote after the end of the Flavian dynasty, the victor in the Civil Wars he describes. As was familiar, the only language in which you could write about the reigning emperor was that of panegyric; anything else was much too dangerous, and enemies alert to accusations of *maiestas*, treason, could get you and your writing into deadly trouble. The moment we read the opening sentence of Procopius' *Wars*, alarm bells must start ringing: 'Procopius of Caesarea wrote the history (*xynegrapsen*) of the wars which Justinian the king of the Romans waged against barbarians both in the East and the West.' The echo of Thucydides is explicit: 'Thucydides the Athenian wrote the history (*xynegrapsen*) of the war of the Peloponnesians and Athenians, how they fought against each other.' But Thucydides could write of the ongoing war during his lifetime, because there was no emperor to fear – or, rather, the Athenian democracy, which had sent him into exile for losing a campaign, represented no threat to free speech. To write the history of Justinian's reign while Justinian was still in power would have been impossible even if he was the most clement of rulers, and not the vindictive monster depicted in the *Secret History*. How could he pull this off?

The answer is that Procopius finds a formula in his history for writing about war without writing about the emperor. He is often represented as highly traditional, writing in a classicising idiom that harked back a millennium, and scarcely fitting the changed circumstances of an all too Christian empire. This is true, but he gives us tradition with a crucial twist, in which the rules of the art, the genre, offer him a perfect alibi. He calls them the wars of Justinian, but as every reader saw, they were the wars of his general Belisarius, and even at an autobiographical level they were wars in which the author participated in person as a member of the general's advisory staff (he says *xymboulos*, the closest Latin would be *consiliarius*). His role is normally interpreted as that of legal advisor, but it should not be excluded that Belisarius, like other ambitious generals (Alexander with Callisthenes,

---

[16] For an argument that Procopius intended the three works as an ensemble, see Signes Codoñer, 'One history ... in several instalments'.

Pompey with Theophanes of Mytilene) actually wanted him to write up his campaigns from the outset.[17] On the face of it, the historian who narrates the wars in which he had personally taken part represents a well-worn tradition: from Thucydides, who held a command in the Athenian navy, to Xenophon, his continuator, himself a military commander, to Polybius, who saw action in at least part of the conflict between Rome and Greece he narrated, to Josephus, a participant in his Jewish Wars, to Ammianus Marcellinus, adviser to Julian's general Ursicinus. It was perhaps more a tradition of Greek historiography than Latin: Ammianus, though writing in Latin, remained a Greek, but neither Sallust, nor Livy, nor Tacitus was a participant in the wars they narrated. This meant that to Procopius' Greek readers, his autobiographical focus was both familiar and conveyed the authority of autopsy.[18]

As interesting as what Procopius writes about is what he does *not* write about. He very much models himself on Thucydides. Thucydides offers not merely military narrative, but one of the most acute analyses in Greek literature of political systems at work. His wars are through and through the product of politics: you can have no meaningful narrative of the Sicilian expedition without the conflict between Nicias and Alcibiades, the row over profanation of the mysteries and its outcomes. The Peloponnesian Wars are fought in the *ekklēsia*, between orator and orator, as much as on the battle-field. The same can be said in varying degrees of the other authors in this tradition: Polybius counts as inferior as a political analyst only to Thucydides. Ammianus Marcellinus too is a historian of wars, of campaigns in which he had himself participated; yet his use of the excursus ensures that he can cover many topics including social history, which the military narrative would not otherwise permit. What is so striking about Procopius' military narrative is its complete divorce from a political narrative. This is precisely what he then reminds us in the *Secret History*: that to understand the causes of what was happening, he needed to talk about matters, political and personal, that would have been impossibly dangerous. The architecture of the *Wars* is designed to conceal this problem. He organises according to the theatre of war, not chronology: first the Persian Wars, then the Vandal Wars in Africa, then the Gothic Wars in Italy – a scheme that only breaks down in the eighth book, which updates the narrative in all theatres. If the focus of interest had been on Justinian's military strategy, this would have made less sense. But because he constantly puts himself and Belisarius (represented here, but not in the *Secret*

---

[17] A suggestion not previously made to my knowledge. For 'legal advisor', see, for example, Greatrex, 'Lawyers and historians'; Rance, 'Wars', p. 73.
[18] On his use of autobiographical references to give authority to the narrative, see Ross, 'Narrator and participant in Procopius' *Wars*'.

History, as an apolitical figure) at the centre of the narration, the sequence of Persia, Africa, Italy makes complete sense.

There are two notable exceptions to the focus on military history: his account of the Nika riots in Constantinople (1.24), and the memorable description of the plague (2.22–23). Not even these are true exceptions. The Nika riots of AD 532 are described as a civil war (*stasis*), comparable in literary terms to Thucydides' account of *stasis* in Corcyra (3.69–85), an integral part of his war narrative; since Belisarius, newly returned from his Persian campaign, is the hero of the hour, rescuing Justinian and Theodora, together with John of Cappodocia and Tribonian, all barricaded against the rioters in the palace, this is effectively a further episode in Belisarius' campaigns. It is the closest the narrative comes to touching palace politics, but since the narrator and his hero are on the right side, he can get away with it. The vivid description of the great plague of AD 542 is even more closely modelled on Thucydides' account of the plague in Athens of 430 BC, resulting from Pericles' policy of gathering the population within the Long Walls (2.47–55); in literary terms, it harks back to the opening of the *Iliad* and the plague sent by Apollo. Since Procopius is happy to ascribe the bubonic plague too to the inexplicable will of God, this is perfectly safe ground.

We may well imagine that Procopius would have liked to write about more than war, but the deliberate self-limitation in the *Wars* was a survival strategy. His ever-frustrated ambition was surely to write a history of Justinian, a massive figure by whom he was obsessed. This could only be done openly as panegyric. He therefore supplements the *Wars* with a work of explicit panegyric. But traditional though this genre was, his *Peri Ktismaton* is something more limited, more original, and more interesting than a standard panegyric. There were rhetorical rules for how this should be done. The rhetorical treatises ascribed to Menander Rhetor, which we encountered earlier (see Chapter 2, p. 44), have much to say on the subject,[19] and virtually every surviving panegyric, from Pliny's of Trajan to the endless panegyrists in both Latin and Greek of Late Antiquity, followed those rules, more or less.[20] Far from a traditional panegyric, Procopius achieves an unique new blend of genres, praise of ruler, praise of cities, *ekphrasis* (description) of buildings, and even geographical description in the periegetic tradition.[21]

---

[19] Menander Rhetor (ed. Russell and Wilson), *Treatise II*, pp. 77–95, 'Basilikos Logos'; see Chapter 2.
[20] See Whitby, *The Propaganda of Power*; Whitby, Procopius' *Buildings* book 1'.
[21] Well brought out by Elsner, 'The rhetoric of buildings'; also Turquois, 'Technical writing, genre and aesthetic in Procopius'. Note that Cameron, 'Writing about Procopius', p. 14 nuances her earlier position of genre.

Procopius chooses to focus on a single aspect – that of building activities – which in any other panegyric occupies scarcely more than a paragraph.[22] Had he wanted to provide a corrective to the *Wars* and the *Secret History* by admitting that Justinian should be credited with some major achievements, he might have given space to his legislative activity. After all, Justinian is probably better known to posterity for his *Digest*, *Code*, and *Novels* than for his building activity.[23] However, the aim is not to give a fairer picture of this hated emperor, but to draw attention to an aspect of imperial activity which he regarded as crucial. Not even the *Secret History*, though easy enough to classify as invective, should be thought of as a typical product of the genre.[24] Attacks on sexuality, and on the subjection of a ruler to female family members, indeed formed a traditional theme.[25] The *Secret History* starts with the unsparing attack not on Justinian but on Belisarius and his wife Antonina, and he makes clear that the aim is not simply to attack Justinian's regime, but to restore what he thought of as the essential personal background that he had been constrained to suppress in his supposedly neutral and truthful military narrative.

For a chapter looking at the city in Procopius, the *Peri Ktismaton* might be the most obvious place to start. The city is a powerful theme that runs right through his oeuvre, yet, before tussling with the problem of what trust we can place in a panegyrical account, it helps to look at the narrative of military campaigns. Here, where war itself is in the foreground, cities (and, indeed, the countryside which forms an integral part of them) are the setting. This background is of enormous and continuous importance: it dictated the very nature of warfare, and it was at the heart of the author's value-system.

Barbarians and Cities

Cities in ancient thought, as we have seen, were what distinguished Greco-Roman civilisation from barbarism. Procopius, as he tells us, recounts wars with barbarians, eastern and western. Yet barbarians were by no means all

---

[22] Whitby, 'Procopius' *Buildings*', pp. 54–56, compares to Augustus' *Res Gestae*, Eusebius' *Life of Constantine*, and panegyrics of Anastasius by Procopius of Gaza and Priscian: in none do buildings have so dominant a role.
[23] On Procopius' familiarity with Justinianic law-making, see Kruse, 'Justinian's laws and Procopius' *Wars*'; and, more generally, Honoré, *Tribonian*.
[24] For a new translation with helpful introduction, see Kaldellis, *Prokopios: The Secret History*; for a critical account of the work, Pfeilschifter, 'The *Secret History*'.
[25] Cameron, *Procopius*, pp. 59–60, compares Claudian's vicious invective against Eutropius.

the same: although Greco-Roman sources are accused of reducing barbarians to literary stereotypes, Procopius goes to some lengths to show that barbarians were different, not just from Romans but from each other.[26] The differences show up in their relations with cities and urbanism. The first book of the *Wars* opens with some oddly anecdotal material on the Persians and their neighbours; here, rather than imitating Thucydides, he seems to recall Herodotus with his introductory stories of Greek relations with Persia in mythology, from Io to the Trojan Wars (*Histories* 1.1–5), and tells stories he himself flags as incredible, like that of the shark and the oyster and the pearl of king Peroz (*Wars* 1.4.17–31). An odd feature of these stories is that rather than providing background for Roman/Persian relations, they explore Persia's relations with its barbarian neighbours to the north. Whatever the historians' motivation,[27] it gives him the chance to set out some basic cultural differences.

Procopius' first focus is on Persia's relations with the Ephthialite Huns, occupying the territory to the north of Persia (*Wars* 1.3). Having identified them as Huns, always regarded as particularly barbarous, he explains that the White Huns, though of the same stock, are very different. He at once mentions that they have a city called Gorgo, which lies on the northern border of Persia – a city that seems not to be entirely mythical, to be identified with Gurgan near the Caspian Sea.[28] That might come as a surprise, given the normal expectation that barbarians were antithetical to urban civilisation, but he explains that, unlike other Huns, they were not nomads. Their skin colour was white and their faces were not ugly; their way of life was unlike the bestial life of their kinsmen, and they had a single king and constitutional government (πολιτείαν ἔννομον) and dealt with each other justly making contracts (δικαίως ξυμβάλλουσιν) – no less, indeed, than the Persians and Romans. We suddenly find ourselves in a looking-glass world where expectations are stood on their head, yet may be reassured to discover that the Ephthialites are not quite so civilised after all, given their habit of burying alive the entire mess-band of twenty or so on the death of the leaders of the bands.

Procopius is putting down a marker. His readers can no longer assume that all the enemies of the Romans were uncivilised brutes: certainly not the

---

[26] For the debate on ethnic stereotyping, see Greatrex, 'Procopius' attitude towards barbarians'; Sarantis, 'Procopius and the different types of northern barbarian'; Wiemer, 'Procopius and the barbarians in the West'.

[27] Kaldellis, *Procopius*, pp. 75–78, sees it as part of a Platonic account of the process of degeneration into tyranny.

[28] See Kaldellis, ibid., p. 244, note 28, comparing the claim in Menander the Protector frag.10.1 that the Ephthialites lived in cities. For Gorgo, Börm, 'Procopius and the East', at pp. 328–332.

Persians, but not even some of the other marginal peoples. He has more to say about Huns in the *Peri Ktismaton*. On the north-eastern border of the Roman Empire in the Crimea, the city of Bosporus (Kerch) that controls the entrance to the sea of Azov had fallen into ruin, 'having long ago been barbarised and lain under the control of the Huns' (3.7.12). Justinian restored it, making the ruinous walls beautiful and safe. Nearby was another city called Dory, inhabited by a segment of Goths who were historic allies of the Romans. Their territory, though on high ground, was fruitful, but here Justinian built no cities or forts, since the people of the area could not endure to be enclosed in walls.

One area on the margins of 'barbaria' to which he gives particular attention is Lazica, the fertile delta of the river Phasis that now forms part of Georgia (classical Colchis). The Lazi, he tells us, had long acknowledged token Roman suzerainty, but without taxes or a Roman military presence, until Justinian decided on military occupation (2.15). Justinian's general, John called Tzibus, persuaded the emperor to build a city called Petra on the coast, which he treated as his acropolis, and, from a strongly fortified position, imposed a monopoly on salt and other staples which the Lazi had previously traded for hides and slaves (2.15.9–11). The Lazi take it ill and complain to the Persian king Chosroes (Khusrau), whom they persuade to invade in their defence (2.15.14–35). That Petra was built *ex novo* emerges as untrue, since the description of its impressive fortifications concedes that there was previously a place 'of no importance' (2.17.3) with fortifications constructed by 'those who previously built the city' (2.17.20). Lazica emerges as already semi-urbanised, and Justinian is trying to push the process further, both with fortification and with the imposition of trading restrictions and taxes which trigger revolt – a familiar feature of the early stages of Romanisation that recalls the revolt of Boudicca in Britain.

As the narrative develops, it becomes clear that 'barbarians' differ amongst themselves in attitudes to cities and how to use them. The Persians are of course urbanised in their own right; their attacks on Roman cities are not, despite their destructive effects, attacks on urbanism, but attempts to seize control. The Goths in Italy, as we will see, are enthusiastic in their support of the urban tradition. Only the Vandals, in his view, seem not quite to have grasped how to make best use of the urban infrastructure they have taken over. Ever since Gaiseric, as Procopius never tires of reminding us, they had systematically torn down city walls, except at Carthage, so laying themselves open to attack not just by Belisarius, but also by raiding Moors. Yet the Vandals had an appreciation of some of the more regrettable features of urban living. They compared poorly to the Moors:

> For of all the ethnic groups we know, the Vandals are the softest, and the Moors the hardiest. Ever since they held Libya, the Vandals have all used the baths on a daily basis and dined off all the sweetest and best produce the earth bears. They generally wore gold, and dressed themselves in the Medic clothing now called silk, and passed their time in theatres and hippodromes and other forms of entertainment, and particularly enjoyed hunting with dogs. (*Wars* 4.6.6–7)

Civilisation is always ambivalent, and these barbarians have literally gone to the dogs. In rather similar language, Procopius reports the mutual criticisms of the barbarian Utigurs and Cutrigurs (8.19.16): the Utigurs protest to Justinian that he is friendly and hospitable to the dastardly Cutrigurs, who have fallen for some of the seductions of civilisation:

> It is not, I think, a fair thing for you to receive hospitably the nation of the Cutrigurs, inviting in a foul set of neighbours, and making people at home with you now whom you have not endured beyond your boundaries. . . . while we eke out our existence in a deserted and thoroughly unproductive land, the Cutrigurs are at liberty to traffic in corn and to revel in their wine-cellars and live off the fat of the land. And doubtless they have access to baths too and are wearing gold – the vagabonds – and have no lack of fine clothes embroidered and overlaid with gold. (*Wars* 8.19.16–17)

Cities in the *Wars*

Cities, then, may come with a cargo of other elements, including laws, taxes, and luxurious living, but what defines the city in Procopius' narrative is the circuit of walls that gives it defence.[29] A striking feature of his accounts of campaigns, whether in Persia/Mesopotamia, North Africa, or Italy, is that they revolve around cities. As a general rule, the barbarian enemy attacks cities and tries to sack them, while the Romans defend them. Of course, things are more complicated in Vandal Africa, where the Vandals are in possession of the cities until Belisarius swiftly drives them out, and in Ostrogothic Italy, where the Goths and Romans alternate in the long and painful pendulum of campaigns between being the attackers and

---

[29] I have found little or no discussion of the theme of cities in the *Wars* in the literature; thus, no chapter on the theme in Meier and Montinaro's *Companion to Procopius*.

the defenders of the cities. This means that among the possible types of war narrative, that of sieges plays a conspicuous role. Indeed, of those episodes which might count as battles in the field, the majority are fought either outside a city or as part of a struggle for it. The great set-piece battles in open countryside are few and tend to cluster towards the end of campaign narratives. In the end, a pitched battle was the only way to impose a decisive defeat on a barbarian army. Indeed, it is the preference of barbarian armies to meet the Romans in the field, for sieges are frustrating and do not play to their strengths; but since the condition of the Roman world is a landscape densely studded with cities, it is inevitably around them that most of the action takes place.[30]

Sieges were a feature of ancient war narratives from the start:[31] Homer sets the model with the protracted siege of Troy, with battles fought around the walls, from the battlements of which the women watch the men fighting and the gruesome spectacle of Hector's body dragged round the walls. Herodotus gives us the sieges of the Ionian revolt, Thucydides gives us the memorable siege of Platea and later that of Periclean Athens, which leads to the outbreak of plague. Conversely, we have the Athenians as besiegers in the campaign against Syracuse. Nevertheless, the staple of ancient military history is the set-piece battle out in the open. Even the siege of Athens reminds us how it *ought* to be done. The Spartans invade and ravage the countryside just as the crops ripen, expecting the Athenians to come out to defend their land and form the long line of hoplites which they are confident of defeating. Pericles' tactic of bringing the countrymen within the walls and sitting out the invasion is made possible by their naval supply line through the Piraeus. That is to say, it is built into the DNA of the cities of antiquity that the citizens take up arms to fight in the open in lines abreast. This continues to some extent throughout antiquity, and the great military historians recount great battles in the open, from Marathon or Zama to Adrianople.

Procopius was a close imitator of Herodotus and especially Thucydides, and he knows how to exploit their models of sieges, and, indeed, of the plague.[32] But if his narrative were determined by imitation of classical models alone, he might have given less prominence to sieges. His focus is

---

[30] Whately, *Battles and Generals: Combat*, pp. 237–243, lists thirty-four engagements, of which roughly half are sieges, but most of the battles around cities; see also Whately, Procopius on Soldiers. I have not seen Whately, 'The beautiful wall: Militarized cityscapes in the age of Justinian'.

[31] Armstrong and Trundle, *Companion to Sieges in the Ancient Mediterranean*.

[32] On Procopian *mimesis*, see Kaldellis, *Procopius*, pp. 17–24 and passim; Basso and Greatrex, 'How to interpret Procopius' preface'.

on the defending, capturing, or recapturing of cities. The nature of warfare has shifted since classical Greece. Above all, the tactics are determined by the collapse of the continuous frontier established by Augustus, which led to unprecedented conditions of peace and the abandonment, neglect, and overbuilding of city walls. The collapse of the frontier meant that every city had to be its own frontier. Neglected walls are reconstructed and reinforced. That leads to the impression that reliance on walls is a sign of late imperial weakness – which, of course, it is – but is also a reversion to the normal functioning of the city. It is the High Empire with its downplaying of walls, not Late Antiquity with their renewed importance, that is historically exceptional.[33]

Procopius' narrative thus reflects and illustrates the crucial importance of walled cities, and with it the importance of ensuring that the systems of fortification were effective. The main narrative of the Persian Wars, once prefatory fables are over, opens with the siege and sacking, and eventual recovery, of Amida (Diyarbakır) in AD 503, reminiscent of the siege and fall of the same city in Ammianus Marcellinus:[34]

> So the city (Amida) was captured by storm on the eightieth day after the beginning of the siege. There followed a great massacre of the townspeople, until one of the citizens – an old man and a priest – approached Cabades as he was riding into the city, and said that it was not a kingly act to slaughter captives. Then Cabades, still moved with passion, replied: 'But why did you decide to fight against me?' And the old man answered quickly: 'Because God willed to give Amida into thy hand not so much because of our decision as of thy valour.' Cabades was pleased by this speech, and permitted no further slaughter, but he bade the Persians plunder the property and make slaves of the survivors, and he directed them to choose out for himself all the notables among them. (*Wars* 1.7.30–35)

It then turns to the foundation of Dara, and to Persian attempts to dislodge the Romans. The next book is dominated by the invasion of Chosroes (Khusrau), which finds the great cities of the Roman Near East undefended: the sack and plundering of Antioch is the most traumatic event. Procopius goes out of his way to underline the importance of this city and the extent of the calamity (2.8). Already, some fourteen years previously in 526, the city had suffered a devastating earthquake:

---

[33] Rizos, *New Cities in Late Antiquity*, pp. 36–38; Dey, *The Aurelian Wall*; Tagliata, Courault, and Barker, *City Walls in Late Antiquity*.
[34] See Lenski, 'Two Sieges of Amida'.

> Accordingly, a little later, when Justinus was ruling over the Romans, the place was visited by an exceedingly violent earthquake, which shook down the whole city and straightway brought to the ground the most and the finest of the buildings, and it is said that at that time three hundred thousand of the population of Antioch perished. (2.14.6)

The number of the earthquake victims is evidently much exaggerated, but that the city repeatedly suffered serious seismic damage is well attested.[35] The astronomic number of victims alleged adds to the picture of the size and importance of the city. Chosroes initially hangs back from attacking and sends a demand for a ransom of ten *centenaria* (ten hundred pounds) of gold; Antioch remains obstinate, but its fall will induce other cities to pay up. The people of Antioch abuse the Persian ambassadors by jeering at them, increasing Chosroes' anger. The Romans fail to spot a weakness in the defences of the walls to the east, where Mount Silpius rises above the city, and a particular rock from which it was possible to fire down on the defensive positions. With the benefit of hindsight, and knowledge of Justinian's later rebuilding of the wall (*Peri Ktismaton* 2.10.2–12), Procopius criticises them for not seizing this rock. As the Persians storm the walls, Chosroes briefly hesitates, nervous that the fleeing Romans will turn back on them

> and thus become an obstacle, as might well happen, in the way of his capturing a city which was both ancient and of great importance and the first of all the cities which the Romans had throughout the East both in wealth and in size and in population and in beauty and in prosperity of every kind. (2.8.22)

The hesitation does not last long, and Chosroes wreaks devastation on Antioch:

> Chosroes commanded the army to capture and enslave the survivors of the population of Antioch, and to plunder all the property, while he himself with the ambassadors descended from the height to the sanctuary which they call a church. There Chosroes found stores of gold and silver so great in amount that, though he took no other part of the booty except these stores, he departed possessed of enormous wealth. And he took down from there many wonderful marbles and ordered them to be deposited outside the fortifications, in order that they might convey these too to the land of Persia. When he had finished these things, he gave orders to the Persians to burn the whole city. (*Wars* 2.9.14–17)

---

[35] *Wars* 2.14.6–7. On the numbers, Liebeschuetz, *Antioch*, p. 94 with note 1.

The narrative makes clear that the Persian king entirely appreciates the importance of a great city. Antioch provides him not only with loot, but with material to build his own Antioch back home:

> Now Chosroes built a city in Assyria in a place one day's journey distant from the city of Ctesiphon, and he named it the Antioch of Chosroes and settled there all the captives from Antioch, constructing for them a bath and a hippodrome and providing that they should have free enjoyment of their other luxuries besides. For he brought with him charioteers and musicians both from Antioch and from the other Roman cities. (2.14.1–2)

If Romans continued to call Persians 'barbarians', they were not the sort who destroyed cities because they did not appreciate them. Antioch is the greatest loss, but far from the only one: Chosroes' army threatens city after city to pay a ransom or be sacked: Apamea (2.11); Callinicum, which has the misfortune to have its walls still under repair when the Persians approach, and is captured and razed (2.21); and, finally, there is the great siege of Edessa, subject of a long and detailed narrative (2.26–27).

The Vandalic Wars throw up a different but related situation. Gaiseric, the conqueror of North Africa, is said to have ordered the destruction of all the walls of the cities of Africa except Carthage, and even these are kept in very poor repair (3.5 and 3.21). On landing, Belisarius finds the city of Syllectus, which has made itself temporary walls against raiding Moors and makes this his base; Procopius takes the opportunity to remind us that, thanks to Gaiseric, the cities of Africa were unwalled (3.15–16). He then advances on Carthage, Gelimer's capital, outmanoeuvres him in the suburb of Decimum, marches into Carthage unopposed, and seizes the Vandal palace, seating himself on Gelimer's throne (3.17–21). His first action is to repair the crumbling walls of the city, which later the captive Gelimer was to admire:

> [Belisarius] built up in a short time the portions of the wall which had suffered, a thing which seemed worthy of wonder not only to the Carthaginians, but also to Gelimer himself at a later time. For when he came as a captive to Carthage, he marvelled when he saw the wall and said that his own negligence had proved the cause of all his present troubles. (3.23.19–21)

Gelimer's army is now without an urban base; he tries to attack Carthage, tearing down a section of the aqueduct, but when nobody comes out to fight, he withdraws (4.1). The final campaign is therefore fought in open countryside at Tricamarum in a set-piece battle; Gelimer takes to flight, and the Romans capture his camp unopposed, and in it the accumulated treasures of the Vandal kingdom – the largest sum ever found together in one place (4.3). The Romans obviously think it is demented to go on the march outside the security of fortifications carrying such vast sums, while the Vandals are allergic to the sort of war that is fought around cities:

> And the Romans, coming up, captured the camp, money and all, with not a man in it; and they pursued the fugitives throughout the whole night, killing all the men upon whom they happened, and making slaves of the women and children. And they found in this camp a quantity of wealth such as has never before been found, at least in one place ... And from this it resulted that their wealth, amounting to an extraordinary sum, returned once more on that day into the hands of the Romans. (*Wars* 4.3.24–28)

The Goths are very different. Belisarius' invasion of Italy is a sequence of sieges, for, thanks to Theoderic, the Goths have fully grasped the advantages of repairing walls.[36] The first great siege is of Naples, with its vivid narrative of the ruse of entry down an aqueduct (5.9). When Belisarius takes Rome, he swiftly grasps the importance of blocking off access by the same route, even if it means cutting off the water supply; a long and ineffectual siege follows till the Goths give up and turn their attention to Milan, which is sacked, allegedly with the massacre of 300,000:

> not one of the soldiers was willing to undergo the danger, and they surrendered both themselves and the city on the terms which the enemy offered. And the barbarians did indeed inflict no harm upon the soldiers, simply putting them under guard with Mundilas, but the city they razed to the ground, killing all the males of every age to the number of not less than three hundred thousand and reducing the women to slavery and then presenting them to the Burgundians by way of repaying them for their alliance. (*Wars* 6.21.38–39)

Witigis also adopts a Vandal-like policy of tearing down some city walls to disadvantage the Romans, but exempted others, including Rome itself:

> For when Witigis was entering upon this war at the very beginning, he did indeed tear down the walls of the coast towns Fanum and Pisaurum, but Rome and the other cities of Italy without exception he exempted, not damaging them in the least. Consequently, while no trouble has come to the Goths from Fanum and Pisaurum, it was because of the circuit-walls of Rome and the other fortified places that trouble came to the Gauls and Wittigis after the manner that is well-known to you. (*Wars* 7.25.7)

---

[36] See Whately, 'Procopius on the siege of Rome'.

With the accession of Totila in place of Witigis, the tables are turned: Totila besieges and captures Rome. Belisarius pleads with Totila not to destroy Rome but to spare it for its beauty:

> Now among all the cities under the sun Rome is agreed to be the greatest and the most noteworthy. For it has not been created by the ability of one man, nor has it attained such greatness and beauty by a power of short duration, but a multitude of monarchs, many companies of the best men, a great lapse of time, and an extraordinary abundance of wealth have availed to bring together in that city all other things that are in the whole world, and skilled workers besides. Thus, little by little, have they built the city, such as you behold it, thereby leaving to future generations memorials of the ability of them all, so that insult to these monuments would properly be considered a great crime against the men of all time; for by such action the men of former generations are robbed of the memorials of their ability, and future generations of the sight of their works. (7.22.9–14)

Although he decides against the sacking of Rome (7.36), Totila burns part of it, especially Trastevere, something he supposedly later comes to regret:

> Not long before this Totila had sent to the ruler of the Franks and requested him to give his daughter in marriage. But the Frankish king spurned the request, declaring that Totila neither was nor ever would be king of Italy, seeing that after capturing Rome he had been utterly unable to hold it, but after tearing down a portion of it had let it fall again into the hands of his enemy. Consequently he made haste on the present occasion to convey supplies into the city, and gave orders to rebuild as quickly as possible everything which he himself had pulled down and destroyed by fire when he captured Rome at the previous time. (7.37.1)

But Totila does not end up wrapped up in sieges and counter-sieges. The Goths try their best to provoke the Romans to open battle (8.28), and the final encounters are precisely of this type, near the little village of Gualdo Tadino (8.32), and then in Campania, near the rumbling Vesuvius, beneath Monte Lattare, the milky produce of which Cassiodorus had so praised (8.35).

Justinian the Founder of Cities

The *Wars* and its numerous sieges provide the essential background to the panegyrical work, *Peri Ktismatōn*. Understanding of this text has been complicated by the demonstration that of the two versions transmitted, one shorter than the other, the shorter is a first draft, rather than an abbreviation; whether or not Procopius was actually commissioned to write it (and, from an emperor, any wink may be a nudge), he was encouraged to bulk it out.[37] Both drafts probably belong to the 550s; the failure to redraft the description of Haghia Sophia after the collapse of the dome in 558 strongly suggests his revisions had finished by then.

This work is conventionally rendered in English as *On Buildings* (in Latin, *de Aedificiis*), yet the translation misses at least half the point. Indeed, the first book describes Justinian's building activity in Constantinople (which he usually calls Byzantium), starting with the spectacular and much-read description of Haghia Sophia, and continuing with his other 'innumerable' buildings, mostly churches in and around the capital. Both the activity of building and the structure is called οἰκοδομία (*oikodomia*) in Procopian Greek. But the *ktismata* of the title (whether it is Procopius' original title or not) has a double meaning which covers the full scope of the text. From Homer onwards, κτίζω refers to the foundation of cities and walls, and only secondarily to that of buildings. Troy is a 'well-founded city', εὐκτίμενον πτολίεθρον. Herodotus represents the Scythians, very much as Procopius represents the Huns, as uncivilised and therefore easy to defeat, because they have 'no founded cities or walls (μήτε ἄστεα μήτε τείχεα ἐκτισμένα), but are all nomads and mounted archers, not living by tilling the soil but by raising cattle and carrying their dwellings on wagons'. The founder of a city is its κτίστης (alternatively its 'settler', οἰκιστής) and may be commemorated by a κτιστεῖον, a founder's sanctuary. Ktisma (κτίσμα, plural κτίσματα) indicates 'foundation'. The advantage of *peri Ktismatōn* ('On Foundations') as a title is that it covers everything from buildings to cities to fortifications.

This matters because, at the beginning of the second book, Procopius flags a shift of subject matter.

> All the new churches which the emperor Justinian built ... as well as other buildings which he put up here have been described in the preceding book. From this point we must go on to the defences with which he surrounded the farthest limits of the territory of the Romans. (2.1.1–2)

He contrasts these defences favourably with the pyramids of Egypt, which are for useless show; Justinian's fortifications, by contrast, saved the empire. The following four books look region by region (book 2, the eastern empire; 3, Armenia; 4, Thrace; 5, North Africa) at cities

---

[37] See Montinaro, 'Power, taste and the outsider'. For a good discussion of the work, see Whitby, 'Procopius' *Buildings* and the panegyric effect'.

strengthened, renewed, or founded from new, and lesser, fortresses which together formed the new defensive system. There is a great deal more to this than churches and other buildings, and the author of the *Wars* makes plain where his emphasis lies.

Indeed, the close relationship between the *Wars* and the *Peri Ktismaton* becomes apparent early in the second book. His first focus is on the city of Daras (Dara) on the Persian border:

> When the Persians retired from the territory of the Romans, selling to them the city of Amida, as I have already shown in my discussion of *Wars*, the emperor Anastasius selected a hitherto insignificant village close to the Persian boundary, Dara by name, and urgently set about enclosing it with a wall and making it into a city which would serve as a bulwark against the enemy. (2.1.4)

The reference to the previous work both flags that they are to be read in parallel with one another and invites us to recall his narrative of the Persian Wars. There, Procopius introduces the city of Dara, which, being close to the Persian border, is to play a key role (1.10). He explains how Anastasius took advantage of the distraction of the Persians, at war with the Huns, to establish a city (*polis*), which was extremely strong and noteworthy, and which bore his name. This did not go down well with the Persians, and it remained a bone of contention, but Anastasius persuades Cabades (Kawad), paying over 'no small sum of gold', to let the city be. Procopius then offers a parenthesis. This was not the only city Anastasius founded, since there was another in Armenia, which had been a village (*kōmē*), and which Theodosius raised to the dignity of a city and put his name on. This Anastasius fortified with a particularly strong wall, which also greatly irritated the Persians.[38]

Explicit in all this is that emperors name cities after themselves: Anastasiopolis and Theodosiopolis. He returns to this theme later in the *Peri Ktismaton*, where he says that what Theodosius built was a fort (*phrourion*), though he named it Theodosiopolis. This was amplified by Anastasius to a much larger city, which included the old fort in its circuit walls:

> And he gave his own name to the city, yet he was quite unable to obliterate that of Theodosius, the earlier founder (*oikistēs*); for though it is always

---

[38] John Malalas 16.10 similarly describes the construction of baths, colonnades, warehouses, and cisterns by Anastasius at the city renamed for him (trans. Jeffreys, *The Chronicle of John Malalas*, p. 224). I thank Suna Çağaptay for this reference.

human nature to innovate established custom, it is not so easy to let go of former names. (3.5.5)

Procopius will make plain in the *Secret History* his dim view of emperors who 'innovate established custom' – one of Justinian's principal failings. He is not so rash in his *Peri Ktismaton* as to criticise Justinian for calling a city Justinianopolis. Rather, he takes safe aim at Anastasius, and mocks the futility of his renaming of a Theodosiopolis. But how dubious he was of the well-established custom of imperial vanity projects in renaming cities is even implicit in his preference for the name of Byzantium for Constantine's new capital.

What the *Peri Ktismaton* achieves, on a vast scale, is to represent Justinian as the greatest of all city founders; indeed, as he puts it when describing the emperor's all too modest birthplace in the village of Taurision in Thrace, he was the 'founder of the civilised world' (ὁ τῆς οἰκουμένης οἰκιστής) (4.1.17; see section on 'Religion and the Ancient City'). That panegyric might exaggerate, even on a grand scale, was well-known to ancient readers too; but, beyond the exaggeration, the interesting point is how important the image of founder of cities was to an emperor. Fustel de Coulanges, as we have seen (Chapter 1), thought it an essential characteristic of the ancient city that it was founded as a deliberate act, and did not simply grow by accretion from a smaller settlement. In fact, many of the late imperial foundations, like Anastasius' Dara, were precisely enlargements of previous villages: what is involved is not an accretive process, but an act of imperial will.

New cities had been founded across the Mediterranean since the earliest 'colonial' period of Greek history in the eighth century BC, but what changes the game decisively is the eastern conquests of Alexander the Great. He and his successors made a regular practice of creating new cities and frequently naming them after themselves or their family members: Alexandria in Egypt was just one of the many foundations of that name.[39] In Syria, the Seleucids, as Libanius proudly explains (Chapter 2), produced a rash of new cities in their names: sixteen Antiochs, nine Seleucias, six Laodiceas, three Apameias, and a Stratonicea;[40] while Cassander in Macedonia founded cities called Cassandreia (on the site of Potideia) and Thessalonike (after his wife). This pattern, once established in the kingdoms of the Hellenistic east, spread to the west too, but with some delay.

---

[39] Jones, *The Greek City*, pp. 2–6, noting, however, that his father Philip set the precedent with Philippopolis.
[40] Jones, *The Greek City*, p. 7.

Rome, which had a centuries-long tradition of founding new cities in Italy, avoided naming cities after the founder, preferring names that brought good luck, such as Bononia, Florentia, Valentia, and so on, though exceptionally the tiny market centres called Forum could carry the founder's names (Forum Cornelii, Forum Julii, etc.) To give your name to a city was to make yourself a king, even a god, and, by no coincidence, Roman practice in city-naming changed at the same time that the portraits of living men appear on the coinage. Augustus leads the way, the most prolific of all Roman city founders: many of his new colonies carry his name, including twenty-one called Colonia Julia and five entitled Colonia Augusta, though often as part of a longer name in which the last might dominate (Colonia Augusta Emerita = Mérida; Colonia Augusta Nemausus = Nîmes; Colonia Augusta Taurinorum = Turin; Colonia Augusta Treverorum = Trier; though the Colonia Augusta Praetoria Salassorum became Aosta). Imperial names are incorporated in adjectival form (Colonia Neroniana Pompeiana), whereas the Greek termination of -opolis is generally avoided in the west (Suetonius records it as one of Nero's madder plans to rename Rome 'Neropolis').[41] Only much later do we find Gratianopolis, the future Grenobles, named for Gratian.

The practice of imperial foundations was continuous throughout the imperial period, though, as A. H. M. Jones demonstrated, it became particularly vigorous in the later period.[42] Constantine sets the standard with his New Rome, Constantinopolis, with four cities called Constantia or Constantine, and one, Helenopolis, named for his wife. Julian had one Julianopolis and one Basilinopolis for his wife; the Valentinians produced three Valentinianopolis, but the family of Theodosius take it to a new level with nineteen foundations bearing their names. There is one Marcianopolis, and one Pulcheriopolis for his wife; five cases of Leopolis, four of Zenopolis, and four of Anastasiopolis. Justinian, in line with the foundational activity attributed to him by Procopius, and thanks to the detailed record of his *Peri Ktismaton*, created fifteen cities called Justinianopolis or, less commonly, Justiniana, plus two cities named for his wife, as Theodoropolis. Just when the city is conventionally supposed to be in decline, we find new examples proliferating.

Indeed, that a king worthy of the name ought to found cities in his name seems to find a partial echo in the post-Roman successor kingdoms. The

---

[41] For Augustan colonies, Brunt, *Italian Manpower*, pp. 608–610; for Neropolis, *Suetonius, Nero* 55.

[42] Jones, *Later Roman Empire*, pp. 718–719. See also *The Greek City*. For a survey of new foundations, Arce, 'La fundación de nuevas ciudades'.

Vandals seem the least likely of city founders, yet they renamed the important city of Hadrumetum, already renamed as Honoriopolis, after Gaiseric's son and successor Huneric, in the form Hunericopolis, playing on the previous name. Theoderic the Great should have been a city founder, and indeed a letter of Cassiodorus gives instructions on the first steps of such a foundation in North Italy in the region of Tridentum (*Variae* 5.9). There is no trace of this order being carried to completion, but the existence of a Theodericopolis is attested by the Anonymous Geographer of Ravenna: its location has been hypothesised in the Alto Adige, Lake Constance, or Switzerland.[43] More convincing are the new cities founded by the Visigoths under Leovigild, of which there are three, including Reccopolis, named for Liuvilgild's second son, Reccared. The site has been at least partially explored and includes a more or less orthogonal layout and an aqueduct (Chapter 9).[44]

There is clear evidence from inscriptions recording imperial decrees that the promotion of new cities was a standard matter of imperial policy. We have long known two inscriptions that spell out in detail the procedure of promotion: from Orcistus in Phrygia under Constantine, and from Tymandus in Pisidia, under an unnamed emperor, probably Diocletian. In each case the emperor is petitioned by a village (*vicus*) which lays out it claims to city status: Orcistus claims it always used to be an independent city with its own councillors (*curiales*) and an abundant population of citizens (*cives*); furthermore, it is positioned on the meeting of four major roads and has an aqueduct with an abundant water supply to the baths, which are decorated with statues of former emperors. Constantine by his *indulgentia* grants the status of *civitas*, which means fiscal independence from the neighbouring Nacolea.[45] The anonymous emperor to whom the people of Tymandus turned underlines that it is a matter of policy, or rather his inborn nature, to increase the number of cities (*cum itaque ingenitum nobis sit, ut per universum orbem nostrum civitatum honor ac numerus augeatur*). Now, by chance, we have a third inscription, for Heraclea Sintica in Bulgaria, also Tetrarchic, with just the same rhetoric:

> Although your city (*civitas vestra*) never previously held the rights of city status (*iura civitatis*), nevertheless, in accord with the zeal native to us toward our state and the favoritism for growth of our new foresight and goodwill, we wish to ennoble your homeland with the ornaments and with

---

[43] Augenti, *Archeologia dell'Italia medievale*, p. 34. [44] Henning et al., 'Reccopolis revealed'.
[45] Constantine to Orcistus (Phrygia): *Monumenta Asiae Minoris Antiqua* 7:305, see Lenski, *Constantine and the Cities*, p. 110.

the right of city status (*ornamentis et iure civitatis*). Wherefore, because you say this same place was [called] the City of the Herculeans (*Civitas Heracleotarum*) already in the past, and now you ask that the rights of city status (*iura civitatis*) be granted to it through our favor, we offer support for your petition quite willingly.[46]

A village could be turned into a city by an act of imperial will; equally, a city could be reduced to a village, as Libanius warned his fellow citizens risking the demotion of Antioch. As the Heracleian inscription makes plain, it is a matter of juridical status, and this mattered intensely, since a city with its *curiales* levied taxes from its territory, and obviously it was preferable to be self-governing, and not dependent on the only too arbitrary power of the neighbouring city, as was Orcistus on Nacolea.[47] But what were the criteria for promotion? At one level, it was simply imperial pleasure or displeasure: if a city can be demoted as a punishment, then other criteria are trumped. At another level it was more objective issues like demography: did the candidate city have a viable level of population, and, in particular, of landowners substantial enough to run it independently? But, at another level, it was a question of physical structures – of the possession of defensive walls and urban amenities – and it is this that is the focus of Procopius' account. Justinian transforms villages into cities by building them up to the required level for autonomous functioning. And it was this transformation that in certain cases gave the emperor naming rights.

We may return to Procopius' text to see this in action. Dara is, as we have seen, his first case study, and closely relates to the text of the *Wars*. As we know from the historical narrative, the Dara episode takes place in 527, when Belisarius had just been appointed to the eastern command, taking Procopius with him as counsellor (*Wars* 1.12.24). So the description of the improvement of the fortifications of Dara is his own eyewitness account, belonging to the first phase of his experience of this campaign. In the *Peri Ktismaton*, by contrast, he says nothing of his own presence, nor of Belisarius. It is the emperor Justinian who, apparently personally, recognises the inadequacy of the old defences, put up by Anastasius in a hurry

---

[46] See Lenski, ibid., pp. 90–91.

[47] The most spectacular example of the wholesale promotion of former centres to cities is Diocletian's reorganisation of Egypt, in which since Augustus only Alexandria had had the juridical status of city; otherwise, the districts called *nomes* had urban centres called *metropoleis*, but these too had magistrates and, from Septimius Severus, also councils, so the difference was technical: Jones, *Cities of the Eastern Roman Empire* pp. 344ff.; for their organisation, Alston, *The City in Roman and Byzantine Egypt*, pp. 185–322.

and under enemy attack, and specifically the danger that the Persians would bring close to the walls elephants carrying wooden towers on their shoulders, from which their archers could shoot downwards at the defenders (it is amazing the detail you can intuit from Constantinople!). He therefore raises the height of the original wall by thirty feet and narrows the battlement apertures to slots suitable for firing arrows through. He buttresses the wall by building a portico against it, then adds towers with a third level. Weaker towers are reinforced by the building of secondary external walls, and so on and so forth. In the context of a normal panegyric, this level of detail would have been entirely superfluous; but Procopius was there and knows the detail, is indeed proud of it, so we have two texts overlaid like a palimpsest: the surface praise of Justinian, and the subtext of the story of his own military adventures. Presumably the knowing reader, but not the emperor, can see the second text shining through and can use it to discount the excessive flattery of the emperor.

The walls of Dara are but the introduction to Procopius' story. He has an enormous amount more to relate about the provision of a reliable water supply to the fortress-city. This is by no means the only occasion on which he shows himself obsessed about details of hydraulic arrangements.[48] Indeed, his concern for hydraulics and other aspects of engineering have led to the suggestion that his background must have been in engineering rather than rhetoric, though this in turn underestimates his rhetorical skills.[49] In fact his elaborate description of how a well was sunk, only to be overwhelmed by a catastrophic flood, which by chance opened up an underground channel carrying excess water far from the city, enabling them eventually to install cisterns to supply the defender with water, while depriving the enemy outside of a water source – all this seems to be riddled with slight contradictions and incoherencies.[50] To say this is not to undermine his credibility as an eyewitness (though it does make it slightly less likely that he had specific engineering skills), for such complex and minute details on the ground are hard to recall, and harder to convey with clarity. His slight incoherence shows he is not simply making it up. But at the same time, the attribution to the all-seeing emperor of the observation and resolution of problems on the ground is made the more absurd by the shortcomings of the eyewitness.

Justinian's ability to intuit a campaign from afar becomes conspicuous in the account of the dam built to control the torrential river that had

---

[48] See Pickett, 'Water and empire in the *de aedificiis* of Procopius'.
[49] Howard-Johnston, 'The education and expertise of Procopius'.
[50] Croke and Crow, 'Procopius and Dara'; Pickett, 'Water and empire', pp. 105–110.

threatened the city. Procopius' narrative in the *Peri Ktismaton* is very curious, both for its odd combination of engineering expertise and divine revelation, and for the ambiguous role played by the emperor (2.3.1–23). First we meet a figure with impeccable engineering qualifications, one Chryses of Alexandria, a skilled mechanical engineer who had previously worked for Justinian. But he is away at the time and, having heard about the disastrous flood, has a solution revealed to him in a dream. Understanding that it 'came from God', he at once writes to the emperor detailing his solution. Meanwhile, the emperor has also heard of the flood and summons his engineers, Anthemius and Isidorus, and asks their advice. Then, while they hesitate, he too has a vision, and although he has not yet seen the letter from Chryses which arrived three days later, 'obviously moved by divine inspiration', he comes up with an identical plan. The two advisors still hesitate, until the letter from Chryses arrives, and they all agree that this proves that the emperor's plan is the right solution. This whole bizarrely contorted narrative underlines that Procopius is not merely attributing to the emperor as a matter of convention those actions which take place under him, but asserts his personal intervention, made possible by a hot line to the deity. And yet, at the same time, the narrative undermines itself: why on earth would Justinian come up with a plan identical to that of Chryses three days in advance, and why do his other advisers hesitate until the letter of Chryses arrives? It feels as if the narrative is designed to be incredible to anyone who did not believe, as Justinian expected of them, that he acted under divine inspiration.

Procopius has it both ways, for diverse audiences. The emperors and his flatterers can read the story at face value; those who shared the sort of views Procopius airs in the *Secret History* will see in it nothing but absurdity. He deflects the emperor's wrath by praising him for actions across the empire of which he was only dimly aware. Of course, it is genuine imperial policy to strengthen the defences of the empire, and to give a network of cities and fortress, new and old, the central role in those defences. And, of course, like any other emperor he had to act through agents he trusted on the ground, such as Belisarius himself. But it is almost as if, having earned potential criticism by attributing too little of the success of the wars to the general, and too little to the emperor, the author now sets out to tell a parallel story in which he attributes all the successes to the emperor, when we know perfectly well it was the same generals at work. (To Dara we will return in Chapter 9.)

The second book of *Peri Ktismaton* continues to run broadly parallel to the war narrative. If in the *Wars* we hear about the besieging and sacking of cities like Antioch (*Wars* 2. 8–9), Edessa, and Callinicum (2.21–27), he can now describe at length their reconstruction (*Ktismaton* 2. 7), and at particular length that of Antioch (2.10). Again, the third book of the *Peri Ktismaton* about Armenia allows him to revisit cities discussed in the *Wars*, like Theodosiopolis/Anastasiopolis (3.4, cf. *Wars* 1.10.18) and, at length, Petra (3.7, cf. *Wars* 2.15; 17; 29–30). Equally, the sixth book, on North Africa, allows him to revisit the narrative of the Vandalic Wars, above all Carthage (6.5, cf. *Wars* 3.23) and Hadrumetum (6.6, cf. *Wars* 3.17.8; 3.27; 4.23 and 27). So, with Carthage he is able to revisit his observations on the folly of the Vandals in demolishing city walls, to save them from the Romans, and repeat his account of Belisarius' rebuilding. But this time he shifts responsibility. Having said that Justinian sent out Belisarius to defeat the Vandals, he continues by saying how 'he' (the emperor) then took thought for Carthage, 'which is now justly called Justinianē', providing it with a church to the Mother of God; stoas around the Maritime Agora; a public bath named the Theodorianae, in honour of the empress; and a monastery on the shore (6.5.8–11). If the agency is ambivalent, the next sentence makes explicit that this is what Justinian did for Carthage. The neurotic renaming of cities after the emperor continues at Hadrumetum, which has already passed through phases of being called Honoriopolis and Hunericopolis:

> Now they call the place Justinianē, thus repaying the emperor for their deliverance and displaying their gratitude simply by the adoption of that name, since they had no other means by which they could requite the Emperor's beneficence, nor did he himself wish other requital. (6.6.7)

Whether it was really useful to call both the major cities of Africa Proconsularis by the same name may be doubted, and we cannot help recalling Procopius' earlier comments on the instability of imperial city names. It is as much an illustration of imperial vanity as of genuine local gratitude.

While the books that overlap with the Persian and Vandalic Wars thus provide a potentially subversive subtext, books 4 and 5, which cover Thrace (4) and Asia Minor and Palestine (5), have no such parallel text. They seem to contrast sharply in degree of personal knowledge. Born in Caesarea in Palestine, and working in Constantinople, Procopius will have known well the cities described in book 5. Some, like the cluster of cities on the far side of the Propontis from Byzantium, Helenopolis, Nicaea, and Nicomedia (5.2–3), were in easy reach of the capital and surely well-known to the author. He emphasises restorations of roads, bridges, aqueducts, and baths.

In the case of Helenopolis he is able to drive home his point about naming rights (5.2.1–5). Constantine had renamed it, but scarcely merited this by his buildings, unlike those of Justinian:

> There is a certain city in Bithynia which bears the name of Helena, mother of the Emperor Constantine, for they say Helena was born in this village, which was formerly of no consequence. But Constantine, by way of repaying the debt of her nurture, endowed this place with the name and dignity of a city. However, he built nothing there in a style of imperial magnificence, but though the place remained outwardly as it had been before, it now would boast merely in the name of a city. (5.2.1–2)

Procopius may exaggerate, but it underlines the point that a village may become a city by a mere act of imperial will. Justinian, by contrast, undertakes the building which made it merit the name of city, without imposing his own name. He provided it with an aqueduct and two bath complexes (one of which existed before, so at least there had been a water supply):

> Moreover, he built here churches and a palace and stoas and lodgings for the magistrates, and in other respects he gave it the appearance of a prosperous city. (5.2.5)

There is indeed a certain monumental formula which defines a city, and we encounter it repeatedly in Justinian's foundations (see pp. 187–192); but the mere act of conveying the juridical status of city can be in itself, without any notable building works, grounds for renaming.

The cities of Bithynia and Asia Minor are likely enough to have been familiar to Procopius. But we might take note of what he has to say about his own province of Palestine (5.6–7). Here he comments only on two cities: Jerusalem and Neapolis. We might have expected something on Caesarea itself, but there is nothing registered. In the case of Jerusalem, there is a major new Justinianic church to talk about, the 'New' Church. This he does in some detail, and since it is partly known to archaeology, we can say that his words fit well with what is on the ground. In particular, his description of the great blocks of stone for the terracing and the columns of locally sourced marble, in flame red, is confirmed by finds.[51] That the only contribution to the holy city of Judaism should be another Christian church passes without comment, though the religious motivation of the emperor is made explicit: this

---

[51] Tsafrir, 'Procopius and the Nea church'.

was an accomplishment not just of human power and technology, but of the force of piety and zeal (5.6.16).

The case of Jerusalem gains added significance from the second city of Palestine with which it is paired, Neapolis. This passage is the more remarkable because it is not a city at all, but a mountain, on which his account focuses (5.7). Mount Garazin, he explains, was the holy mountain of the Samaritans, as important to them as Jerusalem to the Jews, except that the Samaritans built no temple, but simply revered the summit. Or did so until an ugly incident under Zeno, when the Samaritans attacked the Christians in their church in Neapolis at Pentecost, and succeeded in severing the fingers of the bishop, who indignantly appealed to the emperor. Zeno responded by establishing a church to the Mother of God on the summit of Mount Garazin, surrounding it with a stone wall. He thereby fulfilled a biblical prophecy of Jesus, who had told a Samaritan woman that the mountain would cease to be worshipped by the Samaritans, but instead be a place of worship for Christians. If Procopius were the Christian he claimed to be, he might have noted that Jesus is quoted more precisely as saying that Mount Garazin would cease to be a place of worship for the Samaritans and Jerusalem for the Jews, but says nothing of building churches there (*John* 4.8–30), though doubtless that interpretation of the text suited well enough a bishop shaking his mutilated hands under the nose of Zeno. Trouble returned under Anastasius, who omitted to strengthen the surrounding wall, something done instead by Justinian. Fortifications as well as cities are a recurrent concern of the *Peri Ktismaton*, but that Justinian repaired a wall round a church at the top of a mountain is something of a variation on the theme.

Procopius surely wants to twin the accounts of the two holy places of the Jews and Samaritans. If there is no subtext available in the *Wars*, there certainly is in the *Secret History* which, as we have seen, sharply criticises Justinian's violence against non-Orthodox religious targets. As he puts it on another occasion:

> The punishment of the Samaritans and of those called heretics filled the Roman Empire with slaughter. (*Anecdota* 18.34)

Read in this light, the account of Justinian's achievements in Palestine is rather less positive. We may also raise an eyebrow at his account of the two cities, each called Augila, near Boreium in the Libyan Pentapolis.[52] These were

---

[52] For archaeological evidence of Justinianic activity round Augila and Boreion, see Goodchild, 'Boreum of Cyrenaica'; Reynolds, 'Justinian and Procopius in Libya'.

ancient cities whose inhabitants have preserved the practices of antiquity and suffered even into my times from the disease of polytheism. There from ancient times there have been shrines dedicated to Ammon and to Alexander of Macedon. (6.2.15)

Justinian liberates the 'great throng of temple slaves' and converts them to Christianity:

> Indeed he by no means neglected to take thought for their material interests in an exceptional way, and also he has taught them the doctrine of the true faith, making the whole population Christians and bringing about a transformation of their polluted ancestral customs. (6.2.19)

On the surface, the language of disease and pollution suggests nothing but approval for this wholesale conversion, and yet the equal emphasis on the antiquity of their traditions must arouse suspicion in an author who so clearly approves of ancestral practice and hates innovation.

Immediately after the account of the 'polytheist' cities, which boast a long history stretching back even before the visit of Alexander the Great to Ammon, he continues with the city of Boreium, a Jewish settlement of equal antiquity:

> The Jews had lived there from ancient times, and they had an ancient temple there also, which they revered and honoured especially, since it was built, as they say, by Solomon, while he was ruling over the Hebrew nation. But the Emperor Justinian brought it about that all these too changed their ancestral worship and have become Christians, and he transformed their temple into a church. (6.2.22–23)

Here too the repeated invocations of antiquity, complete with a reference to King Solomon as mythical founder, must cast doubt on the implicit brutality with which Justinian attacked pagan and Jewish religion alike.

Procopius' Ideal City

The suggestion that the *Peri Ktismaton* is undercut by a subtext legible from knowledge of Procopius' other writings points to a way of evaluating his panegyric. We are always troubled by whether we can trust panegyric, whether because all such praise tends to the hyperbolical, or because it is evident that the panegyrist drew on a stock of commonplaces. Can we believe that Justinian was indeed such an enthusiastic founder and restorer of cities, or that he built or restored them in the ways the panegyrist represents? We must be attentive, I have argued, to both text and subtext: the text represents Justinian as a great founder of cities in line with Alexander, Augustus, or Constantine; the subtext arouses the suspicion that in his boundless vanity he merely claims credit for the hard work of others, and that his concern, after the strengthening of the empire's defences, was the promotion of his own brand of religious zealotry (all these churches to the Mother of God . . .). But that does not mean that there are not points where the authentic view of the author coincides with the policies of his emperor. It was, we may suggest, an ingenious choice of subject, and a radical innovation in the hoary tradition of imperial panegyric, to focus on a side of imperial activity which matched closely with the author's own experience and values. Experience in three theatres of war taught him the critical difference that a good set of city walls could make: he could illustrate both the fatal tactical error of the Vandals in tearing them down, and the enormous advantage gained by the Goths when they did actually reinforce their defences.

It is evident from the convergence of evidence of his three works that Procopius had a set of ideals for the city. They were of course, as we have seen (Chapter 2), ideals familiar from the rhetorical tradition. What, then, is Procopius' urban ideal like? In the *Peri Ktismaton* he can offer us a rosy picture of Justinianic urbanism at its best. The model, of course, must be his new city of Justiniana Prima. The founder of the civilised world (τῆς οἰκουμένης οἰκιστής) was actually born in a tiny hamlet in Serbia called Taurisium, which he elevated by giving it a wall with four towers, renaming it Tetrapyrgia. His new city he builds nearby. The founder of the city gives it a fine aqueduct and numerous monuments:

> To enumerate the churches is not easy, and it is impossible to tell in words the lodgings for magistrates, the size of the stoas, the beauty of the agoras, the fountains, the streets, the baths and the shops. (4.1.23)

In a word, it is a classic ancient city. As it happens, Justiniana Prima has been well explored by archaeologists, and it emerges as a good deal less impressive and less classically ordered than Procopius suggests (as we will see in Chapter 9, pp. 345–8).[53] But then, it was not a city which he implies he had visited himself, and his praise is understandably generic.

We saw earlier what Justinian did for Helenopolis, that village which Constantine raised to the status of a city without actually making it one (5.2.1). He provided a marvellous aqueduct, ample to supply not only

---

[53] Ivanišević, 'Main patterns of urbanism in Caričin Grad (Justiniana Prima)'.

drinking water but also bathing water, repaired the ruinous baths, and added new ones:

> But he also built churches and stoas and lodgings for the magistrates, and in other respects gave it the appearance of a prosperous city (ἐπιδέδεικται αὐτὴν πόλιν εὐδαίμονα). (5.2.5)

We are beginning to recognise a formula here, one which covers not only churches but also administrative buildings. Later in the text, a fortress in Cappadocia called Mocesus gets a new wall:

> There too he built many churches and hospices and public baths and whatever else points to a prosperous city (ἐνδείκνυται πόλιν εὐδαίμονα). (5.4.17)

In consequence, it rises to the rank of metropolis. There is a clear emphasis in Justinian's programme on walls, churches, and baths; Procopius leaves it to his 'whatever else' to imply stoas and administrative buildings.

In Africa too there are cities to restore. Leptis Magna had been overpowered by the Moors and emptied of its inhabitants.

> In this city the Emperor Justinian also built public baths, and he erected the circuit-wall of the city from its lowest foundations, and by means both of the baths and of all the other improvements gave it the character of a city (ἐς πόλεως σχῆμα). The barbarians who live close by, those called Gadabitani, who up to that time were exceedingly addicted to what is called the Greek form of atheism, he has now made zealous Christians. (6.4.11)

We note that urbanisation also has a civilising power in converting the natives, though whether it is the churches or the baths or the combination of the two is unclear.

In Carthage, as we have seen, he rebuilt the whole circuit wall, dedicated shrines, built stoas on either side of the Marine Forum, and built a public bath named for Theodora (6.5.8–11). Again, we can see Justinian's priorities: walls, aqueducts, baths, but the agora and stoas and magistrates are also there as basic components of a city. One final African example is that of Syllectus/Caputvada in Byzacium. This is where Belisarius made his first landing, and by chance they found a spring and built a camp around it (cf. *Wars* 3.16.9). Justinian decided to commemorate the event by building a new city, and in this he succeeded:

> So the emperor Justinian, by way of bearing witness to the gift of God by means of a permanent testimony – for the most difficult task easily yields to

> his wish – conceived the desire to transform this place forthwith into a city which should be fortified by a wall and distinguished by other appointments as worthy of the dignity of a prosperous city (ἐς πόλεως ὄγκον); and the purpose of the Emperor has been realized, for a wall has been brought to completion, and the condition of the farmland is suddenly transformed. The rustics have thrown aside the plough and live a city life (πολιτικῶς βιοτεύσιν), no longer practising rustic ways but urban ones (ἄγροικον/ ἀστείαν). They spend their days there in the agora (ἀγοράζουσιν) and hold assemblies over their needs (ἐκκλησιάζουσιν) and do business with each other in the agora (συμβάλλουσιν), and they do everything else which brings the dignity of a city (πόλεως ἀξίωμα). (6.6.13–16)

For once, there is no talk of founding churches, though there is a certain ambiguity in the word *ekklēsiazousin*. A reader of Aristophanes like Procopius might instinctively think of meetings of an assembly, as in the women's assembly of the *Ekklesiazousae*; a Christian reader might think more naturally of churches. But *agora*, *ekklēsia*, and contracts define an urbanised community. The mention of contracts might recall the account of the Ephthialite White Huns (above), whose civilised and urbanised ways included the making of contracts (ξυμβάλλουσιν).

Procopius' text represents Justinian as promoter of urban values. For a subtext, we have only to turn to the *Secret History*. Far from improving cities, from this negative perspective, Justinian did everything to damage them. Quite apart from the damage done by barbarian invasions, earthquakes (which levelled eight cities of Asia), and the plague, he dealt a blow to civic culture by cutting support for rhetors, physicians, and teachers, and diverted revenues that had supported civic needs and spectacles, for maintenance of public buildings, and even for street lighting:

> First he decided to abolish the rank of *rhetor*; for he straightway deprived the rhetors of all their competitive prizes in which they had formerly been wont to revel and take pride when they discharged their function as advocates, and he ordered those at variance with one another to litigate directly under oath; and being this scored, the rhetors fell into great despondency ...
>
> Nay more, he also caused physicians and teachers of free-born children to be in want of the necessities of life. For the allowances of free maintenance which former emperors had decreed should be given to men of these professions from public funds he cancelled entirely.
>
> (26.1–2, 5)

This is a declaration of cultural war, at least from Procopius' point of view. How much is true is unclear, but the main charge was the closure of the schools of Athens in 529.[54] The public provision of doctors, teachers and rhetoricians was a basis of urban civilisation. If Athalaric through Cassiodorus could praise *grammatica* as what distinguished Romans from barbarians (see Chapter 4), Justinian is knocking away the very basis of civilisation. But he also assaults urban culture itself:

> Furthermore, all the revenues which the inhabitants of all the cities had been raising locally for their own civic needs and for their public spectacles he transferred and dared to mingle them with the national income. And thereafter neither physicians nor teachers were held in any esteem, nor was anyone able any longer to make provision for public buildings, nor were the public lamps kept burning in the cities, nor was there any other consolation for their inhabitants. For the theatres and hippodromes and circuses were all closed for the most part – the places in which, as it happened, his wife had been born and reared and educated. And later he ordered these spectacles to close down altogether, even in Byzantium, so that the Treasury might not have to supply the usual sums to the numerous and almost countless persons who derived their living from them.
>
> (26.5–7)

The very features of the supposed decline of the ancient city, the abandonment of the institutions that defined its physical appearance, are here blamed squarely on imperial intervention in city finances. One characteristic of the civic taxation system was the 'hypothecation' of taxes, whereby a particular type of tax, or a portion of it, was earmarked for a particular purpose. The expenditures which Procopius indicates – salaries for teachers and doctors, maintenance of buildings, even costs of street lighting – were typically covered by local taxes, not central government. The measures he alleges deprived cities of the last traces of financial independence, as well as their cultural life. The result is a sort of inversion of the image of an ideal city he has conjured up for Byzacium, where the people meet in the agora to do politics and business. Now they meet only to complain about what has been lost:

> And there was both in private and in public sorrow and dejection, as though still another affliction from Heaven had smitten them, and there was no laughter in life for anyone. And no other topic whatever arose in the conversation of the people, whether they were at home or in the

[54] Kaldellis, *Secret History*, p. xxxiv.

> marketplace or were tarrying in the sacred places, than disasters and calamities and misfortunes of novel kind in surpassing degree. (26.10–11).

All of which is a tonic for anyone deluded enough to think that city life flourished under Justinian.

Procopius and the Values of Antiquity

Procopius' ideal city is very much a classical one. Indeed, from one point of view we might think him trapped in the tramlines of the classical: his language that of long-past writers, his values that of long-past literature, and his rosy ideal of the city that of another era. So for Averil Cameron, as we have seen (see Chapter 1, p. 27, n. 54), he was simply out of date, and had not recognised or accepted that the classical city had been replaced by a new model, of winding streets huddled round a fortified citadel and church.[55]

Another generation of archaeology has rendered the confident contrast between the 'classical' and the 'medieval' harder to sustain, in that form at least: there are changes indeed, but many features of the classical city do not merely persist but were actively preserved into the seventh century (see Chapter 9). Nor is it at all clear that Procopius was blind to the new emphasis in urbanism that would define the early middle ages. When he says that, in providing Septem (modern Ceuta) at the straits of Gibraltar with fortifications and a church to the Mother of God, he provided 'the beginnings of a city' (τὰ τῆς πολιτείας προοίμια), he is surely flagging the elements of what we think of as the post-classical city.[56] That Procopius was a traditionalist is beyond question. It is not so much that he has failed to register a sea-change: rather, he sees certain changes only too clearly, and does not approve of them. The clearest, and most generalisable change was the growth of Christian architecture, churches, monasteries, and hospices, at the expense of classical forms, and these he details at length. His panegyric of Justinian makes clear that he sees that change, though he is not rash enough to question it.

Procopius dislikes innovation and actively approves of tradition. His treatment of the city of Rome shows that clearly enough. Like Cassiodorus, as we have seen, he applauds the people of Rome for the patriotic zeal with which they conserve the monuments of their past. Much of the action of the

---

[55] Averil Cameron, *Procopius*, pp. 111–112.
[56] *Buildings* 6.7.16, cited by Cameron, p. 124. Her translation is much preferable to that of Dewey's Loeb, 'the threshold of the empire'.

Gothic war narrative circles round Rome, which is successively seized by Belisarius and besieged by the Goths under Witigis, then later lost to Totila in another siege, then recovered by Belisarius. This gives the historian ample opportunity to share his views of Rome and the impact on it of Gothic rule. One very striking feature of his narrative is the extent to which he shows empathy with the Goths – something all the more surprising given that they not only fell into his category of 'barbarian', but were the enemy against whom he personally fought for several years. Yet, at times, one comes to wonder whether he did not think Gothic rule was not preferable for Rome to conquest by Justinian.

Speeches were the perfect opportunity for a historian to share his thoughts. Of course he had no access to whatever the enemy leaders may have said at the time; but, in the Thucydidean tradition, it was entirely acceptable to reconstruct what in the circumstances, given their situation, they might have said. It also provides the historian with the opportunity to put words into the mouths of others which he might not want to be attributed to himself. At the beginning of his invasion of Italy, Belisarius is approached by a Gothic embassy. They try to strike a deal: he could take Sicily, maybe Campania too, and they could pay tribute. In particular, they defend the record of Gothic rule in Italy. They point out that Theoderic took over Italy from Odoacer at the invitation of the emperor Zeno, and, having done so, he and his successors showed their fidelity to the principles of Roman rule:

> It was in this way, therefore, that we took over the dominion of Italy, and we have preserved both the laws and the form of government as strictly as any who have ever been Roman emperors, and there is absolutely no law, either written or unwritten, introduced by Theoderic or by any of his successors on the throne of the Goths. And we have so scrupulously guarded for the Romans their practices pertaining to the worship of God and faith in Him, that not one of the Italians has changed his belief, either willingly or unwillingly, up to the present day, and when Goths have changed, we have taken no notice of the matter. (6.6.17–18)

The Arian church, that is to say, made no attempt to recruit Catholics. In the light of Procopius' views on the sort of compulsory conversion exercised by Justinian, who concluded his conquest of Italy with the extirpation of the Gothic Arian church, Procopius' sympathies are only too likely. It is precisely the sort of defence which Cassiodorus would have offered.[57]

---

[57] On Procopius' views of the Ostrogothic regime, see Golitz, 'Anspruch und Wirklichkeit'; Pazdernik, 'Reinventing Theoderic in Procopius' *Gothic War*'.

It is always clear that Totila was no Theoderic, and he is represented as constantly tempted to destroy Rome. Having retaken Rome, he ponders on whether to destroy it:

> But when Totila learned this, he decided first to raze Rome to the ground, and then, while leaving the most of his army in that neighbourhood, to march with the rest against John and the Lucanians. Accordingly he tore down the fortifications in many places so that about one third of the defences were destroyed. And he was on the point also of burning the finest and most noteworthy of the buildings and making Rome a sheep-pasture. (7.22.6–8)

At this point Procopius attributes a long letter to Belisarius, pleading the case for Rome (it would be overly optimistic to assume that Procopius had documentary evidence for such a letter, which, just as the speeches, is likely to represent his own thoughts).

> Now among all the cities under the sun Rome is agreed to be the greatest and the most noteworthy. For it has not been created by the ability of one man, nor has it attained such greatness and beauty by a power of short duration, but a multitude of monarchs, many companies of the best men, a great lapse of time, and an extraordinary abundance of wealth have availed to bring together in that city all other things that are in the whole world, and skilled workers besides. Thus, little by little, have they built the city, such as you behold it, thereby leaving to future generations memorials of the ability of them all, so that insult to these monuments would properly be considered a great crime against the men of all time; for by such action the men of former generations are robbed of the memorials of their ability, and future generations of the sight of their works. (7.22.9–14)

Here we have a vision of Rome worthy of Cicero's *de Republica*, which represented the Roman constitution, in contrast to Plato's ideal *politeia*, as a cumulative construction of generations of Romans. It stands in contrast to the sort of instant city produced by Justinian at the flick of a finger across the empire. What makes Rome ideal is not that it has the correct assemblage of classical buildings, let alone an orthogonal street plan, but that it incorporates the historical process itself. We may admire Rome as a city of layers; Procopius admires it as a corporate effort by generations of Romans working to build on what has gone before. Procopius does not exactly have Cassiodorus' concept of the *modernus*: modernity both seeking to preserve antiquity and competing with it. But the effect is not dissimilar: to make the ideal city, you do not need to sweep away the traces of the past, but appreciate them and build on them.

Far from being out of date, Procopius stands at the heart of the ongoing debate of Late Antiquity. The issues he raises are ones of fierce contemporary discussion. Justinian also saw himself as being in the business of restoring the past glories of his Roman empire, and genuinely believed that the correct worship of God would help him achieve his purpose. Procopius saw him as a restless innovator who had no respect for alternative traditions – those of the Jews, the Samaritans, the pagans, the Arians, and the Hellenists. Justinian might well have refused the label of innovator: the words 'we make no innovations' (οὐδὲν καινίζομεν) make frequent appearance in his laws.[58] For Procopius, Rome symbolised respect for the past. If Rome had in the meantime become the most important Christian centre in the west, this was no problem for him. He objected not to faith, but to tearing down established tradition in the name of faith.

---

[58] So Honoré, *Tribonian* p. 27, n. 306.

6 | The City and Its Records

The Ravenna Papyri

Looking back, Italy's period of Ostrogothic rule seems like the Indian Summer of 'the Ancient City'. As evoked by the pen of Cassiodorus, the city seems to have basked in the warm sunshine of the attention of Theoderic and his successors: damaged fabric of vital infrastructure is repaired, restoration of the gleam of antiquity encouraged and supported, the role of the ruling elite given central backing, the joys of urban life promoted, while an ideal of civility mitigates the ever-present threat implicit in the Gothic presence. We will not be taken in by Cassiodorus' spin, and even in his attempts to address problems we can see that problems were there. But for all that, few would doubt that the cities of Italy were in a better state in the four decades and more up to Belisarius' invasion in 535 than in the period that followed Byzantine reconquista. The 'Gothic wars' were fought for fifteen years around and over cities, some, like Rome itself, besieged and sacked repeatedly by both sides. Nor did Justinian's attempt to re-establish law and order in his 'Pragmatic Sanction' of 554 usher in a period of stability. The Lombards under Alboin encountered remarkably little resistance when they invaded in the 560s, and the cities, especially of the north of Italy, suffered heavily. And though the Lombards for the next century, until they were in turn defeated by Charlemagne, based their rule of Italy on the cities, urban prosperity was a distant dream:[1]

> In most areas of Italy, including those that remained in imperial hands and those which fell to the Lombards, most cities survived, albeit at an impoverished level, and urban residence remained the norm as a result of cultural conditioning as much as economic and defensive considerations. This apparent continuity should not obscure the very real changes taking place in urban life.[2]

One way of seeing this process is as a chapter in the 'decline and fall' of the ancient city: the sixth century becomes the final moment of collapse of

---

[1] For the later period, Goodson, 'Urbanism as politics', pp. 198–218. For a critical examination of the sources, Fabbro, *Warfare and the Making of Lombard Italy*.

[2] T. S. Brown, *Gentlemen and Officers*, p. 14.

an institution which had been crumbling long before. It is not just that the fabric of the cities was battered and their population depleted: the institutions which were at the heart of a certain way of life (one so vividly evoked by Cassiodorus) now crumbled. A central part in this narrative is played by the city councils, the *curiae*. As we have seen, A. H. M. Jones identified the decline of the *curiae* as the principal driver of the end of the ancient city (see Chapter 1, pp. 14–20). The flourishing of the cities of the high empire was due to the willingness and competitive enthusiasm of the local elites, composed essentially of larger landowners, to take part in the administration of their cities and invest significant capital in their monumental embellishment. But, over time, this 'patriotic' urge diminished. From the moment, under Diocletian, that service on the local council became a hereditary obligation, policed by the imperial power, local landowners looked for ways to escape their burdens, moving upwards into imperial service, sideways into the church and the legal and rhetorical teaching professions, or downwards by selling their lands or moving out of the city. We can see something of that strain in Cassiodorus, in a case like the family of Agenantia, who at their own request had their names struck off the municipal register of those obligated to serve. Despite the best efforts of the Gothic regime, according to this narrative, the flight of the local elites was unstoppable, and a new pattern emerges whereby real authority at an urban level passes to the bishop and the representatives of central power – the count (*comes*) under the Goths, the duke (*dux*) under the Lombards – and an ill-defined group of 'notables', *honorati*, and large landowners (*possessores*) come to the fore, reducing the old council, the *curia*, in so far as it survived at all, to a mere registry office.[3]

That is one way of telling the story. Another would be to observe with astonishment the ability of the cities and their ancient institutions to survive the collapse of the system of imperial power that created them. The central power of the imperial court and its proliferating army of none-too-honest bureaucrats is often seen as the enemy of the cities; not only did local elites escape municipal obligations by entering imperial service, but the cities found their revenues progressively appropriated by the central power. True, but at the same time, cities and their institutions survived because emperors wanted them to do so: the 186 constitutions of the first chapter of the fifteenth book of the Theodosian Code tell both stories: the multiple ploys of local elites to escape their obligations, and the recurrent insistence of

---

[3] I here summarise, without doing justice to its learning and subtlety, Liebeschuetz, *Decline and Fall*, esp. pp. 104–136.

emperors that they should meet them. Indeed, we should be more surprised that these 'curial' elites survived as long as they did. To make membership of a group both mandatory and hereditary is a system hard to reconcile with the random effects of human reproduction. In few elites can father-to-son succession be sustained beyond a few generations: some have only daughters, some no children at all, some too many sons between whom to divide the inheritance, and, even in times of peace and prosperity, the system is too rigid to survive. Towards the end of the system, we find Justinian desperately legislating to stop the elites from dying out: their landholdings carry curial obligation with them, so that if they pass to a daughter, the obligations pass to her husband; and if there are only illegitimate sons, in inheriting the land, they gain legitimacy and the obligation to serve the council.[4] So, if the control of cities passes from an elite defined in an almost unsustainably rigid way to a less formal and more ill-defined elite, it might be thought a gain, not a collapse.

For Wolf Liebeschuetz, the most eloquent proponent of the 'decline and fall' thesis, what matters is constitutional rule. Rejecting the argument of the late Mark Whittow that the passage from the rule of 'curials' to that of 'notables' made little difference since it was a shift from one elite defined one way to another, and substantially similar, elite of landowners,[5] Liebeschuetz objects that the difference lies in constitutionality:

> the end of curial government also meant the end of government in accordance with a known and accepted constitution. It thus represents the end of an ancient tradition of constitutional politics going back to Solon of Athens and beyond, which had received its classic exposition in Aristotle's *Politics*. (p. 121)

This vision of the ancient city as a bounded organism, with continuous identifying features that stretch across a millennium and more, successfully masks a process of continuous historical change. Despite its *curia/boulê*, the Late Antique city might have seemed deeply alien to Aristotle, a city with no *autonomia*, unable to live by its own laws, but subject to the arbitrary will of what Aristotle might have identified as a tyrant: the emperor. The collapse of imperial power in the west gave cities

---

[4] Justinian, *Novella* 38 (AD 535); cf. *Nov.* 87 (AD 539) banning donations by decurions at death; *Nov.* 101 (AD 539) permits decurions without children to leave estate to outside provided that they assume curial responsibilities; all cited by Liebeschuetz, *Decline and Fall*, p. 104.

[5] Whittow, 'Ruling the late Roman and early Byzantine city', pp. 3–29. The article uses archaeological evidence to suggest that many cities in the east continued to flourish. For the debate, see now Anne-Valerie Pont, *La fin de la cité grecque*.

marginally more autonomy, though only marginally, since kings took the place of emperors.

Let us pose the question a different way. Given that cities had become an instrument of imperial control, how did they respond to and survive the collapse of that system (in the western Empire, that is), which in terms of resilience theory we might regard as a catastrophic impact? With no emperor issuing endless constitutions, mandating a certain hereditary class to undertake challenging and often unwelcome civic burdens, what features of the past did cities choose to retain, and how did they use them to create a new and more sustainable model? Why did not only Theoderic in Italy but Alaric II in Visigothic Spain and Clovis in Francia accept that cities should continue to be run under the old Roman laws and traditions? You can think of it as inertia, the deadweight of the past, a reassurance to the old Roman population that 'barbarian' rule was not the radical change they feared. But it is also a feature of a process of adaptation. The kings, like the emperors before them, found cities extremely useful, a mechanism for organising the population, and in particular for taxing them. In this they were much supported by the church, which had grown up within a system of cities and, for all its talk of a City of God, found that a system of bishops based on the terrestrial cities as administrative centres was a highly effective way of activating the support of the faithful. Neither kings nor church saw any advantage in dismantling cities as a system of social control.

The Ravenna Papyri

How it worked on the ground is revealed to us in fragmentary glimpses by a series of legal documents written on papyrus, the most important of which derive ultimately from the archives of the church of Ravenna and are hence known as the Ravenna papyri, though in fact they show the workings of several Italian cities, including Ravenna's adjoining but independent city Classis, its neighbours Faenza and Rimini, more distant Rieti, Gubbio, Nepi, Syracuse in Sicily, and Rome itself.[6] They have been deployed in the debate about the 'end of the *curia*', though mostly in a twilight zone of anaemic footnotes, compacting them into abbreviated codes (*P.Ital.* 2, etc.), and offered more as unimportant exceptions to the process of decline which they oddly fail to illustrate.[7] In the way of archival documents,

---

[6] Magisterially edited by Tjäder, *Die nichtliterarischen lateinischen Papyri Italiens.*

[7] See Jones, *Later Roman Empire*, vol. 1, p. 761, with note 111 (vol. 2, p. 1313); Liebeschuetz, *Decline and Fall*, p. 127. For a slightly richer use of these papyri, Brown, *Gentlemen and Officers*,

even ones of a highly formulaic and legalistic character, they reveal more about how institutions worked on the ground, offering vivid and surprising snapshots of life at many levels – the lifeblood of the social historian.[8] They do not offer the grand narrative of political history, and yet they intersect with it in surprising ways. Nor are the documents restricted to Italy, for French cities have preserved a collection of similar documents that stretch to AD 804, when Charlemagne had already been crowned emperor. It is worth lingering over them, not so much to demonstrate that an institution that called itself the *curia* persisted for more than three centuries after the collapse of Roman power (though it certainly does so), but to share the insights they offer into life in a series of cities.

We might start with one of the earliest documents from the Ravenna collection, dated to AD 489, when the Roman Empire was freshly 'fallen' (P. 10–11).[9] It involves the man who brought imperial rule in Italy to an end, dismissing Romulus Augustulus to his comfortable exile to the Bay of Naples, and setting himself up as the first of a long series of kings, the Germanic general whom the documents call Odovacar, more familiar in English as Odoacer.[10] AD 489 was not a good year for Odoacer, for despite ruling Italy not ineffectively for more than a decade, Zeno, the Roman emperor in Constantinople, decided it was time to topple him and sent Theoderic for the purpose. Dated to 18th March, five months before his first defeat by Theoderic at the river Isonzo, at the border of Italy near Aquileia, the document shows Odoacer consolidating his support in advance of the crisis by granting a large estate to one of his generals, Pierius, a transaction which one way or another involves several members of the royal court. A year later, on 11 August 490, a decisive defeat was inflicted on Odoacer at the crossing of the river Adda near Milan. The commander of Odoacer's troops was Pierius, the *comes domesticorum*. He perished in the battle, and his likely gravestone has been found nearby in the village of Garlate.[11] We know extraordinarily little about Odoacer or Pierius, for lack of contemporary or later historical accounts.[12] Theoderic

---

pp. 16–17, 75–76. More recent discussions of these documents have re-evaluated their importance: Sansoni, 'I papiri di Ravenna', Everett, 'Lay documents and archives', Pohl, 'Social Cohesion'.

[8] Telling use is made of these papyri by Judith Herrin in a series of passages interwoven into her narrative, *Ravenna*, pp. 27–28, 65–66, 180–181, 194–197, 199, 217–219.

[9] Tjäder vol. 1, pp. 279–293.

[10] See Indelli, *Odocre*; Caliri, *Praecellentissimus rex*, esp. pp. 131–149 on the donation to Pierius.

[11] On Pierius' gravestone, see Sannazaro, 'Un'epigrafe di Garlate'; Caliri, Praecellentissimus Rex, p. 137.

[12] The account of Hodgkin, *Italy and her Invaders*, vol. 3, pp. 122–213, remains valuable for this little-studied but impressive figure.

succeeded in not merely defeating his rival but virtually eliminating him from the historical record. Which makes this papyrus the more precious. Presumably after Pierius' death in battle, Theoderic confiscated his property and donated it to the archbishop of Ravenna, with the happy result that all the paperwork ended up in the archive there.

The document does not cover the main donation, of farms with an annual income of 610 gold *solidi* near Syracuse (why were these in Odoacer's gift? We do not know, but the winner takes much, if not all). In addition, he had thrown in an entire island off the Croatian coast, Melita (now known as Mljet), worth an annual 200 solidi. Still, these donations did not add up to the full 690 annual solidi he had promised, only to 650, and the present donation is of three farms, *fundi*, that formed part of the same massive estate, the Massa Pyramitana, previously donated, together worth 40 solidi, and so bringing the donation up to the amount promised: these are the Fundus Aemilianus, worth 18 solidi; the fundus Budius, worth 15 solidi and 18 siliquae; and part of the Fundus Potaxia, worth 7 solidi (since the total exceeds 40, Pierius made a slight gain of 18 siliquae, there being 24 to the solidus).

If you imagined that a king could simply make a grant by issuing a sort of royal letter patent, that would be to underestimate the complexity of Roman legal procedures. In the first place, the king does not simply sign his own document. He instructs his Master of Offices (a role later held by Cassiodorus), the illustrious and magnificent Andromachus, to sign on his behalf the document drawn up by his notary Marcianus, whose rank of *vir clarissimus* puts him on a par with senators. Nor can signatures simply be taken for granted, for forgeries of documents of such value are rife, and the procedure involves a visit to Marcianus to authenticate the signature of Andromachus. But even with the signature authenticated, we are nowhere near what might be regarded as completion, the legal transfer of the property.

And this is where the *curia* comes in. Roman law required that acts involving transfer of real estate, donations, wills, and sales should be properly registered with the city council. A king Odoacer may be, but it is to the advantage of Pierius that he follow legal procedure. This involves appearing before the council in session, in public (*publicum*), presumably in the council building on the forum. Pierius, as tradition demands, sends a representative to plead on his behalf. In suitably polite terms, the representative addresses the council (*laudabilitas vestra*, Your Praiseworthiness, is the proper language), explains the situation, and requests the presiding magistrate, one Aurelius Virinus, and the council as a whole to embark on the procedure of registration, first verifying the signature of the Master of Offices. This involves the whole council rising and proceeding as a body to His Nobility the notary, presumably in his office in the royal palace nearby. Before they set out, Aurelius Virinus requests a reading of the document, which he treats, as coming from the king, with suitable reverence ('Let the document of the royal generosity offered to us be accepted with the deepest veneration and read out to a competent official'). Once the document has been authenticated by the notary, they return to their public place and set about registration. This involves the scrupulously recorded dialogue that characterises many of these documents (P. 10–11):

> And shortly afterwards having returned to the public, in the presence of the above named, the magistrate said:
>> 'Having received the reply of Marcianus, *vir clarissimus*, what further do the representatives here present wish to be done?'
>
> The representative of the illustrious and magnificent Pierius said:
>> 'We ask Your Praiseworthiness to give instructions to the competent officers to issue the record to us in the customary manner.'
>
> Aurelius Virinus the magistrate said:
>> 'As you request, the record will be issued to you in the customary manner.'
>
> Written below in a second hand:
>> 'I, Melminius Cassianus *vir clarissimus*, on behalf of Aurelius Virinus the magistrate, have verified the proceedings (*gesta*) held before him.' Signed: MELMINIUS
>
> The magistrates said:
>> 'The record shall be attached to the register. Hence, if there are any further actions, they should be added to the proceedings.'

The royal donation is now officially registered in the public archives, but we are far from through with the process, for the estates granted are in another jurisdiction, that of Syracuse. A further royal official now appears, Gregorius, Keeper of the Charters (*chartarium*), having been instructed to take part in the physical handover of the properties. The magistrates give him permission to enter, and he explains that he is required, together with Your Gravity (the chief magistrate) to go together to make the handover in person. The magistrate explains that city business requires him always to be present and he cannot leave (attractive though the prospect of a trip to Sicily might have been), and he deputes the leading councillor (*decemprimus*) Amantius, a *vir perfectissimus*, to go in his stead.

The party sets out together, and they reach the estates near Syracuse which they inspect ritually, 'calling together the tenants and workforce, and perambulating all the boundaries, boundary markers, fields, cultivated or uncultivated, and vineyards', inviting anyone who wished to challenge them. Nobody comes forward to gainsay change of ownership, so on the next day they present themselves to the assembled magistrates and council of Syracuse. Amantius, representing the Council of Ravenna, addresses the chief magistrate of Syracuse, and explains the royal donation and the fact that they have walked round the estates with nobody gainsaying. The magistrate invites the representative of Pierius, the new owner, to comment, and he requests that the name of the former owner be deleted from the public records (*polypticis publicis*) and the name of the new owner entered its place. At this point no fewer than three leading councillors – Flavius Annianus, Zeno, and his perfectissimus Petrus – declare the registration of the document and the account of the subsequent proceedings, and they sign those proceedings (Flavius Annianus doing so on behalf of his son Ennas, leading councillor). The deed is finally done.

Many features may strike us about this record. The first is the highly ritualised nature of proceedings. By no means is it a matter of merely signing the deeds and posting them to the registry office. It is a little drama, albeit of a ceremonial sort. The parties must meet and exchange words: we meet the same dialogue form in document after document, down to AD 804. It is not simply because it is a royal grant that such a fuss is made, for the same fuss is made for many others: bankers, retired soldiers, even a breech maker (*bracarius*).[13] Everybody is referred to in the language that suits their rank, from the glorious king and the magnificent Pierius, his nobility the notary, to their praiseworthinesses the magistrates (also Your Gravity), to Gregorius, sent on the trip to Italy, a *vir devotus*, an address marking a court official or army officer. The proceedings are drawn out in apparently interminable and repetitive exchanges; but these, as later 'formulae' laying out standard procedure reveal, are an essential feature of the ritual. You treat the city magistrate and his council with great respect: you do not simply say what you want, but wait for him to ask what you want, and whether there is anything further you require, though everyone involved is well aware that you simply want a document registered in the city archives. You do not even enter the council chamber without an explicit invitation from the magistrate. But though everything involves personal physical presence and reading aloud, not a mere exchange of written documents, surprisingly many of those involved depute to others,

---

[13] P. 14–15, see below.

from the King who deputes his signature to the Master of Offices, to the devoted Gregorius, deputed to make the journey to Sicily for the royal palace, and Amantius, deputed for the chief magistrate of Ravenna, and even Flavius Annianus, leading councillor of Syracuse, who is acting for his son.

There was doubtless a satisfaction for the members of a council in taking part in these rituals, enacting their place in a society which had long been sensitive to minute gradations in rank. That does not mean that such registrations were purely ceremonial. They had a clear practical purpose, which was of advantage to all parties involved. They were advantageous to the party registering the document. In a world in which forgery was rife, and public officials only too open to corruption, it was important to establish title to property in a way that was beyond question authentic. That is of course why the church of Ravenna, from which many of these documents derive, took care to preserve these documents on papyrus, some of them for centuries. The alternative, and nightmare, scenario, is set out by a law of Justinian dated to AD 535, the first consulship of Belisarius (the year in which the general, having completed his African campaign, launched his invasion of Italy). In the preamble to a law giving new powers to the local officials called *defensores* to maintain a public register in each city, he spells out the difficulties caused by the lack of authority of the *defensores*, their humble social origins, and their dependence on the arbitrary interference of the provincial governor:

> the result is that the officials, the municipal magistrates, and the citizens themselves have not the slightest respect for the *defensores* nor is any confidence reposed in the documents which they execute, and which the *defensores* themselves refuse to draw up if the Governor forbids them to do so; for, being absolutely subjected to his authority, they comply with his slightest inclinations. When documents are drawn up by them in the first place, they only do this for money; and then, as there are no archives in which these documents can be deposited, they are lost; and no monuments of former times are ever found in the possession of those who receive them, but when a demand is made upon their heirs or other successors, they either do not have them, or where any are found they are not worthy of consideration, or have been defaced to such an extent that they can no longer be deciphered. (*Novel* 15, trans. Scott)[14]

Justinian emphasises that the title of *defensor* reflects his duty to defend the rights of the people. It is in their interests to have a reliable public registration office, free from corruption, run by a reliable magistrate with

[14] See now Sarris, *The Novels of Justinian*, trans. Miller, pp. 185ff.

a staff and a physical office. Much of the seemingly redundant ritual of the registration process flows, it may be suggested, from the need to exclude all possibility of corruption and forgery: the fact that proceedings are held in a public place before the highest representatives of the city is a guarantee against malpractice. While reliable registration is in the interests of property owners, it is also very much in the interests of the local council. We know that *curiales* were, at least until a certain moment (doubtless different moments in different areas, and we are never quite sure when) responsible for the collection of taxes. We have met the bitter complaints of Salvian at the way the councillors abused this power and exploited the smaller landowners – *quot curiales, tot tyranni*. We have also met Cassiodorus' stern warning to the family of Agenantia that to have their names removed from the list of *curiales* and to become mere *possessores* is to subject themselves to unwelcome treatment by the those of the rank they have forfeited. To this we may add the voice of Pope Gregory (the Great) at the end of the sixth century, who in two letters to bishops warns them to be very careful whom they appoint to the priesthood, and to exclude people of questionable morals, especially bigamists, illiterates, and those liable to service on the council (*obnoxius curiae*), on the grounds that someone consecrated as a priest should not find themselves obliged to exact taxes.[15]

If the *curia* was indeed responsible for the collection of taxes, in Italy at least till the end of the sixth century, then it relied on keeping a land registry, which recorded not only the names of owners of each farm or estate, but also the annual rental, on which the tax would be based.[16] The proceedings before the council of Syracuse illustrate this process perfectly. It was not enough to register the deeds of ownership of Pierius' new estates at Ravenna: they also needed to go to Syracuse, verify the plots of land involved, present themselves to the council of Syracuse, and have the old owner's name struck from the public record, the *polyptychis publicis* (a polyptych being literally a document with many folds) and the new owner's name entered. Often part of the ceremony of registration is the undertaking by the representatives of the beneficiary to pay the fiscal dues. It is striking in this context how the value of the estates granted by Odoacer to Pierius is represented by their annual return, not their capital value or market price. The king has promised a gift worth 690 solidi of annual rent; of their capital value there is no mention. Each property, each *fundus*, has a precise rental value attached to it: the fundus Budius is

---

[15] Ewald and Hartmann, Pope Gregory, *Registrum Epistolarum*, II.37 (to the bishop of Squillace) and IV.26 (to the bishop of Cagliari).

[16] See Arends, *Fragments from the Past*.

worth 15 solidi and 18 siliquae. This expression of rental value is met repeatedly in the documents. Thus P. 3, a probable registration document of the mid sixth century, lists two batches, each of ten or so properties, the second in the territory of Padua, with rental values varying between 13 solidi and 13 siliquae at the top, and 2 solidi and 2 siliquae at the bottom.[17] Revealingly, the document adds the number of 'voluntary' prestations in kind (*xenia*) the landlord can expect in addition: precise numbers for each *fundus* of pounds of pork, geese, hens, eggs, honey, and milk. The total value of these prestations among all the farms owned is 888 hens, 266 pullets, 8,880 eggs, 3,760 pounds of pork, and 3,450 of honey. Such prestations, unlike the rental, were presumably tax free.

There is a broader point, linked to that about rents and taxes, that concerns the nature of landholding. The documents, including Odoacer's donation, talk about *fundi* and *massae*. These terms correspond neither to 'farms' nor 'estates' in English. The *fundus* is a unit of land ownership that may amount to no more than a few acres. It may or may not come complete with its own buildings, and when there is a farmhouse, a *casale*, the documents tend to specify it.[18] A *massa*, on the other hand, is an amalgamation of *fundi*, normally under single ownership. It may be quite extensive, as the Massa Pyramitana donated to Pierius evidently was. In the early seventh century, P. 17 shows us Flavia Xanthippe, daughter of Megistus, of the imperial department *a secretis*, donating to the church of S. Maria Maggiore in Rome the Massa Paganicense together with all its *fundi* and farm buildings (*casalibus*), and these *fundi* are then itemised, running to thirty in all (we may note that several are called after their buildings: the Casa Porcinare, Casa Viti, Casa Lari, Casa Basili, Casa Gini, and Tris Casas).[19] Much of this language survives to this day in Italy, especially the south, where a plot of land may be a *fondo*, and a large estate a *masseria*, a *casa*, or a *casale*, and even a village may be Trecase, 'three farms' rather than 'three houses'.

While a *massa* was an accumulation of presumably contiguous *fundi*, it was perfectly possible to own a portfolio of scattered *fundi*, even of several *massae*, and not necessarily in the same city's territory.[20] Pierius' holdings, as

---

[17] Tjäder vol. 1, pp. 184–189.
[18] P. 36, late sixth century, Deusdedit sells Hildigernus 6/12ths of the Fundus Genicianus in the territory of Rimini *cum casale* (line 16); P. 44, mid seventh century, the archbishop of Ravenna gives a permanent lease of the Massa Uttianus '*cum omnibus fundis, casalibus vel [a]ppennicibus*; P. 35 of AD572, Domninus sells Deusdedit 5/12ths of the Fundus Custinis in the territory of Rimini and 2/12ths of the casale belonging to it called Bassianum; P. 17, early seventh century, Flavia Xanthippe donates Massa Paganicense *cum fundis et casalibus suis*.
[19] Tjäder vol. 1, pp. 327–334.
[20] On the term *massa*, distinctive of peninsular Italy in Late Antiquity, Vera, '*Massa fundorum*'.

we have seen, were in Sicily and on the Dalmatian island of Melita. In what is probably the earliest surviving specimen of these documentary papyri (P. 1), of AD 445–446, Lauricius, chief chamberlain to Honorius at the court of Ravenna, lists the rents due on his extensive holdings in Sicily, including three *massae* (the Massa Emporitana, at 756 solidi, the massa Fadilianensis at 445, and the massa Cassitana at 500), plus four *fundi* for smaller sums, the whole amounting to 2,175 solidi – a sum that dwarfs the donation to Pierius.[21] At a more modest scale, in a donation to the church of Ravenna dated to 4th April AD 553, a lady with the Gothic name of Ranilo, and a husband called Felithanc, both of very high status (*sublimes*), donate to the church of Ravenna land inherited from her father Aderit, on condition that the church pay an annual income of 15 pounds of silver to her illegitimate half-brother Ademunt, also called Andreas (P. 13).[22] The estates concerned are the Massa Formidiana in the territory of Urbino and another (name lost) in the territory of Lucca; the church is to have six twelfths of these properties, though here the rental value is not stated.

Landholdings could be accumulated; but they could also be divided. The holdings involved are frequently subdivided into twelfths, *unciae*, so that a donation may be of two or four or six *unciae*. This surely does not mean that the land was divided into strips, but that its rental value could be so divided. A *fundus* is a subdivisible unit of ownership or investment, like stocks and shares. Many of those involved in such ownership are by no stretch of the imagination farmers, but rather property owners, bankers, businessmen, and court and army officials. They are *rentiers*, who have no need to live on the land they own, which is worked by slaves or free peasants tied to the land (*adscripti glebae* was the technical term). The owners were free to live in the city, drawing an income from their rents, but enjoying the amenities of city life. If the rich were to flee the city for their country estates, as Cassiodorus feared in Bruttium, they would have to decide which of their portfolio of properties to live on. This is a pattern that survived in Italy tenaciously from Antiquity through the Middle Ages into the Early Modern period, like those Sicilian towns which Leonardo Sciascia evokes, where the local landowners live in palazzi on the main street of the town and meet together in the *circolo* on the main *piazza*, to sort out the life of the town, with or without the help of the *mafia*.

This perception of landholdings as divisible units with known rental values, registered in the *acta* of the local city council, and liable thereby for

---

[21] Tjäder vol. 1, pp. 168–178; Herrin, *Ravenna*, pp. 65–66.
[22] Tjäder vol. 1, pp. 300–308; Herrin, *Ravenna*, p. 194.

tax, might arguably help to explain a well-known puzzle: how did Odoacer and, after him, Theoderic grant one third of the land of Italy to their Gothic followers, even, as Cassiodorus claimed (*Variae* 2.16), dividing the soil between Goths and Romans without provoking the slightest tension between them? Walter Goffart suggested that what the Goths received was one third of the taxes otherwise owed to the treasury.[23] This ingenious solution – that they received taxes not actual land – is hard to reconcile with Cassiodorus' language of division of the soil (*caespitis divisio*). Goffart dismissed the possibility that the revenue of the landholdings itself was divided:

> Besides, how would the 'revenue' of landowners have been determined and checked? Did every piece of Italian property have an officially known rental (in money) of which one third could have been levied? (p. 75)

What the papyri suggest is precisely that: each *curia* kept registers of all landholdings in its territory, together with their rental value. Just as you might donate six twelfths of your estate to the church without putting up a boundary fence, but simply splitting the rent, you might be forced to surrender four twelfths (one third) to the new Gothic landlords. That the old owners should have accepted this cheerfully, as Cassiodorus claims, is hard to believe, but at least it was a division which technically could be carried out.

Land plays the primary role in all exchanges to do with property in the documentary papyri. So much is only to be expected of a principally agrarian economy. But urban property too plays a minor role; houses mattered as well as fields. A respectable lady (*femina spectabilis*) called Maria, newly widowed, writes in January AD 491, when Ravenna is under siege by Theoderic, to donate to the church of Ravenna her home, a house called Domicilium in the territory of Forum Cornelii, modern Imola, outside Ravenna (P. 12).[24] This is a *casa* (*casam iuris mei cui vocabulum Domicilium in Corneliense territorio*), whereas houses in cities are still usually *domus*, and *casa* may often be a plot of land or *fundus* with a house, as in the case of Flavia Xanthippe's holdings. 'Home farm' might catch it better. Distinctly urban, however, is the house sold and registered by Theodorus the banker in AD 616–619 (P. 38–41).[25] What he sold was

---

[23] Goffart, *Barbarians and Romans*, esp. pp. 58–102 for Italy; much disputed, see Halsall, 'The technique of Barbarian settlement'; Porena, *L'insediamento degli Ostrogoti*; Porena and Rivière, *Expropriations et confiscations*. Goffart was well aware of the Ravenna papyri, his interpretation of which was forced: 'From Roman taxation to medieval seigneurie'.

[24] Tjäder vol. 1, pp. 294–299.   [25] Tjäder vol. 2, pp. 126–138.

> six twelfths of a house with upper floors (*domus caenacolata*) with its upper and lower floors and its own ground floor (*solum*) and portico with courtyard and service quarters with upper rooms (*familiarica caenacolata*) with its own ground floor as well as the usage of the well and passageway (*androna*) which stretches to the bank of the river Po, with rights of entrance and exit and all general appurtenances, which came to me in payment of the debt of the late Tzitta, major-domo of John of glorious memory, patrician and exarch of Italy on the judgement of the most eloquent Procopius, counsellor to the most excellent Eleutherius, head of Imperial Protocol.

In Roman law, if you owned the ground (*solum*), you also owned everything built above it, so Theodorus specifies this feature for both the main house and its service quarters.

A very similar, but even grander, city house in Ravenna is leased in perpetuity in the mid seventh century by the archbishop of Ravenna to the prefect in Ravenna, the glorious Theodorus, also known as Calliopa ('Fair Face') (P. 44).[26] The package concerned includes extensive estates, the Massa Uttianus with all its *fundi*, farm houses and appendages, olive groves, woods, meadows, and pastures in the territory of Rimini, plus a town house, or rather half of it:

> Six twelfths of the house (*domus*) situated in the city of Ariminium together with its courtyard, service quarters and all its parts, which house is constructed of mortared limestone up to the rafters, and roofed with tiles and hip tiles, above the forum (*super foro*).

In the repetitive fashion of these documents, the house is described again in greater detail:

> six twelfths of the house together with its upper floors and lower floors (*superioribus et inferioribus*) and six twelfths of the service quarters (*familiarica*), courtyard and small garden plot, and all its appurtenances and dependances, and four twelfths of the bath suite (*balneum*) together with its basin, pipes and all its equipment and the garden of the aforesaid house, which house is constructed in mortared limestone (*calce qaimento*) up to the rafters, with tiles and hip tiles, together with its roofed service quarter, with well and well-head (*puteal*) and a stone chest in the courtyard but also the bakery within the aforesaid service quarters together with oven, grinders and wheel.

The description might well fit some of the grander houses in Pompeii, built of *opus caementicium* with a tiled roof (counting the tiles was a way of

---

[26] Tjäder vol. 2, pp. 172–179.

establishing the size of a council member's house in a Roman city), and not only separate space for slaves, but baths, mills, and an oven. This is a substantial house. All that is missing from the description compared to Pompeii is decoration – frescoes and mosaics – but then Pompeii was at the heart of empire in a period of boom prosperity, and silence at Ravenna is not necessarily absence. Nevertheless, the elite of Ravenna knew how to live in style. The only feature that puzzles is how you can own one half of a house, yet only one third of its bath suite; but this underlines how, like a *fundus*, urban property was an asset divisible into twelfths.

Land and houses are the principal assets met in these documents. But just occasionally, we get a glimpse of the furniture, household items, and objects of value that go to make up a full household inventory. Germana, the widow of Callictus, inherited one third of her husband's estate. In a document registered with the council on 17 July AD 564, she enumerates in unusual detail what that estate consisted of (P. 8).[27] Above all, houses and land: two houses in Ravenna, two twelfths of a *domus* near St. Agatha, four twelfths of another behind the basilica of St. Victor, four twelfths of a country house called the Casa Nova in the territory of Ravenna, two twelfths of the Fundus Savilianus and of the Casale Petronianum in the territory of Bononia (Bologna), one twelfth of the Fundus Veratinanus in the same territory; several other properties of which the details are lost in a lacuna, plus one further house, a *domus* in the territory of Forum Cornelii (Imola). Here again we see how a portfolio could consist of properties, rural and urban, in several different city territories, while at the same time, thanks not least to partible inheritance, the holdings in each case might be only a fraction of the whole. But the particular glory of the document lies in its careful enumeration of household items, valued in all at 45 solidi, 23 siliquae, and 60 gold *nummi*: these include 2 pounds of silver, including 7 spoons; 2 coloured carpets, worth 1 solidus and 1 tremis (third); an embroidered cover worth 1 solidus; a half-silk shirt in scarlet and green worth 3.5 solidi, a short-sleeved silk shirt worth 2 gold siliquae; linen breeches worth 1 siliqua; and so on, with a long list of over 30 items – pots, jugs, lamps, barrels, a grain chest, agricultural tools, chairs, tables – and, at the end of a long list of chattels, one slave called Proiectus. Again, we might easily be in Pompeii with the inventory of finds of a large house made by the excavators.

This is not the end of it, for in addition there is a freed slave (*libertus*) called Guderit who has also died, and who had his own belongings:

---

[27] Tjäder vol. 1, pp. 235–246.

a lockable iron-bound chest worth 2 gold siliquae, another chest worth 1 siliqua and an *asprio* (one can imagine how important such a chest was to a slave, in which to stash away anything of value he acquired over the years); an old iron pot (*cocumella*) with a handle, weighing 1.5 pounds; another pot (*caccavellum*), broken, weighing one pound; a heavy iron chain to hang over the fire; a whetstone; a broken bread-baker; various other pots and tools, some broken; an old dyed silk shirt worth 3 gold siliquae; an embroidered shirt worth 6 siliquae; a cloth (*mappa*) worth 1 asprio-siliqua, an old cloak, and an old travel cloak. The difference between the number, quality, and condition of the possessions of the slave and those of the masters is stark, but it is a rare privilege to know in such detail what the material world of a relatively privileged slave (unlike Proiectus, who has nothing) might look like.

While these documents give us an insight into a world of material possessions – possessions which churches were only too keen to inherit or receive by donation, whence the survival of such records – it was not the only type of business brought before the *curia*, simply the business most likely to survive in the church archives. One exception is P. 7, of AD 557, a record of proceedings before the ordo of Rieti, in which Gundihild, *inlustris femina*, widow of Gudahals, and mother of Lendarit and Landarit, requests the council to appoint tutors for her sons. While their names suggest Gothic background (the husband sounds like an officer in the Gothic army), her high rank points to wealth, and the appointment of a tutor will be because the sons are minors but heirs to significant estates – estates which doubtless eventually ended up in the hands of the church of Ravenna.[28] There is already a legal case over this inheritance, brought by Adiud, *inlustris vir*, and Rosemud known as Faffo. Liberatus, a *vir honestus*, is then invited by the council to take on the role of tutor, and one may guess that, despite his lower social standing than that of Adiud, he succeeded in protecting the sons and their property rights.

Even though the records are largely concerned with property, they illuminate much else, in particular the social spectrum. Naturally, the donors or testators tend to be well-off, with several being of very high social status; but we also meet those they called in as witnesses, and those who took part in the elaborate ritual of registration. We have already met

---

[28] On Gothic names in the papyri, see Herrin, *Ravenna*, pp. 194–195. On Goths in Ravenna, Lazard, 'Goti e Latini in Ravenna'; Amory, *People and Identity*, esp. pp. 86–108 and pp. 348–486 (Prosopographical Index: a prosopography of Goths in Italy). On the disappearance of the Goths in Italy, see Cosentino, 'Social instability'. See Pohl, 'Social Cohesion', pp. 30–31 on the integration of Goths into Roman society documented by the papyri.

a cluster of high-ranking members of the court of Odoacer. In Ravenna – a court centre first for Gothic kings, then for Byzantine exarchs – it is no surprise to run into officials and army officers. When in AD 539 one Thulgilo, honourable lady (*femina honesta*) is left property by her late husband, Pario, she and her children, Domnica and Deutherius, decide to sell 20 *iugera* (c. 5 hectares) of the Fundus Concordiacus in the territory of Faenza and the village (*pagus*) of Painatis, good land planted with trees, for 120 gold solidi. She specifies the neighbours to the land: Secundus, a military speedboat man (*dromonarius*), Witterit, a shield bearer (*scutarius*), and the late Andreas, commander of the speedboat division; evidently, the Gothic command had been distributing land to its loyal supporters, and Goths have become entangled with Romans in the patterns of ownership (P. 30).[29] She also calls in as witnesses those presumably of her husband's social circle: Serapio, *vir strenuus*, military adjutant from the bureau of couriers; Opilio, another *vir strenuus*, guardsman to the prefect; Julianus, banker and stepson of the paint-merchant (*pigmentarius*) Johannes (Julianus signs in Greek); Petrus, *vir honestus*, cashier; and Latinus, *vir honestus*, patron of the corporation of landowners. From their names one might guess that some are Goths, some Romans or Greeks, but Latinus causes pause for thought, for instead of signing 'ego Latinus' for 'I Latinus', he writes '[I]cc', the German 'ich'.[30] Four others, grander in status than the witnesses, have observed proceedings without gainsaying them: Candidianus, *vir laudabilis* (so a *curialis*); Generosus, an Augustalis (a senior official of the prefecture); Armentarius from the prefect's office; and Eusebius, Royal Vittler (*obsonator domini nostri*). It is worth recalling that Cassiodorus himself was praetorian prefect in Ravenna until 538, the year before this transaction. King Witigis surrendered to Belisarius in 540, the year following the transaction. This collection of military officers and officials from the prefect's office must have been well known to Cassiodorus. The Royal Vittler was responsible for providing delicacies (*opsonia*) for the royal table. In view of Cassiodorus' letters encouraging cities to supply such delicacies (*Variae* 12.12), he must have known Eusebius well.

We meet a further cluster of Gothic names in the years following the fall of Witigis. Most striking is a sale of land by the priest of the 'Gothic' (i.e. Arian) church of St. Anastasia, their basilica, to Petrus the *defensor* of the Catholic church in payment of a debt (P. 34).[31] The year is AD 551 (day and month are lost), the year in which Narses was sent by Justinian

---

[29] Tjäder vol. 2, pp. 55–62.   [30] Tjäder vol. 2, p. 260 for the reading Icc.
[31] Tjäder vol. 2, pp. 91–104; Herrin, *Ravenna*, pp. 194–197.

with the new and larger army which finally defeated Totila in the following year. Why the Gothic church is settling debts with the Catholic church is not explained, but they are evidently under pressure. They make over for 180 solidi eight twelfths of the type of wetland typical of the Po delta, a *palus*. Deusdedit, the legal representative (*forensis*) of the city of Classis of Ravenna (home to the Catholic church of S. Apollinare in Classe, dedicated in 549) draws up the document and undertakes to have it registered in the city archives (*alligandi archivialibus gestis*). Then follow the signatures of witnesses, and it is clear that in order to demonstrate the full consent of the Arian church, they ask as many as nineteen of the clergy to sign. This they do, most with Gothic, though some with Latin names. The text gives all names in Latin script, but the signatures are in Latin or Gothic script according to individual choice. There are two priests (*presbyter*), Optarit, signing in Gothic as Ufitahari papa, and Vitalianus signing in Latin. The deacon, Suniefridus, signs in Gothic as Sunjaifrithas diakon. The subdeacon Petrus signs in Latin. Of the two *clerici*, Wiliarit has lost his eyesight to old age and cannot sign; Paulus signs in Latin. Then there are 5 *spodei*, apparently Greek *spoudaioi*, who may be seen as lay members, Minnulus signing as Willienant in Latin, Danihel as Igila also in Latin, Theudila, also in Latin, Mirica signing in Gothic as Merila, then Sindila, being illiterate, signs with a cross. After them there are five *ostiarii*, attendants, none of whom can write: Costila, Gudeclivus, Guderit, Hosbut, and Benenatus; and, finally, two further *spodei* sign: Wiliarit (different from the priest of that name), signing in Gothic as Wiljarith, and Amalatheus, whose signature is lost. Somehow that list of signatories, making over their land to the Catholics shortly before Justinian was to deprive the Gothic church of all its holdings, illuminates the degree to which 'Goths' and 'Romans' were only partially integrated and could keep separate identities.[32]

If Goths could use name-forms, language, and script as well as religion to mark themselves as 'other' in a Roman world, the curial elite could use name-forms to mark themselves as other than less elevated sorts, Goth or Roman. It has been remarked that the 'disappearance of the old order' is most evident 'in the system of name giving', with the old Roman system of multiple names giving way to a single name. So Cassiodorus – in full, Flavius Magnus Aurelius Cassiodorus Senator – is seen as of the last to hold old-style multiple names.[33] Statistically, even the elite adopted the new single-name fashion. But if so, at least in the very formal context of council

---

[32] See Gheller, '"*Identità*" e "*arianesimo gotico*"'.
[33] Brown, *Gentlemen and Officers*, p. 20; cf. Herrin, *Ravenna*, p. 219.

proceedings, the *curiales* clung on to the old ways until the mid sixth century. The best illustration is P. 4–5, an unusual document in which a group of six wills is taken to the Pretorian Prefect in Ravenna for verification.[34] This verification takes place in the mid 550s, after the latest of the wills, dated to 3 January 552, though they go back to the late fifth century, the earliest date being 4 November 474. Some sort of reorganisation seems to be going on in the Catholic church in the aftermath of Narses' defeat of the Goths. The fact that their authenticity might be questioned so many years later illustrates the importance of the whole elaborate procedure of registration in the archives.

In each of these documents, the city magistrates and councillors involved almost invariably bear double names in the traditional fashion, whereas the testators and witness only sometimes do so. In the naming system of the early empire, there were three elements: *praenomen*, *nomen*, and *cognomen* (Marcus Tullius Cicero); of these the *nomen* is the family name, usually in adjectival form (member of the Tullian *gens*), the *cognomen* is more personal and how someone is generally known (Cicero). The use of the *praenomen* had already died out in the early empire.[35] After Caracalla's extension of citizenship, Aurelius became a sort of default *nomen*, often abbreviated to 'Aur.', and little used because so common. After Constantine, Flavius become the default name, abbreviated to Fl. Those with more of a family history made less use of the default names. So we find that in the oldest will in this batch,[36] dated to 5 November 474, and giving Leo Junior as emperor (Leo II became emperor on the death of his grandfather Leo I on 18 January 474, but died on 10 November of the same year, just five days after the date of this document), the testator is a Flavius, Fl. Constantius, *vir honestus*, public dyer to the city (*tinctor publicus*), and the witnesses Fl. Bonifatius, *vir devotus*, the prefect's attendant (*apparitor*), Fl. Probatius, *vir devotus*, and perhaps Fl. Heraclius; they mention as other witnesses not present Simplicius, Exuperantius, Pamonius, and Georgius. If the last three, all *viri devoti*, so probably officials, had a *nomen*, it will have been Flavius. The magistrates and leading councillors, *principales*, offer a contrast. One magistrate is a Flavius, Fl. Proiectus,[37] the other is Pompulius Proiectus Junior, and the councillors are Aelius Marinus, Commodianus Constantius Junior, Tremodius Victor, Popilius Calomniosus, and Melminius Cassianus. This

---

[34] Tjäder vol. 1, pp. 198–217. [35] See Salway, 'What's in a name?'
[36] P. 4–5, lines B.III,8–B.IV,6 (Tjäder pp. 208–210; unfortunately his text does not mark clearly breaks between the different documents).
[37] Proiectus is also named in the fragmentary P. 12 of AD 491 as *quinquennalis*.

attachment to family names makes sense in an elite which was by definition hereditary, and indeed some of these are family names which recur, especially the Pompulii and the all-too dominant Melminii.[38] The attachment of 'Junior' to the name reflects the same social pattern: son followed father on the council, and that was a matter of family pride (just as the emperor might call himself Leo Junior).[39] We may also note that Popilius Calomniosus is following an aristocratic trend of apparently insulting nicknames (like the South Italian *ingiuria*), in the same style as the contemporary senator and consul Inportunus (Cassiodorus *Variae* 1.27).

This pattern becomes more marked with the passage of time. In AD 474, after all, the old Roman order still just about prevailed (if having a Roman emperor, in name at least, symbolically marked that). But even in AD 521, the council looks much the same:[40] the presiding magistrate is Fl. Florianus, *vir laudabilis* (the councillors are always *laudabiles*), acting for his son Severus, the quinquennial magistrate, and the principal councillors in attendance are Firmanus Ursus, Melminius Tranquillus acting for his son Johannes, Studentius (exceptionally without a family name), and Pompulius Severus, acting for Melminius Cassianus Junior. The witnesses are Probinus, *vir spectabilis*, Severus (of the same rank), Amatius and Flavianus, *vir devotus*. The testator is the archbishop himself, who has two names: Caelius Aurelianus.

The last of these wills belongs to AD 552.[41] By now the consulship has been abolished, and the date is fixed as eleven years after the consulship of Basilius Junior and the twenty-fifth year of Justinian's reign (541). Had they given Basilius, last of the annual consuls, his full name, it would be Anicius Faustus Albinus Basilius, with the polyonymy of the high Roman aristocracy. The council is now represented by Melminius Andreas, *vir clarissimus*, the *defensor*; Pompulius Bonifatius the quinquennial magistrate, with present as principal councillors Melminius Cassianus and Melminius Bonifatius, a Theodosius with only one name (unless he too is a Melminius), and Pompulius Plautus. The dominance of the Melminii and Pompulii has become overwhelming. The testator is one Georgius, *vir devotus*, a pure silk merchant (*olosiricoprata*), and his witnesses seem to be drawn from the top echelon of Ravenna's business community: Vitalis the banker (*argentarius*);

---

[38] See Brown, *Gentlemen and Officers*, p. 216 for the Pompulii and Melminii, pointing out that these families are not attested from the seventh century, but this type of evidence also disappears then; see Herrin, *Ravenna* pp. 27–28.

[39] On the use of Junior for consuls' names, see Cameron, 'Junior consuls'.

[40] P. 4–5, lines B.IV,6–B.V,11 (Tjäder pp. 210–212).

[41] P. 4–5, lines B.V,1–B. VII,11 (Tjäder pp. 212–216).

Theodolus, another pure silk merchant; Ammonius, another banker; and Laurentius, a fleece merchant (*gunnarius*).[42] Despite the fact that these evidently rich bankers and merchants had each only one name, the first three of them are labelled as *viri clarissimi*, an address formerly for those of senatorial rank. But the most startling of all these names is that of the Pretorian Prefect before whom these proceedings were held. Initially named as Flavius Aurelianus, when it comes to signing off the document he gives his full name: Flavius Marianus Mihahelius Gabrihelius Petrus Johannes Narses Aurelianus Limenius Stephanus Aurelianus, *vir gloriossimus*. Amidst his collection of biblical and Roman names, one sticks out: that of Narses. A distinctive Perso-Armenian name, its only other bearer in the west known to us was Justinian's general. In a document dated to the very year of his campaign against Totila, one might think it was the general himself, except that, glorious though the position of Pretorian Prefect was, it was too low for Narses, who in any case was too busy at this moment for such proceedings.[43] It looks as if the Pretorian Prefect took his name among his many others as an act of flattery.

Little has changed by 14 February 572 when the breeches maker (*bracarius*) Bonus and his wife Martyria hand over half of all their substance to the church (P. 14–15).[44] By now the council seems to have become the family business of the Melminii. The line-up includes Melminius Bonifatius, Melminius Laurentius, and Melminius Johannes Junior, though there is also one Theodosius. The name of the registry clerk (*exceptor*) by contrast is Gunderit.

Names, as ever, may reveal much about a person: potentially ethnicity and social standing (as well as gender). The use of traditional Roman names in the Council of Ravenna until at least the mid sixth century suggests a pride in the hereditary membership of that body. The rich haul of documents reassures us that plenty of cities of Italy (not just Ravenna, for others like Rimini, Syracuse and Rome were involved) still had functioning city councils, and a practice of formal registration of property transfers, a full century after the last western emperor was deposed. But how long was such a pattern sustained? It is tempting to imagine that the distribution of papyri mirrors the distribution of actual practice, and as the papyri thin out towards the end of the sixth century, to peter out in the early seventh, this reflects an actual disappearance of the old civic institutions on the ground. Unfortunately, our fifty-five or so papyri cannot count as a randomised sample. Nearly all – indeed, perhaps all – these papyri come from the archive of the Archbishop of Ravenna. Yet every

---

[42] Tjäder translates as Fellhändler; cf. Herrin, *Ravenna*, p. 196. [43] See Tjäder vol. 1, p. 202.
[44] P. 14–15, Tjäder vol.1, pp. 308–317.

single Italian city must once have had its archive, as was enjoined in law and illustrated by the registration proceedings. Not one single example of these survives. And what we have from Ravenna is far from a full and curated collection. On the contrary, the Ravenna archive suffered a succession of traumas, with three successive sacks of the city between the seventh and tenth centuries, and a final devastating sack by French troops in 1512. At this point, what survives of the papyrus archive was dispersed, first into the hands of private collectors, then into museums and libraries: the fifty-five papyri of the published Ravenna collection are housed in twenty separate collections, in Italy, France, Great Britain, and Switzerland, and two in the United States (Princeton and Titusville, Pennsylvania), while the Ravenna archive itself preserves only three papyrus fragments.[45] By chance, a fine specimen made its way to the Cambridge University Library (Figure 6.1).

What survives by chance, indeed by fluke. If there are more fragments from the fifth and sixth centuries than from the seventh, it is not safe to infer that such documents ceased to be produced in the seventh century. The last papyrus from the Italian collection to mention registration in the municipal archives is dated to May/June AD 625, when Deusdedit and his wife Melissa donate to the church for the saving of their souls half their

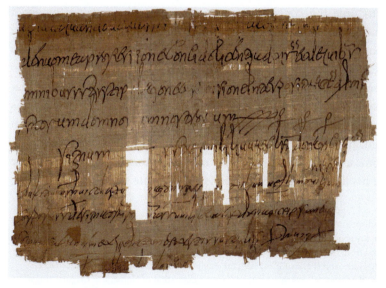

Figure 6.1 Example of papyrus from Ravenna archive, p. 28. Cambridge University Library Add.ms.4076, with permission.

---

[45] A story well told by Sansoni, 'I papiri di Ravenna'.

property, mobile, immobile, and self-propelled (i.e. slaves and animals), including all of their furniture, consisting in a city house next to the gate of St Apollinaris and the arch of St George, together with a small orchard next to the house, with its own entrance and exit, complete with bakery and guest suites with their own courtyard, and the Fundus Carpinianus (P. 25).[46] The proceedings are held before the *curia* because the council secretary, Donus, is quoted addressing 'Your Praiseworthiness' (*laudabilitas vestra*) and asking permission for someone who is standing outside the doors, presumably the representative of Deusdedit, to come in and address them. Unfortunately in its fragmentary state the papyrus does not reveal who was present to hear the act of donation, but at least it confirms that the council and the public registry was still in business.

Curiae and Municipal Records in Gregory the Great

We need to pay attention to evidence beyond the surviving papyri. Pope Gregory the Great, in his abundant collection of letters, takes for granted both the functioning of city council and the process of registration in the municipal archives at the end of the sixth and beginning of the seventh century (590–604).[47] When there is a bishop to be elected and he writes to a city to urge the community to appoint someone suitable (or avoid someone unsuitable), he addresses himself formulaically to 'clergy, council and people' (*clero ordini populo*) of such and such a city. *Ordo* (or *ordo curiae*) is the 'correct' traditional Latin term for a city council. He so addresses some eighteen separate Italian cities.[48] One might suspect that precisely because this form of address for a city community as a whole was formulaic, it did not match up to contemporary realities. But a formula can be varied, and Gregory did on occasion vary his formula: writing to Rimini (but not elsewhere) he puts the local military commander, the *dux*, at the head of his list; writing to Salona in Istria he wrote to 'clergy and nobles';

---

[46] Tjäder vol.1, pp. 376–380; cf. Herrin, *Ravenna*, p. 219.
[47] The indispensable introduction to Gregory is Markus, *Gregory the Great*. Surprisingly, he has little to say about cities in Gregory (his index has no entry for 'city' or 'civitas'). The letters here are cited from the MGH second edition of the *Registrum Epistolarum* by Paul Ewald and Ludwig Hartmann (Berlin 1887–1899); the English translation by Martyn, *The Letters of Gregory the Great*, follows the slightly different numeration of Norberg, *S. Gregorii Magni Registrum Epistolarum*.
[48] I.58 Perusia, I.78 Bevagna, II.12 Naples, II.14 Nepe, II.40 Crotone, III.11 Alba, III.14 Terracina, IV.39 Ortona, V.22 Ravenna, VI.26 Salona, IX.81 Miseno, IX.100 Osimo, IX.185 Todi (read Tudinae for Tadinae), IX.210 Rimini, XIII.17 Palermo, XIII.20 Taurum, Turris and Cosenza. Turris is taken to be Porto Torres in Sardinia, though proximity to Cosenza makes Thurii more likely.

writing to Naples he puts 'clergy, nobles, council and people'; and on one occasion, writing to Ravenna, he elaborates 'to the commanders, nobles, clergy, monks, soldiers in service and people', omitting the council, though we know of course that Ravenna had a *curia* still functioning.[49] The *nobiles* he addresses are surely the members of the *ordo*.

We do not need to judge the civic structures of Italy from the address labels on his correspondence, for the letters themselves offer a rich picture of a world of cities. The word *civitas* is recurrent: he will refer to cities adjectivally, as the *civitas Tarentina*, rather than *Tarentum*; there are no fewer than ninety-two *civitates* so named in his letters, not only in Italy but across the Mediterranean world.[50] The densest cluster of cities is of course in Italy, where some 100 are named either as civitates or as bishoprics, with a further dozen in Sicily. Including the whole Mediterranean, the number rises to some 160.[51] Cities form the network by which he holds together the Catholic church. That web, at the centre of which he sits in Rome, is directly derived from the administrative system of the Roman Empire. If Cassiodorus offers us the image of a late Roman official running the system in the early sixth century, Gregory at the end of that century is every inch a late Roman official running his empire of faith, one rooted in the old empire.[52] *Civitates* are both the most important centres of habitation and the territorial system by which his Catholic empire is articulated: the same word refers to the walled centre, and monasteries and churches may be described as *intra civitatem*, but at the same time it refers to the whole territory for which a bishop has responsibility. Some of these *civitates* are minor settlements, which may be referred to as *castra*, like 'Caesenas castrum', modern Cesena: having a walled settlement of any sort was a major advantage when hostile raiders ravaged the land, especially the feared and hated Lombards. Broadly, the equation bishopric = city works, even if some were small; the names of the vast majority of Gregory's cities are recognisable in the urban map of modern Italy (see Figure 6.2).

---

[49] Addresses include *duci clero ordini et plebi civitatis Ariminensis* (I.56); *clero nobilibus Salonis consistentibus* (VI.26); *clero nobilibus ordini et plebi consistenti Neapolim* (II.5); *ducibus, nobilibus, clericis, monachis, militibus militantibus et populo in Ravenna civitate consistentibus vel ex ea foris degentibus* (VII.42).

[50] See the careful index in the MGH edition of Ewald and Hartmann, vol. II, p. 525, s.v. *civitas*; see also Figure 6.2.

[51] See the index in Hartmann's edition vol. II, p. 494 s.v. Italia: this helpfully lists all the dioceses in Italy mentioned in the letters, drawing attention to the comparable index in the MGH edition of Cassiodorus, p. 505, s.v. Italia, listing the 125 dioceses of Italy represented at the three Roman synods under Theoderic.

[52] Markus, *Gregory the Great*, p. 8, notes that Gregory of Tours exaggerated in attributing his namesake to a 'senatorial' family; but Gregory's use of the term 'senatorial' was imprecise, covering *curiales*, see Chapter 7.

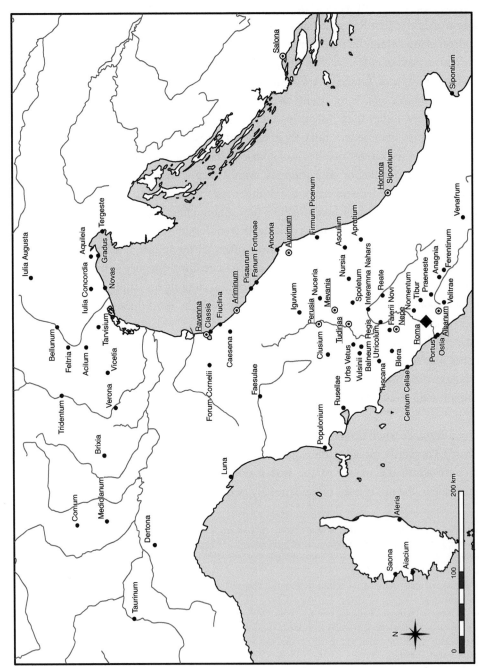

Figure 6.2 Civitates in Gregory the Great's *Registrum* (drawn by Javier Martínez Jiménez).

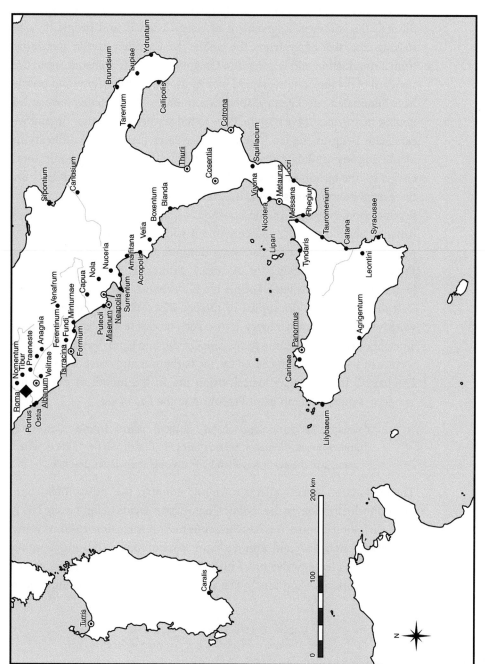

Figure 6.2 (cont.)

Gregory's Italy is anything but peaceful. Many of the bishoprics are unoccupied, and he urges the bishop of some nearby city to act as 'visitor' and set about the appointment of a new bishop, ideally to be achieved through the consensual agreement of clergy, council, and people. In one striking case, that of Syracuse, the 'nobles' have written to him abstaining from a nomination and leaving it to Gregory to identify someone up to the standard of the previous bishop, Maximianus. Meanwhile, clergy and people have nominated one Agathus, about whom the nobles evidently have grave doubts: hence, they leave it to the Pope to judge whether Agathus or another candidate is up to the job.[53] But in other cases there is real difficulty in identifying any candidate at all, who should ideally be chosen from the local clergy; so, the bishop of Agropoli in Puglia is urged to find candidates for three neighbouring cities: Velia, Buxentum, and Blanda.[54] But when there is depopulation, especially in consequence of Lombard raids, it is sometimes better to abandon a city, and combine it with a neighbouring church: so Minturnae, on the coastal flat, is so destitute that the bishop of nearby Formia takes responsibility for the area.[55] Minturnae today is an archaeological site, while castellated Formia is a busy centre.

If the occasional unoccupied or merged dioceses shows an urban network under pressure, Gregory is the very model of resilience: he finds a neighbouring city to come to the aid. On the one hand, he paints a vivid picture of the devastation caused by 'the barbarous and cruel nation of the Lombards'. In the eschatological vision put in the mouth of one of his 'modern' saints, Redemptus of Ferentum in the *Dialogues*,

> Towns (*urbes*) are depopulated, fortified places (*castra*) destroyed, churches burnt, monasteries and nunneries destroyed; fields are deserted by men, and the earth forsaken by the ploughman gapes desolate.[56]

The devastation equally affects town and country, the indissoluble combination which made up the *civitas*. Gregory's answer is to fight back. His is not a shrinking empire. It is he who sends bishop Augustine to convert the Angles of Kent in 597; and within a short space of time, in 601, he is urging Augustine to create twelve more bishops and ruling on the relative precedence of York and London.[57] The urban network of Britain must have

---

[53] V,54 of 595 AD. [54] II,42 of 592 AD to bishop Felix of Agropoli.
[55] I,8 (590 AD): *ecclesiam Menturnensem funditus tam cleri quam plebis destitutam.*
[56] *Dialogi* 3.38, cited by Markus, *Gregory the Great*, p. 52.
[57] XI, 39 of 601 AD on the precedence of York and London, and on instructions to Augustine to create twelve further bishops; on Augustine's mission, see Markus, *Gregory the Great*, pp. 177–187.

survived in however depleted a form for Augustine to move with such speed. At the same time, Gregory is pushing for expansion in Sardinia and Corsica, and negotiating with Frankish kings over the status of parishes in the diocese of Turin, which fell within their kingdom.[58] For all the pressure his network is under, he is pushing back, reinforcing the role of bishops in their cities. He might have been astonished by the suggestion that the centrality of the bishop was undermining the traditional city; he would answer that the church was not only dependent on the old urban network but saving it in the face of attack. The armies of the Byzantine emperor and his Exarch in Ravenna were dubiously successful in pushing back the Lombards; it was Gregory's correspondence with the formidable Lombard queen, Theodelinda,[59] that brought the former barbarians within the fold, just as his correspondence with Leander in Spain and the king Reccared brought the Visigoths (and their many cities) within the Catholic and Roman fold.[60]

'*Nefandissimi barbari*' the Lombards must have seemed, especially when they sacked cities without mercy: Agilulf razed Padua to the ground in 602/3, likewise Cremona and Mantua; Rothari is said to have devastated the cities of Genoa, Albenga, Varigotti, Savona, Oderzo and Luni, and reduced them to the status of villages.[61] Yet that was hostility to enemy cities, not to cities in general: Agilulf celebrated the promotion of his son in the circus at Milan with Byzantine ceremonial, while his wife Theodelinda built her royal palace at Monza; King Cunipert, towards the end of the seventh century, 'restored the half-destroyed city of Mutina to its former glory'; in the next century Liutprand established a new city north of Venice: Cittanova (*Civitas Nova*).[62]

The central importance of bishops was not only spiritual: as the Ravenna papyri illustrate so vividly, the church – or, rather, individual churches – were major landowners. If city councils had always been dominated by the major landowners, it made sense that the bishop played a key role among them, depending on their support for election and using their bureaucracy

---

[58] IX, 214 of 599 to Ursicinus of Turn is backed up by IX, 226 to kings Theuderic and Theudibert; see Markus, *Gregory the Great*, pp. 173–177 for Gregory's relations with the Franks.

[59] See Markus, *Gregory the Great*, pp. 103–107; for the series of letters to Theodelinda, see Ewald and Hartmann's index p. 511 s.v. Theodelinda. The cathedral treasury in Monza preserves gifts sent to the queen by Gregory.

[60] Markus, *Gregory the Great*, pp. 164–168 on Gregory's relations with the Visigoths. On Lombard control of cities, Fabbro, *Warfare and the Making of Early Medieval Italy*.

[61] Brogiolo, 'Ideas of the town', pp. 110–111. Pohl, 'Social Cohesion', p. 33, argues for nuance in Gregory's treatment of Lombard.

[62] Brogiolo, 'Ideas of the town', brings out the contradictions in Lombard's treatment of the cities of Italy.

to safeguard donations. Not only does Gregory assume that city councils will be involved in the election of local bishops, he also assumes that when bishops receive donations, they will need to register them in the municipal archives. He writes in these terms to the bishops of Messina (II.9), Rimini (II.15), Luni (VIII.5), Fermo in the Sabina (IX.58 and 71 and XIII.18), Portus (IX.98), and Tindari (IX.180). They follow closely similar language, a legal formula:

> Gregory to Castor, bishop of Rimini, January 592[63]
>
> Themotea, an illustrious lady, has informed us with the notification of a petition (which is appended hereto) that she has founded an oratory within the city of Rimini in a place owned by her, for the sake of her own devotion, and she desires it to be consecrated in honour of the holy cross. For that reason, dearest brethren, if the aforesaid construction is consistent with your city's regulations, and it is certain that no corpse is buried there, you will solemnly consecrate the aforesaid oratory, without public masses. But first receive the legal donation, that is eight twelfths of her whole property, all goods movable and fixed and self-moving (slaves excepted), their usufruct retained by her for all the days of her life, as registered with the municipal administration (*gestisque municipalibus alligatam*).

When the letters of Pope Gregory cease, at the beginning of the seventh century, one might be tempted to imagine that registration had also ceased. But this is contradicted by a papal book of standard formulae, the *Liber Diurnus Pontificum Romanorum*. Compiled initially in the early seventh century but reaching its present form towards the end of the century, it draws frequently on Gregory for a model of how to write such a letter. Its model of how to register a donation is deeply Gregorian:[64]

> RESPONSE ON DEDICATING AN ORATORY
>
> The applicant has informed us with the notification of a petition (which is appended hereto) that in such and such an estate in such and such a jurisdiction he has founded an oratory for the sake of his own devotion, and he desires it to be consecrated in honour of such and such a saint. For that reason, dearest brethren, if the aforesaid construction is consistent with your city's regulations, and it is certain that no corpse is buried there, first receive the legal donation, that is such and such or such and such, of a value of so many *solidi* free of fiscal dues, registered with the municipal administration (*gestisque municipalibus alligatis*). You will solemnly consecrate the aforesaid oratory, without public masses.

---

[63] II.15 (=Martyn, *The Letters of Gregory the Great* 2.11).   [64] Ed. Foerster, pp. 186–187.

Again, one can imagine scenarios by which standard letters remained in the papal protocol book long after they ceased to be relevant, but it is hard to imagine a matter of such ongoing importance to a church as accepting a donation could be left without necessary updating. As if in confirmation, Pope Zacharias in the mid eighth century reminded Pippin, King of the Franks, that a donation to found an oratory or basilica must be registered in the *gesta municipalia*.[65] Evidence for continued activity by city councils in Italy is rare and scattered, and when it is found, it is treated as an exception to a rule. Both Ravenna and Naples had a civic *curia* as well as an episcopal one into the tenth century – but is this an illustration of a rule or an exception to it?[66]

Municipal Records in Early Medieval Gaul and Spain

In answering this question it is worth looking at the parallel evidence from Visigothic Spain and Merovingian Gaul. It has long been known that both standard formulae and specific documents suggest a practice of recording transactions before magistrates and *curia* in the municipal archives. The evidence was collected for one of those magnificent volumes of the *Monumenta Germaniae Historica* pioneered by Theodor Mommsen at the end of the nineteenth century. Karl Zeumer was responsible for assembling the Merovingian and Carolingian formulae and included those of Visigothic Spain.[67] This material has long been familiar to historians, though there has been much debate over its significance and status. One school of thought sees in the survival of Roman civic institutions and practices a sign of continuity with the Roman past – this is doubtless one reason why Henri Pirenne saw the cities of Merovingian Gaul as a direct continuity with the Roman city, with the real break not coming until Charlemagne.[68] But others have been more sceptical, putting little trust in these documents as proving any real continuity, except of the *curia* as some sort of glorified registration office. So, the great Ferdinand Lot in *Le Fin du monde antique*: 'The "curiales" persisted in Gaul up to the end of the seventh century, but their body is no more than a registration office for private contracts.'[69] A reassessment of the value and significance of these documents has now been made possible by the thorough re-examination of the material by Josiane Barbier, which can leave little doubt that

---

[65] Barbier, *Gesta municipalia*, p. 162. [66] Brown, *Gentlemen and Officers*, pp. 18–19.
[67] See Zeumer, *Formulae Merowingici et Carolini aevi*. [68] Pirenne, *Medieval Cities*.
[69] Lot, *Le Fin du monde antique*, cited by Barbier, p. 54.

a widespread practice of registration of important documents with the municipal records (*gestis municipalibus alligare*) persisted into the early ninth century.[70]

The evidence is particularly abundant from France (the Spanish example will be discussed in Chapter 8, p. 286), and here we have documents preserved in the city archives themselves, in sharp contrast to the Ravenna papyri, which only survive because of the episcopal archive and its interest in preserving the titles to the many properties bequeathed and donated to the church of Ravenna. Stretching in date from the sixth to the early ninth centuries, the formulae and the documents cover a dozen cities spread over Merovingian Gaul; the formulae are found in six cities: Angers (late sixth century), Clermont (late eighth century), Tours (late eighth century), Sens (late eighth century), Bourges (first half of eighth century), Flavigny (late eighth century), plus the formula collection drawn up in the late seventh or early eighth century by a 70-year old monk called Marculfus, whose compilation was heavily drawn on by most of the others.[71] The nine documents that show these formulae in practice come from a similar range of cities: Rouen (probably later sixth century), Le Mans (dated to 616), Poitiers (dated to 677), Autun (dated to 722), the monastery of Murbach (dated to 735/736), Angers (dated to 804), and Paris (dated to 566, though this seems to be a forgery).[72]

Formulae and documents alike tell a remarkably consistent story in terms of the procedures to be followed and the language used in drawing up deeds, wills, and donations, to be formally registered in the city archives. This consistency is no surprise, because the material is interlinked: documents follow the patterns set by the formulae, but the formulae themselves may be based on earlier documents, as presumably in the case of the Angers formula, which dates itself to the fourth year of King Childebert (578–579), where it should have left a blank for the date as it does for the names of the local magistrates. Indeed, the formulae for municipal registration are only part of compilations of formulae for many purposes which constantly copy each other (especially drawing on those of Marculfus, which acted as a sort of school textbook), and are in their turn recopied long after their original dates, stretching into the tenth century.[73] We are looking at a consciously interconnected tradition

---

[70] Barbier, *Archives oubliée*.
[71] See Barbier, *Archives oubliée*, pp. 201–254. For a helpful translation and commentary of two examples, see Rio, *The Formularies of Angers and Marculf*.
[72] Barbier, *Archives oubliée*, pp. 179–199.   [73] Brown, 'The *gesta municipalia*'.

shared by a cluster of cities. Their reliance on set formulae is the principal reason why historians have played down their significance, as if these were meaningless verbiage attached to legal documents. But as the surviving examples make clear, there is a real social ritual involved, parallel to that we have seen in the Ravenna papyri. Indeed, it has been suggested that the enactment of a public ritual had more effectiveness in giving a private document validity than its incorporation in the archives, though surely it is not necessary to draw this distinction, for it was the existence of a physical archive that gave sense to the ritual, and, reciprocally, the ritual that gave social importance to an archive which participants saw as more than a mere registry office.[74]

Numerous features are common to these documents and are shared with the Ravenna papyri. One is the cast of players involved. There is always a representative of the donator or testator called a *prosecutor* who takes the document involved to be registered, together with explicit instructions, the *mandatum*, requiring him to do so. He presents himself to the *curia* with its principal magistrate, the *defensor*.[75] Here we note a difference from the Ravenna examples in which the *curia* is led by a chief magistrate, usually a *quinquennalis*, or simply *magistratus*. The consistent use of *defensor* respects a law issued by Justinian in 535 in one of his New Constitutions (*Novellae*) dated after the completion of the *codex Justinianus* (*Novel* 15, pref.; see Chapter 8, p. 204). The preamble complains of the disintegration of the system of municipal records, which he attributes to lack of respect for the office of *defensor*, who is too junior, too subject to influence by the governor, and too easily bribed. The law reinforces his authority and mandates that every city should have a dedicated building for the record office with a dedicated staff. Ironically, Ravenna, which was under Byzantine control and thus Justinian's latest legislation, continues as before with local magistrates, rather than *defensores*, leading the archive. In Merovingian Gaul, which could follow or ignore imperial legislation as it chose, the role of the *defensor* is constant over three centuries.

Other features which are familiar from Ravenna are the hierarchical titles with which participants are addressed (the curials are always addressed as *laudabiles*) and the repetitive dialogue form in which the ritual is framed. This is best illustrated by one of the fullest surviving specimens of an act of registration: that of the donation by Ansoaldus, bishop of Poitiers, to the monastery of Noirmoutiers of 1 July 677. It falls, as

---

[74] Brown, 'The *gesta municipalia*', pp. 122–124.
[75] Rio, *Two Formularies*, pp. 255–258 (Appendix II. The *Gesta Municipalia*) maintains that these Roman institutions may only have existed in the formularies, not on the ground.

formulaically required, into three documents: donation, mandate, and registration. The donation sets out the substance:

> I Ansoaldus bishop of the city of Poitiers (*Pictavensis urbis*) . . . following the advice and convenience of our venerable brothers, namely our fellow citizens (*civium scilicet nostrorum*), with foresight for the needs both of our brother Abbot Philibert, whom we have established as father of the monastery on the island of Herio (Noirmoutiers), and of his brothers living with him . . . I wish to donate the villa called Ampennus, situated on the seashore, to him or his congregations or the monastery which is established on the island.

Herio or Noirmoutiers is a small island at the mouth of the Loire where Ansoaldus had in 674 established a monastery under Philibert (later a saint and dedicatee of the church), and his donation of an estate seeks to secure its future to ensure the provision of food and clothing for the community. The island was to fall victim to a Viking attack in 799, leading to the dispersal of its archive: the surviving copy is from the priory of Cunault on the Loire, to which presumably some of the monks moved with their precious archive.

Ansoaldus concludes his donation by specifying that in order to have it signed 'by our venerable brothers and the magnificent citizens of Poitiers (*magnificorum civium Pictavensium*)', it should be inserted in the municipal records (*gesta municipalia*) following the custom of Roman law, and that copies should be kept. This document is then signed by Ansoaldus himself ('sinner that I am, bishop'), Romanus ('unworthy that I am, bishop'), Audulfus ('sinner that I am, abbot'), and Abbot Baddo. The following document is the mandatum, in which Ansoaldus instructs his deacon Launegiselus to act as his representative and appear before the *defensor* and *curia* of the city of Poitiers and 'by your pleading (*prosecutio*) before the magnificent and strenuous persons of that city' confirm his donation. The same set of witnesses sign this document too.

The third document records the registration blow by blow and enacts the performance of the civic ritual. It is worth following in detail.

> *Gesta* (1 April 678)
>
> In the second year of the reign of lord Dagobert, most glorious king, on the kalends of April, In the presence of the praiseworthy (*laudabilis*) Defensor and the whole council of the city of Poitiers (*cuncta curia Pictavi civitatis*), the Venerable Launegiselus, deacon, because he saw the public officers present, said:

'I ask you, praiseworthy Defensor, and you, most select councillors (*curiales*), that you may order the public archives (*codices publicos*) to be opened to me, and that you grace to hear my pleading, since there are matters which I wish to be added to the public records (*actis municipalibus*).'

The defensor and all the council said:

'The public records are open to you, continue what you wish to hear.'

Launegiselus, deacon, said:

'Our lord and holy father Bishop Ansoaldus, by the authority of his mandate enjoined me that I should register with your Praisewothiness in the municipal records the document of his donation, which for the remedy of his soul he has made to Philibert abbot of the monastery of Noirmoutiers, in honour of St Peter and the other saints abovementioned, and to the congregation of that place. On this matter I bear a mandate in my hands. I request that you instruct for it to be read out in your presence, for insertion in the municipal records.'

The defensor and the whole council said:

'Let the secretary Lupus receive the mandate which the deacon Launegiselus says he has.'

Secretary Lupus received and read out the mandate:

(he reads out the wording of the mandate, repeated as above.)

When this had been read out, the defensor and all the council said:

'The mandate which secretary Lupus has read out will be added to the record. Whatever else our father Launegislus the deacon wants, he should not hesitate to say.'

Launegiselus said:

'Behold, I have the donation itself here present. I ask that the donation should be reviewed publicly for insertion in the register.'

The defensor and the whole council said:

'Let the secretary Lupus receive the donation which the deacon Launegiselus offers for reading.'

He received it and read it out. After it had been read, the defensor and the whole council said:

> 'Let the archives (*gesta*) keep in custody the donation which the secretary Lupus has read out. Whatever else father Launegiselus the deacon wishes to plead, he should not hesitate to speak.'

Launegiselus said:

> 'Since what my plea contained has been done in the correct manner before God, I request that the proceedings, when they have been written and signed by you and the councillors, following the legal order may be issued and handed to me in the traditional fashion.'

Secretary Lupus signed this record.

> (Further signatures): Daniel, curialis; Bonebertus, curialis; Aldobertus, curialis; Sumdoaldus [read: Gumdoaldus?], curialis; Saligarius, curialis; Adalricus, curialis; Eusichus, curialis.

Dated kalends of April, second year of the reign of King Dagobert.

> Lando wrote and signed.

Implicit in this whole dialogue is a necessary relationship between the written and the spoken. It is never enough to hand over a written document. It must be read out in full in the presence of the councillors, and only then added to the record. This is done separately: first for the mandate (otherwise Launegiselus would not have the authority to represent Ansoaldus) and then for the text of the donation. As we have seen with the Ravenna papyri, it must all be done step by step, in the right order. The *defensor* and his *curiales* never take procedure for granted: at each step they must invite the *prosecutor* to state what he wants, including the final request for a signed copy of the record. Only once each step is ritually completed can the authorities present sign the document and thereby give it validity. In the end it will be a written record (albeit a copy of another written record) which validates the donation, but the writing records the presence of human actors exchanging words. What those words were could be predicted by anyone with a copy of the formula book. But that does not make them pointless; on the contrary – it is a tightly choreographed occasion, and it is the adherence to the choreography that makes it real.

A document like this makes no sense if the performance was never enacted. The witnesses attest not that the document of donation is authentic, but that every necessary element to make it so has been carried out. It makes no sense unless the *curia* was a physical reality: a group of officials who met to represent the citizens of Poitier. Nor can they be dismissed as some sort of lowly secretariat: the whole business is wrapped up in the language of social honour and respect that would have been farcical had they been of low standing: *magnificus* and *strenuus* are not titles to be used at random.[76] Barbier suggests indeed that we can identify two of the witnesses as members of high-placed court families: Addobertus and Sumdoaldus/Gumdoaldus appear as tax farmers in 721 and seem to have links to the court of Dagobert.[77] This may be conjectural, but there is no reason to suppose that our *curiales* are in fact humble people.

It is one thing to accept that these formalities actually took place in late-seventh-century Poitiers, and that something called a *curia* still existed, involving people of high standing in the city, but another entirely to argue that Poitiers was still run by a city council as it had been under the Roman Empire. The documents can give us no hint as to whether this sort of registration was the only sort of function a *curia* would carry out, or one of many other aspects of running the civic administration. It is equally illegitimate to use the documents either to demonstrate that the curial rule continued as in the past, or that it only continued in the restricted circumstances of registration.[78] One key question might be whether there was still a connection to the system of taxation. Under the imperial system, the same set of people keeping the records of property ownership could also establish the taxes owed to central government on those property holdings. Councillors were also *exactores*, tax collectors, which does not so much mean collecting the taxes in person, but assessing what taxes are owed. Merovingian kings still taxed cities in sixth-century Gaul, much to their profit, though taxation seems to have been abandoned in many areas in the seventh century. But, as Chris Wickham observes, it may be no coincidence that the cities in which the activity of the *gesta municipalia* is best attested – Poitiers and Angers – are those which kept up taxation longest.[79]

That things change under Charlemagne is generally accepted.[80] The latest firmly dated example which follows the traditional formula belongs to 8 April 804, 'in the fourth year of the Imperium of Lord Karolus, most serene Augustus' (Charlemagne was crowned emperor in Rome in 800). In it one Harwic (Haruhic), son of Benedict, donates his villa called Odane, in the territory of Angers, to the monastery of St Saviour in the Ardennes

[76] Barbier, *Archives oubliée*, p.167: les responsables des *gesta munipalia* n'étaient pas les guichetiers d'un 'bureau d'enregistrement'.
[77] Barbier, *Archives oubliée*, pp. 93–97.
[78] Rio, 'Merovingian legal cultures', pp. 492–496, points to the limits of what can be inferred.
[79] Wickham, *Framing*, pp. 110–111 for a discussion of the *gesta*; pp. 102–115 for taxation in Gaul/Francia.
[80] Barbier, *Archives oubliée*, pp. 163–164, concludes that the disappearance of the *gesta municipalia* is later than the beginning of the ninth century.

above the River Prumia, as founded by King Pippin and his wife Bertrada. The document survives in the Golden Book of the monastery of Saint-Sauveur de Prüm, not in the municipal archives of Angers, where it was registered.[81] It declares itself to follow Roman legal form, 'since it is written in the books of Theodosianus and Hermogenianus or Papinianus through which the law is contained that handing over (*traditio*) follows a donation' (the knowledge of Roman law is not quite perfect, given that Theodosius' code is described as a book of Theodosian). Three documents – the donation, the tradition, and the mandatum requiring Aganbert to approach the *curia* to register – are duly signed by seven witnesses, of whom the first, Godaldus, is qualified as a *vicarius*. The fourth and last document is the record of registration before Vulfredus the *defensor* and the whole *curia* of the city of Angers. It follows a by now very familiar pattern: the request to the *laudabilis vir defensor* to open the public archives, the reading by Leodegarius the *amanuensis* of the mandate to Aganbertus and the act of donation, the insertion of those documents in the public records, and the request (after the ritual invitation) for a signed copy of the proceedings. The signatories, though described generically as *curiales*, seem to be important civic figures: Nononus the count, Risclenus the *curator*, Vuigfredus the *vicedomus*, two public officials called *centenarii*, Letbaudus and Stabulus, and seven others.

The document was long rejected as a sort of stitch-up, based on copying out passages of Marculfus' formula, and reflecting no actual meeting of any *curia*. Barbier argues that the grounds for rejecting it are baseless.[82] A longstanding difficulty has been caused by a phrase, first met in Marculfus' formula, that has been taken to imply that the *curiales* were too worthless for a registration to be made with them. The key words, *nequaquam curialium vilitate*, are seemingly corrupt, both in the various versions of Marculfus and in the Harwic donation. Not only does the accusation of *vilitas* (worthlessness, even corruption) against the *curiales* go against the unfailingly flattering language normally used of them (*laudabilitas*), it goes against the rest of the dossier, in which the *curiales* are treated with the usual respect, and the documents are indeed registered with them. Barbier notes the variant reading of *augurialium vilitas*, though who these vile augurs might be is left unexplained.[83] Perhaps we could take a hint from the pages of Cassiodorus and read *nequaquam curialium incivilitate*, 'with no trace of lack of civility by the curials'. But whatever

---

[81] Nolden, *Das 'Goldene Buch' von Prüm*.   [82] Barbier, *Archives oubliée*, pp. 99–103.
[83] Barbier, *Archives oubliée*, pp. 101–102, cf. 147.

the truth of this strange and garbled phrase, it is no good reason for believing that the registration as described never took place. We might, on the other hand, believe that the group of civic officials who signed, including no less a man than the count, simply chose to describe themselves as the *curia* in respect for a long tradition that was respected only in the letter.

The Survival of the *Curia*

In bringing to the foreground material too often buried in footnotes in the accounts of the 'end of the ancient city', there can be no point in arguing that, on the contrary, the city survived in its ancient form longer than has been supposed. To do so would be to fall into the same trap. Discussion has been underpinned by two assumptions: first, that the *curia* was the essential and distinctive element of the ancient city; second, that the end of that city must necessarily be marked by the disappearance of the *curia*. It helps sometimes to stand assumptions on their head. The late Roman *curia* was by no means essential to the ancient city, and its survival or otherwise cannot be used as a proof of the survival or otherwise of the ancient city.

What the *curia* was and what it did changed inescapably over the course of time. Late Antiquity has a very precise version of the *curia* which by no means applies to the 'ancient city' in earlier times. We fall into assuming that the *curia* matters so much simply because Late Antiquity set so much store by this particular incarnation of the *curia*, whether in the laments of Libanius or the persistent, if ineffective, attempts by a sequence of emperors from Constantine to Justinian to bolster it by their legislation, or by the eloquent attempts of Cassiodorus to stage a latter-day defence of the system. The significance of the *curia* was hard-baked into later Roman legislation, in the Theodosian and Justinianic Codes and Novels. The post-Roman world, which continued to live in many ways by Roman law, also took as read the importance of the *curia* and found ways ritually to restage its activities. But the survival, or re-enactment, or re-appropriation, of the *curia* does not carry with it the survival of the ancient city.

Of course, a council was a feature of the city going back to archaic Greece, even to the Homeric epics. By an almost mathematical law, Greek theory saw in any society a balance of power between the one (king or senior magistrate), the few (council), and the many (citizen body). In Aristotle's analysis the key variable is not the possession of a constitution, but the balance between these elements. The council might represent the collective power of the rich in an oligarchy; a democracy like that of Athens had numerous expedients to limit the powers of the council, by ensuring that all citizens had access to it by random selection, and by ensuring that its functions were limited to preparing business to the assembly of the full citizen body. The council of Late Antiquity is not easy to fit into an Aristotelian scheme. Its composition – of wealthy landowners sitting for life – looks highly oligarchical; on the other hand, the imposition on its members of services to the community, liturgies, might seem democratic. In fact, the reforms of Diocletian gave city councils an unprecedented character. By making membership not merely a hereditary privilege of the rich, but a mandatory obligation, with the emperor as policeman to block attempts to find loopholes, it not only put wealthy landowners in a position of privilege but subjected them to unwelcome constraints. At the same time, by giving the council the responsibility for collecting taxes on the land, it further trapped the most powerful landowners into service to the state.

This system has the advantages of a certain logic, which we can see at work in the Ravenna documents. If the council is made the public record office, with obligation to register all movements in property, by sale, gift, or inheritance, then it has the knowledge basis for exacting the taxes on land. This system was so advantageous to the state that the kings who inherited the administrative systems of the Roman Empire might well rely on councils both as record offices, and as tax-collecting centres. At the same time, the performance of civic rituals by members of the council was a way of enacting a social hierarchy – one which did not entirely map onto to the growing power of court officials and of the church.

What we see in the continued performance of such rituals, I suggest, is neither a nostalgic attempt to hang on to a lost world, nor the futile attempt of mere members of a registry office to give themselves more importance than they merit, but a mechanism of adaptation. Cities continued after the collapse of Roman power in the west; they continued to be the way to structure territories and societies. If the bishop became a key feature, it was not a constitutional collapse, but a proper reflection of his exceptional influence with the citizen body and of the sheer wealth of the church. To a Roman world built on patronage, the pattern was familiar enough. But the tenacious perception that the *curia* was an essential element of the cities of the past, especially among cities which, like Naples, gave high value to ancient traditions, led to the continuation, in some cities at least in the old Roman west, and in some for surprisingly long, of a set of rituals and practices. What we can see, on the basis of surviving records, is a practice of record keeping. At the same time, bishops and monasteries were equally convinced of the importance of an archive, and not only learnt archival techniques from the *tabelliones* of the cities but found it very convenient to have their own documents validated by them. In the very process of continuing past practices, they made possible the construction of new ways of making the city work.

7 | The City of Bishops

Gregory of Tours and Merovingian Gaul

If an image of the urban world of sixth-century Italy is conjured up by Cassiodorus, expanded by Procopius, and detailed by the Ravenna papyri, the most powerful evocation of the urban world of Gaul is offered by the writings of Gregory of Tours. Close in time, even in distance, Gregory's Gaul may even so seem a world apart from Cassiodorus' Italy. It might be imagined that Gaul, so close to the Rhine frontier which separated off *barbaria* and divided in the fifth century between different kingdoms of Germanic origin, the Visigoths, the Franks, and the Burgundians, would prove very much less stable than an Italy stabilised by Theoderic the Great. Yet thanks not least to the success of the Frankish king Clovis at the battle of Vouillé in AD 507, at which Clovis changed the map of Europe by defeating the Visigoths under Alaric II based on Toulouse, and driving them to Spain, and thanks to the subsequent grinding down of the Burgundians, Gaul enjoyed a surprising degree of stability. Two signs of an underlying stability are the persistence of a hereditary aristocracy with Roman roots, and the persistence of the Roman system of cities. Gregory illustrates both in considerable detail. His *Histories*, taken together with his Saints' Lives which evoke the same world, have long been a prime document for historians like my father working on the Merovingian period;[1] recent decades have seen a flurry of interest, allowing us to fill out a rich picture of urbanism in sixth-century Gaul.[2]

One of the underlying questions of this book (Chapter 1) is whether the late Roman city and the early medieval city can be taken to be 'cities' in the same sense. A good place to start is Gregory's lyrical description of Castrum Divonense or Divio, today's Dijon (*Hist.* 3.19). This was the town where his great-grandfather, Gregory of Langres (*civitas Lingonum*), lived and had his main estate; in his description of his death and funeral, we learn that

---

[1] Interest in Gregory runs throughout his writings: J. M. Wallace-Hadrill, *The Long-Haired Kings*, pp. 49–70; *Early Germanic Kingship*, pp. 47–53, 73–74; *Early Medieval History*, pp. 96–114; *The Frankish Church*, pp. 37–54.
[2] I have benefited from of series of collective volumes: Gautier and Galinié, *Grégoire de Tours*; Mitchell and Wood, *The World of Gregory of Tours*; Murray, *A Companion to Gregory of Tours*; Effros and Moreira, *Handbook of the Merovingian World*.

though he died in Langres, he gave instructions to be buried in Dijon. As his body was being carried to the Basilica of St John, the bier became too heavy to carry and the bearers put it down, just outside the town's prison; the doors of the prison broke open, and the prisoners were freed from their shackles and joined in the funeral. His burial place, where miracles constantly took place, was then extended by his son and successor, Tetricus (*Life of the Fathers* 7, 3–4). Dijon was big enough a town to have a crowded gaol, as well as plenty of others hoping for miracles. It might be no more than a *castrum*, but it was both impressive and delightful:

> It is a stronghold with very solid walls, built in the midst of a plain, a very pleasant place, the lands rich and fruitful, so that after a single ploughing once the seed is sown, a great wealth of produce comes in due season. To the south it has the Ouche, a river very rich in fish, and from the north comes another little stream, which runs in at the gate and flows under a bridge and again passes out by another gate, flowing around the whole fortified place with its quiet waters, and turning with wonderful speed the mills before the gate. The four gates face the four regions of the universe, and thirty-three towers adorn the whole structure, and the wall is thirty feet high and fifteen feet thick, built of squared stones up to twenty feet, and above of small stone. And why it is not called a city I do know. It has all around it abundant springs, and on the west are hills, very fertile and full of vineyards, which produce for the inhabitants such a noble Falernian that they disdain wine of Ascalon. The ancients say this place was built by the emperor Aurelian. (*History of the Franks* 3.19)[3]

Gregory's praise faithfully follows the classic prescriptions for *laudes urbium*: he is well aware of the rules of the rhetorical game (see Chapter 2). But what is it that makes Castrum Divonense less than a city? We note at once that it is a walled settlement, *castrum firmissimis muris*, but in a rural setting of fruitful plain and a river full of fish and driving water mills, and a wine to challenge Falernian (a *synkrisis*). The solid walls of ashlar blocks have the classic features of numerous towers, and four gates are set on the four quarters; it even has a presumptive founder, the emperor Aurelian (who, more plausibly, founded Orléans, which carries his name). It is this combination of fortified urban centre and rich countryside that makes Gregory ask 'why it is not called a city, I do not know', *cur non civitas dicta est, ignoro*. Just as Pausanias famously expressed his puzzlement about Panopeus in Phocis, a *polis* that lacked the defining urban features of

---

[3] For a good translation with a useful index, see Thorpe's Penguin, *Gregory of Tours*. The above translation, however, is my own.

a *polis*,[4] Gregory implies the combination of rural and urban features that defined a *civitas*. But here he was in a bind: only a *civitas* could have a bishop, and, equally, if you did not have a bishop, you could not be a *civitas* (the Penguin translation of Lewis Thorpe runs 'Why Dijon is not elevated to the dignity of a bishopric I cannot imagine', which catches the spirit, though this is not what the text says). The fact that the bishop of Langres so favoured it still did not make Dijon a city.

What makes a city a city is that it has been officially defined as such: the status is the product of an administrative system. A *civitas* was a juridical status and carried with it the right to a bishopric; but unless it had the rank of a *civitas*, it couldn't have a bishop. That isn't simply the decision of the church, but of the history of the urban network inherited from the fourth-century Roman administration and extended along the tramlines of the Roman past. Having impressive walls is indeed one of the defining features of a late Roman city; but walls by themselves were not enough, because a *castrum* too might have walls (just as we find Justinian multiplying *castra* as well as cities; see Procopius, *Peri Ktismaton* 4.4). In the end, it was an administrative decision about the settlement hierarchy of an area, and the Merovingian kings showed little interest in innovating. Maybe in Spain, where cities tended to proliferate, Dijon would have been a *municipium* or a *civitas*; but in Gaul, the *civitates* were thinner on the ground, numbering some 120, as opposed to the 400 or so *municipia* of Spain. Indeed, it was not until 1731 that Dijon was promoted to an episcopal see. It is now (since 2002) one of the metropolitan sees, and the city ranks as 18th in France by population, that vital modern definition.

The Civitates of Merovingian Gaul

A striking continuity is suggested by the survival of the Roman system of *civitates*.[5] Gregory's world is very much one of cities. Cities mattered to two groups in whom Gregory was obsessively interested: kings and bishops. That Gregory's *civitates* were an inheritance from the Late Roman Empire is demonstrated in detail by an extraordinarily valuable document, called the *Notitia Galliarum*, which is a listing of the cities of Gaul, initially some 115 of them, rising to 126 with additions (Figure 7.1). If only we had similar documents for other parts of the Roman Empire, we would understand

---

[4] Pausanias 10.4.1, cited in the opening page of Moses Finley's essay on 'The Ancient City'; see Chapter 1.

[5] Dey, *Afterlife*, pp. 161–178, rightly underlines the centrality of cities in Frankish Gaul.

a good deal more about Roman urbanism. There is a fascinating debate about the *Notitia*. Some maintain that it is in all essentials a fourth-century Roman administrative document, listing the *civitates* into which the seventeen Gallic provinces were divided. Others suggest that it is a rather later document, from the sixth century, generated by the church, and listing the bishoprics. What makes the question hard to answer is that the late Roman organisation of the 'Gauls' (including parts of Belgium, Germany, and Switzerland) into seventeen provinces, each with a capital city or 'metropolis', was the basis for the organisation of the church, with a metropolitan archbishop at the peak of the province and suffragan bishops for individual cities.

The remarkable truth is that this document is both: a late Roman administrative document repurposed as an ecclesiastical document.[6] That can be seen in tiny details. At the end is an appendix, which explains a handful of cities identified in the document by their Roman names and relabelled with their own, more familiar, names. So the civitas Mediomatricum is identified as Mettis, now Metz; the civitas Leucorum as Tullio, now Toul; and the civitas Equestrium as Noviodunus, now Nyon (it is notable that the names, having shifted, then survive today). Clearly standard usage has moved on since the list was first drawn up. The last entry runs as follows: civitas Albensium, nunc Vivarium. But this is different, because Vivarium is not simply a new name for the civitas Albensium or Alba; it is a neighbouring place, Viviers, to which the bishopric was moved by the bishop, Saint Auxonius, around 430 after Alba had been ravaged by barbarians (an episode not in Gregory). So the list was originally produced before 430, and revised thereafter when its principal interest was the location of bishops.

The vast majority of these bishoprics remained as such through the medieval into the modern world. Of the fifteen metropolitan archbishoprics of modern France, six were metropolitan capitals in the *Notitia* (Besançon, Bordeaux, Lyon, Reims, Rouen, and Tours), seven were listed there as *civitates*, but have displaced earlier metropolitans (Clermont replacing Bourges, Marseille replacing Vienne, Paris replacing Sens, Montpellier and Toulouse replacing Narbonne) or have split from the earlier provinces (Poitiers splitting from Bordeaux, Rennes splitting from Tours). All but three of the modern metropolitan sees were *civitates* in Antiquity. Two are medieval foundations, Lille and Montpellier; and one,

---

[6] Harries, 'Church and state in the Notitia Galliarum'; see also Murray, *A Companion to Gregory of Tours*, pp. 583–592, for lists and maps.

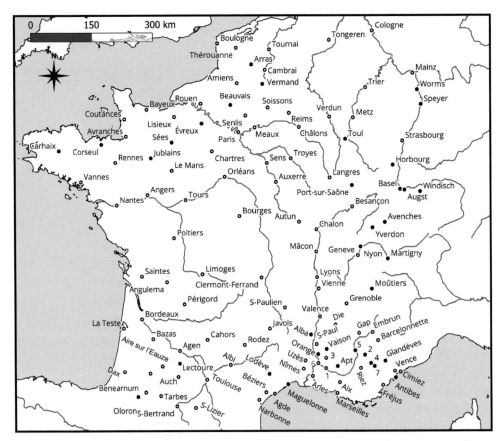

Figure 7.1 Civitates in the Notitia Galliarum, after Harries, 'Church and state', figure 1: 1. Cavaillon; 2. Digne; 3. Carpentras; 4. Senez; 5. Sisteron; 6. Avignon; 7. Castellane. Drawn by Javier Martínez Jiménez.

Dijon, is the very *castrum* which Gregory protested should have been a *civitas* and the seat of a bishop. Of the eighty modern bishoprics beneath metropolitan level, fifty-six were *civitates* listed in the *Notitia*, while seven further *civitates* remain titular bishoprics, and seventeen further *civitates* form part of united sees with a second centre. In all, eighty-five of the *civitates* are still bishoprics today, either in their own right, united with others, or in title. Thus, the network of *civitates* that concerned a fourth-century administrator survived all those waves of barbarian invasion to be the underlying network that defines the ecclesiastical structure of modern France.

Further, there is a close fit between this late fourth-century network and the network we meet in the pages of Gregory. Thanks to the interest of his kings in controlling cities, and his close contacts with a network of

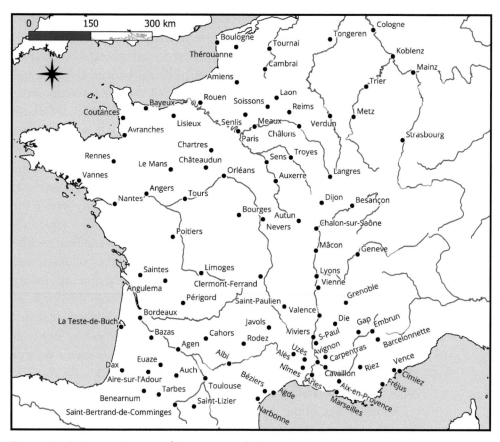

Figure 7.2 Civitates in Gregory of Tours. Drawn by Javier Martínez Jiménez.

bishops based in cities, we find some ninety-four Gallic *civitates* named in the *Histories* or the Saints' Lives (see Figure 7.2).[7] There *are* cities in the *Notitia* which Gregory omits (some three dozen), because he is not like the compiler of the *Notitia* trying to offer an exhaustive list, though it is striking that they are not in his part of central France, but in Switzerland, the German frontier, and the parts of northern France which were the heartland of Frankish rule (see Figure 7.2).[8] Of course, he is not only interested in *civitates*: he has plenty to say about minor settlements, including half a dozen *castra* (fortified towns, including his beloved Dijon), and twenty-five *vici* (ranging from villages to small towns), eighteen of them in the countryside around Tours, as well as *pagi*

---

[7] See also Murray, 'The Merovingian state', esp. pp. 213–217, giving ninety-three as the number of *civitates* named by Gregory (p. 214).

[8] Cf. Goffart, *Narrators*, p. 138: 'The horizon of Gregory of Tours rarely extends north and east of the Loire'.

(districts) and villas.[9] To be interested in *civitates* was not to be interested in cities *rather than* the countryside, so much as cities *in the context of* countryside, a hierarchy of urban centres articulating a rural landscape.

A Gallic *civitas* comprised, on the classical model, both urban centre and countryside, including *castra* and villages. Indeed, the military tactics of the constantly squabbling *civitates* were very much those of classical Greece: you invade the enemy's lands and ravage the crops until they either come out and give battle or cave in. The fate of Poitiers (Pectavum) in 585 is a neat example (*Hist.* 7.24). King Guntram reckons Poitiers is one of his cities, but with the encouragement of bishop Maroveus, it has gone over to Childebert. Guntram calls up those who were liable for military service, for one of the obligations of a city was to provide the king with troops, and, with a force including the people of Orléans (Aurelienses) and Bourges (the Biturigi), marches on Poitiers, loots the land, burns the buildings, and massacres the inhabitants. They ravage the region several times (including Tours in the collateral damage, to Gregory's distress) until the people of Poitiers cave in, albeit with an ill grace. Besieging a city is a heavy military investment (though there is plenty of that too), but the easiest way is to ravage the farmlands: the *regio* is *devastata*, then you approach the walls of the *urbs* and demand surrender. The unity of *urbs* and *regio* in the *civitas* is what enables the familiar classical military tactics.

A further sign of the integration of city and population of the wider territory is in the language Gregory uses to refer to *civitates*. Often the cities themselves have two alternative name-forms: Roman Paris was Lutetia, or Lutetia Parisiorum; Gregory consistently uses the form Parisii. Bayeux was Augustodurum (Baiocassiorum); Gregory prefers Baiocassii. In both these cases, the modern names follow the tribal name. Modern scholars refer to Gallic cities as 'civitas capitals', as they do for Roman Britain; unlike Spain or Italy with their *municipia*, these are thought of as native tribal groupings with an administrative centre. We should be cautious here: at the time of the Roman conquest in the first century BC, the Romans encountered the Gauls as a series of tribal groups, and in urbanising the landscape, set up centres based on these tribal groupings. But by Gregory's day, the Parisii or the Turones were simply the inhabitants of an area defined as being juridically subject to the *civitas* with an urban centre. Gregory's naming practice suggests that he thought the rural population an integral part of the *civitas*: that was compatible with a classical model.

[9] Murray, 'The Merovingian state', p. 216.

Gregory's Senatorial Family

To appreciate Gregory's picture of a world of cities, it is helpful to recognise his own place in a post-Roman social system, about which he has much to tell us. It has been suggested that the impression that Gregory fills his writings with biographical material about himself and his family is something of a myth.[10] While this may be true of his *Histories*, it is certainly not true of his biographical accounts of religious figures, especially the *Life of the Fathers*, written during the composition of the *Histories* in the 570s and 580s.[11] With remarkable frequency, the saints whose lives he narrates are members of his own family – how many others could boast descent from no fewer than three saints? Gregory always draws attention to two contrasting schemes of distinction: the glory of descent from noble families (like his own) in this world, the *saeculum*; and the proximity to God of the saints. His uncle Gallus, brother of his father, Florentius,[12] well illustrates this tension. The Life opens with a little sermon on the contrast between worldly nobility, ever in pursuit of honours and wealth, and those who 'like birds fleeing from a snare and flying up to the skies' escape from such worldly ambitions. Such was Gallus, an inhabitant of Clermont-Ferrand (*Arvernae urbis*), 'whom neither the greatness of his birth nor the elevation of the senatorial order (*celsitudo senatorii ordinis*) nor his immense riches were able to turn away from the worship of God'.[13] But though we are urged to shun earthly nobility, Gregory, who shared it, is not shy about spelling it out. The father of Gallus (Gregory's paternal grandfather) was Georgius, and his mother Leucadia, whose family descended from Vettius Epagathus, the martyr of Lyon. With such noble descent on both sides ('than which nothing could be more well-born and noble'), his father wanted Gallus to marry a suitable girl, the daughter of a senator; but he fled to a monastery, and when he asked to be tonsured, the abbot, learning that he was the son of no less than Georgius the senator, insisted on his seeking his father's permission. With some regret ('He is my first-born, and

---

[10] So the authoritative study of Heinzelmann, *Gregory of Tours*, pp. 7–11; see also Goffart, *The Narrators of Barbarian History*, pp. 191–192. There is a valuable introduction to the author by Ian Wood, *Gregory of Tours*.

[11] For a succinct chronology, Wood, *Gregory*, p. 3. On Gregory's hagiographical works, see esp. Brown, *The Cult of the Saints*; *Society and the Holy in Late Antiquity*, pp. 222–250; Van Dam, *Saints and Their Miracles*.

[12] Heinzelmann, *Gregory*, p. 10 for a tree, and pp. 11–22 for his individual family members.

[13] For Latin text see Krusch, *Gregori Episcopi Turonensis Miracula*, pp. 229–236; for an English translation, James, *Gregory of Tours: Life of the Fathers*, pp. 32–42.

so I wished him to be joined in marriage', implicitly to produce an heir), Georgius agrees to give in gracefully to the will of God.

Gregory may not spell out his own membership of his family, though his full name, Georgius Florentius Gregorius, in fact flagged his descent from both Gallus' father and brother. But the next life in the series, that of Gregory of Langres, is rather more explicit about his descent on the maternal side. Gregory, his great-grandfather, was, exactly like Gallus, one who had humbled himself for his faith: coming 'from the exalted power of the senatorial rank' (*ab excelsa senatorii ordinis potentia*) to a position of humility, he cast aside worldly cares.[14] One of the leading senators of Langres (*civitas Lingonica*) and well educated, he did not, unlike Gallus, forsake the world for a monastery, but embraced public life as the count (*comes*) of the city of Autun (Augustodunum), administering justice with a notable severity that let no guilty man get away. His wife, Armentaria, also from a senatorial family, bore him a number of sons, and it was only after her death, and forty years in public service, that he 'turned to the Lord' (*ad Dominum convertitur*) and was chosen as bishop of his native city. There he distinguished himself by his self-denial (he would secretly eat barley bread at the communion, having served good wheat bread to the others), and by his miracles. One witness to his miraculous power to save was his grand-daughter, Armentaria (the historian's mother), who, as a child suffering from a quartan fever, was cured by lying in the saint's bed. This is a world in which people were tormented by what must have been endemic malaria, and more rarely by bubonic plague, and lying in a saint's bed, or other close contact, was the best remedy for a miracle cure.

It is hard to absolve Gregory of the charge of having his cake and eating it. As a bishop (and himself, in due succession, a saint), he insists on the vanity of worldly pride; but the frequency and emphasis of his claims to high birth and wealth among his family members suggests that he had not wholly cured himself of such pride. And there is more. The following Life is of Saint Nicetius, who was son of Florentinus (distinct from Gallus' father, Florentius) and uncle of the historian's mother, Armentaria.[15] Florentinus was 'one of the senators', married to Artemia. When he was offered the bishopric of Geneva, Artemia, at the time pregnant, begged him to refuse on the grounds that in her womb she bore a future bishop, Nicetius, as proved to be the case. Gregory had fond personal memories of

---

[14] *Vita Patrum* 7 (Krusch, pp. 236–240; James, pp. 43–48).
[15] *Life of the Fathers* 8 (Krusch, pp. 240–252; James, pp. 49–64).

the bishop: at the age of seven, when he was learning letters, he lay in the bed of Nicetius, who, with sweetly paternal affection, propped him up with his elbow, though making sure to have no contact with his flesh, so far was he from any carnal concupiscence. Nicetius too had bishops as well as senators in his blood: he was appointed bishop of Lyon by King Childebert in response to the deathbed wish of his predecessor, Sacerdos, who asked to be succeeded by his *nepos* (nephew or grandson). To Gregory, nepotism was a matter of family pride.

Gregory's rambling family tree boasts both senators and bishop/saints over at least four generations, on both the paternal and maternal sides. As he repeatedly points out, the Gallic elite arranged marriages on dynastic principles. It was a matter of producing heirs to considerable landed wealth, and when a son 'got the call' it could disrupt the smooth pattern of succession. Gallus frustrates his father's dynastic planning, Gregory of Langres avoided the problem by having two careers, and Artemia can't have been the only young wife to beg her husband not to go into the church and thereby deny the family a life of ostentatious wealth. Promising her unborn child to the church was a neat way of buying time, and incidentally reveals the supreme confidence with which members of these powerful families could predict attainment of high office in the church. One could therefore with confidence predict for Gregory himself a distinguished public life or a bishopric. As Venantius Fortunatus, the polished Latinist who was Gregory's close friend,[16] says in his epitaph for another bishop, Chronopius of Périgueux (Petrocorii), his bishopric was his birth right, and on both sides:

> ordo sacerdotum cui fluxit utroque parente:
>   venit ad heredem pontificalis apex.
> hunc tibi iure gradum successio sancta paravit,
>   ut quasi iam merito debitus esset honor.
>
> to him sacerdotal rank flowed from both parents
> a bishop's mitre fell to the heir.
> A sacred succession prepared this step for you
> so that the honour was owed to one who had already merited it.[17]

---

[16] On Venantius see George, *Venantius Fortunatus*, pp. 4–34; Roberts, *Venantius Fortunatus and Gregory of Tours*. For the text, Leo, *Venanti Honori Clementiani Fortunati Presbyteri Italici Opera*.

[17] Venantius, *Poems* 4.8.7–10, cited by Heinzelmann, *Bischofsherrschaft*, p. 215.

Cities and Citizens

It is Gregory's conspicuous place in a social system descended from that of the Roman world that makes him so credible a witness to the social structure of Merovingian Gaul. It is the townsfolk, whether processing round walls, or struggling against listing in tax returns, or being conscripted into the army, whom we need to understand a little better in order to assess how far the city has moved from its classical roots. The continued importance of the *cives* has often been downplayed.[18] Just as Gregory's text is full of mention of *civitates*, it is full of *cives*. Was citizenship of a Merovingian *civitas* anything like citizenship of a classical city? Gregory knew classical authors quite well enough to know that the *civis* classically referred to any free inhabitant of a *civitas*, whether of the *urbs* itself or the territory, who enjoyed rights of participation in the community. He also knew that *populus* referred to the whole body of *cives*: not simply the population (including slaves and foreigners), but members of the community itself. Is there anything of this classical sense in Gregory? It has been maintained that Gregory's usage is more nuanced, and that at least sometimes the *cives* refers to the better-off inhabitants of the city – effectively to what would be called the *curiales*, if only Gregory used that word.[19] It may indeed be the case that named *cives* are better-off people, but this is surely because most of them are bishops. Humble individuals are not often named in a history like this. Durliat suggests that when Gregory wrote to the bishop and citizens (*episcopo et civibus*) of Poitiers urging them not to abandon loyalty to Guntram for Childebert (7.13), the *cives* must be the town council, not the whole citizen body. Maybe, but it is not what Gregory says, and of course he could address a letter to the *cives* knowing well that it would be the council that actioned it.

The absence of the council is indeed strange but it seems to me that *cives* refers overwhelmingly to the citizen body at large – a body with which the bishop has a very special relationship. We have seen that only a *civitas*, not a *castrum* like Dijon, can have a bishop. That is closely connected with the sense that he is elected by and representative of his *cives*. We might start from Gregory's own election. His friend and defender Venantius Fortunatus, one who certainly understood classical usage, addresses a poem (5.3) *ad cives Turonicos de Gregorio episcopo* to celebrate his friend's

---

[18] See my 'Fluidity of an ideal'.   [19] Durliat, 'Episcopus, civis et populus'.

return from the uncomfortable hearing in 580 before Chilperic and a court of bishops at which Venantius had defended him:

> Plaudite, felices populi, nova vota tenentes
>   Praesulis adventu reddite vota deo.
> Hoc puer exertus celebret, hoc curva senectus
>   Hoc commune bonum praedicet omnis homo.
> Spes gregis ecce venit, plebis pater, urbis amator;
>   Munere pastoris laetificantur oves.

Everyone is to rejoice and offer up prayers of thanksgiving to God for Gregory's safe return. He specifies who these happy peoples are – all ages, from boys to bent old men: every man (*omnis homo*) celebrates the good of the community, the *commune bonum*. Gregory is the lover of his city, the father of the common people, the *plebs*, the pastor of his flock. The *cives* whom Venantius addresses are thus constructed as the entire people, including young and old and poor. To reduce these citizens to an elite of the better off goes against the sense of the passage, and indeed the expected relationship of pastor and flock.

The same episode is described by Gregory himself (*Hist.* 5.49). He describes how a priest called Riculf had been stirring up Tours against Gregory and purging the city of the 'rabble from Clermont' (*Arverni populi* – Gregory's lot). Riculf was outgunned:

> The poor fool seems not to have realised that, apart from five, all other bishops who held their appointment in the see of Tours were blood-relations of my family.

Gregory was, we have seen, formidably well connected. Riculf alone fails to take part in the festivities when Gregory returns:

> He did not come out to receive my greeting, as all the other citizens did, but went on threatening me and saying that he would kill me.

Sicut reliqui cives fecerant: the *cives* who come out, in a splendid late Roman *adventus* ceremony, to exchange the *salutatio* with Gregory are the same as the *cives* whom Venantius addressed.[20] Of course, both Gregory and Venantius may be exaggerating wildly in suggesting that ALL the citizens came out to greet their returning hero. But what is represented is an ideal: that the citizen body as a whole is firmly behind the bishop.

These detailed descriptions are consistent with the language repeatedly used of the appointment of bishops, technically by the king, but with the

---

[20] On the *adventus*, see the classic study of MacCormack, *Art and Ceremony in Late Antiquity*.

consensus civium, like Charimeres of Verdun, 'with the consensus of the citizens the authority of the king decreed that he should become bishop',[21] and unlike Waldo of Eauze, who hastens to the king with gifts 'and the consent of the citizens', *et consensu civium*, but finds that Childebert has another candidate in mind (*Hist.* 8.22). We meet the expression *clerici et cives* to represent the two groups, clergy and laity, whose support the bishop needs. When Bishop Aravatius of Tongres dies, he bids farewell first 'to the clergy and remaining citizens of the city',[22] and when Eparchius of Clermont would process to the cathedral with great singing of psalms, it was 'in company of the clergy and citizens'.[23] *Cives* and *populus* are often used interchangeably. Saint Avitus of Clermont is approved as bishop by the king, and then, assembling the citizens (*congregatis in unum civibus*), he is elected by clergy and people (*a clero et populo electus*) (4.35). Of course, no consensus is credible to us without a proper popular vote, yet these people depend on the sort of acclamations and generic manifestations of support that were typical of the late Roman world, since voting had long since disappeared. And, of course, the richer citizens, whom he occasionally calls *seniores civium* or the like, may have played a dominant role in any such manifestations. But that does not diminish the ideology, which is that the whole citizen body is united behind their bishop.

Just occasionally, it becomes credible that all the citizens might benefit from a good bishop. There is the remarkable intervention of Bishop Desideratus of Verdun with King Theudebert (*Hist.* 3.34). He himself had lost all his property because of a quarrel with King Theuderic. He found the inhabitants of Verdun poor and destitute (*valde pauperes et destitutos*), and appeals to Theudebert, a man of well-known charitable disposition. He asks him to grant him a loan to relieve our citizens in distress (*cives nostros*). He says that when the traders, *negotium exercentes*, recover in our *civitas*, as has happened in others, he will be able to pay the king back. He is lent 7,000 gold pieces and, thanks to a distribution among all the *cives*, the traders flourished – and still flourish today. The episode casts a striking light on the effects of episcopal charity: giving to the poor and needy (not just giving grants to start-up enterprises) gives a boost to the entire economy. And it underlines, if this was needed, the importance of trade in the urban economy.[24]

What has happened to the *curiales*, the elite group so often associated with the essence of the Roman city? The word itself occurs not one single

---

[21] *Hist.* 9.23: *cum consensu civium regalis decrevit auctoritas fieri sacerdotem.*
[22] *Hist.* 2.5: *clericis et reliquis civibus urbis.*   [23] *Hist.* 2.21: *comitantibus clericis civibusque.*
[24] Henri Pirenne was well aware of significant references in Gregory: to trade at Verdon and elsewhere, *Medieval Cities*, pp. 8–13.

time, though from contemporary documents and formularies it is quite clear that the *curia* continued to be part of the institutional make-up of a *civitas* (see Chapter 6). The closest Gregory gets to admitting their presence is not in his *Histories* but his book on the *Glory of the Confessors* (20), where he describes his own dedication of an oratory to saints Saturninus and Martin, accompanied by a great procession of singing clerics and people: 'there was no small chorus of priests and levites in white vestments and the distinguished order of honoured citizens (*civium honoratorum ordo praeclarus*) and a great gathering of the people of the next rank (*populi sequentis ordinis magnus conventus*)'. The honoured citizens must be what are normally (or at least under the Late Roman Empire were normally) called *curiales*, especially since they form an *ordo* (the Roman senate was an *ordo*, as were the equestrians, and the decurions or curials of local cities). But he also calls the citizens an *ordo*: not just a crowd of inhabitants, but the formal body of members of the community. When Gregory refers vaguely to the city elites as '*maiores, seniores, priores, honorati, magnifici*' it does indeed seem reasonable to see in them precisely the people who appear in more formal documents as *curiales*.[25]

'Senators' and 'Senatorial Families'

The other group of people Gregory is keen that we should hear about are *senatores*. Given that Roman imperial control of Gaul had collapsed a century before he became a bishop, and that the term had always applied exclusively to the senate in Rome, one might be a little puzzled that post-Roman Gaul seems still to be full of *senatores*. Part of the explanation is of course the intense pride which men like Gregory himself took in being descended from real senators. Already in the high empire, the descendants of a senator could describe themselves as being of senatorial family, if not actually as senators. Gregory, who, as we have seen, could boast that all but five bishops of Tours were his relatives, was intensely proud of his family; his tree is bristling with senators. He describes both his father Florentius and his paternal grandfather as senators (though they lived too late to have been members of the Roman senate). Similarly, his maternal great-grandfather Florentinus is called a senator in Geneva – but not in Rome. (He is not to be confused with the Florentinus from Trier, who in the late fourth century was praetorian prefect in Rome, and of true senatorial

---

[25] So Loseby in *Oxford Handbook of the Merovingian World*, pp. 593–594.

standing.) Even more distinguished is the family of Sidonius Apollinaris, bishop of Clermont after serving as praetorian prefect in Rome. He was son and grandson of Apollinares who served as praetorian prefects in Gaul, father of the Apollinaris who was bishop of Tours, and Arcadius, a senator in the Auvergne.

It is out of families like these that long ago (1948) Karl Stroheker constructed his carefully argued thesis that the great landowning 'senatorial' families who dominated late Roman Gaul continued to dominate long into Merovingian times.[26] Harnessing the 'prosopographical' technique already used by historians of the Roman Republic, notably Friedrich Münzer in his *Römische Adelsparteien und Adelsfamilien*, he drew up a list of the 'nobility' (Adelsfamilien) of fifth- and sixth-century Gaul, tracing the numerous links between them. Ranging from the evidence of Ausonius and especially Sidonius Apollinaris to the historian Gregory, he built up a case for the continuity of rich landowning families from the Late Empire to Gregory's day. Taking his cue from Gregory's repeated use of *senatores* and expressions such as *ex genere senatorio*, he argued that these dominant families took pride in ancestry dating back to the Roman fourth century when their members held senatorial rank in Rome itself – something demonstrably true of Sidonius and his forebears, and of the emperor Avitus, to whose sister Sidonius was married, and from whom Avitus the bishop of Vienne was descended.

Stroheker's picture was subsequently supported and extended by Martin Heinzelmann, later also the author of a major biography of Gregory, in his book on the power of bishops in Gaul; its subtitle proclaimed the theme of continuity of the ruling classes from the fourth to the seventh centuries.[27] Reinforcing Stroheker's argument with further examples of how leading families effectively treated bishoprics as family inheritances, Heinzelmann drew a link between the expression of aristocratic ethos in the funerary epitaphs and *Vitae* (Lives) of these Gallic bishops and the traditions of the Roman republican nobility. He even saw the origins of Gallic epitaphs in the second-century BC tombs of the Scipiones in Rome with their verse epitaphs, initially in the archaic Roman verse form of Saturnians, afterwards in elegiacs, and the funerary laudations traditionally pronounced by young Roman nobles at the death of their family members.

At the very moment when Roman republican historians were falling out of love with Münzer's prosopographical method and its underlying

---

[26] Strokeker, *Der senatorische Adel im spätantiken Gallien*.
[27] Heinzelmann, *Bischofsherrschaft in Gallien*.

assumptions, historians of post-Roman Gaul seem to have embraced it with unquestioning fervour. It assumes a genuine pattern of continuity and tradition in aristocratic families, rather than the attempt by a current generation of competitors for power to bolster their standing by laying claims to ancestry, sometimes plausible and often implausible. Noble status is not simply inherited: it is also artfully produced, as Cicero recognised (*Brutus* 62), by those with an interest in maximising it. Gregory's contemporaries might have been delighted by the claim that they had inherited a Roman republican ethos; sceptics might have pointed out that verse epitaphs had been churned out in their thousands for men far from noble, in a tradition which in the very name 'epitaph' proclaims Greek rather than Roman roots, and that virtues typical of *Vitae* are a Greek tradition as much as a noble Roman one.

The thesis of the great continuity of the Gallo-Roman aristocracy needs to be re-examined with a more sceptical eye. My concern is with the people Gregory calls 'senators'. Stroheker's interpretation of them as descendants of metropolitan Roman senators conflicted with that of the Godefroid Kurth, no less influential an historian (he taught Henri Pirenne).[28] For Kurth the word simply applied to rich landowners, a thesis later revived by Frank Gilliard.[29] That they represented the landowning elite of the cities of Gaul is beyond question, but we still need to explain why they used the language of 'senatorial' to distinguish themselves. There is another possibility, which has seemed so absurd to be dismissed out of hand:

> First, there is virtually no possibility that Gregory's senators were simply the municipal senators, the *curiales* of the Roman *civitates*. It is well known that in the Late Empire *curiales* were commonly referred to as senators, and that their municipal councils, the *curiae*, were called senates. But the *curiae* had almost completely disappeared from the West by the later sixth century; where some did survive in Gaul, they did so only vestigially.[30]

The assumption that the *curiae* had gone (and with them the last vestiges of the 'ancient city') is so tenacious that the possibility that Gregory is talking about them is dismissed out of hand. In the light of Josiane Barbier's vindication of the authenticity of the documents showing *curiae* in action

---

[28] The Belgian Kurth is repeatedly cited by Goffart, himself a Belgian by birth.
[29] Gilliard, 'The senators of sixth-century Gaul', citing Kurth, 'Les sénateurs en Gaule'. (Gilliard seems unaware of Heinzelmann.) There is a closely parallel debate about the meaning of *senatores* in Visigothic Spain: Churchin, 'Senators or curials?' and Chapter 8.
[30] Gilliard, 'The senators of sixth-century Gaul', pp. 687–688.

(discussed in Chapter 6), it is high time to think again. One point that might encourage the idea that 'senator' meant 'someone from a senatorial family' is Gregory's use of the expression *ex genere senatorio*. Stroheker's insistence that descent mattered in the dominant families is unimpeachable. But we might hesitate to ask why, if 'senator' simply meant 'member of a senatorial family', Gregory did not simply call these individuals *senator*, rather than *ex genere senatorio*? Why, for that matter, would he call the presbyter Euphrasius, candidate for the bishopric of Clermont, 'the son of the late senator Euvodius' (*filius quondam senatoris Euvodi*) if 'senator' merely indicated a member of a senatorial family, which would make Euphrasius a senator in his own right? And why are bishops consistently described not as 'senators' but as *de genere senatorio*,[31] or, like Sidonius' relative Ecdicius, as *quidam ex senatoribus* (2.24), or, like the first bishop of Clermont, Urbicus, *ex senatoribus conversus*, 'a convert from senators' (1.44)? Pope Gregory the Great, as we have seen (Chapter 6) explicitly banned priests from holding office as *curiales*; to become a bishop, Urbicus would need to shed curial status, so that he was no longer, in Gregory's language, a 'senator'. If it simply indicated descent from a 'senatorial' family, how could he be converted from it?

One of the main problems with the idea that these people were all descendants of those who once held senatorial rank in Rome itself is that there seem to be a significant number of them, and their numbers increase through time. Stroheker produced three distribution maps of the cities with attested *senatores*, and they increase notably between the fourth century (only thirteen) and the fifth (twenty-three), with only a minor reduction in the sixth century (twenty-one). Gregory frequently refers to them as a group associated with particular cities. A good example is his own natal city of Clermont (*civitas Arvernorum*). He will typically say, not 'a senator from Auvergne', but 'one of the senators of Auvergne', *unus ex senatoribus Arvernis* – language which makes more sense if the Arverni had a local senate.

On other occasions, too, the 'senators' sound like the entire local elite, not just those who happened to descend from Roman senators. When the unspeakable Chramn, son of Lothar I, lived in Clermont, he made himself hated by his arbitrary administration of justice, and by the ugly crowd of youths of low birth he used as counsellors, to the extent that, on their bidding, 'he had the daughters of senators dragged off by force' (*filias*

---

[31] Thus Agricola, bishop of Châlons (*Hist.* 5.45), Eustochius, fifth bishop of Tours (10.31.5), and Volusianus, seventh bishop of the same city (10.31.7)

senatorum vi detrahi iuberet; *Hist.* 4.13). At the great battle of Vouillé (AD 507), the Arvernians, fighting on the losing side under Apollinaris, the son of Bishop Sidonius, suffered heavy casualties: these were both the common people of the Arvernians (*Arvernorum populus*) and *primi qui erant ex senatoribus* (2.37). Were the leaders drawn from the local senate, or were they only those of aristocratic descent? Such families were numerous enough to supply the whole Arvernian officer class. In the context, it sounds like a broad group of local leaders, the 'senators'.

Another case is the conflict between Theuderic and Childebert, two of the sons of Clovis, forever squabbling over which cities they should control (3.15). Theuderic has invaded Arvernian territory after Childebert's attempt to seize Clermont. They patch up a truce, and seal it by an exchange of hostages, *filii senatorum*. But the truce breaks down, and the hostages are reduced, some to public service, others to slavery. Gregory can tell the story because of the involvement of one of his own kinsmen: Attalus, the nephew or grandson of Bishop Gregory of Langres, great-grandfather and namesake of the historian.[32] He goes on to narrate the extraordinary and gripping tale of Attalus' escape from slavery under a Frank based near Trier. Attalus was simply one of a group of young hostages exchanged. Taking hostages from the sons of the local councillors is a way to ensure the council stays loyal.

The incident that most clearly tips the scales in favour of the idea that 'senators' are simply local councillors is the siege of Vienne of AD 500. At the time, Clovis was intervening in the quarrel between the brothers Godigisel and Gundobad for the Burgundian kingdom. Godigisel brings in Clovis and the Franks on his side, promising to make the kingdom pay tribute to Clovis. Gundobad besieges Godigisel and his Frankish allies in Vienne, and enters the city by the old trick of crawling down the aqueduct, thanks to the advice of the local aqueduct engineer. Gundobad then metes out justice to his enemies. Godigisel and his Franks have their lives spared and are sent off in exile to Alaric in Toulouse. But others are shown no mercy and are killed: *interfectis senatoribus Burgundionibus(que) qui Godigiselo consensuerant* (2.33). At this critical juncture, the manuscripts disagree as to whether there is a linking *-que*, 'and': is it senators *and* Burgundians, or Burgundian senators? That the groups were separate is confirmed by the Chronicle of Gregory's contemporary, Marius of Avenches, which records that in 456 the Burgundiones occupied part of Gaul and 'divided the lands with the Gallic senators' (*terrasque cum*

---

[32] Heinzelmann, *Gregory*, pp. 15–16.

Gallicis senatoribus diviserunt).[33] It makes no sense to imagine that the Burgundians' share of land was limited to a share of that of the descendants of Roman senators, whereas the local senators, *curiales*, will, as ever, have constituted major landowners.

That is obviously inconceivable if, as is assumed, there was no *curia* in Vienne to take a vote on such a matter. Is it after all possible that there was a *curia*? As it happens, we have an eyewitness to reassure us that there was one. Bishop Avitus, descendant of the ill-fated emperor of that name, was not only present at the siege, but made a sustained attempt to convert Gundobad from his Arian beliefs to Catholicism. The next chapter in Gregory (Hist. 2.34) is a lengthy account of this attempted conversion, though what emerges from Avitus' own letters is that he was less successful than Gregory liked to imagine.[34] One of the best-known sermons of Avitus, cited with praise by Gregory and paraphrased in the same chapter, is that on the occasion of the annual rogations, a three-day period of prayer and processions after Easter (still celebrated in the Catholic church). Avitus takes the opportunity to explain the origin of the rogations in the mid-fifth century (before 473) under Bishop Mamertus, Avitus' predecessor but one, and the one who officiated at his own baptism.[35] There had been, he narrates, a succession of portentous happenings – fires, earthquakes, plagues, and the like – which culminated in the catastrophic fire of a principal public building (*aedes publica*) set on the highest point of the city (Gregory calls it the palace, *palatium regale*). The bishop checked the fire from spreading to the rest of the city 'not so much by water as by his tears'. Mamertus then conceived the idea of an annual three-day festival of rogations and took his idea to a body which was notorious for opposition to new ideas: the city council. He describes it ('for avoidance of doubt', the lawyers might say) as both *senatus* and *curia*: 'the senate of Vienne, the council of which then flourished with numerous illustrious men'.[36] Since the incident is set in the mid fifth-century, it is no surprise to find an active *curia*; what is significant is that in the sixth century, Avitus still calls it indifferently a *curia* and a *senatus*. That strengthens the likelihood that, at the siege of Vienne in 500, one could still speak of *curiales* as *senatores*. Other evidence suggests that the

---

[33] Marius Aventicensis in *MGH AA* XI, 232, cited by Kurth, 'Grégoire de Tours et les études classiques', p. 109.

[34] Shanzer and Wood, *Avitus of Vienne*, is an exemplary introduction to a neglected author, with translation of the Letters; pp. 13–24 on Avitus' relations with the Burgundians.

[35] On rogations, see Ristuccia, *Christianization and Commonwealth*.

[36] Homilia 6 (MGH AA 6.2 p. 110): *Viennensis senatus cuius tunc numerosis illustribus curia florebat*, cited by Gilliard, 'The senators of sixth-century Gaul', p. 688.

local senate survived well into the sixth century, for a charter of AD 543 refers to the *nobilis senatus Viennensis*.[37]

Gregory's usage in his Saints' Lives bears out that of the *Histories*. There is a clear distinction between those who are described as *senatores* and those who are *ex genere senatorio* of *filii senatoris*.[38] The incident which most clearly reveals the senatorial elite as simply the local elite, and too numerous to be anything else, involves a bishop of Tours, Catianus, one of the glorious confessors (*Glory of the Confessors* 5). Having built himself a reputation in the village of Artonne (*vicus Artonensis*) outside Clermont, he one day leaves the village and heads for Clermont. Word spreads in the city of his approach, causing great excitement, and 'the senators of the city, which at that time was brilliant with descent from Roman nobility' (*nobilitatis Romanae stimmate refulgebat*), come out to meet him. They sound for all the world like Stroheker's descendants of Roman senators, until we observe their sheer numbers. They come out on horseback and in carriages, in carts and in four-wheelers. Hard though it is for us to distinguish a *carruca* from a *currus* from a *rhaeda* (though Isidore of Seville gives some pointers),[39] Gregory's choice of multiple words for means of transport creates the impression of a mighty crowd. That is certainly the impression Catianus gets, and when he sees this procession approach in all its show (*cum his pompis*), he asks who they are that they make all this fuss. Someone replies that they are the Arvernian senators come to escort him in, whereat he turns back (seated as he is on a donkey), and says it is not for him to enter the city with this show.

The senators of Clermont are treating the holy man like a king or a governor. It was customary to celebrate the arrival of someone of great importance with such a procession of notables (and, of course, a panegyric). Who should come out to do the honours? The flower of the local elite, by all means, but the idea that only those of Roman senatorial lineage should take part is absurd. Doubtless they would have been delighted to be thought of as Stroheker's 'Gallo-Roman aristocracy', but

---

[37] Gilliard, 'The senators of sixth-century Gaul', note 12, citing Pardessus, *Diplomata, Chartae, Epistolae*, p. 107. For problems around the Vienne charter, Nimmegeers, *Évêques entre Bourgogne et Provence*.

[38] So the family of Gallus all enjoy *celsitudo senatorii ordinis* in contrast to Georgius, *de primoribus senatoribus* (vit. Patr. 6); Florentinus but not his son Nicetius is *quidam ex senatoribus* (vit. Patr.8); Leobard's family is freeborn but not *genere senatorio* (vit.Patr. 20).

[39] Isidore, *Etymologies* 20.12.1–2, noting that a *reda* is a type of vehicle with four wheels. With similar satirical effect, Emile Zola in the opening of La *Curée* depicts 'tout Paris' out for a ride in the Bois de Boulogne in their differently named vehicles.

it makes no demographic sense that they should be other than the curial elite.

That such an elite should have survived is far from incredible. The Burgundian kings, Gundobad and his son and successor Sigismund, who did convert to Catholicism shortly after the siege, were scarcely less anxious than the Ostrogothic Theoderic to present themselves as legitimate successors to Roman emperors, carrying Roman titles such as *patricius*, issuing (in 517) their own update on Roman laws, and even minting Roman-style coinage.[40] There is no reason to suppose that they were less supportive than was Theoderic of the Roman institutions of civic administration with their *curiae*, the preferred term for the members of which seems to have been *senatores*. If the *senatores* were big local landowners with a hereditary right and obligation to serve on their city's council, it explains why Gregory's senators are so often linked to a specific city (*senatores Arverni* and the like), and why he distinguishes between those who were actual senators and those who were of senatorial descent. The *curiales* of the Late Empire, after all, were a hereditary group based on wealth, and if Stroheker's insight was right that a hereditary aristocracy persisted in fifth- and sixth-century Gaul, its claim to title in local senates, and not the senate in Rome, does not diminish the claim to aristocracy and wealth. Those who could make up a plausibly Roman noble ancestor doubtless did.

Kings and Cities

Gregory's Gaul was dominated by the sprawling family of Clovis, the impressive figure who united the future Francia by conquest of the Visigoths (507) and the Burgundians (534). By a timely conversion from paganism (unlike the Goths, the Franks were not Arians) to Catholicism (*Hist.* 2.29), he both nested Frankish power into the structure of the existing elite and ensured that bishops would be major political as well as ecclesiastical figures. Unlike Theoderic in Italy, he proved successful – indeed, only too successful – in establishing a dynasty of his own blood. Theoderic was left with an underage grandson by his daughter to succeed him; Clovis left four sons: Theuderic, Chlodomer, Childebert, and Lothar. These in their turn produced a batch of grandsons: Theuderic produced Theudebert and Theudebald – the Germanic taste for compound names

---

[40] See Shanzer and Wood, *Avitus of Vienne*, pp. 24–27. For the widespread imitation by kings of Roman imperial ceremony, see Fanning, 'Clovis Augustus and Merovingian *Imitatio Imperii*'.

makes it easier to identify descent, Theud- (people) -ric (kingdom), -bert (bright), -bald (bold) – and Lothar, by four different wives, producing Charibert, Guntram, Sigibert, and Chilperic, as well as Gregory's bête noire, Chramn. Sigibert produced a second Childebert, who in turn fathered a second Theudebert and Theuderic, while Chilperic's ruthless wife Fredegund gave him a second Lothar, who in turn fathered Dagobert. To read Merovingian history is to fight through a thicket of recurring names.[41] They populate the pages of the *Histories*, and, though spectacularly successful as a family in terms of reproduction, were fiercely competitive with each other, constantly fighting, to Gregory's despair, over territory:

> Just think of all that Clovis achieved, Clovis, the founder of your victorious country, who slaughtered those rulers who opposed him, conquered hostile peoples and captured their territories, thus bequeathing to you absolute and unquestioned dominion over them! At the time when he accomplished all this, he possessed neither gold nor silver such as you have in your treasure houses! But you, what are you doing? What are you trying to do? You have everything you want! Your homes are full of luxuries, there are vast supplies of wine, grain and oil in your storehouses, and in your treasuries the gold and silver are piled high. One thing is lacking: you cannot keep peace! (*Hist.* 5. preface)

The eloquence of Gregory's protest (notice the rhetorical trick of apostrophe) has led to the dismal reputation of the Merovingian kings. He goes on to cite Orosius and his Sallustian analysis of Roman power as depending on concord and undermined by civil war; Augustine would have agreed. But where this 'civil war' mattered for Gregory and his Roman contemporaries was that the bone of contention in these endless struggles was control over cities.

As Simon Loseby has nicely shown, cities remained the building blocks, 'like pieces of Merovingian Lego', out of which the territory was made.[42] And there is no mistaking that in Gregory's narrative, it is a world of cities. It was over who got which city that Clovis' descendants squabbled. The feuds put them under strain, but what made cities so desirable was that to control them was to control the territory and cream off whatever profit in taxes or other contributions they could. So the incident in which the

---

[41] For a reliable guide, Wood, *The Merovingian Kingdoms*.
[42] See the fundamental sequence of papers by Loseby, 'Gregory's cities: Urban functions in sixth-century Gaul'; 'Decline and change in the cities of Late Antique Gaul'; and, most recently, 'The role of the city in Merovingian Francia', p. 588 for the quotation.

soldiers of Arles drowned in the river Rhône is just part of a tussle between Sigibert and Guntram for control of the cities of Provence, formerly under Burgundian rule:

> King Sigibert wanted to take over Arles and he ordered the men of Clermont (the *Arverni*) to attack that city. At this time, it was Firminus who was Count of Clermont, and it was he who set out at their head. Meanwhile Audovarius marched on the city with his army from the opposite direction. They entered Arles and exacted oaths of fealty in the name of King Sigibert. When King Guntram heard of this, he in his turn sent the patrician Celsus with an army. Celsus came to Avignon and captured the city. Then he too marched on Arles, surrounded the place and began to assault Sigibert's army. (*Hist.* 4.30, trans. Thorpe)

Not only is it that the kings want to control cities, but they rely on levies from cities to do the fighting. Nor is it enough for the population of a city to acknowledge defeat, for the kings rely on oaths of loyalty, city by city, to consolidate their control. Inescapably, they are sucked into the centre of the maelstrom of Merovingian feuding.

A few chapters later, Sigibert is enmeshed in a three-way struggle with his brothers Chilperic and Guntram. Chilperic sends his son Theudebert to attack the cities of Tours, Poitiers, and others south of the Loire, and ravages the land, burning churches, killing clergy, raping nuns, and causing devastation everywhere (4.47). Then Sigibert marches on Chilperic in the region round Paris, having been given free passage over the Seine by Guntram, which Chilperic regards as an act of treachery. Sigibert threatens battle against Chilperic, who caves in:

> Chilperic was afraid that if their two armies joined in battle, each of their two kingdoms might be destroyed. He sued for peace and handed back Sigibert's cities which Theudebert had so savagely attacked, stipulating that the inhabitants should not be punished, for Theudebert had annexed them forcibly, coercing them with fire and sword. (4.49)

By the seventh century, a series of territorial blocks had emerged: the 'three kingdoms' of Austrasia, Neustria, and Burgundy. It is arguable that this brought a shift away from the city as a unit of territory towards these larger kingdoms.[43] If so, it is far from the case under Gregory's kings, who are still fighting it out city by city. The clearest example is the treaty of Andelot of 588, which Gregory himself played a role in negotiating, and could consequently quote its text verbatim (*Hist.* 9.20). Gregory is

[43] Loseby, 'Lost cities'.

summoned by Childebert to Metz, where he is currently based (Merovingian kings tend to move around) and sent on a mission to his uncle, King Guntram, based at Châlons-sur-Saône, *urbs Cavillonensis*. Guntram tells Gregory straight out that he is not best pleased with Childebert, because he has failed to hand over his part of the city of Senlis. Gregory reassures Guntram he can have his share, and the treaty is read out. What is at issue is a family quarrel over inheritance. Guntram's brothers, kings Charibert and Sigibert, had died some years before; Sigibert had taken the lands previously belonging to Charibert, but had ceded them to Guntram, and now Sigibert's son Childebert was claiming his paternal inheritance back. Childebert is allowed back the third of Paris (*civitas Parisiorum*) with its territory and inhabitants which had been his father Sigibert's. Childebert is allowed Meaux, two thirds of Senlis, Tours, Poitiers, Avranches, Aire, Couserans, Labourd, and Albi. At the same time, Queen Brunhild, the widow of Sigibert, has claimed five cities – Bordeaux, Limoges, Cahors, Lescar, and Cieutat – which she inherited from her sister Galswinth, who on her marriage to Chilperic had been given them as her *Morgengabe*: it is agreed that Brunhild can have Cahors, with its lands and inhabitants, but the rest will be Guntram's until his death when she will inherit them.

For Clovis's descendants, the cities of Gaul were like stocks and shares, to be divided up fairly between all male heirs on death, but also useful for giving as dowries when a son married the daughter of the Visigothic king Athanaric. On the one hand, they are no more than bits of heritable property; on the other, they are well worth quarrelling over. And it is striking how in order to negotiate the family deal, they turn to the bishop of Tours, whom they know to be an honest broker. Mostly each city goes to one member of the family or other. But Paris is too important, and is divided into three shares, as is Senlis, which provoked the present quarrel. And it is of course a massive relief to Gregory when he gets all parties to sign up to the deal, because the alternative is the series of reciprocal invasions that have studded his narrative.

What made cities such valuable assets was their potential for levying both taxes and troops. In the package inherited from the late Empire, as we have seen, cities were the centres where the ownership of land was registered in the *gesta municipalia* and, consequently, where taxes could be levied on that land. While the Roman state levied taxes to pay for the armies that defended the frontiers, military costs were lighter for Merovingian kings, except the costs of their squabbles with one another, and could accumulate significant resources: the stores of wine, oil, and grain, as well as the treasures of gold and silver to which Gregory refers so critically (as noted earlier). Kings felt entitled to tax cities, though of course cities felt entitled to demand exemption or relief. Thus in 579, King Chilperic tries to increase his share:

> King Chilperic decreed that a new series of taxes should be levied throughout the kingdom, and these were extremely heavy. As a result, a great number of people emigrated from their native cities or whatever bits of land they occupied and sought refuge elsewhere, for they preferred to go into exile than endure such punitive taxation. The new tax laws laid it down that a landowner must pay five gallons of wine for every half-acre he possessed. (*Hist.* 5.28, trans. Thorpe)

This leads to rioting in Limoges, where the mob burns the tax books; the king responds by brutal punishments and tortures aimed at the clergy, accused of fomenting the riot.

Gregory had rather more success in Tours (*Hist.* 9.30). Childebert is raising taxes from his cities and sends to Poitiers two tax assessors (*discriptores*), Florentianus and Romulfus, both palace officials, with a list of taxpayers that dated back to the time of his father Sigibert. Thanks to deaths in the intervening time, the lists are badly out of date, but the assessors consider each case in turn to produce a fairer assessment. That the lists could be so out of date shows that tax was not raised annually, or even regularly.[44] The assessors then move on to Tours, where they encounter the objections of its bishop. Gregory explains that his city is exempt from taxation, despite earlier lists of taxpayers. True, they paid tax in the time of King Lothar, but Lothar, who was in awe of St Martin, threw the lists in the fire. On his death, King Charibert promised to respect his father's laws, but the corrupt Count Gaiso taxed Tours anyway. Bishop Euphronius appealed to Charibert, who 'sighed, for he feared the miraculous power of St Martin, and he threw the lists into the fire'. Sigibert took over from Charibert and respected the non-tax agreement. For fourteen years, Childebert his son had made no tax demands. The assessors point out that they have taxation lists. Gregory warns that these must be illegal copies, since the originals had been burnt, and, sure enough, three days later Audinus, who had made the lists, caught a fever and died. You don't mess with St Martin. Childebert promptly sent an official letter

---

[44] Goffart, 'Old and new in Merovingian taxation', showed that the Merovingians only preserved Roman practice in part, and the frequent grants of immunities were un-Roman. The fiscal system of the Merovingians and Carolingians is much debated: Durliat, *Les Finances Publiques*, challenged by Wickham, 'La chute de l'empire romain'; Magnou-Nortier, *Aux origines de la fiscalité moderne*. I thank Ian Wood for guidance.

confirming exemption, doubtless nervous of catching a fatal fever himself. From all of this it emerges that taxation, in so far as the Merovingians could get away with imposing it, was levied *civitas* by *civitas*, as it had been by the Roman administration.

Another sign of the importance of taxation is Merovingian coinage. Gregory has little to say about this, beyond mentioning a moneyer (*monetarius*) who fell gravely ill and was cured by Saint Pelagia (*Glory of the Confessors* 103). It is the coinage itself – in Gregory's day predominantly in gold, later in silver – that bears witness to the hundreds of mints (around 800) and 1,500 different *monetarii* who minted coin. Taxes had to be paid in gold coin. We have met in the Ravenna papyri the insistence on payments being made in good coin, *solidos dominicos probitos, obrizincos, optimos*, 'imperial solidi that are tested, stiff (?), of the best quality' (*P. Ital.* 30, 41). It was only too easy to pay short in worn, debased coin, and the solution was to melt gold down, purify it, and remint it. City mints are constantly minting fresh coinage, initially imitating Byzantine issues, and then in the name of Merovingian kings, and the most obvious context for that minting is payment of taxes:[45]

> Those who minted coins probably engraved so many place names on gold as a means of citing the entities that paid taxes. In other words, cities remained the main political units even through the Merovingian period.[46]

In a later saint's Life – that of St Eligius, bishop of Noyon – we hear that as a boy of great promise he was apprenticed to Abbo, the skilled goldsmith for the public mint for tax payments of the city of Limoges (and, indeed, numerous coins in the name of Abbo survive).[47] Later he was able to intervene miraculously in a minting process when King Dagobert demanded taxes of Limoges. When all the payments had been gathered together, the *monetarius* insisted on melting it all down to ensure that only the purest and most gleaming coinage should reach the royal court. After three or four days of labour at the furnace, they make no progress, not realising that the king had granted Eligius a nearby estate. Eligius then intervenes and completes the task, to general rejoicing. He proceeds to build a monastery on the spot.[48] Reminting gold coins, if you had the skill, was evidently a profitable business.

---

[45] See Garipzanov, 'The coinage of Tours'.
[46] Strothmann, 'The evidence of numismatics', pp. 797–798.
[47] MGH SS rer.Merov. 4, p. 671: *honorabili viro Abbone vocabulo, fabro aurifice probatissimo, qui eo tempore in urbe Lemovicina publicam fiscalis monetae officinam gerebat.*
[48] MGH SS rer.Merov. 4, p. 681: *domesticus simul et monetarius adhuc aurum ipsum fornacis coctionem purgare, ut iuxta ritum purissimus ac rutilus aulae regiae praesentaretur metallus . . .*

Bishops and Cities

The bishop played a key role in a Merovingian city. Gregory is keen to let us know as much, and though he does everything he can to play up the role of the bishop, and correspondingly to play down the role of other figures, we need not doubt its centrality. The bishop, whose election had to be approved by the king, was consequently one who could intervene with the king. We have met Gregory playing the part of royal mediator at Andelot, and also scaring off Childebert from taxing Tours. But while the administrative power of a bishop may flow from the king, and his social power from his membership of the 'senatorial' class and landowning elite, his miraculous power flowed from God, and more specifically from the saints whose cult he promoted locally.[49] There was abundant need of miracles, because cities were tormented by natural disasters, against which there was no other protection.

All in all, we come away with the impression that cities are incredibly fragile – unless, of course, divine assistance is forthcoming. It is not just barbarian invasions they are subject to, but all sorts of earthquakes, fires, floods, famines, plagues, and the like. Neither the physical fabric nor the human inhabitants are ever quite safe. So, the still-busy port city of Marseille suffers from bubonic plague, brought to it in a ship from Spain. First a household of eight who had purchased goods from the ship all died, then it spread to the residential quarter around them, and then, 'like a cornfield set alight', to the entire city. It raged for two months, eventually brought to an end by the incessant prayers of Bishop Theodore, though, even after it had ended, those who had left the city and now returned promptly caught it and died (*Hist.* 9.22).[50] It seems to have returned again a few years later, and, simultaneously, a dire famine affected the cities of Angers, Nantes, and Le Mans (*Hist.* 10.15). Indeed, Gregory tends to gather together these urban afflictions rather as classical historians gathered portents: so, in 580, he explains, the Auvergne was afflicted by terrible flooding, while Bordeaux was badly shaken by an earthquake, nearly flattening the city walls, and causing many of the inhabitants to evacuate. Orléans blazed with a terrible fire, and somewhere near Chartres blood poured forth when a loaf was broken in two. Gregory is clear about the explanation: 'There was no other apparent cause of this fire, and it must have come from God' (*Hist.* 5.33).

---

[49] Van Dam, *Leadership and Community*, pp. 179–201.
[50] On Gregory's account of Marseilles, see Loseby, 'Marseille and the Pirenne thesis'.

Divine intervention can save cities, even from so devastating a force as Attila and his Huns. They first hit Metz on Easter Eve:[51]

> They burned the town to the ground, slaughtered the populace with the sharp edge of their swords, and killed the priests of the Lord in front of their holy altar. No building of the town remained unburnt, except the oratory of St Stephen (*Hist.* 2.6).

At this point Gregory launches into an elaborate account of how, by divine intervention, the oratory was saved, in terms of a vision of St Stephen the Levite intervening with the Apostles Peter and Paul to save the town, which they explain must perish because of the wickedness of its inhabitants, though they grant him the saving of the oratory. Much of Gregory's narrative is designed to bring out the power of divine wrath and divine intervention. Orléans is next up for attack, and is saved by the timely arrival of Aetius, though the bishop, Saint Anianus, has the whole population praying to God, so that when Aetius's army finally comes over the horizon, it is literally an answer to prayer.

In his narrative, urban disasters are messages from God, only to be averted by piety. There emerge some pretty striking elements of continuity of cities which evidently thought of themselves as Roman *civitates* into the late sixth century – which is not, of course, to say that nothing has changed. The most important change is the massive presence of Gregory himself, intervening with dire threats of the wrath of St Martin, in a purely secular business like taxation. Since Frankish kings have taken over from Roman provincial governors, and share the Trinitarian beliefs of the bishops, they are only too subject to threats of divine intervention, making the bishop the scariest person in town. One thinks of the marvellous account of how Zaragoza was saved from an attack by Lothar and Childebert I (3.29). The townsfolk paraded around the walls, followed by their wailing womenfolk, and bearing their most potent relic: the tunic of St Vincent. When the Franks enquired what this black magic was, and learnt it was the tunic of St Vincent, their troops were so scared that they withdrew. Cities are protected by the power of bishops and the power of the saints behind them. This widespread belief is echoed in the changing urban topography that sees cities ringed with places of the cult of saints, supposed to be quite as effective in protecting a city as its walls.

As the narrative draws to a close in book 10, there arrives the belated news of the sack of Antioch in 575 by Chosroes. They hear from an

---

[51] See Brown, *Cult of the Saints*, pp. 73–74.

eyewitness, a bishop called Simon who had himself been led off into captivity. He tells the story of a charitable man who has a vision outside the city gate of half the city being utterly destroyed and the other half spared. When the vision passes, he goes back into the city and finds that half indeed has been totally destroyed, and the other half, including his house and family, spared (*Hist.* 10. 24). Again, city sacking gives Gregory the chance to underline the power of divine intervention and reminds us along the way that the sacking of a city is rarely as total as is claimed: there are survivors.

City Government

By the time Gregory has torn strips off the Merovingian kings, and foregrounded the miraculous powers of bishops, we might be excused for thinking that bishops were the real power in the land. Indeed, that is a complaint which Gregory puts into the mouth of King Chilperic, in his devastating assessment of the failings of that monarch:

> There was nothing he hated so much as he hated the churches. He was perpetually heard to say: 'My treasury is always empty. All our wealth has fallen into the hands of the church. There is no one with any power left except the bishops (*nulli penitus nisi soli episcopi regnant*). Nobody respects me as king: all respect has passed to the bishops.' (*Hist.* 6.46, trans. Thorpe)

There is a symmetry between Chilperic's complaints of the wealth and power of bishops, and Gregory's own attack on the excessive wealth and greed of the kings. There is a danger that the combination of Gregory's partisan account, and the sheer lack of other documentary evidence – except, of course, the formularies which have been dismissed for their implausible picture of *curiae* – leads us to make too much of *Bischofsherrschaft*.[52]

Hand in hand with the assumption that all power now resided with bishops is the impression that local councils, in so far as they survived, had no real importance.[53] It is indeed true that councils lost some of the most

---

[52] Heinzelmann, *Bischofsherrschaft* omits to analyse in what *Herrschaft* consisted. Durliat, *De la ville antique à la ville byzantine'*, pp. 313–319, for wise words of caution on the exaggeration of the role of bishops. On Bischofsherrschaft, see the nuanced discussion of Ian Wood, *The Christian Economy of the Early Medieval West*: I am grateful to the author for an advance view of this book.

[53] Argued in detail by Liebeschuetz, *Decline and Fall*, pp. 137–168.

important functions in local administration: the collection of taxes and the administration of justice; these functions passed not to the bishop but the count (*comes*), appointed for each city by the king.[54] The centrally appointed *comes* was a creation of the Late Roman Empire; we have met the role in the Ostrogothic Italy of Cassiodorus, and it was continued by their Lombard successors. That central government intervened in the running of cities was a well-established late Roman precedent: figures such as imperially appointed *curatores* and *defensores* in cities were a response to complaints of abuse and mismanagement by local councils, a tradition that goes back in a sense to Trajan's appointment of the Younger Pliny in Bithynia to control local abuse.[55] If *curiae* lost their administrative powers, it is part of a long process with its roots in the Roman Empire. Perhaps in Merovingian Gaul, their role was more ceremonial than administrative: but it was still enough to be a strong source of pride, as we can see in Gregory's senators and senatorial families. This group of local landowners continued to dominate cities socially, if not administratively, and it was frequently from their ranks that bishops and counts were drawn – a point which shows their continued influence, rather than their eclipse.

We have already met Gregory's account of his namesake, the bishop of Langres, who spent forty years as *comes* of Autun and administered justice with notable severity before becoming a bishop. He is a perfect illustration of a *senator* who progresses to both secular and ecclesiastical rank. Every now and again, Gregory gives us a glimpse of curial positions. One of those miraculously saved from the quartan fever by Saint Gallus was one Julianus, 'a *defensor*, and later a priest, a man of the sweetest disposition' (*Life of the Fathers* 6). Or we may recall the death of Saint Nicetius, who upset some by failing to leave his property to the church:

> after the days sanctioned by Roman law for the will of the deceased to be read in public [i.e. the standard gap of three days after demise], the testament of this bishop was brought down to the forum (*in foro delatum*), and with a crowd of onlookers was unsealed by the magistrate (*a iudice reseratum*) and read out. (*Life of the Fathers* 8.5)

This *iudex* is exactly the sort of figure we meet in the Ravenna papyri or the Gallic formularies, typically a *defensor*, presiding over the formal opening of a will which will be lodged in the *gesta municipalia*, and constitute the proof of passage of ownership. Ironically, in almost all surviving examples,

---

[54] Murray, *Companion to Gregory of Tours*, pp. 216–217.
[55] For *curatores* and *defensores*, Jones, *Later Roman Empire*, pp. 722–730.

the beneficiary of such a will is the church, but here the bishop and saint proves an exception.

Think in terms not of administrative power but of social ceremonial, and our curial elite is restored to us in all its splendour, rushing from the gates of Clermont in their spectacular carriages to meet the bashful Catianus, or meeting in Vienne to agree three days of rogations to celebrate the saving of their city from the great fire. Every now and again, more is asked of them, as they lead the local contingent on the battlefield of Vouillé, or debate which of two Burgundian brothers their city should side with. We surely see them too in the epic heroism of those who, on their shields, vainly braved the swirling waters of the Rhône (*Hist.* 4.30). It goes without saying that they will have played a key role in the election of bishops, who came from their own class and were expected to use their wealth to endow their cities with fine new buildings.

The Resilience of the Gallic City

There has long been debate, going back to Henri Pirenne and beyond, over how far the cities of Merovingian Gaul should be seen as a continuity with the Roman Empire. To quote a recent voice:

> cities remained the main political units even through the Merovingian period. It is important to acknowledge this role of urban centres in the Merovingian world, which supplemented other facets of Roman tradition, culture, and even language that lived on in the post-Roman period. Indeed, the political culture of the Roman Empire did not cease at all: Antiquity did not end, and there was no 'dawn' of the Middle Ages. Instead, the Merovingian period was a long era of transition.[56]

The debate risks becoming an exercise in optimism, in calculating how much wine is left in the Roman glass. From the perspective of Resilience, we are witnessing the cities of Gaul adapting to their new environment: to waves of 'barbarian' arrivals – Visigoths, Franks, Burgundians, not to mention Alamanni and Lombards – and to the replacement of the imperial system by kingdoms, which nevertheless were appreciative enough of the advantages of *imitatio imperii*. The kings embraced the advantages of an existing system of extracting resources from the land. In the cities, a local landed elite continued to flourish, occupying where it could the key roles of

---

[56] Strohmann, *Handbook of the Merovingian World*, pp. 798–799.

bishop and count, and enjoying the ceremonial prestige of calling themselves senators. But the deliberate retention of many elements from the Roman past does not diminish the fact that these cities had already become something different, just as Gregory's Latin, for all its traditional elements, is something entirely new, a style in which no historian under the Roman Empire could have dreamed of writing.

Afterword: Gregory's Unclassical Style?

One traditional reason for seeing a wide gap between Gregory and the classical world lies in the quirks of his style and Latinity. Gregory takes a certain pleasure in representing himself as some sort of illiterate bumpkin; nobody with an ear for his careful ambivalences should be misled.[57] He opens his *Histories* with a disclaimer (Preface). Literary culture has collapsed in the cities of Gaul (*pereunte ab urbibus Gallicanis liberalium cultura litterarum*), and scarcely anyone is left with adequate grammatical and argumentative skills (*peritus dialectica in arte grammaticus*) to write a history of the times, whether in prose or verse. Yet he cannot bear the story of his times to be buried in silence, however uncouth his style (*etsi incultu effatu*), and, in particular, he is encouraged by the observation that few people can understand a philosophising orator, while many understand the speech of a rustic (*philosophantem rhetorem pauci intellegunt, loquentem rusticum multi*). His carefully balanced antitheses and elegant hyperbata flag to the knowledgeable reader that he is not the bumpkin he claims to be. This tension underpins and defines his style.[58]

His own stylistic shortcoming is a theme to which Gregory returns at the end of the *Histories*, so bracketing the entire work with apologies for his style. The last chapter (10.31), after listing all the bishops of Tours culminating in himself, gives a list of all his writings. Conceding that they may have been written 'in somewhat rustic style' (*licet stilo rusticiore*), he conjures his successors as bishops of Tours by an awful oath before the seat of Final Judgment, to preserve his writings carefully without rewriting

---

[57] For a sensitive re-evaluation of his literary skills, Shanzer, 'Gregory of Tours and poetry'.
[58] Gibbon, unusually, missed the irony of this passage: 'His style is equally devoid of elegance and simplicity. In a conspicuous station he still remained a stranger to his own age and country ... I have tediously acquired, by a painful perusal, the right of pronouncing this unfavourable sentence' (*Decline and Fall*, chapter 38, p. 138 note 117 in Bury's edition). For an excellent analysis, Martínez Pizarro, 'Gregory of Tours and the literary imaginations'.

anything. He then apostrophises an imagined successor (apostrophe was a trick well-known to Cicero's rhetorical toolset):

> But if, O Priest of God, whoever you may be, you are trained by our Martianus in the seven disciplines [and in a long period he proceeds to enumerate the skills of those seven disciplines] and you are so practised in all of these that my style seems rustic to you (*ut tibi stilus noster sit rusticus*), I beg you even so not to rip up what I have written.

As a concession, he suggests it would be fine to versify the *Histories* – a challenge to which not even Venantius could rise, as he had for the Life of St. Martin.

Even as he apologises for his rustic style, he demonstrates that he is anything but uneducated. Martianus Capella's *Wedding of Philology and Mercury* could be taken as the standard textbook since the early fifth century of Late Antique education, covering both the *trivium* of grammar, philosophy, and rhetoric and the *quadrivium* of geometry, arithmetic, astronomy, and music, making up together the seven liberal arts defined by Varro.[59] Gregory not only refers to it with familiarity ('our Martianus', *Martianus noster*) but also shows he knows the contents of the great work. There is a clear warning to anyone who thinks themselves better educated than Gregory not to dare 'correct' him: to take him for a rustic would be a big mistake. (Not that this has deterred generations of scholars from taking him precisely for an ignorant Latinist.)[60] Claims to rusticity must be taken with a large pinch of salt: Venantius Fortunatus, whose urbane polish was the opposite of rusticity, managed to say 'I choose to be recognised as a rustic ... rather than risk offering to the ears of the public anything less than intelligible'.[61]

Gregory, never one to leave a good theme alone, has more to say on this front in his Saints' Lives. In his preface to the *Glory of the Confessors*, he pretends to nervousness in writing, 'because I am without letters, rhetoric and grammatical skill', that some well-educated man will say; '*O rustice et idiota!*' 'You bumpkin and idiot!' '*O rustice*' is exactly what Patroclus' brother has said to him, and the response was to run off to school. So does Gregory, as his critic proceeds to enumerate his technical shortcomings, in daring to count himself as a writer when he has no training in

---

[59] Stahl, *Martianus Capella*; Shanzer, *Commentary on Martianus Capella*.
[60] A nuanced discussion in Goffart, *Narrators*, pp. 145–150; Shanzer, 'Gregory of Tours' vindicates his sophistication.
[61] Venantius, *Life of St Albinus* 4.8; cf. Roberts, 'Venantius Fortunatus and Gregory of Tours', p. 58.

literary skills and cannot even recognise a noun. He confuses masculine, feminine, and neuter, and doesn't know when and where to use a preposition, let alone distinguish an ablative from an accusative. To this Gregory replies that he is making work for the critic himself by his rusticity (*rusticitatem*), and he can now turn his prose into polished verse. The irony is self-evident: how can the critic accuse him of ignorance of grammatical forms when he is capable of spelling them out? And what was Gregory up to at the age of seven if not learning letters with the support of his great-uncle, the bishop and saint Nicetius? His early reading at the saint's elbow may have had a strongly biblical cast, but it did not exclude Virgil.[62]

One sign of his schooling (and his willingness to display it) is his ability to cite Virgil, the staple of Latin education, beloved too, as we have seen, by Augustine, whom Gregory admired.[63] He repeatedly cites Virgil for heightened emotional effect, not only in his *Histories* but in all his writings.[64] He also knows Sallust's *Histories*, which were important similarly for Augustine, and twice cites the preface to the *Catilinarian Conspiracy*.[65] The author is both at the back of Gregory's mind and accessible enough as he writes to pull a copy down from his shelf.[66]

Just as Gregory pretends to the humility of a holy man yet flaunts the noble standing of his family, he pretends to literary rusticity yet flaunts his familiarity with the literature. The preface to the *Life of the Fathers* raises a quite unnecessary philological dispute as to whether he should call it a singular Life, or plural Lives (*Vita* or *Vitae*). Aulus Gellius, he notes, uses the plural; yet the Elder Pliny, in his *Art of Grammar*, says 'the ancients have said "the lives" of each of us, but the grammarians did not believe that the word *vita* has a plural'. Not to be beaten by the pedants, Gregory calls his work *De Vita Patrum*, in the singular. Pliny's work on grammar, which certainly existed, has not survived, so we cannot check Gregory's citation, but he has made it clear that he is as capable as any learned fool of disputing fine grammatical points and citing several authorities. In a word, Gregory's grammatical incompetence is a charade.[67]

---

[62] Van Dam, *Leadership and Community*, p. 221, suggests 'a predominantly biblical education'.

[63] His knowledge of classical literature was discussed by Kurth, 'Grégoire de Tours et les études classiques'.

[64] Kurth, 'Grégoire de Tours et les études classiques', p. 27, lists twenty-two citations in the *Histories*, and twenty-two in his other writings.

[65] On the transmission of Sallust, Reynolds, *Texts and Transmission*, pp. 340–349. Sallust is cited at *Hist.* 4.13 and 6.6.

[66] Kurth, 'Grégoire de Tours et les études classiques', pp. 21–22, on his citations of Sallust, including another from the *Catiline* preface in *Life of the Fathers* 4. pref.

[67] See James, *Gregory of Tours*, pp. xiv and 2. That Gregory did indeed read Gellius is supported by Goffart, *Narrators*, p. 121, n. 42.

This is not to say that Gregory's Latinity is less than challenging to anyone brought up on classical literature, but rather that it is deliberate. Like his uncle Gallus, who threw off the shackles of worldly pride, 'like a bird fleeing from a snare and flying up to the skies', so Gregory shakes off the shackles of grammatical propriety and conventional prose composition, and soars into the empyrean of a style quite of his own. As he repeatedly flags, it is what he considers the language of the people, not of the elite. At the outset of his Life of Saint Martin, he attributes the impulse to write to a repeated vision of his beloved mother, who reproaches him for dragging his heels over writing. He replies, in his dream, 'It doesn't escape you that I am poor in letters and as a fool and idiot (*stultus et idiota*) do not dare to publish such admirable virtues'. His mother will have none of it: 'Do you not realise that for us your colloquial style is held to be excellent because of its popular intelligibility?' His rustic style deliberately shuns the showy rhetoric of the elite – a style familiar also to the Dumnolus, who refused to become bishop of Avignon, preferring his present simplicity to being worn out by sophistic senators and philosophising judges (*inter sophisticos senatores et iudices philosophicos fatigari*) (*Hist.* 6.9).

No classical historian wrote in such a style, but Gregory's embrace of the *sermo rusticus* deliberately and consciously sets up a tension between the world of history (Merovingian kings squabbling) and the world of 'real life'. It may not be good political history, but it is vivid social history, and gives a better idea of what it was like for a Roman aristocrat to live in a world of Franks than any starchier history could. Here his *Histories* have much of the colour of his Saints' Lives. As Peter Brown memorably put it:

> Where can we turn other than to the hagiographic works of Gregory of Tours to learn the truly important facts about Merovingian Gaul: the dimensions of Lac Leman and the superior quality of its trout; the temptations of civet de lapin in the Lenten season; the very first mention of *omelette à la provençale?*[68]

---

[68] Brown, *The Cult of the Saints*, p. 81.

8 | The Grammar of the City

Isidore and Visigothic Spain

> A city (*civitas*) is a multitude of men united by the bond of society (*societas*), called after citizens (*cives*), that is from the residents of the town (*urbs*). For the town is the walls themselves, the city is not stones but inhabitants.
>
> Isidore, *Etymologies* 15.2.1

Paradoxically, the 'classic' definition of the ancient city was written in the early seventh century AD by a Christian bishop in a Spain ruled by Visigothic kings. To grasp his vision of the city, we must constantly engage with the gap between the classical world and Visigothic Spain. But can we trust him? Isidore, who became bishop of Seville in AD 600, give or take a year, so some six years after Gregory's death, was the greatest man of learning of his age. He offers an incomparable window on the idea of the city in Visigothic Spain of the seventh century. To the classically trained reader, Isidore looks like the last in a long tradition of Latin writers about language and what it can tell us about life, stretching from Varro and Verrius Flaccus in the late republican and Augustan periods, through Pompeius Festus in the second century, to the commentators on Virgil, Aelius Donatus and Servius in the fourth/fifth centuries, to culminate in the great compendium of the twenty books of *Etymologies*.[1] So deeply read is he in these earlier writers that one might be forgiven for thinking him a little anachronistic, a classical throwback – 'le dernier philologue de l'antiquité', as Jacques Fontaine put it[2] – not a true representative of the Visigothic Spain of the seventh century. It is a striking observation that his *Etymologiae* are included in the series of Oxford Classical Texts, a privilege denied to most authors of Late Antiquity, including Cassiodorus (the Oxford edition of his *Institutiones* by Roger Mynors does not form part of this series). The place of the *Etymologies* in the OCT series reflects the fact he is constantly used by classical scholars – almost as if he was 'one of them'. Yet, in truth, Isidore is through and through a man of his day, not only the most influential bishop in Spain and friend of successive kings but

---

[1] See the magisterial study of Jacques Fontaine, *Isidore de Séville*.
[2] Fontaine, *Isidore de Séville*, p. 6.

instrumental, with his brother Leander, in persuading the Visigothic rulers to abandon Arianism for the Roman rite.[3]

Isidore demands our attention, if for no other reason, because his account in the *Etymologies* of the city is the fullest discussion of the phenomenon in Latin Literature since Vitruvius; indeed, he can be said to add a dimension that Vitruvius misses, for while the Roman architect is concerned only with the buildings and structures of the city, Isidore is concerned with its social structure, the *cives* that made up the *civitas*, and with the relation of urban centre to countryside – aspects which Vitruvius largely ignores. But, to understand Isidore's take on the city, it is necessary to strip away some of the prejudices that see him as merely recycling past learning,[4] and locate him in his contemporary context.

Between Library and Palace

The twenty books of the *Etymologies* are accompanied in the manuscripts by an exchange of letters between Isidore and his friend and literary executor, Braulio, bishop of Zaragoza. It had been no easy task to persuade Isidore to let go of his manuscript, with which he was, as ever, endlessly tinkering. Indeed, it is a striking feature of many of Isidore's copious publications that they are transmitted to us in two editions, as the scholar, never quite satisfied with what he had written, returned to his texts to polish and supplement.[5] So much is true of many a scholar, but a striking feature of the transmission of Isidore's texts is that so often the first edition is transmitted along with the second. Braulio evidently felt some obligation to address the chaos of his indecisive master's production, to impose something like order, and he does not hesitate to explain that it was his own intervention which sorted the *Etymologies* into twenty books,[6] when what the author offered was simply a series of titles, *tituli* (so Braulio tells us in the biographic notice he appended to Isidore's *On Illustrious Men*).[7] The same Braulio felt it appropriate to share with the public some of the

---

[3] Among recent studies of Isidore, I have benefited from the following collections: *Isidore de Séville et son temps*; Fear and Wood, *Isidore of Seville*; Fear and Wood, *Companion to Isidore of Seville*. Useful too is Merrills, *History and Geography*, pp. 168–228.

[4] Cf. Churchin, 'The role of civic leaders', at p. 287, dismissing references in the *Etymologiae*: 'being based on earlier literature, these have only antiquarian value'.

[5] Well observed by Barrett, 'God's librarian', esp. pp. 60–68.

[6] Inconveniently, the text of Braulio says fifteen books, not twenty, so unleashing much scholarly debate: Elfassi, 'Isidore of Seville', at pp. 247–249.

[7] Braulio of Zaragoza, *Renotatio Isidori*; translation by Barlow, *Iberian Fathers: Braulio*, p. 140.

exchange of letters between himself and Isidore – letters not entirely creditable to the author, which, however, made the contribution of his editor clear.[8] From them emerges a picture of a somewhat ambivalent figure: on the one hand, the man of great learning, distracted and lost in his books, 'God's librarian' indeed;[9] on the other, the important public figure, deep in negotiations with his Visigothic kings.

The correspondence seems to stretch over some decades. Often, their concern is for books: Isidore asks Braulio for a copy of the sixth decade of Augustine's works – a request which must cast some doubt on the holdings of the episcopal library in Seville – and sends him a copy of his book on *Synonyms*, a sort, maybe, of Roget's *Thesaurus* (*Letter* B).[10] But the key text which Braulio is after is the *Etymologies* itself. Braulio is having a tough time. He is worn out by 'the horrible onslaught of plague and enemy attack'. Shaking off a thousand cares, he now demands of copy of Isidore's *mag.op.*:

> I propose, indeed, and I request with every sort of entreaty that you, remembering your promise, will order that the book of *Etymologies* be sent to your servant, as we have heard that, God willing, it has been finished. As I am aware, you have sweated over it in large measure at the request of your servant, and therefore be generous first to me. (Letter II)

That there was much else to distract Isidore emerges from the next paragraph, in which Braulio asks for a copy of the proceedings of the Synod at which Isidore had roasted one Sintharius; we have no further evidence of this Synod or its date, but the Visigothic kings obliged their bishops by summoning frequent synods, often on matters of doctrine.[11] So, Isidore has been busy with matters of national importance, and not just lost in his books.

This impression comes out even more strongly from a following exchange. Isidore writes to Braulio, late in his life (632), probably from Toledo. It is the most extraordinary confession:

> Just at the moment when I received your note a royal servant-boy came to me. I gave it to my chamber-servant, and went straight to the king,

---

[8] For text and translation, Ford, *The Letters of St Isidore of Seville*; a translation of the Braulio exchange is appended to Barney et al., *The Etymologies of Isidore of Seville*.
[9] The expression is that of Barrett, 'God's librarian'.
[10] A comparison suggested by Henderson, *The Medieval World of Isidore of Seville*, pp. ix–xi.
[11] On Visigothic synods, Vives, *Consilios Visigóticos*; for meetings up to 656, Martínez Díez and Rodríguez, *La Colección canónica*; Collins, *Visigothic Spain*, p. 71.

> intending to read through and reply to your letter later. But when I returned from the royal palace, not only could I not find what you had written, but indeed whatever else was among those papers had disappeared. (*Letter* III)

A royal summons sounds like the perfect excuse for distraction, though we must begin to worry about the filing system of God's Librarian if he could so swiftly mislay his correspondence. Possibly, he had a psychological block in play: he was perhaps only too well aware that Braulio was on at him again about the *Etymologies*. Braulio gives it to him straight: 'tearfully' he accuses him of deliberate procrastination:

> Unless I am mistaken, seven years have rolled by since I recall having requested from you your composition, the books of the *Origins*. In various and diverse ways I have been disappointed when in your presence, and you have written nothing back to me when I have been absent. Rather, with subtle delay, you object that the work is not yet finished, or not yet copied out, or that my letters were lost, and a number of other things, until I have come to this day and still have no result from my request.

Braulio's indignation sweeps him along for several pages. The work is a gift of God that he must share with the world. Gradually, it emerges that what especially piques Braulio is that though Isidore won't send him a copy, he has actually shared it with others and allowed it to enter circulation in an imperfect form (and here we have part of the explanation of the pattern of multiple editions of Isidore's works in circulation):

> Therefore I also point out that the books of the *Etymologies*, which I am seeking from you, are already held by many people, even though they have been mutilated and corrupted. For this reason I ask that you deem it suitable to send these to me copied out and in their entirety, emended and well organized, lest I be drawn into evil by eagerness and driven to obtain from others vices instead of virtues. (*Letter* IV)

Throughout this exchange there runs a spirit of good-natured teasing. The two know each other well enough and are fond enough of each other not to take the reproofs amiss. At the same time, Braulio is quite serious, and knows that without heavy pressure, Isidore won't let go of his precious manuscript, but will continue to tinker. And, by including the correspondence, Braulio lets us, the readers, know that he played a major role in ensuring the completion of what was to become one of the most copied works of the Middle Ages (over 450 manuscripts of the *Etymologies* dating between the eighth and eleventh centuries are known, of which 84 are full or substantial versions).[12] Isidore is entirely unfazed by this 'assault'. In return, he plays again his trump card:

> The letter from your holiness found me in Toledo, for I had been summoned on account of the Council. But though the king's command suggested that I should return despite already being on the road, nevertheless I preferred not to cut short the progress of my journey since I was nearer to his own presence than I was to my starting point. I came into the presence of the king and found your deacon there. (*Letter* V)

Isidore is reminding us – and, indeed, Braulio is reminding us – that the great etymologist was no cloistered scholar, but in the thick of affairs of high state. In this sense (if not in many others), he is reminiscent of Gregory of Tours. What all this points to is a double form of authority: he has the authority of the scholar who works long over polishing his text, but he also has the authority of royal approval. This is the writer who had dedicated his *On the Nature of Things* to King Sisebut, who sent in return no minor compliment: a poem of some sixty-one hexametre lines on the same theme from the royal pen.[13] Sisebut and Isidore are each prepared to meet on the other's territory: Isidore will leave his library for the palace, and Sisebut will take a pause from issuing laws to write a learned poem. Isidore clearly intended at some stage (presumably the 'first edition') to dedicate the *Etymologies* to the same Sisebut, for the last letter in the collection Braulio gives us is 'From Isidore to my Lord and son Sisebut':

> See, as I promised, I have sent you the work *On the Origin of certain Things*, compiled from my recollection of readings from antiquity and annotated in certain places as written by the pen of our ancestors. (*Letter* VI)

Sisebut died in 621, and the Toledo Council was over a decade later, so if a copy was sent to Sisebut, it was of the sort of first edition which Braulio deplored. What is striking is the intimacy: Sisebut is 'my son' to Isidore, and the works of classical Latin which he reads and annotates are penned by 'the ancestors' – that is, the king's as well as Isidore's (*stilo maiorum*). A Visigothic king is as much heir to the classical past as a learned bishop.

---

[12] On the 1,000 complete or partial manuscripts of the *Etymologies*, see Elfassi, 'Isidore of Seville', at p. 270, and, in more detail, Steinová, 'The oldest manuscript tradition of the *Etymologiae*'. On Isidore's early impact, Tizzoni, 'Isidore of Seville's early influence'.

[13] For text, see Fontaine, *Isidore de Séville: traité de la nature*; for English translation, Kendall and Wallis, *Isidore of Seville: On the Nature of Things*; for discussion, Fear, 'Putting the pieces back together'; for Sisebut's *de eclipsi lunae*, see Ungvart, 'Clarifying the Eclipse'.

Isidore, Leander, and Visigothic Kings

The close relationship between Isidore, as bishop of Seville, with his contemporary kings is one he inherited from his brother and predecessor as bishop, Leander. Isidore offers a brief notice about Leander in his *De Viris Illustribus*, short biographies *On Illustrious Men*.[14] Among the subjects is his own brother, Leander, though the text gives no hint of the relationship. Isidore's focus throughout is on those authors who effectively refuted Arian doctrines; and it is as author of two books on heretical dogmas, 'in which with a passionate style he exposed the depravity of Arian impiety and ran it through' (28), that Leander earns his place in this company. Isidore goes on to catalogue Leander's other writings: a point-by-point refutation of Arianism; a letter to his sister, Florentina, On Virginity; discourses on the psalter, and much 'sweet-sounding' writing on sacrifices, praises, and psalms. There were also many letters, including that to Pope Gregory and one to 'his brother' (of unspecified identity) on the need not to fear death. There is just a hint of criticism of his epistolary style, for his letters 'even if not particularly splendid in language, were sharp in thought'.

Leander's family do feature – his father Severianus, his sister Florentina, and his little brother – yet Isidore says nothing of the traumatic circumstances in which they left their ancestral home in the province of Cartagena (Carthago Nova, known then as Carthago Spartaria from its esparto grass). For that we must turn to Leander himself. Similarly, he praises Leander for his success in persuading the Goths to turn (he says, 'turn back') from the madness of Arianism to the Catholic creed, without saying anything of the crucial role he played in negotiations with the fiercely Arian king Leovigild and his Catholic-convert sons, Hermenegild and Reccared. The political dangers of those years are only hinted at in his mention of an 'exile', without specifying that it was surely this that took him to Constantinople, where he met the future Pope Gregory and formed such a close bond with him as to become the dedicatee of Gregory's monumental *Homilies on Job*. It is hard to say whether Isidore's reticence is driven by the laws of the genre or, simply, modesty.

Leander himself is considerably more forthcoming. The key text is his letter to Florentina On Virginity.[15] He starts by talking about the wealth he might leave his sister by inheritance but follows the example of Solomon in rejecting the good things of this world, this 'mortal pomp', as vanities; she is

---

[14] For Latin text, Codoñer Merino, *El 'De Viris Illustribus' de Isidoro de Sevilla*.
[15] Barlow, *Iberian Fathers*, vol. 1: *Martin of Braga*, pp. 183–228 for translation.

better off treasuring the things of the spirit in her convent. There follows an essay on the blessing of virginity, and an outline of thirty-one rules for the conduct of nuns. Only at the end (ch. 31) does he turn to the personal circumstances of the family. Like Abraham, she has left '[her] country and [her] kinsfolk'; she must not now look back, like Lot's wife. She must follow the example of their mother, who vowed never to return. It sounds as if Florentina took refuge in a convent, for Leander urges his sister to cling to her mother Dove (Turtur) as a spiritual as well as carnal mother (Mother Superior, maybe). Leander goes on to confess that he had encouraged their brother, Fulgentius, later bishop of Écija (Astigi), close to Seville, but that was a mistake, for he lives in constant dread for his safety:

> He will be safer, however, if you keep safe and pray for him in your absence. You were taken away at such an early age that you cannot remember, even though you, too, were born there. There is no recollection to stir longing in your mind, and you are happy that you do not know what you grieve for. I speak from experience when I say that that country has so completely lost its rank and its beauty that there is not a single free person left in it, not is the land itself as fertile as usual, and that not without the judgement of God. That land, whence citizens were carried off and sent abroad, lost its fertility as soon as it lost its dignity.

There is so much emotion in this passage that we are left longing to know more.[16] Was it the city of Cartagena itself from which the family fled (so much is regularly assumed, and the brother is known as St Fulgentius of Cartagena). In what circumstances were they so brutally deprived of their homeland? Was it the Byzantine conquest of 551, which took the southern strip of Spain from the Visigoths, linking up the key Mediterranean harbour of Cartagena with the African coast? If so, why were Severianus and his family driven out and their land distributed to new settlers? We have no further evidence on the matter, but we may note the familiar language of the *civitas*. Carthago Spartaria was the city to which they belonged, whether they lived in the city or the countryside; they were landowners and *cives*, and the distribution of their land to newcomers left them exiles from their *patria*, forever longing for it even if they were infants when they left, and even if the distance from Cartagena to Seville is not insuperable (some 540k). The city of your birth, for Leander as for Cicero, is where true emotional bonds belong.

---

[16] Discussed by Fontaine and Cazier, 'Qui a chassé de Carthaginoise'; Wood, 'A family affair'.

The little Isidore was left to be raised by his brother. Leander's letter continues:

> Finally, I beg you, dear sister, to remember me in your prayers, and do not forget our younger brother, Isidore, for his parents rejoiced to leave him in the care of God and of his remaining brothers and sister, and when they journeyed to the Lord, they had no fear for his infancy. Although I love him as my own son and would place nothing on earth above my concern for him and would give my life for love of him, you should love him the more dearly and pray to Jesus for him more sincerely because you know that his parents were so tenderly fond of him.

In contrast to Isidore's unemotional picture of Leander, Leander's account of his little brother is all affection. Yet one cannot help wondering what the emotional impact on young Isidore was of losing not only his home but also his parents, to be brought up by a brother in a monastery, while sister and probably mother were sent off to a convent. Loving though Leander was, Isidore seems to have grown up without female affection, and it is hard not to think of him, like some neglected child, left to amuse himself in the monastery library for hours on end, and finding in books the companionship he otherwise lacked.

If Isidore gives little hint of all this in his life of his brother, he also rather underplays the political crisis into which they stepped on arrival in Seville. Leovigild,[17] Visigothic king from 568 to 586, was a major figure in the progressive unification of the kingdom, winning a series of victories against the Suebi in Gallaecia and the Basques (Vascones). In some ways, he presented himself as a Byzantine emperor, issuing gold coinage in his own name, sitting on a throne, and even founding cities.[18] But he was resolutely Arian; and while all Visigoths, like all Ostrogoths, traditionally prided themselves on having a creed that set them apart from the old Latin, Catholic population, they had previously shown no urge to convert them or interfere in their churches. Leovigild both looked for reconciliation, through tweaks to the wording of the creed (the great obstacle was over the role of the Holy Spirit, 'who proceedeth from the father and the Son', a formulation unacceptable to Arians who regarded Christ the Son as subsequent and inferior to the Father), and eventually by putting pressure on Catholics to convert.

---

[17] The form Liuvigild is more correct, given that he was brother of Liuva, but Leovigildus is how Latin sources Latinise him.

[18] On Liuvigild's coinage as claim to status, Pliego, *Figura et potentia*.

To this, Leander, and, following him, Isidore, were passionately opposed, and Leander seems to have exploited the willingness of Leovigild's son, Hermenegild, appointed in 579 as co-regent based in Seville, to join the Catholic side. This ended in civil war between father and son, and later history, even in Isidore's hands, saw Hermenegild as a rebel, one who met the end he deserved. It could well have been after Hermenegild's defeat that Leander left in exile, though it is also possible that what took him to Constantinople was an embassy from Hermenegild to reach an understanding with the Byzantines. Certainly, Pope Gregory said explicitly that it was as an ambassador that Leander met him. But the diplomatic tie which surely mattered above all to Leander was that with Rome rather than Constantinople. When Leovigild's other son, Reccared, succeeded to the throne, he came out openly as a Catholic. At the great church council in Toledo on 4 May 589, at which Reccared proclaimed Catholicism as the religion of his kingdom, and the bishops agreed to accept the Arians 'back' into the bosom of the Catholic church (as if they had always been there and Ulfilas had never made the Goths Arian), Leander preached the concluding homily, the other work to survive from his pen alongside the letter to Florentina.[19] He takes a global perspective: Christ is one, and the church is one, and Spain is now reunited with the whole world (indeed, the Visigoths must have looked isolated, with the Franks turned Catholics since the victory of Clovis, and North Africa Catholic since the defeat of the Vandals):

> There is one Christ the Lord and his Church, a holy possession, is throughout the world ... It remains, then, that we should all with one accord work for one kingdom, and that, both for the stability of the kingdom on earth and for the happiness of the kingdom of heaven, we should pray to God that the kingdom and nation which has glorified Christ on earth shall be glorified by Him, not only on earth, but also in heaven.

It is the soaring rhetoric not of triumph and defeat of the Arian side, but of Unity, 'one nation under God, indivisible'. Just how much personal credit for this goes to Leander is unclear (it was claimed that Leovigild was converted by Leander on his deathbed, and entrusted Reccared to his care, but they would claim that, wouldn't they?). What is certain is that the tenure of the see of Seville by Leander and Isidore puts them at the heart of one of the greatest turning points in Visigothic history. The triumph of the Catholic church was a sort of reincarnation of the Roman Empire.

---

[19] See *Iberian Fathers: Leander*, pp. 229–235.

Isidore on Visigothic Kings

For Isidore's views on Leovigild and other Visigothic kings, we may tun to his *History of the Kings of the Goths, Vandals and Suevi*.[20] The verdict on this slim essay, which comes to us, as so often, in two versions, has frequently been far from favourable. E. A. Thompson, whose *The Goths in Spain* of 1969 was a pioneer of Visigothic studies, famously put it in his opening paragraph like this:

> As a eulogy of the Goths it may have served some purpose. As a history, it is unworthy of the famous savant who wrote it. He could hardly have told us less, except by not writing at all. (p. 7)

It is indeed true that there is little *information* in Isidore that cannot also be found in the succession of chroniclers who, taking up the baton from Eusebius and Jerome, offered year-by-year lists of principal events, from Prosper of Aquitaine to Victor of Tunnuna (one of Isidore's *Illustrious Men*, no. 25) to John of Biclarum, the founder of the monastery of that name. His chronicle covering the thirty-three years from 567 to 590 makes up in lucidity what it lacks through brevity.[21] John too is one of Isidore's Illustrious Men (no. 31), noting that he was a Goth (*natione Gothus*) and learnt both Latin and Greek in Constantinople. Isidore speaks highly of his *Chronica* as a 'really useful history' (*valde utilem historiam*). Isidore also effectively belongs to this tradition of chroniclers, and one can sympathise with the frustration of a historian like Thompson who had to make sense of the Visigoths without the support of a major narrative historian like Procopius. This much Isidore was certainly not. As Thompson complained, his brevity is such that he offers no more information than a chronicler. *Brevitas* is a quality by which Isidore set much store, though he admitted its limits in words that echoed Cicero's rhetorical treatise, the *Brutus*: 'brevity is laudable used occasionally in some part of speaking, but not when in the entire discourse'.[22]

Isidore offers not just a history of the Goths, but a history of how the Goths were first corrupted by Arianism, and then saved – a narrative arc which of course culminates with Leander and Isidore, though he never

---

[20] See Wood, *The Politics of Identity*; also his 'Isidore as a historian'.
[21] For Latin text, see MGH *Chronica Minora* vol. 11; English translation by Wolf, *Conquerors and Chroniclers of Early Medieval Spain*, pp. 51–66. For a translation, Donini and Ford, *Isidore of Seville's History of the Kings of the Goths*; also Wolf, *Conquerors and Chroniclers*, pp. 67–90.
[22] Isidore *de Viris Illustribus* 15, quoting Cicero, *Brutus* 50: *brevitas laus est interdum in aliqua parte dicendi, in universa eloquentia laudem non habet*. On Isidore's brevity, Wood, 'Brevitas in the historical writings of Isidore of Seville'.

mentions their names. He pursues a familiar story (to cut what is not a long tale even shorter) through the sack of Rome by Alaric (15), Athaulf's move of the Goths to Gaul and Spain (19), the participation in the battle against Attila on the plains of Châlons (25), the catastrophic encounter with Clovis' Franks at Vouillé (36), and the consolidation of Visigothic power in Spain, to events which did indeed, just as Isidore expected of true 'history', fall within his lifetime. He touches on the internal conflict which led to the arrival of the Byzantines ('Romans', he consistently calls them) in the south of Spain, but without a hint of the impact this might have had on his family (47). We now meet the king who dominated his early life, and to whom Leander must have been well known: Leovigild, king from 568 to 586 (48–51). His verdict is mixed: Leovigild's conquests in Cantabria and Gallaecia extended Gothic power over most of Spain (49), but his record is blotted with the 'sin of impiety', in his attempts to convert Catholics to Arianism by persecution (50). This account manages to obscure the role of Hermenegild, here seen simply as a 'tyrant' – that is, an illegitimate usurper, both in converting to Catholicism himself and paving the way for his brother's subsequent conversion, in which Leander must have been intimately involved. Leovigild is given credit for founding the city of Reccopolis: he follows John of Biclarum in saying it was named after his son, Reccared, though John also gives the date of the foundation, in 578, and adds the foundation of a second city, Victoriacum, in 581. (We will return to Reccopolis in Chapter 9, pp. 357–362.)

Quite deliberately, Leovigild is represented as a powerful but flawed ruler, as a foil to his son Reccared:

> He was endowed with reverence for religion and was greatly different from his father in character. For the latter was irreligious and very much disposed to war, while he was devout in his faith and renowned for his love of peace (52).

His merit, of course, is his conversion to Catholicism, and his success in persuading other Goths to follow his example, so unifying the two rival churches (53). Again, no word of Leander and his great homily at the synod, but there is careful explanation of what correct doctrine was on the Trinity (53). By contrast, the *Chronicle* of John of Biclarum fully celebrates the role of Leander (under 590). Reccared, the lover of peace, is credited with significant victories, especially against the Franks under his general, Claudius (54). In the final two paragraphs, attention turns to Reccared's open-handedness: restoring church estates confiscated by his father (55) and generosity to individuals (56). It was surely such an act that made Leander able to talk of the great wealth he could leave.

In a word, Isidore is highly partisan in his historical judgements, but at no point steps forward onto the national stage as a participant and eyewitness. Leander's death, and Isidore's elevation to the see of Seville, must have been close in time to Reccared's death in 601. Consequently, as bishop, he is likely to have had at least some contact with each of his successors: his short-lived son Liuva (57); the usurper Witteric, for whom he has no good words (58); his brief successor Gundemar (59); and then, from 612, the king with whom he had particularly close ties, Sisebut (60). Since the first edition of this work was dedicated to Sisebut, one would expect enthusiastic treatment, though there is a note of criticism of his conversion of Jews to Christianity by force rather than persuasion; the preference for persuasion seems to have been the official position of the synod. Sisebut is praised for being 'refined in speech, learned in judgment, and imbued with the knowledge of letters to a large extent', a compliment sufficiently merited by his hexametre verses (61). Yet more generous praise is reserved for his successor Suinthila, who reigned from 621. A general under Sisebut, he is given credit for the defeat of the 'Romans' (Byzantines) and the extension of Gothic control of Spain as far as the strait of Gibraltar: 'with wondrous good fortune he won increased glory for his triumph in comparison with other kings' (62). The tone has changed to one of panegyric, with a listing of his virtues ('faith, intelligence, diligence, vigorous investigation in trials, extraordinary solicitude in ruling the kingdom, generosity to all'; 64). For all these fair words, Isidore was to preside over the IVth Toledo Council which deposed, excommunicated, and exiled Suinthila.

His history is partial from start to finish. It is the account by a Catholic bishop of the conversion of the Arian Visigoths to Catholicism and the unification of Spain under one ruler and one church. It has been argued that his central theme was the happy passing of Spain from Roman hands to Gothic control; indeed, in the 'praises of Spain' with which he prefaces the history, Spain is seen as a beautiful bride, beloved by the Romans, who has passed to the loving hands of the Goths (preface 4).[23] But his praise of the Goths is crucially qualified: in the end, the only truly good Goth is a Catholic Goth. It is a picture of the emergence of the Goths from darkness into light.

---

[23] So Wood, *Politics of Identity*.

A Backdrop of Cities

The Spain of the sixth and seventh centuries is still very much a land articulated by cities, with their surrounding countryside.[24] The importance of cities emerges clearly from the staccato narrative of John of Biclarum: Leovigild's campaigns of conquest are fought over and around cities. We may follow them year by year:

570 Leovigild lays waste to Bastetania and the city of Málaga (*Malacitanae urbis*).
571 L. captures the very strong city of Sidonia (*Ansidoniam fortissimam civitatem*) and returns the town (*urbem*) to Gothic law.
572 L. takes Córdoba (*Cordubam civitatem*) together with many towns and fortresses (*urbes et castella*).
573 L. attacks Sabaria (a region, this time).
574 L. invades Cantabria and occupies Amaia (the city of Amaya).
575 L. invades the Agesensian mountains (no city here!).
576 L. threatens the borders of Suevic territory in Galaecia.
577 L. invades Orespeda (west of Cartagena) and seizes cities and fortresses (*civitates atque castella*).
578 L. founds a new city in Celtiberia called Reccopolis: 'he endowed it with splendid buildings, both within the walls and the suburbs, and he established privileges for the people of the new city (*novae urbis*)'.
579 Hermenegild rebels against his father in Seville (*in Hispali civitate*) and induces other cities and fortresses to rebel (*civitates atque castella*).
580 L. summons a synod in Toledo (*in urbem Toletanam*) and tries doctrinal compromise. No campaigns recorded.
581 L. occupies part of Basque country and founds the city (*civitatem*) of Victoriacum.
582 L. gathers an army against Hermenegild.
583 L. besieges the rebellious Seville.
584 L. restores the walls of the ancient city of Italica (*Italicae antiquae civitatis*), much to the distress of the nearby Seville. He enters Seville and recovers control over the cities and forts that had rebelled.
585 L. lays waste to Galaecia (the region).
586 Death of Leovigild and succession of Reccared.

---

[24] See Kulikowski, *Late Roman Spain and its Cities* for the sixth but not seventh century; Bowes and Kulikowski, *Hispania in Late Antiquity*, esp. pp. 31–76; Dey, *Afterlife*, pp. 140–160 shows the crucial role of cities in the Visigothic kingdom, practically and ritually.

Except in the mountainous north of Galaecia, Cantabria, and the Basque country, campaigns are fought over cities. John seems to use *urbes* and *civitates* indifferently for cities, *castella* for minor fortified settlements. If we had a Procopius at this point, we would doubtless be having gripping accounts of sieges. But, allowing for the telegraphese, the effect is the same. And Leovigild is notably a founder or refounder of new cities, with Reccopolis and Victoriacum to his credit, and Italica, the birthplace of the emperor Hadrian, restored to dignity in order to clip the wings of nearby Seville (it also became a bishopric). In fact, this seems to understate his urban foundations, to which should be added Eio, like Reccopolis an archaeological site, and Ologicus; Amaia too was raised to full city status as a bishopric.[25]

When the Visigoths arrived in Spain, they inherited a landscape with a network of cities. In the 'Golden Age' of empire, especially under the Flavian emperors, Spain was densely studded with cities, of which we know some 400. It is a classic case of overexpansion, and already by the second century AD, some cities were proving unsustainable, leaving handsome ruins in the depths of the countryside like those at Los Bañales, with its aqueduct and baths, giving the site its name.[26] By the Visigothic period the number of cities important enough to have a bishop seems to have fallen to seventy-one.[27] But that, compared to the 100 or so bishoprics in Merovingian Gaul, seems a reasonable number, compared to the overinflated level of the early empire. According to the famous saying of Athaulf reported by Orosius, Gothia was not possible unless the Goths had Roman laws (see Chapter 3, p. 84): the Goths duly continued to use Roman law and the institutions that went with it, including cities and their mode of government.[28] Alaric II shortened the great bulk of the Theodosian Code to an abbreviated form, a *Breviarium*, promulgated in 506; indeed, there are books of the Code (the first five) only known through Alaric's version. Among other elements of continuity were the sections affecting city governance. Cities remained the responsibility of local landowners as *curiales*, even if the elephantine list of 192 imperial constitutions affecting them (12.1.1–192) was trimmed to a more reasonable 9 – enough, however, to bind landowners to the hereditary obligation

---

[25] See Martínez Jiménez, 'Local citizenships and the Visigothic kingdom', at p. 205. On Reccopolis, Olmo Enciso, 'Recopolis: The representation of power' and Chapter 9 pp. 355–362.
[26] See the studies in Andreu and Blanco-Perez, *Signs of Weakness and Crisis*. I am grateful to Javier Andreu for showing me the site of Los Bañales.
[27] Martínez Jiménez, 'Local citizenships', p. 198.
[28] Succinctly set out by Thompson, *Goths in Spain*, pp. 114–131.

of financial service to the community, while allowing them some privileges.[29]

These laws, including those affecting *curiales*, seem to have remained in force until in the mid seventh century (642–672), Chindasuinth and Recceswinth replaced it with a new *lex Visigothorum*, no longer distinguishing between Goths and Romans, probably no longer separate legal categories.[30] But, even then, the institution of *curiales*, landowners legally bound to provide service to the cities, seems to live on. A ruling of King Chindasuinth (V.4.19) bans the alienation of property by *curiales* or *privati*. Who these *privati* are is unclear – presumably, large landowners exempted from service on the *curia*:

> If concern for family property should not [i.e. alienate property], how much more so concern for public benefit, which should always be exercised or increased. Therefore curials or private persons who are accustomed to provide horses or pay dues to the public chest, should never sell their faculty nor donate it nor alienate it by any exchange. It is permissible for the curials themselves or private persons to make sales, donations or exchanges amongst each other, but on condition that the beneficiary does not refuse to pay dues to the public benefit in respect of property acquired. (V.4.19)

This may seem a pallid shadow of the sort of *munera* performed by the curials of the classical city (are the horses provided for the official post? why are they so important to pick out?). The role of the curial seems to be undermined by that of the *privatus*, who, without being a curial, seems to owe the city comparable dues. But just in case we imagine the curials must have entirely evaporated by the mid seventh century, we are reassured of their continued existence.[31]

One role that seems to have continued, as in Merovingian Gaul, was the registration of property transfers in the municipal records. A fragmentary collection of Visigothic laws known as the Fragmenta Gaudenziana, probably from the early sixth century, include the following provision:

> if anyone donate a house (*domus*) or villa to another party, he should confirm his donation with a charter of donation, such that the donator himself sign in his own hand on that donation, and that the donation be

---

[29] Discussed in detail by Churchin, 'The role of civic leaders'; also his 'Curials and local government'.
[30] So Thompson, *Goths in Spain*, p. 120. For the text, Zeumer, *Leges Visigothorum*. Further, King, *Law and Society in the Visigothic Kingdom*.
[31] See Churchin, 'The role of civic leaders', pp. 286–289.

corroborated by not less than three witnesses. But if the donor himself and his witnesses are illiterate, each should mark with a sign in their own hand. And the donation itself should be deposited with the curials. But if no curials can be found in that city, it should be deposited in another city where they are to be found (*Fragmenta Gaudenziana* XV).[32]

This is just the sort of provision that lies behind the Ravenna papyri, and indeed the law seems to be based on the similar provisions of the law of King Theoderic.[33] The prospect of not being able to find local curials is less than reassuring, but in smaller centres their numbers may well have been scarce.

There also survives the equivalent of the sort of formularies that we have met in several cities in Merovingian Gaul, though intervening centuries of Islamic rule have meant that material from the Visigothic period is less likely to survive in municipal archives. But a handsome example from Córdoba makes up for what is otherwise missing.[34] Formula no. 21 exemplifies the formula for registering a will and depositing it in the public records before the council (*apud curiae ordinem gestis publicis facias adcorporare*). Formula no. 25 then sets out the ritual, one familiar to us both from Italy and Gaul:

> In the era (i.e. world date) x, in the year x of our most glorious lord, king X, on the day on the month x, proceedings held at Córdoba (*Patricia Corduba*) before x and y, leading citizens (*principales*), x the *curator*, x and y the magistrates.

The representative of the will-maker asks the magistrates to incorporate it in the public records (*gestis publicis*). The will is accepted by the office of the *curia* and read out. The representative again asks 'that what has been here done or enacted, should remain securely in the public records (*publicis monumentis*)'. The request is granted, and the will duly registered. The same elaborate social ritual is performed as in Italy and Gaul. This was how one kept up the appearance of being a good Roman, following best legal practice. There might have been a shortage of local curials in Visigothic Spain, but this was still the right way to do things under Roman law. How often, and until what date, they were actually done, we cannot possibly tell.

So, what are our chances of finding some *curiales* in the Visigothic landscape? Taking the lead from Gaul, it is worth looking out for those

---

[32] Text in Zeumer, *Leges Visigothorum*, p. 471.   [33] See *Lex Theoderici Regis*, 52.
[34] See Zeumer, *Formulae Merovingici et Karolini Aevi*, pp. 575–595 for Visigothic formulae, p. 585 for no. 21, p. 587 for no. 25. For discussion, Córcolez Olaitz, 'About the origin of the Formulae Wisigothicae'.

calling themselves *senatores* as well as *curiales*. In the *Lives of the Fathers of Emerita* we meet Paul, the noble of senatorial stock in Mérida whose wealth exceeded that of all other senators in Lusitania, and whose estate turned Mérida's into one of the richest churches of Spain.[35] Karl Stroheker was happy to recognise in him a representative of the 'senatorial aristocracy', which, tracing descent from the senators of the Late Empire, played such a dominant role in Merovingian Gaul and suggested that we meet just the same phenomenon in Spain.[36] Others have felt that *senatores* were simply large landowners.[37] But in truth they often look remarkably like what might otherwise be called 'curiales'.[38]

The best test case is the Life of St Aemilianus written by Isidore's friend, Braulio.[39] Aemilianus' activity as a wonderworker is set in Cantabria in the reign of Leovigild, where he established a reputation as the go-to miracle-worker for the better off. Among the numerous beneficiaries of his miracle-working we meet a prominent couple, the senator Nepotianus and his wife, Proseria, suffering jointly from possession by the same demon (22). Yet another victim of demonic possession was Columba, daughter of the *curialis*, Maximus, who is swiftly cured. More of a narrative attaches to the senator Honorius, whose whole house was afflicted by a most wicked demon that stirred up constant trouble, putting the bones of dead animals and manure in the master's dishes. The households to which Aemilianus attends include one of a count (that is, a regal official responsible for a city), three 'senators', and one 'curialis'. The distinction between senator and curialis might imply that the categories did not overlap. But just in terms of the balance of numbers, it would be strange to find three descendants of late Roman senators, as Stroheker imagined, to one local councillor. Further light is cast by the episode at the end of Aemilianus' life (33). During Lent, the doom of Cantabria is revealed to him, so he sends a messenger and instructs the senate to meet on Easter Day. He warns them to repent of their sins, because the end is nigh. Most listened reverently, but the rash Abundantius said the holy man had become senile. It is never a good idea to insult a miracle-worker, and, sure enough, Abundantius was cut down by the avenging sword of Leovigild. That places the incident neatly in 574, when, as John of Biclarum has conveniently told us, Leovigild invaded Cantabria and seized Amaia.

---

[35] The Latin text is edited by Maya Sánchez, *Vitas sanctorum patrum Emeretensium* (Isidore would hardly have approved of the grammar of the modern title), translated by Fear in *Lives of the Visigothic Fathers*, pp. 45–105; see also Dey, *Afterlife*, pp. 151–153.
[36] Stroheker, 'Spanische Senatoren'.   [37] Thompson, *Goths in Spain*, pp. 115–116.
[38] See Churchin, 'Senators or curials?'
[39] For translated text, Fear, *Lives of the Visigothic Fathers*, pp. 15–43.

The most economical reading of this evidence is that the senators who benefited from miracle cures were members of the senate that met on that Easter Day, and that they did so at Amaia. Two unnecessarily convoluted solutions have been offered: that there was an otherwise unheard-of city of Cantabria called Cantabria, and they were members of its senate; alternatively, that Cantabria had an (otherwise unattested) regional senate, of which they were members.[40] Unless the Chronicle of John misleads us, the principal urban centre of this part of Cantabria was Amaia. The 'senators' are simply members of its civic council. If there is a distinction between them and the *curialis* Maximus, it could be that he was a current magistrate, and the senators, the majority, hereditary members of the *curia*. And if this reconstruction is right, the local council did more than register wills and donations: it was the body to which you turned when the enemy approached. Alas, the senators fail to listen to the saint, and Amaia falls to Leovigild.

We cannot build much on the basis of such fragile evidence, but it is enough to show that reports of the demise of the cities and their councils are premature. In this context, it becomes the more interesting to look at what Isidore makes of the city.

The Etymologist's Vision

In trying to derive an Isidorian vision of the city from the *Etymologies*, we are confronted with a double challenge. The first is to deal with an author who is, as we have seen, systematically reticent, whether for psychological or religious reasons, or both, about his own participation, so effectively distancing himself from the subjects he discusses. The second is the nature of the ancient scholarly/philological tradition itself. To dismiss it as 'antiquarian' is an evasion of our duty of nuanced and empathetic interpretation.

The *Etymologies* are the product of a tradition of scholarship, of enquiry into the meanings of words and what they can tell about life, and of close commentary on principal literary texts, that stretches over a full six centuries. The effect can be dismaying for the modern reader: is Isidore telling us what he thinks, or what he has read somewhere, and if so, what has he been reading and of what date? Answers may be frustratingly hard to pin down, for this is a tradition of scholarship that sees no difficulty in the recycling, mostly without acknowledgement, of earlier material, which has itself in all

---

[40] A good discussion in Fear, *Lives*, p. 39, note 107.

probability been recycled from yet earlier texts. Above all, when an author is cited – say, Horace or Sallust – we can have little confidence that Isidore had consulted the author himself. The layers are multiple: not so much a neat archaeological section that can be separated cleanly into numbered strata, but more like a compost or mulch, regularly added to over the years, and periodically turned over with a fork.

At the head of the tradition, for Latin authors, is the great scholar of the first century BC, Varro: his *de Lingua Latina* (*On the Latin Language*) was as fundamental for etymology as were his *Antiquities* for Augustine in trying to understand pagan religion. Appropriately enough, Braulio recycles the Ciceronian encomium of Varro in his *Life of Isidore*: he had rescued his contemporaries, like strangers in their own city, and shown them who they were. *On the Latin Language* is certainly a philological work, as obsessed with the imagined revelations of etymology as was Isidore. But it is simultaneously a work about Roman life, tradition, and identity – Varro also wrote a work *On the Life of the Roman People* in which he was happy to use archaic texts to reconstruct a picture of ancient Rome. That tradition was taken up a century later by Suetonius; we may still regret the loss of his *Prata*, a picking of flowers from the meadow of philology, which was certainly organised by topics, like the calendar, games, terms of insult or even shorthand; and Isidore, who organises his own work thematically, by 'titles', has something of the same aim.[41]

Between Varro and Isidore lie two dense traditions. One is that of commentary on literary texts: Aelius Donatus on Virgil and Terence, used in the fifth century by Servius Honoratus in his massive commentary on Virgil, together with works on grammar, from Donatus to Martianus Capella and Cassiodorus. The second is of biblical exegesis that drew deeply on the grammatical tradition and especially Virgilian commentaries: Jerome, Ambrose, Augustine, Gregory the Great, and many others. Since each of them dipped their buckets deep into the well of classical learning, it can be difficult, if not pointless, to establish who exactly had been reading what, though it is generally the more recent authors whom Isidore demonstrably knows.[42] We can be confident that he read an enormous amount, and his literary appetite was voracious, but the attempt to list his library is full of frustrations. The vital point is surely this: he operates in a tradition six centuries old which sees itself as a continuity. Romans (after Varro, of

---

[41] On Varro and the antiquarian tradition, Wallace-Hadrill, *Rome's Cultural Revolution*, pp. 231–237; on the questionable use of Isidore in reconstructing Suetonius, see Wallace-Hadrill, *Suetonius*, p. 42.

[42] Cf. Elfassi, 'Connaître la bibliothèque'.

course) had been brought up on Virgil and guided by grammarians and commentators, word by word. Augustan Rome might indeed be as distant from Isidore's Visigothic world as is that of Henry VI to our own, but somehow it didn't feel so. One could not have continued to recycle earlier grammatical scholarship, and then incorporate it into the new Christian discourse, if it felt distant and alien. Things changed, of course (Varro said that linguistic practice was in flux, *consuetudo loquendi est in motu*).[43] But they could still recognise themselves in Virgil.

Jacques Fontaine's pioneering study of Isidore opened up a seam of research that a new generation of scholars has been able to mine further, armed with the tools of digital recognition of words and phrases.[44] Far from being an author who would mindlessly follow a single source, Isidore blends an extraordinary richness of multiple sources. 'Originality' is the wrong quality to look for in this genre, but the way he puts together his diverse material makes it his own. Indeed, the *Etymologies* has deep historical roots; but, rather than thinking of this as the work of a dusty antiquarian, out of contact with the language and concerns of his day, we should recognise it as a continuous conversation, generation after generation of Latin authors in contact with each other, looking to the past for insights into a living language – a conversation which may start with Varro and Cicero, but which carries on uninterruptedly through Quintilian, the grammarians, and the commentators, to the leading minds of the Christian church, from Augustine to Gregory the Great, the latter a contemporary whom Isidore deeply respected as a friend of his brother Leander. It was a way of explaining the world through words to which they all cheerfully subscribed.

Cities and Citizens

Seen from this perspective, what Isidore has to say about cities and citizens is of considerable interest, though it is notable that while there has been much recent discussion of the city in Cassiodorus and Gregory of Tours, the city of Isidore seems a non-subject.[45] There are two sections of the *Etymologies* that are highly relevant: the first is a 'title' on the theme of

---

[43] Varro, *Lingua Latina* 9.17. See my *Rome's Cultural Revolution*, pp. 67–68.
[44] Elfassi, 'Isidore and the Etymologies', pp. 265–269. Particularly useful are the book-by-book commentaries in the Belles Lettres series, *Auteurs Latins du Moyen Âge*.
[45] Nothing of relevance in the *Companion to Isidore*, in contrast to discussion of his view on kings or the church.

citizens (*de civibus*) in book 9; the second, the discussion of cities and their context that occupies the whole of book 15. Together they constitute one of the most sustained examinations of the world of cities in any ancient author. It is slightly awkward that the two sections are separated, for they closely interrelate. But this is no problem for Isidore, who is aware of the urge to look at words in closely related clusters. So he sees citizens, and the other status groups of the city, as belonging to a broader picture of social status, following *imperia*, positions of power from kings and consuls to emperors, and *militiae*, ranks in the military. Cities, by contrast, are treated as a geographical and structural phenomenon, in what proves to be a wide-ranging discussion, from cities to countryside to road networks.

A glance at the section of *imperia* reveals his sharp awareness of change through time. He takes kings first, because that is the pattern of Roman history. But, of course, kings for Isidore were also the Gothic kings whom he might reckon himself to know fairly well. He opens (9.3.1–5) with an overview of world history that locates kings and the kingdoms in which they were implicit (*regna* ruled by *reges*): a succession of Assyrians, Medes, Persians, Egyptians, and Greeks, who in his scheme succeed one another, a consciousness of world history typical of Christian authors that is met in similar form, for instance, in Tertullian, blended with an etymology of the words that is straight Augustine.[46] From this perspective, it is natural to treat kings as a universal phenomenon (without drawing distinctions between the seven kings of archaic Rome and the contemporary kings of Spain), and therefore to impose a universal ideology. Kings are named for 'acting rightly': *rex eris quod recte facies*, as Horace puts it (*Epistulae* 1.1.59–60); and he expands this moralising approach by defining which of the many regal virtues (defined as such by the rhetorical tradition) were most important for a king: justice and piety, of which the latter was the most important, since justice was 'somewhat severe'. As if by a sleight of hand, Isidore has taken the virtues attributed to Augustus and exemplified in the *Aeneid*,[47] and expressed them in such a way as to be a relevant lesson to a Visigothic king, whose *pietas* would be seen in his fidelity to the Nicene creed.

From kings he passes to the consuls who in Roman history replaced them, making a contrast between the pomp and arrogance of kings to the

---

[46] Reydellet, *Isidorus*, p. 118, citing Augustine, *City of God* 5.12 for the definition, Tertullian, *to the Nations* 2.17.18–19.

[47] Reydellet, *Isidorus*, p. 122 shows the debt to Servius' commentary on *Aeneid* 1.545, in which he compares these two virtues of Aeneas. On Servius and the longer version of Servius 'Auctus' or 'Danielis', see Fowler, 'The Virgil commentary of Servius'.

benevolence of consuls, whose name indicates 'consultation', specifically of the citizens (*a consulendo civibus*: 9.3.6). Touching swiftly on proconsuls and dictators (9.3.8–11), he comes to the Caesars (was Caesar named after a Caesarean section, or the long hair, *caesaries*, with which he was born? 9.3.12–13). Most attention goes to Augustus and the significance of his titles, *imperator* and *Augustus*, and also to the title he refused, *dominus*, and the anecdote of how he begged the crowd not to use this appellation, given by Suetonius and repeated by Orosius.[48] Considering how this title had become normalised, not just in the so-called Dominate of the Late Empire but even for Trajan, and that *dominus gloriosissimus* was a proper way to refer to a Visigothic king, it might seem surprising Isidore makes such a lot of this anecdote, but his agenda is to take distance from the *superbia dominationis* that Augustine had identified as the central failing of the Roman Empire (see Chapter 3).

The moralisation is not quite finished, for the Greek term *basileus* gives a chance to return to the theme, with an etymology (as in *basis*, base) borrowed directly from Gregory the Great.[49] This takes him to the Greek (and Latin) term, *tyrannus*, and here his sense of change through time is on display. Originally 'tyrant' meant no more than king (he ignores here the sharp distinction drawn by Aristotle and others). He can cite Virgil for a neutral use of the term: Aeneas shook the right hand of Evander, *dextram tetigisse tyranni*, and Servius' commentary wrongly asserts that the word in Greek was neutral.[50] But not anymore!

> Now, subsequently (*iam postea*) it has become usage to name as 'tyrants' the worst and shameless kings who exercise the greed and cruellest domination of luxurious domination over their peoples. (9.3.20)

Isidore's indignant (and repetitive) characterisation of the tyrant is full of the language of Augustine, with phrases like *pessimi atque improbi reges*, let alone *dominatio*.[51] Despite his insistence that this is something recent (*iam postea*), he offers the classic Greek definition of a tyrant, as he would have known if he had read Plato or Aristotle; but he is led astray by a combination of Virgil commentaries and the struggles of Augustine, for all his formidable learning, with the Greek language. If Isidore's account is not completely historical, it is revealing of his attitude. He has put together a heady mixture of Virgil and Horace commentaries, Suetonius filtered through Orosius,

---

[48] Reydellet, *Isidorus*, p. 130, citing Suetonius, *Augustus* 53 and Orosius 6.22.4.
[49] Reydellet, *Isidorus*, p. 130, citing Gregory, *Moralia* 9.15.
[50] Reydellet, *Isidorus*, p. 132, citing Servius on *Aeneid* 7. 266.
[51] Reydellet, *Isidorus*, p. 132, citing *City of God* 5.19.

other Christian writers from Tertullian to Augustine to Pope Gregory, to produce his identikit of kingship. He shows 'truth from words':[52] implicit in the name *rex* is rectitude of behaviour, justice, and piety, the contrary of tyrannical domination driven by greed for power. What he has revealed from his etymology is as relevant to Visigothic kings as to the archaic Rome of Tarquin the Proud: *tyranni* is exactly how he characterises 'bad kings' in his *History of Gothic Kings* – usurpers and tyrants such as Athanagild, Hermenegild, and Witteric.[53] He may dig deep into ancient learning, but for him the deep truth of words is of sharp contemporary relevance.

Consuls, unlike kings, take their name, so Isidore believes, from consulting the citizens (*a consulendo civibus*). But good kings too could consult their citizens, for instance by summoning synods at Toledo. The idea of the citizen is as relevant for Isidore as that of a king. After dealing with commands and the military, he turns to citizens and the 'names of citizens' – that is, civilian positions (9.4.1). First, a definition:

> Citizens are so called because they live 'coming together' (*co-euntes*) in one, with the aim of making communal life more decorative (*ornatior*) and safe. (4.2)

The etymology may be dubious,[54] but it carries with it the evolutionary schema met in Lucretius, Vitruvius, Seneca, and others: human life starts scattered across the land like wild animals, but the social instinct brings them together both for protection and mutual enjoyment in cities. Isidore certainly sees his citizens as living in cities.[55] He goes on with an image of concentric circles: as the house (*domus*) is home to one family, so the city (*urbs*) is to one people (*populus*), and the world to the whole human race. That is pure Lactantius.[56] As in Augustine, the city of God does not render the city of man superfluous, but acts at a higher level, embracing the whole world. This prompts him to define the people (*populus*), identified as inhabitants of the city:

> A people is a coming together of a multitude of humans, associated by consent under the law and shared agreement.
>
> Populus est humanae multitudinis <coetus> iuris consensu et concordi communione sociatus. (4.5)

---

[52] So the punning subtitle of Henderson's *The Medieval World of Isidore of Seville*; p. 133 on kings and citizens.

[53] Reydellet, *Isidorus*, p. 133, citing *History* 46, 47, 49 and 57. For Isidore's views on kingship, see further Fear, 'Isidore of Seville on law and kingship', esp. pp. 339–344.

[54] Reydellet, *Isidorus*, p. 156, citing Ernout–Meillet.

[55] On the Christian use of the classical scheme, Ottewill-Soulsby, 'First cities'.

[56] Reydellet, *Isidorus*, p. 156, citing Lactantius, *Institutions* 2.5.32.

This richly concise definition has a long line of descent: from Cicero's *Republic* (and, of course, the Greek sources behind him, especially the Stoic Chrysippus) to Augustine, who uses it repeatedly in the *City of God*[57] (in words memorably cited by Joe Biden in his inauguration speech, lest there be any doubt regarding how words and ideas may echo through the millennia). One striking feature is the intimate link that exists in Isidore's mind (and vocabulary) between city and people. He does not think of a *populus* in ethnic or in regional terms: there is no room here for a Gothic people or a Spanish people. The Roman people, *populus Romanus*, is of course different: because it consists of Roman citizens who share in *civitas Romana*, it has not become an ethnic or, indeed, a regional concept.[58]

The linkage between citizen and *populus* is further revealed by his definition of *civitas*, though we have to wait for the fifteenth book for this (15.2.1). The definition of a city is almost identical to that of a people:

> Civitas est hominum multitudo societatis vinculo adunata, dicta a civibus, id est ab ipsis incolis urbis.
>
> The city is a multitude of humans united by the bond of society, named after 'citizens', that is the inhabitants of the city themselves.

The source is still Augustine, perhaps closest in this formulation to his *Letters*: 'For what is the city if not a multitude of humans held in a certain bond of concord?'[59] It is striking that Isidore can use virtually identical formulations to define both *populus* and *civitas*, and the urban context of his thinking is made explicit in both passages by the use of *urbs*. To the distinction he draws between *civitas* and *urbs* we will return but, just as we have seen, for instance, in John of Biclarum's *Chronicle*, the terms could be at times virtually interchangeable.

After his broad definition of a *populus*, he turns to the distinction between *populus* and *plebs*. The *populus*, he explains, consists of all the citizens, including the *seniores civitatis*; the *plebs* is the crowd (*vulgus*) and excludes the *seniores* (strictly, 'elders'). The common crowd is the *plebs*. The *plebs* are known for their plurality, for they exceed in number the *seniores* (9.4.6). All this is good Roman law, paralleled in Gaius' *Institutes* and the *Digest*, with a small but significant difference. Gaius defines those

---

[57] Reydellet, *Isidorus*, p. 158, citing *City of God* 2.21; 19.21 and 19.24.
[58] On the changing definition of the Roman, see Pohl, 'Introduction: Early medieval Romanness'.
[59] See Guillaumin and Monat, *Isidore de Séville, Étymologies, Livre XV*, p. 30, citing Augustine, *Letters* 138.10, 'quid est autem civitas nisi hominum multitudo in quoddam vinculum redacta concordiae?'; but also referring to *City of God* 15.8.2, which is equally close.

who are excluded as the *patricii*, technically correct for the Republic; the *Digest* as the *senatores*. Isidore calls them *seniores*, a vague term which eludes the precision of Roman law, but conveniently suits Visigothic Spain by including the *seniores gentis Gothorum* as well as local 'senators'.[60] This subtle change of vocabulary underlines the way Isidore does not think of the city and citizenship as some sort of dated institution to be found in the legal texts, but as a contemporary reality, the truth of which is embedded in its language.

This may encourage us to look again at what Isidore has to say about the leading citizens, without simply assuming that it was irrelevant to his own day (4.8–27). First the *senatores*, who owe their name to the fact that they were *seniores*. This time, the modern etymologist agrees, even if Isidore goes on to offer a far less plausible alternative, from '*sinere*', 'allow'.[61] The etymological link helps to explain how easily he could slip *seniores* into his definition of what the *plebs* excluded. He moves on to the term *patres*, fathers, citing Sallust, whom he knows through Servius' commentary, for the idea of paternal care of the senators for the Republic.[62] But in case we think we are in the world of republican Rome, Isidore rapidly moves on to that of the Late Empire, saying that there were three ranks of senators: *inlustres, spectabiles*, and *clarissimi* (4.12). This very formal distinction of senatorial ranks goes back to the late fourth century, to Valentinian I.[63] Typical of the way Isidore blends different historical periods, it reflects a reality only in part still current, for the use of such titles proliferated in Late Antiquity, as the Ravenna papyri illustrate (see Chapter 6).[64] That practice changed, he is well aware, and he next remarks (4.12) that a son of a Roman senator used to be an *eques Romanus* until he reached maturity, when he received senatorial dignity. This was indeed true under the Republic, until Augustan legislation effectively made senatorial rank hereditary.

Isidore now runs through some magistrates of senatorial rank: censors, a rank he explicitly flags as one of Antiquity (*apud veteres Romanos erant*, 4.13); *iudices*, not the title of a magisterial rank in the classical period, but very much so in Late Antiquity and Isidore's own day;

---

[60] Reydellet, *Isidorus*, p. 158, citing Gaius, *Institutes* 1.3 (*sine patriciis ceteri cives*) and Digest 50.16.238, *plebs est ceteri cives sine senatoribus*. He notes the applicability of *seniores* to contemporary Spain.

[61] Reydellet, *Isidorus*, p. 161, citing Ernout–Meillet, Dictionnaire etymologique de la langue latine: histoire des mots, p. 613.

[62] Reydellet, *Isidorus*, p. 162, the source being Servius on *Aeneid* 5.758.

[63] Reydellet, *Isidorus*, p.162; Jones, *Later Roman Empire*, pp. 528–531.

[64] For Visigothic usage, Álvarez Melero, 'Honesti, clarissimi e illustres'.

praesides for provincial governors, a term that goes back to Diocletian; *praetores* and *quaestores*, good Republican magistracies; and *proceres*, an informal term for leading citizens (*principes civitatis*) attested in Varro.[65] Isidore has evidently no interest here in building up a diachronic picture, but rather of assembling terms for prominent citizens whatever their date. That point comes out more clearly in his next entry, on *tribuni*, whom he rightly dates back to the early years of the Republic,[66] and identifies their function as defending the liberty of the *plebs* against the abuses of the nobility (4.18). But he now makes a revealing comment: that the defence of the *plebs* was also the function of *defensores*, adding that 'nowadays by contrast' (*at contra nunc*), 'the *defensores* are not so much defenders as destroyers (*eversores*)'.

At this point, our faithful commentator observes that *nunc* refers not to sixth-century Spain (or, indeed, seventh), but to the day of the unidentified source.[67] Here we can cast a little more light, for we have already met the Novel of Justinian which in 535 reinforced the role of *defensores* as responsible for municipal registrations (see Chapter 6, p. 204). The Novel opens, as is often the way, with an indignant protest against the contemporary abuses which the new law seeks to address, and lamenting the decline of *defensores*:

> We style them defenders, because they were appointed to defend persons suffering from the acts of wicked men. Now, however (*nunc autem*), the name of defender is treated with contempt in many parts of Our Empire, and is so despised that its use is rather considered an insult than a distinction. (*Novel* 15, preface)

Justinian does not use the word *eversores*, but he clearly provides the model for insistence on the etymological force of the word *defensores*. Whether Isidore read the original Novel, or maybe a Visigothic summary, he was dealing with something still relevant in his world: *defensores* are met in Spain, if rarely,[68] and the parallel of the Merovingian formularies, in which they are met regularly, suggests a similar pattern for Spain.

Isidore now goes on to explore a number of municipal offices which are familiar from Ravenna and Gaul. *Decuriones* are so called from the *curia* (*de ordine curiae*, 4.23); *curiales* are the same as *decuriones* because they

---

[65] Reydellet, *Isidorus*, p. 166: it is Servius on *Aeneid* 1.740 who cites Varro.
[66] Reydellet, *Isidorus*, p. 166: he is using the histories of Eutropius (1.13), but mistakes 16 for 6.
[67] Reydellet, *Isidorus*, pp. 166–167.
[68] Churchin, 'The role of civic leaders', pp. 283–284, citing Severus of Minorca, *Epistula de Judaeis* 6.

serve civic funtions (4.24). *Principales*, *magistrati*, and *duumvirales* are all ranks of *curiales* (4.25); the *tabellio* is the man who carries the *tabellae*, the records; the *exceptor* is the same, as is the *scriba publicus*, because he writes what is published in the records (*quae gestis publicantur*, 4.27). All these are terms current in the registrations in municipal records in Italy and Gaul; so we have the choice of supposing that Isidore reflects a contemporary reality of other areas, or of accepting that they, and the practices they imply, were current in Visigothic Spain itself, as indeed our Córdoba formulary attests.

Dismayed we may be at the apparently casual way in which Isidore shuttles between Republican and Imperial pasts and Visigothic present, but, as already suggested, it reflects his concept of the world of words as a deep continuity across many centuries and political circumstances. Of course, he can differentiate then and now if he finds it relevant, but for him, cities and citizenship, like kings and kingship, are features of life over the *longue durée*, and it is that fundamental continuity that makes it possible to quarry lasting truths from words.

A World of Cities

To these themes he returns in the fifteenth book, but on a broader and more ambitious canvas. As we have seen, cities and citizenship are etymologically entwined, but whereas in book 9 he is concerned with people, in book 15 he addresses places, the most geographical of his titles. He opens with a remarkable survey of cities and their origins; and, because for him the Bible is a source every bit as important as classical literature, there is an emphasis on the East that we might not expect in a classical geographer like Strabo. If ever there was an antidote to the idea of 'the ancient city' meaning restrictively Greco-Roman and classical, it is this overview. His Palestine (or 'Holy Land') is more densely populated with memorable cities than either Greece or Italy (Figure 8.1).

There were, as always, various ways in which Isidore might organise his material: alphabetically (a solution he avoids), or chronologically by date of foundation (but we have already seen that he shows little interests in a strict stratigraphy). Instead, he offers a broadly geographical structure, starting in the East, then sweeping clockwise from Rome to the East, then anticlockwise around the Mediterranean to the West. To this there are two significant modifications. The first is a prefatory remark on the difficulty of determining the origins of cities when these are themselves disputed. The example he offers is Rome itself. For this he looks at three potential

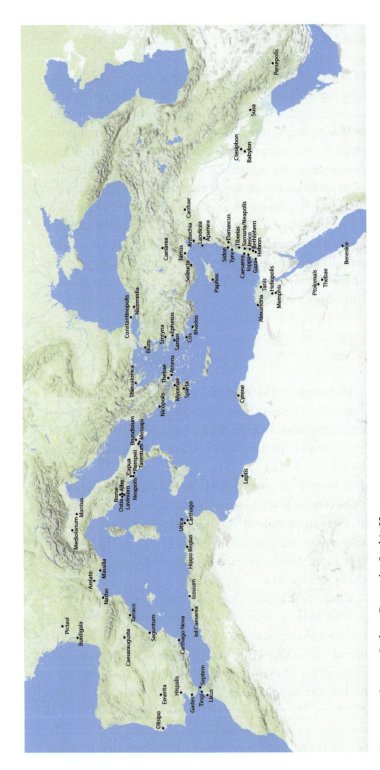

Figure 8.1 Cities in Isidore. Drawn by Sophie Hay.

foundations: Sallust says Rome was founded by the Trojans (i.e. Aeneas) and the 'Aborigines'; Virgil says that Evander founded the citadel of Rome (*Romanae conditor arcis*), but elsewhere he identifies Romulus, under whose auspices the famous Rome (*illa inclita Roma*) was founded. Hence, despite all the importance of Rome (*tantae civitatis*), there is no clear answer, and this, he adds, is the fault of neither the historians nor the commentators because Antiquity itself (*antiquitas ipsa*) generated the error. This he offers as preface to an account of city foundations which are frequently mythological and to us no more than an exercise in shaping identity. There were in fact ways in which he could have dealt with this conundrum in terms of his own distinctions: Aeneas founded the Roman *gens*, the ethnic group not the city; Evander founded the citadel, not the city; Romulus founded the *civitas*, the institution of the city inhabited by the *gens Romana* on the site of Evander's citadel. But he prefers to highlight the doubt, not to resolve the problem. And, whatever his intention (the pursuit of authorial intention being mostly speculative), the effect of this choice is to put Rome, and a statement of its importance, at the head of the survey. In fact, when he comes round to discussing Rome (1.55), he is rather more confident in identifying Romulus as the founder, albeit briefly mentioning Evander.

Rome, then, has managed to steal a place at the head of the queue. But a reader of Augustine's *City of God* could not overlook the clear biblical authority that the first city ever was the city of Enoch founded by Cain, a city populated with the multitude of his own descendants – this, after all, was Augustine's solution to the inherent demographic problem (1.3; see Chapter 3, p. 92).[69] Having started with Cain, it makes sense to open the survey with the biblical Near East. Babylon was the first city after the flood, and for this he identifies, again following Augustine, two founders: the biblical Nimrod (Nemroth), builder of the tower of Babel, and Semiramis, the Herodotean founder of Babylon, who provided it with its great wall of bitumen, so combining Augustine with Hyginus.[70] Of course, Babel and Babylon were not the same, but it allows for an integration of biblical and classical mythology. That indeed is a strong tendency throughout the survey of cities: the biblical and classical are not seen as alternatives, or contrasting ideologies, but as part of a broader whole that needs to be integrated.

The sang-froid with which Isidore will leap from the mythological to the historical must seem one of the strangest features of his writing to the

---

[69] Ottewill-Soulsby, 'First cities'.
[70] Guillaumin, p. 98, citing *City of God* 16.4 and Hyginus, *Fabulae* 223.5.

modern reader. But these are not for him different categories. Myth or history, biblical or classical, remote part or recent past are almost indifferent: what matters are the stories the locals tell about the foundation of their cities. Jerusalem (1.5) passes through a sequence of incarnations. The Jews say it was founded by 'Shem, whom they call Melchizedech' (here he follows Jerome);[71] Solomon renamed it Hierosolyma, as if it were Solomon's Holy City; and then the emperor Hadrian renamed it Aelia after himself. Immediately after these more biblical examples, we have a string of classical mythologies: Dionysus (but Isidore's text has 'Dionysius', man replacing god) founded Nysa on the Indus when conquering India (1.6), Perseus founded Persia and Persepolis (1.8), and Memnon's brother founded Susa (1.10).

Isidore shuttles effortlessly between the historical and the mythological. Carrhae in Mesopotamia was founded by the Parthians but is memorable because the Roman general Crassus met his end there (1.12). Nimrod founded Edessa, formerly called Arach, as well as Chalane, refounded by Seleucus as Seleucia (1.13). This triggers a cluster of (perfectly historical) Seleucid foundations: Antioch, Laodicea, Apamea, and Edessa (1.15). Then we have a Palestinian cluster: Gaza, named after the treasury of Cambyses; and Dor, renamed Caesarea by Herod in honour of Caesar Augustus, the city where the *Acts* (10.1 and 21.8–9) set the houses of Cornelius and Philip (1.18). So easily can one slip between worlds, which for Isidore interlock. Then we meet Joppa, a Palestinian foundation indeed, but this is where you can still see the rock to which Andromeda was chained when Perseus came to rescue her (1.19): this he has from Jerome, who saw the rock.[72] A rich variety of sources are thrown into the Isidorian blender to produce this smoothly homogeneous mix.

The survey continues to sweep round the Mediterranean. After Palestine and Judea (1.22–26), we reach Phoenicia: Tyre, famous for its purple Tyrian dye; Sidon, named after the fish '*sidon*' (1.27–28). The Phoenicians are seen as great city founders (justly so): Utica, Hippo, Leptis, and other cities on the African coast are to their credit (1.18), and above all Carthage, named from the Phoenician for New City (as is indeed the case) by Dido. Scipio destroyed it, but the Romans refounded it (1.30). With the Phoenicians, the survey follows a clockwise course around the Mediterranean, but now we back up, and start to go anticlockwise. There is Egypt, where Alexander the Great and his Alexandria rubs shoulders with Cadmus, founder of Thebes in Egypt as

---

[71] Guillaumin, p. 99, citing Jerome, *Quaestiones Hebraeae*, p. 24.
[72] Guillaumin, p. 106, citing Jerome, *Letter* 108.8.

well as that in Boeotia (1. 332–335). Now we sweep up the coast via Tarsus (this time it is Perseus and St Paul who rub shoulders; 1.38), Smyrna, and Nicomedia to reach Constantinople. At this point, the pace changes, and exceptional status is flagged (1.42):

> Constantine imposed his own name on the Thracian city of Constantinople; it alone is the equal of Rome in importance and power (solam Romae meritis et potentia adaequatam).

After explaining the original foundation of Byzantium by the Spartan king Pausanias (in truth it was a Megarian colony, captured much later by Pausanias), he turns to Constantine:

> Hence Constantine decided to found this most suitable city, so that it would become a haven (*receptaculum*) by land and sea. For this reason it is even today the seat of the Roman Empire and the head of the entire East, as Rome is of the West (unde et nunc Romani imperii sedes et totius caput est orientis, sicut et Roma occidentis).

When Isidore refers to the present (*et nunc*), time, as we have seen, is a little elastic. Constantinople was indeed the seat of the Roman Empire in his day, but to refer to Rome as the equivalent in the west seems more than a century out of date. The same Isidore who in his *History of the Gothic Kings* could celebrate the Visigoths as successors to Roman power could now write as if Rome had never fallen. Is he influenced by the language of some earlier source (unknown),[73] or does he rather think of the western sphere of influence of the Roman papacy? There is no reason to suppose Isidore had ever been to Rome, but we may suspect the influence of family friendship through Leander with Gregory the Great, who did so much to build up the papacy in the west, and who must have seen Leander's conversion of the Goths as their return to the Roman fold.

Constantinople opens the gates to the heartlands of the Greco-Roman city, in Greece and Italy. Athens is given some emphasis, rightly named after Athena/Minerva 'because literature, and the arts of many schools, and philosophy itself have considered Athens as their temple' (1.44) – words closely following those of Augustine in the *City of God* (18.9), though the expression 'temple' (*templum*) is his own. He then rattles off some of the more obvious Greek cities – Corinth, Thebes, Sparta – amongst which he includes Mycenae, a city notoriously abandoned a millennium and a half before his time. But then, there is something timeless about Isidore's cities.

---

[73] Guillaumin, p. 114, offers no comment.

From central Greece, he branches out to a very small selection of colonial foundations, including Rhodes, Thessalonica (wrongly attributed to Thessalus, son of Graecus, instead of Alexander's successor, Cassander), and Brundisium in Italy, alleged to be a Greek foundation named after the Greek for a 'stag's head', *brunda* (1.49). This might have been the moment to give some acknowledgement of the great wave of Greek colonisation of South Italy and Sicily, as would any readers of Thucydides: he manages to pick on a local Messapic foundation, and it is in their language, not Greek, that *brention* means 'stag's head', after the shape of the harbour.[74]

As elsewhere, Isidore's knowledge of the Greek world is distinctly limited. Brundisium has the advantage of taking him to Italy and Latin sources, where he is rather more sure-footed. Interest in mythological origins shines through again, and the first city established is none other than Pompeii, founded by Hercules and named after his triumph (*pompa*); nothing here, though, of Herculaneum, supposedly named after Hercules on the same occasion (1.51). No problem with including Pompeii, like Mycenae, in this timeless carousel. Aeneas and his son are given credit, as legend required, for the foundation of Alba Longa, and thereby Isidore resolves his earlier problem over competing founders of Rome (1.53). Capua too is claimed as an Alban foundation (1.54), and Isidore goes out of his way to underline the importance of this city, 'named with Rome and Carthage as the three greatest cities'. The idea of the three great cities seems to go back to Cicero, who said that their ancestors regarded only three cities as capable of sustaining the weight of empire: Corinth, Carthage, and Capua; but the selection of Rome, Carthage, and Capua comes from Florus, if not from Jordanes' *Gothica*.[75] This third statement of Rome's importance then ushers in the conventional foundation of Rome by Romulus, albeit with another mention of Virgil's line on Evander (1.55).

From Rome, Isidore heads to northern Italy, but he has nothing to say of the numerous Roman colonies there. Instead he focuses on Milan (Mediolanum), seen as a Gallic foundation, and he repeats the etymology popular from Late Antiquity – that it was named for a sow 'woolly in the middle', *medio-lanum*.[76] Mantua (the birth city of Virgil, though he does not mention this) leads to Parthenope/Neapolis (Virgil's place of burial, unmentioned): his source for both will be Servius' commentary on the

---

[74] Guillaumin, p. 20, reports that Hesychius (s.v.) says βρέντιος means stag, but fails to cite Strabo 6.3.6, who explains the origin in Messapic.

[75] Guillaumin, pp. 117–118, citing Cicero, *de lege agraria* 2.87, Florus 1.11.6, possibly interpolated, Jordanes, *Romana* 143.

[76] Guillaumin, p. 119, citing Sidonius Apollinaris, *Letters* 7.17.20 and Claudian, 10.183.

Aeneid, though it was Solinus who unhelpfully persuaded him that it was Augustus who renamed the city Neapolis.[77] Mention of Augustus then allows a leap across the Adriatic to Nicopolis at the site of Actium, another gleaning from Servius (1.61).[78]

It is now time to move west, and in swift succession Isidore looks at Gaul and Spain. In Gaul, the trilingual Massilia (Marseille) is rightly identified as one of the early Greek colonies (it is Varro who observes the trilingual mastery of Greek, Latin, and Gallic); and he briefly adds Narbonne, Arles, Poitiers, and Bordeaux (1.64), skipping Roman colonies like Nîmes or Lyon, and not even flagging the former Visigothic capital of Toulouse. With Spain, he reaches his climax, and he allows himself panegyrics (*laudes urbium*) of two cities: Caesaraugusta (Zaragoza) and Carthago Spartiaria (Cartagena). Because Braulio, who was bishop of Zaragoza, edited his text, there is a strong suspicion that he may have inserted something of his own:

> Caesar Augustus both situated and named Caesaraugusta in the province of Tarragon. With the loveliness of its situation and its charming features it stands out among the cities of Spain and is famous, distinguished for the tombs of its martyrs. (1.66)

The fact that these words are missing from many manuscripts, except those of the 'Spanish family', strengthens the suspicion against Braulio;[79] but it must be said that enthusiasm for an Augustan foundation is Isidorian, and this praise makes a neat contrast with the city that follows, Cartagena:

> The Africans [i.e. Carthaginians], occupying the coasts of Spain under Hannibal, built New Carthage. Later taken and made a colony by the Romans, it gave its name to a province. But now it has been overthrown and reduced to desolation by the Goths. (1.67)

If this is a reference to the capture of the city by Suinthila in 622,[80] this traumatic event took place under the king whom he so warmly praised in the second edition of his *History of the Goths*. Given that Cartagena was the birthplace of Leander and (possibly) Isidore, the regret seems as heartfelt as Leander's complaints at the ruination of his city, though this was many decades earlier. In any case, this chapter shows no enthusiasm for the Goths. He might easily have included Leovigild's foundation of Reccopolis, mentioned in the *History*, or other Gothic foundations such as Victoriacum, or indeed the Gothic capital of Toledo, but of these no hint.

---

[77] Guillaumin, p. 120: Servius on *Aeneid* 10.198 and 4.563; Solinus 2.9.
[78] Guillaumin, p. q20, Servius on *Aeneid* 3.274.
[79] Fontaine, *Isidore* vol. 1, p. 405, raised the doubts.   [80] So Guillaumin, p. 121.

On the other hand, Saguntum, destroyed by the 'Africans' in the Punic Wars, is another example of a no-longer-extant city that finds its way into the survey (1.68). The Augustan colony of Emerita Augusta (Mérida) and the Caesarean colony of Hispalis (Seville) sit alongside Ulisippo (Lisbon), attributed to Ulysses. Isidore's bishopric of Hispalis is treated to one of Isidore's most gloriously implausible etymologies: it was built on deep piles, *his palis* (1.71).

From Cadiz, founded like Cartagena by Phoenicians, we make our way to the Straits of Gibraltar (*Gaditanus fretus*) and Septem (Ceuta) on the African shore, and so to Lixus, Tangiers, Mauretanian Caesarea (another Augustan foundation, just as Palestinian Caesarea, he adds), and, to round it all off, Cyrene (1.74–77). The survey, having already made a foray into North Africa via the Phoenicians, now closes the circle by returning to the same area. Isidore seems to be much more interested in the Phoenician past in Spain, as in North Africa, than in any Visigothic present.

One way and another, it may feel to be a quirkish survey of world cities. The omissions are (inevitably) numerous, and wholly fail to provide a history of either Greek or Roman colonisation (the Phoenicians being better represented on that front). It reflects Isidore's personal choices and interests, whether an interest in the Bible and the Holy Land, or in the Virgilian world of Augustus, or in his own patch of Spain. But an author is entitled to their favourites. What it absolutely fails to do is to suggest that there is anything about the Greco-Roman city that distinguishes it from the biblical city, or that of Persia, or that of the Phoenicians. It is absolutely not a survey of the contemporary cities of his seventh-century world. Dead cities live alongside current ones. There is no sense that the remote and largely mythological past is different in kind from the more recent, 'historical' past. We might conclude that Isidore is lost in his library, blind to the realities of the present, but his complaint about the destruction of Cartagena should disabuse us of that idea. On the contrary: the continuous admixture of mythological and historical, of remote past and present, reinforces the sense that for him the city is something about which we can talk across time and space.

The Anatomy of the City

Neither historically evolving, nor differentiated, whether geographically or ethnically, Isidore's city is a timeless reality that consequently allows itself to be taken apart, stripped down to its verbal elements. Of course, since he approaches the city through words, and those words are Latin (even if he points sometimes to Greek roots), the city he analyses is heavily Roman and has none of the broader scope of the initial survey. Indeed, it may give the impression of being a rather traditional picture of the classical Roman city. But this is to do it less than justice. Intensive research into Isidore's sources has shown in detail, and specifically for this part of the *Etymologies*, that Jacques Fontaine was right to question how far he had direct contact with classical sources at all. He may cite Cato and Varro, Lucilius, Horace, Virgil, and Lucan (all of these in 15.3), but he can be shown to be looking at them filtered by the Virgil commentary of Servius, or compilations such as the third-century *Miracles of the World* (*de Mundi Miraculis*) of Solinus, and, above all, to be using the Christian writers close to his heart: Augustine, Jerome, and Gregory the Great. Where he might have been drawing on Vitruvius, Isidore proves innocent of our principal text on the Roman city. The picture he offers is neither purely antiquarian, stuck in a lost past, nor purely contemporary, the image of a confidently Christian world, but a complex fusion of the two.

Whatever Isidore's sources, we can be confident that his own contribution lies in the organisation and structure of each section. He manages to make it seem so natural as to be self-explanatory, and yet the structure comes from none of his mosaic of sources. Starting from the definition of *civitas*, and the distinctions from *urbs*, *oppidum*, *vicus*, *castellum*, and so forth (15.2.1–15), he passes, as if on foot, from the suburbs through the walls with their battlements and towers (2.16–21), to enter by the gate (2.22). He encounters the roads, with their sheltered porticoes (2.22–26), to arrive at the heart of the city, the Forum, and the principal civic buildings around it (2.27–32). He then ranges through a number of important public buildings, from circuses to baths (2.33–41). These public buildings are followed by private and commercial ones – bars, taverns, and markets (2.42–45) – along with the public institutions to control them: the customs house and the prison (2.45–46). The next chapter, with the unclassical title *de habitaculis*, looks at the private house and its parts (3.1-9), inns, and places of hospitality, including hospitals (3.10–13). The following chapter, with the title 'On sacred buildings', looks at sanctuaries, of whatever religion (4.1–4), monasteries and convents (4.5–6), temples in their various forms (4, 7–12), and the individual elements of religious buildings, from altars to pulpits (4.13–17). The next title is on 'repositories' – storage spaces of various types (5) – followed by places of work (6). Entranceways, including openings like windows, get their own title (7), and just as the gate leads into the city in his account, the doorway leads into the elements of buildings, from foundations to roof-tiles (8). Thence, he moves to fortifications, and the discussion moves beyond the built-up nucleus of the city.

Even this brief summary shows that Isidore's view is not limited to the classical city. Monasteries and hospitals of his contemporary world take their place alongside the circuses and baths (not necessarily defunct) of an earlier world. For the definition of a city, as we have seen, he turns to Augustine and the *City of God*. But there are elements from other Christian authors, too: Cassiodorus, who says the *civitas* is called after its *cives*; Rufinus' translation of Origen, who says it assembles and contains the lives of many; and Jerome, who says the city is 'not stones and buildings, but inhabitants'.[81] Without the advantages of the digital search engine, Isidore must have been collecting these snippets over a long period as he read through various texts, and he now blends them together in a seamless (and much quoted) definition. When he says that the city is 'not stones but the inhabitants', he is drawing, as we have seen (Chapter 2, pp. 34–35) on a longstanding Greek and Roman proverb; but while that proverb normally conveys a protreptic point – that since people matter more than walls, one need not be dismayed by the loss of walls – he is using it for a philological distinction or *differentia*: the word *urbs* refers to the walls – that is, the physical structure of a city – while the word *civitas* refers to the citizen body. That distinction is helpful, but the inherent ambiguity of these terms soon leads to contradiction: the *urbs* derives from *orbis*, because city walls used to be a circuit, cut in a circle by the ploughshare: and yet he says that it was the place of the future *civitas* that was drawn with the plough, so undermining his distinction (15.2.1–4). He is scarcely to be blamed, because that ambivalence, between urban centre and community including the country, is present whenever we speak of 'the ancient city'. He reinforces his distinctions with a sheaf of classical references, to Virgil, Cato, and Horace in quick succession; but he is drawing on a string of passages in Servius' commentary on the *Aeneid*, and ironically, the line of Virgil cited is a compound of two separate lines.[82]

Isidore then proceeds to look at the settlement hierarchy. Because he flattens chronology, vocabulary referring to different periods sits alongside. *Oppidum* is not a term of Roman law and administration, but a general term applied to urban settlements, often in non-Roman contexts

---

[81] Guillaumin, p. 125, citing Cassiodorus, *Exposition of the Psalms* 121.3, Rufinus/Origen, *Homilies on Genesis* 5.5, and Jerome, *On the Gospel of Matthew* 4. The verbal parallels in each case are close.

[82] Guillaumin, pp. 125–126, citing Servius on *Aeneid* 1.12 and 425; 5.755 and 4.212.

(hence, we refer to the 'Iron-age oppida' of Gaul or Britain). Its Isidorian etymology of 'opposing' its walls to threats (2.5–6) makes it a peg on which to hang the evolutionary schema of the emergence of the urban from scattered living, as in Lucretius and Vitruvius. This, then, is not exclusively Greco-Roman. But he then, following the Servius commentary, contrasts *oppidum* by size and possession of walls with the smaller settlements of *vicus*, *castellum*, and *pagus* (roughly, 'village', 'fortress', and 'parish'). These are terms which fit comfortably enough into Visigothic Spain: *castellum*, in particular, which in Classical Antiquity refers principally to military forts, in Late Antiquity becomes common for a fortified settlement smaller than a *civitas*, like the numerous *castra* founded by Justinian and listed by Procopius, or the smaller centres in Gaul like Dijon met in Gregory of Tours.

Isidore's focus now switches to the distinction of *municipia* and *coloniae*, a legal distinction of great importance in the early Empire, since colonies carried full Roman citizenship, whereas *municipia* might have reduced citizen rights, limited, for instance, to magistrates.[83] Since Caracalla's extension of citizen rights in 212, the legal distinction lost its force, and *civitas* was used for any city inhabited by Roman citizens. Isidore reflects the situation of the early empire in contrasting *coloniae*, whose farmer-citizens (*coloni*) came from outside, with *municipia*, founded by their own citizens, though at this point he confusingly uses the contemporary word, *civitates*, for *municipia* (2.8–9). But he then brandishes a bit of Roman law, both referring to status granted by the emperor and by stating that cases involving Roman citizenship 'which start from the emperor' could only be heard in *civitates* (in fact, they were supposed to be heard by the praetor in Rome).[84] That these legal arrangements are not of his day is implied by his remark that *vici*, *castella*, and *pagi* were 'attributed by the ancestors' to *civitates* (2.11), a correct reflection of the imperial tax system whereby minor centres were subsumed to major ones, *civitates*. He stresses the lack of walls in *vici* and *pagi* (2.12–14), and here, with the walled *castella*, we are back in a contemporary landscape.

Discussion of walled and unwalled settlements brings us naturally to the walls of the city, *moenia*, in a definition straight from Servius, as is so much else.[85] There follows his classic image of gates, towers, and

---
[83] See Sherwin-White, *Roman Citizenship*, pp. 205–218.
[84] Guillaumin, p. 129, for references to the lawyers. What Isidore's sources are here is not clear.
[85] Guillaumin, p. 131, citing Servius on *Aeneid* 11.567 and 2.234.

battlements, complete with the implausible etymology that *turris*, tower, comes from *teres*, smooth, though the observation that even square towers look round from a distance goes back to Lucretius.[86] Isidore's image of battlemented walls was to be echoed in many medieval city praises (see Chapter 2, pp. 59–65), and it is likely enough that they had direct access to his much-copied text. Maybe he is also responsible for their insistence on straight roads and broad *plateae*, owed not to Vitruvius, but to a combination of Augustine and Gregory the Great, whose *Reflections on Job* were dedicated to Isidore's brother, Leander (2.23).[87] An image of the city distilled from centuries of literature and passing through Church Fathers was thus powerfully transmitted to the early Middle Ages. But lest we imagine this image is merely classical, the city of the *maiores*, Isidore offers us a term, *promurale*, for a defence before the walls, unknown to classical literature but encountered in ecclesiastical writings (2.21).[88]

Arrived at the heart of the city, this grammarian's grammarian surprises us by using a masculine where a neuter is the norm: not *forum* but *forus*. The latter is possibly a variant on the former.[89] It is not easy to see why Isidore offers a variant on one of the commonest Latin terms, but he returns to the issue several chapters later when discussing places of work (6.8). Having initially defined *forus* as the place of litigation, derived from 'speak', *fari*, he now says the word has many meanings: the place where markets are held, where magistrates give judgement, a treading floor, and an empty space in a ship. Where he gets this from is not revealed by the diligent hunters of his sources, and it is especially odd that he does not offer the double function of forum as marketplace as well as place of judgement when we first encounter it. It may be that, by his day, the central space of the city was now principally a marketplace, and that the seat of judgement was shifting; but in Gaul at least, as we have seen, the forum was where wills were read out, and possibly deeds registered with the *curia*. Isidore places *curia* and *praetorium* by the forum (2. 28–29), though his explanation that the *praetorium* was where the *praetor* gave judgement is misleading, for the praetor's traditional seat was in the forum, whereas the *praetorium* is the seat of imperial

---

[86] Guillaumin, p. 132, citing Lucretius 4.353.
[87] Guillaumin, p. 133, citing Augustine, *Sermon* 10.6, Gregory, *On Job* 14.21, 19.16, 32.22, etc.
[88] Guillaumin, p. 132–133, citing Ernout–Meillet s.v. *murus*.
[89] Guillaumin, *ad loc.* offers no comment, but at p. 162 on the later passage cites Ernout–Meillet s.v. *forus*.

governor, something he would have encountered in the *Acts*, as Herod's seat of judgement.[90]

When Vitruvius sets out the buildings of the city, he moves at once to temples, which, with their orders of architecture, occupy two books (3 and 4). All remaining forms occupy the fifth book: the Forum, and linked to it the basilica, the major civic space (5.1), then Treasury, prison, and *curia* linked to the Forum (5.2); the theatre, detailed at length (5.3–8); linked to the theatre, porticoes, for open-air walking and storage (5.9); then baths and palaestras (5.10–11); and, finally, harbours and shipyards (5.12). Isidore's city has some overlap, but only some: after curia and praetorium, the gymnasium, seen as a Greek educational space (2.30); the Capitolium and citadels (2.31–32 – we might have expected this immediately after the Forum), both as defined by Servius;[91] circus, theatre, and amphitheatre, with etymologies harking back to Servius and Cassiodorus (2.33–35);[92] and then, the least expected and least Vitruvian of his buildings, the labyrinth, the Pharos lighthouse, both of which seem to come from Pliny's *Natural History*, and the column with a spiral staircase or *cochlea*.[93] The first of these curiosities make its way into medieval Praises of Cities (Chapter 2, p. 61), in Verona's misidentification of its amphitheatre with a labyrinth. It is a classical assemblage in many ways, but with an odd Isidorian twist, which owes more to commentaries on the *Aeneid* than to an architectural work like Vitruvius.

Isidore, like Vitruvius, moves from public to domestic buildings (15.3). The title, *de habitaculis*, is a post-classical word (only met in Aulus Gellius for the lair of a lion), but common in the Vulgate.[94]

Lactantius is the source for the idea that a *domus* is the *habitaculum* of one man, as the world is the *domicilium* of the human race, though Isidore, as we have met in book 9, substitutes 'family' for 'one person'.[95] That *domus* comes from the Greek δῶμα is in Varro, but the phrasing seems to come from Jerome.[96] For the elements of the house, like *atrium*, he seems to turn yet again to Servius' commentary, and particularly so for

---

[90] *Acts* 23.35.
[91] Guillaumin, p. 131, citing Servius on *Aeneid* 8.345 (Capitolium) and 1.20 (arx).
[92] Guillaumin, p. 131, citing Servius on *Aeneid* 5.288 and Cassiodorus, *Variae* 5.42.
[93] Guillaumin, pp. 137–138, citing Pliny, *Natural History* 36.83–91, but also Servius on *Aeneid* 5.588.
[94] Lewis and Short s.v., Gellius 5.14.21; du Cange s.v., *Proverbs* 3.33; *1 Kings* 10.5, etc., and Lactantius (below).
[95] Guillaumin, p. 143, citing Lactantius, *Institutes* 2.5.32.
[96] Guillaumin, p. 143, citing Varro, *Latin Language* 5.160 and Jerome, *Letters* 106.63.

the definition of *palatium*, which is straight from Virgil's description of the proto-palace of Evander.[97] That there is a gap between the ways of Antiquity and the present is underlined twice: the *coenaculum* is given a bogus link to *coenobium*, the common life of the monastery, and Isidore claims that 'the ancients used to eat publicly and in common nor did anyone dine on their own, lest delicacies in secret should generate luxury' (3.7); the ancients (*antiqui*) thus come out as moral paragons. Similarly, the *triclinium* of three couches is characterised as a custom of the old days (*veteres*); the custom of the semi-circular *stibadium* had long since taken over.[98] By contrast, the pilgrim centre and hospital, *xenodochium* and *nosocomium* (3.13), take us directly into a contemporary and Christian world.

Without going through every entry, it is clear that Isidore is perfectly aware of the gap between his own world and that of the past, the *antiqui* or *veteres*, as indeed Varro had been when he looked back from the first century BC to the world of the early Republic or the seven kings, half a millennium before him. Just as he wishes to embrace a wider world in his geographical survey, his analysis of the city embraces many periods, and where things have changed, he tries to flag it. So much is particularly evident in the next title: 'On sacred buildings' (15.4). Almost at once, he offers an indication of changing meanings of words: '*sancta* for the ancients were the exterior parts of temples' (4.2). True or not, he is hinting that religion for the ancients was something different. The same sense of gap comes out in his treatment of the word *templum* (4.7). He suggests that for the ancients, a *templum* was any vast space. He refines this dubious claim by an accurate account of the temple as a conceptual space, dividing the heavens into four quarters according to Etruscan ritual, something he could find, if not in Varro himself, in the grammarian Hyginus.[99] Isidore is curious about where pagan religion may have anticipated features of Christianity: the ancients called shrines with running water *delubra* from *diluo*, 'I wash away' (a bogus etymology, needless to say); 'nowadays' (*nunc*) there are shrines with sacred springs 'where the faithful wash away their sins' (4.9). What is so fascinating is Isidore's urge to create a link between the present and antiquity, and a forced etymology smooths his path. Similarly, when we come to the word *basilica*, there is both a gap and a connection:

---

[97] Guillaumin, p. 144, citing Servius on *Aeneid* 1.726 (atrium) and 8.51 (Pallanteum).
[98] Dunbabin, *The Roman Banquet*.
[99] Guillaumin, p. 154, citing Varro, *Latin language* 7.7, Hyginus Grommaticus 1.4, etc.

> Basilicas were formerly (*prius*) the dwelling-places (*habitacula*) of kings, from which they take their name: for *basileus* meant king, and *basilica* meant royal dwellings. But now (*nunc autem*) divine temples are called 'basilicas' for the reason that their cult and sacrifice is offered to God the King of all. (4.11)

The modern architectural historian might offer a somewhat different story: that the Romans, in adopting the model of the Greek stoa, named it after one of the most famous specimens in Athens, the Stoa Basilikē; and that the Roman architectural form of the basilica was then used as the model for Christian churches.[100] Whatever the story, there *is* a link, and the Christian world builds on the foundations of the pagan world, echoing its language, a message Isidore is happy to convey.

Town and Country

Isidore's city is one of public and private buildings, of sacred and profane; but it is also a city of commerce. In the city itself there are bars, *popinae*, especially located near baths, named for drinking, *propinare* (2.42); shops, *tabernae*, originally constructed of planks, *tabulae* (2.43);[101] the meat-market, *macellum*, where meat is butchered (*mactare*); the general market, *mercatum*, where commerce, *commercium*, takes place; and the customs house, *teloneum*, where taxes are charged. All very traditional, except that the last of the terms, *teloneum*, a Greek loan word, is met first in Christian writings, and is an architectural form unknown to Classical Antiquity.[102]

Isidore returns to this commercial theme in his title, 'On places of work' (*de operariis*: 15.6). Here we meet the *ergastulum*, rightly identified as having a Greek root, 'where condemned men are sent for some type of labour, as is normal for gladiators and exiles, who cut marble and even so are kept under guard in chains' (6.2). Possibly taken from Jerome, the observation reflects a late imperial world of punishment and forced labour.[103] Then there are wool-working establishments called *gynaecea* from the women who work there; mills and bakeries; winepresses and treading floors (6.3–8). Isidore's gaze moves naturally beyond the city

---

[100] See, for example, Sear, *Roman Architecture*, pp. 28–29.
[101] Guillaumin, pp. 140–141: Isidore follows Festus, even if Ernout–Meillet rejects this etymology.
[102] Guillaumin, p. 141.
[103] Guillaumin, p. 161, citing Jerome, *Commentary on the Letter to the Ephesians* 3. For the practice, Gustafson, 'Condemnation to the mines'.

walls to the countryside, which is the focus of several chapters that follow. 'Fortifications' are not just military, but include the walls around vineyards, *maceria*, hedges, and sheepfolds (9.4–6). Passing via the graveyards, which traditionally mark the transition zone between town and country (11), we reach rural buildings, including the modest huts, *tugurium*, *capanna*, and the like (12), and the fields themselves (13), with their villas and estates, *fundus* and *praedium*, familiar from the Ravenna papyri as part of a contemporary world. He can draw on the literature of land-surveying to define *limites*, and the classic division of *decumanus* and *cardo* (14–15). Finally, he passes from such field boundaries to the road system, of streets, paths, drove roads, junctions, and mountain paths (16), mountains as ever being the furthest circle from the civilised centre of the city.

It is helpful to think of the entirety of book 15 as being about the city, in its broad sense as a community living under shared laws, for the countryside is as integral to that community as the walled city, and the fields and their produce as integral to the economy as the shops and workshops of the centre. The road network is no mere afterthought: it is the road network that both links the town to its surrounding countryside, and which links one city to another. We only need think of the Peutinger Map for an image of the Roman Empire as a network of urban centres linked by a road network.[104] The same network is as relevant to Visigothic Spain as to the Roman Empire.

In a word, Isidore offers us a credible picture of what the idea of a city could mean to a bishop in early-seventh-century Spain. We should abandon the image of the *Etymologies* as a sort of faded daguerreotype of a lost past. Isidore is indeed fascinated by the distant past, though he seems to access it not so much directly from classical literature, like Varro or Vitruvius, as filtered through fourth-century commentaries on Virgil and an abundance of Christian writing, from Lactantius and Jerome and Augustine to his contemporary and family friend, Pope Gregory. But Isidore is interested in how the past world relates to the present, something regularly flagged by the contrast between the ancients, *antiqui* or *veteres*, and the (rather flexible) present, *nunc*. Where he does not point to such a contrast, he implies a continuous reality. All sorts of details may change over time, but the underlying structure of the city is, for Isidore, timeless.

A crucial element of resilience theory is the idea that in adapting to change and stress, sometimes catastrophic, one mechanism of adaptation is

---

[104] See Talbert, *Rome's World*; Albu, *The Medieval Peutinger Map*.

the transmission of memories of the past as a basis for future change. Perhaps better than any other writer, Isidore shows how it is possible to draw on a deep store of knowledge about the past to make sense of the present. The *Etymologies* was one of the most copied texts of the Middle Ages: it was a principal route by which old ideas of the city were projected into a new world.

9 | The Fabric of the City

The Idea Embodied

Up to this point, this book has paid little or no attention to the physical fabric of cities as they survive or are rediscovered by archaeology. It is a book about ideas, not structures. Yet this distinction is in part false, for buildings embody ideas just as much as do texts. For the last generation there has been extensive discussion among archaeologists and historians of the physical remains of cities in the late Roman and early medieval periods.[1] At issue is whether they tell a story of urban decline, or of transformation from one typology ('the classical city') to another ('the medieval city'). It is as if the physical evidence could be read as a sort of barometer: on the one hand, the steady decline of the essence of the classical, with its open spaces, central forum, and well-paved roads, with its great buildings of religion (pagan temples), of public administration (basilicas and council houses), and of entertainment (baths, theatres, amphitheatres, circuses); on the other, the growth of new churches, baptisteries, cemeteries, bishop's palaces, and regal palaces that mark the emergence of the Christianised medieval. This chapter bypasses that debate. That the sort of changes indicated took place is obvious enough and needs no repeating. But, beyond that, there is the constant danger of using archaeological evidence to prove or disprove hypotheses that are not archaeological in origin. I have argued throughout this book that despite the impression to the contrary, a series of writers from the fourth to the seventh centuries continued to assume that 'the city' was central to the societies they knew, and to assume a continuity with antiquity, while at the same time showing themselves well aware how different their own worlds were from that of antiquity. In turning now to the archaeological evidence, I wish to measure neither decline nor change, but to ask how the changing built environment of Late Antiquity embodied ideas of what it meant to live in a world of cities. The main part of the chapter will be an examination of new foundations of Late Antiquity in the hopes of teasing

---

[1] For surveys of a burgeoning bibliography, see Lavan, *Recent Research on Late-Antique Urbanism*, Grig, 'Cities in the "long" Late Antiquity', and Humphries, *Cities and Meanings in Late Antiquity*.

out the idea of a city that underpinned them. To do so means to look at the physical realities as we know them. But the fabric of a city is also an expression of underlying ideas: ideas shape buildings and buildings shape ideas.[2] First, however, some influential but, in my view, flawed readings of the evidence must be addressed.

Sauvaget's Suq

The deeply engrained notion that the classical city in Late Antiquity underwent a profound change in its very nature is most vividly embodied in Jean Sauvaget's much reproduced diagram of the transformation of a colonnaded street to a suq (Figure 9.1).

Sauvaget made his pioneering study of the cities of Syria (a French protectorate between 1923 and 1946), including Aleppo, Damascus, and Latakia. His major study of Aleppo, constituting his doctoral thesis, was to be published a few years later,[3] but in 1934 he offered an analysis of Latakia, the ancient Laodicea.[4] This he did without excavation, but by the perfectly sound method of analysis of the modern street plan and the relation to it of surviving remains from antiquity. Latakia's plan showed the elements of an impressively regular grid; and surprisingly many columns, still half buried, aligned perfectly with the street grid and implied the presence in antiquity of the sort of colonnaded street that was fashionable in Syria in the Roman

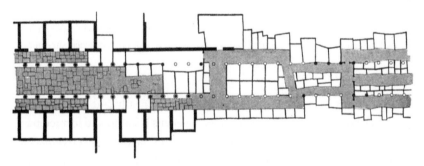

Figure 9.1 Sauvaget's diagram showing supposed breakdown of a colonnaded street into a suq. Sauvaget, 'le plan de Laodiceée-sur-mer', fig.7, also *Alep* p. 104, fig. 25.

---

[2] See Lefebvre, *La production de l'espace*.
[3] Sauvaget, *Alep, essai sur le développment d'une grande ville syrienne*; revisited by Neglia, *Aleppo*.
[4] Sauvaget, 'Le plan de Laodiceée-sur-mer'.

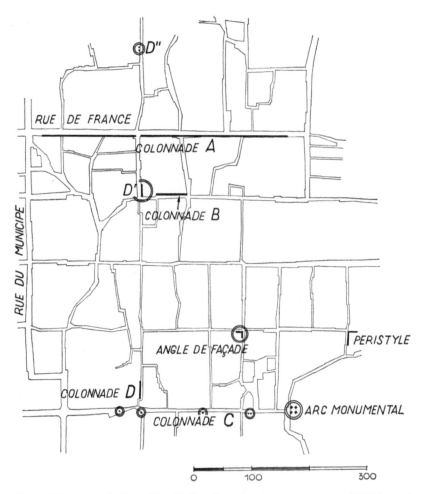

Figure 9.2 Sauvaget's plan of Latakia/Laodicea showing contemporary (1930s) street plan and placement of classical colonnades. Sauvaget, 'le plan de Laodiceée-sur-mer', fig.1.

period.[5] On this basis he was able to hypothesise a neatly laid-out grid plan for Laodicea that went back to its founder, Seleucus Nicator, and formed part of a family of Syrian cities of comparable size and layout. The colonnades, however, were unlikely to be a Seleucid feature, and were introduced in the period of Roman rule when many cities of Syria enjoyed an economic boom.

Sauvaget's analysis of Latakia may be said to have stood the test of time. There has been only minimal subsequent excavation, particularly

---

[5] See Burns, *The Origins of the Colonnaded Streets*, esp. pp. 288–293 on Latakia. I am particularly grateful to Ross Burns for advice on this question.

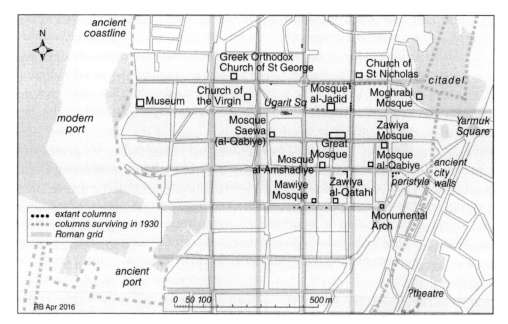

Figure 9.3 Plan of present-day (2010s) Latakia with hypothetical ancient street grid. Plan by Ross Burns, with permission.

a German project to expose fully the 'monumental arch', now known as the Tetraporticus, at the south-east corner of the city. Some of the granite columns that belonged to Sauvaget's Colonnade B have been dug up and re-installed on the edge of Ugarit Square. This east/west road – or Decumanus, to give it the modern archaeological label – now known as Al-Quds/Abdel Rahman, has been restored as a major road, ending to the west in the National Museum, and to the east in Yarmuk Square. Overall, the road layout, which in Sauvaget's careful plan shows many uneven edges caused by the protrusion of buildings, has been 'cleaned up', so that the Latakia of today is even closer to its Hellenistic predecessor than it was in Sauvaget's day (Figures 9.2 and 9.3).[6]

What conclusions can we draw from Sauvaget's findings? In cities in Northern Italy, where, famously, ancient street plans are preserved in the fabric of the modern cities, persistence of street plans is seen as a measure of continuity.[7] Streets represent a dividing line between public space, shared by the community, and the private space of individual property owners. Continuity of street lines implies some sort of continuity of the community

---

[6] For the plan, Sauvaget, 'Le plan de Laodiceée-sur-mer', p. 83, fig. 1.
[7] Bryan Ward-Perkins, *From Classical Antiquity to the Middle Ages*, esp. pp. 179–186.

of inhabitants, just as variations in the street line, generated by the protrusion of private properties into public space, represent some sort of discontinuity or disruption, though such protrusions may be not so much an indication of the weakened control by the community as of the ability of powerful individuals to influence communal decisions. Latakia's impressive preservation of a Hellenistic street layout argues, on the face of it, for a significant degree of continuity.

Yet Sauvaget chose to emphasise the opposite message. The progressive breakdown of a wide public street flanked by elegant colonnades into the supposedly tangled congestion of a suq, with up to three narrow passageways replacing the ancient thoroughfare, becomes the image of the disintegration of a civilisation. It is curious that in the street as Sauvaget plans it, distinguished by his Colonnade B, there is no sign at all of the street breaking down into multiple lanes, though it is clear that in its eastern stretch, the facades of the houses no longer align neatly, so that the road edge jags in and out. In fact, it seems that Sauvaget based his diagram not on Latakia but on Aleppo, where we do indeed see the central east/west road between the Antioch Gate and the Citadel split into suqs with three narrow lanes, illustrated by his careful reconstruction of the nineteenth-century city (Figure 9.4). But even in Aleppo, the suqs, which he dates to the Seljuk period, after the sack of the city by Nicephoros Phocas in AD 962, do not appear to be the product of a gradual breakdown of the colonnade, but of a managed and regular organisation by the city authorities. The pattern, carefully documented in Sauvaget's map, is of strings of units dedicated to the same trade – something likely to be achieved by conscious organisation by the market authorities, not by chaotic or even organic growth. Sauvaget gives no hint of any archaeological evidence on which he has based his Latakia diagram, because what he wants to offer us is a generalisation: this is what generally, in the post-Roman Islamic world, happens to broad, colonnaded roads, which 'disintegrate' into suqs. His image may indeed have some basis in reality, though as a contrast of an end result rather than a process; what matters about it is that it successfully inscribes a deep-rooted western prejudice, a hatred of the 'chaos' and even 'barbarism' of Islamic cities with narrow winding roads (yet not even in Sauvaget's diagram are the streets winding), and an exaltation of the moral values of the 'straight' and regular and the grid plan so firmly endorsed by Haverfield.

It was not Haverfield who first identified the grid with civilisation and the non-grid with barbarism, though he certainly managed to formulate the contrast in a singularly prejudicial way ('the savage, inconsistent in his moral life, is equally inconsistent, equally unable to "keep straight" in his

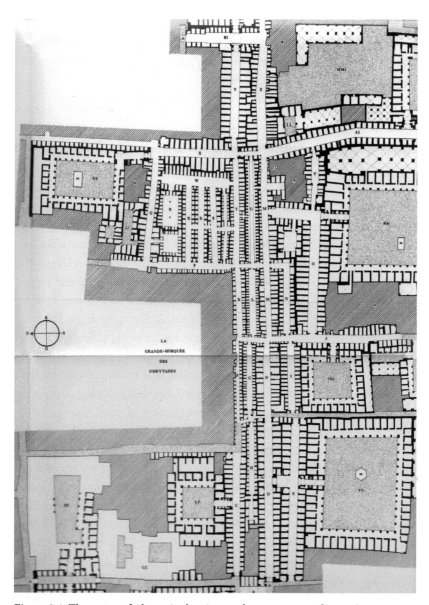

Figure 9.4 The centre of Aleppo in the nineteenth century, according to Sauvaget, showing 2/3 rows of shops in former classical colonnaded street. Sauvaget, *Alep*. pl. LXV.

house-building and road-making'; p. 14). Such attitudes had been widely shared in Europe for at least a century. Particularly significant is the reaction of Greece to liberation from Ottoman rule in 1827.[8] There was

---

[8] See Hastaoglou-Martinidis, 'City form and national identity', pp. 99–123; Koumaridis, 'Urban transformation and de-Ottomanization in Greece'.

a quite explicit campaign of 'de-Ottomanisation', to sweep away the apparently chaotic tangle of streets of a traditional 'Ottoman' town and to rebuild in the 'rational' image of western Europe. As a contemporary newspaper of 1830 put it:

> Architecture is all the time engaged in this aim, opening up streets, leveling, and rectifying as much as possible everywhere, in order to correct the city's former ugliness which can please only barbarians, and to contribute here, indeed, to the nursing of the place.[9]

Greece could take pride in a sort of reverse cultural borrowing, a 'counterloan':[10] it could reach back to the plans of its own antiquity, and the figure of Hippodamus, to reimpose a genuinely Greek identity on the city in place of Ottoman barbarism. Just as in the same century Italian planners discovered the power of the Roman past to enable them to 'modernise' their cities and shake off the legacy of the medieval and papal past,[11] the new independent kingdom planned as many as 170 'new towns' in a neo-Classical idiom: 'The straight line and the right angle became symbols of independence'.[12] A century later, in the newly colonised Syria, Sauvaget is engaged in a similar mission of de-Ottomanisation. His diagram, with all the scientific precision of a medical drawing, sets out the disease to which the classical colonnade has supposedly fallen victim.

That picture, and specifically the identification of such change with Islam, has long been called into question. Hugh Kennedy, in his classic account 'From *polis* to *madina*', argued that the breakdown of the colonnade dates back to the period of Byzantine rule and an impoverishment of the city. Subsequent work has tended to confirm his chronology;[13] the credibility of 'the Islamic city' as a consistent phenomenon has been challenged from all sides.[14] But even the typological distinction between *polis* and *madina* misrepresents a more fluid and complex reality. Colonnades persisted under Umayyad rule; not only did earlier ones survive, but when early Umayyad rulers built themselves new cities, notably that of 'Anjar (to be discussed later in the chapter), they created new colonnaded streets. The classical aesthetic was inherited and adapted, not

---

[9] Cited by Hastaoglou-Martinidis, 'City form and national identity', p. 103 from the *Ephemeris tēs Kybernēseōs* 16 (1830), p. 24.
[10] Hastaoglou-Martinidis, 'City form and national identity', p. 104.
[11] Greaves, 'Roman planning as a model'.
[12] Hastaoglou-Martinidis, 'City form and national identity', p. 105.
[13] See Avni, 'From Polis to Madina revisited'; *The Byzantine-Islamic Transition in Palestine*.
[14] Raymond, 'Islamic City, Arab City'; Valérian, 'Middle East: 7th–15th centuries'.

rejected.[15] More recently, two major studies have re-evaluated the maintenance of aesthetic values in the public spaces of Late Antique cities, tending to push as late as the seventh century any widespread collapse of the classical image of the city.[16] Nor should the blocking of a colonnade be taken as a collapse of civilised living. In the early seventh century, Demosthenes, governor of Osroene, responded to a famine in Edessa by walling in colonnades in order to provide refugees with places to sleep: that is a response to crisis, but not an abandonment of civic ideals.[17] Before getting sucked into a dispute over just when and to what extent colonnades were neglected, encroached upon, blocked up, and built over, it is worth asking how we think these spaces were used in antiquity.

In the late 1970s, Tim Potter took part in an excavation in the heart of Cherchel in Algeria, the Juban capital of Iol Caesarea. The excavation covered a part of the ancient Forum. In the corner of the Forum, just beyond the northern colonnade, which seems to have been converted to a Christian basilica in the fifth century, Potter's scrupulous excavation revealed some faint traces, which he interpreted as markings for some sort of market stalls. On the basis of fourth-century coins abandoned in the cracks in the paving in this area, he proposed that the stalls belonged to the fifth century, like the church (Figure 9.5). From this he inferred a continuity of commercial activity in the forum of Iol Caesarea into the fifth century, though in a thorough survey of other cities of North Africa he suggested that a more typical pattern was abandonment in the fourth century.

What may strike us here, in addition to the skill of the archaeologist, is the tenuity of the traces from which such interesting conclusions might be drawn. As Potter himself emphasises, he almost missed the pattern in the markings:

> It should be said at once that it took some time during the excavation to recognise them for what they were: only in the raking light of the early evening did they show as a distinct pattern, and it required a certain amount of luck to realise their nature.[18]

For Potter, this explained the failure to identify similar markings in other cities: unless you know what you are looking for, you are not likely to come upon such subtle evidence. The traces were also a sign for Potter of what he

---

[15] See Cabiale, 'La lunga durata delle vie colonnate'.
[16] Jacobs, *Aesthetic Maintenance of Civic Space*; Lavan, *Public Space in the Late Antique City*, pp. 374ff., for a radical review of Sauvaget.
[17] Jones, *Later Roman Empire*, pp. 810–811. [18] Potter, *Towns in Late Antiquity*, p. 75.

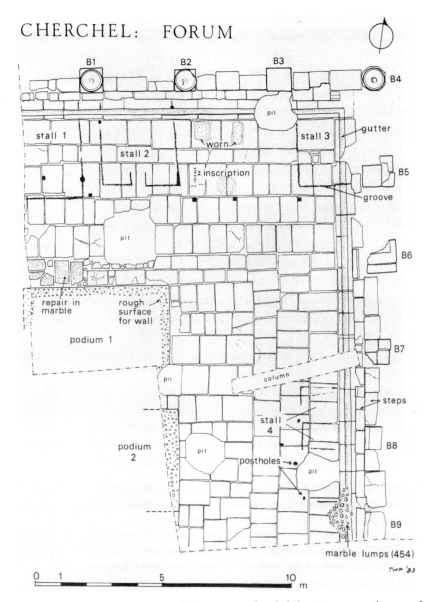

Figure 9.5 Corner of the Forum of Iol Caesarea/Cherchel showing supposed traces of stalls. Potter, *Towns in Late Antiquity*, fig. 17. Reproduced with the permission of the Trustees of the Ian Sanders Memorial Fund.

clearly regarded as a deterioration of the classical city; he evidently has the Islamic world in mind:

> It is not unrealistic to reconstruct these stalls as structures with wooden frames, covered over with suitably decorative awnings, and selling a wide

variety of market goods; one might envisage a somewhat souk-like appearance.[19]

As elsewhere, the imagination of the archaeologist can conjure up an image from very slight traces. One might wonder indeed how a series of shallow grooves would support the structure of a wooden stall, which might rather demand deeper post-holes.

Potter's interpretation might serve as a caution: if traces of stalls are so hard to see, how do we know that they were not similar wooden stalls in classical colonnades? Potter himself suggests as a model the painting of traders in the Forum of Pompeii (a fresco found in the house of Julia Felix), yet no trace of such traders has been found archaeologically in the Forum of Pompeii itself, which reminds us how much human activity must remain archaeologically invisible. Hence the value of written descriptions by ancient authors of the activities in public spaces: without the descriptions of Libanius or his contemporary John Chrysostom, or the life of St Symeon the Fool of Emesa (Homs), all deployed to good effect by Luke Lavan, we would have little idea of how the public spaces of Syrian cities were used.[20] As we have seen (Chapter 2, pp. 50–51), Libanius regarded the central colonnaded street of Antioch as a source of particular urban pride. He celebrates its convenience in allowing pedestrians to circulate, protected from sun and rain. He is especially enthusiastic about its commercial potential. There is room for a shop in front of every house, and 'if anyone gets hold of a square yard or two on the edge, it straightaway becomes a tailor's shop or something like that, and they hang on to their stall like grim death' (254). It was a matter of pride for him that commerce was not restricted to the agora but spread along the colonnades right through the city. Why characterise such patterns as 'Islamic' or 'medieval'?

The image of the classical colonnade as an empty space, valued for its aesthetic impact, and serving only as a space for civic processions and ceremonials,[21] is strongly influenced by the way in which archaeological remains have been scrubbed down to impress tourists.[22] Libanius' description of Antioch allows life and colour to flood back to the colonnade. One may ask indeed whether this was not always a primary function of a colonnade over the pavement outside a private house. It has been noted

---

[19] Ibid. p. 36.
[20] Lavan, *Public Space*, chp. 3, pp. 235–262, is a particularly valuable examination of such sources.
[21] An aspect underlined by Dey, *Afterlife of the Roman City*; also, with rich detail, Lavan, *Public Space*, pp. 150–234.
[22] Excellent discussion in Jacobs, 'Encroachment in the eastern Mediterranean' and 'Late Antique encroachment'.

in Pompeii that the make-up of pavements, and any porticoes over them, seems to change with property boundaries.[23] Whereas the road itself was by definition public space, the pavement occupied a liminal zone between public and private, and though the city authorities could insist on the passageway being kept clear for pedestrians,[24] the private properties behind them could benefit, both by building balconies over the pavement and by allowing their commercial activities to spill out onto the street.

This much is made explicit by the epigrammatist Martial's poem of celebration of the purging of the pavements of Rome by Domitian (Martial, *Epigrams* 12.57):

> The shopkeeper had taken away the entire city
>   And on its threshold was no threshold.
> Germanicus, you bade the narrow side-streets grow
>   and where there had been a path became a road.
> No more pillars draped with jars on chains
>   no more forcing the praetor to step in the mud.
> No more drawing razors blind in thick crowds
>   No more filthy pubs blocking the whole road.
> Barber, innkeeper, cook, butcher each keeps to his threshold
>   Now it is Rome again, not one vast shopping centre.

Rather than thinking of the encroachment of the commercial as a sign of decline limited to Late Antiquity, we might rather think of this as a natural feature of urban life.[25] Domitian was only the first emperor we hear of who tried to clear away stalls from the pavements: Late Antique emperors continue a sort of trench warfare against such encroachment. So in 389, Valentinian, Theodosius, and Arcadius order the City Prefect of Constantinople to clear the streets:

> It is disgraceful that the ornaments of public splendour should be ruined by attachment thereto of private buildings, and that those structures which have arisen for the decoration of Our distinguished City, either in Our time or in the time of a previous age, should be associated with eagerness for acquiring money. Hence Your Sublime Eminence shall order to be removed whatever structure you find wrongfully erected through such fraudulent cunning, if it produces a deterioration in the aspect of public elegance, whether this rash lawlessness was committed by voluntary presumption or the violator expressly obtained the occasion for

---

[23] Saliou, *Les lois des bâtiments*.   [24] Robinson, *Ancient Rome*, pp. 59–76.
[25] Lavan, *Public Space*, p. 373.

fraud, pursuant to an extorted imperial annotation. We leave to your discretion to decide what shall be spared and what shall be removed.[26]

Commercial premises want to maximise their opportunities to attract the passer-by, and where the road and its pavements are wide enough, bars and restaurants to this day spill out into the street. It would take the subtle eye of a Potter to pick up all their traces in the built fabric. That is to say, in our anxiety to create a contrast between the classical and Islamic cities, we have greatly exaggerated the lack of commercial activity that must already have characterised the classical colonnade.

In fact, Potter's observations of possible wooden stalls in Cherchel have been paralleled and given greater conviction by Luke Lavan's re-examination of the agora of Sagalassos. Not only has he identified a series of post-holes in the paving strongly suggesting wooden stalls, but four *'topos'* inscriptions accompanying them seemingly marking the owners of each 'pitch'. The phase of the agora at Sagalassos is dated as late as the sixth century. Other cities of Turkey, including Laodicea ad Lycum, offer similar evidence of *topos* inscriptions.[27] These traces had been entirely missed in the initial excavations: it is only when the archaeologists' eye is on the alert for such things that they are noticed, just like the graffiti of board games and the Christian crosses that also characterise such public spaces.[28] In a word, the sharp contrast between the supposedly unencumbered classical colonnade and the busy commercial suq overlooks the extensive commercial activities of the colonnade, which only become easy for the archaeologist to trace when wooden stalls are replaced by stone walls. The pattern of commercial activity of Late Antiquity indicates deep continuity with Classical Antiquity.[29] We may indeed be witnessing an increase in the commercialisation of city centres in the fourth to sixth centuries; it is not a product of Islamic rule.[30]

The Built City as Idea: Constantine's New Rome

The physical fabric of a city as revealed by archaeology does indeed cast a bright light both on episodes of urban decline/abandonment and on the construction that comes with new priorities: the Crypta Balbi in Rome, as excavated by Daniele Manacorda, can tell a vivid story of how a great

---

[26] *Codex Theodosianus* 15.1.25, cited by Jacobs, 'Late Antique encroachment', pp. 8–9.
[27] Lavan, *Public Space*, pp. 377–379.   [28] See Talloen, 'Rolling the dice'.
[29] Lavan, *Public Space*, p. 407.   [30] Lavan, *Public Space*, p. 415.

theatre falls into disuse, and finds itself surrounded by the early middle ages by horticultural plots instead of dense housing;[31] the city of Brescia, as explored over fifteen years by stratigraphic excavation of a series of sites by Gian Pietro Brogiolo, can show the contraction of the Roman city to the *curia regis* and *curta regia* at either end of the old city, separated by ten hectares of pasture land covering the former city.[32] Archaeology is good at documenting decay. But decay has many causes: a shrinking economy, a shrinking population, changed priorities of political masters, the growing dominance of the church; but it is not so easy to infer from that how the idea of the city has changed, and we may be surprised at the mismatch between the archaeological record and the rosy aspirations expressed by contemporary writers.[33] Indeed, we are in danger of pursuing in the 'urban ideal' a will-o'-the-wisp: the 'idea' of the city may derive not so much from a coherently theorised form as from experience of cities on the ground, cities which inescapably have grown over centuries and only respond to changing circumstances over time. If we want to see an ideal, it is better, rather than registering modifications in old urban fabric, to look at cities built from new; and even if these too are impregnated with the cities of the past, they may mark new perceptions and ideals.

In this context, the model is set by Constantinople: a new city which was not entirely new, but an extension of a long existing city, and one which looked to the Roman past in order to make its future.[34] It is exactly this ambivalent relationship between past and present, between models derived from historical experience and aspirations of a new future, which must lie at the heart of any ideal of the city. Constantine's project was very explicit: whether or not 'New Rome' was from the start incorporated in the name of his foundation, it was how contemporary panegyrists like Themistius celebrated it, and how future observers understood it.[35] Whether or not we unthink the label of 'Byzantine' and call the empire controlled by the New Rome as 'Roman', they thought of themselves as Romans, Ῥωμαῖοι.[36]

[31] Manacorda, *Archeologia urbana a Roma*; Manacorda and Arena, *Museo Nazionale Romano: Crypta Balbi*.
[32] Brogiolo, 'Ideas of the town in Italy'.
[33] So Brogiolo, 'Ideas of the town in Italy', p. 100, on the oscillation 'between a pessimistic view of a dying world' and 'a propagandistic view in which the activity of kings and military commanders reverses disaster'.
[34] On this theme, see Grig and Kelly, *Two Romes: Rome and Constantinople*.
[35] For the evidence, Grig and Kelly, *Two Romes*, 'Introduction', pp. 11–12: Themistius, *Oration* 184a in AD 357 calls the city 'a Second Rome'; Porphyrius, *Carmina* 4.6 and 18.34 after 324 speaks of *altera Roma*.
[36] So Kaldellis, 'From Rome to New Rome'. Berger, 'Urban development', rightly underlines the gradual process.

The Built City as Idea: Constantine's New Rome

In urban terms, Constantine's project – one which takes a good two centuries up to Justinian to reach its fullest form – was to turn old Byzantium into a city recognisable as Rome.[37]

The first, and easiest, observation to make is that Constantinople was not, any more than Rome itself, a grid city. That form was convenient enough for a colonial foundation, especially one where the topographic context of a plain like the Po valley permitted it; from Aosta to Timgad we can see the military regularity of the checkerboard offering a statement of a particular type of Roman identity. It was not, as Thomas Ashby, who thought little of the cult of straight lines and right angles, emphatically pointed out, the case of Rome itself.[38] Nor was it the case with Constantinople. The determinant element of the urban design of the New Rome was its hilly topography on a rocky peninsula: indeed, by no coincidence, it numbered precisely seven hills like its model, though we have to wait for the extension beyond Constantine's initial wall to the definitive walls of Theodosius II before seven hills can be convincingly counted.[39] Unlike the hills of Rome, identified by names which allowed much ambiguity and changing identification,[40] the hills of Constantinople were numbered, so that nobody could miss the point (Figure 9.6).[41]

To impose a regular grid even on one hill, as in San Francisco, requires a feat of engineering; seven hills must defeat even the most ambitious engineer. Rome's system of roads is dictated by the alternation of hill and valley, by the watercourses running off the hills to the lowest point in the Forum, which had to be raised and drained to become a usable space. Hence, the roads form a pattern of convergence, and only in the flat lands beyond the hills, on the flood plain of the Campus Martius or that of Trastevere, were localised grid systems possible. The topography of Constantinople is in a sense the inverse of that of Rome. Rather than valleys converging on a central point by the Tiber, the hills of Constantinople are

---

[37] Helpful recent introductions to the city include Basset, *The Urban Image of Late Antique Constantinople*, and Freely and Çakmak, *Byzantine Monuments of Istanbul*. The pioneering modern work is Cyril Mango, *Le développement urbain de Constantinople*; the indispensable reference work is Müller-Wiener, *Bildlexikon zur Topographie Istanbuls*. For a recent overview, see the chapters in Bassett, *The Cambridge Companion to Constantinople*, esp. Berger, 'Urban development and decline', pp. 33–49. For Constantinople in context among old and new cities, Ćurčić, *Architecture in the Balkans*, pp. 54–59. On the transformation of Byzantium by Constantine, Magdalino, 'From Byzantium to Constantinople'.

[38] See Chapter 1 on the impact of the *Town Planning Conference London*, 10–15 October 1910.

[39] Berger, 'Urban development and design', p. 41 cautions that 'seven hills' are not explicitly attested until seventh- and eighth-century texts.

[40] Vout, *The Hills of Rome*, pp. 57–80.

[41] Berger, 'Urban development', p. 41, notes that the evidence for numbering the seven hills is late.

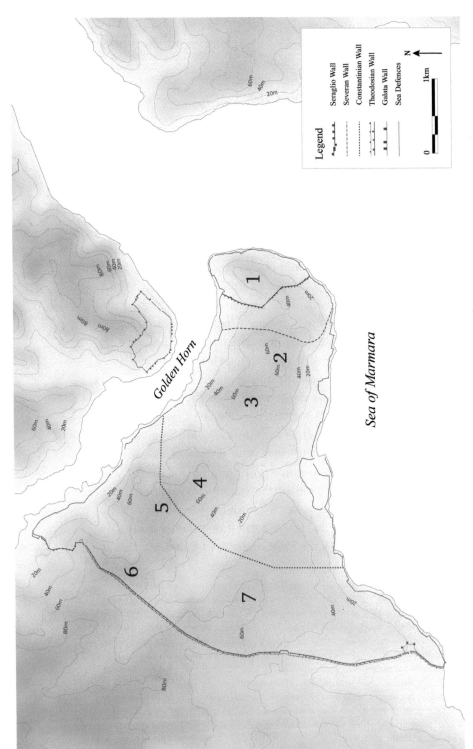

Figure 9.6 Plan of Constantinople with contours to show the seven hills. Drawn by Dr Sophie Hay.

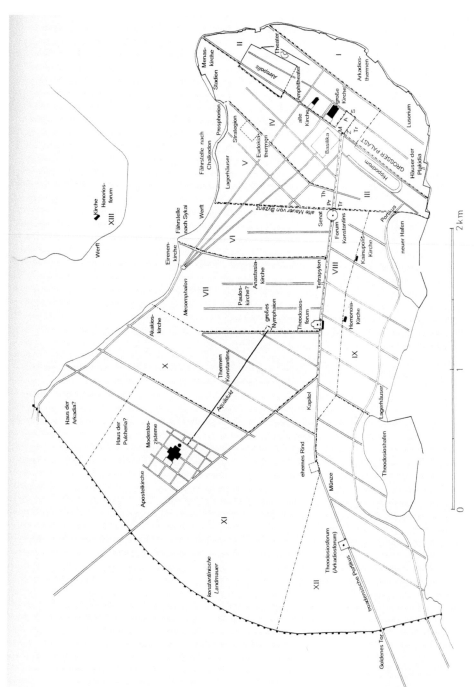

Figure 9.7 Street plan of Constantinople as a regular grid according to Berger. Reproduced with permission of Prof. Albrecht Berger.

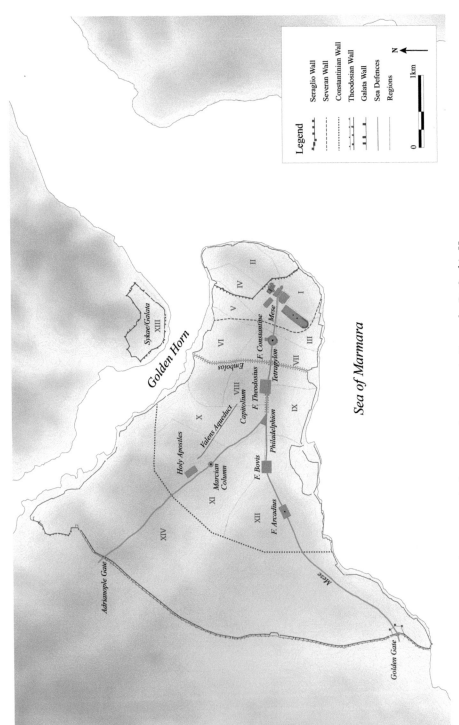

Figure 9.8 Plan of Constantinople showing principal streets and monuments. Drawn by Dr Sophie Hay.

The Built City as Idea: Constantine's New Rome

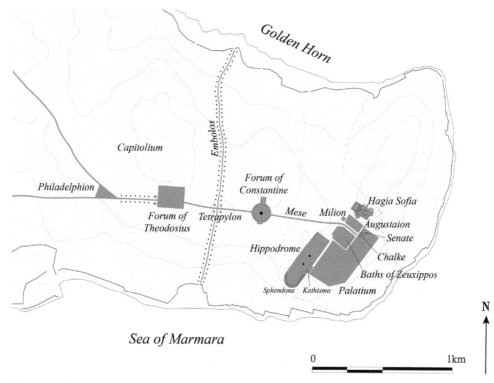

Figure 9.9 Eastern tip of Constantinople with monumental complex. Drawn by Dr Sophie Hay.

the variations in a single spine, which sheds not inwards but outwards to the Golden Horn and the sea of Marmara.

How the road network of the Constantinian city worked is ill understood, and the case has been made that there was a high degree of orthogonal planning. The case rests necessarily on guesswork, for lack of archaeological exploration in the heart of the city, and on a series of inferences from the orientation of buildings. Even the most optimistic plan offered by Albrecht Berger is far removed from a grid city, and any plan of this city which does not offer contour lines risks ignoring the topographical complexity of the peninsula (Figure 9.7).[42] Only the modern conviction that the grid defined Roman identity leads scholars to impose straight lines on this hilly terrain. What was needed to make the New Rome like the old one was never a grid.

The core of the road system of Constantinople was the arterial route leading to the tip of the peninsula. This was a Roman consular road of great

---

[42] Berger, 'Streets and public spaces in Constantinople'; for its methodological weaknesses, see Dark, 'Houses, streets and shops in Byzantine Constantinople', esp. pp. 100–107; also Dark and Özgümüş, *Constantinople*, pp. 32–35.

significance, the *via Egnatia*, which constituted the principal land route from Italy and the western provinces, running almost exactly west to east, from Dyrrhacium and the sea-crossing from Brundisium, via Thessalonike to Byzantium and the crossing of the Bosphorus to Asia. In broad terms, it is the route of the Simplon-Orient Express of the early twentieth century, originating in Paris, then running from Venice to Istanbul; the route too in more recent times that of the A2 motorway, called the Egnatia Odos, that cuts across northern Greece from Igoumenitsa via Thessalonike to the Turkish border. If you need to shift an army fast from the Adriatic to Asia Minor, as Constantine well knew, Byzantium is a key point in your route. It is highly appropriate that this road, in its intra-urban guise as the Mesē, Centre Road, should be the defining spine of the city plan (Figure 9.8).[43]

This underlying structure was already present in the pre-Constantinian city. The point at which the *via Egnatia* reached the settlement on the tip of the peninsula was the heart of the city as reconstructed by Septimius Severus after the destructive effects of civil war (Figure 9.9). Already there was a cluster of key buildings, including a hippodrome and the Baths of Zeuxippos, around the square called the Tetrastôon for its four-sided colonnade.[44] At least part of the *via Egnatia/Mesē*, as it approached the Tetrastôon, was itself colonnaded. To the west, the road must already have split into its characteristic Y shape, with the southern branch forming the *via Egnatia*, following the coast of the Sea of Marmara and heading west, and the northern branch running parallel to the Golden Horn, following the ridge of the hills. The wedge-shaped form of the peninsula dictates that this pattern of Y-junctions as you head westwards reproduces itself in the modern road map, and surely did so already in antiquity: roads successively branch off the *via Egnatia* route to the northwest, to reach the gates of the Theodosian wall.

If this is the underlying structure Constantine inherited, the challenge to him was to transform it into what could be recognised as a New Rome.[45] Imposing a grid forms no part of the plan. Instead, he created a series of monumental spaces which mirrored Old Rome. The Tetrastôon was replaced by a new space called the Augustaion;[46] its initial form was that of an open Forum,[47] though later it became an enclosed space associated with

---

[43] The role of the Mesē is well brought out by Dey, *Afterlife of the Roman City*, pp. 77–84.
[44] Mango, *Le développement*, p. 19; Basset, *Urban Image*, pp. 18–22; Russell, 'Before Constantinople'.
[45] The designation, 'New Rome' may not originate with Constantine himself: Berger, 'Urban development and decline', p. 35.
[46] Spelling varies, Augusteion also being common. [47] Mango, *The Brazen House*, pp. 42–47.

Haghia Sophia (known to us in its Justinianic form: the 'Great Church' was consecrated in 360 to Constantius II, but surely goes back to Constantine).[48] To its north was a four-way arch, the Miliarium Aureum (or, in Greek, Milion), marked by its name if not its form as the equivalent of Rome's Golden Milestone, and so by implication marking the Augustaion as the equivalent of the Forum Romanum, underlined by the placing of what was explicitly a senate house (*Senaton*) rather than the Bouleuterion of a Greek Council House. It also gave onto the entrance to the palace called the Bronze House (*Chalkē*).[49] The north-eastern tip of the already existing Hippodrome reached the Augustaion; but the Hippodrome, in addition to being extended, was transformed into the Circus Maximus by the placing on its east side of the Palatium. Palace, Circus, Senate, and Forum point to Rome; but while the Forum Romanum occupies a valley between two hills, Capitoline and Palatine, the Augustaion is on the top of the second hill, and the Palatium slopes away towards the sea, so that the hippodrome/Circus and its Imperial Box, the Kathisma, could only be reached from below by a spiral staircase, the Cochlear. The inversion is also clear in the substructure called the Sphendonē which carries the south-western end of the hippodrome above the slope below; the contrast is with Rome's Circus Maximus, occupying a natural valley, to which the emperor descended from the Palatium.

These sharp contrasts in topography do not impede a determined attempt to create a symbolic mirror of Rome. If there is no Capitoline and Palatine, there is a Palatium and a Capitolium. The latter is one of the hardest monuments of Constantinople to understand.[50] It seems to have been located at the point at which the Mesē splits in its Y junction. This was also the location of a monument called the Philadelphion, a celebration of brotherly love from which came the porphyry sculptures, now on the

---

[48] Mathews, *The Early Churches of Constantinople*, pp. 11–18.

[49] Mango, *The Brazen House*, pp. 36–72, discusses in detail not only the Palace but all the buildings around the Augustaion.

[50] The location of the Capitolium remains a puzzle. In earlier discussion it was identified with the Third Hill, where the present university has its administrative building, neatly coinciding with the function of the Capitolium as a seat of learning, attested in the Theodosian Code (14.9.3 and 15.1.53). This was challenged by Janin, *Constantinople Byzantine* (1950; 2nd ed. 1964). The *Notitia Urbia Constantinopolitanae* places the Capitolium in Region VIII, the long, narrow region that ran alongside the Mesē. This was traditionally located north of the Mesē; Janin challenged this on the grounds that it was 'on the right hand side', though that expression is ambiguous, and placed Region VIII south of the Mesē. But this makes no topographic sense, since the ground drops steeply to the sea to the south and a division half way down the hill makes no sense; a long, narrow strip makes better sense on the relatively level ground to the north of the Mesē. In the accompanying maps, I have rejected Janin's arguments; placed Region VIII to the north of the Mesē, which includes the Third Hill; and suggest that the Capitolium belongs there. But this is controversial.

corner of St Mark's in Venice, showing two pairs of figures in military uniform embracing. Traditionally called the 'tetrarchs', they have been argued to have been the children of Constantine, though the new discovery of painted reliefs of the tetrarchs from Diocletian's palace in Nicomedia supports the traditional identification.[51] The discovery of a porphyry heel near this location (more precisely at the site of the Myrelaion, later the Bodrum Camii) confirms the origin of the Venetian sculptures.[52] Separate from the Philadephion was the Capitolium, about which the sources tell us virtually nothing. Cyril Mango, to whom we owe so much of our understanding of Constantine's city, thought that it must, as elsewhere, be a temple of Jupiter Optimus Maximus and betray the imperfect impact of Christianisation on Constantine (Zosimus says he erected on the Augustaion temples to Rhea and Fortuna).[53] But if you can call a four-way arch the Golden Milestone, there is no knowing what you can call the Capitolium. From legal sources, we gather it acted as the seat of the professors paid by the state, and the contemporary university is in a similar location.[54] There is still something to be said for placing the Capitolium in its former location on the Second Hill. The point surely is that the central stretch of the colonnaded Mese ran between Capitolium and Palatium. However implausibly, Rome was reproduced. We might even imagine that the twinning of Philadelphion and Capitolium echoed the temple of Concordia beneath the Capitolium in Rome.

If in Rome beneath the twin peaks of Capitoline and Palatine lay not only the Forum Romanum, but the entire cluster of imperial Fora, named for successive emperors from Caesar though Augustus, the Flavians, Nerva, and Trajan, so the Mese became over time a long string of imperial Fora. Constantine initiates the process with his own Forum, an oval or circular colonnaded space with a diameter of 140 metres, and the porphyry column at its centre, perhaps 40 metres high, bearing a colossal statue of Constantine as Sun God (Nero had a similar statue in Rome).[55] The column still stands, albeit much repaired, the statue long gone (Figure 9.10).[56] On this Forum of

---

[51] See Ağtürk, *The Painted Tetrachic Reliefs of Nicomedia*. I am grateful to the author for arranging my visit to this site.
[52] Mango, *Le développement*, pp. 28–30; Müller-Wiener, *Bildlexikon*, pp. 266–268.
[53] Mango, *Le développement*, p. 30; 'The triumphal way of Constantinople', p. 177.
[54] Codex Theodosianus XIV.9.3 and XV.1.53. See Gaul, 'Schools and learning', pp. 265–266 on the Theodosian reform of the schools.
[55] Müller-Wiener, *Bildlexikon*, pp. 255–257; Arslan, 'Towards a new honorific column' for a study of this and other columns. Kaldellis, 'The Forum of Constantine in Constantinople'.
[56] On the afterlife of the column, Ousterhout, 'Visualising Constantinople as a palimpsest', and Akyürek, 'New history for old Istanbul'.

The Built City as Idea: Constantine's New Rome

Figure 9.10 Peutinger Map (Codex Vindobonensis 324), detail of Constantinople with the column of Constantine. From Konrad Miller (ed), *Die Peutingersche Tafel* (Stuttgart 1929).

Constantine was a second *Senaton* or senate house. It is one of the most striking features of Constantine's desire to make his city a New Rome that he gave it a senate, with empire-wide and not simply local powers, though it was not until the reign of Constantius II that it was raised to parity with the senate of Rome;[57] but the importance of this was embodied in the creation of two senate houses: one on the Augustaion beside the palace, and the other in the new Forum of Constantine. In this, he went one better than Rome.[58]

Constantine's new Forum, set on the second hill over what had been a necropolis for the old Byzantium (burials were discovered in excavations below the column), was only the first of the string of new Fora set along the Mesē. The next west, the Forum Theodosi/Tauri, was monumentalised by Theodosius I, though Constantine may have started the process of clearing the old necropolis there for a piazza. The triple-naved building of the Basilica Theodosiana and the honorific column with a spiral of reliefs, and bearing a silver equestrian statue of Theodosius (erected in 386) suggest a conscious evocation of the Forum of Trajan in

---

[57] Dagron, *Naissance d'une capitale*, pp. 119–146.
[58] It is possible that Julian was responsible for the Augustaion senate: Mango, *Brazen House*, p. 57.

Rome (Figure 9.11).[59] Enough architectural fragments have been recovered to reconstruct the triple arch that straddled the Mesē (as elsewhere, the central arch for traffic, the side arches for pedestrians following the colonnade). The edge of the modern road is littered with architectural fragments from the colonnade. Next came the Philadephion, with its images of brotherly love, and the parting of the ways: it was along the southerly route, the *via Egnatia*, that other emperors added further Fora. The Forum Bovis was created by Julian, with a possible function as a Forum Boarium suggested not only by its statue of an ox (*Bous*) but by the halls and workshops around it.[60] Arcadius, son of Theodosius I, added a further Forum on the southern route, with an honorific column bearing a statue of his father, until his own son, Theodosius II, substituted it with a statue of Arcadius himself. Again, a spiral relief evoked the model of Trajan's Forum, which, though gone now except for its base, remained standing for seventeenth-century travellers to record.[61]

While the Fora followed the southern branch of the Mesē, the northern branch was no less significant as a processional route. The principal Constantinian monument to which it led was the Church of the Holy Apostles, located precisely where Mehmed the Conqueror built the Fatih mosque.[62] Constantine built it as his own circular mausoleum, his burial place surrounded by twelve tombs of the apostles (he was seen as the thirteenth): Mehmet's mosque, in turn, was to be his own mausoleum. We know nothing of the architecture of Constantine's building, but an imperial mausoleum must evoke its Roman model.[63] The mausoleum of Augustus was set on the northern edge of Rome, a little inside what was later defined as the city wall, separated from the Capitoline by 2 kilometres of the *Via Flaminia*, the closest Rome came to a straight processional route. The Church of the Holy Apostles stood towards the north-western edge of the Constantinian city, a little short of his original walls. Consciously or not, the echo is there.

If it was Constantine's intention to reproduce Rome, it was a programme to which his successors signed up with enthusiasm. The sequence of Fora, from the Augustaion to the Forum of Arcadius, with their triumphal columns modelled on Trajan's in Rome, took a century to evolve, but once the idea of a simulacrum of the imperial Fora of Rome was set by

---

[59] Müller-Wiener, *Bildlexikon*, pp. 258–263. [60] Müller-Wiener, *Bildlexikon*, pp. 253–254.
[61] Müller-Wiener, *Bildlexikon*, pp. 250–253.
[62] Dark and Özgümüş, *Constantinople*, pp. 83–96 argue (controversially) that the mosque follows the outline of the Byzantine church.
[63] Dark and Özgümüş, *Constantinople*, p. 85 cites a letter of Manuel Chrysolaras comparing the circular mausoleum to those in Rome.

The Built City as Idea: Constantine's New Rome

Figure 9.11 View of Constantinople from manuscript (MS Canonici Misc 378, fols 84r-87r) of the *Notitia Urbis Constantinopolitanae* in the Bodleian library, University of Oxford, with permission. Note the equestrian statue of Justinian on a column, next to the dome of Haghia Sophia

Constantine, it could be embellished, in a process that leads to Justinian's restorations of the Augustaion after the Nika riots, with the creation of a new column 35 metres high, bearing his own colossal image on horseback, one which survived until the fifteenth century as the symbol of the city. But while these Fora and their honorific columns use a language that is recognisably Roman, the effect of the Mesē with its long colonnades, protected from disfigurement by imperial edict, and articulated by a sequence of piazzas, has no parallel in Rome, and stands rather in the tradition of the colonnaded streets of the eastern cities, from Antioch to Jerash and Palmyra, which also allow for multiple piazzas, often curved (a form unknown in Rome).[64] The ideal of reproducing Rome can marry comfortably with a urban model familiar in the Greek East.

Topographical differences meant that Constantinople could never be a literal reproduction of Rome: it reproduces an *idea* of Rome rather than the reality. Yet that did not stop Constantine and his successors from

[64] Burns, *Origins of the Colonnaded Steets*; Dey, *Afterlife of the Roman City*; Lavan, *Public Space*; Mango, 'The porticoed street at Constantinople'.

competing with Rome and ensuring that their new city lacked nothing of which the Old Rome could boast.[65] Rome, since Aurelian, had been famous for its wall circuit. The peninsula of Byzantium required no circuit, but a single land-wall cutting it off from the Thracian mainland. The walls were built initially by Constantine, then, significantly further out, and lasting for a millennium, by Theodosius II, around 413, a defensive structure 6.44 kilometres in length, every bit as impressive as Rome's.[66] An even longer defence was built further out by Anastasius I.[67]

Aqueducts were very much a feature of the Old Rome, and one which Roman conquest spread to many other cities. Since Byzantium before Constantine had major public baths in the Baths of Zeuxippos, it relied on some sort of water supply, but the need greatly increased as the new capital grew, and it is Valens who takes credit for the still visible aqueduct; but this too was the work of generations, reaching at its full extent some 250 kilometres in its winding course.[68] Here, again, the topographic contrast shows. Rome was famous not only for its aqueducts, but for its sewers, rapturously described by Cassiodorus as one of Rome's wonders:

> the splendid sewers of the City of Rome, which strike visitors with such amazement as to exceed the wonders of other cities ... For which other city dares compete with your heights, O Rome, when they cannot even offer a match for your depths? (*Variae* 3.30)

Constantinople had indeed a maze of sewers and water channels, but a city built on a ridge, unlike one built in a valley, has few problems with water disposal. Rather, the challenge is water storage, and it is the cisterns of Constantinople, 160 of them and counting, which strike the visitor with amazement.[69] Here what Rome and Constantinople have in common is the consequences of being a megalopolis – an engorged capital that, unlike the Aristotelian ideal, cannot rely on its own hinterland. That was even more so with the food supply, and the procurement and distribution of a regular supply of grain was achieved by mechanisms derived from those of Rome.[70] The physical correlate of the supply line was the

---

[65] See the point-by-point comparison of Bryan Ward-Werkins, 'Old and New Rome compared'; also Grig, 'Competing capitals, competing representations', pp. 31–53.
[66] Ward-Perkins, 'Old and New Rome', pp. 62–63; the main study is Krischen, *Die Landmauer von Konstantinopel*.
[67] Crow, 'The long walls of Thrace'.
[68] Crow, Bardill, and Bayliss, *The Water Supply of Byzantine Constantinople*; Crow, 'Water and Late Antique Constantinople'; Crow, 'Water for a capital'.
[69] Bardill, *The Water Supply*, pp. 125–156; Crow, 'Water for a capital', pp. 74–77.
[70] Durliat, 'L'approvisionnement de Constantinople'; Van Dam, 'The supply of food to Constantinople'.

high number of bakeries and *gradus*, steps from which free rations were doled out.

Over the century from Constantine's foundation to Theodosius II, the features that not only competed with Rome, but aspired to turn the urban fabric into a simulacrum of Rome, accumulated. It is at this point that a document, the *Notitia Urbis Constantinopolitanae* (Regionary Catalogue of Constantinople), attempts, in conscious imitation of a similar document for Rome, to list out these very Roman features.[71] By now, the city not only sits on seven hills, but is even divided into fourteen regions. Each region is described following a standard pattern. Thus, the first region contains the following:

> The First Region reaches out in length before those leaving the lower part of the palace in the direction of the Great Theatre. It is on level ground and becomes progressively narrower, while on its right flank it descends downhill to the sea. It is distinguished by the residences of the royal family and the nobility.

Contained in it are:

> The aforesaid Great Palace
> Lusorium
> Palace of Placidia
> House of Placidia Augusta
> House of the Most Noble Marina
> Baths of Arcadius
> Streets or alleys, twenty-nine
> Houses, one hundred & eighteen
> Continuous colonnades, two
> Private baths, fifteen
> Public bakeries, four
> Private bakeries, fifteen
> Steps (gradūs), four
> One curator, with responsibility for the whole Region
> One public slave, who serves the general needs of the Region and is its messenger
> Twenty-five collegiati appointed from among the various guilds, whose duty is to bring assistance in cases of fire
> Five vicomagistri, to whom is entrusted the night watch of the city.

---

[71] Translated and discussed by Matthews, 'The Notitia Urbis Constantinopolitanae'. Drakoulis, 'The functional organization of early Byzantine Constantinople' attempts to map the regions. See also Berger, 'Urban development', pp. 40–42.

In the same way – indeed, in the same manuscript[72] – the *Notitia Urbis Romae* (Regionary Catalogue of Rome) lists the monuments of each region, including the temples (exceptionally absent from Region I); the houses of the famous (though this is rare); the number of *vici*, which in Rome represent not simply streets, but the parishes through which the region is organised (by contrast in Constantinople, each region has only five *vicomagistri*, rather than the four per *vicus* of Rome); private houses (the Roman list distinguishes *domus* from *insulae*, property blocks, and the numbers run higher by an order of magnitude); bakeries, public and private (Rome does not make this distinction); *gradus* for grain distribution (Rome has fewer distribution points); curators and their staff (Rome too has one curator per region); and the firewatch (at Rome, the *vigiles*, with one barracks to cover two regions; here, 'guilds' at one per region). One can point to minor variations between the buildings and organisations that make up a region in the two cities; what is evident is the desire to structure the cities as similarly as possible, and at a scale and with features that no other city could match. What the *Notitia* does not tell us about are the other features of organisation in which the New Rome mirrored the Old: a City Prefect (*praefectus urbi*), a prefect of the grain supply (*praefectus annonae*), a senate (though it lists the Senate Houses in Regions 2 and 6), and, perhaps most significant, a patriarch with equal standing to the Pope in Rome.

The pattern of consistent emulation by Constantinople of Rome, not just under its founder, Constantine, but sustained by his successors, can hardly be missed. But how does this illuminate the 'idea of the city'? Had Constantine wished to build an 'ideal city', he might have hunted down a copy of Hippodamus' treatise; but it is unlikely he would have been impressed by his demands for orthogonal layout and mathematical equality, let alone the odd social structure supposed to go with it. Hippodamus might have urged him to find a more level site than the Byzantine peninsula. Constantine had no need for Hippodamus. His vision was driven by military strategy: from Byzantium he could control the crossing between Europe and Asia, and it is a tribute to his understanding that so long as Constantinople controlled that crossing, for some eleven centuries no barbarian army from northern Europe threatened the cities of Asia, and no Asian army, Persian, Arab, or Ottoman Turkish, could threaten northern Europe, until Mehmed made the city

---

[72] See the edition of Unterkircher, *Notitiae Regionum Urbis Romae et Urbis Constantinopolitanae*, offering a facsimile of a ninth-century Fulda manuscript. I owe this point to Rosamond McKitterick.

his own. Strategy dictated a site surrounded on three sides by water, and from which the crossing between the Mediterranean and the Black Sea was entirely controlled. Choice of site took priority over orthogonal planning.[73] What else had Aristotle and Vitruvius recommended as the first priority for building a city if not choice of site?

What Constantine then did with the rocky peninsula was driven by two ideas. The first was to make his city a New Rome by mirroring the structures of the Old Rome: the linkage of emperor, senate, and people expressed in the cluster of Palatium, Circus Maximus, and Curia; and, with them, the church, embodied in the Great Church of Haghia Sophia; and then all the infrastructure of a city of (eventually) seven hills and fourteen regions, its aqueducts and cisterns, its fire brigades, its streets, houses, and bakeries. But married to this idea was a traditional idea of the Roman cities of the Greek East (far more rarely found in the West): the colonnaded processional route. The Mesē was equally suitable for imperial, triumphal processions, and ecclesiastical ones; and, as the detailed account of Constantine Porphyrogenitus' *Book of Ceremonials* spells out, the two could blend, passing through the series of Fora with their commemorations of past imperial victories to arrive at a culmination of the Augustaion, with Haghia Sophia on the left and the Chalkē, the vestibule of the Palace, to the right.[74] The account of the accession ceremonial in AD 457 of Leo I as paraphrased by Gilbert Dagron shows how topography turned the city into Rome, and the former officer into a Roman emperor. The procession starts at the seventh milestone from the Milion, the Hebdomon, where there was a military parade ground outside the walls called the Campus Martius (the starting point in Rome for military ceremonial):

> On leaving the tribunal of the Campus Martius, the emperor proceeded on foot to the nearly church of the Hebdomon, removed his crown and said a prayer... The second stage took the emperor, riding on a white horse and again wearing his crown and escorted by dignitaries, to a sanctuary of St John the Baptist, which was probably by the Golden Gate, the monumental gate of Theodosius II built into the Theodosian walls... A third stage took the procession, still on horseback, to the quarter of the Helenianai, where the keeper of the Palace came to prostrate himself before the emperor... Here he dismounted and entered a *metatorion* to put on a purple *chlamys*,

---

[73] Van Dam, *Rome and Constantinople*, pp. 50–51, points out there were downsides to the site too, but ones for which the Theodosian Wall amply compensated: it resisted Attila's attack.

[74] On the Mesē as ceremonial route, see Mango, *Brazen House*, pp. 78–81; *Le développement*, pp. 27–31; 'The triumphal way of Constantinople'.

a white *divetesion* and consular sandals, the *kampagia*; it was in these new robes that, mounted on a chariot, in the middle of a civil and military procession, he passed through the 'gate' of the ancient walls to reach the Forum of Constantine, where he was received by the city prefect and the senate. The 'first' of the senate handed him the traditional 'golden wreath' ... He climbed back into the chariot alone, senators and dignitaries lining the route as far as the Augustaion, the Horologion and the atrium and narthex of St Sophia ... He then proceeded to the place prepared for him in the south aisle, heard the Gospels and, if he wished, attended the office. Lastly, he received the crown again from the hands of the patriarch ... The final stages took place inside the Consistorium, where the prefects, senators and dignitaries assembled, in the chamber (*cubiculum/kouboukleion*) into which only the patricians followed the emperor, in the Great Triklinos, where a banquet was held, and, next day, at the Hippodrome, where the emperor decreed there would be races, if the Christian calendar permitted.[75]

It is a journey simultaneously through the city, from the seventh milestone (from where else to approach a city of seven hills?), passing through the walls of Theodosius and Constantine, and the Fora both of Constantine and the Augustaion, to church, palace, and, finally, Hippodrome; and, at the same time, a journey through the orders of Roman society, from the army outside the walls, through senators and dignitaries, the patriarch, the patricians with whom to dine, and the next day, the people in the Hippodrome. Each step that makes Leo emperor also makes Constantinople Rome.

Justinian's New Cities

The old story that cities were neglected in Late Antiquity and ceased to be an imperial priority will not stand up to a new generation of archaeology. The continued creation of 'new cities' is a phenomenon that stretches from the fourth into the seventh centuries: not only did a succession of emperors take pride in putting their names to 'new' cities, as we have seen (see Chapter 5), but they sank considerable resources into the project.[76] Already the third and fourth centuries see a series of new foundations, often concentrated in frontier zones: that their defensive works are a prominent feature is no surprise, but one may also note the emergence

---

[75] Dagron, *Emperor and Priest*, pp. 61–63.
[76] See the excellent survey of Rizos, *New Cities in Late Antiquity*.

of a typology of cities with garrisons, in contrast to the largely garrison-free cities of the high empire.[77] These include both cities with more or less regular rectilinear wall circuits and signs of a regular grid of roads, like Diocletianopolis/Hisarya in Thrace,[78] and others with highly irregular circuits and seemingly random placement of buildings. There was never just one model for a city plan. The process tends to gather pace with Constantine's successors, reaching a notable climax under Justinian (who was happy to take credit for the work of his predecessors, especially Anastasius). Justinian's new cities make a particularly revealing case study, thanks to the coincidence of ample literary description by Procopius, both in his panegyrical *Peri Ktismaton* and in his historical narratives (see Chapter 5), and a number of well-excavated and studied sites. We may look briefly at four of them: Justiniana Prima at Caričin Grad in northern Illyricum (modern Serbia); and three cities on the Mesopotamian frontier Dara/Anastasiopolis, Zenobia/Halabyia, and Sergiopolis/Rusafa.[79]

Justiniana Prima

Justiniana Prima (Figure 9.12), unlike the majority of late imperial foundations that were concentrated on the eastern frontier zone of Armenia, Mesopotamia, and Arabia, owes its location to the chance of the emperor's own birthplace: away from the main road network, it served no real defensive function. As Procopius explains, Justinian was born in the tiny village of Taurisium, which he subsequently fortified with a circuit with four towers (unimaginatively renamed Tetrapyrgium); it was not this but a place nearby which he chose to elevate to the status of the first city of Illyricum – 'Prima', as Procopius elaborately explains, being the Latin for 'first', indicated its outstanding rank, which was sealed by making it the seat of the Archbishop of Illyricum. He might have added that it became the base of the Praetorian Prefect of Illyricum. And just as Justinian took intense pride in the place of his birth, so the new city took intense pride in having been built by him (*Peri Ktismaton* 4.1.17–27). The panegyrist forebears to describe it in all its detail, for no words could measure up to a city so personal to the emperor (*Peri Ktismaton* 4.1. 27).

---

[77] Rizos, 'New cities and new urban ideals'; see also his 'No colonies and no grids'.
[78] Rizos, 'New cities and new urban ideals', p. 28.
[79] These four cities are the focus of an illuminating study by Zanini, 'The urban ideal and urban planning in Byzantine new cities'.

Where Procopius breathlessly fails for words, archaeology can offer us a more focused picture, and Caričin Grad has benefited from decades of intense excavation.[80] The choice of site for a city intended to act as a provincial capital might seem a surprise: not only off the principal routes of communication but avoiding the advantages (at least in terms of easy construction) of the plain. It occupies the top of a long, finger-like promontory looking down on the plain to its north, with a river winding round three sides, broadening to a lake to the east. The long hilltop is broadly flat, though it rises to its north-west to an acropolis, which was surrounded by its own wall (this seems to be a secondary addition) and occupied by the Cathedral Basilica, Consistorium, and archiepiscopal complex. In the Upper Town are situated the Principia, horreum, and three churches. The Lower town contains the baths, a large cistern, various public buildings, and three more churches. Both Upper and Lower towns can be dated to Justinian's reign, though there are modifications in that period, particularly the southward extension of the Lower town.[81] The city as a whole is surrounded by a further defensive wall, following the contours of the ridge, which drops away steeply on three sides, leaving it relatively accessible only by a short stretch to the south. The terrain then dictates the layout of the town, divided between its 'upper town', the acropolis, and the lower town around and below it.[82]

Had Justinian had any intention of making as his own symbol an orthogonally planned grid city, this was not the location to choose. Yet so ingrained is the notion that classical cities must be orthogonal that it has been suggested that there was an original design, involving a straight north/south road along the length of the ridge, crosscut at right angles by an east/west road leading straight through the acropolis (Figure 9.13). Not only is it hard to explain why such a plan, if orthogonality mattered to Justinian, should have been modified (to fit better with a terrain which the planners knew from the outset, if they did their job), but even within the acropolis itself there are buildings which fail to respect a rectilinear design (Figure 9.14).[83] Even so, Vasić's diagram is a helpful illustration of a different contrast: between the city as mapped by ourselves and the city as experienced by its users. The ancient visitor, who will not have had the advantage of a city map, will have perceived the colonnaded street leading

---

[80] Ivanišević, 'Main patterns of urbanism in Caričin Grad', gives a helpful update. The principal publication is the three volumes of Duval and Popović, *Caričin Grad*, esp. vol. III. For the new city in context, Ćurčič, *Architecture in the Balkans*, pp. 209–214.
[81] Ivanišević, 'Main patterns of urbanism', pp. 224–225.
[82] Dey, *Afterlife*, pp. 104–108, brings out the importance of the colonnaded route.
[83] Ivanišević, 'Main patterns of urbanism', p. 225–227.

from the gate to the centre as straight; reaching the circular Forum, they will not have seen that the turn to the left to the acropolis was not a perfect right angle. The gate into the walls of the acropolis similarly masked from them a further kink. They will have had the impression of a perfectly orthogonal layout: to give such impressions was always part of the toolkit of the Roman architect. Deviations were not a failure when success was defined by what you experienced.

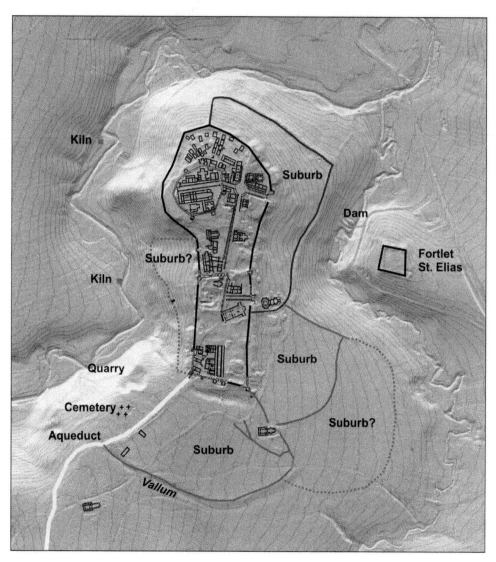

Figure 9.12 Plan of Justiniana Prima, from Ivanišević, 'Main patterns of urbanism in Caričin Grad'. Reproduced with permission of Prof. Vujadin Ivanišević.

Figure 9.13 Photo of circular Forum and colonnades of Justiniana Prima. From Ivanišević, 'Main patterns of urbanism in Caričin Grad'. Reproduced with permission of Prof. Vujadin Ivanišević.

If Rome and the New Rome are the main models, right angles are not the most important consideration. There is a case for seeing Justiniana Prima as a sort of Constantinople in the miniature. The site is hilly, and surrounded on three sides by water; its shape is elongated, along a hilly spine. The main north/south road fulfils the same function as the Mesē, leading from the main gates to the heart of the city. At that heart is an impressive circular piazza, decorated, like Constantine's Forum in his new foundation, with a bronze statue of the founder, and surrounded by colonnades, which then extend down the four approach roads; consciously or not, it evokes the circular Forum of Constantine.[84] Moreover, the road that heads westwards (but not at a right angle!) to the acropolis makes for the cathedral, as does the Mesē for Haghia Sophia and the palace. The wall circuit follows the natural defensive

---

[84] Zanini, 'Urban ideal', p. 211 and Ivanišević, 'Main patterns of urbanism', p. 227, both make the comparison with Constantinople.

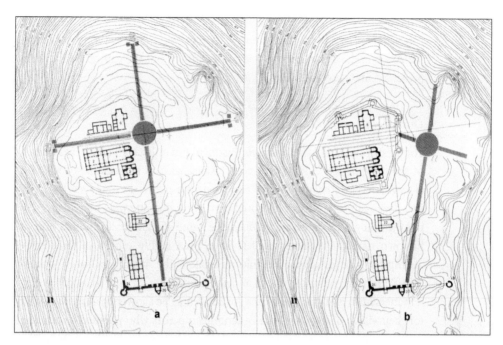

Figure 9.14 Hypothetical initial plan (a) and plan as constructed (b) according to Vasić, from Ivanišević, 'Main patterns of urbanism in Caričin Grad'. Reproduced with permission of Prof. Vujadin Ivanišević.

topography, as does that of Constantinople, except on one side. It is from this (southern) side that the long aqueduct enters, coming up from the south, a stretch of some 30 km.[85]

If the New Rome is your model for a new city, Justiniana Prima, with its mere 7.4 ha – tiny for any city, let alone a provincial capital – succeeds in miniaturising several of the salient features. Procopius' way of summarising it is to say that it had churches too numerous to list (indeed, there were at least six), lodgings for magistrates (various buildings have been identified as Principia), large stoas and beautiful agoras (this will be the circular Forum), fountains, streets, baths, and shops (all features that can be confirmed). He inflates, and his description gives no hint of the tiny scale of the city, but breathless prose ('a city both great and populous and fortunate as fits the metropolis of the whole country') is expected of the panegyrist. He may mislead as to the scale, but not as to the urban form of Justiniana Prima. We may add (what Procopius omits) that the city evidently was closely linked to its hinterland, protected by two forts, with an artificial lake made possible by

---

[85] Zanini, 'Urban ideal', p. 212 gives 30 km, Ivanišević, 'Main patterns of urbanism', p. 223, says 20km.

a dam, surely enabling water mills, and clear signs of suburban settlement spreading beyond the fortifications.[86] The city was not to last long, sacked by the Avars and Slavs in the early seventh century, but the gain to us is a well-preserved archaeological site.

Dara/Anastasiopolis

For the city of Dara/Anastasiopolis, Justinian can only claim credit by a stretch of the imagination.[87] His predecessor Anastasius, as its renaming indicates, claimed credit for enlarging what had been a simple village to the level of a city (we have seen how Procopius could wax ironical at attempts by emperors to put their names on cities, and, indeed, the name of Dara stuck, and not only in his own narrative). Some scholars have been highly critical of Procopius' attempts to give Justinian a key role in remaking the city; others have defended him.[88] From the point of view of understanding sixth-century ideas of the city, it matters little, and Anastasius and Justinian may be allowed to share the credit for their vision of the city: both Byzantine emperors who pursued a common frontier policy, and for whom Constantinople was a reference point. The building up of a village so close to the Persian frontier and Nisibis was a conscious challenge to Sasanid power, and it made the optimisation of defences critical. But the new city had clear aspirations to be more than a military strong point. The discovery of a villa with an impressive mosaic 200 metres outside the city walls points to the spread of the sort of more luxurious living that marked a city. The inscription in the mosaic not only gives a precise date, of AD 514, but celebrates Anastasius, and names his Praetoria Prefect, Daethus; the most holy bishop of Anastasiopolis, Eutychianus; and the presbyters, Abraamos and Thomas, who administered the city.[89] This much in turn bears out the account in the chronicle of Pseudo-Zachariah of the role of Thomas and Eutychian in the building of Anastasius' city.[90]

Procopius' account, as we have seen, emphasises two elements: walls and water supply. His account is not easy to follow without grasping the unusual topography of the site (Figure 9.15). The walls encompass three steep hills (a city, then, not of seven hills like the New Rome, but at least on its very much

---

[86] Ivanišević, 'Main patterns of urbanism', pp. 231–232.
[87] For an excellent survey of recent work on the site, Keser-Kayaalp and Erdoğan, 'Recent research on Dara/Anastasiopolis'.
[88] Croke and Crow, ' Procopius and Dara'; Picket, 'Water and empire', pp. 105–110; Michael Whitby, 'Procopius' description of Dara'.
[89] Keser-Kayaalp and Erdoğan, 'Recent research', pp. 165–167.
[90] Greatrex, *The Chronicle of Pseudo-Zachariah Rhetor*, vii.6.f–g, cited by Keser-Kayaalp and Erdoğan, 'Recent research', p. 167.

Figure 9.15 Plan of Dara/Anastasiopolis. From Zanini, 'Urban development', fig. 2, after Italo Furlan. Reproduced with permission of Prof. Enrico Zanini.

reduced scale of three). Rather than being surrounded by water (like Constantinople or Justiniana Prima), it was bisected by a torrent, entering from the north-east in the cleavage between two hills, passing to the south-west, where it was deflected by the third hill to leave by the south gate. Justinian's engineering works were all about how to control the flow of this torrent by building a dam upstream, and by canalising the stream as it passes through and leaves the city, and to conserve the water by building cisterns (again, like Constantinople, this is a city that relies on cisterns for its water). The broad lines of Procopius' account are convincing, as one might expect of an eyewitness.

John Malalas has more to say than Procopius about the urban amenities built by Anastasius: 'two public baths, churches, colonnades, warehouses for storing grain and cisterns for water'; archaeological exploration has duly found traces of churches, a colonnade, a structure identified as a tetrapylon, a monumental complex, perhaps more likely to be episcopal than a Praetorium, and cisterns. Malalas' list represents, as Enrico Zanini showed, the basic building recipe of a sixth-century new city.[91] We may add, at the risk of labouring the point, that these were all features of Constantinople itself. It is not that the New Rome was the sole model of urbanism, for similar features were to be found in numerous cities; but

---

[91] Zanini, 'Urban ideal', p. 209; Keser-Kayaalp and Erdoğan, 'Recent research', p. 154.

a model with such features was clearly present in the imperial mind, as is made explicit in Justinian's legislation.[92] In two *Novels*, addressed to the newly created praetors of Lycaonia and Thrace, the emperor includes in his list of responsibilities for the Praetor of Lycaonia the maintenance of urban fabric, following orders given to various officials:

> which orders sometimes have reference to the repair of walls, highways, statues, bridges, and harbours; or provide for the renovation of public water-courses, and the cleaning of public places; as well as the demolition of buildings which have been erected where this ought not to have been done, and other matters of this kind which are extremely annoying to Our subjects; but the Praetor himself must discharge this duty, and cause the necessary labour to be performed without any expense to those under his authority. (Novel 25.4.1)

Similarly the Praetor of Thrace is mandated:

> The Praetor of Thrace shall see that the public works do not suffer any damage, for instance, the harbors, walls, bridges, and highways; but he himself must provide for all necessary repairs where the civil revenues are sufficient, and if any greater expenditures are necessary, he must inform Us of the fact, and accounts must be rendered, just as has already been prescribed by one of Our laws. Nor do We wish that persons who are ordinarily charged with the inspection of watercourses, and the repair of gardens, walls, pictures, and other things of this kind, should be sent from your prefecture (which indeed We have already prohibited) into the province; but the Praetor himself must ascertain what should be done, and render an account of the expenditures for repairs, in accordance with Our Constitution. (*Novel* 26.4)

Justinian shows his concern, in his legislation as in his activities as reported by Procopius, with urban infrastructure. Again, if we are hoping to find in Dara a model of orthogonal planning, we are bound to be disappointed, for a city set on three hills will always defeat the grid planner.[93] But if, like Cassiodorus, we see the Roman achievement of infrastructure in its sewerage system as more impressive than its other monuments, we may adopt a different perspective. Urban geographers such as Ash Amin and Nigel Thrift have identified infrastructure as the vital element in successful urbanism:[94] it is as much part of the ancient legacy as orthogonal

---

[92] See Zanini, 'Urban ideal', p. 199.
[93] Keser-Kayaalp and Erdoğan, 'Recent research', p. 155, notes the tradition in Mesopotamian cities of orthogonal street grids.
[94] Amin and Thrift, *Seeing like a City*, esp. pp. 152–156.

planning. Justinian also cared about superstructure, and for him places of worship were as vital for the defence of the city as its walls. These are the indispensable elements out of which the new city can be constructed.

Zenobia

Zenobia (modern Halabiya) is another city for which Procopius almost entirely credits Justinian, noting indeed that the Palmyrene queen Zenobia had made a small city there, which had fallen almost entirely into ruin (*Peri Ktismaton* 2.8). What he omits to mention is that Anastasius had already undertaken defensive works there, though recent excavation confirms that Justinian extended the circuit wall to the north and included the hill top to the west, which became a sort of acropolis (Figure 9.16).[95] If, as at Dara, Justinian was building on Anastasius' initiative, it remains a fine example of an early sixth-century 'new city'.[96] Like Dara, the site is chosen for its strategic significance: an isolated hill rising immediately from the west

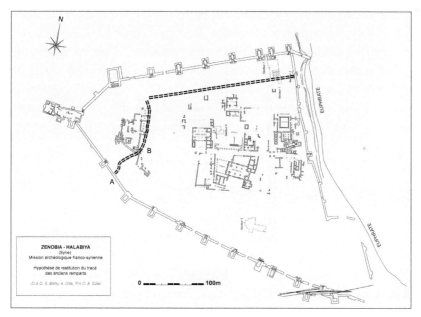

Figure 9.16 Plan of Zénobia-Halabiya. From Blétry, 'L'urbanisme et l'habitat de la ville de Zénobia-Halabiya', copyright ©Mission archéologique franco-syrienne à Halabiya.

---

[95] Blétry, 'L'urbanisme et l'habitat de la ville de Zénobia-Halabiya' is an update on recent excavations. The main publication of earlier excavations is Lauffray, *Halabiyya-Zénobia*.
[96] Zanini, 'Urban ideal', pp. 204–206; also Cyril Mango, *Byzantine Architecture*, p. 38 for plan. See too Dey, *Afterlife*, pp. 103–104.

bank of the Euphrates, it controlled a vital crossing. Zenobia, if we can follow Procopius, had only fortified the lower reaches above the steep banks of the river: Justinian (and Anastasius) take full advantage of the contours, including the steeper ground rising to a sharp peak, and building down from it a circuit wall 'like wings', which still give the site a dramatic aspect.

We have a familiar combination falling into the typology of Constantinople: hilly terrain, water, and strong fortification. The layout of the city is known well enough to say that it is based on a cross-like intersection of two roads: one from the north gate to the south, the other from the river gate extending westwards towards (without reaching) the acropolis. At the intersection was a tetrapylon, the four-way arch typical not just of Constantinople but many eastern Greek cities. The surrounding layout may be described as 'a dense orthogonal network',[97] but not only is the intersection less than precisely rectilinear, the buildings within this grid, particularly the episcopal complex to the south-east, make little effort to conform to the road system. The excavator, Lauffray, identified the area to the north of this episcopal complex as the Forum, though more recent exploration has found it at least in part built over with housing. In the western part of the north wall, just below the acropolis, is a rectangular structure identified as a Praetorium. We can be reasonably confident that here, as elsewhere, there was provision for both ecclesiastical and civil/military authorities; but the city also provided private housing and workshops of a small but lively settlement. The combination of dramatic site, impressive walls, and at least broadly orthogonal layout means that it makes an impression out of proportion to its size, a mere 12 hectares.

Sergiopolis/Rusafa

Among our quartet of Justinianic 'new' cities, Resafa/Sergiopolis is the exception in purely topographic terms, for the terrain is anything but hilly (Figure 9.17). Set in the flat desert steppe 20 kilometres south of the Euphrates, it became in the sixth century a key crossing point of routes between Persia, Arabia, and Syria, an area known to Greek-speakers for its Arabic-speaking inhabitants as the 'barbarian plain'.[98] On the edge of a wadi, this watering hole (rather than oasis) was a welcome stopping-off point for caravans and armies. The site of a small fort established by

[97] Zanini, 'Urban ideal', p. 204.
[98] Elizabeth Key Fowden, *The Barbarian Plain*, not only traces the growth of the cult of Sergius but vividly evokes the setting of Rusafa (pp. 60–100). I am grateful to the author, my colleague, for guidance.

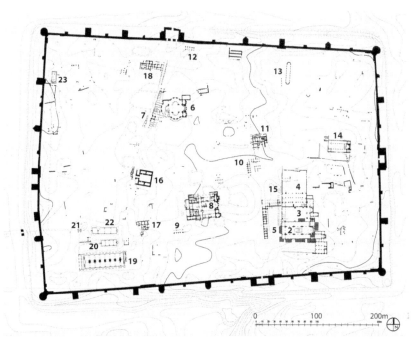

Figure 9.17 Plan of Resafa/Sergiopolis. Reproduced from Gussone and Sack, 'Resafa/Syrien', with permission. Abb.2 Resafa. Stadtplan (*M.Gussone–G. Hell 2010. Mitarbeit N. Erbe, I. Salman*). 1 al-Mundhir-Bau; 2 Basilika A; 3 Nordhof; 4 Große Moschee; 5 Westhof Basilika A - Suq; 6 Zentralbau; 7 Zentralbau-Suq; 8 Basilika B; 9 Straßenbogen (II) - Basilika B; 10 Pfeilermonument (I) - Basilika D; 11 Basilika D; 12 Straßenbogen (III) - Nordtor; 13 Doppelabsidenbau; 14 Basilika C; 15 Kuppelbau vor Großer Moschee; 16 Khan; 17 Hausgräbung; 18 maison arabe; 19 Große Zisterne; 20 Kleine Zisterne; 21 Wasserverteiler; 22 Kuppel-Zisterne; 23 Nordwest-Zisterne.

Diocletian, it owed much of its growth in the fifth century to the cult of the martyr Sergius, executed before the gates of the fort. The cult acquired physical form of a martyrium built by Bishop Alexander of Heliopolis in the early fifth century, beneath what was to be rebuilt as a major basilica. Even if Justinian rightly grasped its strategic significance, Anastasius was again there before him, both in giving the city metropolitan status, reflected in the new name of Anastasiopolis, and in taking a thumb bone of the martyr to Constantinople (the church of Sergius and Bacchus near the imperial palace is one of the most charming Justinianic buildings). As ever, it is difficult to distinguish which emperor was responsible for what, and Procopius attributes all to Justinian (*Peri Ktismaton* 2.9), but between them they turned Sergiopolis into a significant city.[99]

---

[99] The Arabic name is variously transliterated Resafa, Rusafa, Rosapha, and so forth.

The crucial features of sixth-century urbanisation are, as elsewhere, walls and water supply.[100] The massive gypsum circuit walls rise to a height of 14 metres on a rhomboidal rather than rectangular plan, with fifteen towers and four major gates, one in each side, plus two minor gates. The lack of interest in strictly orthogonal planning shows not only in the disparity of lengths of the opposite sides, but in the failure of the gates to dictate a grid. The excavators omitted to establish the exact positions of the roads (the site cries out for geophysical prospection), but it is agreed that there was one central east/west road, and two north/south roads, dividing the town into six segments. These roads seem to be dictated by an earlier convergence of routes from outside, and the one stretch of road that has been excavated by the north gate enters at an angle.[101] The placing of the major buildings, including three basilicas and the cisterns, broadly respect an east/west orientation, but without being precisely aligned with each other. But, as at Justiniana Prima, maybe appearances mattered more than mathematical plans, and it is frustrating that the excavators in their focus on major buildings have not illuminated the layout better (was there a central colonnaded road? a tetrapylon or a circular piazza?).

Water supply is critical, but in the arid conditions of the steppe, the technology looks rather different from the aqueducts of Constantinople or Justiniana Prima, or the dammed torrent of Dara. Water was brought in from the wadi by a series of long channels and cleaned of sand by filters and decanting tanks, to be stored in a series of large cisterns in the south-western corner of the city.[102] Without such a water supply, the city would surely have died of thirst. Procopius celebrates defensive wall and water supply, but adds that he 'added to the place houses and stoas and the other buildings which are the usual embellishments of a city' (*Peri Ktismaton* 2.9.7), and archaeology confirms small fragments of stoas (to the south-west and north-east of Basilica B and to the west of Basilica C) without giving much idea of the urban landscape that surrounded the cult of Sergius.

The foundation must count as a success, and it had a long post-Roman history under the Umayyads and later, seen in the mosque built alongside Basilica A, the khan in the centre, and the remains to the south of the city beyond the walls of the settlement created by Caliph Hisham b. Abd al/Malik (724–743) who took up residence here. Not only did the cult of St Sergius continue to flourish, but the city's role as a point of exchange in a frontier zone between different geographical and cultural worlds retained its importance.

---

[100] Fowden, *Barbarian Plain*, pp. 77–80, and Zanini, 'Urban ideal', p. 206–207 for the plan. Gussone and Sack, 'Resafa/Syrien' offers an update on the archaeology.

[101] Gussone and Sack, 'Resafa/Syrien', pp. 125–129 for the gradual incorporation of older routes.

[102] Zanini, 'Urban ideal', p. 213.

These four Justinianic 'new cities' cannot be taken to stand for the entirety of the sixth-century idea of the city: by the side of Constantinople itself, always the ultimate expression of the eastern Roman ideal, these were sideshows. But they show a certain consistency of priorities: of strategic function, defence, and water supply; of religious buildings and institutions; and of an urban aesthetic in which the colonnade and the viewshed were more important than 'the straight line and the right angle'. As Enrico Zanini well put it:

> At this time in the late antique West, and even in a large part of Italy, urban centres – and with them the very ideal of the city – were seriously risking extinction. In the eastern part of the Graeco-Roman world, the birth of a new generation of cities testifies to the continuity of the urban tradition here and, at the same time, of the shaping of a new ideal of the city, in the proto-Byzantine empire.[103]

Reccopolis and the Visigothic West

This new flowering of urbanism in the East should not blind us to the tenacious attachment to city life in at least some parts of the West. While the East continues to witness many new city foundations, these are rare in the West. But when there are exceptions, they are eloquent. Visigothic Spain may not have a panegyrist to match Procopius, but it had in Isidore of Seville, as we have seen (Chapter 8), a commentator for whom cities were still central. It also had a series of kings, starting with Leovigild, who cared enough about cities to found new ones: Reccopolis in 578, then Victoriacum in Basque territory in 581, followed later by Ologicus in the same area founded by Swinthila in the 620s (reported by Isidore).[104] A fourth city not mentioned by the sources is that at Tolmo de Minateda, identified as Eio, the subject of considerable archaeological investigation.[105] Among these, Reccopolis stands out as a city both mentioned by several sources and the focus of extensive archaeological investigation in recent years.[106]

Already the name of Reccopolis is eloquent. As John of Biclar puts it under the year 578 (see Chapter 8, p. 283),

---

[103] Zanini, 'Urban ideal', p. 201.
[104] Isidore, *History of the Goths*, p. 63. Dey, *Afterlife*, pp. 140–160 well brings out the central role of cities in the Visigothic kingdom; pp. 147–149 on Reccopolis.
[105] See Martínez Jiménez, '*Civitatem condidit*'. I owe my knowledge of these Spanish sites to my colleague, Javier Martínez Jiménez. See also Arce, 'La fundación de nuevas ciudades'.
[106] See the volume edited by Olmo Enciso, *Recópolis y la ciudad en la epoca visigoda*, especially his own paper, 'Recópolis: una ciudad en época de transformaciones'. The results of important new geophysical survey are reported in Henning et al., 'Reccopolis revealed'.

> He (Leovigild) founded a city (*civitas*) in Celtiberia named after his son, which he called Reccopolis, which he endowed with wonderful works within the walls and in the suburbs, and he established privileges for the people of the new city (urbs).

Isidore offers a similar account in his *History of the Goths* (51), similarly explaining the name as in honour of his son, Reccared. Doubts have been cast, suggesting that the root Recc-, corresponding to the Germanic 'Reich', celebrates the kingdom rather than the family, but, certainly, when he succeeded to the throne Reccared was happy enough to promote the idea of the family name.[107] However, it is not just the Recc- root that is striking, but the Greek termination, -opolis. It is very much a feature of new foundations in the Greek east, but quite exceptional in the Latin west – one can point to Gratianopolis, a name surviving as Grenoble, and to the renaming of Hadrumetum in Africa as Honoriopolis, and later, under the Vandals, Hunericopolis. This form of dynastic naming points to direct influence from Constantinople.

In one sense, Visigothic Spain is as far removed as it could be, geographically and culturally, from Constantinople; yet ever since Justinian's troops seized control of the south coast of Spain, including the Cartagena from which Isidore's family fled, the Visigothic kingdom had a land border with the Byzantine, or rather, Roman, empire. Leovigild may have been at war with the Eastern Roman emperors, but war does not preclude close contact. When his son Hermenegild rebelled, he turned to the Romans for support – though he found himself deserted at a crucial moment by his allies, to whom Leovigild had paid a ransom of 30,000 gold *solidi*. The best way to defeat an enemy may be to imitate them, and *imitatio imperii* is a recurrent feature of Leovigild's reign.[108] Isidore characterises Leovigild in these terms:

> He was the first to increase the treasury and fisc, and the first to sit among his courtiers on a throne, dressed in regal clothing, for before him kings wore the same clothing and used the same seats as his people. However, he founded a city in Celtiberis which he called Reccopolis after the name of his son. (*History of the Goths* 51)

He was evidently borrowing court ceremonial from Constantinople. The clearest sign of direct imitation is in the gold coinage: before Leovigild, Visigothic mints issued imitations of Byzantine coinage, never mentioning

---

[107] Collins, *Visigothic Spain*, p. 56, for doubts.
[108] Diaz and Valverde, 'The theoretical strength and practical weakness of the Visigothic monarchy'.

the king's name; then, with Leovigild, starts an impressive series of gold tremisses, which carry the head of the king on the obverse, albeit represented by a sort of shorthand more reminiscent of emoticons than of portraiture, and the legend in Latin, LIVVIGILDVS REX (Figure 9.18).[109] The types are based on those of the contemporary Byzantine mints, and gradually the king's titulature becomes more elaborate, including the epithets PIUS and INCLITUS. The coinage is an expression of a deeper transformation: Leovigild is turning his kingdom into a state modelled on at least some elements of the Roman Empire.

The founding of new cities was thus part of an expression of a state that raised taxes and maintained a well-paid army.[110] The coinage was issued by cities, which spelled out their names on the reverse: RECCOPOLIS had a busy mint under Leovigild and Reccared (Figure 9.18). Just as the coinage of the Frankish kingdom was issued from a multiplicity of mints, driven by the need to pay taxes is fresh coin (we have seen the role of St Eligius in this process; see Chapter 7, p. 261), taxation, coinage, and cities were closely linked in the new-look kingdom, though, unlike the situation in Francia, the Spanish mints were under royal control. In this context, it is no surprise that the dynastic naming of Reccopolis should form part of extensive *imitatio imperii*. But what of the urban form of the new city? Can we detect here too an idea of the city related to the eastern empire? This is precisely what the excavators suggest.

The site of Reccopolis is set in a loop of the river Tagus, as is indeed the case with the Visigothic capital of Toledo, from which it is some

Figure 9.18 Golden tremissis of Reccopolis. Obv. stylised head of Leovigild facing right with paludamentum, LIVVIGILDVS REX; rev. cross on four steps, RECCOPOLIS CONOB. From Ruth Pliego, *La moneda visigoda*, Sevilla, 2009, t. II, nº 36b, with the author's permission.

---

[109] Catalogued by Pliego Vázquez, *La Moneda Visigoda*; cf. Pliego, 'Figura et potentia'; see too Kurt, *Minting, State, and Economy in the Visigothic Kingdom*.
[110] Kurt, *Minting*, pp. 173–230, for discussion of the reasons for minting.

65 kilometres distant. It stands on a hill, rising steeply from the bank of the river to its north (Figure 9.19). The summit of the hill, rising to 60 metres, forms a natural acropolis, artificially levelled to a plateau, while below it spreads the lower city, surrounded on the edge of a steep rise by a wall.[111] For decades, excavation has focused on the summit, though more recent geophysical survey has shown the lower part of the city to be densely occupied by buildings (Figures 9.20 and 9.21).[112] At the top, on the lip of a spectacular drop to the Tagus, allowing dramatic views, is a building complex that is identified as a palace (Figure 9.22). This forms a series of buildings on two storeys set around an open piazza; the longest of the buildings, following the lip of the hill, is 133 metres long. What survives is a basement floor, evidently purposed for storage, especially of grain: the reception rooms will have been above, with a commanding view over both city and countryside. High-quality building material and sculpted decorative elements, combined with size and location, point to a building designed to be seen from afar, and to impress. To the east of the piazza is a church in a form based on a Latin Cross, with an apse at its east end, and

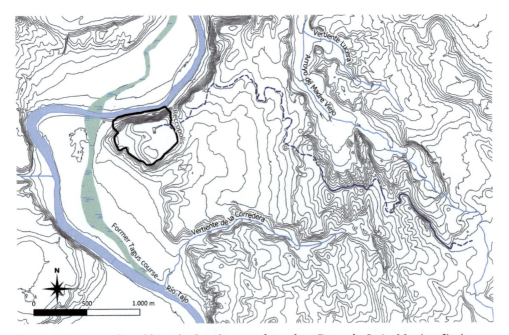

Figure 9.19 Reccopolis and hinterland, with route of aqueduct. Drawn by Javier Martínez Jiménez.

[111] For the walls, Gómez de la Torre-Verdejo, 'La muralla de Recópolis'.
[112] Henning et al., 'Reccopolis revealed'.

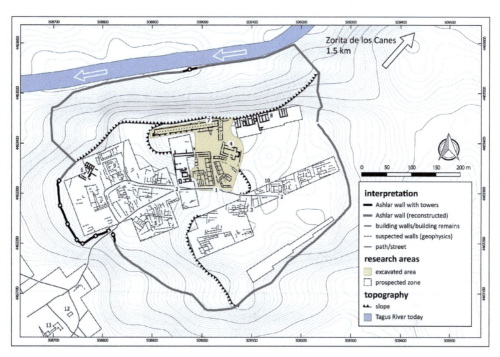

Figure 9.20 Reccopolis with results of geophysical prospection. Henning et al., 'Reccopolis revealed', reproduced with permission.

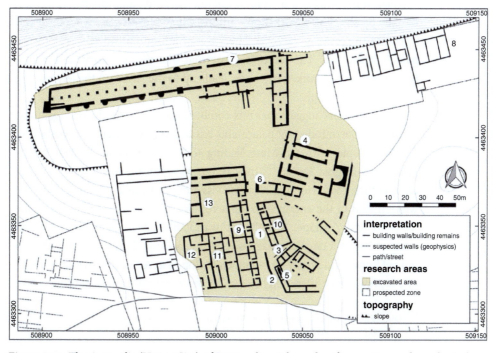

Figure 9.21 The Acropolis (Upper City) of Reccopolis, with results of excavation and geophysical prospection. Henning et al., 'Reccopolis revealed', reproduced with permission.

Figure 9.22 View from Royal Palace of Reccopolis over Tagus valley. Author's photo.

a narthex and baptistery at the west end, which is unique in Spain and seems to be based on the Holy Apostles in Constantinople.[113] Entrance to the piazza is controlled by a monumental gateway, and an approach road flanked by shops and workshops, among which were a glass workshop and a goldsmithy (see Figure 9.23). These were high-end businesses serving the palace at the top. The effect is somewhat like that of Norman Lincoln, where Steep Hill, flanked by shops, leads up to the castle on the left and the cathedral on the right.

The excavators suggest that this combination of approach road, gateway, and piazza surrounded by palace and basilica was a conscious evocation of Constantinople, with the Mesē leading to the Augustaion, flanked by the Palace and Haghia Sophia.[114] Indeed, the survey of the area below indicates an approach road, running more or less straight from the main gate in the western wall to the entrance to the acropolis, even more reminiscent of the Mesē for its Y shape. Whether it was flanked by colonnades and had a tetrapylon or a circular piazza where it turned uphill to the summit we do not yet know, and it may be too much to hope for. An echo, however remote, of the New Rome there might seem to be. Were the ancient visitor to take

---

[113] Olmo Enciso, *Recópolis: un paseo por la cuidad visigoda*, p. 65.
[114] So Olmo Enciso, *Recópolis*.

Figure 9.23 View of housing in Reccopolis and road leading to acropolis. Author's photo.

a plan of Constantinople and compare it to that of Reccopolis, they might strain to see the comparison. But plans were a thing of the future, and what mattered was impressions – the 'wow' factor. We know that Goths could be impressed by Constantinople. We have met Athanaric, in Cassiodorus' description, 'exclaiming in wonder, "Lo, now I see what I have often heard of with unbelieving ears", meaning the great and famous city'.[115] Colonnades, vistas, glittering buildings, the setting by the sea ... Our visitor to Reccopolis might let out a scarcely less muted 'wow' when they passed through the city gates and followed the way up to the summit, the palace conspicuous from every angle, then looked down on the loop of the river below.

Another striking feature of Reccopolis is the construction of an aqueduct, the first known to have been built in the Iberian peninsula since the third century, and at a time when the necessary technology seems to have collapsed.[116] Aqueduct construction is a clear sign of aspiration to imperial models, and the source of inspiration is likely to have been, more than the Roman past in Spain, Constantinople itself, which could also have supplied

---

[115] Cassiodorus, *History of the Goths*, p. 143; also see Chapter 4, p. 135.
[116] Martínez Jiménez, 'Water supply in the Visigothic urban foundations', esp. 238–239; Martínez Jiménez, *Aqueducts and Urbanism in Post-Roman Hispania*, esp. pp. 203–210.

the engineering skills necessary.[117] Reccopolis was also equipped with at least one cistern, and it has been suggested that this 'mixed' system of aqueduct and cisterns is a sign of the inadequacy of the aqueduct.[118] Nevertheless, the combination of aqueduct and cisterns is characteristic, as we have seen, of Constantinople itself, and here too we must suspect a Justinianic model.

Whether or not there is a conscious evocation of Constantinople here, we are surely looking at an idea of the city held in common. In fact, a closer parallel is Justiniana Prima, with its location on the loop of a river, and its use of a natural ridge to create a contrast between Upper and Lower Town. If what we see in both Justiniana and Reccopolis is an idea of a city based on Constantinople, it is as distant from the original as the highly stylised and reductive portrait of Leovigild on a gold tremissis is distant from the classicising portraiture of a Byzantine coin. This is surely the point. It is not that the idea of the city has been replaced by some medieval alternative idea. Rather, just as the idea of Rome is transformed when applied in the new context of Constantinople, such that the *imitatio* produces a completely new outcome, so the idea of Constantinople is transformed when applied to the context of a Syrian frontier fort, a remote Balkan village, or a Visigothic hill top. The idea Leovigild had when he minted his own coins was an *imitatio imperii*; but the outcome might have seemed to Roman eyes quite alien, not to say barbarous. The irony, and the revelation, is that the new cities of Late Antiquity are shaped not by the desire to be different, but by the desire to follow what they understood as a classical tradition.

Umayyad ʿAnjar

There is no sign in the new cities we have considered of a desire for strict orthogonal design. There were doubtless some streets that ran parallel in Constantinople, but to describe the city plan as a whole as orthogonal would be a major distortion of a complex landscape. There are some cases, as in the circular piazza of Justiniana Prima, where the viewer might have perceived a layout as more regular than in fact it was. There were of course plenty of cities surviving from earlier periods for which the grid plan was an essential feature: Antioch, Apamea, and Laodicea are fine examples. But Justinian's new foundations felt no obligation to find their model in them. In this context, it is all the more striking to find an example of grid planning

---

[117] Martínez Jiménez, *Aqueducts*, pp. 50–55. [118] Olmo, 'Recópolis', p. 55.

of considerable mathematical precision in one of the earliest Islamic 'new cities', the palace-city of the Umayyad Caliph al-Walid I, the construction of which is dated fairly securely to around 714 by graffiti left in the quarries for its stone.[119]

The layout forms a precise rectangle measuring 370 by 310 metres, so enclosing an area of just under 11.5 hectares (Figure 9.24).[120] As Hillenbrand observes, 'the concept of a rectilinear grid underpins virtually every detail of the plan'. It goes far beyond mere grid planning. The design is based on symmetry on two axes, a pattern that starts with the city walls, but reproduces itself in a fractal fashion down to the design of individual houses.[121] Particularly important for the design are the forty towers regularly spaced along the walls. The number forty may have had special significance in the Islamic world;[122] but it also has a direct consequence for the plan. This number of towers distributed around the four sides of a square would result in an uneven number on each side, and consequently a pair of towers flanks the gateway set centrally in each wall. 'Anjar has, in addition to its four corner towers (each circular with a spiral stair), ten solid semi-circular towers on its north and south walls, but only eight on its east and west walls.

This type of arrangement is also met in early Islamic al-Aqabar where, in addition to four circular corner towers, the north-west and south-east walls have six semi-circular towers, whereas the north-east and south-west have only four.[123] The plan derives directly from that of Roman military *castra* on the Syrian frontier. The clearest example is el-Lejjun (Betthorus) in Lebanon, its name preserving the Legio originally stationed there. There too the walls are of unequal length, with four circular towers at the corners, four semi-circular towers on the north and south walls, and six on the east and west. There can surely be no doubt that 'Anjar is self-consciously modelled on a Roman legionary fort, albeit on a larger scale. Whether, as Hillenbrand suggests, in following a 'Roman' model the Umayyads were distancing themselves from their enemies the Byzantines depends on whether they perceived any contrast between old Romans and new.[124] Perhaps it is better to say that they took the model of a military power which they had defeated in the past and had every intention of defeating in the future.

[119] See the illuminating discussion by Hillenbrand, "'Anjar and early Islamic urbanism'.
[120] Hillenbrand, "'Anjar', p. 61, gives the area as 11,470 square metres, but this is out by a factor of 10.
[121] Finster, 'Researches in 'Anjar: I. Preliminary report' is now basic on the design.
[122] Hillenbrand, "'Anjar', p. 61 note 11.   [123] Hillenbrand, "'Anjar', p. 74.
[124] Hillenbrand, "'Anjar', p. 94, suggests that Umayyad art followed Roman models and distanced itself from the Byzantine in other respects.

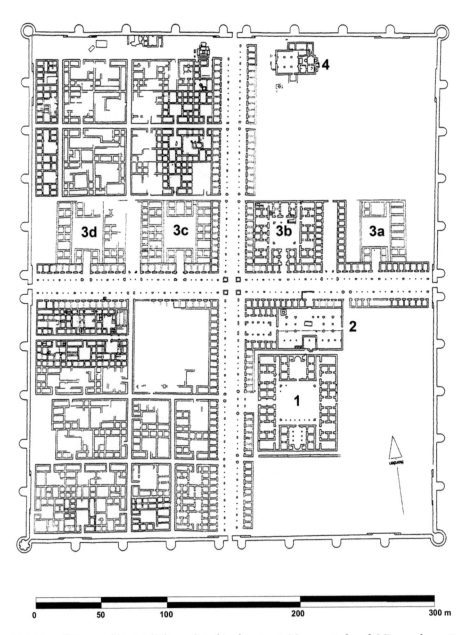

Figure 9.24 Plan of Umayyad ʿAnjar (Lebanon). 1. dār-al-imāra; 2. Mosque; 3a-b-c-d. Minor palaces; 4. Hammām. From Finster, 'Researches in ʿAnjar', reproduced with the author's kind permission.

The forty towers then determine the rest of the interior layout. Gates flanked by towers precisely bisect each of the walls, and lead to broad avenues 20 metres wide, flanked by colonnades, and meeting at their intersection with a *tetrapylon* four-way arch. The four avenues (the false Roman labels of 'decumanus' and 'cardo' have been applied to these) divide the city into four quarters, in their turn subdivided by much narrower alleys, which form a grid within each quarter; they do not, however, extend across the city as a whole, since there is an evident desire to differentiate hierarchically by size, from the caliphal palace at one extreme through blocks of residential housing to the shops/workshops that line the central streets, reaching a total of more than 200 units.[125]

There is a clear hierarchy of housing. The dominant building is the caliphal palace, arranged with symmetry on two axes around a central court. A door in the north wall of the palace leads directly across the street to the mosque, entered next to the minbar.[126] There are four further 'palaces', arranged symmetrically to the north of the central east/west avenue: these are of identical design, each forming a square, symmetrical on both axes.[127] To their north are four blocks of housing, each consisting of six houses of standard symmetrical design. In the south-west quadrant of the city are further residential blocks, on two modules, with four pairs of slightly larger houses, three blocks divided into six houses, and one half-block divided into three.[128] It is evident that all this is the product not of private enterprise, but of rigid central planning that envisaged a range of inhabitants beneath caliphal level: some very grand, some relatively spacious, some rather less so, and a great majority of one-room shop units forming the suqs that line the axial roads. If the style is reminiscent of military planning, it is not a purely military population envisaged.

Another recognisably 'Roman' feature is the bath block in the north-eastern quadrant, close to the city walls. Again, its design is symmetrical, with a sequence of *frigidarium*, *tepidarium*, and *calidarium* set in a grid of four squares.[129] But lest we imagine that this is some sort of ghostly Roman city repurposed by the Umayyads, the mosque forms an essential part of the design and follows similar symmetries on two axes.[130] Indeed, there are signs of different phases in the building of the mosque, and it has been suggested it may have replaced an earlier monastery.[131] A monastery set in

---

[125] Hillenbrand, "Anjar', counted 116 shops, Finster's new survey more than 200.
[126] Finster, 'Researches in 'Anjar', pp. 218–223 on the design. For the connection to the mosque, see Santi, 'Anjar in the shadow of the church?'
[127] Finster, 'Researches in 'Anjar', pp. 223–227.
[128] Finster, 'Researches in 'Anjar', pp. 232–236.
[129] Finster, 'Researches in 'Anjar', pp. 227–228.
[130] Finster, 'Researches in 'Anjar', pp. 229–232.
[131] See Santi, "Anjar in the shadow of the church?'

a Roman *castrum* with so many houses and shops is a tall order, and we should not be tempted to deprive a proud Umayyad caliph of the credit for this extraordinary site.

Is it right to call 'Anjar a 'city'? Hillenbrand raises doubts, which have been echoed by others, but if it is not a city, it is hard to say what it is.[132] It is more than a palace, though the cluster of palatial quarters, mosque, and baths might suit a palatial complex. There are other examples of Umayyad elite residences, but not remotely on this scale.[133] More than 200 shops point to other commercial and productive functions, and while the number of residential units (just over 50) is small, it is designed with a thoroughness of conception rarely met in a classical city for a minutely differentiated society.[134] By now we should acknowledge that the city eludes rigid definitions. The more so, it is vain to produce any single model of 'the Islamic city'. The cities of the Islamic world take many forms, including that of organic growth around private residences which are given maximum privacy, and hence generate the sort of narrow streets and end-stopping that characterise a city like Fez in Morocco.[135] In the matter of scale, 11.5 hectares is large enough for a small but respectable city in the classical world, like Herculaneum which was probably no more than 12 hectares, with 15 as the outer limit. Nothing is solved by denying 'Anjar to be a city and making an exception of it. What is certain is that an early caliph such as al-Walid saw the regularity of a Roman military fort as a way of expressing his own power and prestige. 'Anjar is the first in a long tradition of Islamic foundations that relied on strict orthogonality to express such prestige: in tenth-century Umayyad Spain, the first caliph, abd ar-Rahman III, was to express his own glory by building near Córdoba a new city of spectacular orthogonality, the Madinat al-Zahra, though its 112 hectares dwarfed 'Anjar.

Charlemagne's New Rome?

As a coda, we might look at what some contemporaries at least claimed to be new cities founded by Charlemagne, especially his 'new Rome', Aachen. The idea of the city, I have tried to suggest, is not just an abstraction subject

---

[132] Leal, "Anjar: an Umayyad image of urbanism and its afterlife'.
[133] See Genequand, *Les établissements des élites omeyyades*.
[134] Hillenbrand, "Anjar' counted twenty-six residential units; the new plan by Finster allows us to double that number.
[135] See Ennahid, 'Access regulation in Islamic urbanism'. I thank the author for sharing this with me.

to some process of transformation driven by changes in social structure,[136] but a conscious attempt to apply the models of the cities of the past to changing contexts. If Constantinople is consciously modelled on Rome, Justinian's new cities are consciously modelled on Constantinople, and Leovigild's on Justinian's. Nor can we speak of a collapse of classical ideals in the face of barbarism, as suggested by Haverfield. If orthogonality and grid-planning cease to be priorities in Late Antique cities, it is Constantine and his successors who had different priorities. Ironically, for those who fancy that the 'Islamic' city developed a model antithetical to the classical, it was a Muslim caliph who built the most convincing grid city of the eighth century.

In a world of rulers of new kingdoms who drew on the classical past for inspiration and authority, Charlemagne stands out: the first of the 'barbarian' kings to take the imperial titles of Imperator and Augustus, formally conferred on him by Pope Leo in 800. KAROLVS IMP AVG appears on his coinage; and, in his charters and capitularies, he changes from 'Carolus gratia Dei Rex Francorum et Langobardorum ac Patricius Romanorum' to become 'Karolus serenissus Augustus a deo coronatus Magnus Pacificus Imperator Romanorum gubernans imperium'.[137] The new titulature is not wholly classical, but it states plainly enough his claim to be successor to the Roman emperors and ruler of their empire. Little wonder the emperors in Byzantium were less than happy at this invasion of their imaginary territory. Authority is located both in the past and in the present of papal unction. Culturally too he drew on the past and the model of Augustus: the intellectuals with whom he surrounded himself in his court – Alcuin and Einhard, and authors like Angilbert, Theodulf, and Modoin – went out of their way to present themselves as following an 'Augustan' model, whether in Einhard's *Life of Charlemagne* so closely modelled on Suetonius' *Life of Augustus*, or in the classicising poetry replete with citation of Virgil and Ovid.[138] The classicising nicknames of the circle, however, were at odds with their actual reading, with Alcuin as (Horatius) Flaccus, Angilbert as Homer, Theodulf as Pindar, and Modoin as (Ovidius) Naso: only the last can be shown to have read the poet after whom he was known.[139]

We might expect a Charlemagne who paraded as a new Augustus to have been a founder of cities. This, in the sense that Justinian or even Leovigild were, Charlemagne was not. Nevertheless, it was one way of seeing him,

---

[136] For this idea, Olmo Enciso, *Recópolis*. [137] McKitterick, *Charlemagne*, p. 116.
[138] Godman, *Poets and Emperors*, pp. 38–92, for the poets; Townend, 'Suetonius and his influence', pp. 98–106 for Einhard's use of Suetonius.
[139] Raby, *Secular Latin Poetry in the Middle Ages*, pp. 178–209.

and most spectacularly so in the epic poem by one of the circle of court poets (which one, scholars cannot agree) going under the title 'Karolus Magnus et Leo Papa'.[140] The poem is not, at 536 lines, a short one, yet it is probably only a fragment, for its account of the meeting of Charlemagne and Pope Leo III at Paderborn in 799 would lead naturally to Charles' visit to Rome in 800 and his coronation by Papa Leo as Emperor on Christmas day. It opens with a panegyrical passage on the virtues of Karolus, the beacon of Europe (*Europae ... pharus*) and the new David (12–14). After a round-up of his virtues, including an inflated view of his literary talents, putting him on a level with Cato, Cicero, and Homer (70–74), the poet, spoilt for material for praise, highlights him at work building a new city, in a very Roman capacity:

> Europae venerandus apex, pater optimus, heros,
> Augustus: sed et urbe potens, ubi Roma secunda
> Flore novo, ingenti, magna consurgit ad alta
> mole, tholis muro praecelsis sidera tangens.

> The venerable summit of Europe, best father, hero,
> Augustus: but mighty too in his city, where a second Rome
> with a new bloom, vast, rises to the heights with great effort,
> touching the stars with the towering peaks of its wall. (93–96)

To generate this impression of an Augustan city founder, the poet turns to the proto-Augustan hero, Aeneas, and drawing closely (but not exclusively) on the first book of the *Aeneid*, mirrors the account in which, not Aeneas, but Dido is found building her own 'New City' (as Isidore knew, the Punic qrt-ḥdšt means 'new city'). Virgil captures much building in a few lines (*Aeneid* 1.420–440). Aeneas is amazed by the great mass (*molem*, a word which the Carolingian poem picks up insistently); readers might also remember the much-cited Virgilian line, *tantae molis erat Romanam condere gentem*. Virgil swiftly enumerates gates, roads, walls, and citadel; magistrates and senate; port and theatre; and then, in a striking simile borrowed from his own *Georgics*, compares the building site to a hive of bees. Aeneas then finds Dido in a clearing supervising the construction of a temple, the doors of which are decorated with scenes from the Trojan war, which the Trojans linger over at length (441–493). There is scarcely an element from this description of (a purely imaginary) Carthage which is

---

[140] Dümmler, *Poetae Latini Aevi Carolini*, no. 799, pp. 366–379, there attributed to Angilbert, by others to Alcuin or Modoin, see Godman, *Poets and Emperors*, pp. 82–83, McKitterick, *Charlemagne*, p. 140.

not promptly recycled as Karolus surveys the site of the future Rome (*venturae moenia Romae*, 98): Forum and senate, port and theatre (99–105), and also the temple (111–120). If this is supposed to be Aachen, we may wonder whether any Carolingian city was supposed to have a senate house or a theatre – though surely we are not asked to read this literally, but rather as an evocation of Virgil, on the understanding that he too was not describing a real Carthage so much as an Augustan image of an ideal city.

Yet one element obtrudes in this borrowing that is not Virgilian, and that has every right to be seen as an image of the real Aachen:

> hic alii thermas calidas reperire laborant,
> balnea sponte sua ferventia mole recludunt,
> marmoreis gradibus speciosa sedilia pangunt.
> Fons nimio bullentis aquae fervere calore
> non cessat: partes rivos deducit in omnes/urbis.

> Here others work to discover hot baths;
> with effort they open up hot springs boiling spontaneously,
> they form beautiful seating with marble steps.
> The source of all too boiling water never ceases to heat:
> it produces streams in all parts of the city. (106–111)

The lack of Virgilian precedent underlines the genuine local colour. Aachen, Roman Aquae Grani, was named for its hot springs; Einhard assures us that Charlemagne took particular pleasure in 'the vapours of naturally hot baths' and was such a good swimmer than nobody excelled him (*vita Karoli* 22.5). The description of the building work is then rounded off with a reworking of the beehive simile that manages to blend in further elements from the *Georgics* and even the *Eclogues*. As in Virgil, the simile gives a powerful impression of high levels of activity and coordination, and tacitly points to the role of the Queen or King Bee, for Virgil, Dido, and now Charlemagne.

Another poet, Modoin ('Naso'), opens his *Eclogues*, cobbled together from Virgilian citations, with a dialogue between an old poet and a young one. The 'boy' reports seeing the 'New Rome':

> Prospicit alta novae Romae meus arce Palaemon
> cuncta suo imperio consistere regna triumpho.
> rursus in antiquos mutataque saecula mores
> aurea Roma iterum renovata renascitur orbi.

> My Palaemon looks out from the high citadel of the New Rome
> that all the kingdoms in his empire stand in triumph,

and an age transformed into ancient ways.
Golden Rome renewed again is reborn for the world.[141]

The boy is challenged by the old poet:

> huc tibi, stulte puer, quae causa palatia tanta
> Quae fuit alta novae cernendi moenia Romae?

> Foolish boy, what was the cause for seeing such a palace,
> the high walls of the New Rome? (1.30–31)

The boy reiterates his assertion that this palace is the New Rome:

> quo caput orbis erit, Roma vocitare licebit

> Where the capital of the world will be may be called Rome. (1.40)

Call Charlemagne's palace a city or the dream of one, it is a reproduction of Rome as much as the poems are reproductions of Augustan poets.

Can we use these poems as evidence that either Charlemagne or his courtiers seriously took Aachen (or indeed Paderborn) for a new city? If so, Einhard was not one of them. He regards his Karolus as a great builder and picks out the basilica at Aachen as a wonder, and points to his outstanding palaces, mentioning one at Ingilheim near Mainz and a second at Nijmegen, though he says nothing of Paderborn (*Vita* 17.2–3). He sees Charlemagne as a builder of palaces, not cities. It is true that the chroniclers speak of an Urbs Karoli or Karlsburg near Paderborn, but this was a short-lived experiment, and it was burnt down by the Saxons.[142] If we meet a Carolopolis in tenth-century sources, it is a city founded by his grandson, Charles the Bald, and there is no evidence that, at the time, any Frankish king experimented with the naming patterns of eastern emperors, as did Leovigild at Reccopolis.[143]

Charlemagne's Aachen is magnificent, but it is not a city.[144] The palatial complex is built round a symmetrically planned square and

---

[141] Modoin, *Ecloga* 1.24ff (Dümmler p. 385).

[142] The Annals of Pettau for 776 report the building of a *civitatem quae vocatur Urbs Caroli*, the Annals of Moselle for the same year call it Karlsburg, the Annales Maximiniani call it 'Urbs Caroli et Francorum'. Its burning by the Saxons is reported (Annals of Pettau) under 778. I am grateful to Sam Ottewill-Soulsby for guidance and references.

[143] Bertoldo, 'Le città carolinge battezzate con il nome di un sovrano'. The first reference to Carlopolis is in the Holder-Egger, *Ex sermone in tumulatio*, pp. 271–273, a reference I owe to Sam Ottewill-Soulsby.

[144] For recent discussions, Nelson, 'Aachen as a place of power'; Rollason, 'Charlemagne's Palace'; and the three-volume 2014 exhibition catalogue, *Karl der Große: Orte der Macht* (ed. F. Pohle). I am grateful to both Rosamond McKitterick and Sam Ottewill-Soulsby for guidance, bibliographically and on site.

Figure 9.25 View of central dome of the octagon of the Aachen Palace Basilica; the mosaics are not original. Author's photo.

Figure 9.26 View of the central dome of the octagon of S. Vitale in Ravenna. Author's photo.

triangle, bisected on its axis by a road, the Principia (Hauptfeldstrasse) intersecting at a tower gate with the passage that links Chapel and Royal Hall, now the Rathaus. It is not hard to see this as a descendant of the sort of axial planning of roads intersecting at a *tetrapylon*. Beyond doubt, it is a fine example of orthogonal planning. And, beyond doubt, Charlemagne was looking to classical models, particularly Ravenna and Rome, from which he took ample building material.[145] The octagonal chapel is inconceivable without close knowledge of S. Vitale in Ravenna and matches it in beauty (Figures 9.25–9.26): Charlemagne twice visited Ravenna, and put its bishop under pressure to supply him with marbles. He also helped himself to the equestrian statue of Theoderic that had decorated his palace. The links with Constantinople are weaker – the church of Saints Sergius and Bacchus is suggested as a model but is not a true octagon. In a rather broader sense, the influence of the New Rome can be detected in the model of palace/square/basilica. It is in this sense that the core of the Byzantine New Rome is the ultimate core of the city which Aachen's New Rome was yet to become.

Can the epic of 'Karolus Magnus and Papa Leo' be taken as evidence for a serious desire to present Aachen (or any other palace complex) as a new city? It is risky to read too literally a poem so full of witty allusion to classical texts, so much an in-joke between the learned members of the court. With the same amused detachment with which they called each other Homer, Ovid, Horace, and Pindar, even without necessarily knowing those works, they could rely on each other to recognise in the picture of the New Rome of Karolus a brilliant *jeu-d'esprit*. Behind the wit, there is also something serious: the recognition that Charlemagne had entered into competition with the past, and, in the best tradition of *imitatio imperii*, was capable of matching it in quality. That the new emperor valued cities is confirmed by his will, as reported by Einhard, in which he left two-thirds of his wealth to be divided between the twenty-one *civitates metropolitanae* of his realm. Aachen was less of a city than Reccopolis; but, as an architectural achievement, the Frankish palace far outshone Leovigild's urban essay. The classical idea of the city survived and inspired innovation not just in cities, but in an astonishing attempt to relaunch the Roman Empire.

---

[145] See Nelson, 'Charlemagne and Ravenna'; Herrin, *Ravenna*, pp. 375–385.

10 | Decline and Resilience

Shall we then conclude that the 'ancient city' did not, after all 'decline and fall' as Wolf Liebeschuetz argued? That, this book has tried to show, was not the way in which contemporaries, from Cassiodorus to Isidore, saw the matter. It is not that they did not see the world as transformed, rather, it was transformed by Christianity, not by a change in the nature of the city. Like Isidore, or the verses of praise for Verona, they could contrast the world of the pagan ancients, the *antiqui,* to the Christian world of the present, *nunc*; but their city existed across space and time, from the biblical city of Enoch to the new foundations of the Visigothic kings. It would be wrong to use this perception to contradict the clear evidence of the material remains that the fabric of the city was changing in some fundamental ways. It is not helpful to privilege written sources over archaeological remains. What it illuminates, rather, is a process of resilience, the use of the memories of the past for adaptation and survival. Even as material reality, and the social and economic structures within which it is formed, reveals a process of change, the perception that what, say, Cicero had to say about cities and citizenship was still valid helped them fashion a future that was, as Cassiodorus might have put it, truly *modernus* while respectful of, even in competition with, the past. The Ostrogothic Theoderic could draw even on broken fragments of the classical past to fashion a new image of power in Ravenna; and Charlemagne symbolically helped himself to both the marble of Ravenna and the statue of Theoderic to build his new image of power in Aachen. I turn again, in conclusion, to the theory of resilience to ask how it may illuminate our understanding.

Resilience Theory

The ecological theory that has had most influence in recent times is not one of collapse, or even of transformation, but of resilience. Ever since the introduction of the concept of resilience in the 1970s by C. S. (Buzz)

Holling,[1] his model has been seized on in numerous disciplines, from ecology to the social sciences and psychology.[2] Indeed, its influence has spread far beyond the academic sphere, and it has become central to discussions of modern urbanism as a tool of public policy, promoted, for instance, by the initiative pioneered by the Rockefeller Foundation, 100 Resilient Cities.[3] The contemporary city stands at risk of potential 'collapse' in numerous ways, ranging from historically inflated multi-million populations, dependent on fragile supply chains, to overreliance on digital technologies vulnerable equally to hacking and to sunspots. In addition, there is a range of additional threats: both ecological, like global warming, and not least pandemics spreading uncontrolled across the globe, and social, including migration, failures of social justice, civil war, and breakdown of political order. Models of resilience are sought which might at least mitigate the devastating impact of these potential urban catastrophes. The 'good news' is that cities have proved resilient in the past and are capable of doing so again in the future.

Yet before we are tempted to turn Late Antiquity into a message of 'good news', it is worth looking more closely at what resilience involves at a theoretical level, and whether it may offer a way of looking at the complex, confused, and contradictory evidence of the past. Resilience theory goes far beyond a cheerful message that ecological systems, or human societies, or cities, or, at a psychological level, individuals, are capable of 'bouncing back' and recovering from disaster. It offers a model of the complex relationship between growth, prosperity, and stability, on the one hand, and crisis, break down, adaptation, and rebuilding on the other. Memory plays a crucial role in adaptation through what Andersson and Barthel have called 'social memory carriers'; historical memory may underpin reconstruction.[4] Rather than seeing stability or equilibrium as a norm and breakdown as a failure, it proposes a continuously fluid movement between phases at different speeds – typically, a long and slow period of growth and consolidation followed by a rapid sequence of breakdown and rebuilding. In the classic formulation offered by Gunderson and Holling, there is a continuous figure-of-eight loop between four states, on a quadrant of two axes, from an 'exploitation' phase (designated as 'r', as in the rate of spread of a virus) moving slowly to consolidation (designated as 'K') to a rapid breakdown or 'release' phase ('Ω'), swiftly followed by

---

[1] Holling, 'Resilience and stability of ecological systems'; Holling and Gunderson, 'Resilience and adaptive cycles'.

[2] Bollig, 'Resilience–analytical tool, bridging concept or development goal?'

[3] See www.resilientcitiesnetwork.org.   [4] Andersson and Barthel, 'Memory carriers'.

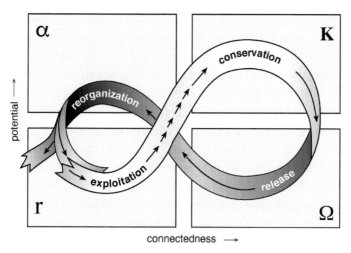

Figure 10.1 Stylised representation of the four ecosystem functions from Holling and Gunderson, 'Resilience and adaptive cycles'. Reproduced with permission of Island Press.

reorganisation ('α'), ushering in a new phase of exploitation (Figure 10.1). The resilience of such a system is not a given, but a variable: depending on the degree of resilience, it will move more easily from one phase to another.

Moreover, it may move between phases on different levels and at different rhythms over time. On a long timescale, you might think of the Roman Empire as following a single long loop: from expansion under the Republic (the 'r' phase), to consolidation under the empire ('K'), to a more rapid phase of breakdown and reorganisation in Late Antiquity ('Ω'/ 'α'), leading to new phases of exploitation and consolidation in the emergence of the successor kingdoms in the West, and of the Byzantine Empire in the East. Alternatively, you could think of the Roman Empire as a remarkably resilient system, cycling continuously between phases of growth and consolidation, breakdown and reorganisation. Thus, the expansion of empire after the Punic Wars leads to consolidation of a new imperial pattern with the *nobilitas* as its elite in the late Republic, which breaks down and is reorganised by Caesar, breaks down again and is more definitely reorganised by Augustus, but even then is subject to repeated crises and civil wars which break down old elites and reform them. A deeper phase of breakdown develops in the third century, leading to reorganisation of the system under Diocletian, swiftly followed by another breakdown and reorganisation by Constantine. This imports a new basis of stability in the adoption of Christianity, ushering in a new phase of stability that lasts till the crisis of the battle of Adrianople and the successful penetration of Germanic war bands, producing the collapse of Rome as a centre of power ('Ω') and a reorganisation that puts Byzantium at the centre of the old power system ('α') and a new consolidation ('K') that reaches its peak, but also the verge of collapse, under Justinian. From this point of view the repeated civil wars and power shifts that mark the history of the empire are a sign not of weakness, but of the resilient ability to dismantle and replace some features of the system, while maintaining an overall continuity that allows us to see it as a single structure. It may be very different by the end, but it still sees itself as part of a continuous 'Roman Empire', even under rule from Constantinople.

The potential for archaeology of resilience theory as developed by ecologists was seen by the leading American archaeologist, Charles Redman.[5] Because of the potential of archaeology to study human societies and their interaction with the changing environment over a long timescale, archaeology allows us to study the entire adaptive cycle and its changing rhythms: not just looking for stability and the collapse that brings it to an end, but patterns of adaptation in response to crisis in which survival in the long term is defined by resilience and adaptability, not by stability itself. This sort of alliance between the long-term view offered by archaeology and the shorter-term systems view offered by ecology is what made it possible for Jared Diamond to evolve his picture of ecological collapse caused by human choices. If the most vigorous application of resilience theory has been in New World archaeology, it has also had a growing impact on the archaeology of the Greek and Roman world. Alan Walmsley first applied it to his study of Late Antique and early Islamic Syria.[6] Reacting against traditions of archaeology that assumed that Islamic conquest simply represented the collapse of the urban systems of antiquity, he showed from sites like Jarash that a remarkable degree of urban continuity could sit alongside dramatic changes. Cities adapted to new conditions rather than collapsing. More recently, he and Louise Blanke have shown how a trio of neighbouring cities on either side of the Jordan valley – Baysān/Scythopolis, Fihl/Pella and Jarash/Gerasa – can be re-read not as 'abruptly and vindictively' collapsing at the end of antiquity, but as adapting successfully to the changed circumstances of Arab conquest of 634–638.[7] Jarash, with its conspicuous colonnades of the second century, saw transformation of its major monuments, hippodrome, theatre, and temples through the Christianisation of the fourth and fifth centuries. The Umayyad Caliphate brought not collapse but new

---

[5] Redman and Kinzig, 'Resilience of past landscapes'; most accessibly in Redman, 'Resilience theory in archaeology'.
[6] Walmsley, *Early Islamic Syria*, pp. 146–147.   [7] Blanke and Walmsley, 'Resilient cities'.

importance, with the construction of a major congregational mosque at the centre of the city. The greatest damage, at Jarash as in the other two cities, was caused not by warfare but by earthquakes, especially that of 749. Yet, in the face of claims of the total abandonment of Jarash after the earthquake, new excavation shows rebuilding and reconfiguration of both the mosque and the adjoining commercial area. The supposed collapse after Late Antiquity is due to the preconceptions of the archaeologists, not the physical evidence. In this context, it should be remembered that A. H. M. Jones, whose vision of the decline of the ancient city has had such formative influence, frequently visited the site of Jarash (see Chapter 1).

Another fruitful application of resilience theory, this time to longer-term patterns in the Byzantine world, has been developed in a series of papers by John Haldon and his colleagues.[8] The sixth century and the peak of Mediterranean reconquest under Justinian is seen as a growth or exploitation phase (r) leading to a phase in the early seventh century when the networks are overconnected (i.e. conservative and rigid, K); war with Persian and then Arab–Islamic conquests bring crisis (Ω), followed by reorganisation in the eighth century producing a new equilibrium (α).[9] This model of an adaptive cycle, it is emphasised, is different from the model of transformation. Adaptability, in this scenario, involves human agency, the capacity of humans to manage change and respond to crisis; while adaptation and resilience allow a system 'to retain its fundamental shape and defining characteristics'; transformation, by contrast, 'occurs when external forces … stimulate responses that generate 'non-linear' changes in systems and social or ecological environments, thus driving the system to become fundamentally new and different'.[10]

Resilience and Transformation

We may think again of the story of the Seven Sleepers of Ephesus which Peter Brown so vividly used to mark what he saw as the transformation of Late Antiquity (see Chapter 1). The refugees from the third-century persecution of Decius find their city transformed by a cross above the gate, men praising Christ in the streets, and the presence of churches. Of course for these fervent Christians, as indeed for Gregory of Tours in narrating the episode, the conversion of the city from pagan to Christian is a radical

---

[8] Especially Haldon et al., 'Lessons from the past, policies for the future'.
[9] Haldon and Rosen, 'Society and environment in the East Mediterranean'.
[10] Haldon and Rosen, 'Society and environment in the East Mediterranean', p. 277.

transformation. Yet the city gates are still the same city gates, despite the presence of a cross, the streets they walk through are the same streets, and in the city central place where they present themselves to the magistrates, brandishing their out-of-date coins, are all the old city structures. The transformation is one of perception and belief, not of fabric (except in so far as temples give way to churches). By all means, we can call this a transformation; but, from the viewpoint of an adaptive change cycle, the city as system may be thought to have retained its fundamental shape.[11]

Herein lies the question: are the cities of the post-Roman, Byzantine, or Islamic worlds something different in their nature, a wholly new system, or are they an adaptation of the cities from which they emerged? Whether or not they 'declined and fell', have they undergone a transformation so fundamental as to be something new? Have they undergone the 'sea-change' of Ariel's song in the *Tempest* (Act 1, scene ii)?

> Full fathom five thy father lies;
> Of his bones are coral made;
> Those are pearls that were his eyes;
> Nothing of him that doth fade,
> But doth suffer a sea-change
> Into something rich and strange.

Or, for another image of transformation, we can think of an Ovidian metamorphosis: the nymph Daphne pursued by the amorous Apollo is transformed, limb by limb, finger to twig, hair to leaves (*Metamorphoses* 1. 545–552). The laurel tree she becomes is no longer 'the same structure' as the nymph, but a profound transformation.

There can be no clear or definitive answer to this question, only an acknowledgement that the issue is complex and depends on our own perceptions. Wolf Liebeschuetz, rather like Gregory of Tours, felt that a city controlled by bishops was something fundamentally different from the classical city – only that Gregory felt that this was how things should be, and exaggerated the role of the bishop, while Liebeschuetz lamented the end of what he saw as a 'secular' city, underplaying the role of the priest in the pagan city. Fustel de Coulanges, as we have seen, thought that religion of a specific sort was a necessary characteristic of his ancient city, giving it a particularism which was incompatible with the global ambitions of Christianity. On the contrary, it is not difficult to argue that bishops inherited and extended the system of local administration developed by

---

[11] The distinction between adaptation and transformation cannot be pressed too hard, but see for an attempt at distinction Blanke and Walmsley, 'Resilient cities', p. 71.

the imperial authorities, and that the bristling ranks of local saints in which cities like Verona and Milan rejoiced gave each city as powerful a local particularity as any collection of pagan deities.

Resilience, then, cannot be the only way of looking at the cities of the Antique and post-Antique worlds, but it offers a framework within which to look afresh at complex historical changes. Recently, Greg Woolf has remarked on the striking continuities that mark the cities of the ancient world between 500 BC and AD 500.[12] For all our difficulties of cataloguing and counting them, the cities of Classical Greece are those that survive into the late empire, except that their numbers and areas have expanded (were there now 2,000? Or as few as 1,400?). Woolf sees resilience as a characteristic of these cities. There were failures, but they were pruned out: those that survived were stronger. Woolf sees two factors to their resilience: their generally small size, with the majority being of 5,000 inhabitants or fewer, and the networking, locally and criss-crossing the Mediterranean, that held them together. While everyone in antiquity was painfully aware that individual cities, like men, could 'die', seen as a system they survived remarkably well, and did so thanks to their adaptability.

This in turn raises the question of their survival after the collapse, by a painfully slow process over the century between Adrianople in 378 and the abdication of the last western Roman emperor in 476, of the system of imperial power that had supported them in the West.[13] Here was a shock to the system to match any environmental catastrophe: does that mean that the cities lost the resilience that had seen some of them through a millennium of change, and does it mean that any adaptive changes that happened now were so different as to change their fundamental nature, a transformation in the hard sense rather than resilient adaptation? Those who wish to underline the contrasts – economic, social, and cultural – between the ancient world and the Middle Ages may prefer to talk of transformation; those who underline the continuities may point to resilience.

Variations on a Theme: Antioch

To speak of resilience is not to suggest a generalised pattern. The idea of an 'adaptive cycle' acknowledges that cities, as other organisms, respond to localised environmental changes in specific and localised ways. The

---

[12] Woolf, *Life and Death of Ancient Cities*; also 'Locating resilience in ancient urban networks'. I am grateful to the author for sharing the latter with me ahead of publication.
[13] See Salzman, *Falls of Rome*, for the long cycle of set-backs and recoveries.

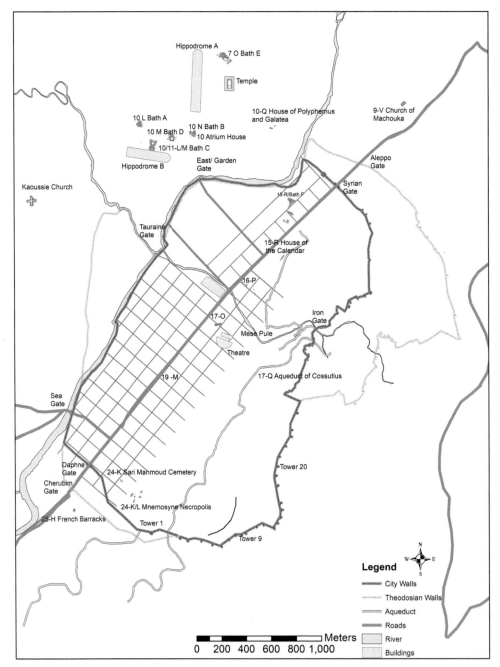

Figure 10.2 Plan of ancient Antioch after Justinian, drawn by Stephen Batiuk. From De Giorgi & Eger, *Antioch*, figure 4.7, with the authors' permission.

Variations on a Theme: Antioch 381

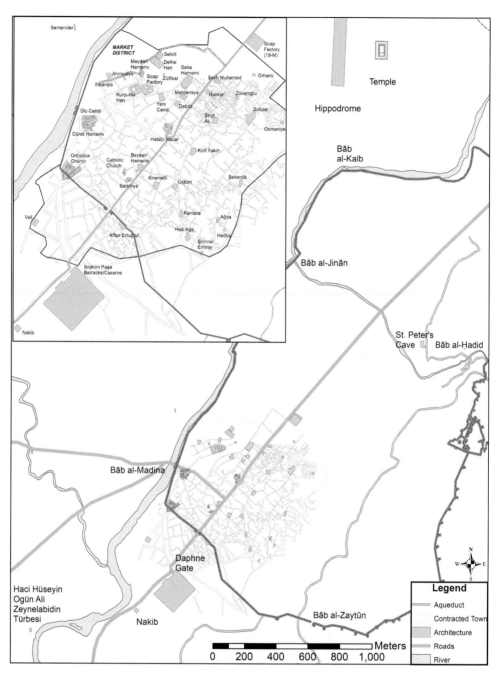

Figure 10.3 Plan of Ottoman Antioch, created by Steve Batiuk. From De Giorgi & Eger, *Antioch*, figure 10.2, with the authors' permission.

Figure 10.4 View of southern end of Antioch viewed from Mt. Silpius. Author's photo.

resilience of Greek and Roman cities lies in the fact that they are not locked into one set of geopolitical and social structures, but adapt individually: some disappear entirely after antiquity (as they had long before), but surprisingly many find rich and complex new futures. At issue is not merely the ability of cities to survive and change, but our own perceptions: an underlying conviction that nothing could ever be the same again after the period we call 'Antiquity'.

A powerful example of changing perceptions is Antioch – the Antiocheia of antiquity, the Antakya of today. Antioch was one of the 'apex' cities of the ancient Mediterranean, founded as capital of a Hellenistic kingdom that stretched initially from Syria to Mesopotamia and Persia, and achieving a renewed significance in Late Antiquity as the imperial base of operations against Persia. We have met it already as the city rosily but evocatively praised by Libanius (Chapter 2, pp. 47–51), and as the focus of the campaigns of Chosroes described by Procopius, in his text a striking example of resilience in the face of repeated earthquakes and Persian sacking, then rebuilt by Justinian (Chapter 5, pp. 171–173). The archaeological campaign of the 1930s led by Princeton University was unsurprisingly aimed at recovering the traces of the ancient city, described in some detail not only by Libanius and Procopius, but also several other

Figure 10.5 View of Antakya hotel/museum. Author's photo.

sources, such as John Malalas. Yet the city was not easily explored archaeologically, being buried under the deep layers of post-Antique occupation. One should not underestimate the challenges of recovering archaeological traces of a city lying in a deep valley bottom, subject to constant silting, and occupied continuously after antiquity. As the brilliant archival researches of Andrea De Giorgi and Asa Eger have shown, while the excavators inevitably found, and at least partially documented, those post-Antique layers, in terms of publication the emphasis of the Princeton team was entirely on antiquity, and especially on the spectacular mosaics which enriched museums across the world: there was no interest in telling the story of the later city.[14] Hence, the definitive account of Glanville

[14] De Giorgi and Eger, *Antioch*.

Downey was of what he defined as a 900 year history, 'from Seleucus to the Arab Conquest', a story he regarded as ending finally with that conquest.[15] Almost all other publications followed the same pattern, and even if it was acknowledged that Antioch did not entirely disappear, it was regarded as too much of a come-down from antiquity to be worth discussing.[16] A combination of archival study and new research has shown that 'the city continued to thrive and transform well into the Islamic/medieval periods as a religious, intellectual, and economic centre'.[17] That claim is abundantly borne out by the detailed account of the successive phases of the city in the 'forgotten' periods: 'Early Islamic (638–969), Middle Byzantine (969–1084), Saljūq (1084–1098), Crusader (1098–1268), Mamlūk (1269–1516), and Ottoman (1516–1920)'.[18] Even to list the periods is to observe the strong fluctuations between eastern and western influence that a city built to bridge the spheres embodies, and consequently the ability of the city to adapt to deep changes. The mapping of the city in each of these phases shows both striking continuities and no less striking periods of contraction (Figures 10.2 and 10.4). That it inescapably 'declined' after its Late-Antique peak does not mean that it ceased to be inhabited or to have (constantly changing) significance. The authors offer it as a model of resilience.[19] They note too that at all periods the inhabitants were conscious of their pasts:

> In many instances, the city's classical past is evident in its medieval and early modern incarnations, consciously expressed, remembered, and etched into the buildings and walls themselves.[20]

A symbol of that continuity is the central avenue that defines the city, much praised in antiquity by Libanius for its long colonnades (Chapter 2, pp. 50–51), and still today visible from the viewpoint of Mount Silpius above (Figure 10.3). That conscious remembering applies at no time more so than the present, when the ancient mosaics offer a tourist attraction, and the largest mosaic yet exposed lies under a luxury hotel (Figure 10.5).[21]

---

[15] Downey, *A History of Antioch in Syria from Seleucus to the Arab Conquest*.
[16] De Giorgi and Eger, *Antioch*, p. 2.   [17] De Giorgi and Eger, *Antioch*, p. 5.
[18] De Giorgi and Eger, *Antioch*, p. 4.   [19] De Giorgi and Eger, *Antioch*, pp. 8–10.
[20] De Giorgi and Eger, *Antioch*, p. 12.
[21] The theme of memory is explored in detail in Martínez Jiménez and Ottewill-Soulsby, *Remembering and Forgetting the Ancient City*.

Mérida

At the opposite end of the Mediterranean world, Mérida in Spain offers a similar model of resilience, though, as in Antakya, the modern visitor, bowled away by theatre, amphitheatre, aqueduct, bridge, and an exceptionally effective museum of antiquities, might scarcely notice that the period intervening between past and present has a rich story of its own to tell. Just as Antioch starts as a deliberate foundation as capital of the Seleucid empire, Augusta Emerita starts as an Augustan colonial foundation designed to be the regional capital of Lusitania, and its footprint, quite visible today, has the familiar hallmarks of a Roman colonial foundation, from the gridded plan to the monuments that attract the modern visitor (Figure 10.6). The survival, at least in part, of the grid points to a degree of continuous inhabitation.[22] But Mérida, like Antioch, is a city repeatedly conquered and adapted, with significant Visigothic and Islamic phases, though the separation of the Visigothic material in a museum separate from the Roman reflects a modern desire to emphasise the Roman past which can be a hot political issue.[23]

Mérida has benefited from more intense archaeological investigation than Antioch, allowing us to be more precise about the timing of the ups and downs characteristic of a resilience cycle.[24] Already in the fourth century, despite retaining significance as a territorial capital, and despite clear signs of prosperity, we can detect the shifting urban priorities of the Late Antique city. The major pagan monuments show signs of degradation and neglect: litter accumulates in the previously vast public space (5 hectares, no less) of the Colonial Forum (Figure 10.7), and private houses intrude on the quadriporticus of the theatre and the pavements of some streets (notably to the south of the city in the Morería area, where modern redevelopment has exposed extensive remains of Roman housing). A shift in priorities leads the still-wealthy local elite to invest in palatial mansions and churches, rather than temples and theatres. By the early fifth century, there are clearer signs of economic downturn, and the arrival of the Visigoths in the 440s (associated, it seems, with signs of burning and destruction) brings a revival. The city walls are repaired, and there are attempts, though not up to the standards of Roman technology, to repair the aqueduct.[25] The great bridge (1 kilometre in length)

---

[22] On the colonial grid, Greaves and Wallace-Hadrill, *Rome and the Colonial City*.
[23] Martínez Jiménez and Ottewill-Soulsby, *Remembering and Forgetting*, pp. 327–332.
[24] See Osland, 'Abuse or reuse? Public space in late antique Emerita'.
[25] See Martínez Jiménez, *Aqueducts and Urbanism in Post-Roman Hispania*, pp. 42–43.

is restored and celebrated in a verse inscription, in not entirely classical elegaics:

> solb(v)erat antiquas moles ruinosa vetustas
> lapsum et senio ruptum pendebat opus.
>
> Ruinous old age had undermined the ancient piers/ and the structure was sagging, collapsed and broken up through age (trans. Osland).[26]

It goes on to celebrate the restoration under 'the mighty king of Goths', Ervig (probably we should read 'Euric'), supported by the local *dux*, Salla, and the bishop Zeno.[27] The collaboration between royal and episcopal powers is familiar from Merovingian Gaul, as depicted by Gregory of Tours (Chapter 7). The growth of the cult of St Eulalia gave a new importance to Mérida; the *Lives of the Fathers of Emerita* spell out clearly how some of the wealth of the local landed elite passed to the church, making it one of the richest in Spain. Bishop Zeno, with his Greek name, not only acts

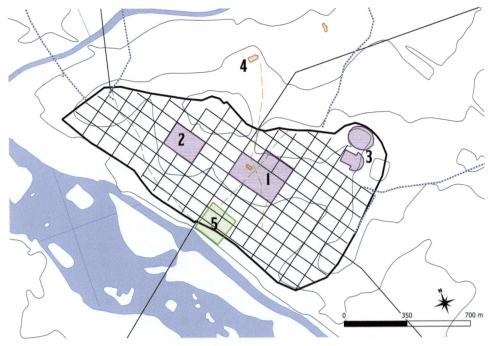

Figure 10.6 Plan of ancient Mérida: 1. Forum/temple of Diana; 2. Colonial Forum; 3. Theatre/amphitheatre; 4. St Eulalia; 5. Alcabazar/Umayyad citadel. Drawn by Javier Martínez Jiménez.

---

[26] The second line of each couplet ends as if a pentametre, but fails to sustain the scansion.
[27] The text is discussed in detail by Osland, 'Text and context'.

Figure 10.7 View of temple of Diana area. Author's photo.

like the old elite in care for the urban infrastructure but passes on the torch of classical education in his brave if imperfect versification.

However much things change, we can detect vitality in Visigothic Emerita.[28] The Umayyad conquest of 713 spells a distinct diminution of the city. The destruction of the Roman wall and gate, and the well-built garrison of the Alcazaba controlling the head of the bridge (Figure 10.8), flags tensions between the Moorish occupiers and the local population; the creation of an alternative regional centre at Badajoz deprived Mérida of its regional importance, and it is clear that there is gradual demographic and economic decline. The defeat of the Almohads by Alfonso IX in 1260 restored the city's role as a Christian centre, and there are signs of new wave of investment in the seventeenth century, when a remarkable entrance loggia for the church of St Eulalia was created out of the remains

---

[28] Osland, 'Abuse or reuse?', pp. 89–90.

Figure 10.8 View of bridge and Alcazaba of Mérida. Author's photo.

Figure 10.9 Porch of S Eulalia, constructed in the sixteenth century from remains of Roman temple of Mars. Author's photo.

of classical architraves, including the dedicatory inscription, MARTI SACRVM (Figure 10.9). The now unusable aqueduct was replaced by a technically more modest masonry canal. It is, however, in the twentieth century that the city most overtly embraces its classical past, rebuilding the *scaenae frons* of its theatre and sealing its claim to Roman status in 1986 with a major National Museum of Roman Art designed by Rafael Moneo. The political choice to emphasise links to Rome is seen again in the 1990s, when a statue of the wolf and twins, donated by the Comune di Roma, was set in the middle of a roundabout at the head of the bridge.[29]

Naples

Mérida shows us a city always conscious of its Roman past, sometimes restoring it, transforming it, sometimes suppressing it. Both Mérida and Antioch are cases of what can be called 'decline' after antiquity – a clear reduction of their wealth and wider importance, though neither disappears from the map at any stage. Naples, by contrast, is a conspicuous example of 'continuity' after antiquity (Figure 10.10). By the classic measure of the survival of a street grid, Naples clings to its sixth-century BC layout more tenaciously even than the cities of North Italy. Some of that continuity is imagined: the three principal east–west streets are today referred to as the 'decumani', though rather than a term surviving from antiquity (when 'plataeae' is the only documented term), this is a modern imposition of the questionable Latin label favoured by modern archaeology.[30] Physically, it is clear that there is a close continuity in the street layout, most tangibly illustrated by the excavations under S. Lorenzo Maggiore, where phases from the Greek colonial foundation through the city of the Roman period up to Late Antiquity deep below the modern street surface nevertheless follow the same line.[31] Such continuities are real, but belie a continuous process of adaptation and refashioning. What in antiquity seems to have served as a market is entirely refashioned as a monastic foundation, and it is unclear whether the deep layers of earth that cover up the ancient levels (so preserving them so well) are the result, as the excavators suggested, of a natural process of silting, or of deliberate backfilling and burial. Either way, the medieval structures are disconnected from the ancient in all but the street line. And proud though modern Naples may be of its *centro storico* with its picturesquely narrow streets lined with stalls, the area has

---

[29] See Martínez Jiménez and Ottewill-Soulsby, *Remembering and Forgetting*, pp. 328–329.

[30] See my 'Ancient ideals and modern interpretations', at p. 55; Kaiser, *Roman Street Networks*, pp. 24–25.

[31] Arthur, *Naples: from Roman Town to City-State*, pp. 31–58, for the urban continuities; pp. 42–44 for S. Lorenzo.

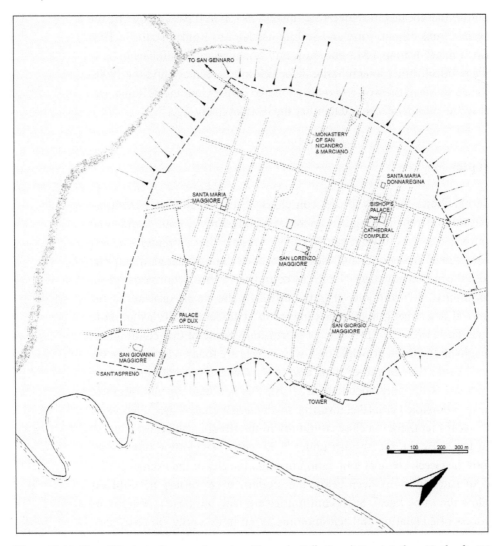

Figure 10.10 Plan of Naples in the seventh century (drawn by Sally Cann). From Arthur, *Naples*, fig. 3.3, with permission of the British School at Rome.

been historically a deep embarrassment to the city authorities, the unhealthy slums densely packed with the poor. The broad boulevard of the via Umberto I, known as the Rettifilo, was the product of the abortive effort in the nineteenth century to let light and air into the slums, on the model of Baron Haussmann's transformation of Paris, above all to bring devastating outbreaks of cholera under control.[32] The kings and viceroys of

---

[32] Snowden, *Naples in the Time of Cholera*.

Naples avoided the historic centre, moving away from the Norman fortress of the Castel Capuano at the east gate of the city: the Federican Castel dell'Ovo, the thirteenth-century Angevin castle (Maschio Angioino), and the Bourbon Palazzo Reale are set to the south-west of the ancient grid, and the via Toledo, built by the Spanish Viceroy Pedro de Toledo in 1536, slicing to the west of the ancient city off the line of the grid, also served to keep the slums to its east under control with the garrison stationed in the new grid of the Quartieri Spagnoli.

This too is a city always conscious and proud of its Greek and Roman past. Yet the presentations of continuity are again illusory. The Maschio Angioino, with its dark volcanic stonework, was transformed in the fifteenth century under Aragonese rule by Alfonso V, with the addition of a gateway in the form of a bright marble triumphal arch, featuring relief work in Roman style by the Renaissance architect Francesco Laurana, advertising a fresh start and a return to ancient ideals. Perhaps the most conspicuous 'revival' was the 'recreation' of the Roman aqueduct as part of the late-nineteenth-century campaign against cholera: a thorough piece of research by an engineer at the time established the exact route and technology of the Augustan aqueduct, and though the new aqueduct differed both in route and technology, it was advertised as part of a return to Roman ideals of urban sanitation.[33]

The tendency is always to think of the fate of cities after antiquity as one of 'decline'. Naples certainly underwent profound changes in the early Middle Ages, but whether these constitute 'decline' is a moot point. In many ways, the Neapolis of antiquity was limited by its setting among competing cities with varied functions: Cumae as the original colonial foundation, Puteoli as what became in the late Republic the most important commercial harbour in Italy, and also Misenum as the base for the main navy of the western Mediterranean, let alone minor neighbours such as Herculaneum and Pompeii.[34] Capua too retained a position of dominance in the Campanian plain. Already by the sixth century, the Naples besieged by Belisarius in Procopius' narrative is a major regional centre (see Chapter 5, p. 174), and at the end of the century, when Pope Gregory writes, as he does frequently, to Naples, he emphasises the importance of the *nobilitas*, suggesting that the major landowners of the region were clustering there, as they were to in later centuries.[35] After antiquity, as the centre of Dukes originally dependent on the Byzantine Exarchate of

---

[33] Greaves, 'Roman planning as a model for urban modernity in Liberal Naples'.
[34] D'Arms, *Romans on the Bay of Naples*, is the enduring classic.
[35] See Chapter 6. For the *nobiles* of Naples, see *Letters* II.5, II.13, and III.35.

Ravenna, and then as an independent Duchy, Naples considerably extended its territory to reach as much as 1,500 km^2 – a figure 300 times higher than its extent in antiquity.[36] If in the Roman period Neapolis was tolerated, even encouraged, as a sort of museum of Greek culture, albeit one of limited economic or political importance, in Late Antiquity and the Early Middle Ages it became one of a special set of Italian coastal cities strong enough to resist the Lombards, and, subsequently, under Angevin, Aragonese, and Spanish rule it became the dominant city of South Italy. It flourished not because of its antique credentials, but because its position on the Bay of Naples allowed it to grow in changing geopolitical configurations: nevertheless, its antique credentials were important to display.[37]

Resilience and the Idea of the City

We could catalogue the numerous cities of antiquity which, like the three discussed, have long afterlives, along with many, in north Africa and elsewhere, which did not.[38] That exercise might show that ancient cities were more resilient than we thought, but if so would only show that we had underestimated the extent of resilience. More important, it would show that there is no one model of resilience: each city has its own biography, determined by a range of contingent factors. The aim of this book is not to show how resilient they were, nor even how they were resilient, but to explore the resilience of the *idea* of the city after antiquity, and to ask how *contemporary participants* saw them. It is exactly the perception of fundamental change in the city that seems to me to be absent from those contemporary observers who have most to say about the city. Cassiodorus, as spokesman for the Ostrogothic regime, is emphatic about the importance his government attached to conserving and reviving the traditional urban fabric of Italy, both in its physical structure and in its institutions (see Chapter 4). We may regard him as a biased witness, whether as a propagandist, determined to demonstrate to critics both in Rome and Constantinople that Gothic rule was compatible with preservation of a Roman imperial tradition, or as a conservative, descendant of the high Roman aristocracy and defender of their cultural values. Both these

---

[36] Arthur, *Naples*, p. 83.   [37] Well summarised by Arthur, *Naples*, pp. 14–51.
[38] Rome itself would make an illuminating case study but would require a book to itself; see now Dey, *The Making of Medieval Rome*. For Late Antiquity, the theme of resilience is illuminatingly discussed by Salzman, *The Falls of Rome*. Constantinople/Istanbul merits discussion at the same level: see now the essays in Fowden et al., *Cities as Palimpsests*.

points may hold true, but he is interesting not as a witness to the facts on the ground (of course cities, including Rome itself, and institutions, including curial rule, and even the residential preferences of the landowning elite, may have fallen well short of his ideals). He is witness not so much to facts as to perceptions. His reversion to the past for models of how things should be speaks not of transformation but of resilient adaptation, in which memories of the past are a necessary feature of the reorganisation that allows the system to survive changed circumstances. It was the deliberate choice of the Gothic rulers to employ a spokesman steeped in Roman tradition, because it allowed them to present their rule not as a transformation but as a continuity with the past.

Procopius too is both conservative and propagandist, though in this case his propaganda is balanced by encomium for and invective against the regime of Justinian (see Chapter 6). It has been suggested that he was so steeped in classical literature, voicing the language and thoughts of the fifth century BC, that he was unable to see or represent the real changes in his world, and specifically in cities.[39] His image of Rome as the city most dedicated to preserving its past sits ironically alongside his narrative of the damage done to Rome's fabric by Witigis and Totila, and of the desperate pleas of Belisarius to Totila not to destroy the object of universal admiration, that could only enhance his reputation by sparing it. Procopius' ideals are quite expressly conservative. So are Justinian's. Seen by his critics (including Procopius) as a restless innovator, Justinian was in the business of recapturing past glories, whether in rebuilding the Roman Empire by reconquests of the areas that had fallen to barbarians or of restoring and enhancing the urban fabric of his empire. Here too the memory of the past serves the purposes of adaptive resilience rather than transformation. This does not mean that Justinian's new cities were quite the same as the new foundations of the high empire – quite the contrary (Chapter 9, 'Justinian's New Cities'). They served a new context but drew on the language and components of the urban past to do so.

Isidore too is easily dismissed as an antiquarian, too immersed in his library to bear witness to the realities of his Visigothic world (Chapter 8). His career, and his deep involvement with the Visigothic court and its religious policies, are enough to show he was no mere antiquarian. His search in ancient writings for the true meaning of things is an exercise in using the past to improve the present. He may look like a throwback from the Augustan world of Virgil, but it is a Virgilian world already

---

[39] Averil Cameron, *Procopius* (see Chapter 1, p. 27.).

reinterpreted by Augustine and other church fathers. He can use the wisdom of the past to instruct Visigothic kings what the true meaning of kingship is (piety and justice) and instruct the successors of Leovigild and Reccared who took pride in the ability to build a new city what the components of a true city were. How can you build the cities of the future if you do not have an instruction book on how the cities of the past were built?

Ask the poets and prose authors to praise their cities, whether in the fourth or eighth or even twelfth centuries, and they have no difficulty in accommodating their praise to the prescriptions drawn up by authors of rhetorical handbooks in the third or fourth centuries (Chapter 2). Ask Alcuin to praise York, or the anonymous author of the epic of Charlemagne and Pope Leo to evoke Charlemagne's Aachen, and they effortlessly do so in classical terms. This is not to say that York or Aachen were not different in many ways from classical cities; it is to say that they were perceived as part of a continuous tradition. Paradoxically, it is the differences that show resilience at work.

Too much stress has been laid on the survival of one specific aspect of the classical city, itself heavily reformulated by Diocletian and his successors: the rule of a hereditary elite of landowners named *curiales*. The rigid (and seemingly ineffective) rules around them are on display at interminable length in the *Theodosian Code*, and survive into Justinian's legislation, not to be finally repealed until Leo the Wise in the tenth century. They served imperial convenience, as a mechanism for delegating the burden of tax collection, together with the registration of property on which they depended, to those in the cities rich enough to act as unwilling guarantors should the tax returns fall short. There was no need for the successor kingdoms, in Italy under the Ostrogoths, in Spain under the Visigoths, and in Gaul under the Franks, to continue such a system. Yet the documents, when not dismissed as forgeries or simply ignored, suggest that old rituals continued in all three, and longest in Gaul (Chapter 5). This may be only a pale echo of the curials of the imperial city, but it is eloquent of a determination at least to preserve forms. Behind it lies the survival of the landed aristocracy itself. The suggestion that those who appear in the sources as *senatores* in Gaul or Spain were all descendants of the senatorial elite of the late empire is not only demographically implausible, it masks from us the vigorous survival of the local landed elites: the sort of families to which Gregory of Tours himself was proud to belong (Chapter 7).

Gregory himself may serve as a symbol of the difference between resilience and transformation. His apparent rejection of the classical rules of style and grammar make him easier to recruit (unlike Isidore) as an authentically 'medieval' voice. Yet Gregory's rejection of classical rules is at best ambivalent: it is done not by any means in ignorance, or through lack of education, but as an attempt to create a new idiom accessible to a supposedly 'rustic' audience. Descended from 'senators' and saints, Gregory has still much in him of the late Roman aristocrat. Where the deep continuity with the past shows is in his loyalty to the idea of the city, and in his use of the role of bishop to fight the cause of the city in the fissile courts of the Merovingians.

The End of the Ancient City?

What, then, does it mean to speak of 'the end of the ancient city'? It is quite legitimate if we want to treat the 'ancient city' as a bounded phenomenon, one with a beginning, a middle, and an end, and different in kind from the cities that followed it, the 'medieval' and 'Islamic' cities. As Moses Finley put it:

> I hold it to be methodologically correct to retain the ancient city as a type.[40]

We can construct typologies to suit our favoured narratives. Historians of the Islamic world are now much more cautious about assuming there is a typology of the 'oriental town'. Historians of the Classical world might be a little more reflective about what ideological assumptions are smuggled into the idea of the 'ancient city' and the anti-medieval and anti-Islamic rhetoric for which it has been employed: do we want to join Francis Haverfield in his message to town-planners of the inherent civilised values of the ancient town plan, or rather to give ear to Thomas Ashby, who thought the cult of the straight line and the rectangle was overdone?

The idea of the ancient city as a phenomenon with an end offers a cleaner narrative and a satisfying sense of closure. But it comes at a cost. That is already visible in the lack of clarity over when in fact the end came: as early as Constantine, with the official adoption of Christianity, or at some ever-receding horizon between the fifth and the eighth centuries – indeed, the whole territory now seen as 'Late Antiquity'?[41] That can been seen in the narratives of A. H. M. Jones and Wolf Liebeschuetz of the gradual demise of

---

[40] Finley, 'The ancient city', p. 23, cited in Chapter 1, p. 5.
[41] For a balanced discussion of the 'end of the ancient city', see Zuiderhoek, *The Ancient City*, pp. 167–185.

the *curiales*. They never seem to want to lie down and die, and their death agonies stretch over some four centuries. That sort of pace of change seems hardly compatible with a story of profound and radical transformation. It may be that 'structurally ... they had changed so profoundly that we can no longer call them ancient cities'.[42] Look a little closer, and this 'they' blurs: we are talking of the cities of the West from the fifth century and of the East from the sixth and seventh centuries, leaving us with a margin of uncertainty of a full three centuries.

Where the idea of resilience might help is in accounting for a change, or set of changes, that are drawn out over a long period, a process of continuous adaptation rather than a rapid metamorphosis from one state to another. If the secret of the ancient city, as Greg Woolf suggests, lies in its resilience, then we are not looking at a stable phenomenon that persists over a millennium, but a process of constant adaptation to changing circumstances. Claude Mossé (to give one example among many) thought that the end of Athenian democracy in the fourth century BC was part of a wider decline of the ancient city.[43] Once Aristotle had defined what the *polis* truly was, it is hard not to see everything after Aristotle as a decline. Alternatively, the decline is a resilient adaptation to changed circumstances. Athens had to cope with its defeat by Philip and Alexander, as it later did with its defeat by Rome. The city persists, even if the sort of university and tourist centre it became under the Roman Empire is hard to recognise in Aristotle. Later, when the schools of philosophy were closed by Christian emperors, it felt as if this, not democracy, was what had defined Athens. From such a viewpoint, the constant adaptive cycles of Late Antiquity represent not the breakdown but the continuation of the adaptive cycles that preceded them.

None of this is to deny the severity of the trauma that afflicted the Roman world from the late fourth century on. Bryan Ward-Perkins has reminded us that the breakdown of an imperial system necessarily had negative consequences: economically, socially, and culturally. Cities were brutally sacked in this period at an unprecedented rate; some recovered, many did not. Nor it is reasonable to imagine that if the unification of the Mediterranean under Roman rule had the effect of facilitating and increasing exchange – of people, goods, and ideas – the breakdown of that system could have other than dampening effects. But the question about cities is not the same as the question about an empire, which evidently did 'decline and fall' in a western Mediterranean no longer united under an imperial

---

[42] See Zuiderhoek, *The Ancient City*, p. 185.   [43] Mossé, *La fin de la démocratie athénienne*.

power. The question is how the network of cities which the empire had promoted and reduplicated survived under changed circumstances. The answer is that they survived, in so far as they did so, by the sort of adaptive strategies that had always characterised cities. If, for instance, their generally small size was a factor in their resilience in the classical period, it might equally be so in the post-classical period.

It is the privilege of the historian-narrator to begin and end a story where they choose: it is a choice to present Late Antiquity as a breakdown and dissolution of what had gone before, and it adds pathos to the story if what went before is seen through rosy spectacles as an ideal, and what comes after as a tragic loss. But it is not a choice made by the authors of Late Antiquity who are most concerned with the city. Just as much as classical authors, they continued to take the city for granted. Not even Christian critics like Augustine or Salvian dreamt of doing away with the city: at most, they wished to see cities follow the model of the heavenly city. Salvian's city might be a hotbed of vice, but that is an argument for moral reformation, not abolition. As for Augustine's *civitas terrestris*, his target was not urbanism but an empire built on conquest, and if there was one feature of it he admired, it was the idea of citizenship, a model for the superior citizenship of the City of God (Chapter 3).

Not just writers, from Cassiodorus to Isidore, but also the rulers they served took cities for granted. It was the only conceivable way to organise civilised life, and the definitions offered by Cicero continued to be valid for them. Memory is a basic feature of the adaptive cycle, and they drew constantly on memories of the classical city. Rather than an exercise in reactionary conservatism, it was the means by which they could allow their resilient cities to survive, develop, and, in the longer term, flourish.

Bibliography

Abu-Lughod, Janet L., 'The Islamic city', *International Journal of Middle Eastern Studies* 19 (1987), pp. 155–176.

Adshead, Kate, 'Procopius and the Samaritans', in P. Allen and E. Jeffreys (eds.), *The Sixth Century: End or Beginning?* (Brisbane, 1996), pp. 35–41.

Ağtürk, Tuna Şare, *The Painted Tetrachic Reliefs of Nicomedia: Uncovering the Colourful Life of Diocletian's Forgotten Capital* (Turnhout, 2021).

Akyürek, Göksun, 'New history for old Istanbul', in Elizabeth K. Fowden, Suna Çağaptay, Edward Zychowicz-Coghill and Louise Blanke (eds.), *Cities as Palimpsests: Responses to Antiquity in Eastern Mediterranean Urbanism (Impact of the Ancient City, vol. 1)* (Oxford, 2022), pp. 307–326.

Albu, Emily, *The Medieval Peutinger Map: Imperial Roman Revival in a German Empire* (Cambridge, 2014).

Alston, Richard, *The City in Roman and Byzantine Egypt* (London, 2002).

Álvarez Melero, Anthony, 'Honesti, clarissimi e illustres en la Hispania tardoantigua (ss. IV–VIII)', in Sabine Panzram (ed.), *Oppidum-civitas-urbs: Städtforschung auf der iberischen Halbinsel zwischen Rom und al-Andalus* (Münster, 2017), pp. 107–130.

Amin, Ash and Nigel Thrift, *Seeing Like a City* (Cambridge, 2017).

Amory, Patrick, *People and Identity in Ostrogothic Italy, 489–55* (Cambridge, 1997).

Andersson, Eril and Stephan Barthel, 'Memory carriers and stewardship of metropolitan landscapes', *Ecological Indicators* 70 (2016), pp. 606–614.

Ando, Clifford, 'The children of Cain', in Asuman Lätzer-Lasar and Emiliano Rubens Urciuoli (eds.), *Urban Religion in Late Antiquity* (Berlin, 2021), pp. 51–68.

Andreu, Javier and Aitor Blanco-Perez (eds.), *Signs of Weakness and Crisis in the Western Cities of the Roman Empire (c.II–III AD)* (Stuttgart, 2019).

Andrews, Frances, *The Early Humiliati* (Cambridge, 1999).

Arce, Javier, 'La fundación de nuevas ciudades en el Imperio romano tardío: de Diocleciano a Justiniano', *Memorias de la Real Academia de Buenas Letras de Barcelona* 25 (2000), pp. 31–62.

Arends, Niels Paul, *Fragments from the Past: A Social-Economic Survey of the Landholding System in the Ravenna Papyri* (Leiden, unpublished thesis 2018).

Armstrong, Jeremy and Matthew Trundle (eds.), *Brill's Companion to Sieges in the Ancient Mediterranean* (Leiden, 2019).

Arnold, Jonathan J., M. Shane Bjornlie, Kristina Sessaet (eds.), *A Companion to Ostrogothic Italy* (Leiden, 2016).

Arnold, Jonathan J., *Theoderic and Roman Imperial Restoration* (Cambridge, 2014).

Arslan, Pelin Yoncaci, 'Towards a new honorific column: The column of Constantine in early Byzantine urban landscape', *METU JFA* 33.1 (2016), pp. 121–145.

Arthur, Paul, *Naples: From Roman Town to City-State* (London, 2002).

Arzone, Antonella and Ettore Napione (eds.), *La più antica veduta di Verona: l'Iconografia Rateriana. L'archetipo e l'immagine tramandata. Atti del seminario di studio 7 maggio 2011 Museo di Castelvecchio* (Verona, 2012).

Atkins, E. M. and R. J. Dodaro, *Augustine: The Political Writings* (Cambridge, 2001).

Auerbach, Erich, *Literary Language and Its Public in Late Latin Antiquity and in the Early Middle Ages* (trans. Ralph Manheim) (London, 1965).

Augenti, Andrea, *Archeologia dell'Italia medievale* (2018).

Avni, Gideon, 'From Polis to Madina revisited: Urban change in Byzantine and early Islamic Palestine', *Journal of the Royal Asiatic Society* 3rd series, 21 (2011), pp. 300–329.

Avni, Gideon, *The Byzantine-Islamic Transition in Palestine: An Archaeological Approach* (Oxford, 2014).

Badewien, J., *Geschichtstheologie und Sozialkritik im Werk Salvians von Marseilles* (Göttingen, 1980).

Bakirtzis, Nikolas, 'Perceptions, histories and urban realities of Thessaloniki's layered past', in Elizabeth K. Fowden, Suna Çağaptay, Edward Zychowicz-Coghill and Louise Blanke (eds.), *Cities as Palimpsests: Responses to Antiquity in Eastern Mediterranean Urbanism (Impact of the Ancient City, vol. 1)* (Oxford, 2022), pp. 199–221.

Balzaretti, Ross, Julia Barrow, and Patricia Skinner (eds.), *Italy and Early Medieval Europe: Papers for Chris Wickham* (Oxford, 2018).

Barbier, Josiane, *Archives oubliées du haut Moyen Âge: Les Gesta municipalia en Gaule franque, VIe–IXe siècle* (Paris, 2014).

Barlow, Claude (trans.), *Iberian Fathers: Braulio of Saragossa and Fructuosus of Braga*, The Fathers of the Church vol. 63 (Washington DC, 1969).

Barlow, Claude W. (trans.), *Iberian Fathers Vol. 1: Martin of Braga, Pachasius of Dumium and Leander of Seville* (Catholic University of America Press, 1969).

Barney, Stephen A., W. J. Lewis, J. A. Beach, and Oliver Berghof *The Etymologies of Isidore of Seville*, translated with introduction and notes (Cambridge, 2006).

Barnish, Sam, *Selected Variae of Magnus Aurelius Cassiodorus Senator* (Liverpool, 1992).

Barnish, S. J. B., 'The work of Cassiodorus after his conversion', *Latomus* 48 (1989), pp. 57–87.

Barnish, Sam, 'Roman responses to an unstable world: Cassiodorus' Variae in context', in S. Barnish, L. Cracco Ruggini, L. Cuppo, R. Marchese, and M. Breu (eds.), *Vivarium in Context: Essays* (Vicenza, 2008).

Barrett, Graham, 'God's librarian: Isidore of Sevilla and his literary agenda', in Andrew Fear and Jamie Wood (eds.), *A Companion to Isidore of Seville* (Leiden, 2020), pp. 42–100.

Bassett, Sarah (ed.), *The Cambridge Companion to Constantinople* (Cambridge, 2022).

Bassett, Sarah, *The Urban Image of Late Antique Constantinople* (Cambridge, 2004).

Basso, Franco and Geoffrey Greatrex, 'How to interpret Procopius' preface to the Wars', in Christopher Lillington-Martin, and Elodie Turquois (eds.), *Procopius of Caesarea: Literary and Historical Interpretations* (London, 2018), pp. 59–72.

Beneš, Carrie E., *Urban Legends: Civic Identity and the Classical Past in Northern Italy, 1250–1350* (University Park, 2011).

Bennison Amira, K. and Alison Gascoigne, *Cities in the Pre-Modern Islamic World: The Urban Impact of Religion, State and Society* (London, 2007).

Berger, Albrecht, 'Streets and public spaces in Constantinople', *Dumbarton Oaks Papers* 54 (2000), pp. 161–172.

Berger, Albrecht, 'Urban development and decline, fourth to fifteenth centuries', in Sarah Bassett (ed.), *The Cambridge Companion to Constantinople* (Cambridge, 2022), pp. 33–49.

Bertelli, Carlo, 'Visual images of the town in Late Antiquity and the early Middle Ages', in Gian Pietro Brogiolo and Bryan Ward-Perkins (eds.), *The Idea and Ideal of the Town in Late Antiquity and the Early Middle Ages* (Leiden, 1999), pp. 127–146.

Bertoldo, Laura, 'Le città carolinge battezzate con il nome di un sovrano nell'alto medioevo (secoli VIII–IX): continuità di un toponimo classico', *Archeologia medievale* 21 (1994), pp. 657–664.

Bjornlie, M. Shane, *Cassiodorus, The Variae: The Complete Translation* (University of California Press, 2019).

Bjornlie, M. Shane, *Politics and Tradition Between Rome, Ravenna and Constantinople: A Study of Cassiodorus and the Variae, 527–554* (Cambridge, 2012).

Bjornlie, M. Shane, 'What have elephants to do with sixth-century politics? A reappraisal of the "official" governmental dossier of Cassiodorus', *Journal of Late Antiquity* 2 (2009), pp. 143–171.

Blanke, Louise and Alan Walmsley, 'Resilient cities: Renewal after disaster in three late antique towns of the Eastern Mediterranean', in Javier Martínez Jiménez and Sam Ottewill Souslby (eds.), *Remembering and Forgetting the Ancient City* (Oxford, 2022), pp. 69–107.

Blétry, Sylvie, 'L'urbanisme et l'habitat de la ville de Zénobia-Halabiya: résultats de la mission Franco-Syrienne', in Efthymios Rizos (ed.), *New Cities in Late Antiquity. Documents and Archaeology* (Turnhout, 2017), pp. 137–152.

Blok, Josine 'A covenant between Gods and men: *Hiera kai hosia* and the Greek Polis', in Claudia Rapp and H. A. Drake (eds.), *The City in the Classical and Post-Classical World: Changing Contexts of Power and Identity* (Cambridge, 2014), pp. 14–37.

Blok, Josine, *Citizenship in Classical Athens* (Cambridge, 2017).

Boerefijn, Wim, The foundation, planning and building of new towns in the 13th and 14th centuries in Europe: An architectural-Historical research into urban form and its creation (unpublished PhD thesis, 2010).

Bollig, Michael, 'Resilience–analytical tool, bridging concept or development goal? Anthropological perspectives on a border object', *Zeitschrift für Ethnologie* 139 (2014), pp. 253–279.

Börm, Henning, 'Procopius and the East', in Mischa Meier and Federico Montinaro (eds.), *A Companion to Procopius of Caesarea* (Leiden, 2022), pp. 310–336.

Bowes, Kim and Michael Kulikowski (eds.), *Hispania in Late Antiquity: Current Perspectives* (Leiden, 2005).

Bresson, Arnaud, 'Fifty years before the Antonine Constitution', in Lucia Cecchet and Anna Busetto (eds.), *Citizens in the Greco-Roman World. Aspects of the Citizenship from the Archaic Period to AD 212* (Brill, 2017), pp. 199–220.

Brodka, Dariusz, 'Prokopios von Kaisareia und die Abgarlegende', *Eos* 100 (2013), pp. 349–360.

Brogiolo, Gian Piero 'Ideas of the town in Italy during the transition from Antiquity to the Middle Ages', in Gian Piero Brogiolo and Bryan Ward-Perkins (eds.), *The Idea and Ideal of the Town between Late Antiquity and the Early Middle Ages* (Brill, 1999), pp. 99–128.

Brown, Peter, *Augustine of Hippo: A Biography* (Berkeley, 1967).

Brown, Peter, *The Cult of the Saints: Its Rise and Function in Latin Christianity* (Chicago, 1981).

Brown, Peter, *The Making of Late Antiquity* (Cambridge, 1978).

Brown, Peter, *The Rise of Western Christendom: Triumph and Diversity, AD 200 – 1000* (10th ed., Chichester, 2013).

Brown, Peter, *Salvian of Marseilles: Theology and Social Criticism in the Last Century of the Western Empire* (Oxford, 2012).

Brown, Peter, *Society and the Holy in Late Antiquity* (London, 1982).

Brown, Peter, *Through the Eye of a Needle: Wealth, the Fall of Rome, and the Making of Christianity in the West, 350–550 AD* (Princeton, 2012).

Brown, T. S., *Gentlemen and Officers. Imperial Administration and Aristocratic Power in Byzantine Italy AD 554–800* (London, 1984).

Brown, Warren, 'The *gesta municipalia* and the public validation of documents in Frankish Europe', in Matthew Innes, Adam J. Kosto, Warren Brown, and

Marios Costambeys, *Documentary Culture and the Laity in the Early Middle Ages* (Cambridge, 2013), pp. 95–124.

Browning, Robert. 'The riot of AD 387 in Antioch', *Journal of Roman Studies* 42 (1952), pp. 13–20.

Brunt, P. A., *Italian Manpower* (Oxford, 1971).

Buchberger, Erica, *Shifting Ethnic Identities in Spain and Gaul, 500–700: From Romans to Goths and Franks* (Amsterdam, 2017).

Bullough, Donald, *Alcuin: Achievement and Reputation* (Leiden, 2004).

Burns, Ross, *The Origins of the Colonnaded Streets in the Cities of the Roman East* (Oxford, 2017).

Burton, Philip, 'Augustine and language', in Mark Vessey (ed.), *A Companion to Augustine* (Chichester, 2012), pp. 111–124.

Buzzi, Giulio, 'La Curia arcivescovile e la Curia cittadina di Ravenna dall'850 al 1118', *Bullettino dell'Istituto Storico Italiano* 35 (1915), pp. 7–187.

Cabiale, Valentina, 'La lunga durata delle via colonnate nella regione siro-palestinese. Dai Bizantini agli Omayyadi', *Archeologia Medievale* 40 (2013), pp. 321–336.

Caliri, Elena, *Praecellentissimus Rex: Odoacre tra storia e storiografia* (Rome, 2017).

Cameron, Alan, *Circus Factions: Blues and Greens at Rome and Byzantium* (Oxford, 1976).

Cameron, Alan, *Claudian: Poetry and Propaganda at the Court of Honorius* (Oxford, 1970).

Cameron, Alan, 'Junior consuls', *Zeitschrift für Papyrologie und Epigraphik* 56 (1984), pp. 159–172.

Cameron, Averil, *Procopius and the Sixth Century* (London: 1985).

Cameron, Averil, 'Writing about Procopius then and now', in Christopher Lillington-Martin and Elodie Turquois (eds.), *Procopius of Caesarea: Literary and Historical Interpretations* (London, 2018), pp. 13–25.

Campbell, J. B., *The Writings of the Roman Land Surveyors: Introduction, Text, Translation and Commentary* (London, 2000).

Carile, Maria Cristina, 'Production, promotion and reception: The visual culture of Ravenna between late antiquity and the middle ages', in Judith Herrin and Jinty Nelson (eds.), *Ravenna: Its Rome in Earlier Medieval Change and Exchange* (London, 2016), pp. 53–85.

Castagnoli, Ferdinando, *Ippodamo di Mileto e l'urbanistica a pianta ortogonale* (Rome, 1956).

Cecconi, Giovanni Alberto, 'Honorati, possessores, curiales: competenze istituzionali e gerarchie di rango nell'età tardoantica', in Rita Lizzi Testa (ed.), *Le trasformazioni delle élites nell'età tardoantica* (Rome, 2006), pp. 41–64.

Chernin, Liubov, 'Visigothic Jewish converts: A life in between', *Visigothic Symposia* 3 (2018), pp. 1–18.

Chiesa, Paolo (ed.), *Bonvesin de la Riva, De Magnalibus Mediolani. Meraviglie di Milano. Testo critico, traduzione e note* (Milan, 1997).

Chouquer, Gérard and François Favory, *Les arpenteurs romains. Théorie et pratique* (Paris, 1992).
Christie, Neil, 'Ostrogothic Italy: Questioning the archaeologies of settlement', in Hans Ulrich Wiemer (ed.), *Theoderich der Große und das gotische Königreich in Italien* (Munich, 2021), pp. 125–153.
Churchin, L., 'Curials and local government in Visigothic Hispania', *Antiquité Tardive* 26 (2018), pp. 225–240.
Churchin, L., 'The role of civic leaders in late antique Hispania', *Studia historica. Historia antigua* 32 (2014), pp. 281–304.
Churchin, Leonard A. 'Senators or curials? Some debatable *nobiles* in late antique Hispania', *Hispania Antiqua* 37–38 (2013–2014), pp. 129–135.
Clark, Gillian, 'City of Books: Augustine and the World as Texts', in William Klingshirn and Linda Safran (eds.), *The Early Christian Book* (Washington, 2007), pp. 117–138.
Clark, Peter (ed.), *The Oxford Handbook of Cities in World History* (Oxford, 2013).
Classen, Carl Joachim, *Die Stadt im Spiegel der Descriptiones und Laudes Urbium* (Hildesheim, 1980).
Coates, Simon. 'The bishop as benefactor and civic patron: Alcuin, York, and episcopal authority in Anglo-Saxon England', *Speculum* 71 (1996), pp. 529–558.
Codoñer Merino, Carmen, *El "De Viris Illustribus" de Isidoro de Sevilla. Estudio y Edition critica* (Salamanca, 1964).
Collins, Roger, *Visigothic Spain, 407–711* (Oxford, 2006).
Conant, Jonathan, *Staying Roman: Conquest and Identity in Africa and the Mediterranean, 439–700* (Cambridge, 2012).
Conterno, Maria, 'Procopius and non-Chalcedonian Christians: A loud silence?', in Geoffrey Greatrex and Sylvain Janniard (eds.), *Le Monde de Procope/The World of Procopius* (Paris, 2018), pp. 95–111.
Conybeare, Catherine, 'The city of Augustine: On the interpretation of *civitas*', in Carol Harrison, Caroline Humfress, and Isabella Sandwell (eds.), *Being Christian in Late Antiquity. A Festschrift for Gillian Clark* (Oxford, 2014), pp. 139–154.
Cooper, Kate, 'The heroine and the historian: Procopius of Caesarea on the troubled reign of Queen Amalasuentha', in Jonathan Arnold, Shane Bjornlie, and Kristina Sessa (eds.), *A Companion to Ostrogothic Italy* (Leiden, 2016), pp. 296–315.
Córcolez Olaitz, Edorta, 'About the origin of the Formulae Wisigothicae', *Annuario Facultade de Dereito da Universidade de Coruña* 12 (2008), pp. 199–221.
Cormack, Robin, 'Exploring Thessaloniki – A mismatch of art history and urban history', in Liz James, Oliver Nicholson, and Roger Scott (eds.), *After the Text: Byzantine Enquiries in Honour of Margaret Mullett* (London, 2021), pp. 317–327.
Cosentino, Salvatore, 'Social instability and economic decline of the Ostrogothic community in the aftermath of the imperial victory: The papyri evidence', in

Judith Herrin and Jinty Nelson (eds.), *Ravenna: Its Rome in Earlier Medieval Change and Exchange* (London, 2016), pp. 133–149.

Costambeys, Marios, 'The legacy of Theoderic', *Journal of Roman Studies* 106 (2016), pp. 249–263.

Cracco Ruggini, Lellia 'The Italian city from the Third to the Sixth century: "Broken History" or "Ever-changing kaleidoscope"?', in Carole Straw and Richard Lim (eds.), *The Past Before Us: The Challenge of Historiographies of Late Antiquity* (2004), pp. 33–48.

Cracco Ruggini, Lellia and Giorgio Cracco, 'Changing fortunes of the Italian city from late antiquity to the early Middle Ages', *Rivista di Filologia ed Istruzione Classica* 105 (1977), pp. 448–475.

Crawford, Michael H. et al (eds.), *Roman Statutes* (London, 1996).

Cristini, Marco, *La politica esterna dei successori di Teoderico* (Rome, 2023).

Croke, Brian and James Crow, 'Procopius and Dara', *Journal of Roman Studies* 73 (1983), pp. 143–159.

Croke, Brian, 'The search for harmony in Procopius' works', in Mischa Meier and Federico Montinaro (eds.), *A Companion to Procopius of Caesarea* (Leiden, 2022), pp. 28–58.

Crow, James G., 'The long walls of Thrace', in Cyril Mango and Gilbert Dagron (eds.), *Constantinople and Its Hinterland* (Aldershot, 1995), pp. 109–124.

Crow, James, 'Water and late antique Constantinople', in Lucy Grig and Gavin Kelly (eds.), *Two Romes: Rome and Constantinople in Late Antiquity* (Oxford, 2012), pp. 116–135.

Crow, James, Jonathan Bardill, and Richard Bayliss, *The Water Supply of Byzantine Constantinople* (London, 2008).

Crow, James, 'Water for a capital: Hydraulic infrastructure and use in Byzantine Constantinople', in Sarah Bassett (ed.), *The Cambridge Companion to Constantinople* (Cambridge, 2022), pp. 67–86.

Ćurčić, Slobodan, *Architecture in the Balkans from Diocletian to Süleyman the Magnificent* (New Haven, 2010).

D'Arms, John, *Romans on the Bay of Naples* (Cambridge, 1970).

Dagron, Gilbert, *Emperor and Priest: The Imperial Office in Byzantium* (Cambridge, 2003).

Dagron, Gilbert, *Naissance d'une capitale: Constantinople et ses istitutions de 330 à 451* (Paris, 1974).

Dark, K. R., 'Houses, streets and shops in Byzantine Constantinople from the fifth to the twelfth centuries', *Journal of Medieval History* 30 (2004), pp. 83–107.

Dark, Ken and Ferudun Özgümüş, *Constantinople: Archaeology of a Byzantine Megapolis* (Oxford, 2013).

De Aedificiis: le texte de Procope et les réalités, *Antiquité Tardive* vol. 8 (2000).

De Giorgi, Andrea U. and A. Asa Eger, *Antioch. A History* (Abingdon, 2021).

de Ste. Croix, G. E. M., *The Class Struggle in the Ancient Greek World* (London, 1981).

Devecka, Martin, 'White elephant gifts: Classicism in Ostrogothic policy and in Variae 10.30', *Journal of Late Antiquity*, 9 (2016), pp. 195–217.

Dey, Hendrik W., *The Aurelian Wall and the Refashioning of Imperial Rome, AD 271–855* (Cambridge, 2011).

Dey, Hendrik, 'Politics, patronage and the transmission of construction techniques in early Medieval Rome, c. 650–750', *Papers of the British School at Rome* 87 (2019), pp. 177–205.

Dey, Hendrik, *The Afterlife of the Roman City: Architecture and Ceremony in Late Antiquity and the Early Middle Ages* (Cambridge, 2015).

Dey, Hendrick, *The Making of Medieval Rome. A New Profile of the City, 400–1450* (Cambridge, 2021).

Dey, Hendrik and Fabrizio Oppedisano (eds.), *Justinian's Legacy. The Last War of Roman Italy? L'eredità di Giustiniano. L'ultima guerra dell'Italia romana* (Rome, 2024).

Diaz, Pablo C. and M. R. Valverde, 'The theoretical strength and practical weakness of the Visigothic monarchy in Toledo', in Franz Thews and Janet L. Nelson (eds.), *Rituals of Power from Late Antiquity to the Early Middle Ages* (Brill, 2000), pp. 59–94.

Dodaro, Robert, 'Augustine's secular city', in Robert Dodaro and George Lawless (eds.), *Augustine and His Critics* (London, 2000), pp. 231–259.

Dodaro, Robert, *Christ and the Just Society in the Thought of Augustine* (Cambridge, 2004).

Donini, Guido and Gordon B. Ford (trans.), *Isidore of Seville's History of the Kings of the Goths, Vandals, and Suevi* (Leiden, 1996).

Downey, Glanville, *A History of Antioch in Syria from Seleucus to the Arab Conquest* (Princeton, 1961).

Drakoulis, Dimitris P., 'The functional organization of early Byzantine Constantinople, according to the *Notitia Urbis Constantinopolitanae*', in Theodoros Korres et al. (eds.), *Openness. Studies in honour of Vasiliki Papoulia* (Thessaloniki, 2012), pp. 153–183.

Drinkwater, John, 'The Bacaudae of fifth-century Gaul', in John Drinkwater and Hugh Elton (eds.), *Fifth-Century Gaul: A Crisis of Identity?* (1992), pp. 208–217.

Dubouloz, Julien, 'Acception et défense des loca publica, d'après les Variae de Cassiodore. Un point de vue juridique sur les cités d'Italie au VIe siècle', in Massimiliano Ghilardi, Christophe J. Goddard and Pierfrancesco Porena (eds.), *Les cités de l'Italie rado-antique (IVe-VIe siècle). Institutions, économie, société, culture et religion* (Rome, 2006), pp. 53–74.

Dümmler, Ernestus, *Poetae Latini aevi Carolini* (MGH Berlin, 1881).

Dunbabin, Katherine, *The Roman Banquet: Images of Conviviality* (Cambridge, 2003).

Duplouy, Alain, 'Citizenship as performance', in Alain Duplouy and Roger Brock (eds.), *Defining Citizenship in Archaic Greece* (Oxford, 2018), pp. 249–274.

Durliat, Jean, *Les Finances publiques de Dioclétien aux Carolingiens (284–888)* (Sigmaringen, 1990).

Durliat, Jean, 'Episcopus, civis et populus dans les Historiarum Libri de Grégoire', in Nancy Gautier and Henri Galinié (eds.), *Grégoire de Tours et l'espace gaulois* (Tours, 1997), pp. 185–193.

Durliat, Jean, 'L'approvisionnement de Constantinople', in Cyril Mango and Gilbert Dagron (eds.), *Constantinople and Its Hinterland* (Aldershot, 1995), pp. 19–33.

Durliat, Jean, *De la ville antique à la ville byzantine: Le problème des subsistances* (Rome, 1990).

Duval, Noël and Vladislav P opović (eds.), *Caričin Grad*, 3 vols (Rome, 2010).

Edwards, Catharine, *Writing Rome: Textual Approaches to the City* (Cambridge, 1996).

Effros, Bonnie, 'The enduring attraction of the Pirenne thesis', *Speculum* 92 (2017), pp. 184–208.

Effros, Bonnie and Isabel Moreira (eds.), *The Oxford Handbook of the Merovingian World* (Oxford, 2020).

Elfassi, Jacques, 'Connaître la bibliothèque pour connaître les sources: Isidore de Séville', in *Isidore de Séville et son temps* (*Antiquité Tardive* 23, 2015), pp. 59–66.

Elfassi, Jacques, 'Isidore of Seville and the Etymologies', Andrew Fear and Jamie Wood (eds.), *A Companion to Isidore of Seville* (Leiden, 2020), pp. 245–278.

Elm, Susanna, 'Salvian of Marseilles *On the Governance of God*', *Journal of Early Christian Studies* 25.1 (2017), pp. 1–28.

Elsner, Jaś, 'The rhetoric of buildings in the *De Aedificiis* of Procopius', in Liz James (ed.), *Art and Text in Byzantine Culture* (Cambridge, 2007), pp. 33–57.

Ennahid, Said, 'Access regulation in Islamic urbanism: The case of medieval Fès', *Journal of North African Studies* 7 (2002), pp. 119–134.

Ennahid, Said, 'Searching for Rome: French colonial archaeology and urban planning in Morocco', in Sofia Greaves and Andrew Wallace-Hadrill (eds.), *Rome and the Colonial City. Rethinking the Grid* (Oxford, 2022), pp. 367–388.

Ernout, A. and A. Meillet, *Dictionnaire etymologique de la langue latine: histoire des mots* (3rd ed., Paris, 1951).

Everett, Nicholas, 'Lay documents and archives in early medieval Spain and Italy, c. 400-700', in Matthew Innes, Adam J. Kosto, Warren Brown, and Marios Costambeys (eds.), *Documentary Culture and the Laity in the Early Middle Ages* (Cambridge, 2013), pp. 63–94.

Ewald, Paulus and Ludovicus M. Hartmann (eds.), *Pope Gregory, Registrum Epistolarum* (MGH Berlin, 1857).

Fabbro, Eduardo, *Warfare and the Making of Early Medieval Italy (568-652)* (London, 2021).

Fanning, S., 'Clovis Augustus and Merovingian Imitatio Imperii', in Kathleen Mitchell and Ian Wood (eds.), *The World of Gregory of Tours* (Leiden, 2002), pp. 321–335.

Fasoli, Gina and Francesca Bocchi, *La città medievale italiana* (Florence, 1973).

Fasoli, Gina, 'La coscienza civica nelle "*Laudes Civitatum*", in *Scritti di storia medievale*, ed. F. Bocchi, A. Carile, and A. I. Pini (Bologna, 1974), pp. 42–74.

Fauvinet-Ranson, Valérie, *Decor civitatis, decor Italiae: monument, travaux publics et spectacles au VIe siècle d'apres les Variae de Cassiodore* (Bari, 2006).

Fauvinet-Ranson, Valérie, 'Les valeurs idéologiques de la parure monumentaldes cités en Italie chez Cassiodore', in Hervé Ingelbert (ed.), *Idéologies et valeurs civiques dans le monde romain. Hommages à Claude Lepelley* (Nanterre, 2000), pp. 231–240.

Fear, Andrew T., *Orosius Seven Books of History against the Pagans* (Liverpool, 2010).

Fear, Andrew (trans.), *Lives of the Visigothic Fathers* (Liverpool, 1997).

Fear, Andrew and Jamie Wood (eds.), *A Companion to Isidore of Seville* (Leiden, 2020).

Fear, Andrew and Jamie Wood (eds.), *Isidore of Seville and His Reception in the Early Middle Ages: Transmitting and Transforming Knowledge* (Amsterdam, 2016).

Fear, Andrew, 'Isidore of Seville on law and kingship', Andrew Fear and Jamie Wood (eds.), *A Companion to Isidore of Seville* (Leiden, 2020), pp. 332–358.

Fear, Andrew, 'Putting the pieces back together: Isidore and De Natura Rerum', in *Isidore of Sevilla and His Reception*, pp. 75–92 (Amsterdam, 2016).

Fenwick, Corisande, 'From Africa to Ifrīqiya: Settlement and society in early medieval North Africa (650–800), *Al-Masāq* 25 (2013), pp. 9–33.

Fernández, D., *Aristocrats and Statehood in Western Iberia, 300–600 CE* (Philadelphia, 2017).

Filippi, Dunia (ed.), *Rethinking the Roman City. The Spatial Turn and the Archaeology of Roman Italy* (London, 2022).

Finley, Moses I. 'The ancient city', in Brent D. Shaw and Richard P. Saller (eds.), *Economy and Society in Ancient Greece* (London, 1981), pp. 3–23, reprinted from *Comparative Studies in Society and History* 19 (1977), pp. 305–327.

Finster, Barbara, 'Researches in ʿAnjar: I. Preliminary report on the architecture of ʿAnjar', *Bulletin d'Archéologie et d'Architecture Libanaises* 7 (2003), pp. 209–244.

Flierman, Robert and Els Rose, 'Banished from the company of the good: Christians and aliens in fifth-century Rome', in J. Martínez Jiménez and S. Ottewell-Soulsby (eds.), *Cities and Citizenship after Rome. Al-Masaq special edition* (2020), pp. 64–86.

Folin, Marco and Monica Preti, *Wounded Cities: The Representation of Urban Disasters in European Art (14th to 20th centuries)* (Brill, 2015).

Fontaine, Jacques and P. Cazier, 'Qui a chassé de Carthaginoise Sévérianus et les siens. Observations sur l'histoire familiale d'Isidore de Séville', reprinted in *Fontaine's Tradition et actualité chez Isidore de Séville* (London, 1988), I pp. 349–400.

Fontaine, Jacques, *Isidore de Séville et la culture classique dans l'Espagne wisigothique*, 2 vols (Paris, 1959).

Fontaine, Jacques, *Isidore de Séville: traité de la nature* (Paris, 1960).

Fontaine, Jacques, *Tradition et actualité chez Isidore de Séville* (London, 1988).

Ford Jr., G. B., *The Letters of St. Isidore of Seville* (Amsterdam, 1970).

Foss, Clive, *Ephesus after Antiquity: A late Antique, Byzantine and Turkish city* (Cambridge, 1979).

Fowden, Elizabeth Key, *The Barbarian Plain: Saint Sergius between Rome and Iran* (University of California Press, 1999).

Fowden, Elizabeth K., Suna Çağaptay, Edward Zychowicz-Coghill and Louise Blanke (eds.), *Cities as Palimpsests: Responses to Antiquity in Eastern Mediterranean Urbanism (Impact of the Ancient City, vol. 1)* (Oxford, 2022).

Fowden, Garth, 'Gibbon and Islam', *English Historical Review* 131 (2016), pp. 261–292.

Fowler, Don, 'The Virgil commentary of Servius', in Charles Martindale (eds.), *The Cambridge Companion to Virgil* (Cambridge, 1997), pp. 73–78.

Freely, John and Ahmet S. Çakmak, *Byzantine Monuments of Istanbul* (Cambridge, 2004).

Freeman, P. W. M., *The Best Training Ground for Archaeologist. Francis Haverfield and the Invention of Romano-British Archaeology* (Oxford, 2007).

Frezza, Paolo, *L'influsso del diritto romano giustinianeo nelle formule e nello prassi in Italia (Ius Romanum Medii Aevi* pt.1.2, c, ee: Milan, 1974).

Frugoni, Chiara, *A Distant City: Images of Urban Experience in the Medieval World*, translated by W. McCuaig (Princeton, 1991).

Fustel de Coulanges, Numa Denis, *The Ancient City: A Study on the Religion, Laws, and Institutions of Greece and Rome*; with a new foreword by Arnaldo Momigliano and S. C. Humphreys (Baltimore, 1980).

Gantner, Clemens and Pohl, Walter (eds.). *After Charlemagne: Carolingian Italy and Its Rulers* (Cambridge, 2020).

Gardner, Jane, *Being a Roman Citizen* (London, 1993).

Garipzanov, Ildar H., 'The coinage of Tours in the Merovingian period', *Revue Belge de Numismatique* 147 (2001), pp. 79–118.

Garzya, Antonio, 'Cassiodoro e la grecità', in *Flavio Magno Aurelio Cassiodoro. Atti della settimana di studi, Cosenza-Squillace 19–24 settembre 1983* (Catanzaro, 1986), pp. 118–134.

Gaul, Niels, 'Schools and learning', in Sarah Bassett (eds.), *The Cambridge Companion to Constantinople* (Cambridge, 2022), pp. 263–276.

Gautier, Nancy and Henri Galinié (eds.), *Grégoire de Tours et l'espace gaulois* (Tours, 1997).

Genequand, Denis, *Les établissements des élites omeyyades en Palmyrène et au Proche-Orient* (Beyrouth, 2012).

George, Judith W., *Venantius Fortunatus. A Poet in Merovingian Gaul* (Oxford, 1992).

Gheller, Viola, *"Identità" e "arianesimo gotico": genesi di un topos storiografico'* (Bologna, 2017).

Giardina, Andrea, Giovanni Alberto Cecconi, Ignazio Tantillo, and Fabrizio Oppedisano (eds.), *Flavio Magno Aurelio Cassiodoro Senatore, Varie* (Rome) vol. II (2014), vol. III (2015), vol. IV (2016), vol. V (2015); vols I and VI (forthcoming).

Giardina, Andrea, *Cassiodoro politico* (Rome, 2006).

Gibbon, Edward, *The History of the Decline and Fall of the Roman Empire*, ed. J. B. Bury, 7 vols (London, 1896-1900).

Gibbon, Edward, *Memoirs of my Life and Writings, Illustrated from his Letters, with Occasional Notes and Narrative, by John, Lord Sheffield* (London, 1837).

Gilliard, Frank, 'The senators of sixth-century Gaul', *Speculum* 54 (1979), pp. 685-697.

Glinister, Fay and Clare Woods (eds.), *Verrius, Festus, & Paul: Lexicography, Scholarship, and Society* (BICS Supplement 93, London, 2007).

Godman, Peter, *Poets and Emperors. Frankish Politics and Carolingian Poetry* (Oxford, 1987).

Godman, Peter, *The Poetry of the Carolingian Renaissance* (London, 1985).

Goffart, Walter, 'From Roman taxation to medieval seigneurie: Three notes (Part II)', *Speculum* 47 (1972), pp. 373-394.

Goffart, 'Walter, 'Old and new in Merovingian taxation', *Past and Present* 96 (1982), pp. 3-21.

Goffart, Walter, *Barbarians and Romans AD 418-584: The Techniques of Accommodation* (Princeton, 1980).

Goffart, Walter, *The Narrators of Barbarian History (AD 550-800)* (2nd ed., Notre Dame, 2005).

Golitz, Andreas, 'Anspruch und Wirklichkeit–Überlegungen zu Prokops Darstellung ostgotischer Herrscher und Herscherinnen', in Geoffrey Greatrex, and Sylvain Janniard (eds.), *Le Monde de Procope/The World of Procopius* (Paris, 2018), pp. 285-310.

Gómez de la Torre-Verdejo, Amaya, 'La muralla de Récopolis', in Lauro Olmo Enciso, *Recópolis y la ciudad en la epoca visigoda* (Alcalá, 2008), pp. 76-86.

Goodchild, R. G., 'Boreum of Cyrenaica', *Journal of Roman Studies* 41 (1951), pp. 11-16.

Goodson, Caroline, 'Urbanism as politics in ninth-century Italy', in C. Gantner (ed.), *After Charlemagne: Carolingian Italy and Its Rulers* (Cambridge, 2020), pp. 198-218.

Granier, Thomas, 'La *renovatio* du modèle rhétorique antique dans les éloges urbains de l'Italie du haut Moyen Âge', in Michel Balard and Michel Sot (eds.), *Au Moyen Âge entre tradition antique et innovation* (Paris, 2009), pp. 35-56.

Gray, Ben, *Stasis and Stability: Exile, the Polis, and Political Thought, c. 404-146 BC* (Oxford, 2015).

Gray, Cam, 'Salvian, the ideal Christian community and the fate of the poor in fifth-century Gaul', in Margaret Atkins and Robin Osborne (eds.), *Poverty in the Roman World* (Cambridge, 2006), pp. 162-182.

Greatrex, Geoffrey (ed.), *The Chronicle of Pseudo-Zachariah Rhetor* (Liverpool, 2011).

Greatrex, Geoffrey and Hugh Elton (eds.), *Shifting Genres in Late Antiquity* (Farnham, 2015).

Greatrex, Geoffrey and Sylvain Janniard (eds.), *Le Monde de Procope/The World of Procopius* (Paris, 2018).

Greatrex, Geoffrey, 'Lawyers and historians in Late Antiquity', in Ralph W. Mathisen (ed.), *Law, Society and Authority in Late Antiquity* (Oxford, 2001), pp. 148–161.

Greatrex, Geoffrey, 'L'historien Procope et la vie à Césarée au VIe siècle', in Geoffrey Greatrex and Sylvain Janniard (eds.), *Le Monde de Procope/The World of Procopius* (Paris, 2018), pp. 15–38.

Greatrex, Geoffrey, 'Perceptions of Procopius in recent scholarship', *Histos* 8 (2014), pp. 76–121.

Greatrex, Geoffrey, 'Procopius' attitude towards barbarians', in Geoffrey Greatrex and Sylvain Janniard (eds.), *Le Monde de Procope/The World of Procopius* (Paris, 2018), pp. 327–354.

Greatrex, Geoffrey, 'The date of Procopius' *Buildings* in the light of recent scholarship', *Estudios bizantinos* 1 (2013), pp. 13–29.

Greatrex, Geoffrey, 'The dates of Procopius' works', *Byzantine and Modern Greek Studies* 18 (1994), pp. 101–114.

Greatrex, Geoffrey, 'Procopius: Life and works', in Mischa Meier and Federico Montinaro (eds.), *A Companion to Procopius of Caesarea* (Leiden, 2022), pp. 61–69.

Greaves, Sofia, 'Ildefonso Cerdà and the Eixample grid plan', in Sofia Greaves and Andrew Wallace-Hadrill (eds.), *Rome and the Colonial City: Rethinking the Grid* (Oxford, 2022), pp. 327–352.

Greaves, Sofia, 'Roman planning as a model for urban modernity in Liberal Naples', in Javier Martínez Jiménez and Sam Ottewill Souslby (eds.), *Remembering and Forgetting the Ancient City* (Oxford, 2022), pp. 137–164.

Greaves, Sofia and Andrew Wallace-Hadrill, 'Introduction: Decolonising the Roman grid', in Sofia Greaves and Andrew Wallace-Hadrill (eds.), *Rome and the Colonial City: Rethinking the Grid* (Oxford, 2022), pp. 1–24.

Greaves, Sofia and Andrew Wallace-Hadrill (eds.), *Rome and the Colonial City. Rethinking the Grid* (Oxford, 2022).

Green, R. P. H., *The Works of Ausonius*, edited with introduction and commentary (Oxford, 1991).

Grig, Lucy, 'Cities in the "long" Late Antiquity, 2000–2012 – a survey essay', *Urban History* 40 (2012), pp. 554–566.

Grig, Lucy, 'Competing capitals, competing representations', in Lucy Grig and Gavin Kelly (eds.), *Two Romes: Rome and Constantinople in Late Antiquity* (Oxford, 2012), pp. 31–53.

Grig, Lucy and Gavin Kelly (eds.), *Two Romes: Rome and Constantinople in Late Antiquity* (Oxford, 2012).

Guillaumin, Jean-Yves and Pierre Monat, *Isidore de Séville, Étymologies, Livre XV, Les constructions et les terres* (Paris, 2016).

Gussone, Martin and Dorothée Sack, 'Resafa/Syrien. Städtebauliche Entwicklung zwischen Kultort und Herrschaft', in Efthymios Rizos (ed.), *New Cities in Late Antiquity. Documents and Archaeology* (Turnhout, 2017), pp. 117–136.

Gustafson, Mark, 'Condemnation to the Mines in the Later Roman Empire', *Harvard Theological Review* 87 (1994), pp. 421–433.

Hagendahl, Harald, *Augustine and the Latin Classics* (Göteborg, 1967).

Haldon, John and Arlene Rosen, 'Society and environment in the East Mediterranean ca 300–1800 CE. Problems of resilience, adaptation and transformation. Introductory essay', *Human Ecology* 46 (2018), pp. 275–290.

Haldon, John, Merle Eisenberg, Lee Mordechai, Adam Izdebski, and Sam White, 'Lessons from the past, policies for the future: Resilience and sustainability in past crises', *Environment Systems and Decisions* 40 (2020), pp. 287–297.

Halporn, James W. and Mark Vessey, *Cassiodorus. Institutions of Divine and Secular Learning* (Liverpool, 2004).

Halsall, G., 'The technique of Barbarian settlement in the fifth century', *Journal of Late Antiquity* 3 (2010), pp. 99–112.

Halton, Thomas P., *The Fathers of the Church. Jerome, On Illustrious Men* (Catholic University of America Press, 1999).

Hammer, William. 'The Concept of the New or Second Rome in the Middle Ages', *Speculum*, 19, (1944), pp. 50–62.

Harries, Jill, 'Church and state in the Notitia Galliarum', *Journal of Roman Studies* 68 (1978), pp. 26–43.

Harries, Jill, *Sidonius Apollinaris and the Fall of Rome, AD 407–485* (Oxford, 1994).

Hastaoglou-Martinidis, Vilna, 'City form and national identity: Urban designs in nineteenth-century Greece', *Journal of Modern Greek Studies* 13 (1995), pp. 99–123.

Haverfield, Francis, 'An Inaugural Address Delivered before the First Annual General Meeting of the Society, 11th May, 1911', *Journal Of Roman Studies* 1 (1911), pp. xi–xx.

Haverfield, Francis, 'Town planning in the Roman world', in *Transactions of the RIBA Town Planning Conference* (London, 1911), pp. 122–133.

Haverfield, Francis, *Ancient Town-Planning* (Oxford, 1913).

Heather, Peter, 'Merely an ideology? Gothic identity in Ostrogothic Italy', in S. J. Barnish and F. Marazzi (eds.), *The Ostrogoths from the Migration Period to the Sixth Century: An Ethnographic Perspective* (Woodbridge, 2007), pp. 31–79.

Heather, Peter, 'A tale of two cities: Rome and Ravenna under Gothic rule', in Judith Herrin and Jinty Nelson (eds.), *Ravenna: Its Rome in Earlier Medieval Change and Exchange* (London, 2016), pp. 19–37.

Heather, Peter, *The Fall of the Roman Empire: A New History of Rome and the Barbarians* (Oxford, 2005).

Heinzelmann, Martin, *Bischofsherrschaft in Gallien: zur Kontinuität römischer Führungsschichten vom 4. bis zum 7. Jahrhundert: soziale, prosopographische und bildungsgeschichtliche Aspekte* (Munich, 1976).

Heinzelmann, Martin, *Gregory of Tours. History and Society in the Sixth Century* (Eng. translation by Christopher Carroll, (Cambridge, 2001).

Henderson, John, *The Medieval World of Isidore of Seville: Truth from Words* (Cambridge, 2007).

Henning, J. et al., 'Reccopolis revealed: First geomagnetic mapping of the early medieval Visigothic royal town,' *Antiquity* 93 (2019), pp. 735–751.

Herdt, Jennifer, 'The theatre of the virtues: Augustine's critique of pagan mimesis', in James Wetzel (ed.), *Augustine's City of God: A Critical Guide* (Cambridge, 2012), pp. 111–129.

Hermanowicz, Erika T., 'Possidius on Augustine', in Tarmo Toom (ed.), *Augustine in Context* (Cambridge, 2017), pp. 30–36.

Herrin, Judith and Jinty Nelson (eds.), *Ravenna: Its Rome in Earlier Medieval Change and Exchange* (London, 2016).

Herrin, Judith, *Ravenna. Capital of Empire, Crucible of Europe* (Penguin, 2020).

Hillenbrand, Robert, "Anjar and early Islamic urbanism', in Gian Pietro Brogiolo and Bryan Ward-Perkins (eds.), *The Idea and Ideal of the Town in Late Antiquity and the Early Middle Ages* (Leiden, 1999), pp. 59–98.

Hingley, R., *Roman Officers and Gentlemen: The Imperial Origins of Roman Archaeology* (London, 2000).

Hodges, Richard and David Whitehead (eds.), *Mohammed, Charlemagne & the Origins of Europe: Archaeology and the Pirenne Thesis* (London, 1983).

Hodges, Richard, *Visions of Rome: Thomas Ashby, Archaeologist* (London, 2000).

Hodgkin, Thomas, *Italy and her Invaders 476–535* 8 vols., 2nd ed. (Oxford, 1892–1899).

Holder-Egger, O., *Ex sermone in tumulatio e SS Quintini, Victorici, Cassiani, MGH ss* 15 (Hanover, 1888).

Holling, C. S., 'Resilience and stability of ecological systems', *Annual Review of Ecology and Systematics* 4 (1973), pp. 1–23.

Holling, C. S. and Lance H. Gunderson, 'Resilience and Adaptive Cycles', in Lance H. Gunderson and C. S. Holling (eds.), *Panarchy: Understanding Transformations in Human and Natural Systems* (Washington, DC, 2002), pp. 25–62.

Homo, L., *Rome impériale et l'urbanisme dans l'antiquité* (Paris, 1951).

Honoré, Tony, *Tribonian* (London, 1978).

Hopkins, Keith, *Death and Renewal. Sociological Studies in Roman History*, volume 2 (Cambridge, 1983).

Howard-Johnston, James, 'The education and expertise of Procopius', *Antiquité Tardive* 8 (2000), pp. 19–30.

Humfress, Caroline, 'Citizens and heretics. Late Roman lawyers on Christian heresy', in E. Iricinschi and H. Zellentin (eds.), *Heresy and Identity in Late Antiquity* (Tübingen, 2008), pp. 128–142.

Humfress, Caroline, *Orthodoxy and the Courts in Late Antiquity* (Oxford, 2007).

Humphries, Mark 'The rhetorical construction of a Christian Empire in the Theodosian Code', in R. Flower and M. Ludlow (eds.), *Rhetoric and Religious Identity in Late Antiquity* (Oxford, 2020), pp. 145–159.

Humphries, Mark, *Cities and Meanings in Late Antiquity*, Ancient History 2.4 (2019), pp. 1–112.

Hyde, J. K. 'Medieval descriptions of cities, *Bulletin of the John Rylands Library* 48 (1965–66), pp. 308–340.

Indelli, Tommaso, *Odoacre. La fine di un impero (476 d.C.)* (ViVa Liber, 2014).

Isidore de Séville et son temps (Antiquité Tardive 23, 2015), pp. 43–268.

Ivanišević, Vujadin, 'Main patterns of urbanism in Caričin Grad (Justiniana Prima)', in Efthymios Rizos (ed.), *New Cities in Late Antiquity. Documents and Archaeology* (Turnhout, 2017), pp. 221–232.

Jacobs, Ine, *Aesthetic Maintenance of Civic Space. The 'Classical' City from the 4th to the 7th c. AD* (Leuven, 2013).

Jacobs, Ine, 'Encroachment in the Eastern Mediterranean between the fourth and seventh century AD', *Ancient Society* 39 (2009), pp. 203–243.

Jacobs, Ine, 'Late Antique encroachment in the City centres of Asia Minor. Economic bustle and socio-political significance', in Rudolf Haensch and Philipp von Rummel (eds.), *Himmelwärts und erdverbunden? Religiöse und wirtschaftliche Aspekte spätantiker Lebensrealität* (Berlin, 2021), pp. 87–100.

Jäggi, Carola, *Ravenna: Kunst und Kultur einer spätantiken Residenzstadt: die Bauten und Mosaiken des 5. und 6. Jahrhunderts* (Regensburg, 2013).

James, Edward (trans.), *Gregory of Tours: Life of the Fathers* (2nd ed. Liverpool, 1991).

Janin, Raymond, *Constantinople Byzantine. Développement urbain et répertoire topographique*, 2nd ed. (Paris, 1964).

Janvier, Yves *La legislation du Bas-Empire Romain sur les édifices publiques* (Aix-en-Provence, 1969).

Jeffreys, Elizabeth, Michael Jeffreys, Roger Scott, et al. *The Chronicle of John Malalas: A Translation* (Melbourne, 1986).

Johnson, Mark, 'Towards a history of Theoderic's building program', *Dumbarton Oaks Papers* 42 (1988), pp. 73–96.

Jones, A. H. M., *The Cities of the Eastern Roman Empire* (Oxford, 1937).

Jones, A. H. M., *The Greek City from Alexander to Justinian* (Oxford, 1939).

Jones, A. H. M., *The Later Roman Empire 284–602: A Social Economic and Administrative Survey* (Oxford, 1973).

Jones, Philip, *The Italian City-State: From Commune to Signoria* (Oxford, 1999).

Jordanes, *Romana and Getica*; translated with an introduction and notes by Peter Van Nuffelen and Lieve Van Hoof (Liverpool, 2020).

Kaiser, Alan, *Roman Street Networks* (New York, 2011).

Kaldellis, Anthony, 'From Rome to New Rome, from empire to nation-state', in Lucy Grig and Gavin Kelly (eds.), *Two Romes: Rome and Constantinople in Late Antiquity* (Oxford, 2012), pp. 387–403.

Kaldellis, Anthony, 'The Forum of Constantine in Constantinople: What do we know about its original architecture and adornment?' *Greek, Roman, and Byzantine Studies* 56 (2016), pp. 714–739.

Kaldellis, Anthony, *Procopius of Caesarea: Tyranny, History, and Philosophy at the End of Antiquity* (Philadelphia, 2004).

Kaldellis, Anthony, *Prokopios: The Secret History with Related Texts* (Indianapolis, 2010).

Kaldellis, Anthony, *Romanland: Ethnicity and Empire in Byzantium* (Cambridge, 2019).

Kaster, Robert, *Suetonius De Grammaticis et Rhetoribus*, edited with a translation, introduction and commentary (Oxford, 1995).

Kelly, Christopher, 'Political history: The later Roman Empire', in Mark Vessey (ed.), *A Companion to Augustine* (Chichester, 2012), pp. 11–23.

Kendall, Calvin B and Faith Wallis, *Isidore of Seville: On the Nature of Things*, translated with introduction, notes, and commentary (Liverpool, 2016).

Keser-Kayaalp, Elif and Nihat Erdoğan, 'Recent research on Dara/Anastasiopolis', in Efthymios Rizos (ed.), *New Cities in Late Antiquity. Documents and Archaeology* (Turnhout, 2017), pp. 153–175.

King, P. D., *Law and Society in the Visigothic Kingdom* (Cambridge, 1972).

Klingshirn, William E., 'Cultural geography: Roman North Africa', in Mark Vessey (ed.), *A Companion to Augustine* (Chichester, 2012), pp. 24–39.

Koumaridis, Yorgos, 'Urban transformation and de-Ottomanization in Greece', *East Central Europe* 33 (2006), pp. 213–241.

Krischen, Fritz, *Die Landmauer von Konstantinopel* (Berlin, 1938).

Krusch, Bruno (ed.), *Gregori Episcopi Turonensis Miracula et opera minora*, MGH Scriptores Rerum Merovingicarum I, 2 (Hannover, 1885).

Kruse, Marion, 'Justinian's laws and Procopius' *Wars*', in Christopher Lillington-Martin and Elodie Turquois (eds.), *Procopius of Caesarea: Literary and Historical Interpretations* (London, 2018), pp. 186–200.

Kulikowski, Michael, *Late Roman Spain and Its Cities* (Baltimore, 2004).

Kurt, Andrew, *Minting, State, and Economy in the Visigothic Kingdom* (Amsterdam, 2020).

Kurth, Godefroid, 'Grégoire de Tours et les études classiques au VIe siècle', in his *Études Franques* (Paris, 1919), vol. 1, pp. 1–29.

Kurth, Godefroid, 'Les sénateurs en Gaule au VIe siècle', in his *Études franques* vol. 2 (Paris, 1919), pp. 97–115.

La Rocca, Adolfo and Fabrizio Oppedisano, *Il senato romano nell'Italia ostrogota* (Rome, 2016).

La Rocca, Cristina, '*Mores tuos fabricatae loquunturI* building activity and the rhetoric of power in Ostrogothic Italy', *The Hoskins Society Journal* 26 (2014), pp. 1–13.

La Rocca, Cristina, 'Una prudente maschera "antiqua": La politica edilizia di Teoderico', in *Tederico il Grande e i Goti d'Italia* (Spoleto, 1993), pp. 451–515.

La Rocca, Cristina, 'An arena of abuses and competing powers: Rome in Cassiodorus' *Variae*', in Ross Balzaretti, Julia Barrow, and Patricia Skinner (eds.), *Italy and Early Medieval Europe: Papers for Chris Wickham* (Oxford, 2018), pp. 201–212.

La Rocca, Cristina, 'Urban change in Northern Italy', in J. Rich (ed.), *The City in Late Antiquity* (London, 1992), pp. 161–180.

La Rocca, Cristina, 'Cassiodoro, Teodato e il restauro degli elefanti di bronzo della Via Sacra', *Reti medievali rivista*, 11 (2010), pp. 25–44.

La Rocca, Eugenio, 'L'affresco con veduta di città dal Colle Oppio', in Elizabeth Fentress (ed.), *Romanization and the City: Creation, Transformations, and Failures* (Portsmouth, 2000), pp. 57–72.

Lafferty, Sean D. W., *Law and Society in the Age of Theoderic the Great: A Study of the Edictum Theoderici* (Cambridge, 2013).

Lambert, David, 'Uses of decay: History in Salvian's *De gubernatione Dei*', *Augustinian Studies* 30:2 (1999), pp. 115–130.

Lauffray, Jean, *Halabiyya-Zénobia: Place forte du limes oriental et la haute Mésopotamie au VIe siècle* (vol. 1, Paris, 1983, vol. 2 Paris, 1991).

Lavan, Luke, 'A. H. M. Jones and "the cities" 1964–2004', in *A. H. M. Jones and the Later Roman Empire* (Leiden, 2008), pp. 167–191.

Lavan, Luke, 'The late-antique city: A bibliographic essay', in Luke Lavan (ed.), *Recent Research on Late-Antique Urbanism* (*Journal of Roman Archaeology* Supp.), 42 (2001), pp. 9–26.

Lavan, Luke, *Public Space in the late Antique City* (Leiden, 2020).

Lavan, Luke (ed.), 'Recent Research on Late-Antique Urbanism', *Journal of Roman Archaeology*, Suppl. 42, (2002).

Lavan, Myles, 'The spread of Roman citizenship, 14–212 CE: Quantification in the face of high uncertainty', *Past & Present* 230 (2016), pp. 3–46.

Lazard, Sylvanie, 'Goti e Latini in Ravenna', in A. Caville (ed.), *Storia di Ravenna* II/1 (1991), pp. 109–143.

Le Roux, Patrick, 'L'amour patriae dans les cités de l'empire romain', in H. Ingelbert (ed.), *Idéologies et valeurs civiques dans le monde romain. Hommages à C. Lepelley* (Paris, 2002), pp. 143–161 (reprinted in *La toge et les armes. Rome entre Méditerranée et Océan* (Rennes, 2011), pp. 565–581.

Leal, Bea, "Anjar: An Umayyad image of urbanism and its afterlife', in John Mitchell, John Moreland, and Bea Leal (eds.), *Encounters, Excavations and Argosies. Essays for Richard Hodges* (Oxford, 2017), pp. 172–189.

Lefebvre, Henri, *La production de l'espace* (Paris, 1974).

Lenski, Noel, *Constantine and the Cities: Imperial Authority and City Politics* (Philadelphia, 2016).

Lenski, Noel, 'Two Sieges of Amida (AD 359 and 502–503) and the Experience of Combat in the Late Roman Near East', in Ariel S. Lewin and Pietrina Pellegrini (eds.), *The Late Roman Army in the Near East from Diocletian to the Arab Conquest* (Oxford, 2007), pp. 219–236.

Leo, Friedrich, *Venanti Honori Clementiani Fortunati Presbyteri Italici Opera Poetica, MGH Auctores Antiquissimi* 4, 1: (Berlin, 1881).

Lepelley, Claude, 'La survie de l'idée de cité républicaine en Italie au début di VIe siècle, dans un édit d'Athalaric rédigé par Cassiodore (Variae, IX,2), in Claude Lepelley (ed.), *La fin de la cité antique et le débutde la cité médiéval: de la fin di IIIe siècle à l'avènement de Charlemagne* (Bari, 1996), pp. 71–84.

Lepelley, Claude, 'Un éloge nostalgique de la cité classique dans les *Variaei de Cassiodore*', in Claude Lepelley, Michel Sot, and Pierre Riché (eds.), *Haut Moyen-Age: Culture, éducation et société* (Nanterre, 1990), pp. 33–47.

Lepelley, Claude, *Les Cités de l'Afrique romaine au Bas-Empire*, 2 vols (Paris, 1979, 1981).

Liebeschuetz, J. H. W. G., *Antioch: City and imperial administration in the later Roman Empire* (Oxford, 1972).

Liebeschuetz, J. H. W. G., *The Decline and Fall of the Roman City* (Oxford, 2001).

Liebeschuetz, J. H. W. G., 'Goths and Romans in the leges Visigothorum', in Gerda de Kleijn and Stéphane Benoist (eds.), *Integration in Rome and in the Roman World: Proceedings of the Tenth Workshop of the International Network Impact of Empire (Lille, June 23–25, 2011)* (Leiden, 2014) pp. 89–104.

Liebeschuetz, J.H.W.G, 'Making a Gothic history: Does the *Getica* of Jordanes preserve genuinely Gothic traditions?', *Journal of Late Antiquity* 4 (2011), pp. 185–216.

Lilley, Keith, *City and Cosmos: The Medieval World in Urban Form* (London, 2009).

Lillington-Martin, Christopher and Elodie Turquois (eds.), *Procopius of Caesarea: Literary and Historical Interpretations* (London, 2018).

Lim, Richard, 'Augustine and Roman public spectacles', in Mark Vessey (ed.), *A Companion to Augustine* (Chichester, 2012), pp. 138–150.

Liverani, Mario, 'Power and citizenship', in Peter Clark (ed.), *The Oxford Handbook of Cities in World History* (2013), pp. 164–180.

Loseby, Simon T., 'Lost Cities. The End of the Civitas-System in Frankish Gaul', in S. Diefenbach and G. M. Müller (eds.), *Gallien in Spätantike und Frühmittelalter. Kulturgeschichte einer Region* (Berlin, 2013), pp. 223–252.

Loseby, Simon T., 'Decline and Change in the Cities of Late Antique Gaul', in Jens-Uwe Krause and Christian Witschel (eds.), *Die Stadt in der Spätantike – Niedergang oder Wandel? Historia Einzelschriften* 190, Stuttgart, 2006), pp. 67–104.

Loseby, Simon T., 'Gregory's cities: Urban functions in sixth-century Gaul', in Ian Wood (ed.), *Franks and Alamanni in the Merovingian Period: An Ethnographic Perspective* (Woodbridge, 1998), pp. 239–270.

Loseby, Simon T., 'Marseille and the Pirenne thesis, i: Gregory of Tours, the Merovingian Kings, and "un grand port"', in Richard Hodges and William Bowden (eds.), *The Sixth Century: Production, Distribution and Demand (Transformation of the Roman World*, vol. 3) (Leiden, 1998), pp. 203–229.

Loseby, Simon T., 'The role of the city in Merovingian Francia', in Bonnie Effros and Isabel Moreira (eds.), *The Oxford Handbook of the Merovingian World* (Oxford, 2020), pp. 583–610.

Loseby, Simon, *Marseille in Late Antiquity and the Early Middle Ages* (Oxford, 1993).

Loseby, Simon T., 'Reflections on urban space: Streets through time', review article on *Le trasformazioni dello spazio urbano nell'alto medio-evo (secoli V–VIII). Città mediterranee a confronto, reti Medievali Rivista* 11 (2010), p. 2.

Lot, Ferdinand, *Le Fin du monde antique et le début du moyen âge* (Paris, 1st ed. 1927, 2nd ed. 1968).

Lovejoy, Arthur O. and George Boas, *Primitivism and Related Ideas in Antiquity* (Johns Hopkins Press 1935, reprinted New York, 1973).

Lugaresi, L., *Il teatro di Dio: il problema degli spettacoli nel cristianesimo antico (II-IV secolo)* (Brescia, 2008).

Maas, M., 'Ethnicity, orthodoxy and community in Salvian of Marseilles', in J. Drinkwater and H. Elton (eds.), *Fifth-Century Gaul: A Crisis of Identity?* (Cambridge, 1992), pp. 275–284.

MacCormack, Sabine G., *Art and Ceremony in Late Antiquity* (Berkeley, 1981).

MacCormack, Sabine, *The Shadows of Poetry: Vergil in the Mind of Augustine* (Berkeley, 1998).

Machado, Carlos, *Urban Space & Aristocratic Power in Late Antique Rome AD 270–535* (Oxford, 2019).

Magdalino, Paul, 'From Byzantion to Constantinople', in Elizabeth K. Fowden, Suna Çağaptay, Edward Zychowicz-Coghill and Louise Blanke (eds.), *Cities as Palimpsests: Responses to Antiquity in Eastern Mediterranean Urbanism (Impact of the Ancient City*, vol. 1) (Oxford, 2022), pp. 225–246.

Magnou-Nortier, Elisabeth, *Aux origines de la fiscalité moderne: le système fiscal et sa gestion dans le royaume des Francs à l'épreuve des sources (Ve–XIe siècles)* (Geneva, 2012).

Maire Vigueur, Jean-Claude, *Cavaliers et citoyens* (Paris, 2003).

Malkin, Irad, *A Small Greek World: Networks in the Ancient Mediterranean* (Oxford, 2013).

Manacorda, Daniele and Maria Stella Arena, *Museo Nazionale Romano: Crypta Balbi* (Rome, 2000).

Manacorda, Daniele, *Archeologia urbana a Roma : il progetto della Crypta Balbi* (Florence, 1982).

Mango, Cyril and Gilbert Dagron (eds.), *Constantinople and Its Hinterland* (Aldershot, 1995).

Mango, Cyril, *Byzantine Architecture* (New York, 1976).

Mango, Cyril, *Le développement urbain de Constantinople (IVe – VIIe siècles)* (Paris, 1985).

Mango, Cyril, *The Brazen House. A Study of the Vestibule of the Imperial Palace of Constantinople* (Copenhagen, 1959).

Mango, Cyril, 'The triumphal way of Constantinople and the Golden Gate', *Dumbarton Oaks Papers* 54 (2000), pp. 173–188.

Mango, Marlia Mundell, 'The porticoed street at Constantinople', in Nevra Necipoğlu (ed.), *Byzantine Constantinople: Monuments, Topography and Everyday Life* (Leiden, 2001), pp. 29–51.

Marazzi, Federico, 'Ostrogothic cities', in Jonathan Arnold, Shane Bjornlie, and Kristina Sessa (eds.), *A Companion to Ostrogothic Italy* (Leiden, 2016), pp. 98–120.

Marconi, G., *Ennodio e la nobiltà gallo-romana nell'Italia ostrogota* (Spoleto, 2013).

Marcus, Joyce and Jeremy A. Sabloff (eds.), *The Ancient City: New Perspectives on Urbanism in the Old and New World* (Santa Fe, 2008).

Markus, Robert A., *Saeculum: History and Society in the Theology of St Augustine* (Cambridge, 1970).

Markus, Robert A., *The End of Ancient Christianity* (Cambridge, 1991).

Markus, Robert A., *Gregory the Great and His World* (Cambridge, 1997).

Marrou, Henri, *Saint Augustin et le fin de la culture antique* (Paris, 1949).

Martin, Roland, *L'urbanisme dans la Grèce antique* (Paris, 1975).

Martínez Díez, Gonzalo and Felix Rodríguez (eds.), *La Colección canónica Hispana* (6 vols, 1966–92).

Martínez Jiménez, Javier and Sam Ottewill-Soulsby (eds.), *Remembering and Forgetting the Ancient City* (Oxford, 2022).

Martínez Jiménez, Javier, 'Civitatem condidit. City building and community formation in the new Visigothic foundations', in Carlos Machado, Rowan Munnery, and Rebecca Sweetman (eds.), *The Routledge Companion to Lived Spaces in Late Antiquity* (London, 2024), pp. 213–234.

Martínez Jiménez, Javier, 'Local citizenships and the Visigothic kingdom', in Sabine Panzram and Paulo Pachá (eds.), *The Visigothic Kingdom. The Negotiation of power in Post-Roman Iberia* (Amsterdam, 2020), pp. 195–212.

Martínez Jiménez, Javier, 'Water supply in the Visigothic urban foundations of Eio (El Tolmo de Minateda) and Reccopolis', in Efthymios Rizos (ed.), *New Cities in Late Antiquity. Documents and Archaeology* (Turnhout, 2017), pp. 233–245.

Martínez Jiménez, Javier, *Aqueducts and Urbanism in Post-Roman Hispania* (Piscataway, 2019).

Martínez Pizarro, Joaquín, 'Gregory of Tours and the literary imaginations: Genre, narrative style, sources and models in the *Histories*', in Alexander Callandar Murray (ed.), *A Companion to Gregory of Tours* (Leiden, 2015), pp. 338–374.

Martyn, John R. C., *The Letters of Gregory the Great*, 3 vols (Pontifical Institute of Medieval Studies, 2004).

Marzano, Annalisa, *Roman Villas in Central Italy: A Social and Economic History* (Boston, 2007).

Mathews, Thomas F., *The Early Churches of Constantinople: Architecture and Liturgy* (Pennsylvania, 1971).

Matthews, John, 'The Notitia Urbis Constantinopolitanae', in Lucy Grig and Gavin Kelly (eds.), *Two Romes: Rome and Constantinople in Late Antiquity* (Oxford, 2012), pp. 81–115.

Mathisen, Ralph W. and Danuta R. Shanzer (eds.), *Romans, Barbarians, and the Transformation of the Roman World : Cultural Interaction and the Creation of Identity in Late Antiquity* (London, 2016).

McCormick, Michael, *The Origins of the European Economy. Communications and Commerce, AD 300–900* (Cambridge, 2001).

McKitterick, Rosamond, *Charlemagne: The Formation of a European Identity* (Cambridge, 2008).

McKitterick, Rosamond, *Rome and the Invention of the Papacy: The Liber Pontificalis* (Cambridge, 2020).

Meier, Mischa and Federico Montinaro (eds.), *A Companion to Procopius of Caesarea* (Leiden, 2022).

Meiggs, Russell, 'Arnold Hugh Martin Jones', *Journal of Roman Studies* 60 (1970), pp. 186–187.

Merrills, Andrew H., *History and Geography in Late Antiquity* (Cambridge, 2005).

Mierow, Charles Christopher, *The Gothic History of Jordanes* (Cambridge, 1915).

Mitchell, Kathleen and Ian Wood (eds.), *The World of Gregory of Tours* (Leiden, 2002).

Momigliano, Arnaldo, 'The ancient city of Fustel de Coulanges', in *Essays in Ancient and Modern Historiography* (Oxford, 1977), pp. 325–343.

Mommsen, Theodore (ed.), *Chronica Minora: Saec. IV.V.VI.VII vol. 2, MGH Auctores antiqui vol. 11*, (Berlin, 1894).

Montinaro, Federico, 'Power, taste and the outsider: Procopius and the Buildings revisited', in Geoffrey Greatrex and Hugh Elton (eds.), *Shifting Genres in Late Antiquity* (Farnham, 2015), pp. 191–206.

Moreno Martin, Francisco, 'Espacios públicos y espacios de uso común en los primeros monasteros hispanos', in Amélie de las Heras, Florian Gallon, and Nicolas Pluchot (eds.), *Oeuvrer pour le salut. Moines, chanoines et frères dans la péninsule ibérique au Moyen Age* (Madrid, 2019), pp. 165–186.

Moorhead, John, 'The word modernus', *Latomus* 25 (2006), pp. 425–433.

Moorhead, John, *Theoderic in Italy* (Oxford, 1992).

Mossé, Claude, *La fin de la démocratie athénienne: Aspects sociaux et politiques du déclin de la cité grecque au IVe siècle avant J.-C.* (Paris, 1962).

Müller-Wiener, Wolfgang, *Bildlexikon zur Topographie Istanbuls* (Tübingen, 1977).

Münzer, Friedrich, *Römische Adelsparteien und Adelsfamilien* (Stuttgart, 1920).

Murray, Alexander Callandar (ed.), *A Companion to Gregory of Tours* (Leiden, 2015).

Murray, Alexander Callandar, 'The Merovingian state and administration in the times of Gregory of Tours', in Alexander Callandar Murray (ed.), *A Companion to Gregory of Tours* (Leiden, 2015), pp. 191–231.

Murray, James, 'Procopius and Boethius: Christian philosophy in the *Persian Wars*', in Christopher Lillington-Martin, and Elodie Turquois (eds.), *Procopius of Caesarea: Literary and Historical Interpretations* (London, 2018), pp. 104–119.

Necipoğlu, Nevra (ed.), *Byzantine Constantinople: Monuments, Topography and Everyday Life* (Leiden, 2001).

Neglia, Giulia Annalinda, *Aleppo: Processes of Formation of the Medieval Islamic City* (Bari, 2009).

Nelson, Jinty, 'Charlemagne and Ravenna', in Judith Herrin and Jinty Nelson (eds.), *Ravenna: Its Rome in Earlier Medieval Change and Exchange* (London, 2016), pp. 239–252.

Nelson, Jinty, 'Aachen as a place of power', in Mayke de Jong and Francis Theuws (eds.), *Topographies of Power in the Early Middle Ages* (Leiden, 2001), pp. 217–242.

Nicolet, Claude, *The World of the Citizen in Republican Rome*, trans. P. S. Falla (London, 1980).

Nimmegeers, Nathanaël, *Évêques entre Bourgogne et Provence : Ve-XIe siècle : la province ecclésiastique de Vienne au haut Moyen Âge* (Rennes, 2014).

Nippel, Wilfried, *Public Order in Ancient Rome* (Cambridge, 1995).

Nippel, Wilfried, 'Webers "Stadt". Entstehung–Struktur der Argumentation–Rezeption', in Hinnerk Bruhns and Wilfried Nippel (eds.), *Max Weber und die Stadt im Kulturvergleich* (Göttingen, 2000), pp. 11–38.

Nisbet, R. G. M. and Niall Rudd (eds.), *A Commentary on Horace: Odes, Book III* (Oxford, 2007).

Nolden, Reiner (ed.), *Das "Goldene Buch" von Prüm (Liber aureus Prumiensis): Faksimile, Übersetzung der Urkunden, Einband* (Prüm, 1997).

Norberg, Dag, *S. Gregorii Magni Registrum Epistolarum* (Corpus Christianorum Series Latina 140, Turnhout, 1982).

Norman, A.F., *Antioch as a Centre of Hellenic Culture as Observed by Libanius* (Liverpool, 2000).

Noyé, Gislaine, 'Villes, économie et société dans la province de Bruttium-Lucania', in Riccardo Francovich and Gislaine Noyé (eds.), *La storia dell'alto medioevo italiano (VI-X secolo) alla luce dell'archeologia* (Florence, 1994), pp. 693–733.

O'Daly, Gerard, *Augustine's City of God: A Reader's Guide* (Oxford, 1999).

O'Donnell, James J., 'Salvian and Augustine', *Augustinian Studies* 14, (1983), pp. 25–34.

O'Donnell, James J., *Augustine: A New Biography* (New York, 2005).

O'Donnell, James J., *Cassiodorus* (Berkeley, 1979).

Oldfield, Paul, *Urban Panegyric & the Transformation of the Medieval City, 1100–1300* (Oxford, 2019).

Oldfield, Paul, 'To destroy a city so great and remarkable: Lamentation, panegyric, and the idea of the medieval city', in Ross Balzaretti, Julia Barrow, and Patricia Skinner (eds.), *Italy and Early Medieval Europe* (Oxford, 2018), pp. 291–302.

Olmo Enciso, Lauro, *Recópolis y la ciudad en la epoca visigoda* (Alcalá, 2008).

Olmo Enciso, Lauro, 'Recópolis: una ciudad en época de transformaciones', in *Recópolis y la ciudad en la epoca visigoda* (Alcalá, 2008), pp. 40–63.

Olmo Enciso, Lauro, *Recópolis: un paseo por la cuidad visigoda* (Museo Arqueológico Nacional n.d.).

Olmo Enciso, Lauro, 'Recopolis: The representation of power in a complex landscape', in Sabine Panzram and Paulo Pachá (eds.), *The Visigothic Kingdom. The Negotiation of power in Post-Roman Iberia* (Amsterdam, 2020), pp. 215–233.

Osborne, John, *The Marvels of Rome/Master Gregorius*, translated with an introduction and commentary (Toronto, 1987).

Osborne, Robin and Andrew Wallace-Hadrill, 'Cities of the ancient Mediterranean', in Peter Clark (ed.), *The Oxford Handbook of Cities in World History* (Oxford, 2013), pp. 49–65.

Osland, Daniel, 'Text and context. Patronage in late antique Mérida', *Studies in Late Antiquity* 3 (2019), pp. 581–625.

Osland, Daniel, 'Abuse or reuse? Public space in late antique Emerita', *American Journal of Archaeology* 120 (2016), pp. 67–97.

Östenberg, Ida, Simon Malmberg, and Jonas Bjørnebye (eds.), *The Moving City: Processions, Passages and Promenades in Ancient Rome* (London, 2016).

Ottewill-Soulsby, Sam, 'First Cities in Late Antique Christian Thought', *Journal of Early Christian Studies* 30 (2022), pp. 379–387.

Ottewill-Soulsby, Sam, '"Hunting diligently through the volumes of the Ancients": Frechulf of Lisieux on the first city and the end of innocence', in J. Martínez Jiménez and S. Ottewill-Soulsby (eds.), *Remembering and Forgetting the Ancient City* (Oxford, 2022), pp. 225–245.

Ousterhout, Robert, 'Visualising Constantinople as a palimpsest', in Elizabeth K. Fowden, Suna Çağaptay, Edward Zychowicz-Coghill, and Louise Blanke (eds.), *Cities as Palimpsests: Responses to Antiquity in Eastern Mediterranean Urbanism (Impact of the Ancient City, vol. 1)* (Oxford, 2022), pp. 47–59.

Panzram, Sabine and Paulo Pachá (eds.), *The Visigothic Kingdom. The Negotiation of Power in Post-Roman Iberia* (Amsterdam, 2020).

Pardessus, Jean Marie, *Diplomata, Chartae, Epistolae, Leges, aliaque instrumenta ad res gallo-francicas spectantes* (Paris, 1843, repr. Darmstadt, 1969).

Pazdernik, Charles, 'Reinventing Theoderic in Procopius' *Gothic War*', in Christopher Lillington-Martin and Elodie Turquois (eds.), *Procopius of Caesarea: Literary and Historical Interpretations* (London, 2018), pp. 137–153.

Peck, Alexander, *The Conceptualisation, Function and Nature of* Patria *in the Roman World* (University of Warwick, PhD thesis, 2016).

Pergoli Campanelli, A. *Cassiodoro alle origini dell'idea di restauro* (Trevi, 2013).

Pfeilschifter, Rene, 'The *Secret History*', in Mischa Meier and Federico Montinaro (eds.), *A Companion to Procopius of Caesarea* (Leiden, 2022), pp. 121–136.

Pharr, Clyde, *The Theodosian Code and Novels and the Sirmondian Constitutions* (Princeton, 1952).

Pickett, Jordan, 'Water and empire in the *de aedificiis* of Procopius', *Dumbarton Oaks Papers* 71 (2017), pp. 95–126.

Pirenne, Henri, *Medieval Cities: Their Origin and the Revival of Trade* trans. Frank D. Halsey (first ed. 1925, with introduction by Michael McCormick Princeton, 2014).

Pliego, Ruth, '*Figura et potentia*. Coin and power in the Visigothic kingdom', in Sabine Panzram and Paulo Pachá (eds.), *The Visigothic Kingdom. The Negotiation of Power in Post-Roman Iberia* (Amsterdam, 2020), pp. 235–255.

Pliego Vázquez, Ruth, *La Moneda Visigoda* (2 vols, Seville, 2009).

Pohl, Walter, 'Telling the difference: Signs of ethnic identity', in Walter Pohl and Helmut Reimitz (eds.), *Strategies of Distinction: The Construction of Ethnic Communities, 300–800*, (Leiden, 1998), pp. 17–69.

Pohl, Walter, 'Social Cohesion, Breaks, and Transformations in Italy, 535–600', in Balzaretti et al. (eds.), *Italy and Early Medieval Europe* (Oxford, 2018), pp. 19–38.

Pohl, Walter, 'Introduction: Early medieval Romanness: A multiple identity', in Walter Pohl, Clemens Gantner, Cinzia Grifoni, and Marianne Pollheimer-Mohaupt (eds.), *Transformations of Romanness: Early Medieval Regions and Identities* (Berlin, 2018), pp. 3–40.

Pohle, Frank (ed.), *Karl der Große charlemagne: Orte der Macht* 3 vols (Aachen, 2014).

Pont, Anne-Valérie, *La fin de la cité grecque: métamorphoses et disparition d'un modèle politique et institutionelle local en Asie Mineure, de Dèce à Constantin* (Geneva, 2020).

Porena, Pierfrancesco, 'Gioco di ombre a Costantinopoli: Cassiodoro, papa Vigilio, Giustiniano'. Seminar 30 April 2021, in the series Seminari Cassiodorei. *Variae*.

Porena, Pierfrancesco, *L'insediamento degli Ostrogoti in Italia* (Rome, 2012).

Porena, Pierfrancesco and Yann Rivière, *Expropriations et confiscations dans les royaumes barbares* (Rome, 2013).

Potter, Tim, *Towns in Late Antiquity: Iol Caesarea and Its Context* (Sheffield, 1995).

Purcell, Nicholas, 'Literate games: Roman urban society and the game of alea', *Past&Present* 147 (1995), pp. 3–35.

Raby, F. J. E., *A History of Christian-Latin Poetry from the Beginnings to the Close of the Middle Ages* (Oxford, 1927).

Raby, F. J. E., *Secular Latin Poetry in the Middle Ages* (Oxford, 1934).

Rance, Philip, 'Wars', in Mischa Meier and Federico Montinaro (eds.), *A Companion to Procopius of Caesarea* (Leiden, 2022), pp. 70–120.

Rapp, Claudia, 'City and citizenship as Christian concepts', in Bonnie Effros and Isabel Moreira (eds.), *The City in the Classical and Post-Classical World: Changing Contexts of Power and Identity* (Cambridge, 2014), pp. 153–166.

Raymond, André, 'The spatial organization of the city', in Salma K. Jayyusi, et al. (ed.), *The City in the Islamic World* (Boston, 2008), pp. 47–70.

Raymond, André, 'Islamic city, Arab city: Orientalist myths and recent views', *British Journal of Middle Eastern Studies* 21/1 (1994), pp. 3–18.

Raymond, Irving Woodwort, *Seven Books of History against the Pagans: The Apology of Paulus Orosius*, translated with introduction and notes (New York, 1936).

Rebillard, Éric, *Christians and Their Many Identities in Late Antiquity, North Africa, 200–450 CE* (Ithaca, 2017).

Redman, Charles L. and Anne P. Kinzig, 'Resilience of past landscapes: Resilience theory, society and the Longue Durée', *Conservation Ecology* 7 (1): 14 (2003). http://www.consecol.org/vol7/iss1/art14/.

Redman, Charles L., 'Resilience theory in archaeology', *American Anthropologist* 107 (2005), pp. 70–77.

Resilient Cities, Resilient Lives, with lessons from the 100 Cities Network. www.rockefellerfoundation.org/100-resilient-cities/.

Reydellet, Marc, *Isidorus Hispalensis Etymologiae IX* (Paris, 1984).

Reynolds, Joyce, 'Justinian and Procopius in Libya', *Antiquité Tardive* 8 (2000), pp. 173–175.

Reynolds, L. D. (ed.), *Texts and Transmission. A Survey of the Latin Classics* (Oxford, 1983).

Richter, Gisela, *Three Critical Periods in Greek Sculpture* (Oxford, 1951).

Rio, Alice, *The Formularies of Angers and Marculf: Two Merovingian Legal Handbooks*, translated with an introduction and notes (Liverpool, 2008).

Rio, Alice, 'Merovingian legal cultures', in Bonnie Effros and Isabel Moreira (eds.), *The Oxford Handbook of the Merovingian World* (Oxford, 2020), pp. 489–506.

Ristuccia, Nathan J., *Christianization and Commonwealth in Early Medieval Europe: A Ritual Interpretation* (Oxford, 2018).

Rizos, Efthymios (ed.), *New Cities in Late Antiquity. Documents and Archaeology* (Turnhout, 2017).

Rizos, Efthymios, 'New cities and new urban ideals, AD 250–350', in Efthymios Rizos (ed.), *New Cities in Late Antiquity. Documents and Archaeology* (Turnhout, 2017), pp. 19–38.

Rizos, Efthymios, 'No colonies and no grids: New cities in the Roman east and the decline of the colonial urban paragigm from Augustus to Justinian', in Sofia Greaves and Andrew Wallace-Hadrill (eds.), *Rome and the Colonial City. Rethinking the Grid* (Oxford, 2022), pp. 209–238.

Roberts, Michael, 'Venantius Fortunatus and Gregory of Tours: Poetry and patronage', in Alexander Callandar Murray (ed.), *A Companion to Gregory of Tours* (Leiden, 2015), pp. 35–59.

Robinson, O. F., *Ancient Rome. City Planning and Administration* (London, 1992).

Rollason, David, 'Charlemagne's Palace', *The Archaeological Journal* 172 (2015), pp. 443–448.

Romagnoli, Daniela, 'La coscienza civica nella città comunale italiana: il caso di Milano', in F. Sabaté (ed.), *El mercat: un món de contactes i intercanvis* (Lleida, 2014), pp. 57–75.

Rose, Else, Robert Flierman, and Merel de Bruin-van de Beek, *City, Citizens, Citizenship 400-1500: a Comparative Approach* (Cham, 2024).

Ross, Alan J., 'Narrator and participant in Procopius' *Wars*', in Christopher Lillington-Martin and Elodie Turquois (eds.), *Procopius of Caesarea: Literary and Historical Interpretations* (London, 2018), pp. 73–90.

Roussel, Denis, *Tribu et cité: Études sur les groupes sociaux dans les cités grecques aux époques archaïque et classique* (Paris, 1976).

Ruth, Jeffrey S. *Urban Honor in Spain. The Laus Urbis from Antiquity through Humanism* (Lewiston, 2011).

Russell, D. A. and N. G. Wilson, *Menander Rhetor*, edited with translation and commentary (Oxford, 1981).

Russell, Thomas, 'Before Costantinople', in Sarah Bassett (ed.), *The Cambridge Companion to Constantinople* (Cambridge, 2022), pp. 17–32.

Saitta, Biagio, *La civilitas di Teodorico: rigore amministrativo, 'tolleranza' religiosa e recupero dell'antico nell'Italia ostrogota* (Rome, 1993).

Saliou, Catherine, *Les lois des bâtiments: Voisinage et habitat urbain dans l'empire romain; Recherches sur les rapports entre le droit et la construction privée du siècle d'Auguste au siècle de Justinien* (Beyrouth, 1994).

Salzman, Michele Renée, 'Apocalypse then? Jerome and the fall of Rome in 410', in *Maxima debetur magistro reverentia. Essays on Rome and the Roman Tradition in honor of Russell T. Scott*, ed. Paul B. Harvey, Jr. and Catherine Conybeare, *Biblioteca do Athenaeum* 54 (2009), pp. 172–192.

Salzman, Michele Renée, 'From a Classical to a Christian city: Civic euergetism and charity in Late Antique Rome', *Studies in Late Antiquity* (2017) 1, pp. 65–85.

Salzman, Michele Renée, *The Falls of Rome. Crises, Resilience, and Resurgence in Late Antiquity* (Cambridge, 2021).

Salway, Benet, 'What's in a name? A survey of Roman onomastic practice from c. 700 BC to AD 700', *Journal of Roman Studies* 84 (1994), pp. 124–145.

Sánchez, A. Maya, *Vitas sanctorum patrum Emeretensium* (CPL 2069: Turnhout, 1992).

Sandford, Eva M. (trans.), *On the Governance of God by Salvian* (New York, 1966).

Sannazaro, Marco, 'Un'epigrafe di Garlate: il *comes domesticorum* Pierius e la battaglia dell'Adda del 490', *MEFRA* 105 (1993), pp. 189–219.

Sansoni, Francesca, 'I papiri di Ravenna: *gesta municipalia* e procedure di insinuazione', in J. M Martin, A. Peters-Custet, and V. Prigent (eds.), *L'héritage byzantin en Italie (VIIIe -XIIe siècle). I. la fabrique documentaire* (Rome, 2011), pp. 9–32.

Santi, Aila, 'Anjar in the shadow of the church? New insights on an Umayyad urban experiment in the Biqā' Valley, *Levant*, 50:2 (2018), pp. 267–280.

Saradi, Helen G., 'The city in Byzantine hagiography', in Stephanos Efthymiades (ed.), *The Ashgate Research Companion to Byzantine Hagiography. Vol.II, Genres and Contexts* (Farnham, 2014), pp. 419–452.

Saradi, Helen G., *The Byzantine City in the Sixth Century: Literary Images and Historical Reality* (Athens, 2006).

Sarantis, Alexander, 'Procopius and the different types of northern barbarian', in Geoffrey Greatrex, and Sylvain Janniard (eds.), *Le Monde de Procope/The World of Procopius* (Paris, 2018), pp. 355–378.

Sarris, Peter (ed.), *The Novels of Justinian*, trans. David J. D. Miller (Cambridge, 2018).

Sauvaget, Jean, 'Le plan de Laodicée-sur-Mer', *Bulletin Études Orientales* 4 (1934), pp. 81–114.

Sauvaget, Jean, *Alep, essai sur le développment d'une grande ville syrienne des origines au milieu du XIXème siècle*, 2 vols, (Paris, 1941).

Scivoletto, Nicola, 'Cassiodoro e la retorica della città', in *Filologia e cultura latina* (Naples, 2000), pp. 325–344.

Sear, Frank, *Roman Architecture* (2nd ed., London, 2021).

Shanzer, Danuta and Ian Wood, *Avitus of Vienne* (Liverpool, 2002).

Shanzer, Danuta, *A Philosophical and Literary Commentary on Martianus Capella's De nuptiis Philologiae et Mercuri* (Berkeley, 1986).

Shanzer, Danuta, 'Augustine and the Latin classics', in Mark Vessey (ed.), *A Companion to Augustine* (Chichester, 2012), pp. 161–174.

Shanzer, Danuta, 'Gregory of Tours and poetry: Prose into verse and verse into prose', *Proceedings of the British Academy* 129 (2005), pp. 303–319.

Sherwin-White, A. N., *The Roman Citizenship* (Oxford, 1st ed. 1939, 2nd ed. 1973).

Signes Codoñer, Juan, 'One history ... in several instalments. Dating and genre in Procopius' works', *Studi Bizantini e Neoellenici* 54 (2017), pp. 3–26.

Snowden, Frank M., *Naples in the Time of Cholera, 1884–1911* (Cambridge, 1995).

Sommer, Michael, 'Die "entzauberte" Antike: Max Webers Fragment Die Stadt als Entwurf einer verstehenden Altertumswissenschaft', *Oldenburger Universitätsreden* 207 (Oldenburg, 2015).

Spevak, Olga, *Isidorus Hispalensis Etymologiae I* (Paris, 2020).

Stahl, William Harris, *Martianus Capella and the Seven Liberal Arts* (Columbia 1971, 1991).

Steinová, Evina, 'The oldest manuscript tradition of the Etymologiae (eighty years after A.E. Anspach)', in *Visigothic Symposium* 4 (2020-2021), ed. Dolores Castro and Michael J. Kelly, pp. 100–143.

Stella, Francesco, *La poesia Carolingia a tema biblico* (Spoleto, 1993).

Stickler, Timo, 'Procopius and Christian historical thought', in Mischa Meier and Federico Montinaro (eds.), *A Companion to Procopius of Caesarea* (Leiden, 2022), pp. 212–230.

Storoni Mazzolani, Lidia, *The Idea of the City in Roman Thought: From Walled City to Spiritual Commonwealth*, translated from the Italian (*L'idea della città nel mondo romano: l'evoluzione nel pensiro politico di Roma*, 1967) by S. O'Donnell (London, 1970).

Stroheker, Karl, *Der senatorische Adel im spätantiken Gallien* (Darmstadt, 1948, reprinted 1970).

Stroheker, Karl, 'Spanische Senatoren der spätrömischen und westgotischen Zeit', *Madrider Mitteilungen* 4 (1963), pp. 107–132, reproduced in his *Germanentum und Spätantike* (Zurich, 1965), pp. 54–87.

Strothmann, Jürgen, 'The evidence of numismatics: "Merovingian" coinage and the place of Frankish Gaul and its cities in an "invincible" Roman Empire', in Bonnie Effros and Isabel Moreira (eds.), *The Oxford Handbook of the Merovingian World* (Oxford, 2020), pp. 797–818.

Strousma, Guy, 'Augustine and books', in Mark Vessey (ed.), *A Companion to Augustine* (Chichester, 2012), pp. 151–157.

Tabata, Kayoko, *Città dell'Italia nel VI secolo d.C.* (Rome, 2009).

Tagliata, Emanuele, Christopher Courault, and Simon Barker (eds.), *City Walls in Late Antiquity. An Empire-wide Perspective* (Oxford, 2020).

Talbert, Richard J. A., *Rome's world: The Peutinger Map Reconsidered* (Cambridge, 2010).

Talloen, Peter, 'Rolling the dice: Public game boards from Sagalassos', *Herom* 7 (2018), pp. 97–132.

Tarpin, Michel 'Strangers in Paradise', in Tesse Stek and Jeromia Pelgrom (eds.), *Roman Republican Colonization* (KNIR, Rome, 2014), pp. 164–191.

Thompson, E. A., *The Goths in Spain* (Oxford, 1969).

Thorpe, Lewis, *Gregory of Tours. The History of the Franks*, trans. with introduction (Harmondsworth, 1974).

Tizzoni, Mark Lewis, 'Isidore of Seville's early influence and dissemination (636–711)', in Andrew Fear and Jamie Wood (eds.), *A Companion to Isidore of Seville* (Leiden, 2020), pp. 397–423.

Tjäder, Jan-Olof, *Die nichtliterarischen lateinischen Papyri Italiens, 445–700* (Lund, vol. 1, 1955, vol. 2, 1982).

Town Planning Conference London, 10–15 October 1910, Transactions (London, 1911); partly reissued with introductory essay by William Whyte (London, 2012).

Townend, Gavin, 'Suetonius and his influence', in T. A. Dorey (ed.), *Latin Biography* (London, 1967), pp. 98–106.

Tsafrir, Yoram, 'Procopius and the Nea church in Jerusalem', *Antiquité Tardive* 8 (2000), pp. 149–164.

Tucci, Pierluigi, 'Dove erano il tempio di Nettuno e la nave di Enea?', *Bullettino della Commissione Archeologica Comunale di Roma* 98 (1997), pp. 15–42.

Tucci, Pierluigi, 'Nave di Enea', *Lexicon Topographicum Urbis Romae* vol. 5 (Rome, 1999), pp. 278–29.

Turner, Bryan S. 'Revisiting Weber and Islam', *British Journal of Sociology* 61 (2010), 161–166.

Turquois, Elodie, 'Technical writing, genre and aesthetic in Procopius', in Geoffrey Greatrex and Hugh Elton (eds.), *Shifting Genres in Late Antiquity* (Farnham, 2015), pp. 219–231.

Ungvart, David, 'Clarifying the Eclipse: Ascetics, Politics, and the Poetics of Power in Post-Roman Iberia', in *Vigiliae Christianae* 73 (2019), pp. 531–563.

Unterkircher, F. (ed.), *Notitiae Regionum Urbis Romae et Urbis Constantinopolitanae: Glossarium latino-theotiscum. Codex vindobonensis 162* (Amsterdam, 1960).

Urbano, Arthur, 'Donatio, dedication, and *damnatio memoriae*: The Catholic reconciliation of Ravenna and the church of Sant'Apollinare Nuovo', *Journal of Early Christian Studies* 13:1 (2005), pp. 71–110.

Valérian, Dominique, 'Middle East: 7th–15th centuries', in Peter Clark (ed.), *The Oxford Handbook of Cities in World History* (Oxford, 2013), pp. 258–274.

Van Dam, Ray, *Leadership and Community in Late Antique Gaul* (Berkeley, 1985).

Van Dam, Ray, *Rome and Constantinople. Rewriting Roman History during Late Antiquity* (Waco, 2010).

Van Dam, Ray, *Saints and Their Miracles in Late Antique Gaul* (Princeton, 1993).

Van Dam, Ray, 'The supply of food to Constantinople', in Sarah Bassett (ed.), *The Cambridge Companion to Constantinople* (Cambridge, 2022), pp. 87–101.

Van der Graaff, Ivo, *The Fortifications of Pompeii and Ancient Italy* (Abingdon, 2019).

Van Nuffelen, Peter, *Orosius and the Rhetoric of History* (Oxford, 2012).

Van Nuffelen, Peter and Lieve Van Hoof, *Romana and Getica / Jordanes*, translated with an introduction and notes (Liverpool, 2020).

Van Renswoude, Irene, 'The sincerity of fiction: Rather of Verona and the quest for self-knowledge', in Richard Corradini, Matthew Gillis, Rosamond McKitterick, and Irene van Renswoude (eds.), *Ego trouble: Authors and Their Identities in the Early Middle Ages* (Vienna, 2010), pp. 309–334.

Van Slyke, Daniel G., 'The Devil and his Pomp in Fifth-century Carthage: Renouncing *spectacula* with spectacular imagery', *Dumbarton Oaks Papers* 59 (2005), pp. 53–72.

Vera, Domenico. '*Massa fundorum*. Forme della grande proprietà e poteri della città in Italia fra Costantino e Gregorio Magno', *Mélanges de l'École française de Rome. Antiquité*, 111 (1999), pp. 991–1025.

Verhulst, Adriaan E., *The Rise of Cities in North-West Europe* (Cambridge, 1999).

Vessey, Mark (ed.), *A Companion to Augustine* (Chichester, 2012).

Vessey, Mark, 'The history of the book: Augustine's City of God and post-Roman cultural memory', in James Wetzel (ed.), *Augustine's City of God: A Critical Guide* (Cambridge, 2012), pp. 14–32.

Vives, José (ed.), *Consilios Visigóticos e Hispano-Romanos* (Barcelona, 1963).

Vocino, Giorgia, 'Between the Palace, the School and the Forum: Rhetoric and Court Culture in Late Lombard and Carolingian Italy', in C. Gantner (ed.), *After Charlemagne: Carolingian Italy and Its Rulers* (Cambridge, 2020), pp. 250–274.

Vout, Caroline, *The Hills of Rome: Signature of an Eternal City* (Cambridge, 2012).

Wallace-Hadrill, Andrew, 'Ancient ideals and modern interpretations', in Sofia Greaves and Andrew Wallace-Hadrill (eds.), *Rome and the Colonial City. Rethinking the Grid* (Oxford, 2022), pp. 41–49.

Wallace-Hadrill, Andrew, 'Antiqua in nitorem pristinum contineas et nova simili antiquitate producas: Restoration and modernization in the Rome of Cassiodorus', in Bruno Bonomo, Charles Davoine, and Cécile Trodes (eds.), *Reconstruire Rome: La restauration comme politique urbaine de l'Antiquité à nos jours* (École Française de Rome, 2024), pp. 403–419.

Wallace-Hadrill, Andrew, 'Back to M. I. Finley's ancient city: Town and country, landowners and the rest at Pompeii', *Journal of Roman Archaeology* 32 (2019), pp. 718–723, reviewing Wilson and Flohr, *The Economy of Pompeii*.

Wallace-Hadrill, Andrew, 'The cities of Cassiodorus: The resilience of urban values', in J. Martínez Jiménez and S. Ottewill Souslby (eds.), *Remembering and Forgetting the Ancient City* (Oxford, 2022), pp. 23–34.

Wallace-Hadrill, Andrew, '*Civilis princeps*: Between citizen and king', *Journal of Roman Studies* 72 (1982) pp. 32–48.

Wallace-Hadrill, Andrew, '*Civitas Romana*: The fluidity of an ideal', in J. Martínez Jiménez and S. Ottewell-Soulsby (eds.), *Cities and Citizenship after Rome. Al-Masaq special edition* (2020), pp. 18–33.

Wallace-Hadrill, Andrew, 'Elites and trade in the Roman town', in John W. Rich and Andrew Wallace-Hadrill (eds.), *City and Country in the Ancient World* (London, 1991), pp. 241–272.

Wallace-Hadrill, Andrew, *Herculaneum. Past and Future* (London, 2011).

Wallace-Hadrill, Andrew, *Houses and Society in Pompeii and Herculaneum* (Princeton, 1994).

Wallace-Hadrill, Andrew, *Rome's Cultural Revolution* (Cambridge, 2008).

Wallace-Hadrill, Andrew, 'Salvian of Marseilles and the end of the ancient city', in Javier Andreu and Aitor Blanco-Perez (eds.), *Signs of Weakness and Crisis in the Western Cities of the Roman Empire (c.II–III AD)* (Stuttgart, 2019), pp. 223–232.

Wallace-Hadrill, Andrew, *Suetonius: The Scholar and His Caesars* (London, 1984).

Wallace-Hadrill, J. M., 'The bloodfeud of the Franks', in *Long-Haired Kings and Other Studies in Frankish History* (London, 1962), pp. 121–147.

Wallace-Hadrill, J. M., *Early Germanic Kingship in England and on the Continent* (Oxford, 1971).

Wallace-Hadrill, J. M., *Early Medieval History* (Oxford, 1975).

Wallace-Hadrill, J. M., *The Frankish Church* (Oxford, 1983).

Wallace-Hadrill, J. M., *The Long-Haired Kings and Other Studies in Frankish History* (London, 1962).

Walmsley, Alan, *Early Islamic Syria: An Archaeological Assessment* (London, 2007).

Walser, Gerold (ed.), *Die Einsiedler Inschriftensammlung und der Pilgerführer durch Rom (Codex Einsidlensis 326): Facsimile, Umschrift, Übersetzung und Kommentar* (Stuttgart, 1987).

Ward-Perkins, Bryan, *From Classical Antiquity to the Middle Ages. Urban and Public Building in Northern and Central Italy AD 300–850* (Oxford, 1984).
Ward-Perkins, Bryan, *The Fall of Rome and the End of Civilization* (Oxford, 2005).
Ward-Werkins, Bryan, 'Old and New Rome compared', in Lucy Grig and Gavin Kelly (eds.), *Two Romes: Rome and Constantinople in Late Antiquity* (Oxford, 2012), pp. 54–78.
Ward-Perkins, J. B., *Cities of Ancient Greece and Italy. Planning in Classical Antiquity* (London, 1974).
Weber, Max, 'Die Stadt', *Archiv für Sozialwissenschaft und Sozialpolitik* 47 (1921), pp. 621–772, cited from the English translation of Don Martindale and Gertrud Neuwirth, *The City* (New York, 1958).
Weingarten, Susan, *The Saint's Saints: Hagiography and Geography in Jerome* (Brill, 2005).
Welton, Megan, 'The city speaks: Cities, citizens and civic discourse in Late Antiquity and the early Middle Ages', *Traditio* 75 (2020), pp. 1–37.
Wetzel, James (ed.), *Augustine's City of God. A Critical Guide* (Cambridge, 2012).
Whateley, Conor, *Battles and Generals: Combat, Culture, and Didacticism in Procopius' Wars* (Leiden, 2016).
Whateley, Conor, 'Procopius on the siege of Rome in AD 537/538', in Jeremy Armstrong and Matthew Trundle (eds.), *Brill's Companion to Sieges in the Ancient Mediterranean* (Leiden, 2019), pp. 265–284.
Whateley, Conor, *Procopius on Soldiers and Military Institutions in the Sixth-Century Roman Empire* (Leiden, 2021).
Whateley, Conor, 'The beautiful wall: Militarized cityscapes in the age of Justinian', in E. Turquois and M. Ritter (eds.), *Imagery and Aesthetics of Late Antique Cityscapes* (Mainz, forthcoming).
Whitby, Mary, 'Procopius' *Buildings* book 1: A panegyrical perspective', in *Antiquité Tardive* 8 (2000), pp. 45–57.
Whitby, Mary, *The Propaganda of Power: The Role of Panegyric in Late Antiquity* (Leiden, 1998).
Whitby, Michael, 'Procopius' description of Dara', in Philip Freeman and David Kennedy (eds.), *The Defence of the Roman and Byzantine East* (Oxford, 1986), pp. 737–783.
Whitby, Michael, 'Procopius' *Buildings* and the panegyrical effect', in Mischa Meier and Federico Montinaro (eds.), *A Companion to Procopius of Caesarea* (Leiden, 2022), pp. 136–151.
Whittow, Mark, 'Ruling the late Roman and early Byzantine city', *Past & Present* 103 (1990), pp. 3–29.
Wickham, Chris, *Early Medieval Italy: Central Power and Local Society, 400–1000* (Ann Arbor, 1981).
Wickham, Chris, 'La chûte de l'empire romain n'aura pas lieu', *Le Moyen Âge* 99 (1993), pp. 88–119.

Wickham, Chris, *Framing the Early Middle Ages: Europe and the Mediterranean 400–800* (Oxford, 2006).

Wickham, Chris, *Sleepwalking into a New World: The Emergence of Italian City Communes in the Twelfth Century* (Princeton, 2015).

Wiemer, Hans-Ulrich, 'Procopius and the barbarians in the West', in Mischa Meier and Federico Montinaro (eds.), *A Companion to Procopius of Caesarea* (Leiden, 2022), pp. 275–309.

Winterbottom, Michael, *Oxford Medieval Texts: William of Malmesbury: Gesta Pontificum Anglorum: The History of the English Bishops, Vol. 1: Text and Translation* (Oxford, 2007).

Wiseman, T. P. *A Short History of the British School at Rome* (London, 1990).

Wolf, Kenneth Baxter (trans.), *Conquerors and Chroniclers of Early Medieval Spain* (Liverpool, 1990).

Wolfram, Herwig, *History of the Goths*, trans T. J. Dunlap (Berkeley, 1988).

Wood, Ian, *Gregory of Tours* (Headstart, 1994).

Wood, Ian, *The Merovingian Kingdoms 470–751* (London, 1994).

Wood, Ian, 'Ethnicity and language in medieval and modern versions of the Attalus story', in Walter Pohl and Bernhard Zeller (eds.), *Sprache und Identität im frühen Mittelalter* (Vienna, 2012), pp. 65–75.

Wood, Ian, *The Christian Economy of the Early Medieval West: Towards a Temple Society* (Binghamton, 2022).

Wood, Jamie, 'A family affair. Leander, Isidore and the legacy of Gregory the Great in Spain', in Andrew Fear and Jamie Wood (eds.), *A Companion to Isidore of Seville* (Leiden, 2020), pp. 31–56.

Wood, Jamie, 'Brevitas in the historical writings of Isidore of Seville', in Alan Deyermond and Martin J. Ryan (eds.), *Early Medieval Spain: A Symposium* (London, 2010), pp. 37–53.

Wood, Jamie, 'Isidore as a historian', Andrew Fear and Jamie Wood (eds.), *A Companion to Isidore of Seville* (Leiden, 2020), pp. 153–181.

Wood, Jamie, *The Politics of Identity in Visigothic Spain: Religion and Power in the Histories of Isidore of Seville* (Leiden, 2012).

Woolf, Greg, *The Life and Death of Ancient Cities: A Natural History* (Oxford, 2020).

Woolf, Greg, 'Locating Resilience in Ancient Urban Networks', in Simon Malmberg, Eivind Heldaas Seland and Christopher Prescott (eds.), *City, Hinterland and Environment: Urban Resilience during the First Millennium Transition* (Acta 34 no. 22 n.s. 2022), pp. 3–13.

Wycherley, R. E., *How the Greeks Built Cities* (London, 1973).

Zanini, Enrico, 'The urban ideal and urban planning in Byzantine new cities in the sixth century AD', in Luke Lavan and William Bowden (eds.), *Theory and Practice in Late Antique Archaeology* (Leiden, 2003), pp. 196–223.

Zeumer, Karl (ed.), *Formulae Merowingici et Karolini Aevi: accedunt Ordines Iudiciorum Dei* (*MGH Leges* Hanover 1886).

Zeumer, Karl (ed.), *Leges Visigothorum Antiquiores* (*MGH* Hanover/Leipzig, 1894).

Zimmermann, Odo John, *The Late Latin Vocabulary of Cassiodorus* (Hildesheim, 1944; reprint, 1967).

Zubaida, Sami, 'Max Weber's "The City" and the Islamic city', *Max Weber Studies* 6.1 (2006), pp. 111–118.

Zuiderhoek, Arjan, *The Ancient City* (Cambridge, 2017).

Zumbo, Antonino, 'Sugli excursus zoologici nelle Variae di Cassiodoro', in Sandro Leanza (ed.), *Cassiodoro. Dalla corte di Ravenna al Vivarium di Squillace. Atti del convegno internazionale di studi – Squillace, 25–27 ottobre 1990* (Catanzaro, 1993), pp. 191–197.

Index

Aachen
    as new city, 370
    as New Rome, 372
    praise of, 394
Agilulf, 223
agrimensores (land surveyors), 37
Alaric II, 199, 236, 253
    law code of, 284
Alaric II, king of Spain, 19
Alaric, sack of Rome, 1, 34, 74, 75, 281
Alboin, 196
Alcaeus, lyric poet, 2, 34, 43
Alcuin
    praise of York, 64
Aleppo, 315, 318
Alexander the Great
    and democracy, 16, 28
    as pirate, 94
    commissions history, 163
    conquests change world, 16
    defeat of Athens, 396
    founder of cities, 48, 52, 178, 188, 300
    shrine to, 187
Alexandria, 49, 52, 300
    named for Alexander, 178
Amalasunta, 121
    murder of, 134
    trilingualism of, 121, 122, 158
Ambrose *Hexameron*, 115, 146
Amida (Diyarbakır), 177
    siege of, 171
Andelot, treaty of, 258, 262
'Anjar, 362–366
    a city?, 366
    modelled on Roman fort, 363
Antioch, 4, 18
    as Christian city, 51
    boulē, 48
    city of immigrants, 49
    colonnaded street, 49, 50–51, 323, 337
    continuity of, 380–381
    earthquake, 171
    foundation of, 300, 381
    grid plan, 362
    praise of, 41–42, 47–51, 68, 323
    reconstruction of, 57–58, 184
    reduced to village, 181
    rioting at, 75
    sack of, 3, 171–173, 263
    town/country symbiosis, 50
    Tyche of, 42
Aquileia, 43, 62
    praise of, 52
    sack of, 46
Aquinas, Thomas
    de regimine principum, 71
Arcadius, emperor, 117, 138, 139, 143, 324
    baths of, 339
    Forum of, 336
    statue of, 336
Aristides, orator, 34
Aristotle *Politics*, 8–9, 14–15, 16, 27, 34, 71, 87, 198, 233–234, 396
Arles
    as Rome of Gaul, 52
Ashby, Thomas, 22, 23–24, 26, 327, 395
Athalaric, Ostrogothic king, 115, 128
    death of, 122, 133
    edicts of, 138, 140, 145, 147, 153, 155
    education of, 158, 191
    on importance of grammar, 122
Athanaric, 259
    amazed by Constantinople, 135, 361
Athaulf, 284
Athens, 234
    city of arts, 52, 301
    constitution of, 198
    etymology, 45
    immigrants in, 49
    no street grid, 27
    Parthenon, 15
    plague of, 165
    praise of, 46
    resilience of, 396
    schools of, 49, 191

siege of, 170
stoa basilikē, 311
Attila
    battle of Châlons, 281
    sack of Aquileia, 46
Augustine
    City of God, 2, 85–99
    death of, 99
    Letters, 74–77
    On the Sack of Rome, 1–2, 34
    praise for Roman citizenship, 95
    use of Cicero, 87–89
    use of Varro, 90
    use of Virgil, 86–87, 89, 94
Augustus
    founder of cities, 179
    titles of, 292
Ausonius, 51–54
Autun (Augustodunum), 226, 244, 265
Avezzano, relief, 35
Avitus of Vienne, 254

Babylon, 64, 97, 299
Bacaudae, 106
basilica
    change of meaning, 310
Belisarius, 1
    attacked in *Secret History*, 166
    commissions Procopius, 163
Boethius, philosopher, 119, 141
    downfall of, 129, 133
    murder of, 122
Bononia (Bologna), 210
Bonvesin de la Riva, 47, 65–69, 70
Bordeaux (Burdigala), 51, 73, 239, 259, 303
    earthquake, 262
    praise of, 53–54
Bourges (Biturigi), 226, 239, 242
Braulio, 272–275, 287, 289
Britain
    urban network of, 222
Brown, Peter, 4, 29, 100, 102, 270, 377
Brundisium (Brindisi)
    Messapic origin, 302

Caesarea in Palestine, 159, 185, 304
    birthplace of Procopius, 184
    renamed by Herod, 300
    Samaritan population, 160
Calama, 74–76, 98
Capua, 302, 391
    one of three great cities, 302
    praise of, 52

Caracalla
    Constitutio Antoniniana, 77, 107, 307
Cartagena (Carthago Nova), 276, 277, 283, 303, 304
Carthage
    built by Dido, 300, 369
    leading city, 302
    model city, 111
    passion for games, 110, 112
    rebuilt by Justinian, 189
    renamed Justiniane, 184
    sack of, 86, 99, 112
    second city of empire, 52
Cassiodorus
    as bridge builder, 119–128
    as Praetorian Prefect, 132–133
    official roles, 129
    on cities as civilisation, 134–135
    role as Quaestor, 129–131
Cassiodorus, *Variae*
    as propaganda, 134
    civic values in, 149
    date of publication, 131, 134, 141
    on *civilitas*, 151–156
    on SPQR, 149–151
    on urban fabric, 136–143
    rhetoric of, 118, 132
    theme of, 118
    voices of, 128–134
castra v. cities, 43, 219, 222, 238, 241, 307, 363
Cesena, 219
Charlemagne, 14, 63, 196, 200, 225
    as city builder, 372
    crowned emperor, 231
    coronation as Emperor, 368
    meets Pope Leo III, 368
    title Imperator et Augustus, 367
Chester, praise of, 71
Childebert, son of Clovis, 253, 263
Childebert, son of Sigibert, 226, 259, 260, 262
Chilperic, son of Lothar, 247, 257, 258, 259, 260, 264
Chosroes (Khusrau), 168
    sack of Antioch, 3, 57, 171, 172–173, 263, 380
Chramn, son of Lothar, 252, 257
Christianity
    impact of city on, 72
Cicero
    as letter writer, 131
    Brutus, 251, 280
    civic conscience, 77
    de lege agraria, 302
    de Republica, 76–77, 86, 87–89, 194, 294

Cicero (cont.)
  definition of the state, 2, 76, 93, 94, 98, 116
  linguistic model, 142
  on civilisation, 35, 397
  on patriotism, 277
  on Varro, 90, 289, 290
  rhetorical tricks, 268
cities
  and barbarians, 104–105, 134–135, 159, 166–169
  and civilisation, 189–190, 191
  cities, number of, 16
  Gallic, as stocks and shares, 259
  how to build, 394
  walls do not make, 1, 2, 21, 34, 55, 271, 306
citizenship
  as performance, 78
  political participation, 15
citizenship, Roman
  changing, 104
  end of ideal, 98
  exclusion from, 78–82
  in imperial legislation, 77–82
  infames, 79
  overlap with Christianity, 83–84
  respect due to, 149–151
  right to live in cities, 81
  rights of inheritance, 78
  v. barbarians, 103–107
  value of, 106
city
  'Oriental', 5
  advantages of city life, 115–116
  city, as root of civilisation, 35
  city, as universal human phenomenon, 35
  Enoch as first, 92
  representation of, 33–43
  streets, 112
civilitas
  Augustan coinage, 152
  demanded of Goths, 156
  in Ennodius, 152
  reformulated by Cassiodorus, 136, 151–156
  towards Jews, 153
civitas
  body of *cives*, 246, 272, 306
  city and country, 242
  definition of, 43, 72, 99, 116, 238, 240, 246, 271, 294, 305, 307
  Gallic, 242
  ideological charge, 69
  in Gregory the Great, 219

in Notitia Civitatum, 239
  status of, 180, 238
  v. *urbs*, 2
  v. *vicus*, 75
  values of, 106
civitas Romana. See citizenship, Roman
Classis, 199, 213
  S.Apollinare, 213
Claudian
  On Stilicho's consulship, 84
Clermont-Ferrand (Arverni), 226, 239, 243, 247, 248, 250–253, 255, 258, 266
  birthplace of Gregory of Tours, 252
Clovis, 199, 236, 253, 257, 279
  family of, 253, 256, 257, 259
Codex Theodosianus, 79, 80, 117, 138
  misnamed, 232
  model for Gothic law, 19
conscience, civic (*coscienza cittadina*), 73
Constantine
  adoption of Christianity, 10, 395
  end of antiquity, 27, 33
  founder of cities, 179
  founds Constantinople, 52, 96, 301, 325–342
  founds Helenopolis, 188
  limits elite marriage, 79
  on citizenship, 79
  promotes Orcistus, 180
  protects municipal buildings, 138
  reorganises empire, 375
Constantinople
  aqueducts, 338
  as New Rome, 96, 326–342
  Capitolium, 334
  Forum, 332–333, 334–336
  Forum of Constantine, 346
  fourteen regions, 339
  Haghia Sophia, 57, 341, 342, 346
  Haghia Sophia, rebuilt, 176
  hilly topography, 327
  Mausoleum of Constantine, 336
  Mesē as processional route, 342
  Mesē as spine, 334–337
  Mesē colonnaded, 332, 337
  Mesē/via Egnatia, 331–332
  Nika riots, 165, 337
  no grid, 327
  Palatium, 333
  Regionary Catalogue, 47, 339–340
  Senaton, 333, 335
  strategic position, 332, 340
  topography inverse of Rome, 327
  twin capital with Rome, 301

Córdoba (Corduba), 52, 283, 286, 297
  praise of, 52
Corinth
  sack of, 86
Cremona
  sack of, 223
curia (boule, council)
  as system of governance, 17–20
curia (palazzo comunale), 65
curia regis, 326
curiae
  collection of taxes by, 205
  decline of, 197
  groupings of *gentes*, 8
  in Gregory the Great, 225
  in Merovingian Gaul, 264–265
  in Spain, 225–226
  location of, 308
  ordo curiae technical term, 218
  Ostrogoths support, 143–144
  registration by in France, 232–233
  registration by in Italy, 201–211
  supposed decline, 143–144
  survival of, 145–148, 200
curials
  as sinews of the cities, 146
  as tyrants, 104
  behaviour of, 108–109
  called senators, 251–256
  civic devotion of, 137–138
  etymology of, 297
  exemption, 147
  flogging of, 146
  in Gregory of Tours, 246, 248–249
  in Visigothic Spain, 288
  local elite as, 265–266
  naming patterns of, 213–216
  provide spectacles, 112
  punishment of, 75
  residence in cities, 118
Cyprian
  criticism of, 122
  trilingualism of, 121

Dara
  as new city, 348–351
  fortification of, 181–183
  foundation of, 171, 177–178
  founded by Anastasius, 177, 178
  renamed Anastasiopolis and
    Theodosiopolis, 177
defensor
  meaning of title, 204
  role of, 227, 296

Dijon (Divio), 72, 236–238, 240, 241, 246, 307
Diocletian
  creates *praesides*, 296
  founds fort, 353
  makes service on council compulsory, 197, 234
  palace in Nicomedia, 334
  promotes cities, 180
  punishes council of Antioch, 49
  reformulates council, 394
  reorganises empire, 375
Domitian, 152
  clears streets of Rome, 324

Einhard, *Life of Charlemagne*, 370, 372
  Suetonius as model, 367
Emerita Augusta (Mérida), 179, 287, 304, 381–389
Ennodius of Pavia, 127, 135, 152
Enoch, city of, 299
Ephesus, Seven Sleepers of, 29, 377

Faenza, 199
Finley, Moses, 4–5, 11, 21, 69, 395
Formia, 222
forum
  variant *forus*, 308
Fustel de Coulanges, Numa Denis, 7, 8–10, 11, 28, 72, 78, 178, 378

Gaiseric, 168
  demolishes walls, 173
  sack of Rome, 1
Geneva, 244, 249
Genoa
  sack of, 223
  synagogue, 153
Gerasa (Jarash), 19, 376–377
gesta municipalia
  in France, 232–233, 259, 265
  in Visigothic Spain, 285–286
Gibbon, Edward, 4, 6–7
Goths
  and civility, 154
  and duelling, 155
  and rule of law, 84, 156, 284
  conversion of, 276, 279, 282, 301
  distinctive names of, 213
  history of, 120, 121, 280, 303, 356
  land grants in Italy, 115, 208
  live in cities, 148
  support tradition, 168
Gregory of Langres, 244, 245, 253, 265

Gregory of Tours
 curiales not mentioned, 248–249
 family of, 245
 Glory of the Confessors, 249, 255, 268
 Histories, 236
 Histories, style of, 267–270
 Life of the Fathers, 237, 243, 265
 on bishops of Tours, 267
 on citizens, 248
 on city government, 264–266
 on *civitates*, 240–242
 on power of bishops, 262–264
 on senators and senatorial families, 249–256
Gregory the Great, 252, 289
 and Leander, 276, 279, 290, 301, 308
 as imperial administrator, 219
 Dialogues, 222
 Homilies on Job, 276
 source of Isidore, 292, 293, 305, 312
 writes to cities, 218–225
 writes to Naples, 219, 391
Gubbio, 199
Gundobad, 253, 254, 256

Hadrumetum
 renamed Honoriopolis, 356
 renamed Hunericopolis, 180, 356
 renamed Justiniane, 184
Haussmann, Baron, 7, 9
Haverfield, Francis, 21–25, 318, 367, 395
Helenopolis, 188
 named for mother of Constantine, 185
Herculaneum
 named for Hercules, 302
Hermenegild, 279
Hermogenes
 Progymnasmata, 45
Herodotus, 34
Hippodamus, 25, 320, 340
Honorius, emperor, 74, 75, 81, 84, 99, 117, 123, 138, 139, 207
Horace
 Ars Poetica, 132
 Epistulae, 291
 Odes, 95
Huns, Ephthialite
 and cities, 167

Iol Caesarea, 304, 321–323
Isidore
 and antiquarian tradition, 271, 288–290
 and Visigothic kings, 276–282
 antiquarism of, 393
 brevitas of, 280
 De Viris Illustribus, 272, 276, 280
 defines *civitas*, 271, 272, 294, 305, 306
 History of the Gothic Kings, 280, 301
 influence of Augustine, 291, 292–294, 299, 301, 305, 306, 308, 312
 Jerome as source, 305, 311, 312
 on Arians, 276–279
 on cities and citizens, 61, 290–297
 On the Nature of Things, 275
 synods attended, 273
 Synonyms, 273

Jerome
 source of Isidore, 289, 300, 306, 309
Jerusalem, 41, 185–186, 300
 heavenly, 71, 91, 100
 New Church, 185
John Chrysostom, 51
John of Biclarum, 280, 281, 283–284
Jones, A. H. M., 4, 15–20, 28, 144–145, 179, 197, 377, 395
Jordanes *Gothica*, 120, 134, 302
Justinian
 abolishes Arian church, 193, 213
 and innovation, 142, 195, 393
 and Lazica, 168
 and Ravenna, 123, 125
 builds *castra*, 238, 307
 equestrian statue of, 337
 founder of cities, 16, 26, 57–58, 175–187, 194, 342–355, 393
 history of reign, 165
 history of reign impossible, 163
 imposition of orthodoxy, 161
 invasion of Italy, 158
 invasion of Spain, 356
 law codes of, 144, 166, 204, 233, 394
 law codes, *Novels*, 204, 227, 296, 350
 marks end of era, 16
 persecution of heretics, 186
 Pragmatic Sanction of, 162, 196
 rebuilds Antioch, 380
 rebuilds Haghia Sophia, 333
 supports city elites, 198
Justiniana Prima, 188, 343–348

labyrinth
 in Isidore, 61, 309
Langres (*Lingones*), 236, 244
Laodicea (Latakia), 300, 315–318, 362
 colonnades of, 317
 continuity of, 315–318
 founded by Seleucus, 316
Latinity, Junian
 survival of, 79
laudes urbium, 33, 43–73, 303

Greek tradition, 46, 47
rhetorical tradition, 43, 44–45, 47, 52, 55, 59, 73, 237
Leander, 223, 276–279
Lefebvre, Henri, 2
Leovigild, 280, 281, 283–284, 287–288
   Arianism of, 278
   coinage of, 278
   coins of, 362
   conversion of, 279
   founder of cities, 180
   founds Reccopolis, 281, 284, 303, 355, 356–357, 367, 370, 372
   reign of, 278
Leptis Magna
   rebuilt by Justinian, 189
Libanius
   complaints over councils, 233
   family of, 75
   on council, 72
   on risks of riots, 181
   praise of Antioch, 18, 47–51, 65, 323, 380
   praise of colonnades, 381
   protests at flogging of councillors, 146
   rhetorical tradition, 47, 54
Liebeschuetz, Wolf, 3–4, 20, 21, 33, 77, 148, 198, 373, 378, 395
Lisbon (Ulisippo), 304
Lorenzetti, *Allegory of Good and Bad Government*, 36
Lothar, 263
   awe of St Martin, 260
Lyon (Lugdunum), 243, 245, 303

Madaba, mosaic, 41
Majorian, emperor, 146
Mantua
   sack of, 223
Marseille (Massilia), 100, 239
   foundation of, 303
   plague of, 262
Martial, *Epigrams*, 324
Martianus Capella, 268, 289
Menander Rhetor, 44, 48, 165
Metz (Mettis), 71, 72, 239, 259
   praise of, 43, 64
   sack of, 263
Milan
   as metropolis, 60
   as second Rome, 68
   circus of, 223
   civil conflicts, 72
   forum of, 71

   praise of, 43, 52, 58–62, 65–69, 70
   protected by saints, 60, 379
   sack of, 174
   synagogue, 153
Milan (Mediolanum)
   etymology of, 302
Minturnae, 222
Modena, 43
modernus v. *antiquus*, 142, 194, 373
Modoin, *Eclogues*, 369

Naples, 7
   council of, 219, 225
   praise of, 43
   resilience of, 392
   siege of, 174
Narbonne (Narbo), 155, 239, 303
   praise of, 53
Narses, 212, 214, 216
Neapolis in Palestine
   Samaritan capital, 186
Nectarius, 74–77, 98
Nepi, 199
Nicomedia, 184, 301
   Diocletian's Palace, 334

Odoacer, 119, 121, 193, 212
   donation by, 200–201
   grant of land to Goths, 208
Orléans (Aurelienses), 242, 262, 263
   founded by Aurelian, 237
Orosius, 82–85, 93, 101, 113, 257

Padua
   sack of, 223
Paris
   Haussmann's, 7, 9, 390
Paris (Parisii), 226, 239, 242, 258, 259
patria, 95, 116
   exile from, 277
   heavenly, 77, 84
   ideological charge, 69
   patriotism, 53, 76, 89, 99, 136, 137
Patria Constantinopoleos, 57
Pausanias
   on Panopeus, 21, 237
Peutinger Map, 312, 335
Pierius, 200
Pippin, 225
Pirenne, Henri, 14, 225, 266
Plato *Laws*, 34
Pliny, the Elder, 35, 46, 269, 309

Pliny, the Younger, 142
   Letters, 265
   Panegyric of Trajan, 152, 165
Poitiers (Pictavi), 226, 228–231, 239, 246, 258, 259, 303
   curia of, 228
   ravaged, 242
   taxation of, 231, 260
politeuma en ouranô, 78, 91
Pompeii
   Forum of, 323
   Pompeii, house of Sacerdos Amandus, 37
Procopius
   and Christianity, 162, 186
   genre of writings, 163
   genre, manipulation of, 163
   ideal of city, 187–192
   imitation of Thucydides, 164, 165, 170
   links to Cassiodorus, 158
   on city foundation, 175–187
   on doctrinal disputes, 160
   on Jews, 187
   on Roman passion for conservation, 158, 192
   on Rome as exceptional, 175
   on Samaritans, 160, 186
   peri Ktismaton, 343
   peri Ktismaton as panegyric, 165
   peri Ktismaton, meaning of title, 162, 176
   relationship of writings, 162
   role as *consiliarius*, 163
   Secret History as invective, 162
Psalms, book of, 91

Ratherius (Rather), bishop of Verona, 39, 61
Ravenna
   Anonymous Geographer of, 180
   aqueducts of, 140
   archbishop of, 201, 209, 216
   archives, 19, 131, 217, 234
   Arian baptistery, 123
   business community of, 215
   church of, 199, 204, 207, 208, 211, 226
   court of, 100, 121, 123–125, 131, 134, 207, 212
   curia of, 203, 216, 219, 225, 296
   elite of, 210, 213–216
   houses in, 208, 209, 210
   mausoleum of Galla Placidia, 99, 123
   mausoleum of Theoderic, 125
   mosaics of, 121, 123–125
   Palatium, 123
   papyri, 199–218, 223, 227, 236, 261, 265, 286, 295, 312
   praise of, 62
   Prefect/exarch in, 209, 214, 223, 392
   San Vitale, 372
   siege of, 208
   supplies marble for Charlemagne, 372
   theatre of, 110
   Theoderic's capital, 137, 142
Ravenna Papyri
   p. 1, 207
   p. 3, 206
   P. 4–5, 214, 215
   p. 7, 211
   p. 8, 210
   p. 10–11, 204
   p. 12, 208
   p. 13, 207
   p. 14–15, 216
   p. 17, 206
   p. 25, 218
   p. 30, 212
   p. 34, 212
   p. 38–41, 208
   p. 44, 209
Reccared, 223, 279, 281–282, 283, 394
   Catholicism of, 279
   naming of Reccopolis, 180, 356
Reccopolis, 281, 283, 372
   aqueduct, 361
   foundation of, 284, 356
   mint of, 357
   site of, 284, 357–362
resilience v. transformation, 377–379
resilience, theory of, 30, 76, 114, 118, 157, 199, 266, 312, 373–374
Ricimer, sack of Rome, 1
Rieti, 199, 211
Rimini, 199, 224
Rome
   city as second Rome, 46, 65, 69, 326–342, 368–370
   foundation of, 299
   papyri from, 199
   praise of, 84, 85
   Regionary Catalogue, 47, 339–340
   repair of walls, 137
   Rome, Colle Oppio frieze, 38
   sack of (Alaric), 86, 100, 114
   sack of (Gallic), 86
   second Rome, 64–65
   ship of Aeneas, 159
   synagogue, 153
Romulus Augustus
   deposed, 119

Sagalassos
   agora, 325
Salvian, *On the Governance of God*, 100–113
   on curials, 108–109
   on vices of cities, 109–112
Sauvaget, Jean, 315–320
Scyllaceum (Squillace), 43, 54–56, 116, 118, 133
Seleucia
   founded by Seleucus, 300
Seleucids
   founders of cities, 178
Seleucus Nicator, 48
Sergiopolis/Rustafa, 352–355
Seville (Hispalis)
   arrival of Isidore, 278
   Caesarean colony, 304
   episcopal library, 273
   praise of, 52
   punished by Leovigild, 283–284
   seat of Hermenegild, 279, 283
   see of, 271, 276, 279, 282
Sigibert of Gembloux
   praises Metz, 64
Sigibert, son of Lothar, 257–259
Sisebut, 275, 282
Sophocles, 34
Stroheker, Karl, 250–252, 255–256, 287
Suetonius, *Lives of the Caesars*, 152
suq, 365
   colonnade transformed to, 26–27, 51, 315–318, 321–323, 325
Syracuse, 199, 201–203, 205, 222
   sack of, 86

Tacitus *Agricola*, 108
Tarentum
   sack of, 86
Tarragona
   arena, 113
Themistius, 326
Theodahad, 122
   deposition of, 134
   reign of, 128
   reproof of, 133, 153, 156
Theodelinda, 223
Theoderic
   common Gothic name, 128
Theoderic, king of Italy, 118, 236
   achievement of, 196
   and Rome, 135–138, 159
   buildings in Ravenna, 123–125

education of, 121
eliminates Odoacer, 200
equestrian statue, 372
founds city, 180
grants land to Goths, 208
history of, 127
ideal of *civilitas*, 156
laws of, 128, 286
legitimacy, 193
on SPQR, 151
panegyric of, 120, 152
politics of continuity, 118–119
policy of conservation, 139
politics of continuity, 127, 256
promotes *civilitas*, 130
repair of statues, 143
repair of walls, 174
repairs water supply, 141
resistance to, 122
succession, 256
supports cities, 199
Theodosian Code, 18, 128, 138, 197, 233, 284, 394
Theodosius II, emperor, 29, 81, 336, 339
   codex of. See Codex Theodosianus
   wall of, 327, 338, 341
Theodosius the Great, emperor, 75, 96, 99, 123, 135, 139, 143, 324
   family of, 179
   Forum of, 335
   names Theodosiopolis, 177
   persecution of heretics, 80
   Trinitarian, 75
Thessalonike (Thessalonica), 7, 302
   named for wife of Cassander, 178
Theuderic, son of Childebert, 257
Theuderic, son of Clovis, 248, 253, 256
Thucydides, 34, 46
   model of Procopius, 163
Toledo
   Council of, 275, 279, 282, 283, 293
   Visigothic capital, 303, 357
topos inscriptions, 325
Totila, 1, 175
   campaign against, 216
   defeat of, 213
   persuaded to spare Rome, 194
   tears down walls, 393
Toulouse (Tolosa), 54, 121, 236, 239, 253
   praise of, 52
   Visigothic capital, 303

Tournai
　as second Rome, 65
Tours (Turones), 239, 241, 246, 247, 249, 255, 258, 259
　list of bishops, 267
　taxed, 260, 262
Town Planning Conference of 1910, 22
Trier, 249, 253
　Augustan foundation, 179
　commerce of, 54
　demands circus, 109
　leading city, 52
　origin of Salvian, 100
　sack of, 108
　second Rome, 46

Valentinian I, emperor, 80, 117, 143, 295, 324
Valentinian III, emperor, 81, 99, 123
Valentinian, emperors, 179
Vandals
　as city founders, 180
　attitude to cities, 168
　tear down walls, 188
　treasures of exceptional, 174
Varro, 271, 289, 290, 296, 303, 305, 309, 310, 312
Venantius Fortunatus, 245, 247, 268
Verdun
　economy boosted, 248
Verona
　Arena, 41
　arena as labyrinth, 46, 61, 64, 309
　depiction of, 39–41
　forum of, 62, 71
　praise of, 43, 58, 61–62
　protected by saints, 62, 72, 379
Vienne (Vienna), 239, 250, 266
　curia of, 254
　siege of, 253, 254

Virgil
　Aeneid, 75, 89, 291, 299, 306, 368
　Aeneid, model for Carolingian poets, 369
　birthplace Mantua, 302
　cited by Augustine, 86–87, 90, 94, 95
　cited by Carolingian poets, 367
　cited by Gregory of Tours, 269
　cited in *laudes urbium*, 46
　commentators on used by Isidore, 271, 289, 292, 305, 310, 312
　Georgics, as model, 368
Vitruvius, 309
　influence of, 305, 308, 309, 312
　on cities, 35, 37, 50, 71, 272, 341
　on evolution, 293, 307
Vouillé, battle of, 236, 253, 266, 281

walls
　define cities, 33–43, 52, 54, 58, 59, 63, 64, 141, 171, 181, 237, 238, 307, 348
　heretics excluded from, 82
　protected by saints, 60, 263
Weber, Max, 4, 5, 11–14, 20, 69
　Weber, 'ideal type', 11
William of Malmesbury, 44
Witigis
　fall of, 131, 134, 212
　reign of, 129
　siege of Rome, 193
　tears down walls, 174, 393

York (Eburacum), 63–64, 222
　praise of, 43, 72, 394

Zaragoza (Caesaraugusta), 272
　praise of, 303
　siege of, 60, 263
Zeno, 200
Zenobia (Halabyia), 351–352